Cults and New Religions

Sources for Study of Nonconventional
Religious Groups in Nineteenth-and
Twentieth-Century America

A collection of
reprinted books, pamphlets, articles, and ephemera
documenting the development of nonconventional religion in America

Edited by
J. GORDON MELTON

Director
Institute for the Study of American Religion
Santa Barbara

A Garland Series

The Peoples Temple and Jim Jones

Broadening Our Perspective

Edited with an introduction by

J. GORDON MELTON

Director
Institute for the Study of American Religion

GARLAND PUBLISHING
NEW YORK   LONDON
1990

Publisher's Note:

many of the photographs which appeared with these magazine
and newspaper articles have not been reproduced in this volume.

Library of Congress Cataloging-in-Publication Data

The Peoples Temple and Jim Jones ; broadening our perspective /
edited with an introduction by J. Gordon Melton.
p. cm. — (Cults and new religions)
A reprint of articles and pamphlets.
Includes bibliographical references.
ISBN 0-8240-4498-3 (alk. paper)
1. Peoples Temple. 2. Jones, Jim, 1931–1978. I. Melton, J. Gordon. II. Series.
BP605.P46P45 1990
289.9—dc20   89-49666

Printed on acid-free, 250-year-life paper.

Manufactured in the United States of America.

CONTENTS

Acknowledgments

The editor and publisher are grateful to the following for permission to reproduce material in this volume:

The Untold Story of the Jonestown Massacre, © Histrionics Publications, Inc., 1979; "The Cult of Death," © Newsweek, Inc., 1978; "The Making of a Madman," "Jim Jones: The Seduction of San Francisco," © *New West*, 1978; "The Freedom Abusers," © *Inquiry*, 1979; "Cult Wars on Capitol Hill," © Time Inc., 1979; "The Twisted Roots of Jonestown," © *Mother Jones*, 1979; "Jim Jones: Deadly Hypnotist," © *Science News*, 1979; "Black Panther Party Statement on Jonestown Massacre," "Researcher Charges News Reporters in Guyana C.I.A. Agents," "Dick Gregory Charges Conspiracy at Jonestown," © *The Black Panther*, 1978, 1979; "Why Alienated Blacks are the Easiest Prey," "Papers Reveal Role of Cult in Guyana Politics," "My Daughters Died in Guyana," "U.S. Lists Jonestown Victims Who Lack Kin," "Jones' Son Admits Killing of 4 Cultists," "One Year After Jonestown Cults Still Unchecked," "Some Jones Followers Still Believe in Him," "Kids are Author's One-Man Crusade," © *Chicago Sun-Times*, 1978, 1979; "Gregory Charges Conspiracy," © *New Observer*, 1979; "Black Reflections on the Jonestown Holocaust," © *IBW Monthly Reporter*, 1979; "Churchman Hunts Clues on Cult's Lure for Blacks," © *Christianity Today*, 1979; "Peoples Temple Colony 'Harassed'," "The Long Night of Fear at Guyana Airstrip," "Government's Jonestown Role Being Investigated," © *San Francisco Examiner*, 1978; "Newsmen Shot in Guyana/Congressman Feared Slain," "Jones Wasn't the Man They Used to Know," "New Revelation of Jonestown Deaths Shocks Remnant of Peoples Temple," "Lawsuits Expected in Cult Deaths," "Peoples Temple to Dissolve Itself," "Grand Jury Calls 17 from Temple," "Peoples Congregation is Dissolving Church," "Jim Jones Had a Charisma That Could Take Anybody In," "Jonestown Escapee Followed 'Moses' 22 Miles to Safety," "Suit Says U.S. Conspired in Massive Cult Deaths," "Final Accounting Near for Peoples Temple," © United Press International, 1978, 1981, 1985; "U.S. Monitored Cult But Took Little Action," © *Los Angeles Herald Examiner*; "Faith in the Extreme," "Sanity—A Condition of Survival," "Sect Request Denied," "First Cult Bodies Leave Air Base," "Cult Kept Huge Cache of Mind Warping Drugs," "Probe Urged," "Claim Against Temple Assets Denied," "A Reply on Jonestown," "Temple Member is Home," "Another Part of Peoples Temple Story Ends," "Probe of Cult Termed Inadequate," "Guyana Trial Opens," © *Milwaukee Journal*, 1978, 1980, 1982, 1983, 1987; "Day by Day, A New Stunning Horror," "Jim Jones: Portrait of a Madman," "Key to Cult: Man Was Paranoid," "U.S. Had No Proof of Cult Danger," "Cult Intended to Give Millions to Russ[ia]," "'Remember Jim Jones? I'm His Son'," "Survivor: A Decade After Jonestown Horrified the World . . .," © *Chicago Tribune*, 1978, 1984, 1988; "Senseless Orgy," © *Chicago Daily Defender*, 1978; "Jones Burial to be in Indiana," "U.S., Fearing Rights Violations, Ruled Out Investigating Cults," "Pain is Still Intense 10 Years After Jonestown," "Jonestown Myths Leave People Unaware, Vulnerable," © The Associated Press, 1978, 1988; "A Deadly Cult," © *The Pilot*, 1978; "US Probes New Tale of Cult Escapees," "Cult Funds Put at $10 Million," "70 at Jonestown Got Injections," "Jim Jones' Memoirs Reveal He Believed in Communism," "'Those People Should Have Lived'," "By Death Possessed," "Jonestown Has Many Precedents," "Church Leaders Come to Defense of Fringe Groups," "38 More Survivors Released in Guyana," "Medical Examiners Criticize Actions on Cult Bodies," "U.S. Acting to Secure Temple's $10 Million in 3 Banks in Panama," "Body of Cult's Leader Cremated in Jersey," "Profiles of Seven Whose Faith in Jim Jones Carried Them to Death in Guyana," © New York Times Company, 1978, 1988; "South Florida Cults," © *Miami Herald*, 1978; "Cultists Were Not Unusual," "Jones Cult Spotlights Freedom of Religion," © *Indianapolis News*, 1978; "Jonestown," © *Christian Citizen*, 1978; "After Jonestown—Six Family Portraits," "Jonestown Physician Called a Sadist by Settlement Survivor," © Washington Post Company, 1978; "Rev. Jones Promised Utopia—Delivered Death," © *Boston Herald-American*, 1978; "'Moonies' Lawyer Calls for Jonestown Probe," © *San Francisco Chronicle*, 1978; "'How Did Your Children Become Involved in Peoples Temple?'," "10 Years After, Jonestown Remembered," © *United Methodist Reporter*, 1978, 1988; "After Loss of Three Children, Father Looks at Cult in Different Perspective," "Church Tried to Help Guyana Cult Members," "Pressure for Supression of Cults Likely in Wake of Jonestown Horror," © Catholic News Service, 1978; "Federal Crackdown on Cultists Could Threaten Religious Liberty," © *Our Sunday Visitor*, 1978; "Jonestown Retrieval Criticized," © *Fort Worth Star-Telegram*, 1978; "Minister Looking for Answers at Jonestown," © *Birmingham News*, 1978; "Lessons for Society from the Jonestown Tragedy," © *Alabama Christian Advisor*, 1979; "Body of Massacre Victim Returned to Evanston," © *Evanston Review*, 1979; "How Jim Jones 'Conditioned' His Sheep for Death," © *National Catholic Register*, 1980; "CIA Charged with Aiding Jim Jones," © *Star*, 1980; "Jonestown: Only a Bad Memory," © Knight-Ridder News Service, 1981; "$1.6 Million Settlement Near in Cult Deaths," "Final Accounting Near for Peoples Temple,"© *Milwaukee Sentinal*, 1982, 1985; "Layton Sentenced to Life in Ryan's Death," "10 Years Later, Jonestown is a Site of Silent Desolation," "Church Officials Ponder Lesson of Guyana Events," © Los Angeles Times Company, 1978, 1987, 1988; "Cult News Had Wide Following," © George Gallup, 1978.

INTRODUCTION

On Broadening Our Perspective
on the People's Temple

In the weeks following the deaths of hundreds of members of the Peoples Temple in Guyana in November of 1978, the group became the symbol of all that was wrong in new religious movements. The pictures of the bodies rotting in the tropical sun became full-color portraits of all of the fears surrounding the controversial unconventional religious groups. Integral to the attack upon new religions such as the Unification Church or the Hare Krishnas was the constant imputation of guilt by association with Jonestown and the condemnation of their leaders by comparison to Jim Jones. When critics of a strange new religious group in the neighborhood have lacked any substantive rationale for their hostility to the group, they could simply state their belief that the group was a potential Jonestown. Such a comment said it all without saying anything.

Over twenty books have been written about Jonestown, the Peoples Temple, and Jones (see list at the end of this essay). One could certainly suppose that all that needed to be said has been said, but the contrary seems to be the case. Overall, the Jonestown literature has adopted a very narrow focus. Authors of the several "quicky" books, published within weeks of the event, needed an immediate explanation. They settled on the superficially available one: the Peoples Temple was a cult. Their labeling provided a set of questions for future writers and largely determined the perspective of those who followed. and those who wanted to probe beyond mere labeling and reach a more satisfying appraisal of the deaths have been hampered by the government investigation of the death of congressman Leo J. Ryan. To date, eleven years after Ryan murder, the vast storehouse of documents about the Peoples Temple from which a broader perspective could be gained remains under lock and key. The significant number of missing pieces (contained in the documents being held by the congressional investigating committee) attending any attempt to put together the jigsaw puzzle of the Guyana deaths has allowed the secular anti-cult movement to seize the event and exploit it for their cause. The movement has been able to turn Jonestown into the ultimate cult nightmare. Annually, it has memorialized the deaths and given a "Leo J. Ryan Award" to an outstanding worker in the anti-cult wars.

However, a number of facts about the case suggest that reducing Jonestown to the image of an evil cult is to trivialize an intensely serious event and to miss the evil that actually occurred that hot and sticky day in the jungle. The fact that the majority of records concerning Jonestown have remained unavailable for public scrutiny indicates that the United States government and/or the Guyanese government may have had a more significant level of involvement in the life of the community than we have been led to believe. The fact that the Peoples Temple was so involved in the political and religious life of San Francisco and Northern California indicates that it was far more than just a culturally-marginal congregation. That the Peoples Temple was a full and valued congregation in a major American denomination, and that it was able to recruit many liberal Protestants into its ranks indicates that answers to the Jonestown enigma are to be sought at the midstream of America's religious life, not its boundaries.

On the other hand, the Peoples Temple does not resemble any of the other contemporary controversial new religions. The Temple found its home within the black community of San Francisco. It was an activist group so honored for its efforts that both local and national politicians sought identification with it. While its membership consisted primarily of poorer middle aged black people, Jones recruited many of the leaders from among the pool of white liberal Protestant social idealists (who placed so much emphasis on social justice that they were quite willing to overlook Jones' personal faults, especially his sexual life). This profile suggests that the primary questions of the Peoples Temple do not relate to the "cult" question but concern the possibility of perverting the very acceptable program of a mainline church. To pursue such a question, however, leads one into an examination of the life of the congregation, the worship it offered, the programs it promoted, the goals its set and fatal flaw(s) that destroyed it. In stark contrast to the Temple, the new "cults" which so concern the anti-cult movement today are predominantly white in membership. Leadership is drawn from the groups, but is generally focused in a single leader who has foreign (Oriental or Indian) origins. Members tend to be middle to upper-middle class. Rejecting their parents religion and more familiar religious ties, the cults pursue a most strange and unconventional spiritual path. While a courageous politician might on occasion defend the rights of a new religion, none would seek to be identified with them. In other words, the new religious offer few, if any, points of similarity with the Peoples Temple.

It is not the purpose of this volume, or this brief essay, to complete the Peoples Temple puzzle, only to add a few missing pieces here and there. The author has some insight derived from his original encounter with the Temple in 1971, his cursory monitoring of it over the remaining years of its existence, and his efforts to gather data about it in the years since its disbanding. The first encounter began in the summer of 1971 at Benjamin Franklin High School in San Francisco.

A Personal Experience

During the summer of 1971, I was a visiting lecturer at the University of San Francisco. My class being during the first period each morning, I had the rest of the day to visit all of the new religions which I had only heard about from my home base in Chicago. Thus, I found myself the subject of healing treatments in storefront temples, squatting on the floor before strange altars, and gathering literature on Telegraph Avenue in Berkeley from a wide variety of evangelists. As people discovered my particular interest in spiritual healing, they began to tell me, "You must go see Jim Jones!" From their descriptions, he seemed like just another Pentecostal deliverance evangelist, and at first I did not take the suggestions seriously. What was another Pentecostal preacher when compared to a new exotic guru? But, finally, after the fourth or fifth suggestion to go to a service at the Peoples Temple, I told myself, "Maybe there is something there I should see".

It was a Sunday morning in July. Several thousand people crowded into the high school auditorium. A gospel choir was on the stage. In front of them, seated at a pulpit was the Rev. Jones. The service, which lasted for several hours, certainly took its basic thrust from Pentecostalism. There was spirited singing, intense exhortation from the pulpit, and, of course, healing. Two events stand out.

Jones looked over his congregation through a pair of sunglasses. As he began the healing services, he leaned over the pulpit and informed the uninitiated why he wore the glasses. It seemed that he had very powerful radiations emanating from his eyes, and if exposed to the full strength of the rays, we mere mortals could be harmed rather than healed.

The healing service was conducted from his distant place apart from the congregation. He did not lay his hands on any for prayer, but dealt with them where they were seated in the audience. He called upon people and pronounced their healing accomplished one after the other. One healing was particularly memorable. Jones pointed out a woman but two rows directly in front of me, and as he called upon her, she rose from her seat. He began to tell her that he could see that she was being eaten up with cancer, that if she walked out of the auditorium to an x-ray machine at that moment, she would be able to document her condition. It had reached a fatal stage. the woman was dumbstruck, but before she was able to fully react, Jones continued.

He told her that she need not worry, he had called her out in order to heal her. At that moment, her complete, miraculous, life-saving healing was being completed. It took only a matter of seconds for the woman to grasp what had just occurred. She was on her way to an untimely death and was not even aware of her condition. But Jones had saved her life by his intervention. She raised her voice with words of thanksgiving to her pastor, the miracle-worker in the pulpit. "Thank you, Rev. Jones!" echoed throughout the auditorium as she raised her hand, and members of the audience joined in the celebration of her healing. I left the auditorium trying to rationalize the manipulation of these people by Jones. I never succeeded, and the incident was scorched into my memory.

Over the next few years, in Chicago, I continued to receive the mailings from the temple, but thought little of them. Jones invited participation in his work by mailing out blessed prayer cloths and other items which contained a healing potency because he had prayed over them. I thought little more of Jones until the next year when the newspaper columnist and Episcopal priest Lester Kinsolving attacked him with a series of stories not at all pleasing to the Temple's membership. The Temple mobilized and forced the *San Francisco Examiner* to drop the series in the middle. It was an impressive show of power. The Kinsolving episode became but the first of a number of stories that would appear periodically over the next years. Rather than simply attack some of the Temple's practices and miraculous claims, these latter stories would suggest high crimes and misdemeanors committed by Temple members at Jones' instigation. As evidence of wrongdoing within the Temple mounted, and pressure from both media attacks and official investigations increased, Jones would flee investigations and promised legal action to Guyana. The next act in the story, of course, led to over 900 deaths.

Documenting the Story

The materials in this collection supply additional documentation of the Peoples Temple which should be useful to any researcher. First, a set of publications *produced by* the Temple during the 1970s will introduce the student to the life of the several congregations in California, their outreach to cities around the United States, and their hopes of developing an "agricultural project" in South America. The second set of materials *written about* the temple appeared over the ten years following the deaths at Jonestown and relate aspects of the story usually missed in the books. Most notable are the continued reflection upon the deaths by people involved in the Temple who survived the killings. The speculation about the reasons for the deaths has been wide-ranging and include the unique problem presented to the black community which is somewhat similar to the problem which the Holocaust presents to the Jewish community.

The mailings from the Temple for the years 1971 to 1974 provide a glimpse of the Peoples Temple at the time it was becoming controversial. Jones moved among the three congregations in Ukiah, San Francisco, and Los Angeles, and led an outreach which wanted to build other congregations along the West Coast, the Midwest (especially Indianapolis), and the rest of the country. Social action and individual miracles formed the two-pronged emphasis. The single issue of *The Temple Reporter* (produced to counter criticism) from the summer of 1973 described the many points at which the Temple members penetrated the communities in which they lived.

The two booklets from 1977 and 1978 describe in some detail the hopeful beginning of the agricultural project (Jonestown) in Guyana. There is every reason to believe that the disparity between the image presented in these booklets and the reality of life in the colony was not nearly so wide in its early years as it became after Jones moved there and took personal control of its day-to-day schedule.

Of particular importance in this collection of material generated from within the Temple are the two letters from Timothy Oliver Stoen and Michael J. Prokes. Together they illustrate the close ties between the temple and both the Dis-

ciples of Christ and the local political structures. These two letters lead directly into the two documents distributed from the national office of the Christian Church (Disciple of Christ) in March 1979. As might be expected, the church was embarrassed and distressed by the events at Jonestown and attempted as far as possible to distance itself Jones' work. The Church, which operates as a loosely affiliated association, was caught in a double bind. It was under pressure to develop machinery to kick congregations out of its fellowship. It felt pressure from religious critics who emphasized the Temple's relation to the denomination. While it had no use for cults, it did not agree with government attempts to define religion as a means of getting to cults. The obvious hope that the issue would just go away (and hence they should not have to deal with the Protestant community) was realized in this case when the anti-cult forces stole the issue away and effectively turned the Peoples Temple into a cult.

The second block of material in this collection includes some of the important, but now difficult to retrieve, coverage of Jonestown from the days immediately after the deaths through the tenth anniversary remembrance. The reports in the December 4, 1978 issues of *Newsweek* and *People* convey the flavor of the media's coverage of the event and their need to explain this group about which few had ever heard. More informative and a step above most of its media competition was *New West* whose coverage of Jones had helped motivate his move from California to Guyana in the first place.

The remaining articles, most from newspapers, document the steps by which the Temple assets were seized, the corporation finally dissolved (though rumors persist that some surviving members in California have quietly stayed together as a worshiping community), and survivors have tried to pick up their lives. The events in Guyana, as could be expected, generated numerous legal actions, both civil and criminal. Possibly the most drawn-out proceedings were those of Larry Layton which were only resolved in recent months. Of particular importance in the collection are the stories of the numerous survivors. A few people at Jonestown did not die and have lived to tell the story. A larger number of Temple members who had not moved to Jonestown are also counted among the survivors, as are the people, such as Timothy Stoen, whose son died at Guyana. Jim Jones' son also survived and five years after Jonestown told his side of the story.

A Final solution

A Resolution of the major problems posed by the Jonestown deaths will await the decision of Congress to release the pertinent documents and the revelation of the discoveries of the numerous investigations that have made the Peoples Temple one of the most thoroughly documented religious communities that ever existed. In the meantime, we can only offer some partial reflections from the information available. This collection on Jonestown, placed as it is at the end of a set of volumes on the "cults," symbolizes in part the resolution of at least one issue; i.e., the relation of Jonestown to the larger question of new religions in Western society. *Jonestown simply has nothing to do with those groups labeled cults by popular anti-cult movements.* There is no reason to believe that groups such as the Unification Church, the International Society for Krishna Consciousness, or the Church of Scientology are in any way similar to the Peoples Temple or destined to reenact its fate. These newer groups are distinct at almost every point.

Experience both before and since Jonestown should also suggest what types of religious association might be moving toward the kind of deadly future properly symbolized by Jonestown. The group in the highest risk category is the small informally organized group of which the Manson family and the drug cult at Matamoras are the most prominent examples. Such groups are, unfortunately, so informal as to escape detection until tragedy occurs. From the few groups which have been discovered over the years, we can legitimately hypothesize both that a small number of these "cults" exist at any given moment and that most will dissolve before any real disaster occurs. We also know that we have yet to discover a way to locate and monitor such groups. Certainly, such groups as the Cult Awareness Network have proved of no assistance in this regard.

A second high risk group would be a former congregation of an established religious body which is undergoing a radical change in questionable directions. Examples are not lacking of congregations with a prior community acceptance (possibly by association with a larger conventional denominational body) who have traveled a significant distance along a destructive path before anyone was willing to admit to what has been gradually occurring.

Jonestown was an extreme example of this process; more was at stake. Jones was a high-profile public figure, and was accused of capital crimes. His entire realm of influence was under attack, and by using his power, he was able, for a period at least, to stifle criticism and to extend the time for the process of disintegration within the Temple to operate. Then, with the law about to close in upon him, he had the opportunity to move into a self-imposed exile in a foreign land.

Because of the unusual circumstances surrounding the Peoples Temple disaster, it is highly unlikely that we will live to see another Jonestown. It is possible, however, that we might on a rare occasion see previously-stable conventional congregations begin a search for a better way, only to adopt new well-meaning directions that lead them not to revival but to destruction. The first step is a subtle one, but seems to be that event in which some hurt against one is sanctioned in the name of the good it will bring to the whole group.

In Conclusion

Jonestown, Jim Jones, and the Peoples Temple raise important questions about the relation of evil and religion for both the academic student of religion and the wider community of religious people. The questions are too important to leave to the shallow and exploitive uses of the anti-cult movement, or to ignore by dismissing the People Temple as just a "cult." It is hoped that this compilation will assist the reader, however minutely, in the consideration of these basic moral and spiritual issues.

J. Gordon Melton

A Bibliography of Books on the Peoples Temple, Jim Jones, and Jonestown
Compiled by James R. Lewis

Note: The literature about Jonestown varies widely from personal accounts of involvement, to government documents, to scholarly analysis. Among the volumes which stand out as most valuable are those by journalist Tim Reiterman, religious scholar John R. Hall, and Rebecca Moore and Fielding M. McGahee's *New Religious Movements, Mass Suicide, and Peoples Temple: Scholarly Perspectives on a Tragedy.*

Ahlberg, Sture. *Messianic Movements: A Comparative Analysis of the Sabbatians, the People's Temple, and the Unification Church.* Stockholm: Almqvist & Wiksell International, 1986.

The Assassination of Representative Leo J. Ryan and the Jonestown Tragedy: Report of a Staff Investigative Group to the Committee of Foreign Affairs U.S. House of Representatives. Washington: U.S. Government Printing Office, 1979.

California Attorney General's Office. *Report of Investigation of People's Temple*. Sacramento: Office of the Attorney General, 1980.

California Department of Social Services, Fraud Prevention Unit. *Investigation Report on People's Temple*. Sacramento: The Department of Social Services, 1979.

Carpozi, George, Jr. *The Suicide Cult*. New York: Manor, 1978.

Chidester, David. *Salvation and Suicide: An Interpretation of Jim Jones, the People's Temple, and Jonestown*. Bloomington: Indiana University Press, 1988.

The Death of Representative Leo J. Ryan, People's Temple, and Jonestown: Understanding a Tragedy: Hearing before the Committee on Foreign Affairs, House of Representatives, Ninety-Sixth Congress, First Session. Washington: U.S. Government Printing Office, 1979.

Feinsod, Ethan. *Awake in a Nightmare: Jonestown: The Only Eyewitness Account*. New York: W. W. Norton & Co., 1981.

Hall, John R. *Gone from the Promised Land: Jonestown in American Cultural History*. New Brunswick, New Jersey: Transaction, 1987.

Kerns, Phil with Dough Wead. *People's Temple/People's Tomb*. Plainfield, Connecticut: Logos International, 1979.

Kilduff, Marshall and Ron Javers. *The Suicide Cult: The Inside Story of the Peoples Temple and the Massacre in Guyana*. New York: Bantam, 1978.

Klineman, George and Sherman Butler. *The Cult that Died: The Tragedy of Jim Jones and the People's Temple*. New York: G.P. Putnam's Sons, 1979.

Krause, Charles A. *Guyana Massacre: The Eyewitness Account*. New York: Berkley Publishing, 1978.

Lane, Mark. *The Strongest Poison*. New York: Hawthorn, 1980.

Levi, Ken, ed. *Violence and Religious Commitment: Implications of Jim Jones' People's Temple*. University Park, Pennsylvania: State University Press, 1982.

Lewis, Gordon K. *"Gather with the Saints at the River": The Jonestown Guyana Holocaust of 1978: A Descriptive and Interpretative Essay on its Ultimate Meaning from a Caribbean Viewpoint*. Rio Piedras, Puerto Rico: Institute of Caribbean Studies, University of Puerto Rico, 1979.

Maguire, John and Mary Lee Dunn. *Hold Hands and Die! The Incredibly True Story of the People's Temple, Reverend Jim Jones and the Tragedy in Guyana*. New York: Dale, 1978.

McCoy, Alan W. *The Guyana Murders*. San Francisco: Highland House, 1988.

Mills, Jeannie. *Six Years with God: Life Inside Rev. Jim Jones' Peoples Temple*. New York: A & W Publishers, 1979.

Moore, Rebecca. *A Sympathetic History of Jonestown: the Moore Family Involvement in Peoples Temple*. Lewiston, New York: Edwin Mellen, 1985.

———. *The Jonestown Letters: Correspondence of the Moore Family, 1970–1985*. Lewiston, New York: Edwin Mellen, 1986.

———. *In Defense of People's Temple—and other Essays*. Lewiston, New York: Edwin Mellen, 1988.

Moore, Rebecca and Fielding M. McGehee III, eds. *The Need for a Second Look at Jonestown*. Lewiston, New York: Edwin Mellen, 1989.

———. *New Religious Movements, Mass Suicide, and Peoples Temple: Scholarly Perspectives on a Tragedy*. Lewiston, New York: Edwin Mellen, 1989.

Naipaul, Shiva. *Journey to Nowhere: A New World Tragedy*. New York: Simon and Schuster, 1981.

———. *Black and White*. London: H. Hamilton, 1980.

Nichols, Norma. *Pot-pouri with a Taste of Cult*. Georgetown, Guyana?: s.n., 1979 or 1980.

Reiterman, Tim with John Jacobs. *Raven: The Untold Story of the Rev. Jim Jones and His People*. New York: Dutton, 1982.

Reston, James, Jr. *Our Father Who Art in Hell: The Life and Death of Jim Jones*. New York: Times Books, 1981.

Rose, Steve. *Jesus and Jim Jones: Behind Jonestown*. New York: Pilgrim Press, 1979.

Thielmann, Bonnie with Dean Merrill. *The Broken God: Jim Jones' Onetime "Daughter" Tells Her Inside Story of Peoples Temple . . . and Why She Left*. Elgin, Illinois: David C. Cook Publishing, 1979.

Weightman, Judith Mary. *Making Sense of the Jonestown Suicides: A Sociological History of the Peoples Temple*. Lewiston, New York: Edwin Mellen, 1987.

White, Mel. *Deceived*. Old Tappan, New Jersey: Spire Books, 1979.

Wooden, Kenneth. *The Children of Jonestown*. New York: McGraw-Hill, 1981.

Vee, Min S. & Thomas N. Layton. *In My Father's House: The Story of the Layton Family and the Reverend Jim Jones*. New York: Holt, Rinehart and Winston, 1981.

I

Publications of the Peoples Temple

Response of the Christian Churches

Box 214
Redwood Valley, California
July 21, 1971

Dearest Friends,

Pastor James Jones and his enthusiastic rainbow family are coming east to
visit our old friends and members of People's Temple, and to extend our missionary
work. We will be holding miraculous healing services at 7:30 on the evenings of Tuesday,
July 27 and Wednesday July 28, at the old site of the People's Temple Christian
Church, at 10th and North Delaware Streets, Indianapolis, Indiana. Pastor Jones
is taking a nationwide trip spreading his prophetic words to all with ears ready
to listen: "How can we hear without a Prophet, and how can he preach lest he be
sent?"

Just last week in a San Francisco healing service, our Prophet James Jones
meditated for over 450 people plagued with arthritis, and hundreds of them were cured
instantly. As well as his healing ministry, Pastor Jones has established a fellowship of thousands, who have given up alcohol, drugs and tobacco so that they can
better follow His truth. He shows his love for us each day and in countless ways.

In friendship,

Laura Johnston, in behalf of
People's Temple Christian Church
of the Disciples of Christ
Denomination.

1

Cordy   nov. 26
elderly   84   cipriani
1½   Pierre — went back
Long lives   Fa & 92
Sis passed 17 yrs
Pneumonia   5 yrs ago
Avoid something in rest

      few days

nurse — personal

don't tell
  mother
Relation because
not dwell on
negative

Almond   soy   nuts
sesame   oils
millet   cereals
greens — greatest natives
      of health

Raw shredded best with
lunch & dinner meals dark
in salad in one spoon is kept
if you boil is sufficient

      3 min when
        bruise dry
        before store

St. Pierre no meeting them

So many people doubt them

he's in need to me

PEOPLE'S TEMPLE
P.O. BOX 214
Redwood Valley, Calif. 95470

Mrs. Marjorie H. Crosby
3610 - 28th Ave.
San Francisco, Calif.
94121

Nonprofit Org.
U.S. Postage
1.7 ¢ PAID
San Francisco, Calif.
Permit No. 9729

2

JUNE 12 AND 13 PASTOR JIM JONES WILL CONDUCT A HUMANITARIAN
AND HEALING MEETING AT BENJAMIN FRANKLIN JUNIOR HIGH SCHOOL
ON THE CORNER OF SCOTT & GEARY. THE SATURDAY NIGHT MEETING WILL
START AT 7:30 PM AND THE SUNDAY MEETING WILL BEGIN AT 11:00 A.M.

<u>SEE MESSAGE BEGINNING PAGE 2</u>

RADIO BROADCAST ON KFAX

Be sure to tune in to our radio broadcast on KFAX, 1100 on the dial from 10:00 to 10:30 AM every Saturday and Sunday morning to hear the inspiring words of Jim Jones.

People's Temple continues to expand its vast human service ministry following the precept that "The highest worship to God and Christ is service to our fellow man."

We are presently in the process of trying to purchase a multi-facility child-care home on extensive acreage with room for a large garden and a number acres of orchards and grape vineyards. In this way we can serve the needs of many young people. But in order to achieve this worthy goal everyone must make a very special effort to help!

Also, the Temple has purchased a college dormitory home for the forty-five Temple college youth whom we sponsor and provide dormitories for in Santa Rosa while they receive their college education subsidized by the Temple.

In addition to this we continue to provide an aged home, the fellowship house, manse and our youth center with its indoor heated swimming pool, an animal refuge shelter for homeless pets of all kinds; also, we have the great task of maintaining three large commercial air conditioned busses especially comfortable for trips for our aged members and our **young** people.

Recently Temple members were assisting around-the-clock in help and supervision of young persons coming off drugs. Over 85 of our Temple youth have been converted to a life of Christian service from the misery of a life in the drug world. Although <u>none</u> of the youth reared in the Temple family has ever turned to drug use, many young people coming into the Temple as teenagers or young adults came to us from the drug world and none who has become a part of the Temple family has ever returned to this kind of life. Most of these youth are in college in our church-sponsored dormitories or the others have very responsible jobs in the community.

If you would like to help in any of these most worthy endeavors, please send your gift to P. O. Box 214, Redwood Valley, Calif. <u>THE FINANCIAL NEED IS CRITICAL AT THIS TIME!</u> You can also be a sponsor of a college student, helping him financially receive his education and he or she will keep in close communication with you writing you of the activities he or she as a student is undertaking.

BOAT CRUISE! Don't miss our exciting boat cruise departing from Pier 43-1/2 at Fisherman's Wharf, June 12th starting at 4:00 PM. Our Temple Band will be on hand for entertainment as well as a full course banquet meal for all.

<u>PLEASE SEND STAMPS</u>: Due to our immense correspondence of over 2000 letters a week, we are in need of postal stamps, since every letter is answered. Please include postal stamps in your letters to the Temple or Pastor Jones.

SPECIAL GRADUATION PARTY AND BIRTHDAY CELEBRATION: The regular Birthday **Party** celebration will be changed to June 19 at 7:00 PM, but with this a gala graduation celebration for all those who have just completed high school and college will take place. Don't miss this event.

<u>TO RECEIVE THE NEWSLETTER</u>: Only those who write us and keep in constant communication with us will receive this newsletter which will provide important protection in the stormy times ahead. If you have not received the newsletter and you want to receive it just write the Temple, P. O. Box 214, Redwood Valley and let us know. Even members of our own staff who have not written within the last three months will not be getting the newsletter this month. **Please** send financial assistance or some valid explanation as to why you can't assist (i.e., **if** you have not sent an offering for the newsletter recently.)

HEALING MINISTRY

We often receive questions related to our healing ministry. The healing ministry of **Pastor** Jones is in <u>no way</u> opposed to medical science. In fact, in over 82 documented cases

3

through the direct encouragement of our Pastor, individuals who had previously refused to seek medical help, went to their own doctors and were saved from serious and fatal conditions in this way. (Cases such as those of Mr. Jim Pugh of Redwood Valley and Mrs. Edith Cordell showed the total remission of what had been diagnosed as cancer.) It is our belief as the scripture states "All good things come down from above." Medical science and the special healing ministry we have witnessed time after time work hand-in-hand for good.

Astounding healings are increasing in number in every service as in the case of Mrs. Fannie E. Johnson of 2211 4th Ave., San Francisco, who was called out by the Divine Gift of God working through Pastor Jones. She was told that she once lived at 24th and College and that her neighbor had sold her something over a year ago of which no one but Pastor Jones and Mrs. Johnson knew. Jim Jones also told her of the illness of cancer which took her mother and of details about her family in Louisiana. He called her out (and placed his hand upon the exact spot (as they did in the early Apostolic days) where she was having severe pain and she then passed a cancerous growth before the eyes of the hundreds present. Ever since that September day in 1970 she has been free of pain and been active in her work and now she attends school in addition to her other work. She has not needed the service of one doctor since that time.

In another astounding case within the last couple of weeks Mrs. Alberta McDead of Route 2, Box 144, Livingston, Texas was called out by name as a visitor to our meeting and told by Pastor Jones that she had four children. She was told of a condition she had in her legs and of an accident that caused a back injury. She was told many, many more details which no one could have known including exact details about items she carried inside a purse she owned and a watch was described vividly which she wasn't even wearing or had in her possession at that time! As Pastor Jones meditated all pain in her back immediately left. She rejoiced freely for the entire rest of the service so grateful that she was free of pain at last.

Of even more wonder are the miraculous protections and warnings given people in each service. Recently, Mrs. Margaret Elsey of 105 S. Idaho St., San Mateo was called out and told the exact address of a house she owned but did not live in. She was told intimate details of her family back in Baton Rouge, Louisiana. She was told the specific condition which took her father and through the meditations of Pastor Jones those same areas of pain were completely relieved and she was protected from the condition which took her father. In still another situation a Mrs. Ann Hammonds of Harrison St. in San Francisco was spared from what would-have-been a fatal car accident as she was called out and told of the aunt who had reared her of which only she knew, and of her relatives in Georgia. As in the cases of Mrs. Albert Stahl and Mrs. Carolyn Layton, precise details of situations to avoid and instructions were given which by the testimony of each enabled them to avoid fatal accidents.

Last week the daughter of Rev. Harry Williams, 858 Arkansas, San Francisco, was miraculousy spared from death in an accident that had been described in detail by a prophecy given by Jim Jones days before the near tragedy took place.

Come and see for yourself the dynamic and astounding miracles of God through His Messenger Jim Jones in every service. In the past two weeks alone we have seen the crippled walk, all kinds of known conditions and illnesses healed, and we have even seen the elements change before our very eyes. We have seen peoples' lives change as they become filled with Christian love and concern for others. Come and be a part of this wonderful humanitarian and Christ-centered work.

Don't miss the radio broadcast every Saturday and Sunday morning starting at 10:00 AM to 10:30 AM on KFAX, 1100 on the radio dial. Hear the inspiring words of Jim Jones!

MESSAGE

Ancient scripture declares "Give no place to the devil." It also emphasizes that "As a man thinketh in his mind so is he." A great deal of scientific evidence has been presented by several American and European research centers and university laboratories as well as eminent psychiatric authorities which give us valid reason to conclude that this is not merely religious subjective opinion, but a scientific rationale based on realistic research. Psychiatrists are bringing to light, daily, information that proves that one can lower his own blood pressure, alter his pulse beat, actually mentally control how much oxygen the body needs to sustain its physiological processes of life. Furthermore, research indicates that one can through trauma alter metabolism, change the color of one's hair and through hypno-suggestion cause breasts to grow to the proper shape idealized by the woman concerned. Case after case has been documented by the world's most eminent psychiatrists of cancer remission

-2-

and the control and actually healing of crippling diseases through mind therapy and/or psych-
analysis. The negative side of the coin also reveals people can pre-determine the date of
their death even to the exact minute as was brought out by Dr. Flanders Dunbar in a case study
where one woman determined that she would die on her own birthday as a sort of symbolic
punishment to her mother for bringing her into the world. This attitude was cultivated in
this particular case study mentioned by Dr. Dunbar from the woman in question hearing her
mother tell the father to "get that brat out of her, I hate her," when the child was still in
the crib. That shows you the power of mind and how early it begins its strong impressions.
Whatever the theological explanations of evil, we have nothing to gain by thinking about the
power of evil in the universe. As the New Testament declares, our only hope is to think on
whatsoever things are pure, lovely and of good report, and so assert, as has been the creed
of all the world's great religions, that you're in the I Am, that you have a healthy mind.
    We have thousands of testimonies in our Temple files that reveal that this attitude of
mind demonstrated by Jim Jones will cause permanent remission and cure of fatal diseases!
When you say I Am you assert the reality of your true existence, not the reality of mere
physical existence which is but temporary and relative as was indicated in the scripture
figuratively by the example of Moses putting his hand into his bosom and drawing it out white
as snow with the dread disease of leprosy and then shortly thereafter restoring his hand to
natural healthy condition by the same process of mind over matter. Your real existence is
Mind. Science shows that the most substantial metal in our universe is composed of nothing
more than energy, atoms, protons, neutrons, electrons. Thus, assert the real I Am that is
independent of body and material circumstances. The body is now scientifically proved to be
merely the vehicle of your mind's expression. If your mind is negative in attitude, medical
science is proving it will produce disease and likewise if positive there is a great deal of
information to indicate that one can almost obtain eternal youth, the cessation of cellular
death (actually cellular life is being controlled in several hypno-therapy studies throughout
the world.) If you so believe, your mind cannot die nor become annihilated. It may change the
form of its expression as Malachi 4:5 shows Elias later became John the Baptist by Jesus'
own words in Matthew 11:14. Yes, you shall if you affirm it, always remain the I Am of health
and peace. You can be a bit of the great ocean of love and power that atomizes the true
consciousness of the highest spiritual unfoldment. Do not think of yourself as material,
but as Mind. Some will say this is an illusion, but even if it were so you have much more to
gain by thinking that you are Mind than you do by thinking you are only matter or under the
control of some diabolical negative demoniac force in the universe. If you do not wish to take
our word for this, come and study the case examples that we have in our Temple to prove the
dynamic of believing in the principle that "This mind can be in you which was also in Christ
Jesus!"

FUTURE SAN FRANCISCO MEETINGS are scheduled June 12 & 13, July 10 & 11, and August 7 & 8
at the Benjamin Franklin Junior High School Auditorium at Geary & Scott Sts. Services start
Saturday night at 7:30 PM and Sunday morning at 11:00 with a free meal following Sunday service.

JULY 10 AND 11 PASTOR JIM JONES WILL CONDUCT A HUMANITARIAN
AND HEALING MEETING AT BENJAMIN FRANKLIN JUNIOR HIGH SCHOOL
ON THE CORNER OF SCOTT & GEARY. THE SATURDAY NIGHT MEETING WILL
START AT 7:30 PM AND THE SUNDAY MEETING WILL BEGIN AT 11:00 A.M.
SEE MESSAGE PAGE 2

NEWS FLASH: We now have confirmation of the Los Angeles meeting. See Page 3 for particulars.

This summer the Temple youth and qualified adults will be taking an extended camping trip in our large commercial busses to provide a worthwhile outing for the youth.

As still another part of our Christian missionary outreach, the Temple pastor, choirs and many members will be conducting services in Los Angeles, Portland, Seattle, and even as far as Vancouver, B.C. We will keep you posted as to future dates and times so that you may contact all your friends in that area and let them know of the inspirational healing and humanitarian service ministry of Pastor Jim Jones.

The Temple has recently purchased a beautiful college dormitory home to house half of the forty-five Temple college young men and women whom we subsidize as they further their education at Santa Rosa Junior College, Sonoma State College and associated nursing schools.

In addition to this we continue to provide an aged home, the fellowship house, manse and our youth center with its indoor heated swimming pool, an animal refuge shelter for homeless pets of all kinds; also, we have the great task of maintaining three large commercial air conditioned busses especially comfortable for trips for our senior citizen members and all our Temple people.

Recently Temple members were assisting around-the-clock in help and supervision of young persons coming off drugs. Over 100 of our Temple youth have been converted to a life of Christian service from the misery of a life in the drug world. Although none of the youth reared in the Temple family has ever turned to drug use, many young people coming into the Temple as teenagers or young adults came to us from the drug world and none who has become a part of the Temple family has ever returned to this kind of life. Most of these youth are in college in our church-sponsored dormitories or the others have very responsible jobs in the community.

If you would like to help in any of these most worthy endeavors, please send your gift to P. O. Box 214, Redwood Valley, California. THE FINANCIAL NEED IS CRITICAL AT THIS TIME! You can also be a sponsor of a college student, helping him financially receive his education and he or she will keep in close communication with you writing you of the activities he or she as a student is undertaking.

BOAT CRUISE! Don't miss our exciting boat cruise departing from Pier 43-1/2 at Fisherman's Wharf, August 7 at 4:00 PM Our Temple Band will be on hand for entertainment as well as a full course banquet meal for all. Tickets may be obtained by calling Mrs. Bessie Johnson at 655-2586 or Mrs. Dorothy Harris at 334-2663.

PLEASE SEND STAMPS: Due to our immense correspondence of over 2000 letters a week, we are in need of postal stamps, since every letter is answered. Please include postal stamps in your letters to the Temple or Pastor Jones.

TO RECEIVE THE NEWSLETTER: Only those who write us and keep in constant communication with us will receive this newsletter which will provide important protection in the stormy times ahead. If you have not received the newsletter and you want to receive it just write the Temple, P. O. Box 214, Redwood Valley and let us know. Even members of our own staff who have not written within the last three months will not be getting the newsletter this month. Please send financial assistance or some valid explanation as to why you can't assist (i.e., if you have not sent an offering for the newsletter recently.)

HEALING MINISTRY

We often receive questions related to our healing ministry. The ministry of Pastor Jones is in no way opposed to medical science. In fact, in over 82 documented cases through the direct encouragement of our Pastor, individuals who had previously refused to seek medical help, went to their own doctors and were saved from serious and fatal conditions in this way. (Cases such as those of Mr. Jim Pugh of Redwood Valley and Mrs. Edith Cordell showed the total remission of what had been diagnosed as cancer.) It is our belief as the scripture states "All good things come down from above." Medical science and the special healing ministry we have witnessed time after time work hand-in-hand for good.

In every service for over twenty years Peoples Temple members and visitors have witnessed scores of healings, special protections and special warnings which have saved lives in the most seemingly hopeless situations.

6

One of the most touching healings was tha' of Mrs. Rosa Ijames, Guest Home owner of Rt. 1, Box 223M, Redwood Valley, Calif. Mrs. Ijames had already had a stroke when she came into Pastor Jones's meeting. Jim Jones called her out by name giving precise details about events happening in her life. As he meditated for her, all symptoms of excruciating pain in her head disappeared and she was delivered from fatal hypertensive stroke through the miraculous power of God healing through Jim Jones.

The greatest miracles witnessed are often the healings of the mind as in the case of Mrs. Faith Kice of 619 Willow Ave., Ukiah, Calif. Psychiatrist, Dr. Shipley of the Child Guidance Center in Indianapolis, Indiana, pronounced her a hopeless schizophrenic and said it was useless to try to work with her. Through the meditation of Pastor Jones, Mrs. Kice is a happily married licensed nurse who is in every way whole of mind and body. She received excellent grades in studies in her field of nursing and is now a responsible and contributing member of society.

In still another case the mind was again restored from hopeless brain damage caused by extensive drug use. Larry Schactt of 1678 Dutton Ave., Santa Rosa, Calif. was delivered from a totally meaningless life and his mind was made "every whit whole" following the meditations of Jim Jones. He is now a college student receiving honors in school and living in one of our church-sponsored dormitories.

We have seen children spared of fatal diseases in scores of instances as in the case of Kathy Richardson. Pastor Jones called out her mother, Mrs. Virginia Richardson, of Box 950, Redwood Valley, Calif. and told her of the lumps on her daughter's chest which she and her daughter had told to no one. Pastor Jones said they would disappear at the end of two weeks and there would be no more sign of that dread disease of cancer. Just exactly as Pastor Jones had stated the lumps had totally vanished at the end of the two week period to the amazement and extreme gratitude of the entire family. This condition has never returned to the child from the date Jim Jones said it would be gone.

A most astounding miracle occurred when Mrs. Rose Shelton, former instructor of cosmotology at the Regina Beauty College in San Francisco, was called out by Pastor Jones and told to immediately stop work or she would have a stroke. She did not heed this warning and one week later as she was conducting her Theory Class, her right side became very, very weak and she could not use her right hand at all. The next morning her right side was totally paralyzed and she could not walk. However, the very next day Pastor Jones contacted her and meditated for her and all ability to use her right side was totally restored and she is perfectly healed to this day. She writes us that "I owe it all to the mighty power of God that works through this modern-day Prophet Jim Jones.

This astounding gift of God healing in every service without fail and the special protection which has spared numerous lives from fatal accidents and illnesses of all types is so vast we could mention only a small number of them and have room in the newsletter for other activities. Lives have totally changed as they have become a part of this wonderful Christ-centered, humanitarian work. Come and see for yourself!

"Message"

Now hear the words of Jesus "These things shall you do and greater because I go to the Father! It is written that ye are Gods and Sons of the most high." Another passage declares that "We are the Temples of the Living God, and As a man thinketh in his mind so is he." I would like to give you a demonstration that took place in Rockefeller Institute where they conducted a series of tests with parasites found on plants which showed that even the lowest order of creatures had the power to call upon Universal Supply for the resources to meet any unusual need. In order to obtain the material, a pot of rose bushes were brought into a room and placed in front of a closed window. If the plants were allowed to dry out, the aphides (parasites), previously wingless, changed to winged insects. After the metamorphosis, the animals leave the plants, fly to the window and then creep upward on the glass. The scientists concluded, it is evident that these tiny insects found that the plants on which they had been thriving were dead and that they could therefore secure nothing more to eat and drink from this source. The only method by which they could save themselves from starvation was to grow temporary wings and fly, which they did. In short, when the source of this primitive life form's sustinence was shut off and they had to find the means of migrating or perish, Universal Mind furnished the means for migration. If this mind, which "I Am" inculcating can thus provide for the meanest of its creatures, is it not logical to suppose that it will do more for us, the highest product of creation, if we but call upon it - if we will but have the faith of a grain of a mustard seed. Determining with Jesus as he said in Sonship Degree, though he was thought to be a servant, he considered it not robbery to be equal with God. In

-2-

that affirmation we have seen thousands healed every month and literally several restored to life, not to mention all the practical demonstrations for human service that have been brought about even on the date we decided and affirmed by Infinite Mind. We have declared we shall not wait for the imaginary and suppositional God in the heavens for the sky is nowhere and is nothing, but everywhere where there is nothing. We shall lift our minds from superstition and bring our conscious concepts concerning heaven into our recognition of something that is no longer superstitious, but as the revelations declared, we've heard a great voice, (a great revolutionary cry) out of the imaginary heaven, saying "Behold the tabernacle or Temple of God is with men, and He will dwell with them and they shall be His people and God himself shall be with them and be their God." And this God, Principle shall wipe away all tears from our eyes and there shall be no more death as a final consumate, neither sorrow, nor crying, neither shall there be any more pain for the former things with this actual recognition of the continual presence of God will be passed away eternally!

Newsletter Writer's Comment

Today one young man, Carl Barnett by name, who was in a local hospital from severe injuries received in an accident which caused neurological involvement and prospective brain damage; decided to affirm this principle "Lo, I am with you always, even unto the end of the world." He did so by seeing Jim Jones as a Fundamental Principle bearer and as a result, he was immediately able to walk with restored health and full return of his vision!

FUTURE SAN FRANCISCO MEETINGS! are scheduled July 10 and 11, and August 7 and 8 at the Benjamin Franklin Junior High School Auditorium at Geary & Scott Sts. Services start Saturday night at 7:30 PM and Sunday morning at 11:00 with a free meal following Sunday's service.

REGULAR SERVICES of People's Temple begin at 11:00 AM Sunday in Redwood Valley with a free banquet communion dinner following each morning service. Our evening service begins at 6:00PM Pastor Jones has been and will be ministering in all of our regular services. Sunday night services close out at 9:30 every Sunday. On Tuesday evening starting at 7:00 PM there is a congregational meeting at the Temple in Redwood Valley. These are Deeper Life Catharsis meetings for development of our spiritual growth. If you would like to spend the weekend in Redwood Valley, you can arrange for housing with one of our families by calling Judy Flowers in San Francisco 864-7113 or by calling Mrs. Neva Sly in Redwood Valley 462-9495.

GREEN AND BLUE CHIP STAMPS ARE URGENTLY NEEDED in order to acquire needed items for the church. Stamps and any canned goods or good used clothing which you would like to donate for use by many needy families can be donated by calling Leona Collier 626-3365 in San Francisco

LEGAL QUESTIONS should be addressed to the attorney who is a public official in our area and an active member of our church. Address your letters to: c/o Attorney, Peoples Temple, P. O. Box 214, Redwood Valley, California 95470.

RESERVATIONS FOR BUS SERVICE to Redwood Valley can be made by calling Caroline Reese in San Francisco at 586-3378 or Regina's Beauty College 346-9879. The bus leaves 1415 Divisadero at 7:30 AM each Sunday morning.

XXXXXXXXXXXXXXXXXXXXXXXXXXXXXXXXXXXXXXXXXXXXXXXXXXXXXXXXXXXXXXXXXXXXXXXXXXXXXXXX
XXXXXXXXXXXXXXXXXXXXXXXXXXXXXXXXXXXXXXXXXXXXXXXXXXXXXXXXXXXXXXXXXXXXXXXXXXXXXXXX
XXXXXXXXXXXXXXXXXXXXXXXXXXXXXXXXXXXXXXXXXXXXXXXXXXXXXXXXXXXXXXXXXXXXXXXXXXXXXXXX
XXXXXXXXXXXXXXXXXXXXXXXXXXXXXXXXXXXXXXXXXXXXXXXXXXXXXXXXXXXXXXXXXXXXXXXXXXXXXXXX

WE NOW HAVE A DEFINITE SCHEDULE FOR A HEALING CAMPAIGN IN LOS ANGELES. THE MEETINGS WILL TAKE PLACE AT FREMONT HIGH SCHOOL AUDITORIUM, 7600 S. SAN PEDRO, LOS ANGELES, CALIFORNIA (OFF OF SLAUSEN) ON SATURDAY, JULY 3 AT 7:30 PM AND SUNDAY JULY 4 AT 2:00 PM. MIRACLE PURPOSES TO EACH OF YOUR LIVES AND THOSE OF YOUR LOVED ONES. IT IS IMPERATIVE ALL INDIVIDUALS PARTICIPATE IN THIS CAMPAIGN.

-3-

SEPTEMBER 11 AND 12 PASTOR JIM JONES WILL CONDUCT A HUMANITARIAN
AND HEALING MEETING AT THE BENJAMIN FRANKLIN JUNIOR HIGH SCHOOL
ON THE CORNER OF SCOTT & GEARY. THE SATURDAY NIGHT MEETING WILL
START AT 7:30 PM AND THE SUNDAY MEETING WILL BEGIN AT 11:00 A.M.

SEE MESSAGE BEGINNING PAGE 2

RADIO BROADCAST ON KFAX - CHANGE OF TIME

Be sure to tune in to our radio broadcast on KFAX 1100 on the dial on Saturday from 10:00
to 10:30 AM and Sunday morning at 7:00 AM to hear the inspiring words of Jim Jones.

VAST EXPANSION AT PEOPLE'S TEMPLE

People's Temple continues to expand its extensive outreach throughout the West Coast. One
thousand three hundred and thirty-six people turned out for our tremendously successful
Indianapolis rally in our huge Temple-owned auditorium there in July. Healings were too
numerous to mention except for a few like that of Mr. George Johnson of 3412 Chicamanga St.,
Dayton, Ohio who had been operated on unsuccessfully for cancer six months before. He was in
immense pain. He was called out by Jim Jones and he passed a growth for all to see. The
excruciating pain in his spine was instantly relieved and he states that he is feeling wonderful still. In another instance a most touching miracle occurred when the relative of
Mrs. Odessa Jones, a 13 year old girl who had had severe epileptic seizures for years was
beginning a seizure. Pastor Jones walked to her saying a few words to here and he put his
fingers in her mouth and she could no longer bite and nash her teeth together as he had
prophesized. Her seizure stopped immediately and she danced and rejoiced in gratitude throughout the entire service.
In another case the Spirit of God in Pastor Jones called out Mrs. Cleo Dwight, 2057 Lafaye
Rd., Lafayette, Indiana, who could barely see anything. After Jim Jones' meditation she was
able to read the print of the Bible to the entire congregation. Truly, the Glory of God is
manifest as the blind regain sight, the crippled walk and growths are expectorated before the
eyes of all present in every service. All these miracles were witnessed in Indianapolis as in
every service. We are now conducting regular services in Indianapolis.
On the week-end of August 14 and 15 three bus loads and numerous cars came up to worship
at our Redwood Valley Center from Los Angeles, Fresno, Stockton, and Sacramento, as well as our
regular busses coming from San Francisco. Scores were healed and protected in this inspirational rally.
On September 4th we will hold a meeting in Vancouver at the John Oliver Secondary School
beginning at 7:00 PM, and on September 5th we will be holding meetings in Seattle at the
Paramount Theater at 11:00 AM, 2:00 PM and 7:30 PM. Be sure to write your friends and relative:
in those areas and tell them of our meetings. In October Pastor Jim Jones will again be
holding meetings in Philadelphia and Indianapolis on the following dates: October 7th, 8th
and 9th in Philadelphia, and October 10th, 11th, 12th and 13th in Indianapolis at People's
Temple on 10th and Delaware Sts. Please write People's Temple, P. O. Box 214, Redwood Valley
with the names and addresses and phone numbers of anyone in these areas so that we can send
them special brochures of our meetings.
In addition to this we continue to provide an aged home, fellowship house, manse and our
youth center with its indoor heated swimming pool, an animal refuge shelter for homeless pets
of all kinds, an organic garden, an orchard, and two college dormitories for the forty-five
college youth whom we sponsor and provide dormitories for in San Francisco while
they receive their college education subsidized by the Temple. If you would like to help in
any of these most worthy endeavors, please send your gift to P.O. Box 214, Redwood Valley,
Calif. THE FINANCIAL NEED IS CRITICAL FOR SUCH MEANINGFUL WORK! You may also be a sponsor of
college student, helping him financially receive his education and he or she will keep in close
communication with you writing you of the activities being undertaken, and recognize you
publically and privately as his or her sponsor.

HEALING MINISTRY

In every service the wonderful Christ that operates through Pastor Jones has such care and
concern for each of us that scores are called out by name, given intimate details of their live:
and healed of all types of disorders. This healing ministry of Pastor Jones in no way opposes
medical science. In fact, in many instances through the direct encouragement of our Pastor,

individuals who had previously refused to seek medical help, went to their own doctors and were saved from serious and even fatal conditions. Medical science and the special healing ministry we have witnessed time after time work hand-in-hand for good. Recently, Mrs. Doxsee Swaney, 280 North Oak, Ukiah was called out in the services while she was at work in another city. The congregation heard many revelations from this Source of Knowledge and Healing including even precise details of a medication she had taken every day for seven years. One of the members of the congregation was so touched and awed by this wonderful force of love that she called Mrs. Swaney at her work and told her of the revelations. She confirmed the many details given of her family members thousands of miles away and all the other facts given by this marvelous and All-knowing powerful Gift in our midst. That very evening she testified that the revelations she was given by Pastor Jones spared her very life!

In another instance, Mrs. Edna Logan of 2452 South Lilly Street, Fresno, was called out by name through Pastor Jones' extraordinary gift of discernment. She was told many things about her life, things so detailed that only a Divine source could reveal them to her. Very importantly, she was told of an operation she had had and that for her health, there was still work to be done. At that very instant, as she confirmed, the wonderful Christ that operates through Jim Jones sent the healing force flowing into her body and she was healed of the horrid cancer that was present.

MESSAGE

As we have been led to believe the radical is left, the conservative establishes himself to the right of the dividing line of political and philosophical thought, but the liberal attempts to pitch his tent seemingly in both camps. The liberal is neither hot nor cold, neither red nor white, just a soft faint almost indistinguishable mixture of the two - a delicate pink, that invariably bleaches when exposed to the rigors of the atmosphere. Verily, tis easy to bleach him, but difficult to increase the life in his makeup. Behold this "yes man", this suave soul perched so calmly upon the fence, aneel in all of his watery glory was never more elusive than he. This shifty straggler sitting with one foot resting lightly in the meadow on each side of the partition. He is the true phenomenon man. He is the one example of an object occupying two places in space at the same time. The liberal can see both sides to every issue and embrace either with equal sincerity. He can defend fervently either side in debate. He wants to hunt with the hounds and run with the rabbits. He is broad and unbiased, so broad in fact that one can never get a grip on his whole person; so unbiased that he never knows what side he is on or when he is on it. He respects everyone's views whether they be lies or the truth. In him knowledge and action are so nicely balanced he cannot act for thinking. Nor can he think lest his thought might lead to action. He sees all sides, hears all sides and speaks on all sides of the subject. The liberal is a puzzle to his fellows and a tragedy to himself for he is unsteadfast and all believing. It is written all Christ-like believers must know in whom they have believed and be persuaded that Christ is able to keep everything that is committed unto Him against that day. We are not in need of liberals who stand for nothing and fall for everything. We need those who will have a definite conviction about their God and their principles, but of course first we must establish where our God is and how to love God. It is written in Scripture one must love God with all their heart, mind, soul, and strength. I declare that it is impossible for one to love an abstract theological spirit or thought. In order to love God and to begin your growth in principle, you must find and know the Word made flesh. Yea, the living God is embodied in human form in the most pure love and unselfed devotion. After all God is love. So, therefore, the instrumentality that embraces the most of God becomes the vehicle or incarnation of God in the earth plane.

It's very important to find your God for "they that know their God will do exploits." It's impossible to achieve anything in the realms of faith until you have determined who your God is and of what His nature and character consists. Remember, anyone that comes to God "Must believe that He is, and that He is the rewarder of those that diligently seek Him." In the realm of People's Temple, men and women of every race and creed are finding their God and they are indeed doing exploits! They are realizing that God in His principle and love is being embodied even in our day and as a result of their faith the cripples are walking, the blind are seeing, the deaf hear and the poor have this anointed Gospel ministered unto him. Signs and wonders of every variety take place every hour on this beautiful acreage of our garden of Eden. We recommend that you find your God and know Him for to "know Him aright is life eternal." This is the satisfaction that we are finding, not only health for our bodies, but immortality that has even worked in the Temples that has literally brought people back from the dead such as Mrs. Emily Leonard, the wife of a former agricultural commissioner and Miss Sherri Richardson

- 2 -

and Mrs. Simpson and Mrs. Esther Mueller, all of Redwood Valley who were literally clinically dead, but were revived by this principle, this Apostolic equalitarian principle and motivated by our Messenger of God to live and to have eternal life within.

We would like to give you one of the benefits of our Divinely inspired conviction and hope that you will search to find the God that you can love with all your heart, mind, soul and strength, and one that you can believe in. I ask do you believe in the God that has been taught in the churches of the past via the theological concepts of yester-year. If you do not believe in your God whole-heartedly, you can achieve nothing, but if you believe in God harmoniously and sympathetically and completely enthusiastically there is nothing that will be denied you which you imagined to do. All things are possible to them that believe! Sincere people find it impossible to believe in an abstract theological idea, but when the Word is made flesh and swells amongst us, then it is indeed possible to believe with all of your heart, mind, soul and strength and to gain the victory over health, Hell and the grave.

TO RECEIVE THE NEWSLETTER: Only those who write us and keep in constant communication with us will receive this newsletter which will provide important protection in the stormy times ahead. If you have not received the newsletter and you want to receive it just write the Temple, P.O. Box 214, Redwood Valley and let us know. Even members of our own staff who have not written within the last three months will not be getting the newsletter this month. Please send financial assistance or some valid explanation as to why you can't assist (i.e., if you have not sent an offering for the newsletter recently.)

PLEASE SEND STAMPS: Due to our immense correspondence of over 2000 letters a week, we are in need of postal stamps, since every letter is answered. Please include postal stamps in your letters to the Temple or Pastor Jones.

DON'T MISS THE RADIO BROADCAST EVERY SATURDAY MORNING STARTING AT 10:00 AM TO 10:30 AM ON KFAX, 1100 ON THE RADIO DIAL AND AT 7:00 AM EACH SUNDAY MORNING. TUNE IN AND HEAR THE INSPIRING WORDS OF JIM JONES!

FUTURE SAN FRANCISCO MEETINGS are scheduled for September 11th and 12th, October 16th and 17th, November 6th and 7th and December 4th and 5th at the Benjamin Franklin Junior High School Auditorium at Geary and Scott Sts. Services start Satuday night at 7:30 PM and Sunday morning at 11:00 with a free meal following the Sunday service.

REGULAR SERVICES of People's Temple begin at 11:00 AM Sunday in Redwood Valley with a free banquet communion dinner following each morning service. Our evening service begins at 6:00 PM. Pastor Jones has been and will be ministering in all of our regular services. Sunday night services close out at 9:30 every Sunday. Every other Wednesday evening starting at 7:00 PM there is a congregational meeting at the Temple in Redwood Valley. These are Deeper Life Catharsis meetings for development of our spiritual growth. If you would like to spend the weekend in Redwood Valley, you can arrange for housing with one of our families by calling Judy Flowers in San Francisco 864-7113 or by calling Mrs. Neva Sly in Ukiah 462-9495.

GREEN AND BLUE CHIP STAMPS ARE URGENTLY NEEDED in order to acquire needed items for the church. Stamps and any canned goods or good used clothing which you would like to donate for use by many needy families can be donated by calling Leona Collier 626-3365 in San Francisco.

LEGAL QUESTIONS should be addressed to the attorney who is a public official in our area and an active member of our church. Address your letters to: c/o Attorney, People's Temple, P. O. Box 214, Redwood Valley, California 95470.

RESERVATIONS FOR BUS SERVICE to Redwood Valley can be made by calling Carolina Reese in San Francisco at 586-3378 or Regina's Beauty College 346-9879. The bus leaves 1415 Divisadero at 7:30 AM each Sunday morning.

- 4 -

11

PEOPLES' TEMPLE
P. O. Box 214
Redwood Valley, Calif. 95470

Nonprofit Organization
U. S. Postage
1.7¢ PAID
San Francisco, Calif.
Permit No. 9729

12

OCTOBER 16 AND 17 PASTOR JIM JONES WILL HOLD A HUMANITARIAN AND HEALING MEETING IN SAN FRANCISCO AT THE BENJAMIN FRANKLIN JR HI SCHOOL ON THE CORNER OF SCOTT AND GEARY. THE SATURDAY MEETING WILL START AT 7:30 PM AND THE SUNDAY MEETING WILL BEGIN AT 11:00 AM (See dates below for other meetings across the country) COME AND ENJOY THE MANY FACILITIES ON OUR BEAUTIFUL 21 ACRES CONNECTED WITH OUR MOTHER CHURCH IN REDWOOD VALLEY, CA. WE HOLD AN ALL DAY HEALING SERVICE EVERY SUNDAY EXCEPT WHEN WE ARE IN SAN FRANCISCO.

Keep tuned to KFAX RADIO STATION in San Francisco to receive information regarding a change in time and schedule so that you will not miss any inspiring words of Pastor Jones. At present, our broadcasts are Sat. morning 10:00 AM to 10:30 AM and Sunday morning 7:00 AM to 7:30 AM.

RADIO BROADCASTS SPREAD ACROSS THE COUNTRY: If you have friends or relatives within receiving distance of any of the following radio stations, please tell them of our broadcasts so they too can hear the "Living Word." SEATTLE, WASHINGTON: Tune in to KHLE 10:30 to 11:00 AM Sat., 1050 on the dial. BLAINE, WASHINGTON: (Reaches into Canada) Tune in to KARI 7:30 to 7:45 AM Sat. 550 on the dial. MIDDLETOWN, OHIO: Tune in to WPFB 8:00 to 8:30 AM Sun. 910 on the dial. INDIANAPOLIS, INDIANA: WBRI 7:30 to 8:00 AM Sat. morning 1500 on the dial and/or WGEE 7:30 to 8:00 AM Sunday 1590 on the dial AM and 103.3 FM. . MEDIA, PENN: (Reaches into Philadelphia) Tune in to WXUR, 4:30 to 4:45 PM Monday thru Friday 690 on the dial.

FUTURE PHILADELPHIA AND INDIANAPOLIS MEETINGS: October 7th and 8th at 7:30 and October 9 at 2:00 PM and 7:00 PM Jim Jones will again be holding meetings in Philadelphia at the Benjamin Franklin Senior Hi School, Green and Broad Sts., Philadelphia, Pa., and in Indianapolis, Ind. October 10 at 2:30 and 7:00 and Oct. 11th, 12th and 13th 2:30 PM and 7:30 PM at the People's Temple, 10th and Delaware Sts., Indianapolis. Please write People's Temple, P.O. Box 214, Redwood Valley, Calif. with the names and addresses and phone numbers of anyone in these areas so that we can send them special brochures of our meetings.

THE WORD IS MADE FLESH: God manifests himself through our Beloved Prophet as we continually receive word of healings from all parts of the world and even this week we were given word of the touching extent of this work in Africa where one follower, Mrs. Eucharia Nzerem, Woano Postal Agency, East Central State, Nigeria, was instantly healed of cancer so metastasized it had eaten away one of her legs. Mrs. Kathy Tropp of P.O. Box 326, Redwood Valley, Ca. testifies "Pastor Jones called me out by name and told me many many intricate details of my life which I had told no one. Revelation revealed a female infection I had two years ago and the exact thought I had at the time that I could never have cancer, but a doctor's examination had proved otherwise. The Prophet spoke the Living Word to me and the cancer was passed from my body for all to bear witness with their own eyes. Eight people in our vast attendance in our Seattle and Vancouver meetings experienced the instant restoration of sight and many who were deaf regained their hearing. If we only could convey to you the beautiful deliverances of the touch of God as one man totally blind in Seattle stood in the back of an assembly crowded with 2,500 people and he was able to tell from far away the exact number of fingers that Pastor Jones held up.

Some weeks ago Pastor Jones was shot by a racist before our eyes. He picked himself up covered by blood and went into the service and healed hundreds of people without any thought for himself. The shot left injuries so extensive, that when we witnessed some put their fingers in the wounds, we could no longer see the fingers for the depth of the wounds. In the past, we have seen our pastor knifed, shot and attacked by bigots. On one occasion some time ago a knife wound instantly closed before our eyes. In every service our local membership of over two thousand witness for themselves undeniable miracles. AS ALL GOOD THINGS COME FROM GOD the healing work of our Pastor does not oppose the field of medicine in any way.

WE ALL MAKE UP THE BODY OF CHRIST Jim Jones, our constant shepherd, leads us in a daily service work that has created an atmosphere of refuge and salvation. But we need every hand in this worthy endeavor so please send your donations as you, too, may have cause to call upon your only true friends in times of crises. We now have three dormitories, senior citizens homes and two other residences that need your support urgently.

BUS SERVICE: Make reservations to come to Redwood Valley on our San Francisco and Oakland buses by calling Caroline Reese in San Francisco 586-3378 or Regina's Beauty College 346-9879. The San Francisco bus leaves 1415 Divisadero at 7:30 each Sunday morning, and our Oakland bus leaves from Ashby and San Pablo at 7:30 AM Sunday morning. People in Richmond or Berkeley who want bus transportation should write People's Temple to make connections with the East Bay bus.

SERVICES IN REDWOOD VALLEY start at 11:00 AM Sunday mornings with a free banquet communion dinner following the service. The evening service begins at 6:00 PM and ends at 8:00 PM. All buses will leave Redwood Valley promptly at 8:00 PM and frequently earlier .

853 people were converted to our Savior in meetings at the Temple this month alone.

PEOPLES' TEMPLE
P. O. Box 214
Redwood Valley, Calif. 95470

Non-Profit Organization
U.S. Postage
PAID
San ____, Calif.
Permit No. 9729

NOVEMBER 6 AND 7 PASTOR JIM JONES WILL HOLD A HUMANITARIAN AND HEALING MEETING
IN SAN FRANCISCO AT THE BENJAMIN FRANKLIN JR HI SCHOOL ON THE CORNER OF SCOTT
AND GEARY. THE SATURDAY MEETING WILL START AT 7:30 PM AND THE SUNDAY MEETING
WILL BEGIN AT 11:00 AM. COME AND ENJOY THE MANY FACILITIES ON OUR BEAUTIFUL
21 ACRES CONNECTED WITH OUR MOTHER CHURCH IN REDWOOD VALLEY, CA. WE HOLD AN
ALL DAY HEALING SERVICE EVERY SUNDAY EXCEPT WHEN WE ARE IN SAN FRANCISCO.
Circulation of this month of October newsletter was 36,000

Keep tuned to KFAX RADIO STATION in San Francisco to receive information regarding changes
in time and schedule so that you will not miss any inspiring words of Pastor Jones. At present,
our broadcasts are Sat. morning 10:00 to 10:30 AM and weekdays from 5:30 to 5:45 AM.
RADIO BROADCASTS SPREAD ACROSS THE COUNTRY: If you have friends or relatives within receiv-
ing distance of any of the following radio stations, please tell them of our broadcasts so they
too can hear the "Living Word." SEATTLE, WASHINGTON: KBLE - 1050 on the dial 10:30 to 11:00 AM
Saturday. BLAINE, WASHINGTON: (Reaches into Canada) KARI - 550 on the dial 7:30 to 7:45 AM
Saturday. MIDDLETOWN, OHIO: WPFB - 910 on the dial 8:00 to 8:30 AM Sunday. INDIANAPOLIS, IND.:
WTLC - 105 FM on the dial 12:00 to 12:15 Sunday midnight. LOS ANGELES, CALIF.: XPRS (formerly
XERB) - 1090 AM on the dial 7:30 to 8:00 AM Sunday and KTYM - 103.9 FM 8:00 to 8:30 AM Sunday.
MEDIA, PENN: (Reaches into Philadelphia) WXUR - 690 on the dial 4:30 to 4:45 PM Monday thru
Friday.
FUTURE LOS ANGELES AND INDIANAPOLIS MEETINGS: Nov. 26, 27 & 28 Pastor Jim Jones will conduct
meetings at the Embassy Auditorium, 9th & Grand Sts., Los Angeles, Calif. The Friday night
meeting will begin at 7:30 PM; the Saturday meetings at 2:00 PM and 7:30 PM, and the Sunday
services at 11:00 AM and 4:00 PM. ******** Pastor Jones will return to Indianapolis Dec.
10th & 11th (2 services each day at 2:30 PM and 7:00 PM) at the People's Temple, 10th & Delaware
Sts, Indpls. Please write People's Temple, P.O. Box 214, Redwood Valley, Calif. with the names,
addresses and phone numbers of anyone in these areas so that we can send them special brochures
of our meetings.
Our Philadelphia and Indianapolis campaigns were a resounding success as scores upon scores
were healed in each service. One of the many dynamic healings is that of Mrs. Ella Mae Kirby of
617 N. East St., Indianapolis who was warned that very evening of those who were planning assault
against her person. She writes that all of the circumstances described to her by this Prophetic
Voice (Oracle) took place exactly as stated, but she was marvelously protected from brutal
attack just as Pastor Jim Jones said she would be. She rejoices with gratefulness.
In our last San Francisco meeting where thousands were in attendance, Mrs. Etta Nixon,
1622 Ingalls was literally raised from the dead. Even after she was given her prescribed nitro-
glycerine by the nurses, there was no response in pulse or heart. It was not until God working
within Jim Jones strolled down to her calmly and meditated for her that she was restored to life
and the normal body functions began to re-appear. Within seconds she was jumping to her feet
with energy in gratitude. In still another astounding example of the Christ within our midst,
Miss Jane Mutschman of 1010 FellSt., San Francisco was called out by name and given exact and
intimate details of her life that no one could know lest God Reveal It. After the Word was sent
by Pastor Jones her body was immediately relieved of the excruciating pain of a cancerous growth
which had plagued her for many months. In every service those in attendance witness the blind
regain sight, the crippled walk, protections of every kind are given to scores including the
marvelous protection from what would-have-been a fatal accident in which all four of the children
of Mrs. Bonnie Beck of 400 Empire, Ukiah, Calif. would have been lost. Due to this Divine
Protection every child was totally made whole when doctors had grave concern for their well-
being. Pastor Jones, who was thousands of miles away at the time of the accident, told others
on the bus of his concern of the Becks back in California to the detail of the exact place on
the road, where danger await them. He said all would be alright and no one would have serious
injury. It is interesting to note that a warning was given months before by Jim Jones never to
travel any distance on a holiday without special permission and this incident did occur on a
holiday. This healing ministry in no way opposes medical science, but rather works hand in hand
with it. In over 82 cases as a result of Pastor Jones special insight and encouragement, fatal
diseases were discovered in persons who would otherwise not have gone to their physicians.
MESSAGE FROM THE PROPHET: If one is interested in coming into the full Sonship after my
example he must be jealous of none; a fount of mercy, treat friend and foe alike; never allow
emotions to rule; have no special loves - treat all alike (love all men but none too much).
Our actions should be of such a character as not to cause dread. Renounce all accomplishments
from the fruit of your work. (Do nothing for reward - but rather for the sheer joy of doing.)
WE ARE IN THE BODY OF CHRIST DISPENSATION: Jim Jones, our constant shepherd, leads us in a

(over)

daily service work that has created an atmosphere of refuge and salvation. But we need every hand in this worthy endeavor so please send your donations as you, too, may have cause to call upon your only true friends in times of crises. We now have three dormitories, senior citizens homes and two other residences that need your support urgently.

BUS SERVICE: Make reservations to come to Redwood Valley on our San Francisco and Oakland buses by calling Caroline Reese in Oakland 635-9761 or Leona Collier in San Francisco 626-3365. The San Francisco bus leaves 1415 Divisadero at 7:30 each Sunday morning, and our Oakland bus leaves from Ashby and San Pablo at 7:30 AM Sunday morning. People in Richmond or Berkeley who want bus transportation should write People's Temple to make connections with the East Bay bus.

SERVICES IN REDWOOD VALLEY start at 11:00 AM Sunday mornings with a free banquet communion dinner following the service. The evening service begins at 6:00 PM and ends at 8:00 PM. All buses will leave Redwood Valley promptly at 8:00 PM and frequently earlier.

Our vast human service ministry provides an aged home, three college dormitories in Santa Rosa and San Francisco, a fellowship hall and manse, and ministers to the needs of hundreds in legal difficulties, with hospital costs, with care during times of family crises such as unemployment and illness and many activities in our youth center with heated indoor pool and recreation area.

Nonprofit Organization
U.S. Postage
1.74 PAID
San Francisco Calif.
Permit No. 9729

PEOPLES' TEMPLE
P.O. Box 214
Redwood Valley, Calif. 95470

BEAUTIFUL COLOR PRINT OF PASTOR JIM JONES - SEE OVER.

JANUARY 15 AND 16 PASTOR JIM JONES WILL HOLD A HUMANITARIAN AND HEALING
MEETING IN SAN FRANCISCO AT THE BENJAMIN FRANKLIN JUNIOR HIGH SCHOOL ON
THE CORNER OF SCOTT AND GEARY. THE SATURDAY MEETING WILL BEGIN AT
7:30 PM AND THE SUNDAY MEETING AT 11:00 AM.

RADIO BROADCASTS

Be sure to tune in to the radio broadcast in your area. We have had reports that
the broadcast on XPRS out of Los Angeles is being heard nation-wide all the way from
Canada to the Gulf of Mexico.

SCHEDULE OF FUTURE MEETINGS

SAN FRANCISCO: The next scheduled meetings at Benjamin Franklin Junior High School
in San Francisco will be January 15 and 16, and February 19 and 20.

LOS ANGELES: On January 8, 1972 at 6:00 AM our buses will load and depart for
Redwood Valley from in front of the Embassy Auditorium, 9th and Grand Sts. in Los
Angeles. We have reservations already for seven buses so get your reservation in as
soon as possible. Reserve seats by writing P.O. Box 214, Redwood Valley 95470.
Roundtrip fare will be $15.00 for adults - one-half fare for children.

On January 22nd and 23rd Pastor Jones will return to Los Angeles at the Embassy
Auditorium, 9th and Grand Sts. The Saturday meetings will be held at 2 and 7 PM and
the Sunday meetings will be held 11 AM and 4 PM. In our last Los Angeles campaign
amongst many other healings we saw a lady who had been crippled for 12 years drop her
crutches and run away rejoicing. We also saw others leave their wheelchairs. In our
Indianapolis campaign we saw healing of many who were crippled, deaf, and blind.

PSYCHIATRIST CONFIRMS HEALINGS ARE REAL!!

Dr. I.H. Perkins, Director of the Drug Abuse Program at Camarillo State Hospital
and former Director of the Drug Abuse Program at Mendocino State Hospital, stated
recently: "The healings of Pastor Jones are undeniably real, marvelous. When you see
them with your own eyes there is no question about it. Jim Jones is a wonderful person
and he's doing great work." He said we certainly have his permission to quote him.
Karen Layton, 765A Apple Ave., Ukiah, Calif. 95482.

TEMPLE ACTIVITIES

The regular worship services at the mother church and community center on our
beautiful acreage in Redwood Valley are now all free communion banquets held on Wednesday
at 7:30 PM and Sunday at 11:00 AM. Come and enjoy the many facilities on the acreage
here. Our vast human service ministry provides a senior citizens' home, a community
and youth center with large indoor heated swimming pool and recreation area, a drug
rehabilitation center, a fellowship hall, manse and animal refuge. This semester the
Temple is sponsoring 58 young people attending college, most of whom are living in the
four college dormitories of the Temple. Seven of these students are studying to be
medical doctors. The Temple has also acquired a new convalescent home to enable us to
meet the geriatric needs of our senior citizens if and when they arise.

Because of the many animals which have been left for us to care for, our animal
refuge shelter continues to grow. If you have a special concern for animals and would
like to donate food for the animal shelter, please bring or send it to the Valley.

Any canned goods or food which you would like to donate to be used by needy families
of all races and religions can also be brought to the mother church in Redwood Valley.

URGENT   The many facets of this wonderful service ministry need your blue and
green trading stamps. We need to furnish our children's home, the
new convalescent home and our community center as well as the college   URGENT
dormitories. We also need postage stamps in our vast mailing program.
Every letter received is personally answered. Few stamps are included
in correspondence to us, so include as many as you can spare.

DON'T MISS THE BEAUTIFUL COLOR PRINT OF PASTOR JIM JONES - SEE OVER.

17

Nonprofit Organization
U.S. Postage
1.74 PAID
San Francisco, CA
Permit No. 9729

People's Temple
P.O. Box 214
Redwood Valley, CA 95470

PEOPLE'S TEMPLE RADIO BROADCAST SCHEDULE
Don't miss the Living Word spoken on the air!
The Voice of People's Temple can now be heard over most of the United States, Canada, and Mexico.

NATIONAL	XPRS (Formerly XERB)	1090 KC	Sunday	
			Pacific Standard Time	9:00 PM
			Mountain Standard Time	10:00 PM
			Central Standard Time	11:00 PM
			Eastern Standard Time	Midnight
SAN FRANCISCO	KFAX	1100 KC	Monday through Friday	5:30 AM
			Saturday	10:00 AM
SEATTLE	KBLE	1050 KC	Saturday	10:30 AM
	KBLE-FM	93.3 MC	Monday through Friday	5:45 PM
BLAINE, WASH.	KARI	550 KC	Saturday	7:30 AM
INDIANAPOLIS	WTLC-FM	105 MC	Sunday	Midnight
MIDDLETOWN, OHIO	WPFB	910 KC	Sunday	8:00 AM

BE SURE TO TAKE ADVANTAGE OF OUR BEAUTIFUL COLOR PRINT OFFER

FEBRUARY 19 AND 20 PASTOR JIM JONES WILL HOLD A HUMANITARIAN AND HEALING MEETING IN
SAN FRANCISCO AT THE BENJAMIN FRANKLIN JUNIOR HIGH SCHOOL ON THE CORNER OF SCOTT AND
GEARY. THE SATURDAY MEETING WILL BEGIN AT 7:30 PM AND THE SUNDAY MEETING AT 11:00 AM.

RADIO BROADCASTS
The Voice of People's Temple can be heard throughout the nation on XPRS out of Los
Angeles and on several other stations locally. Be sure to tune in to the broadcast in your
area.

MIRACULOUS HEALINGS
Our meetings in Los Angeles January 22nd and 23rd were a spectacular success! Every
seat in all four balconies and on the main floor was filled and there was standing room
only in the Embassy Auditorium as we watched, among other healings, 15 people come out of
wheelchairs. Every single one of them had been hopelessly crippled for years. Mrs. Mary
Aikens of 642 N. Poinsettia Ave., Compton 90221, was suffering from a fatal kidney
disease, a nervous disorder and had been chairbound for many years. Her daughter, who
was with her, had been a disbeliever, but God spoke the healing Word through Pastor Jones
and Mrs. Aikens was instantly released from her wheelchair and began walking down the
aisle, totally healed, walking for the first time in over 10 years. The next morning she
got up and cooked breakfast. So surprised was her daughter that she phoned Pastor Jones
in Redwood Valley to apologize for not believing the miraculous work Christ manifested
through him, and she is now a believer in this marvelous power.
At our last campaign in Seattle every seat on the lower floor of the Moore Theater
and many in the balcony were filled. Not only were the people there in numbers, but
they were also there in mind and spirit. While Pastor Jones ministered in person to the
needs of his congregation in Redwood Valley, many in Seattle were called out through his
workers there, told intimate details of their lives and were delivered of every kind of
disease and ailment -- this while Pastor Jones was a thousand miles to the south!

MAKE YOUR RESERVATIONS NOW!!
Everyone interested in coming to our San Francisco meetings the 19th and 20th and to
Redwood Valley the 26th and 27th please contact Mrs. Corine Liggins at 232-1749, 180 E.
30th, Los Angeles, California 90011, or Mrs. Melvina Green at 266-7854, 2274 S. Lotus,
Fresno, California 93706. Also, please write us at P.O. Box 214, Redwood Valley,
California 95470, to reserve a seat. Our buses will load and leave from in front of the
Embassy Auditorium at 6 AM on the 19th and on the 26th.
The next scheduled meeting at Benjamin Franklin Junior High School in San Francisco
will be March 18th and 19th.
All of our friends in the Pacific Northwest are invited to come to Redwood Valley,
California March 11. Please make reservations through our Seattle coordinators, Mr. and
Mrs. Harold Flowers, 3405 E. Pine, Seattle, Washington 98122, EA3 5836, and by writing
P.O. Box 214, Redwood Valley. Buses will load and leave from in front of the Moore
Theater in Seattle at 12 noon Saturday, March 11th.

TEMPLE ACTIVITIES
We are currently in the process of purchasing a Children's Home which houses 14 guests
on 39 acres of lovely Redwood Valley land. We are also purchasing three new Senior
Citizens' Homes. Only this week a caucasian and just last week a black lady moved into
our Senior Citizens' Homes. Where there is need we take in those who are not members.
These homes are also available to our own members should the need arise. To date we have
had no need to utilize these facilities.
To help defray these costs we would greatly appreciate your contribution. Do not
send us money because of our spiritual healing work but because you wish to support the
Christian service we render to needy humanity. Your blue and green trading stamps and
any postage stamps you can send to help with our vast mailing program would also be
greatly appreciated. Many blessings follow those who support this ministry.

BEAUTIFUL COLOR PRINT OF PASTOR JIM JONES - SEE OVER.

SPECIAL OFFER

We have available two beautiful color prints of Pastor Jones for $5.00 each, one taken on the steps of the Capitol Building as we were taking 225 of our youngsters to interview our congressman on the very floor of the House of Representatives. The other was taken in front of the Temple in Redwood Valley. Proceeds from the sale of these prints will support our Christian Service Ministry which includes 4 church-sponsored dormitories where most of our 58 college students are housed. The pictures have been a blessing to many. Scores of testimonies have stressed that they are very effective reminders of the wonderful deliverance and healing power and Christ-like attributes which characterize the ministry of this outstanding Prophet of God. Our supply is limited, so please write soon.

Nonprofit Organization
U.S. Postage
1.7¢ PAID
San Francisco CA
Permit No. 9729

People's Temple
P.O. Box 214
Redwood Valley, CA 95470

PEOPLE'S TEMPLE RADIO BROADCAST SCHEDULE
Don't miss the Living Word spoken on the air!
The Voice of People's Temple can now be heard over most of the United States, Canada, and Mexico.

NATIONAL	XPRS (Formerly XERB)	1090 KC	Sunday	
			Pacific Standard Time	9:00 PM
			Mountain Standard Time	10:00 PM
			Central Standard Time	11:00 PM
			Eastern Standard Time	Midnight
SAN FRANCISCO	KFAX	1100 KC	Monday through Friday	5:30 AM
			Saturday	10:00 AM
SEATTLE	KBLE	1050 KC	Saturday	10:30 AM
	KBLE-FM	93.3 MC	Monday through Friday	5:45 PM
BLAINE, WASH.	KARI	550 KC	Saturday	7:30 AM
MIDDLETOWN, OHIO	WPFB	910 KC	Sunday	8:00 AM

20

MARCH 18 AND 19 PASTOR JONES WILL HOLD A HUMANITARIAN AND HEALING SERVICE IN SAN FRANCISCO AT THE BENJAMIN FRANKLIN JUNIOR HIGH SCHOOL ON THE CORNER OF SCOTT AND GEARY. THE SATURDAY MEETING WILL BEGIN AT 7:30 PM AND THE SUNDAY MEETING AT 11:00 AM.

RADIO BROADCASTS. Be sure to tune in to the life-saving Voice of People's Temple broadcast in your area. XPRS out of Los Angeles can be heard throughout many parts of the country. Our broadcast on KFAX has been changed from 10:00 to 10:30 to 11:00 to 11:30 Saturday mornings. beginning March 4.

MAKE YOUR RESERVATIONS NOW!! Those wishing to come to our Los Angeles meetings March 25 and 26 please make reservations with the bus coodinators nearest you listed on the other side. (NOTE: BUSES WILL NOT BE SENT TO SAN JOSE AND SEATTLE.) Those from Fresno wishing to come to our San Francisco meetings March 18 and 19 please contact Mrs. Melvina Green. Our next San Francisco Rally will be April 8 and 9. Our next campaign in Seattle will be April 15 and 16.

ATTENTION! We are planning now for another trip East from June 19 through the week of July 3. More details later. Our last trip East was a real joy for us all. The highlight of the trip was an educational visit to Washington, D.C. to see historical sites and meet our Representatives, who conducted us on tours through Congress.

SCORES HEALED IN EVERY SERVICE. The lame are made to walk, the blind to see and people suffering with nearly every affliction known to man are beautifully healed of their conditions. Come and see for yourself, as did thousands in our January Los Angeles meetings and thousands more in our February San Francisco meetings. Fifteen left wheelchairs in Los Angeles alone, and cripples have been healed in every service since. In San Francisco every seat on every floor was filled; chairs were placed in the aisles. Many of the faithful regular members lined the walls, in some places several deep. There was very little standing room left. Among the many spectacular miracles in our Los Angeles campaign was the healing of 6-year-old Larry Rocqremore of Los Angeles, who was healed instantly of an extremely severe asthmatic condition. The mighty power of God moved through Pastor Jim Jones, who called the child out and immediately this distressing condition vanished. After running all the way down from the balcony at Pastor Jones' command to "come running to me," he showed absolutely no distressing symptoms and was not even out of breath! In our last San Francisco meeting more than 2,000 watched as God through Pastor Jones called Mrs. Lodie Harris out of her wheelchair. A broken bone that previously would not mend was miraculously healed. She had despaired because she had not been able to work for so long. When the Word of Life was spoken by God's anointed Prophet, she left her wheelchair and ran down the aisle screaming "I can walk, I can walk!" then "I can dance!" She danced for everyone to see. She was as jubilant and bouncy as a child who had never experienced pain. In another astounding incident of protection, Rev. Mabel Davis of San Jose was called out from her seat way in the rear of the balcony and told of a precise item that belonged to her but she did not have in her possession at that time. She was told many details of her life and spared from a broken neck by special prophetic warning. She later confirmed to the exact detail that what this prophet of God spoke to her had indeed spared her life. PLEASE SEND THE NAMES AND ADDRESSES OF YOUR RELATIVES IN YOUR AREA TO P.O. BOX 214, REDWOOD VALLEY, SO WE CAN TELL THEM OF THIS WONDERFUL LIFE-GIVING MINISTRY OF GOD WORKING THROUGH OUR BELOVED PASTOR JIM JONES.

REDWOOD VALLEY ACTIVITIES. Our ministry is flourishing as People's Temple continues to acquire property in Redwood Valley. Our loving Pastor has promised quiet resting places for those in their golden years and for rejected and abused children. Free banquet services begin on Sundays at 11 AM and on Wednesdays promptly at 7 PM. All should attend as many meetings as possible as you never know when God will reach your condition through the Spirit of Prophecy and Healing. Please call the coordinator in your area for details of bus transportation. Also, be sure to ask the secretary in your area for details of our midweek Deeper Life Service.

BEAUTIFUL COLOR PRINTS AVAILABLE. We now have available several beautiful color prints of Pastor Jim Jones. You may choose one of him wearing a robe or one of him wearing a suit. Your donation of $5 per print will help support our Christian Service Ministry, which includes sponsoring 58 college students in our guaranteed education program. Remember, many people have reported deliverance from illness and accidents by thinking on the Divine Love personified in these pictures.

THIS SANE SPIRITUAL HEALING MINISTRY IN NO WAY OPPOSES MEDICAL SCIENCE, for "all good things come down from above." Many people have sought medical attention (of their own choosing) for the first time because they were encouraged to do so by this Divine Prophet of God, often with the result that they were spared of illnesses and potentially fatal conditions.

To help defray the costs of our extensive human service ministry, we would greatly appreciate any contribution you can make. Our animal refuge that takes in every stray, our 4 college dorms, and our various retirement homes all continue to serve the needs of the community but at great expense. Do not send us money because of our spiritual healing work but because you wish to support the Christian service we render to needy humanity.

BUS COORDINATORS

San Francisco	Miss Jane Mutschmann	(415) 864-7113
		(415) 863-3290
	Mrs. Leona Collier	(415) 626-3365
Oakland	Mrs. Elsie Maddox	(415) 444-1857
Berkeley	Mrs. Mattie Wimberly	(415) 654-3829
Richmond	Mrs. Mary Green	(415) 235-3209
San Mateo	Mrs. Margaret Elsey	(415) 343-0722
Palo Alto	Mrs. Mary Lindo	(415) 325-2589
San Jose	Mrs. Mabel Davis	(415) 272-0871
Fresno	Mrs. Melvina Green	(209) 266-7854
Los Angeles	Mrs. Corine Liggins	(213) 232-1749
Seattle	Mr.&Mrs. Harold Flowers	(206) 323-5836
	Mrs. Darnell	(206) 323-8222
	Mr.&Mrs. John Kostelnik	(604) 929-8107

REMINDER: Your blue and green trading stamps and any postage stamps you can send to help with our vast and growing mailing program will be appreciated. Many blessings follow those who support this ministry!

PEOPLE'S TEMPLE RADIO BROADCAST SCHEDULE
Don't miss the Living Word spoken on the air!
The Voice of People's Temple can now be heard over most of the United States, Canada, and Mexico.

NATIONAL	XPRS (Formerly XERB)	1090 KC	Sunday	
			Pacific Standard Time	9:00 PM
			Mountain Standard Time	10:00 PM
			Central Standard Time	11:00 PM
			Eastern Standard Time	Midnight
SAN FRANCISCO	KFAX	1100 KC	Monday through Friday	5:30 AM
			Saturday	11:00 AM
SEATTLE	KBLE	1050 KC	Saturday	10:30 AM
	KBLE-FM	93.3 MC	Monday through Friday	5:45 PM
BLAINE, WASH.	KARI	550 KC	Saturday	7:30 AM
MIDDLETOWN, Ohio	WPFB	910 KC	Sunday	8:00 AM

APRIL 8 AND 9 PASTOR JONES WILL HOLD A HUMANITARIAN AND HEALING SERVICE IN SAN FRANCISCO AT THE BENJAMIN FRANKLIN JUNIOR HIGH SCHOOL ON THE CORNER OF SCOTT AND GEARY. THE SATURDAY MEETING WILL BEGIN AT 7:30 PM AND THE SUNDAY MEETING AT 11:00 AM.

REDWOOD VALLEY. April 1 and 2 we will be in Redwood Valley instead of Sacramento as planned. SEATTLE. Those wishing to attend our Seattle meetings on Saturday, April 15 (2:30 and 7:00 PM) and Sunday, April 16 (10:30 AM) at the Masonic Temple at 801 E. Pine St., make your reservations now. If anyone from the Los Angeles or Fresno areas is interested in coming up a few days early and going to Seattle with us, please let us know through your bus coordinators. SAN FRANCISCO. We will hold two weekend rallies in San Francisco, one on April 8 and 9, and another on April 22 and 23. Those from Fresno who plan to attend either of these weekends, please contact Mrs. Melvina Green at (209) 266-7854. Those from other areas, including Los Angeles and Sacramento, contact the coordinator nearest you. SPECIAL NOTE: April 8 at 3:30 PM there is a boat ride leaving from Pier 43 1/2 in San Francisco with Pastor Jones planning to lead it. You may call your coordinators or write P.O. Box 214, Redwood Valley, Calif. 95470, for reservations. LOS ANGELES. We will be in Los Angeles again April 29 and 30. Please contact your bus coordinator for details of time and place because we may not be at the Embassy Auditorium.

MAY: The Word has spread to Sacramento! We will hold services there the 1st week in May, details to follow. On May 21 and 22 we will again be in San Francisco at Benjamin Franklin Junior High School. On May 27 and 28, we will again be in Los Angeles, at the Embassy Auditorium.

JUNE: Plan now to bring the good news of Christ to the East Coast with us when we return there June 19 through July 4. Details of this trip will be released.

THE MOST MIRACULOUS MINISTRY ON THE FACE OF THE EARTH

Meeting after meeting, month after month, there is standing room only left in our services as Divine Compassion reaches out to every infirmity, every affliction, to ease the heavy burden of suffering. This Divine Compassion gives precise revelations that no man could possibly know, often of events that took place many years in the past or that are currently taking place many miles from the meeting. Often it even tells of events that are yet to happen. Fifteen hopelessly crippled people were healed in our last Los Angeles campaign alone. In addition to all the other miracles, the crippled have been healed in every meeting since. Just last Sunday (March 12) in Redwood Valley, the marvelous God-given gift of discernment working through Pastor Jones called out Sister Myrtle Ritchie, who had suffered a terrible stroke that paralyzed the left side of her body. Pastor Jones told her that she was originally from St. Louis and that she had been having trouble with her high blood pressure for the last 2 hours. He described a picture she had in her house of Jesus praying in Gethsemane. He told her how many sisters and brothers she had; that she had lost a loved one in World War I; that she sometimes visited a specific residence. He named her precise birthday, and he even told her the brand names of several of the foods she liked to eat. She confirmed each revelation as it was given to her. Finally she was told to come running as fast as she could. She did and was instantly healed of her paralysis! The dear woman was filled with joy. In the same meeting Christ working through Pastor Jones called a woman out by her house number, asking if 1204 were her address. It was. The Holy Spirit then revealed the very type of gold figurine she had in her home; that she had a blue buttoned-down sweater; that she had 3 children; and described an exact picture of Jesus she had on display. Pastor Jones told her she suffered from severe arthritis and rheumatism. Finally he told her to come running out to him. She did, and, like Mrs. Ritchie, she was instantly made ever whit whole. Pastor Jones told her, "No rheumatism in your body now. Try it, it's done!" She cried and rejoiced "Amazing! Amazing!"

The end of the rainbow is at Redwood Valley. Senior citizens relax in their own church-owned residences. Neglected or abused children find a haven in our Children's Homes. No stray is turned away from our animal shelter, where we now have over 40 cats and a wide variety of other animals. Our Community Center provides a heated indoor swimming pool for therapy as well as recreation. Free banquet meals are served in every Wednesday meeting in Redwood Valley so as to bring back the spirit of the early church.

BEAUTIFUL COLOR PRINTS AVAILABLE.. We now have available several beautiful color prints of Pastor Jim Jones. You may choose one of him wearing a robe or one of him wearing a suit. Your donation of $5 per print will help support our Christian Service Ministry, which includes sponsoring 58 college students in our guaranteed education program. Remember, many people have reported deliverance from illness and accidents by thinking on the Divine Love personified in these pictures.

THIS SANE SPIRITUAL HEALING MINISTRY IN NO WAY OPPOSES MEDICAL SCIENCE, for "all good things come down from above." Many people have sought medical attention for the first time because they were encouraged to do so by this Divine Prophet of God, often with the result that they were spared of illnesses and potentially fatal conditions.

To help defray the costs of our extensive human service ministry, we would greatly appreciate any contribution you can make. Do not send us money because of our spiritual healing work but because you wish to support the Christian service we render to needy humanity. Many blessings follow those who support this ministry!

REMINDER: Your blue and green trading stamps and any postage stamps you can send to help with our vast and growing mailing program will be much appreciated.

REGULAR SERVICES

Services in Redwood Valley start at 11AM every Sunday morning when no out-of-town meeting is scheduled. A free banquet communion dinner follows the service. The evening service begins at 6PM, and all busses will leave Redwood Valley immediately after evening service and frequently earlier.

BUS SERVICE

You can make reservations to come to almost all of our services, in Redwood Valley and elsewhere, on our modern air-conditioned Greyhound-type buses. If you are in or near the cities listed, call:

San Francisco	Mrs. Leona Collier	(415) 626-3365
San Francisco	Miss Jane Mutschman	(415) 863-3290
Oakland	Mrs. Elsie Maddox	(415) 444-1857
Berkeley	Mrs. Mattie Wimberly	(415) 654-3829
Richmond	Mrs. Mary Green	(415) 235-3209
San Rafael	Mrs. Bea Morton	(415) 457-3530
San Mateo	Mrs. Margaret Elsey	(415) 343-0722
Palo Alto	Mrs. Mary Lindo	(415) 325-2589
San Jose	Mrs. Mable Davis	(415) 272-0871
Sacramento	Mrs. E. Tennerson	(916) 383-8735
Fresno	Mrs. Melvina Green	(209) 266-7854
Los Angeles	Mrs. Corine Liggins	(213) 232-1749
Seattle	Mr. & Mrs. Harold Flowers	(206) 323-5836
	Mrs. Darnell	(206) 323-8222
	Mr. & Mrs. John Kostelnik	(206) 784-3045

Elsewhere, write to People's Temple to make connections with the nearest of our large fleet of busses.

Nonprofit Organization
U.S. Postage
1.74 PAID
San Francisco, CA
Permit No. 9729

People's Temple
P.O. Box 214
Redwood Valley, CA 95470

PEOPLE'S TEMPLE RADIO BROADCAST SCHEDULE

Don't miss the Living Word spoken on the air!

The Voice of People's Temple can now be heard over most of the United States, Canada, and Mexico.

NATIONAL	XPRS (Formerly XERB)	1090 KC	Sunday	
			Pacific Standard Time	9:00 PM
			Mountain Standard Time	10:00 PM
			Central Standard Time	11:00 PM
			Eastern Standard Time	Midnight
SAN FRANCISCO	KFAX	1100 KC	Monday through Friday	5:30 AM
			Saturday	11:00 AM
SEATTLE	KBLE	1050 KC	Saturday	10:30 AM
	KBLE-FM	93.3 MC	Monday through Friday	5:45 PM
BLAINE, WASH.	KARI	550 KC	Saturday	7:30 AM
MIDDLETOWN, OHIO	WPFB	910 KC	Sunday	8:00 AM

PROPHETIC REVELATION AND HEALING

It is almost impossible to imagine the dynamic miracles we have witnessed in every service, as in our recent services when Mrs. Rosetta Lewis, 303 Oak Street, San Francisco got up off her crutches and walked at the Word of the Pastor. She had not been able to take a step without her crutches for over 1½ years due to a serious accident. But immediately upon the meditation of Pastor Jim Jones she arose and literally *ran* around the room rejoicing and crying "I can walk, I can walk!" In still another instance Mrs. Maude Smith of 801 Haight Street, San Francisco, was called out by name and told intricate details of her home, of her past, and of relatives thousands of miles away. Mrs. Smith was then immediately healed of her serious condition and was able to throw down her crutch and danced freely in the Spirit, where before she could not even walk without the aid of a crutch.

Yet another stunning example of the power of the Spirit is that of the healing of Mrs. Marceline LeTourneau, a prominent teacher formerly of the Assemblies of God. Sister LeTourneau, who came out to California in our modern busses to be a part of the ministry of Pastor Jones, was instantly healed of an equilibrium problem which had plagued her for many years. She now resides in our Senior Residence Home, teaches the entire congregation about the Sonship ministry, and now dances in the Spirit when inspired, which she reports she had not been able to do for years due to her invalid condition. Sister LeTourneau recently brought to our services a friend of hers, Mrs. Cecil Pipkin of Modesto, who was dying. She was called out and numerous details of her life were revealed to her by the Prophetic Voice of Jim Jones. Miraculously she is now walking around with health and energy, thanks to the meditations of Pastor Jim Jones. One could go on and on describing the astounding protection and healings of all kinds of ailments wrought to scores of those in attendance.

KNOW THE SERVANT OF GOD

As the Apostles said of old, "I speak in the person of Christ." Our Pastor has declared that he comes in that same Spirit. Follow Him as He manifests Christ and He will lead you into the promised land (into a Heaven beyond your fondest dream or imagination). Who else in these times fulfills the scripture so well (that they who live Godly in Christ Jesus shall suffer persecutions) and who else demonstrates the gifts and the fruits of the Holy Spirit so beautifully? *Know this Servant of God who labors so remarkably in your midst.* Many can say because of Him and the Christ that works through Him that though I were dead, yet do I live; though I were blind, now do I see.

MINISTRY OF SERVICE TO ALL

Our vast human service ministry provides a senior citizens' home, a community and youth center with large indoor heated swimming pool and recreation area, a drug rehabilitation center where 108 have been rescued from meaningless lives of drugs, a fellowship hall, manse, and animal refuge. This semester the Temple is sponsoring 58 young people attending college, most of whom are living in the four college dormitories we own and operate. We regularly minister to the needs of hundreds in legal difficulties, with hospital costs, and with care during times of family crisis such as unemployment and illness. We need every hand in this worthy endeavor, so please keep your donations coming as you, too, may need to call upon your only true friends in times of crisis.

IMPORTANT ANNOUNCEMENT

We need to hear from people with supportive letters if you wish us to continue to come regularly to your area. In many areas we don't even take an offering; thus, it is *vital,* considering that no church could do more to help mankind, that you write *soon.*

PEOPLE'S TEMPLE OUT-OF-TOWN MEETINGS

LOS ANGELES	EMBASSY AUDITORIUM 9th & Grand Streets	Friday, November 26 . . . . 7:00PM Saturday, November 27 . . . . . .2:00 & 7:00PM Sunday, November 28 . . . . .11:00AM . . . . 2:00, 4:00, & 7:00PM
SAN FRANCISCO	BENJAMIN FRANKLIN J. H. S. Auditorium Scott & Geary Streets	Saturday, December 4 . . . . 7:00PM Sunday, December 5 . . . . .11:00AM
INDIANAPOLIS	PEOPLE'S TEMPLE 10th & Delaware Streets	Friday, December 10 . . . . . . .2:30 & 7:00PM Saturday, December 11 . . . . . .2:30 & 7:00PM
VANCOUVER, B.C.	JOHN OLIVER SCHOOL 530 East 41st Avenue	Sunday, December 26 . . . . 7:30PM Monday, December 27 . . . . . .2:00 & 7:30PM Tuesday, December 28 . . . . . .2:00 & 7:30PM
SEATTLE	MOORE THEATER 2nd Avenue & Virginia Street	Wednesday, December 29 . . . . .4:00 & 7:00PM Thursday, December 30 . . . . .4:00 & 7:00PM Friday, December 31 . . . . . . .4:00 & 7:00PM

BE SURE TO ATTEND THE MEETINGS IN YOUR AREA!

BUS SERVICE

You can make reservations to come to almost all of our services, in Redwood Valley and elsewhere, on our modern air-conditioned Greyhound-type buses. If you are in or near the cities listed, call:

San Francisco	Mrs. Leona Collier	(415) 626-3365
Oakland	Mrs. Elsie Maddox	(415) 444-1857
Berkeley	Mrs. Mattie Wimberly	(415) 654-3829
Fresno	Mrs. Melvina Green	(209) 266-7854
Los Angeles	Mrs. Corine Liggins	(213) 232-1749

Elsewhere, write to People's Temple to make connections with the nearest of our large fleet of busses.

REGULAR SERVICES

Services in Redwood Valley start at 11AM every Sunday morning when no out-of-town meeting is scheduled. A free banquet communion dinner follows the service. The evening service begins at 6PM and ends at 8PM. All busses will leave Redwood Valley promptly at 8PM and frequently earlier.

Nonprofit Organization
U.S. Postage
PAID 1.7¢
San Francisco, CA
Permit No. 9729

People's Temple
P.O. Box 214
Redwood Valley, CA 95470

PEOPLE'S TEMPLE RADIO BROADCAST SCHEDULE
Don't miss the Living Word spoken on the air!
The Voice of People's Temple can now be heard over most of the United States, Canada, and Mexico.

NATIONAL	XPRS (Formerly XERB)	1090 KC	Sunday	
			Pacific Standard Time	9:00 PM
			Mountain Standard Time	10:00 PM
			Central Standard Time	11:00 PM
			Eastern Standard Time	Midnight
SAN FRANCISCO	KFAX	1100 KC	Monday through Friday	5:30 AM
			Saturday	10:00 AM
SEATTLE	KBLE	1050 KC	Saturday	10:30 AM
	KBLE-FM	93.3 MC	Monday through Friday	5:45 PM
BLAINE, WASH.	KARI	550 KC	Saturday	7:30 AM
INDIANAPOLIS	WTLC-FM	105 MC	Sunday	Midnight
MIDDLETOWN, OHIO	WPFB	910 KC	Sunday	8:00 AM
MEDIA, PA.	WXUR	690 KC	Monday through Friday	4:30 PM

WRITE: NEWSLETTER FILE, PEOPLE'S TEMPLE, P.O. BOX 214, REDWOOD VALLEY, CALIF. 95470

If you wish to continue receiving our newsletter, please send us a special request for it and a donation to help pay printing and mailing expenses. Remember--in the future, these newsletters will contain prophesies and guidance from Pastor Jim Jones vital to all our lives!! Bear in mind that these newsletters will become more extensive every month and may contain messages pertaining to all of our outpost areas, including your own. Even if you are a regular member you must write to be placed on our (new) newsletter mailing list!! If you are unable to contribute anything toward these costs, please write and let us know why not. Of course there will be no hard feelings if you cannot contribute.

IMPORTANT, ADDRESS ENVELOPES TO:

Newsletter File
People's Temple Christian Church
P.O. Box 214
Redwood Valley, California 95470

Please note: Nothing will go out to those who do not write us except perhaps brief notices of our meeting dates and places, so please sit down and write immediately. Be sure to give us your complete name and return address, including your zip code.

WRITE: NEWSLETTER FILE, PEOPLE'S TEMPLE, P.O. BOX 214, REDWOOD VALLEY, CALIF. 95470

PEOPLE'S TEMPLE
P.O. Box 163, Redwood Valley, Calif. 95470

WRITE TODAY FOR YOUR ANNOINTED GIFT. MAKE YOUR CHOICE FROM THE SELECTIONS DESCRIBED BELOW, AND FILL IN THE INFORMATION REQUESTED. YOUR GIFT WILL BE SENT BY RETURN MAIL.

GIFTS 3, 4, 5 AND 7 are 5" x 7" color pictures of Pastor Jones.

PASTOR JONES annointing oil in a recent meeting.

      3   4   5   7

GIFT 20 is a container of ANNOINTED OIL.

GIFTS 21, 22 AND 23 are lovely lockets, each with a picture of Pastor Jones in it.

GIFT 24 is a keychain with a picture of Pastor Jones enclosed.

GIFT 25 is a packet of personalized Temple Stationery with a pen and a small picture enclosed.

"Cheerful givers are the ones God prizes. God is able to make it up to you by giving you everything you need and more, so that there will not only be enough for your own needs, but plenty left over to give joyfully to others. It is as the Scriptures say: 'The godly man gives generously to the poor'." 2 Cor. 9:7-9, THE LIVING BIBLE

- -

Dear Pastor Jones:

    I understand that these blessed gifts work only by faith, as it was in the days of scripture. I also understand that there is no charge for the blessed gift, and since there is a limited supply I should order soon.

    Please send me Gift Number ___ for my blessing. Here is my offering.

$5____ $10____ $20____ $50____ $100____   OTHER_____

NAME_____   ADDRESS_____

CITY_____   STATE_____   ZIP_____   PHONE_____

    SEND TO: PEOPLE'S TEMPLE   ____*Please place my name on your*
              P.O. BOX 163   *mailing list.*
              REDWOOD VALLEY, CALIF. 95470

PEOPLES TEMPLE CHRISTIAN CHURCH

P.O. Box 163, Redwood Valley, Calif 95470

*WRITE TODAY FOR YOUR ANNOINTED GIFT. MAKE YOUR
CHOICE FROM THE SELECTIONS DESCRIBED BELOW, AND
FILL IN THE INFORMATION REQUESTED. YOUR GIFT
WILL BE SENT BY RETURN MAIL. ALL THE HEALINGS
AND PROTECTIONS FROM THESE GIFTS COME FROM
ALMIGHTY GOD AND DEPEND EXCLUSIVELY ON PRAYER.*

GIFT 10 IS AN ANNOINTED PRAYER CLOTH
which has been blessed for special
protection to the wearer when it is
used in faith.

GIFT 21 IS A LOVELY LOCKET WITH A
picture of Pastor Jones in it.

*PASTOR JONES annointing PRAYER CLOTHS
by Divine Revelation in a recent
meeting.*

GIFT 20 IS A CONTAINER OF
ANNOINTED OIL

GIFT 24 IS A KEYCHAIN WITH AN
annointed picture of Pastor Jones in it

GIFT 30 IS A CHILD'S LOCKET
which has been blessed for
PROTECTION AND SAFETY FOR CHILDREN

PASTOR JONES annointing the OIL

GIFT 25 IS A SPECIAL LOCKET WHICH
Pastor Jones has annointed for
PROTECTION FROM EVIL. This locket
has a picture of Pastor Jones in
it which has been annointed by him,
-and then closed with this annointing-
untouched by anyone else. This locket
your own personal birthstone on the
outside of it, if you will tell us
which month you were born.

*PASTOR JONES annointing the special
locket which is blessed for
PROTECTION FROM EVIL.*

- -

PEOPLES TEMPLE, P.O. BOX 163, REDWOOD VALLEY, CALIF. 95470

*Dear Pastor Jim Jones, I understand that these blessed gifts work only by faith, as it was
in the days of scripture. I also understand that there is no charge for the blessed gift,
and since there is a limited supply I should order soon.* MY BIRTH MONTH_____

Please send me GIFT NUMBER ____ for my blessing. HERE IS MY LOVE OFFERING.

$5___ $10___ $15___ $20___ $25___ $50___ $100___ OTHER $_____

NAME_____ ADDRESS_____

CITY_____ STATE_____ ZIP_____ PHONE_____

HUNDREDS OF LETTERS ARE COMING IN EACH WEEK FROM ALL OVER THE COUNTRY TELLING OF MIRACLES AND BLESSINGS THE PEOPLE ARE RECEIVING FROM USING THE ANNOINTED GIFTS IN FAITH. ALL OF THESE MIRACLES AND BLESSINGS DEPEND EXCLUSIVELY UPON PRAYER. HERE ARE JUST A FEW OF THESE AMAZING TESTIMONIES.

"I put the annointed cloth on my daughter's chest and her fever left. She was able to get up and eat."
                                        A. Guillary, Los Angeles

"I received the literature and the prayer cloth, and I thank you very much for these. So far I have received money which I needed very much."
                                        D. Hughes, Texas

"My son-in-law was in Community Hospital. Doctors gave him up to die from lung collapse. My daughter called to tell me about it. When I got there he said his stomach hurt, so I placed the Annointed Picture on his stomach. The next morning the picture was on his back. He put it on his leg which he couldn't use, and it moved down to his ankles. One week later he came home - completely well. He called me and told me that I could come get the picture. The picture of Pastor Jones had come completely off of the paper and had disappeared as the healing went into his body. The papers were blank photographic paper where Jim Jones' picture had been before! I'll tell everyone I see that if they don't have these annointed pictures, they should get one."
                                        A. Johnson, Fresno, Calif.

"The Annointed Oil I got from you has healed my feet. I thank God for the Oil and for you."
                                        Albertha McClay, Louisiana

"I was at your meeting in 1972 when I was getting ready to move to Texas. I just had to see you before I left, and I'm glad I did. I got the Annointed Locket while I was there. We drove from San Diego to Texas and I kept that locket around my neck. The car started to smoke once. I caught hold of that locket and began to call on God who works through you. The car stopped smoking and we drove all the way there. We got to Texas Sunday morning about 2:30 a.m., and went to bed. The next morning that car didn't do anything when I stepped on the starter. I say 'Thank you' to God. The car could have stopped on the road!"
                                        F. Peel, Texas

"Three years ago a young boy abandoned my little dog when she was only one month old. I had her only two days when she got diarrhea so bad I had to take her to the Veterinarian. He told me that the only thing to do was to put this little dog to sleep, as she had been infected with rabies virus distemper. He said she would have leg and muscle spasms as long as she lived, which would not be long.

"In November while I was at the Sunday meeting I got an Annointed Picture and locket. In January whenever Pastor Jones came on the radio I would put the locket and picture on this little dog. She has been healed now and has no more spasms or any sign of the condition she had for more than three years."
                                        Mrs. D. Kent, Oakland, Calif.

"My right knee had swollen. I tried hot packs but they didn't seem to help me. Then the Holy Spirit reminded me of your picture. I placed it on my knee and the swelling instantly went down.

"Also I have a miniature persimmon tree that was dying. Again I used your Annointed Picture and called on the Christ that is in you. Now it is a healthy tree."
                                        E. Watkins, Los Angeles, Calif.

Peoples Temple, P.O. Box 163, Redwood Valley, Calif. 95470

PEOPLE'S TEMPLE, P.O. Box 163, Redwood Valley, California 95470

WRITE TODAY FOR YOUR ANNOINTED GIFT. MAKE YOUR CHOICE FROM THE SELECTIONS DESCRIBED BELOW AND FILL IN THE INFORMATION REQUESTED. YOUR GIFT WILL BE SENT BY RETURN MAIL.

- - - - - - - - - -

GIFTS 3, 4 AND 5 are 5"x7" color pictures of Pastor Jim Jones.

GIFT 20 is a container of ANNOINTED OIL

GIFTS 21, 22 AND 23 are lovely lockets, each with a picture of Pastor Jones in it.

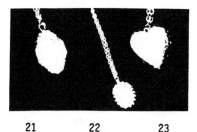

21   22   23

GIFT 24 is a keychain with a picture of Pastor Jones enclosed.

GIFT 25 is a packet of personalized Temple Stationery with a pen and a small picture enclosed.

GIFT 33 is a keychain which has been blessed for SAFETY ON THE ROAD by Pastor Jones, and a two-minute timer for the meditation which Pastor Jones has advised all motorists to observe before going anywhere in a car.

Dear Pastor Jones:

I greet you in peace, love, and oh so much thanksgiving. I feel I must tell you of the past two weeks. Tuesday my 12 year old son was sent home from school with what we thought was a head cold. Friday morning his temperature went to 103, his neck stiffened and the pain became unbearable. Saturday at the hospital the doctors did two examinations and they said MENINGITIS. I almost died. That is a horrible crippling, blinding disease. I could not accept this. He was so sick you could almost smell the fever. They tapped his back for spinal fluid, and said "Yes", it was Meningitis, no doubt about it. I was in shock all day and night. Sunday morning I went to the hospital armed with your picture for Child Protection. I rubbed his neck and head with it. He jumped and wanted to know what I had put on him. I told him something cool. He said it wasn't cold, it was hot! All that temperature and the picture in plastic was hot on his skin!

Well, they did another tap Sunday night to find out what type of Meningitis he had, but they couldn't find anything. By Wednesday, after they had tested him every way they knew how, I brought him home. I put your Key Chain Picture in his pocket and Monday he went back for another examination. The doctors were shocked at his recovery. Tuesday he went back to school, and today I have a well and happy child.

This past weekend my offerings were really given from my heart. Sacrifice? Yes, but willing gladly and with thanksgiving and praise. I couldn't wait any longer to tell you this wonderful story. I thank and praise God through you.

Eleanor Muldrow - Los Angeles

GIFTS 30, 31 AND 32 are annointed gifts in which are enclosed the picture that Pastor Jones has blessed for Protection and Safety for Children.
   30 - Child's Locket
   31 - Medallion Neck Chain
   32 - Keychain and Small Picture

"No one will ever attain perfection until they are willing to share what they have"
                                        Pastor Jim Jones

"Jesus said unto him, If thou wilt be perfect, go and sell what thou hast, and give to the poor, and thou shalt have treasure in heaven."   *Matthew 19:21*

- -

Dear Pastor Jones:

   I understand that these blessed gifts work only by faith, as it was in the days of scripture. I also understand that there is no charge for the blessed gift, and since there is a limited supply I should order soon.

   Please send me my gift number ___ for my blessing. Here is my offering.

$5____ $10____ $15____ $20____ $25____ $50____ $100____   OTHER $____

NAME_____ ADDRESS_____

CITY_____ STATE_____ ZIP_____ PHONE_____

SEND TO: PEOPLE'S TEMPLE, P.O. BOX 163, REDWOOD VALLEY, CALIFORNIA 95470

32

URGENT NEED - PLEASE HELP!

PEOPLE'S TEMPLE
P. O. Box 163
Redwood Valley, Cal.
95470

Marceline Jones has been the wife and companion of our beloved Pastor Jim Jones for 23 years, and during that time she has lived a completely selfless life, devoted to the people that Pastor Jim ministered to. During these years she and her husband have adopted children of all races and had one of their own. They have traveled all over the world - always helping and ministering to people.

Because of the high principles of Pastor Jim, they have never owned a new car, (or anything else new except for a very few clothes) but they have used whatever they could get second-hand from others. It has caused many hardships and trials to them with their busy church work schedule, but they felt that the needs of the people were too great for them to afford the luxury of a new car.

Due to the ever increasing responsibilities of Jim and Marcie it has recently become more and more apparent that this is now unsafe and unwise, especially in view of the fact that in recent weeks Jim Jones has had to meditate five times to save Marceline from danger and death on the highway.

Besides working full time on a very responsible job, Marceline also carries the extremely heavy responsibility of being Mother to three large churches in Los Angeles, San Francisco and Redwood Valley. She holds services in the temples when Pastor Jim cannot be there, even calling out people that Jim has told her ahead of time will be there - and healing them in the power of God that works through Jim Jones. Her character and dedication to the Christian principles have shown that she is truly worthy to be Mother to the church, as Pastor Jim is unquestionably our loyal and loving Father.

The church has voted for reasons of safety and practicality to buy a car which will be safe on the roads as a staff car, one which will be used by Marceline and also by other staff people to carry on the work of the church in the world. They wanted to make it a direct gift to the Jones's, but Jim and Marcie's principles of convictions would not allow them to accept it as a personal gift.

If you share our concern for the safety of the Pastor's wife and staff, and would like to contribute sacrificially toward a safe car, your gift will be appreciated by Pastor Jim as a token of your love for him and his family.

* * *

So many of our family members have taken in children, many of whom are unable to contribute anything toward their support, that it has become necessary to appeal for help from members in our congregation who are unable to take in children, but would like to be a part of this important ministry. Many of these children have come from the courts, from homes where the fathers have deserted them, or from lives of drugs and lawlessness. They have been given homes where love is shown so that they are rehabilitated and live productive lives. Surely each person should feel obligated to help these children - who have never had an opportunity to know a good life until the love of Pastor Jim Jones made a way for them to have good homes.

- -

I would like to help by giving sacrificially, as I know Pastor Jim has given of himself sacrificially all his life.

I pledge $_____ toward the automobile for Marceline to use, and $_____ to help support the children who have been given homes through the love of Jim Jones.

I enclose $_____ today and will send more next month_____.

NAME_____

ADDRESS_____

CITY_____ STATE_____

ZIP CODE _____ TELEPHONE_____

Return to:
PEOPLE'S TEMPLE
P. O. BOX 163
REDWOOD VALLEY, CALIF. 95470

Every week we receive hundreds of testimonies from people all over the country who are experiencing MIRACLES AND BLESSINGS through this miraculous ministry.

Here are just a few, from people who have learned that the promises of old about sharing and giving are very true - that we do indeed receive a hundred fold when we give all we can.

* * *

"I received your blessed picture which I was so thankful for. My house feels so much better now - like Pastor Jones is present all through the house. I was blessed Christmas Day when I didn't have but $6.00 to my name. I had food but no money to buy gifts for anyone. I was blessed with $10.00, then with $25.00, and then God blessed me with $41.00 to give gifts to others - all this when I only had $6.00 of my own. I am thanking God for your picture.

"Also some money was to come to me - securities we had put away four years ago. I was turned down from receiving my husbands securities, and then my lawyer called and told me I will get it all - so I received the securities. Thank God!"

Mary Cottinghan
New York

"I have some very good news to tell you! The first donation I gave to help the senior citizens and children - well you said God would return it to me. The very next day I found $20.00. The next time I found $40.00. I do believe you tell the truth."

Blanche Armour
Los Angeles

"The Lord has blessed me since I met Pastor Jones. I can pay bills and house note. I've had a roof put on my house that was given to me. This Christmas I had a new outfit, and I haven't had one since I was a girl. Thank God for it and thank Him for letting me find Pastor Jim Jones."

Naomi Riggins
Seattle, Washington

"I was in Oakland last week telling a friend of mine about my healing by Pastor Jones. The next morning after my healing I didn't have any money, but I had $5.00 which was for my son. I mailed it to People's Temple. When the postman passed, he had a $50.00 check for me which I hadn't expected. Praise God that $50.00 check came."

Ethel Broussard
Los Angeles

"WE ALL THANK GOD FOR SUCH A WONDERFUL PASTOR AND FOR OUR BLESSINGS. I CANNOT TELL ALL MY BLESSINGS. I CAN SAY THAT SINCE I WENT TO PASTOR JONES' MEETINGS WHILE VISITING IN CALIFORNIA I HAVE MADE MORE MONEY THAN I EVER MADE IN MY LIFE."

JESSIE POLITE
TEXAS

"I have been blessed in my Social Security being restored last month after I was cut off."

V. Tutt
Los Angeles

"I was drawing compensation and they cut me off of it. Then I received one of your small pictures and I put it in my billfold and carried it with me when I went back to the compensation office. It really was a blessing to me because before I had taken the picture with me the manager told me I would not receive any more. Now I have it back!"

M. Allford
Illinois

PASTOR JIM JONES

NEW SCHEDULE FOR ALL CHURCHES*

SAN FRANCISCO TEMPLE 1859 Geary Boulevard (former WAY Club Bldg)	Sundays	11:00 AM 7:00 PM	Singspirational Worship Apostolic Worship
LOS ANGELES TEMPLE 1366 South Alvarado (near Hoover)	Sundays Wednesdays	11:00 AM 7:00 PM 7:30 PM	Singspirational Worship Apostolic Worship Business (Membership) Meeting
REDWOOD VALLEY TEMPLE East Road 9 miles north of Ukiah	Sundays Wednesdays	11:00 AM 6:00 PM 7:30 PM	Singspirational Worship Apostolic Worship COMBINED CONGREGATIONS Business (Membership) Meeting

* The above is a regular schedule for all churches when Church Ministers OTHER THAN PASTOR JIM JONES are conducting services. See following schedule for times when PASTOR JONES will be conducting the services.

Monday	January	1	12 NOON	REDWOOD VALLEY	Gift Distribution & Family Party
Wednesday	January	3	7:30 PM	REDWOOD VALLEY	COMBINED CONGREGATIONS Business (Membership) Meeting
Friday	January	5	8:00 PM	SAN FRANCISCO	Singspiration Worship & Healing
Saturday	January	6	2 & 4 PM	LOS ANGELES	Dynamic Healing and Worship
Sunday	January	7	11:00 AM & 2:00 PM	LOS ANGELES	Spiritual Healing and Worship
Wednesday	January	10	7:30 PM	REDWOOD VALLEY	COMBINED CONGREGATIONS Business (Membership) Meeting
Friday	January	12	8:00 PM	SAN FRANCISCO	Singspiration Worship & Healing
Saturday	January	13	7:30 PM	SAN FRANCISCO	Dynamic Healing and Worship
Sunday	January	14	11:00 AM 8:00 PM	SAN FRANCISCO REDWOOD VALLEY	Spiritual Healing and Worship Apostolic Worship and Healing
Wednesday	January	17	7:30 PM	REDWOOD VALLEY	COMBINED CONGREGATIONS Business (Membership) Meeting
Friday	January	19	8:00 PM	SAN FRANCISCO	Singspiration Worship & Healing
Saturday	January	20	2 & 4 PM	LOS ANGELES	Dynamic Healing and Worship
Sunday	January	21	11:00 AM & 2:00 PM	LOS ANGELES	Spiritual Healing and Worship
Wednesday	January	24	7:30 PM	REDWOOD VALLEY	COMBINED CONGREGATIONS Business (Membership) Meeting
Friday	January	26	8:00 PM	SAN FRANCISCO	Singspiration Worship & Healing
Saturday	January	27	7:30 PM	SAN FRANCISCO	Dynamic Healing and Worship
Sunday	January	28	11:00 AM 8:00 PM	SAN FRANCISCO REDWOOD VALLEY	Spiritual Healing and Worship Apostolic Worship and Healing
Wednesday	January	31	7:30 PM	REDWOOD VALLEY	COMBINED CONGREGATIONS Business (Membership) Meeting
Friday	February	2	8:00 PM	SAN FRANCISCO	Holiday Worship and Healing
Saturday	February	3	2 & 4 PM	LOS ANGELES	Dynamic Healing and Worship
Sunday	February	4	11:00 AM & 2:00 PM	LOS ANGELES	Spiritual Worship and Healing

Plan to be in your seats thirty minutes ahead, since Pastor Jones usually ministers to everyone who arrives early.

ALL OF THESE MEETINGS WILL PERTAIN TO APOSTOLIC HUMAN SERVICE TO PEOPLE IN THE COMMUNITY WHO HAVE NEEDS, FOLLOWING THE ADMONITION OF JESUS IN ST. MATTHEW 25.

LOS ANGELES TEMPLE

SAN FRANCISCO TEMPLE

REDWOOD VALLEY TEMPLE

35

THE MESSAGE OF JIM JONES:

Jesus said,
"What I am so shall ye be. These things shall ye do and greater because I go to the Father."

I have built on this ideal and, thus, have made Christ real to those who are ready for the Sonship ministry. I have come to demonstrate to you that God can abide in these temples of clay, that God *can reign* in our bodies, for we are, indeed, Temples of the Holy Ghost! Some have never actually come to terms with what this sacred teaching signifies! Yea, it is written, that the Captain of our Salvation, Jesus Christ, was *made* perfect through His suffering. I have taken to heart the instruction in Philippians (2:5-7) to *"Let this mind be in you, which was also in Christ Jesus: Who, being in the form of God, thought it not robbery to be equal with God: But made himself of no reputation, and took upon him the form of a servant, and was made in the likeness of men,"* and have come to declare that *you* can have as much of God as you are willing to pay for with the dedication and sacrifice of your life in service to others.

(. . .excerpts from sermon)

PEOPLES TEMPLE CHRISTIAN CHURCH has extensions in many cities, and provides transportation to and from all its meetings. Call your local secretaries for information about meetings and transportation. They are:

Redwood Valley	Mrs. Edith Bogue	(707)	485-7765
	Mrs. Rita Tupper	(707)	462-6291
Bay Area	Mrs. Leona Collier	(415)	626-3365
San Francisco	Miss Jane Mutschman	(415)	863-3290
Oakland East Bay	Mrs. Mattie Wimberly	(415)	654-3829
Richmond	Mrs. Mary Green	(415)	235-3209
Pittsburg	Mrs. Theresa Nickerson	(415)	439-1678
San Mateo	Mrs. Margaret Elsey	(415)	343-0722
Palo Alto	Mrs. Mary Lendo	(415)	325-2589
San Jose	Rev. Mabel Davis	(408)	272-0871
Fresno	Mrs. Melvina Green	(209)	266-7854
Sacramento	Mr. & Mrs. Louis Tennerson	(916)	383-8735
Los Angeles	Mrs. Corine Liggins	(213)	232-1749
	Mrs. Irene White	(213)	384-3604
	Mrs. Julie Beres	(213)	384-3604
Seattle	Mr. & Mrs. Harold Flowers	(206)	323-5836
	Mrs. Davis	(206)	325-4661
	Mrs. Darnell	(206)	763-0919
	Mr. & Mrs. John Kostelnik	(206)	784-3045
Renton, Washington	Mrs. Wroten	(206)	228-6092

PEOPLES TEMPLE, Los Angeles	. . . . . 1366 So. Alvarado	(213)	384-3604
PEOPLES TEMPLE, San Francisco	. . . . 1859 Geary Blvd .	(415)	346-0385
PEOPLES TEMPLE, Redwood Valley	. . East Road	(707)	485-7219

People's Temple
P.O. Box 214
Redwood Valley, CA 95470

Nonprofit Organization
U.S. Postage
1.7d PAID
San Francisco, CA
Permit No. 9729

PASTOR JIM JONES

NEW SCHEDULE FOR ALL CHURCHES*

SAN FRANCISCO TEMPLE 1859 Geary Boulevard (former WAY Club Bldg)	Sundays	11:00 AM 7:00 PM	Singspirational Worship Apostolic Worship
LOS ANGELES TEMPLE 1366 South Alvarado (near Hoover)	Sundays Wednesdays	11:00 AM 7:00 PM 7:30 PM	Singspirational Worship Apostolic Worship Business (Membership) Meeting
REDWOOD VALLEY TEMPLE East Road 9 miles north of Ukiah	Sundays Wednesdays	11:00 AM 6:00 PM 7:30 PM	Singspirational Worship Apostolic Worship COMBINED CONGREGATIONS Business (Membership) Meeting

* The above is a regular schedule for all churches when Church Ministers OTHER THAN PASTOR JIM JONES are conducting services. See following schedule for times when PASTOR JONES will be conducting the services.

Thursday	February	1	7:30	PM	LOS ANGELES	MIRACLE Healing and Deliverance Service
Friday	February	2	8:00	PM	SAN FRANCISCO	Singspiration Worship & Healing
Saturday	February	3	2 & 4	PM	LOS ANGELES	Dynamic Healing and Worship
Sunday	February	4	11:00	AM &		
			2:00	PM	LOS ANGELES	Spiritual Healing and Worship
Wednesday	February	7	7:30	PM	REDWOOD VALLEY	COMBINED CONGREGATIONS Business (Membership) Meeting
Thursday	February	8	7:30	PM	LOS ANGELES	MIRACLE Healing and Deliverance Service
Friday	February	9	8:00	PM	SAN FRANCISCO	Singspiration Worship & Healing
Saturday	February	10	7:30	PM	SAN FRANCISCO	Dynamic Healing and Worship
Sunday	February	11	11:00	AM	SAN FRANCISCO	Spiritual Healing and Worship
			8:00	PM	REDWOOD VALLEY	Apostolic Worship and Healing
Wednesday	February	14	7:30	PM	REDWOOD VALLEY	COMBINED CONGREGATIONS Business (Membership) Meeting
Thursday	February	15	7:30	PM	LOS ANGELES	MIRACLE Healing and Deliverance Service
Friday	February	16	8:00	PM	SAN FRANCISCO	Singspiration Worship & Healing
Saturday	February	17	2 & 4	PM	LOS ANGELES	Dynamic Healing and Worship
Sunday	February	18	11:00	AM &		
			2:00	PM	LOS ANGELES	Spiritual Healing and Worship
Wednesday	February	21	7:30	PM	REDWOOD VALLEY	COMBINED CONGREGATIONS Business (Membership) Meeting
Thursday	February	22	7:30	PM	LOS ANGELES	MIRACLE Healing and Deliverance Service
Friday	February	23	8:00	PM	SAN FRANCISCO	Singspiration Worship & Healing
Saturday	February	24	7:30	PM	SAN FRANCISCO	Dynamic Healing and Worship
Sunday	February	25	11:00	AM	SAN FRANCISCO	Spiritual Healing and Worship
			8:00	PM	REDWOOD VALLEY	Apostolic Worship and Healing
Wednesday	February	28	7:30	PM	REDWOOD VALLEY	COMBINED CONGREGATIONS Business (Membership) Meeting
Thursday	March	1	7:30	PM	LOS ANGELES	MIRACLE Healing and Deliverance Service
Friday	March	2	8:00	PM	SAN FRANCISCO	Singspiration Worship & Healing
Saturday	March	3	2 & 4	PM	LOS ANGELES	Dynamic Healing and Worship
Sunday	March	4	11:00	AM &		
			2:00	PM	LOS ANGELES	Spiritual Worship and Healing

NEW . . . IN LOS ANGELES . . . Every Thursday at 7:30 PM, Pastor Jones will be coming . . . ally to conduct MIRACLE HEALING AND DELIVERANCE SERVICES . . .

LOS ANGELES TEMPLE

SAN FRANCISCO TEMPLE

REDWOOD VALLEY TEMPLE

Plan to be in your seats thirty minutes ahead, since Pastor Jones usually ministers to everyone who arrives early.

THE MESSAGE OF JIM JONES:

Jesus said,
"What I am so shall ye be. These things shall ye do and greater because I go to the Father."

I have built on this ideal and, thus, have made Christ real to those who are ready for the Sonship ministry. I have come to demonstrate to you that God can abide in these temples of clay, that God *can reign* in our bodies, for we are, indeed, Temples of the Holy Ghost! Some have never actually come to terms with what this sacred teaching signifies! Yea, it is written, that the Captain of our Salvation, Jesus Christ, was *made* perfect through His suffering. I have taken to heart the instruction in Philippians (2:5-7) to *"Let this mind be in you, which was also in Christ Jesus: Who, being in the form of God, thought it not robbery to be equal with God: But made himself of no reputation, and took upon him the form of a servant, and was made in the likeness of men,"* and have come to declare that *you* can have as much of God as you are willing to pay for with the dedication and sacrifice of your life in service to others.

(. . .excerpts from sermon)

PEOPLES TEMPLE CHRISTIAN CHURCH has extensions in many cities, and provides transportation to and from all its meetings. Call your local secretaries for information about meetings and transportation. They are:

Redwood Valley	Mrs. Edith Bogue	(707) 485-7765
	Mrs. Rita Tupper	(707) 462-6291
Bay Area	Mrs. Leona Collier	(415) 626-3365
San Francisco	Miss Jane Mutschman	(415) 567-0925
Oakland-East Bay	Mrs. Mattie Wimberly	(415) 654-3829
Richmond	Mrs. Mary Green	(415) 235-3209
Pittsburg	Mrs. Theresa Nickerson	(415) 439-1678
San Mateo	Mrs. Margaret Elsey	(415) 343-0722
Palo Alto	Mrs. Mary Lendo	(415) 325-2589
San Jose	Rev. Mabel Davis	(408) 272-0871
Fresno	Mrs. Melvina Green	(209) 266-7854
Sacramento	Mr. & Mrs. Louis Tennerson	(916) 383-8735
Los Angeles	Mrs. Corine Liggins	(213) 232-1749
	Mrs. Irene White	(213) 384-3604
	Mrs. Julie Beres	(213) 384-3604
Seattle	Mr. & Mrs. Harold Flowers	(206) 323-5836
	Mrs. Davis	(206) 325-4661
	Mrs. Darnell	(206) 763-0919
	Mr. & Mrs. John Kostelnik	(206) 784-3045
Renton, Washington	Mrs. Wroten	(206) 228-6092
Vancouver, BC	Mrs. Ursula Dabrowska	Canada 255-1418

PEOPLES TEMPLE, Los Angeles	1366 So. Alvarado	(213) 384-3604
PEOPLES TEMPLE, San Francisco	1859 Geary Blvd.	(415) 346-0385
PEOPLES TEMPLE, Redwood Valley	East Road	(707) 485-7219

People's Temple
P.O. Box 214
Redwood Valley, CA 95470

Nonprofit Organization
U.S. Postage
1.7¢ PAID
San Francisco, CA
Permit No. 9729

38

PASTOR JIM JONES

NEW SCHEDULE FOR ALL CHURCHES*

SAN FRANCISCO TEMPLE 1859 Geary Boulevard (former WAY Club Bldg)	Sundays	11:00 AM 7:00 PM	Singspirational Worship Apostolic Worship
LOS ANGELES TEMPLE 1366 South Alvarado (near Hoover)	Sundays Wednesdays	11:00 AM 7:00 PM 7:30 PM	Singspirational Worship Apostolic Worship Business (Membership) Meeting
REDWOOD VALLEY TEMPLE East Road 9 miles north of Ukiah	Sundays Wednesdays	11:00 AM 6:00 PM 7:30 PM	Singspirational Worship Apostolic Worship COMBINED CONGREGATIONS Business (Membership) Meeting

* The above is a regular schedule for all churches when Church Ministers OTHER THAN PASTOR JIM JONES are conducting services. See following schedule for times when PASTOR JONES will be conducting the services.

Thursday	March	1	7:30	PM	LOS ANGELES	MIRACLE Healing and Deliverance Service
Friday	March	2	8:00	PM	SAN FRANCISCO	Singspiration Worship & Healing
Saturday	March	3	2 & 4	PM	LOS ANGELES	Dynamic Healing and Worship
Sunday	March	4	11:00	AM &		
			2:00	PM	LOS ANGELES	Spiritual Worship and Healing
Wednesday	March	7	7:30	PM	REDWOOD VALLEY	COMBINED CONGREGATIONS Business (Membership) Meeting
Thursday	March	8	7:30	PM	LOS ANGELES	MIRACLE Healing and Deliverance Service
Friday	March	9	8:00	PM	SAN FRANCISCO	Singspiration Worship & Healing
Saturday	March	10	7:30	PM	SAN FRANCISCO	Dynamic Healing and Worship
Sunday	March	11	11:00	AM	SAN FRANCISCO	Spiritual Healing and Worship
			8:00	PM	REDWOOD VALLEY	Apostolic Worship and Healing
Wednesday	March	14	7:30	PM	REDWOOD VALLEY	COMBINED CONGREGATIONS Business (Membership) Meeting
Thursday	March	15	7:30	PM	LOS ANGELES	MIRACLE Healing and Deliverance Service
Friday	March	16	8:00	PM	SAN FRANCISCO	Singspiration Worship & Healing
Saturday	March	17	2 & 4	PM	LOS ANGELES	Dynamic Healing and Worship
Sunday	March	18	11:00	AM &		
			2:00	PM	LOS ANGELES	Spiritual Healing and Worship
Wednesday	March	21	7:30	PM	REDWOOD VALLEY	COMBINED CONGREGATIONS Business (Membership) Meeting
Thursday	March	22	7:30	PM	LOS ANGELES	MIRACLE Healing and Deliverance Service
Friday	March	23	8:00	PM	SAN FRANCISCO	Singspiration Worship & Healing
Saturday	March	24	7:30	PM	SAN FRANCISCO	Dynamic Healing and Worship
Sunday	March	25	11:00	AM	SAN FRANCSICO	Spiritual Healing and Worship
			8:00	PM	REDWOOD VALLEY	Apostolic Worship and Healing
Wednesday	March	28	7:30	PM	REDWOOD VALLEY	COMBINED CONGREGATIONS Business (Membership) Meeting
Thursday	March	29	7:30	PM	LOS ANGELES	MIRACLE Healing and Deliverance Service
Friday	March	30	8:00	PM	SAN FRANCISCO	Singspiration Worship & Healing
Saturday	March	31	2 & 4	PM	LOS ANGELES	Dynamic Healing and Worship
Sunday	April	1	11:00	AM &		
			2:00	PM	LOS ANGELES	Spiritual Healing and Worship
Wednesday	April	4	7:30	PM	REDWOOD VALLEY	COMBINED CONGREGATIONS Business (Membership) Meeting
Thursday	April	5	7:30	PM	LOS ANGELES	MIRACLE Healing and Deliverance service
Friday	April	6	8:00	PM	SAN FRANCISCO	Singspiration Worship & Healing
Saturday	April	7	7:30	PM	SAN FRANCISCO	Dynamic Healing and Worship
Sunday	April	8	11:00	AM	SAN FRANCISCO	Spiritual Healing and Worship
			8:00	PM	REDWOOD VALLEY	Apostolic Worship and Healing

NEW . . . IN LOS ANGELES . . . Every Thursday at 7:30 PM, Pastor Jones will be coming personally to conduct MIRACLE HEALING AND DELIVERANCE SERVICES . . .

Plan to be in your seats thirty minutes ahead, since Pastor Jones usually ministers to everyone who arrives early.

LOS ANGELES TEMPLE

SAN FRANCISCO TEMPLE

REDWOOD VALLEY TEMPLE

THE MESSAGE OF JIM JONES:

Jesus said,
"What I am so shall ye be. These things shall ye do and greater because I go to the Father."

I have built on this ideal and, thus, have made Christ real to those who are ready for the Sonship ministry. I have come to demonstrate to you that God can abide in these temples of clay, that God *can reign* in our bodies, for we are, indeed, Temples of the Holy Ghost! Some have never actually come to terms with what this sacred teaching signifies! Yea, it is written, that the Captain of our Salvation, Jesus Christ, was *made* perfect through His suffering. I have taken to heart the instruction in Philippians (2:5-7) to *"Let this mind be in you, which was also in Christ Jesus: Who, being in the form of God, thought it not robbery to be equal with God: But made himself of no reputation, and took upon him the form of a servant, and was made in the likeness of men,"* and have come to declare that *you* can have as much of God as you are willing to pay for with the dedication and sacrifice of your life in service to others.

(. . .excerpts from sermon)

PEOPLES TEMPLE CHRISTIAN CHURCH has many extensions and provides transportation to and from its meetings. Local secretaries and Associate Pastors may be called for information or guidance:

Redwood Valley	Mrs. Edith Bogue	(707) 485-7765
	Mrs. Rita Tupper	(707) 462-6291
Bay Area	Mrs. Leona Collier	(415) 626-3365
San Francisco	Miss Jane Mutschman	(415) 567-0925
Oakland-East Bay	Mrs. Mattie Wimberly	(415) 654-3829
Richmond	Mrs. Mary Green	(415) 235-3209
Pittsburg	Mrs. Theresa Nickerson	(415) 439-1678
San Mateo	Mrs. Margaret Elsey	(415) 343-0722
Palo Alto	Mrs. Mary Lendo	(415) 325-2589
San Jose	Rev. Mabel Davis	(408) 272-0871
Fresno	Mrs. Melvina Green	(209) 266-7854
Sacramento	Mr. & Mrs. Louis Tennerson	(916) 383-8735
Los Angeles	Mrs. Corine Liggins	(213) 232-1749
	Mrs. Irene White	(213) 384-3604
	Mrs. Julie Beres	(213) 384-3604
Seattle	Mr. & Mrs. Harold Flowers	(206) 323-5836
	Mrs. Davis	(206) 325-4661
	Mrs. Darnell	(206) 763-0919
	Mr. & Mrs. John Kostelnik	(206) 784-3045
Renton, Washington	Mrs. Wroten	(206) 228-6092
Vancouver, BC	Mrs. Ursula Dabrowska	Canada 255-1418

PEOPLES TEMPLE, Los Angeles . . . . . 1366 So. Alvarado   (213) 384-3604
  David Wise, Los Angeles Associate Pastor   (213) 384-0854
PEOPLES TEMPLE, San Francisco. . . . . 1859 Geary Blvd.   (415) 346-0385
  John Brown, San Francisco Associate Pastor   (415) 431-7968
  Michael Cartmell, Oakland Associate Pastor   (415) 465-8220
PEOPLES TEMPLE, Redwood Valley . . East Road   (707) 485-7310

People's Temple
P.O. Box 214
Redwood Valley, CA 95470

Nonprofit Organization
U.S. Postage
1.7¢ PAID
San Francisco, CA
Permit No. 9729

40

PASTOR JIM JONES

NEW SCHEDULE FOR ALL CHURCHES*

SAN FRANCISCO TEMPLE 1859 Geary Boulevard (former WAY Club Bldg)	Sundays	11:00 AM 7:00 PM		Singspirational Worship Apostolic Worship
LOS ANGELES TEMPLE 1366 South Alvarado (near Hoover)	Sundays Wednesdays	11:00 AM 7:00 PM 7:30 PM		Singspirational Worship Apostolic Worship Business (Membership) Meeting
REDWOOD VALLEY TEMPLE East Road 9 miles north of Ukiah	Sundays Wednesdays	11:00 AM 6:00 PM 7:30 PM		Singspirational Worship Apostolic Worship COMBINED CONGREGATIONS Business (Membership) Meeting

* The above is a regular schedule for all churches when Church Ministers OTHER THAN PASTOR JIM JONES are conducting services. See following schedule for times when PASTOR JONES will be conducting the services.

Sunday	April	1	11:00 2:00	AM & PM	LOS ANGELES	Spiritual Healing and Worship
Wednesday	April	4	7:30	PM	REDWOOD VALLEY	COMBINED CONGREGATIONS Business (Membership) Meeting
Thursday	April	5	7:30	PM	LOS ANGELES	MIRACLE Healing and Deliverance Service
Friday	April	6	8:00	PM	SAN FRANCISCO	Singspiration Worship & Healing
Saturday	April	7	7:30	PM	SAN FRANCISCO	Dynamic Healing and Worship
Sunday	April	8	11:00 8:00	AM PM	SAN FRANCISCO REDWOOD VALLEY	Spiritual Healing and Worship Apostolic Worship and Healing
Wednesday	April	11	7:30	PM	REDWOOD VALLEY	COMBINED CONGREGATIONS Business (Membership) Meeting
Thursday	April	12	7:30	PM	LOS ANGELES	MIRACLE Healing and Deliverance Service
Friday	April	13	8:00	PM	SAN FRANCISCO	Singspiration Worship & Healing
Saturday	April	14	2 & 4	PM	LOS ANGELES	Dynamic Healing and Worship
Sunday	April	15	11:00 2:00	AM & PM	 LOS ANGELES	 Spiritual Worship and Healing
Wednesday	April	18	7:30	PM	REDWOOD VALLEY	COMBINED CONGREGATIONS Business (Membership) Meeting
Thursday	April	19	7:30	PM	LOS ANGELES	MIRACLE Healing and Deliverance Service
Friday	April	20	8:00	PM	SAN FRANCISCO	Singspiration Worship & Healing
Saturday	April	21	7:30	PM	SAN FRANCISCO	Dynamic Healing and Worship
Sunday	April	22	11:00 8:00	AM PM	SAN FRANCISCO REDWOOD VALLEY	Spiritual Healing and Worship Apostolic Worship and Healing
Wednesday	April	25	7:30	PM	REDWOOD VALLEY	COMBINED CONGREGATIONS Business (Membership) Meeting
Thursday	April	26	7:30	PM	LOS ANGELES	MIRACLE Healing and Deliverance Service
Friday	April	27	8:00	PM	SAN FRANCISCO	Singspiration Worship & Healing
Saturday	April	28	2 & 4	PM	LOS ANGELES	Dynamic Healing and Worship
Sunday	April	29	11:00 2:00	AM & PM	 LOS ANGELES	 Spiritual Worship and Healing
Wednesday	May	2	7:30	PM	REDWOOD VALLEY	COMBINED CONGREGATIONS Business (Membership) Meeting
Thursday	May	3	7:30	PM	LOS ANGELES	MIRACLE Healing and Deliverance Service
Friday	May	4	8:00	PM	SAN FRANCISCO	Singspiration Worship & Healing
Saturday	May	5	7:30	PM	SAN FRANCISCO	Dynamic Healing and Worship
Sunday	May	6	11:00 8:00	AM PM	SAN FRANCISCO REDWOOD VALLEY	Spiritual Healing and Worship Apostolic Worship and Healing

NEW . . . IN LOS ANGELES . . . Every Thursday at 7:30 PM, Pastor Jones will be coming personally to conduct MIRACLE HEALING AND DELIVERANCE SERVICES . . .

Plan to be in your seats thirty minutes ahead. since Pastor Jones usually ministers to everyone who arrives early.

LOS ANGELES TEMPLE

SAN FRANCISCO TEMPLE

REDWOOD VALLEY TEMPLE

THE MESSAGE OF JIM JONES:

Jesus said,
"What I am so shall ye be. These things shall ye do and greater because I go to the Father."

I have built on this ideal and, thus, have made Christ real to those who are ready for the Sonship ministry. I have come to demonstrate to you that God can abide in these temples of clay, that God *can reign* in our bodies, for we are, indeed, Temples of the Holy Ghost! Some have never actually come to terms with what this sacred teaching signifies! Yea, it is written, that the Captain of our Salvation, Jesus Christ, was *made* perfect through His suffering. I have taken to heart the instruction in Philippians (2:5-7) to *"Let this mind be in you, which was also in Christ Jesus: Who, being in the form of God, thought it not robbery to be equal with God: But made himself of no reputation, and took upon him the form of a servant, and was made in the likeness of men,"* and have come to declare that *you* can have as much of God as you are willing to pay for with the dedication and sacrifice of your life in service to others.

(. . .excerpts from sermon)

PEOPLES TEMPLE CHRISTIAN CHURCH has many extensions and provides transportation to and from its meetings. Local secretaries and Associate Pastors may be called for information or guidance:

Redwood Valley	Mrs. Edith Bogue	(707)	485-7765
	Mrs. Rita Tupper	(707)	462-6291
Bay Area	Mrs. Leona Collier	(415)	626-3365
San Francisco	Miss Jane Mutschman	(415)	567-0925
Oakland-East Bay	Mrs. Mattie Wimberly	(415)	654-3829
Richmond	Mrs. Mary Green	(415)	235-3209
Pittsburg	Mrs. Theresa Nickerson	(415)	439-1678
San Mateo	Mrs. Margaret Elsey	(415)	343-0722
Palo Alto	Mrs. Mary Lendo	(415)	325-2589
San Jose	Rev. Mabel Davis	(408)	272-0871
Fresno	Mrs. Melvina Green	(209)	266-7854
Sacramento	Mr. & Mrs. Louis Tennerson	(916)	383-8735
Los Angeles	Mrs. Corine Liggins	(213)	232-1749
	Mrs. Irene White	(213)	384-3604
	Mrs. Julie Beres	(213)	384-3604
Seattle	Mr. & Mrs. Harold Flowers	(206)	323-5836
	Mrs. Davis	(206)	325-4661
	Mrs. Darnell	(206)	763-0919
	Mr. & Mrs. John Kostelnik	(206)	784-3045
Renton, Washington	Mrs. Wroten	(206)	228-6092
Vancouver, BC	Mrs. Ursula Dabrowska	Canada	255-1418

PEOPLES TEMPLE, Los Angeles . . . . . 1366 So. Alvarado   (213) 384-3604
   David Wise, Los Angeles Associate Pastor   (213) 384-0854
PEOPLES TEMPLE, San Francisco. . . . 1859 Geary Blvd.   (415) 346-0385
   John Brown, San Francisco Associate Pastor   (415) 431-7968
   Michael Cartmell, Oakland Associate Pastor   (415) 465-8220
PEOPLES TEMPLE, Redwood Valley East Road   (707)

People's Temple
P.O. Box 214
Redwood Valley, CA 95470

Nonprofit Organization
U.S. Postage
1.7¢ PAID
San Francisco, CA
Permit No. 9729

PASTOR JIM JONES

NEW SCHEDULE FOR ALL CHURCHES*

SAN FRANCISCO TEMPLE 1859 Geary Boulevard (former WAY Club Bldg)	Sundays	11:00 AM 7:00 PM	Singspirational Worship Apostolic Worship
LOS ANGELES TEMPLE 1366 South Alvarado (near Hoover)	Sundays Wednesdays	11:00 AM 7:00 PM 7:30 PM	Singspirational Worship Apostolic Worship Business (Membership) Meeting
REDWOOD VALLEY TEMPLE East Road 9 miles north of Ukiah	Sundays Wednesdays	11:00 AM 6:00 PM 7:30 PM	Singspirational Worship Apostolic Worship COMBINED CONGREGATIONS Business (Membership) Meeting

* The above is a regular schedule for all churches when Church Ministers OTHER THAN PASTOR JIM JONES are conducting services. See following schedule for times when PASTOR JONES will be conducting the services.

Day	Date	Time	Location	Service
Wednesday	May 30	7:30 PM	REDWOOD VALLEY	COMBINED CONGREGATIONS Business (Membership) Meeting
Thursday	May 31	7:30 PM	LOS ANGELES	MIRACLE Healing and Deliverance Service
Friday	June 1	8:00 PM	SAN FRANCISCO	Singspiration Worship & Healing
Saturday	June 2	7:30 PM	SAN FRANCISCO	Dynamic Healing and Worship
Sunday	June 3	11:00 AM	SAN FRANCISCO	Spiritual Healing and Worship
		8:00 PM	REDWOOD VALLEY	Apostolic Worship and Healing
Wednesday	June 6	7:30 PM	REDWOOD VALLEY	COMBINED CONGREGATIONS Business (Membership) Meeting
Thursday	June 7	7:30 PM	LOS ANGELES	MIRACLE Healing and Deliverance Service
Friday	June 8	8:00 PM	SAN FRANCISCO	Singspiration Worship & Healing
Saturday	June 9	2 & 4 PM	LOS ANGELES	Dynamic Healing and Worship
Sunday	June 10	11:00 AM &		
		2:00 PM	LOS ANGELES	Spiritual Worship and Healing
Wednesday	June 13	7:30 PM	REDWOOD VALLEY	COMBINED CONGREGATIONS Business (Membership) Meeting
Thursday	June 14	7:30 PM	LOS ANGELES	MIRACLE Healing and Deliverance Service
Friday	June 15	8:00 PM	SAN FRANCISCO	Singspiration Worship & Healing
Saturday	June 16	7:30 PM	SAN FRANCISCO	Dynamic Healing and Worship
Sunday	June 17	11:00 AM	SAN FRANCISCO	Spiritual Healing and Worship
		8:00 PM	REDWOOD VALLEY	Apostolic Worship and Healing
Wednesday	June 20	7:30 PM	REDWOOD VALLEY	COMBINED CONGREGATIONS Business (Membership) Meeting
Thursday	June 21	7:30 PM	LOS ANGELES	MIRACLE Healing and Deliverance Service
Friday	June 22	8:00 PM	SAN FRANCISCO	Singspiration Worship & Healing
Saturday	June 23	2 & 4 PM	LOS ANGELES	Dynamic Healing and Worship
Sunday	June 24	11:00 AM &		
		2:00 PM	LOS ANGELES	Spiritual Worship and Healing
Wednesday	June 27	7:30 PM	REDWOOD VALLEY	COMBINED CONGREGATIONS Business (Membership) Meeting
Thursday	June 28	7:30 PM	LOS ANGELES	MIRACLE Healing and Deliverance Service
Friday	June 29	8:00 PM	SAN FRANCISCO	Singspiration Worship & Healing
Saturday	June 30	7:30 PM	SAN FRANCISCO	Dynamic Healing and Worship
Sunday	July 1	11:00 AM	SAN FRANCISCO	Spiritual Healing and Worship
		8:00 PM	REDWOOD VALLEY	Apostolic Worship and Healing

NEW . . . IN LOS ANGELES . . . Every Thursday at 7:30 PM, Pastor Jones will be coming personally to conduct MIRACLE HEALING AND DELIVERANCE SERVICES . . .

Plan to be in your seats thirty minutes ahead, since Pastor Jones usually ministers to everyone who arrives early.

LOS ANGELES TEMPLE

SAN FRANCISCO TEMPLE

REDWOOD VALLEY TEMPLE

THE MESSAGE OF JIM JONES:

Jesus said,
"What I am so shall ye be. These things shall ye do and greater because I go to the Father."

I have built on this ideal and, thus, have made Christ real to those who are ready for the Sonship ministry. I have come to demonstrate to you that God can abide in these temples of clay, that God *can reign* in our bodies, for we are, indeed, Temples of the Holy Ghost! Some have never actually come to terms with what this sacred teaching signifies! Yea, it is written, that the Captain of our Salvation, Jesus Christ, was *made* perfect through His suffering. I have taken to heart the instruction in Philippians (2:5-7) to *"Let this mind be in you, which was also in Christ Jesus: Who, being in the form of God, thought it not robbery to be equal with God: But made himself of no reputation, and took upon him the form of a servant, and was made in the likeness of men,"* and have come to declare that *you* can have as much of God as you are willing to pay for with the dedication and sacrifice of your life in service to others.

(. . .excerpts from sermon)

PEOPLES TEMPLE CHRISTIAN CHURCH has many extensions and provides transportation to and from its meetings. Local secretaries and Associate Pastors may be called for information or guidance:

Redwood Valley	Mrs. Edith Bogue	(707) 485-7765
	Mrs. Rita Tupper	(707) 485-7877
Bay Area	Mrs. Leona Collier	(415) 626-3365
San Francisco	Miss Jane Mutschman	(415) 567-0925
Oakland-East Bay	Mrs. Mattie Wimberly	(415) 654-3829
Richmond	Mrs. Mary Green	(415) 235-3209
Pittsburg	Mrs. Theresa Nickerson	(415) 439-1678
San Mateo	Mrs. Margaret Elsey	(415) 343-0722
Palo Alto	Mrs. Mary Lendo	(415) 325-2589
San Jose	Rev. Mabel Davis	(408) 272-0871
Fresno	Mrs. Melvina Green	(209) 266-7854
Sacramento	Mr. & Mrs. Louis Tennerson	
		(916) 383-8735
Los Angeles	Mrs. Corine Liggins	(213) 384-3604
	Mrs. Clara Johnson,	
	Coordinator	(213) 299-0284
	Mrs. Julie Beres	(213) 384-3604
	Mrs. Irene White	(213) 384-3604
Pasadena	Mrs. Virginia Taylor	(213) 798-6530
Seattle-Vancouver	Mrs. Dorothy Suggs	(206) 725-1836
	Mrs. Genevieve Fye	(206) 362-3309
	Mr. Harold Flowers	(206) 323-5836
Renton, Washington	Mrs. Wroten	(206) 228-6092

PEOPLES TEMPLE, Los Angeles . . . . . 1366 So. Alvarado — (213) 384-3604
David Wise, Los Angeles Associate Pastor — (213) 384-0854
PEOPLES TEMPLE, San Francisco . . . . . . 1859 Geary Blvd. — (415) 346-0385
John Brown, San Francisco Associate Pastor — (415) 431-7968
Michael Cartmell, Oakland Associate Pastor — (415) 465-8220
PEOPLES TEMPLE, Redwood Valley ... East Road — (707) 485-7219

PASTOR JIM JONES

NEW SCHEDULE FOR ALL CHURCHES*

SAN FRANCISCO TEMPLE 1859 Geary Boulevard (former WAY Club Bldg)	Sundays	11:00 AM 7:00 PM	Singspirational Worship Apostolic Worship
LOS ANGELES TEMPLE 1366 South Alvarado (near Hoover)	Sundays Wednesdays	11:00 AM 7:00 PM 7:30 PM	Singspirational Worship Apostolic Worship Business (Membership) Meeting
REDWOOD VALLEY TEMPLE East Road 9 miles north of Ukiah	Sundays Wednesdays	11:00 AM 6:00 PM 7:30 PM	Singspirational Worship Apostolic Worship COMBINED CONGREGATIONS Business (Membership) Meeting

* The above is a regular schedule for all churches when Church Ministers OTHER THAN PASTOR JIM JONES are conducting services. See following schedule for times when PASTOR JONES will be conducting the services.

Day	Date	Time		Location	Service
Friday	*JUNE 29*	8:00	PM	SAN FRANCISCO	Singspiration Worship & Healing
Saturday	*JUNE 30*	7:30	PM	SAN FRANCISCO	Dynamic Healing and Worship
Sunday	*JULY 1*	11:00	AM	SAN FRANCISCO	Spiritual Healing and Worship
		8:00	PM	REDWOOD VALLEY	Apostolic Worship and Healing
Wednesday	*JULY 4*	7:30	PM	REDWOOD VALLEY	COMBINED CONGREGATIONS Business (Membership) Meeting
Thursday	*JULY 5*	7:30	PM	LOS ANGELES	MIRACLE Healing and Deliverance Service
Friday	*JULY 6*	8:00	PM	SAN FRANCISCO	Singspiration Worship & Healing
Saturday	*JULY 7*	2 & 4	PM	LOS ANGELES	Dynamic Healing and Worship
Sunday	*JULY 8*	11:00	AM &		
		2:00	PM	LOS ANGELES	Spiritual Worship and Healing
Wednesday	*JULY 11*	7:30	PM	REDWOOD VALLEY	COMBINED CONGREGATIONS Business (Membership) Meeting
Thursday	*JULY 12*	7:30	PM	LOS ANGELES	MIRACLE Healing and Deliverance Service
Friday	*JULY 13*	8:00	PM	SAN FRANCISCO	Singspiration Worship & Healing
Saturday	*JULY 14*	7:30	PM	SAN FRANCISCO	Dynamic Healing and Worship
Sunday	*JULY 15*	11:00	AM	SAN FRANCISCO	Spiritual Healing and Worship
		8:00	PM	REDWOOD VALLEY	Apostolic Worship and Healing
Wednesday	*JULY 18*	7:30	PM	REDWOOD VALLEY	COMBINED CONGREGATIONS Business (Membership) Meeting
Thursday	*JULY 19*	7:30	PM	LOS ANGELES	MIRACLE Healing and Deliverance Service
Friday	*JULY 20*	8:00	PM	SAN FRANCISCO	Singspiration Worship & Healing
Saturday	*JULY 21*	2 & 4	PM	LOS ANGELES	Dynamic Healing and Worship
Sunday	*JULY 22*	11:00	AM &		
		2:00	PM	LOS ANGELES	Spiritual Worship and Healing
Wednesday	*JULY 25*	7:30	PM	REDWOOD VALLEY	COMBINED CONGREGATIONS Business (Membership) Meeting
Thursday	*JULY 26*	7:30	PM	LOS ANGELES	MIRACLE Healing and Deliverance Service
Friday	*JULY 27*	8:00	PM	SAN FRANCISCO	Singspiration Worship & Healing
Saturday	*JULY 28*	7:30	PM	SAN FRANCISCO	Dynamic Healing and Worship
Sunday	*JULY 29*	11:00	AM	SAN FRANCISCO	Spiritual Healing and Worship
		8:00	PM	REDWOOD VALLEY	Apostolic Worship and Healing

NEW . . . IN LOS ANGELES . . . Every Thursday at 7:30 PM, Pastor Jones will be coming personally to conduct MIRACLE HEALING AND DELIVERANCE SERVICES . . .

Plan to be in your seats thirty minutes ahead, since Pastor Jones usually ministers to everyone who arrives early.

LOS ANGELES TEMPLE

SAN FRANCISCO TEMPLE

REDWOOD VALLEY TEMPLE

EQUAL VACATIONS TOGETHER

While Pastor Jim Jones has been offered vacation facilities at many luxury locations, he goes only where he can take the ENTIRE PEOPLES TEMPLE FAMILY. He takes no privilege for himself that the family cannot share! Last year we vacationed up and down the West Coast, into the rain forests of Canada and down into the deserts and beaches of Mexico. Meetings were held along the way, spreading the gospel of the LIVING WORD and bringing many wonderful healings to many sweet souls touched by our Pastor.

Wonders followed us wherever we went. Even the elements of nature seemed pleased with the coming of our pastor. When rainclouds covered the Northland, the sun broke through forests that would have been impenetrable and dark as night. When the rains came down so heavily in another instance so that our bus drivers became worried, Pastor Jones said not to worry, it would let-up in a few minutes. The rains stopped almost immediately thereafter. God's name be praised!

When we arrived at the beaches of Mexico, all were disappointed at the heavy clouds that hovered over the beaches blotting out the sunlight. Our pastor said that the sun would come out and it did. However, it came out only over that patch of beach where we were encamped. Others came from miles north and south of us to share the sunlight that came and went with our caravan of busses. He said after this miraculous phenomena that it seems on occasion that Divine Love and pure motivations even move clouds of natural -- as well as spiritual obscurity.

Great protection was witnessed throughout the journey, Sharks menaced the beaches of Mexico, but none of those killer-fish came near any of the places our children bathed. When our pastor said all would be well, it was. And there were those of us who saw him literally rise on the waves, not to show off or be seen of men, but to save a little child who would have drowned.

SUMMER IS HERE AGAIN. . . AND SO IS THE FAMILY VACATION. Beginning on August 3rd, we will again gather into our busses with our pastor and vacation together. Those wishing to join Pastor Jones in this wonderful EQUAL VACATION should immediately get in touch with the secretaries of their local areas.

THE MESSAGE OF JIM JONES:

Jesus said,
"What I am so shall ye be. These things shall ye do and greater because I go to the Father."
I have built on this ideal and, thus, have made Christ real to those who are ready for the Sonship ministry. I have come to demonstrate to you that God can abide in these temples of clay, that God *can reign* in our bodies, for we are, indeed, Temples of the Holy Ghost! Some have never actually come to terms with what this sacred teaching signifies! Yea, it is written, that the Captain of our Salvation, Jesus Christ, was *made* perfect through His suffering. I have taken to heart the instruction in Philippians (2:5-7) to *"Let this mind be in you, which was also in Christ Jesus: Who, being in the form of God, thought it not robbery to be equal with God: But made himself of no reputation, and took upon him the form of a servant, and was made in the likeness of men,"* and have come to declare that *you* can have as much of God as you are willing to pay for with the dedication and sacrifice of your life in service to others.

(. . .excerpts from sermon)

Redwood Valley	Mrs. Edith Bogue	(707) 485-7765
	Mrs. Rita Tupper	(707) 485-7877
Bay Area	Mrs. Leona Collier	(415) 626-3365
San Francisco	Miss Jane Mutschman	(415) 567-0925
Oakland-East Bay	Mrs. Mattie Wimberly	(415) 654-3829
Richmond	Mrs. Mary Green	(415) 235-3209
Pittsburg	Mrs. Theresa Nickerson	(415) 439-1678
San Mateo	Mrs. Margaret Elsey	(415) 343-0722
Palo Alto	Mrs. Mary Lendo	(415) 325-2589
San Jose	Rev. Mabel Davis	(408) 272-0871
Fresno	Mrs. Melvina Green	(209) 266-7854
Sacramento	Mr. & Mrs. Louis Tennerson	
		(916) 383-8735
Los Angeles	Mrs. Corine Liggins	(213) 384-3604
	Mrs. Clara Johnson,	
	Coordinator	(213) 299-0284
	Mrs. Julie Beres	(213) 384-3604
	Mrs. Irene White	(213) 384-3604
Pasadena	Mrs. Virginia Taylor	(213) 798-6530
Seattle -Vancouver	Mrs. Dorothy Suggs	(206) 725-1836
	Mrs. Genevieve Fye	(206) 362-3309
	Mr. Harold Flowers	(206) 323-5836
Renton, Washington	Mrs. Wroten	(206) 228-6092

PEOPLES TEMPLE, Los Angeles . . . . . 1366 So. Alvarado	(213) 384-3604
David Wise, Los Angeles Associate Pastor	(213) 384-0854
PEOPLES TEMPLE, San Francisco . . . . . 1859 Geary Blvd.	(415) 346-0385
John Brown, San Francisco Associate Pastor	(415) 431-7968
Michael Cartmell, Oakland Associate Pastor	(415) 465-8220
PEOPLES TEMPLE, Redwood Valley ... East Road	(707) 485-7219

PASTOR JIM JONES

NEW SCHEDULE FOR ALL CHURCHES*

SAN FRANCISCO TEMPLE 1859 Geary Boulevard (former WAY Club Bldg)	Sundays	11:00 AM 7:00 PM		Singspirational Worship Apostolic Worship
LOS ANGELES TEMPLE 1366 South Alvarado (near Hoover)	Sundays Wednesdays	11:00 AM 7:00 PM 7:30 PM		Singspirational Worship Apostolic Worship Business (Membership) Meeting
REDWOOD VALLEY TEMPLE East Road 9 miles north of Ukiah	Sundays Wednesdays	11:00 AM 6:00 PM 7:30 PM		Singspirational Worship Apostolic Worship COMBINED CONGREGATIONS Business (Membership) Meeting

* The above is a regular schedule for all churches when Church Ministers OTHER THAN PASTOR JIM JONES are conducting services. See following schedule for times when PASTOR JONES will be conducting the services.

Wednesday	AUGUST 1	7:30	PM	REDWOOD VALLEY	COMBINED CONGREGATIONS Business (Membership) Meeting
Thursday	AUGUST 2	7:30	PM	LOS ANGELES	MIRACLE Healing and Deliverance Service
Friday	AUGUST 3	8:00	PM	SAN FRANCISCO	Singspiration Worship & Healing
Saturday	AUGUST 4	2 & 4	PM	LOS ANGELES	Dynamic Healing and Worship
Sunday	AUGUST 5	11:00 AM & 2:00	PM	LOS ANGELES	Spiritual Worship and Healing
Wednesday	AUGUST 8	7:30	PM	REDWOOD VALLEY	COMBINED CONGREGATIONS Business (Membership) Meeting
Thursday	AUGUST 9	7:30	PM	LOS ANGELES	MIRACLE Healing and Deliverance Service
Friday	AUGUST 10	8:00	PM	SAN FRANCISCO	Singspiration Worship & Healing
Saturday	AUGUST 11	7:30	PM	SAN FRANCISCO	Dynamic Healing and Worship
Sunday	AUGUST 12	11:00	AM	SAN FRANCISCO	Spiritual Healing and Worship
		8:00	PM	REDWOOD VALLEY	Apostolic Worship and Healing
Wednesday	AUGUST 15	7:30	PM	REDWOOD VALLEY	COMBINED CONGREGATIONS Business (Membership) Meeting
Thursday	AUGUST 16	7:30	PM	LOS ANGELES	MIRACLE Healing and Deliverance Service
Friday	AUGUST 17	8:00	PM	SAN FRANCISCO	Singspiration Worship & Healing
Saturday	AUGUST 18	2 & 4	PM	LOS ANGELES	Dynamic Healing and Worship
Sunday	AUGUST 19	11:00 AM & 2:00	PM	LOS ANGELES	Spiritual Worship and Healing
Wednesday	AUGUST 22	7:30	PM	REDWOOD VALLEY	COMBINED CONGREGATIONS Business (Membership) Meeting
Thursday	AUGUST 23	7:30	PM	LOS ANGELES	MIRACLE Healing and Deliverance Service
Friday	AUGUST 24	8:00	PM	SAN FRANCISCO	Singspiration Worship & Healing
Saturday	AUGUST 25	7:30	PM	SAN FRANCISCO	Dynamic Healing and Worship
Sunday	AUGUST 26	11:00	AM	SAN FRANCISCO	Spiritual Healing and Worship
		8:00	PM	REDWOOD VALLEY	Apostolic Worship and Healing
Wednesday	AUGUST 29	7:30	PM	REDWOOD VALLEY	COMBINED CONGREGATIONS Business (Membership) Meeting
Thursday	AUGUST 30	7:30	PM	LOS ANGELES	MIRACLE Healing and Deliverance Service
Friday	AUGUST 31	8:00	PM	SAN FRANCISCO	Singspiration Worship & Healing
Saturday	SEPT. 1	2 & 4	PM	LOS ANGELES	Dynamic Healing and Worship
Sunday	SEPT. 2	11:00 AM & 2:00	PM	LOS ANGELES	Spiritual Worship and Healing

FAMILY VACATION TO MEXICO... Tentative for Week Beginning August 3, 1973
Verify with local church secretaries. RESERVATIONS ARE A MUST.

Plan to be in your seats thirty minutes ahead, since Pastor Jones usually ministers to everyone who arrives early.

LOS ANGELES TEMPLE

SAN FRANCISCO TEMPLE

REDWOOD VALLEY TEMPLE

47

PASTOR JIM JONES
SPIRITUAL HEALING &
HUMAN SERVICE MINISTRY
SCHEDULE OF MEETINGS

Wednesday	SEPTEMBER 12	7:30	PM	REDWOOD VALLEY	COMBINED CONGREGATIONS Business (Membership) Meeting
Thursday	SEPTEMBER 13	7:30	PM	LOS ANGELES	MIRACLE Healing and Deliverance Service
Friday	SEPTEMBER 14	8:00	PM	SAN FRANCISCO	Singspiration Worship & Healing
Saturday	SEPTEMBER 15	2 & 4	PM	LOS ANGELES	Dynamic Healing and Worship
Sunday	SEPTEMBER 16	11:00	AM &		
		2:00	PM	LOS ANGELES	Spiritual Worship and Healing
Wednesday	SEPTEMBER 19	7:30	PM	REDWOOD VALLEY	COMBINED CONGREGATIONS Business (Membership) Meeting
Thursday	SEPTEMBER 20	7:30	PM	LOS ANGELES	MIRACLE Healing and Deliverance Service
Friday	SEPTEMBER 21	8:00	PM	SAN FRANCISCO	Singspiration Worship & Healing
Saturday	SEPTEMBER 22	7:30	PM	SAN FRANCISCO	Dynamic Healing and Worship
Sunday	SEPTEMBER 23	11:00	AM	SAN FRANCISCO	Spiritual Healing and Worship
		8:00	PM	REDWOOD VALLEY	Apostolic Worship and Healing
Wednesday	SEPTEMBER 26	7:30	PM	REDWOOD VALLEY	COMBINED CONGREGATIONS Business (Membership) Meeting
Thursday	SEPTEMBER 27	7:30	PM	LOS ANGELES	MIRACLE Healing and Deliverance Service
Friday	SEPTEMBER 28	8:00	PM	SAN FRANCISCO	Singspiration Worship & Healing
Saturday	SEPTEMBER 29	2 & 4	PM	LOS ANGELES	Dynamic Healing and Worship
Sunday	SEPTEMBER 30	11:00	AM &		
		2:00	PM	LOS ANGELES	Spiritual Worship and Healing
Wednesday	OCTOBER 3	7:30	PM	REDWOOD VALLEY	COMBINED CONGREGATIONS Business (Membership) Meeting
Thursday	OCTOBER 4	7:30	PM	LOS ANGELES	MIRACLE Healing and Deliverance Service
Friday	OCTOBER 5	8:00	PM	SAN FRANCISCO	Singspiration Worship & Healing
Saturday	OCTOBER 6	7:30	PM	SAN FRANCISCO	Dynamic Healing and Worship
Sunday	OCTOBER 7	11:00	AM	SAN FRANCISCO	Spiritual Healing and Worship
		8:00	PM	REDWOOD VALLEY	Apostolic Worship and Healing

The following is a regular schedule for all churches when Church Ministers OTHER THAN PASTOR JIM JONES are conducting services.

SAN FRANCISCO CHURCH
Now meeting at
BEN. FRANKLIN JR. HIGH
SCOTT AND GEARY BLVDS.

Sundays	11:00 AM	Singspirational Worship
	7:00 PM	Apostolic Worship

LOS ANGELES TEMPLE
1366 South Alvarado
(Near Hoover)

Sundays	11:00 AM	Singspirational Worship
	7:00 PM	Apostolic Worship
Wednesdays	7:30 PM	Business (Membership) Meeting

REDWOOD VALLEY TEMPLE
7600 East Road
9 mi. north of Ukiah

Sundays	11:00 AM	Singspirational Worship
	6:00 PM	Apostolic Worship
Wednesdays	7:30 PM	COMBINED CONGREGATIONS Business (membership) meeting

SPECIAL GIFT

This August Pastor Jim Jones took 12 buses full of members of Peoples Temple on a vacation trip through the United States. These members, ranging in age from infants to 98 years, enjoyed a full program of recreation, education and inspiring meetings.

This large group went through the town where Pastor Jim was born and grew up. We saw many of the places that he knew as a child. We also went to the White House in Washington, D.C. and toured through the Capitol buildings.

Many pictures were taken of this historic trip. As a souvenir of this trip, we have put together several Anointed Pictures of Pastor Jim Jones on this vacation that are of historical significance, and we are offering them to you as an OCTOBER ANOINTED GIFT.

PASTOR JIM JONES

NEW SCHEDULE FOR ALL CHURCHES*

SAN FRANCISCO TEMPLE 1859 Geary Boulevard (former WAY Club Bldg)	Sundays	11:00 AM 7:00 PM	Singspirational Worship Apostolic Worship
LOS ANGELES TEMPLE 1366 South Alvarado (near Hoover)	Sundays Wednesdays	11:00 AM 7:00 PM 7:30 PM	Singspirational Worship Apostolic Worship Business (Membership) Meeting
REDWOOD VALLEY TEMPLE East Road 9 miles north of Ukiah	Sundays Wednesdays	11:00 AM 6:00 PM 7:30 PM	Singspirational Worship Apostolic Worship COMBINED CONGREGATIONS Business (Membership) Meeting

* The above is a regular schedule for all churches when Church Ministers OTHER THAN PASTOR JIM JONES are conducting services. See following schedule for times when PASTOR JONES will be conducting the services.

Wednesday	October 25	7:30	PM	REDWOOD VALLEY	COMBINED CONGREGATIONS Business (Membership) Meeting
Friday	October 27	8:00	PM	SAN FRANCISCO	Spiritual Healing and Worship
Saturday	October 28	2 & 4	PM	LOS ANGELES	Dynamic Healing and Worship
Sunday	October 29	11:00	AM &		
		3:00	PM	LOS ANGELES	Spiritual Healing and Worship
Wednesday	November 1	7:30	PM	REDWOOD VALLEY	COMBINED CONGREGATIONS Business (Membership) Meeting
Friday	November 3	8:00	PM	SAN FRANCISCO	Singspiration Worship & Healing
Saturday	November 4	7:30	PM	SAN FRANCISCO	Dynamic Healing and Worship
Sunday	November 5	11:00	AM	SAN FRANCISCO	Spiritual Healing and Worship
		7:30	PM	REDWOOD VALLEY	Apostolic Worship and Healing
Wednesday	November 8	7:30	PM	REDWOOD VALLEY	COMBINED CONGREGATIONS Business (Membership) Meeting
Friday	November 10	8:00	PM	SAN FRANCISCO	Singspiration Worship & Healing
Saturday	November 11	2 & 4	PM	LOS ANGELES	Dynamic Healing and Worship
Sunday	November 12	11:00	AM &		
		3:00	PM	LOS ANGELES	Spiritual Healing and Worship
Wednesday	November 15	7:30	PM	REDWOOD VALLEY	COMBINED CONGREGATIONS Business (Membership) Meeting
Friday	November 17	8:00	PM	SAN FRANCISCO	Singspiration Worship & Healing
Saturday	November 18	7:30	PM	SAN FRANCISCO	Dynamic Healing and Worship
Sunday	November 19	11:00	AM	SAN FRANCISCO	Spiritual Healing and Worship
		7:30	PM	REDWOOD VALLEY	Apostolic Worship and Healing
Wednesday	November 22	7:30	PM	REDWOOD VALLEY	COMBINED CONGREGATIONS Business (Membership) Meeting
Friday	November 24	8:00	PM	SAN FRANCISCO	Singspiration Worship & Healing
Saturday	November 25	2 & 4	PM	LOS ANGELES	Dynamic Healing and Worship
Sunday	November 26	11:00	AM &		
		3:00	PM	LOS ANGELES	Spiritual Healing and Worship
Wednesday	November 29	7:30	PM	REDWOOD VALLEY	COMBINED CONGREGATIONS Business (Membership) Meeting
Friday	December 1	8:00	PM	SAN FRANCISCO	Singspiration Worship & Healing
Saturday	December 2	7:30	PM	SAN FRANCISCO	Dynamic Healing and Worship
Sunday	December 3	11:00	AM	SAN FRANCISCO	Spiritual Healing and Worship
		7:30	PM	REDWOOD VALLEY	Apostolic Worship and Healing

ALL OF THESE MEETINGS WILL PERTAIN TO APOSTOLIC HUMAN SERVICE TO PEOPLE IN THE COMMUNITY WHO HAVE NEEDS, FOLLOWING THE ADMONITION OF JESUS IN ST. MATTHEW 25.

LOS ANGELES TEMPLE   SAN FRANCISCO TEMPLE   REDWOOD VALLEY TEMPLE

PASTOR JIM JONES

NEW SCHEDULE FOR ALL CHURCHES*

SAN FRANCISCO TEMPLE	Sundays	11:00 AM	Singspirational Worship
1859 Geary Boulevard		7:00 PM	Apostolic Worship
(former WAY Club Bldg)			
LOS ANGELES TEMPLE	Sundays	11:00 AM	Singspirational Worship
1366 South Alvarado		7:00 PM	Apostolic Worship
(near Hoover)	Wednesdays	7:30 PM	Business (Membership) Meeting
REDWOOD VALLEY TEMPLE	Sundays	11:00 AM	Singspirational Worship
East Road		6:00 PM	Apostolic Worship
9 miles north of Ukiah	Wednesdays	7:30 PM	COMBINED CONGREGATIONS
			Business (Membership) Meeting

* The above is a regular schedule for all churches when Church Ministers OTHER THAN PASTOR JIM JONES are conducting services. See following schedule for times when PASTOR JONES will be conducting the services.

Friday	December 1	8:00	PM	SAN FRANCISCO	Singspiration Worship & Healing
Saturday	December 2	7:30	PM	SAN FRANCISCO	Dynamic Healing and Worship
Sunday	December 3	11:00	AM	SAN FRANCISCO	Spiritual Healing and Worship
		8:00	PM	REDWOOD VALLEY	Apostolic Worship and Healing
Wednesday	December 6	7:30	PM	REDWOOD VALLEY	COMBINED CONGREGATIONS Business (Membership) Meeting
Friday	December 8	8:00	PM	SAN FRANCISCO	Singspiration Worship & Healing
Saturday	December 9	2 & 4	PM	LOS ANGELES	Dynamic Healing and Worship
Sunday	December 10	11:00	AM &		
		3:00	PM	LOS ANGELES	Spiritual Healing and Worship
Wednesday	December 13	7:30	PM	REDWOOD VALLEY	COMBINED CONGREGATIONS Business (Membership) Meeting
Friday	December 15	8:00	PM	SAN FRANCISCO	Singspiration Worship & Healing
Saturday	December 16	7:30	PM	SAN FRANCISCO	Dynamic Healing and Worship
Sunday	December 17	11:00	AM	SAN FRANCISCO	Spiritual Healing and Worship
		8:00	PM	REDWOOD VALLEY	Apostolic Worship and Healing
Wednesday	December 20	7:30	PM	REDWOOD VALLEY	COMBINED CONGREGATIONS Business (Membership) Meeting
Friday	December 22	8:00	PM	SAN FRANCISCO	Holiday Worship and Healing
Saturday	December 23	2 & 4	PM	LOS ANGELES	Dynamic Healing and Worship
Sunday	December 24	11:00	AM &		
		3:00	PM	LOS ANGELES	Holiday Worship and Healing
Monday	December 25	12	NOON	REDWOOD VALLEY	Family CHRISTMAS DINNER
Wednesday	December 27	7:30	PM	REDWOOD VALLEY	COMBINED CONGREGATIONS Business (Membership) Meeting
Friday	December 29	8:00	PM	SAN FRANCISCO	Singspiration Worship & Healing
Saturday	December 30	7:30	PM	SAN FRANCISCO	Dynamic Healing and Worship
Sunday	December 31	11:00	AM	SAN FRANCISCO	Apostolic Worship and Healing
		8:00	PM	REDWOOD VALLEY	NEW YEARS EVE SERVICE
Monday	January 1	12	NOON	REDWOOD VALLEY	Gift Distribution & Family Party
Wednesday	January 3	7:30	PM	REDWOOD VALLEY	COMBINED CONGREGATIONS Business (Membership) Meeting
Friday	January 5	8:00	PM	SAN FRANCISCO	Singspiration Worship & Healing
Saturday	January 6	2 & 4	PM	LOS ANGELES	Dynamic Healing and Worship
Sunday	January 7	11:00	AM &		
		3:00	PM	LOS ANGELES	Spiritual Healing and Worship

ALL OF THESE MEETINGS WILL PERTAIN TO APOSTOLIC HUMAN SERVICE TO PEOPLE IN THE COMMUNITY WHO HAVE NEEDS, FOLLOWING THE ADMONITION OF JESUS IN ST. MATTHEW 25.

LOS ANGELES TEMPLE

SAN FRANCISCO TEMPLE

REDWOOD VALLEY TEMPLE

THE MESSAGE OF JIM JONES:

Jesus said,
"What I am so shall ye be. These things shall ye do and greater because I go to the Father."

I have built on this ideal and, thus, have made Christ real to those who are ready for the Sonship ministry. I have come to demonstrate to you that God can abide in these temples of clay, that God *can reign* in our bodies, for we are, indeed, Temples of the Holy Ghost! Some have never actually come to terms with what this sacred teaching signifies! Yea, it is written, that the Captain of our Salvation, Jesus Christ, was *made* perfect through His suffering. I have taken to heart the instruction in Philippians (2:5-7) to *"Let this mind be in you, which was also in Christ Jesus: Who, being in the form of God, thought it not robbery to be equal with God: But made himself of no reputation, and took upon him the form of a servant, and was made in the likeness of men,"* and have come to declare that *you* can have as much of God as you are willing to pay for with the dedication and sacrifice of your life in service to others.

(...excerpts from sermon)

PEOPLES TEMPLE CHRISTIAN CHURCH has extensions in many cities, and provides transportation to and from all its meetings. Call your local secretaries for information about meetings and transportation. They are:

Redwood Valley	Mrs. Edith Bogue	(707) 485-7765
	Mrs. Rita Tupper	(707) 462-6291
Bay Area	Mrs. Leona Collier	(415) 626-3365
San Francisco	Miss Jane Mutschman	(415) 863-3290
Oakland-East Bay	Mrs. Mattie Wimberly	(415) 654-3829
Richmond	Mrs. Mary Green	(415) 235-3209
Pittsburg	Mrs. Theresa Nickerson	(415) 439-1678
San Mateo	Mrs. Margaret Elsey	(415) 343-0722
Palo Alto	Mrs. Mary Lendo	(415) 325-2589
San Jose	Rev. Mabel Davis	(408) 272-0871
Fresno	Mrs. Melvina Green	(209) 266-7854
Sacramento	Mr. & Mrs. Louis Tennerson	(916) 383-8735
Los Angeles	Mrs. Corine Liggins	(213) 232-1749
	Mrs. Irene White	(213) 234-1143
	Mrs. Julie Beres	(213) 242-1287
Seattle	Mr. & Mrs. Harold Flowers	(206) 323-5836
	Mrs. Davis	(206) 325-4661
	Mrs. Darnell	(206) 763-0919
	Mr. & Mrs. John Kostelnik	(206) 784-3045
Renton, Washington	Mrs. Wroten	(206) 228-6092

PEOPLES TEMPLE, Los Angeles	1366 So. Alvarado	(213) 384-3604
PEOPLES TEMPLE, San Francisco	1859 Geary Blvd.	(415) 346-0385
PEOPLES TEMPLE, Redwood Valley	East Road	(707) 485-7219

People's Temple
P.O. Box 214
Redwood Valley, CA 95470

PEOPLES
Temple
Report

FEBRUARY, 1973

Led by our Pastor, JIM JONES, PEOPLES TEMPLE is on the march... Our Pastor's evangelical mission is expanding throughout the United States and into foreign lands. We want you, our members and friends, to be a part of these wonderful happenings reflecting the GLORY OF GOD in earth today... WITNESS THIS LAST MONTH:

SAN FRANCISCO CHRONICLE PRAISES TEMPLE. . . In their January 17, 1973, edition, one of the largest newspapers in the United States, printed an article praising our Pastor and Peoples Temple as being:

> ". . .highly regarded for its social works which include housing and feeding senior citizens and medical convalescents, maintaining a home for retarded boys, rehabilitating youthful drug users and assisting non-members as well as members of the faith through college and legal difficulties."

This article was an inspiration for countless thousands of readers...

A GREAT NEW TEXAS CAMPAIGN. . . A Baptist official in Texas has invited us there for a great campaign this spring. While still in Texas this man was healed of a heart condition. He was brought by air in a wheel chair to our Los Angeles temple, and was delivered from blindness as he was miraculously called by Pastor Jones and healed of his many afflictions. He came out of his wheel chair and is now a rallying force for thousands in this great, expanding missionary program.

NOTED NEWSPAPER EDITOR UNITES WITH PEOPLES TEMPLE. . . E. P. Alexander is the editor of the HERALD-DISPATCH, a prominent newspaper circulated around the globe. She has elected to unite with Peoples Temple. . .In her newspaper editorial of January 18, 1973, she writes:

> ". . .I want all...to become members of The Peoples Temple —— and be exposed to the teachings of Pastor Jim Jones. I think Pastor Jim Jones is Godly —— and I plan to become a member of the temple in Los Angeles. I can relate to his teachings. . ."

Her voice, in praise of our Pastor has already been heard around the world.

A FEDERAL CREDIT UNION —— FOR . . .MEMBERS. . .ONLY. . . Now, in addition to legal, nursing and social services, Peoples Temple is establishing a Federal Credit Union, available to MEMBERS ONLY. This will provide loans for the needy at LOW rates, provide group insurance at the lowest cost, and other money saving advantages. .at the same time paying HIGH INTEREST on savings accounts FULLY INSURED up to $20,000. by an agency of the FEDERAL GOVERN— MENT.

MEETINGS, EXPANSION AND MIRACLES CONTINUE. . . In every meeting, growths are removed, persons throw away crutches and come out of wheel chairs —— some having been crippled for many years. The blind see again, the deaf hear. . . and all shout joyous praise of CHRIST MANIFESTED THROUGH PASTOR JIM JONES. Thousands of testimonies have been received of miraculous healings through pictures, prayer cloths and anointed oil. We joyfully PRAISE GOD for these great, miraculous events that have marked the beginning of 1973 and wish to share our joy in work and praise with you during this coming year. . .

COMING SOON. . .THE LIVING WORD. . . begins a continuous new series as of the end of February when a new publication contract has been arranged. Earlier subscribers will receive 12 monthly issues at no additional cost. SUBSCRIPTION INFORMATION will be published in our next bulletin.

The Temple Reporter

Published as a community service by Peoples Temple Christian Church (Disciples of Christ), as part of its mission to help bring about God's Kingdom "On Earth" and the American dream of "Freedom and Justice for All."

Vol. I, No. I   Summer 1973

Board of Supervisors Tentatively Approve Rehabilitation Center

"The aura of the jail is one of a zoo, with bleak, tobacco stained walls, cold concrete floors, the smell of body odors, and the dim lighting that emphasizes the gloomy lives of the occupants. There is no privacy from peer-ing eyes, or from the constant dull noises of distant talking, a blaring radio, and the almost constant sound of opening and closing steel doors. There is no place to retreat."

The quote is from a recent study for the proposed Mendocino County Regional Comprehensive Rehabilitation Center (MC/RCRC). The project, which has been approved by the Board of Supervisors, subject to being funded 75 percent from a

(Continued on Page 4)

FREEDOM OF THE PRESS

The current threat to freedom of the press and the rights of the people to know the affairs of state is unprecedented in America's history and represents, perhaps, the most serious danger ever known to the liberty of our collective citizenry. Last year more reporters were jailed or threatened with jail for refusing to reveal confidential sources and informaton than in any previous year. In June of 1971 prior restraint was exercised for the first time ever when a court order stopped two of the nation's leading newspapers (The New York Times and Washington Post) from printing specific articles on the Pentagon Papers. Although the action was subsequently overturned, a U. S. Circuit Court of Appeals ruled that such censorship orders must be obeyed until they are determined illegal by a court. These actions threaten the very basis of press freedom guaranteed by the First Amendment, upon which the survival of this country as a democracy depends.

The case for confidential sources should be obvious. If newsmen in the past could not have guaranteed that they would protect the identity of their sources, few reports could have been made public exposing government corruption. Confidential sources must be protected simply because they reveal vital information that otherwise could not be obtained -- information responsible for winning many Pulitzer Prizes.

COLLISION WITH ERROR

A fundamental premise of our democratic form of government has been that, given a wide range of opinions, facts and information the people will somehow make the right decision. The premise takes for granted that some of the information will be false, but it also assumes an unrestricted access to the informational sources so that a fair balance of information and ideas may be reported. As long as the unlimited access to information remained intact, truth

(Continued on Page 5)

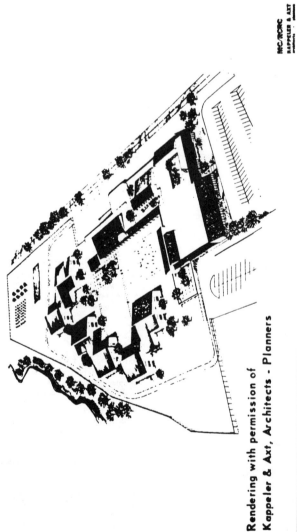

Rendering with permission of Kappeler & Axt, Architects - Planners

MC/RCRC
KAPPELER & AXT

54

PEOPLES TEMPLE in the Congressional Record

United States of America

PROCEEDINGS AND DEBATES OF THE 93^d CONGRESS, FIRST SESSION

June, 1973

Editor's Note: Peoples Temple Christian Church, which is affiliated with the Disciples of Christ denomination, and has a statewide membership in excess of 10,000, last month received a highly significant and unsolicited commendation from a prominent Caucasian Congressman. Documenting the Congressman's remarks to the House of Representatives, the Record tells of how Rev. James W. Jones, "has sparked a campaign in defense of the First Amendment to the Constitution." Because of the critical Constitutional issues involved, the statement is being presented here, exactly as it appeared in the Congressional Record.

PEOPLES TEMPLE CHRISTIAN CHURCH SUPPORTS FIRST AMENDMENT

IN THE HOUSE OF REPRESENTATIVES

Mr. Speaker, I was recently made aware of the fact that the congregation of the Peoples Temple Christian Church of Redwood Valley, Calif., has donated a total of $4,400 for the defense of William Farr and other reporters jailed for refusing to reveal their sources of information. I would like to commend the Rev. James W. Jones, who is pastor of the church, and every member of his congregation for this outstanding demonstration of their commitment to the principles on which this country was founded.

I would like to include in the Record at this point a few items which appeared in the press recently about Peoples Temple. The first is an article from the IAPA News, which is published bimonthly by the Inter American Press Association. This item appeared in the February-March edition, and reads as follows:

CHURCH DONATION AIDS FIGHT FOR PRESS FREEDOM

The Inter American Press Association, we all know, operates strictly on dues paid by members and does not solicit outside contributions for its main task of defending and promoting freedom of information in the Americas. Recently, however, we received an unsolicited contribution that moved us deeply. We accepted it with gratitude and full appreciation of the high principles that moved the donors.

The donation of $250 came from the congregation of the Peoples Temple Christian Church, of Redwood Valley, California, whose pastor, the Reverend James W. Jones, has sparked a campaign in defense of the First Amendment to the constitution.

"We believe," wrote James R. Pugh, in behalf of the Board of Elders, "that the American way of life is being threatened by the recent jailings of news reporters for refusal to reveal their sources. As a church, we feel a responsibility to defend the free speech clause of the First Amendment, for without it America will have lost freedom of conscience and the climate will become ripe for totalitarianism."

The elders voted the donation after hearing the Rev. Jones read "to an overflow congregation" excerpts from a report on the state of the press in the U.S. made by Brady Black, editor of the Cincinnati Enquirer, and regional vice chairman of the IAPA's Committee on Freedom of the Press, at the IAPA's annual meeting last October in Chile. Mr. Black," the covering letter said, "gave a lucid and convincing account of developments in our country constituting a threat to the people's right to know." The letter was addressed to Francis Dale, Publisher of The Enquirer.

Mr. Pugh reported that a grand total of $4,400 had been contributed by the congregation, made up of "ordinary working people of all backgrounds," for the defense of William Farr and other reporters jailed for refusing to reveal their sources of information.

"No acknowledgement for this contribution is necessary," wrote Mr. Pugh. "We wish simply to demonstrate ... that there are churches and other groups in society which are not connected with the institutional press who do indeed care about this threat to freedom of speech, press and conscience."

He said the donation was "to be used as you see fit in defense of a free press."

The Peoples Temple Christian Church, under the Rev. Jones does not only take a stand on constitutional rights. The church also has established a drug rehabilitation program, two convalescent homes, a 40-acre home for mentally retarded boys, three senior citizen's homes and an animal shelter.

The next item appeared in the San Francisco Chronicle of January 17 of this year, and without further introduction, I place it in the Record:

A CHURCH GIVES $4,400 TO THE PRESS

Twelve newspapers—among them The Chronicle—and a newsmagazine and a television station have been awarded grants totaling $4400 by Peoples Temple Christian Church of the Disciples of Christ for use "in the defense of a free press."

Announcement of the grants was made yesterday in Ukiah, Mendocino county, by the board of trustees of the church, which has a statewide membership of more than 7500.

THREAT

Speaking for the board, trustee James R. Pugh said:

"We believe the American way of life is being threatened by the recent jailings of news reporters for refusal to reveal their sources.

"As a church, we feel a responsibility to defend the free speech clause of the First Amendment, for without it America will have lost freedom of conscience and the climate will become ripe for totalitarianism."

Pugh said the church's pastor, the Rev. Jim Jones, had "publicly commended" The Chronicle and its "fine editorial staff" for taking a strong editorial position in defense of the First Amendment and for "the high quality of the newspaper."

"The San Francisco Chronicle has shown itself to be fair, lucid, comprehensive and courageous in confronting many issues head on," trustee Pugh said.

SOCIAL

Called less formally Peoples Temple, the church is best known and highly regarded for its social works which include housing and feeding senior citizens and medical convalescents, maintaining a home for retarded boys, rehabilitating youthful drug users, and assisting non-members as well as members of the faith through college and legal difficulties.

In accepting the grant in behalf of The Chronicle, Charles de Young Thieriot, editor and publisher, expressed his thanks to the Peoples Temple Christian Church.

Thieriot said the $500 awarded to The Chronicle will be turned over to Sigma Delta Chi, the professional journalistic society, which is active in defense of freedom of the press.

And next I would like to share with our colleagues the text of a resolution which the Christian Church of Northern California-Nevada—Disciples of Christ—passed by an overwhelming margin on May 19 at their 1973 annual meeting. The resolution was offered by the First Christian Church of San Jose and won broad support from the 230 delegates attending the convention at the First Christian Church of Modesto, Calif. The delegates represented about 16,000 members from 79 congregations.

The text of the resolution follows:

Whereas, the church stands for freedom, and the free flow of information, and

Whereas, the public media, namely the press, is under increased challenge as to its exercising freedom in news and programming, as guaranteed by the First Amendment of the Constitution, and

Whereas, one of our congregation, Peoples Temple Christian Church, Redwood Valley, California, has made a financial contribution for use in defense of a free press as guaranteed by the First Amendment;

Therefore, be it resolved that the Christian Church of Northern California-Nevada (Disciples of Christ) meeting in its Annual Meeting May 18, 19 and 20, 1973, at First Christian Church, Modesto, California, encourage its member congregations to make their voice heard in support of a free and responsible press by either making financial contributions to insure a free and responsible press or by letting our elected officials, representatives of the communications media, and others know that we oppose any action which infringes on the First Amendment.

And be it further resolved that the Christian Church of Northern California-Nevada (Disciples of Christ), meeting in its Annual Meeting, May 18, 19 and 20, 1973 at First Christian Church, Modesto, California, make known to our elected officials, representatives of communications media, and others our support of a free and responsible press and our commitment to that position and our rejection of any action which infringes on the First Amendment.

The Church Board, First Christian Church San Jose, California.

PEOPLES TEMPLE VOLUNTEERS PAINT Redwood Valley School

"In the classic American tradition of churches acting to alleviate the burdens of government, Rev. James W. Jones, pastor of Peoples Temple Christian Church, organized a crew of 20 to 25 Temple members to spend the weekend of July 28 - 29th painting the Redwood Valley Elementary School and the Redwood Valley Junior High School. Arriving at 8:00 AM and working for many hours, the crew painted all of the wainscoting and most of the exterior stucco on ten of the eleven buildings making up the school complex. They also painted the yellow stripes on the parking lot, repaired holes in some of the walls, and painted all six restrooms. They applied four coats to the butler storage building and painted the duct and refrigeration units in one of the buildings.

Wallace Bralich, principal of Redwood Valley Junior High School, took paint brush in hand and worked side by side during the whole time. Persons associated with the school, including Denny Parks and Frances Lamb, as well as Vivian Yurko, provided lunch and dinner, to the pleasure and surprise of the workers.

The volunteers from Peoples Temple included two professional painting crews, one from Hayward and the other from Fresno. They were joined by local members, black and white, men and women, young and old. All of them came off their regular weekend projects to help the schools out. As one Temple member described it, "Jim Jones has always praised Mr. Bralich, the staff and teachers of Redwood Valley School."

Surveying the work accomplished at the end of the job, a professional painting contractor estimated the value of the work done, thus constituting a savings to the taxpayers of the Redwood Valley Union School District, of two thousand eight hundred dollars ($2,800.00).

PRINCIPAL WALLACE BRALICH (third from left) joins Peoples Temple painting crew

UVARC: An Alternative for the Handicapped

DOREEN BRADY, Director of Ukiah Valley Rehabilitation Workshop

In the sprawling network of modern urban America, individuals with their problems and frustrations are often lost in the high-pressure shuffle. This is particularly the case for the mentally retarded or physically handicapped. Too often considered merely irritating reminders of unpleasant reality, these people are left alone to make their way as best they can. They do not fit into the busy pattern of city life, and we find ourselves guiltily wishing they would go away.

In Mendocino County, however, the story is different. For the past eight years, an organization has existed in our area that has courageously worked to lighten the burden of the handicapped and mentally retarded. With great sensitivity, the Ukiah Valley Association for the Retarded (UVARC), under the energetic leadership of Doreen Brady, has consistently provided the handicapped with alternatives to loneliness and isolation. Its well coordinated monstrated their sense of social concern and community responsibility by engaging in work contracts with UVARC, but more contracts are desperately needed. It is now clear that in order for the workshop to continue, local businesses and organizations must actively participate by contracting with the center.

The skills and services offered are many and are of the highest quality. In addition, by designing, producing, and marketing a hand weaving loom, the trainees have been directed in machine tool operation. They engage in wood-production trades; craft training and textile work; and office skills, including collating, addressograph machine operation, packaging and shipping. During the past three years the workshop has averaged better than twenty placements per year of its trainees into full time jobs. This represents a yearly placement record of over 22 percent -- a figure that ranks impressively high in comparison with similar programs for the handicapped.

program includes job training, counseling for parents of the disabled, and community education on the needs and special problems of mental retardation. The training program involves work evaluation, work adjustment, and work experience covering periods of training, to bring multiple and severely disabled adults to their highest possible level of job skill efficiency. The result is, in our county at least, that the disabled need no longer fear shame and anxiety as the unwanted and outcast members of society.

THE CRISIS

Currently, the program is facing a crisis. Quite simply, it needs the help of our community to continue its operation. In the past, the workshop has succeeded in obtaining contracts from local and nationwide industries, as well as public agencies. United Airlines, the Post Office, Masonite, and several other area manufacturers, have de-

a style of living that we have worked hard to earn.

But there are others in our valley, the mentally retarded, who are unable to compete in the daily struggle -- although their dreams of happiness are no different from our own. The workshop gives them a chance, a chance to fulfill these dreams, a chance to gain that most precious American right -- the right to human dignity. Support of the workshop gives them their opportunity. And it gives us a chance too -- a chance to be our brother's keeper.

THEY DREAM TOO

But perhaps the best reason for supporting the workshop is the human reason. Most of us are fortunate people. We live in a lush and beautiful valley, a valley untouched by the choking smog and deafening clatter of city living. We need not walk down a maze of cracked and ragged sidewalks, greeted at every turn by the stench of overflowing garbage, or by the open sores of cast-off poverty. Drunks lying in the gutters do not offend our eyes. We live in comfortable homes, surrounded by well-kept gardens; neat, clipped, and clean. We enjoy

Mendocino College
A SECOND CHANCE IN EDUCATION

"I like to see people get a second chance educationally," says Peter De Vries, the highly qualified president of Mendocino College. Mr. De Vries is a man on the lookout for the best methods and means for meeting the needs of his new students. It is a quality that other top officials of the institution share. Judging from the comments of Tom McMillan, the young Dean of Student Personnel, Walter Robie, Business Manager, and Paul Alcantra, Dean of Instruction, Mendocino College will not want for enthusiastic yet reasonable men to set the academic guidelines. All are genuinely interested in seeing that each student will receive constructive help in realizing his or her highest potential.

Human Potential Approach

With 11 years of experience in the field, Mr. McMillan has demonstrated concern for the problems of students who possess the capabilities for high achievement, but who fail to make the grades. His doctoral thesis, a sensitive study of school dropouts, is indicative of his ability to approach students on a one-to-one basis. As he sees it, the greatest difficulty a student faces is the inability to define his personal values and goals. McMillan feels the college should help. Mendocino College will offer a positive, "Human Potential Approach," designed to determine a student's strengths, as well as those factors that will motivate him towards achievement.

Frustrated Grads

Paul Alcantra, Dean of Instruction, explains it this way: "Grads can't find jobs because education has been too specialized. I don't like to see someone go through school and get a master's degree, then end up frustrated. This is what we want to change." If the prospective program for the upcoming fall is any indication, change is, indeed, in the offing. At this time there are twelve approved majors for transfer to four year institutions, nineteen majors that will lead to a Certificate of Achievement in one year, or an Associate Degree in two years. In the first year of operation about 150 different courses in the day and evening programs will be available, reflecting a wide range of academic interests and vocational goals.

700 this fall

Currently housed in temporary quarters at the Twelth District Fairgrounds, the college is searching for a permanent site. Walter Robie notes that interest presently centers around a possible location in the area near the junction of Highways 20 and 101, but that property as far north as Willits is also under scrutiny. Mr. Robie, formerly assistant business manager for Sierra College, and the father of four children, expects that the college will be at the Fairgrounds for two to three years. The main concern at the present time is getting portable classrooms set up and ready for the

PETER De VRIES, President Mendocino College

opening of the fall semester on September 11th. With an anticipated enrollment of seven to eight hundred students this fall, the need for classrooms is apparent. The State Senate Bill No. 6, presently under consideration by the legislature and expected to be passed into law, will relieve the financial burden by providing additional funds for educational purposes.

Teaching quality at the new community college will be well above average. All faculty members must have a master's degree or its equivalent to teach in a subject matter field, and most will have had prior teaching experience at another California Community College. Formerly Vice President and Dean of Instruction at Butte College, President Peter De Vries is scouring campuses for top quality instructors who care about people as well as books. Asked if he is satisfied that he's getting the caliber of instructor the College needs and he desires, he confidently replied, "You bet!" After taking a look at Mr. De Vries and the rest of the administrative staff, we would say it is a safe gamble.

BIG BROTHER PROGRAM

To Begin In Mendocino County

MARK RAYMOND

Fatherless boys who have been deprived of the friendship and guidance only a man can provide will have the opportunity to regain that friendship soon because of the efforts of a group of citizens who have been working to start a Big Brother organization in Mendocino County.

The theory of the program is simple: to match one boy with one man, a man who has demonstrated he has the time and the love to share with a youngster who is in need of that priceless commodity.

The Big Brother program idea is not new to this county. Several have thought of starting or have actually taken the first steps in beginning to organize a Big Brother chapter. Their efforts though noble fell short of the goal. However, some have joined the new movement - which is not only off the ground, but getting close to the date when the first Little Brother - Big Brother match is to be made.

Mark Raymond, who was elected chairman of the board of directors of Big Brothers of Mendocino County in March, was a Big Brother in Sonoma County. When he moved to Ukiah in September of last year, he discovered there was no Big Broth-

er organization here, and decided to do something about it. Working with the Ukiah Jaycees, of which he is a member and officer, he and a handful of Jaycee members set about recruiting dedicated and responsive individuals to serve on the board of the organization.

Among those persons who have pledged to give of their time in this effort, are County Welfare Director Dennis Denny, Supervisor Burgess Williams, Ukiah Mayor Jack Simpson, Probation Officer Bob McAllister, Ukiah businessman Jim McArthur, Children's Service Workers Ray Ellis and Jim Armstrong, Juvenile Hall Superintendent Jim Kolesar, school psychologist Bob Ripke, high school counselor Chet Hardin, Officer Paul McCoey of the Ukiah Police Department, Jaycees Rick Woolworth and Jim Rhodes, and Bob Cavender.

Simpson heads the all-important Selection Committee, Armstrong is chairman of the Budget Committee, and McCoey has been appointed head of the Public Relations Committee. A fund-raising chairman has ten-

tatively been appointed, but this is not yet confirmed.

The preliminary steps which must be taken before a match can be made, are painstaking and complex, yet essential to the success of the program. When a Little Brother comes to the attention of the organization, whether through school, church, probation or children's services, parent or friend, the child and his mother or guardian come to the Big Brothers for an application and interview. The child's interests and problems are discussed with the mother, and a file completed on the potential Little Brother. This work is done by a part-time secretary, and by the board's Selection Committee.

Selection of a Big Brother applicant is much more detailed. After the applicant, who can be 18 years or older in age, has filled out an application, a police record and background reference check is made by Big Brothers' staff. The potential Big Brother is then interviewed by the Selection Committee to determine if he would be a capable Big Brother. Care is taken to exclude those with possible emotional problems, and those who have boys in the same age group where a Little Brother match may interfere with the man's family life.

After a file has been completed on the Big Brother, his interests and strong points will be reviewed, and if they seem to be compatible with one of the Little Brother applicants on file, the match process will begin.

First, the mother is contacted and told about the potential Big Brother for her son. Then the man is contacted and briefed about his potential Little

Brother. Either may reject the match before it starts. Once accepted, however, a counselor (a volunteer who has some background in dealing with people) is assigned to the match and will arrange for the Little Brother and Big Brother to be introduced.

The counselor is an important link in the match process. He or she will keep in touch with the Big Brother and Little Brother's mother to ensure the match is progressing well. If any problems arise, the Counselor will attempt to resolve them.

Any expenses incurred by the Big Brother for his Little Brother come from his own pocket, whether it be for a camping or fishing trip, taking in a movie, going to a ballgame, grabbing a milkshake, or just driving around enjoying the countryside. Some of the best experiences occur when no expense is involved: sitting in the park and talking friend-to-friend.

A Big Brother is asked to spend at least four hours a week with his Little Brother, or at least be in contact by phone. The match will hopefully last at least one year, since short-term matches have relatively little benefit for the boy. Some matches have lasted from the time the boy was 8 until he graduated from high school.

As Big Brothers of Mendocino County is a non-profit, volunteer organization, funding for necessary expenses must come from membership, contributors, clubs, and organizations, and other outside sources. United Way has accepted Big Brothers to include in its annual fund drive, but that will supply

only a portion of the budget, which this year is $6,700. The remainder must come from one fund-raising activity, and from memberships.

Operating expenses include salary for a part-time secretary, expenses involved in operating an office, and miscellaneous expenses for insurance, office supplies, printing, and an activity fund for an annual get-together of all Big and Little Brothers.

At this point, the organization is beginning to gear up for the first match. An office is being sought, a telephone has been installed with an answering service to take phone messages, forms are being printed for applications. Big Brothers are now being sought to apply and be interviewed. All correspondence, donations, and requests for Big Brother application forms should be directed to: Big Brothers of Mendocino County, P.O. Box 362, Ukiah CA 95482. You may also get information by phoning 462-5545.

Little Brother referrals are also being accepted for the first matches, hopefully by the end of August.

Initially, the organization will serve the greater Ukiah area to include Redwood Valley Potter Valley, Willits, Talmage and Hopland. As the operation expands, and more funding is available, Big Brothers will expand to serve all parts of Mendocino County, supplying a vital service which has proven to be effective in the prevention of juvenile delinquency.

A Big Brother executive in Los Angeles hit the heart of the matter when he recently stated, "There are no big rewards for becoming a Big Brother; just the knowledge that when a boy reached his hand out for help, yours was there to receive it."

TRINITY SCHOOL: ...*Suffer The Little Children...*

STEVEN KATSARIS, Director

Trinity School's guiding philosophy is to create a warm and friendly atmosphere where-in battered, neglected, abandoned, and educationally handicapped children may overcome their emotional and adjustment problems. A non-sectarian facility, run under the auspices of the Greek Orthodox Church, and the very able supervision of Steven Katsaris, Trinity uniquely features an educational and clinical staff who work closely together to provide a consistent therapeutic approach to the problems of each child.

There are 58 children in the school (40 boys and 18 girls) in living groups of eight or ten. The needs of each child are met by child care workers, a housemother, teachers, teachers' aides, and group social workers who supervise the group program. The student-staff ratio is almost one to one.

Working in class groups of no more than twelve, the teachers' aides strive to alter the children's negative attitudes towards learning and schools.

The classrooms are open and ungraded. Each child is encouraged to work to his own level of ability. When a child has reached a level where he is able to benefit from a more academically oriented program, he is transferred to a transitional class, preparatory to his returning to public school. Children are not confined to the subjects available at the school itself. Field trips, movie-going, Little League baseball, Scouting and related experiences allow the children to participate in a broad range of learning activities. Under the intense guidance and direction of the staff, the children share in outside experiences that have a therapeutic, as well as recreational value.

Further information regarding the school is available by calling 462-8721, or by dropping by for a visit at 915 West Church Street, Ukiah.

CHIMP IN THE VALLEY

MR. MUGGS AND HIS ADOPTED MOM, JOYCE TOUCHETTE

Pictured above is Mr. Muggs, our local chimpanzee-in-residence, together with his adopted mom, Joyce Touchette. Grossly mistreated, Muggs was rescued by Rev. Jim Jones and patiently nursed back to health.

Only 18 months old, he has the intelligence of a four year old child. He will be full grown at five years, will weigh 200 lbs.,

and have the strength of ten men. Muggs loves children and animals, but is wary of adults, especially strangers. His reasons deserve our sympathy. For every baby chimp that is brought to the U.S., one mother chimp is killed. Out of seven thousand chimps exported to the United States, only seven hundred survive the taxing journey. Quite naturally, Muggs distrusts strangers, and is always alert when they are around. It may sound anthropomorphic, but Muggs will follow every command of Pastor Jones, and will defend him even when anyone comes up casually to pet the chimpanzee. Muggs likes to be in church services, and will keep rhythm to the music by tapping his feet. A modern, spacious habitat is presently being built near the animal shelter at the Temple, to house Muggs when he grows a little older.

Mrs. Touchette was one of the many who offered to keep and care for Mr. Muggs, and his antics have made him the delight of her family. Muggs is a gourmet. On his list of favorite foods: salad with garlic dressing, lasagna, whipped cream, "Mounds" candy bars, nuts, bolts, screws, and rocks. A somewhat particular eater, Muggs prefers rocks found on the roof of the Touchette house to those lying on the ground. When asked his opinion of life at the Touchette's, Mr. Muggs grinned and replied: "Wahoo!"

JIM JONES will be on The JIM DUNBAR Show

Station KGO-TV, Channel 7
Tuesday, August 28, 1973, 7:08-7:40 am

Mendocino County Peace Officers:

SAVED FROM PARALYSIS BY CHP OFFICER BRAVERY

Highway Patrolman Terry Moses was awarded a Certificate of Commendation recently for his actions last November which saved the life of a San Francisco woman. Moses was on patrol when he came upon the overturned stationwagon of Mrs. Sandra Wessling who was trapped inside with her three-year old son. Taking no heed to the great rush of fire, Moses broke through a window and pulled out the child, then crawled inside to help Mrs. Wessling. She was pinned under the steering wheel and was having trouble breathing. Moses ascertained that her neck was broken. He gently positioned her head so she could breathe more easily, then called for an ambulance.

The commendation reads, "As a result of Officer Moses' action, the victim was rescued from possible suffocation and probable paralysis due to neck injuries. The officer's actions have proven to be an example of the high degree of professional competence resulting in a saved life. . . and high regard for this department."

Moses has been with the California Highway Patrol since 1966, serving the public in an arduous, and for the most part thankless, position of responsibility.

Your CHP & Operation Evidence: A SUCCESS

For the first time in the California Highway Patrol's history, a joint, tri-county effort was made to avoid needless accidents and injuries over the recent Memorial Day weekend.

California Highway Patrol commanders, Captain Hays Hickey of Mendocino County, Lieutenant Merle Dailey of the Garberville Substation, and Captain W. O. Roberts of Humboldt County, cooperated to make over 250 miles of Highway 101 safer for that critical holiday period. Captain Hickey said: "The three counties tripled the number of patrol cars on US 101 beginning the afternoon of May 25th and running through the evening of May 29th. Thus, there was a patrol car on duty for each 8½ miles of the highway from the Oregon border to Cloverdale."

To further identify the patrol cars, they travelled with their headlights on, and with a large fluorescent pennant flying from their radio antennas. Captain Hickey explained the purpose as two-fold. "We provide safer highways for travelers just with our presence, and,

Chief Saulsbury: A HUMAN BEING HAS DIGNITY

In a time when so many law-officers are incensed about the relatively new laws which appear to get criminals "off-the-hook," Ukiah Chief of Police, Donn Saulsbury remains calmly philosophical. He says the disregard for individual rights up until 1955 brought about those tough Supreme Court decisions which set many suspects free when an officer fails to follow strictly the statutory procedure.

"We brought this on ourselves," says Saulsbury, not sounding too unhappy about it. "I think people are now beginning to get their money's worth in law enforcement because serving under the new statutes requires a much more professional officer, one who is more sensitive to the rights of the individual. The officer must also be able to read and comprehend laws more clearly than ever before because of their technical nature."

Saulsbury's officers apparently go along with his belief in the need for better educated law enforcers. Forty-three percent of the sworn staff in the Ukiah Police Department attended community college or took university classes on their own initiative. Twenty-eight percent already have college degrees.

What about the local police record under the newer and more restrictive statutes? Criminal offenses per capita are about the same as in other communities, but over half of them are committed by the transient population, indicating that the local citizenry are unusually law-abiding. Also, about 50 percent of the felonies committed locally are cleared by arrests of the persons responsible for the crime, which is at least double that of most areas.

"That's the advantage of a small town, especially Ukiah, where people know each other and are quick to notice and report law-breaking activity," says Saulsbury.

If the community sentiment in Ukiah is representative of other areas, and if the chief has read the local pulse correctly, the pendulum may be starting to swing the other way as far as public apathy and even hostility to law officers is concerned. He sees various segments making concerted efforts to understand law enforcement problems and help solve them.

"People are more concerned about God and country now than they have been in the last five years," Saulsbury believes. "They're fed up and irate with groups that preach violence and revolutionary tactics and now they want to do something about it."

Chief Saulsbury is giving the community a chance to do something through several police-community relations programs, which are also designed to be relevant for youth. In fact Ukiah police have been welcomed into the schools where they are teaching pedestrian and bicycle safety, showing films on law enforcement, and conducting open-air discussions with students. A ride-along program, "Operation Understanding,"

for 9th through 12th graders, has proven extremely successful and may be extended to adults. Students who now ride with officers on patrol are often right at the scene of a crime and arrest. Saulsbury says this gives them the opportunity to see what is done and why. They can also see the arrests in their total context, not just the inhuman-looking act of arrest itself. This has enabled the young person to see the compassionate, human qualities of a police officer who, unfortunately, is not always seen in this light.

Saulsbury has had 27 years of experience in law enforcement, most of them in Southern California. But he likes the slower pace and more personal feeling of working in a small town where it is not as easy to become desensitized to the needs and personalities of others.

"Many of our officers have lived here a long time and often know the people they are dealing with in a professional capacity, and know how to best handle them," he says.

One statement, perhaps, tells more about the Ukiah Chief of Police than any other. When asked about his philosophy of law enforcement, the chief gently replied, "A human being has dignity, so why not try to let him retain it?"

secondly, the lights and pennants increased the visibility of our cars." The operation was not conceived as an all-out effort to issue citations, but rather as a deterrent to excessive speeding. The effort was a marked succes, as there were no fatalities over the weekend in the patrolled area, and a significant decrease in accidents as well.

Rehabilitation Center

(Continued from Front Page)

grant under Section 306 of the Omnibus Crime Control and Safe Street Act of 1968, has been headed by Sheriff Reno Bartolomie. It is a remarkably innovative, yet realistic program -- an approach that attempts to avoid the common pitfalls of rehabilitation systems (six months in front of a TV set and out on the street again) while keeping in mind that all techniques are merely transitional means to the final objective -- complete rehabilitation. Thus, the project is defined within the borders of reality, in that techniques are limited by community standards and social needs, factors which are subject to change. Therefore, the program remains flexible.

ADVISORY COUNCIL

In keeping with more recent concepts of community responsibility for criminal rehabilitation, an Advisory Council to the Center will be established to assist in the establishment and determination of policies and techniques used at the Center. It is hoped that by doing so, the facility will remain in a more practical, constant contact with the requirements of the community at large. In turn, the community may become more responsive to the needs of the Center. The Sheriff, District Attorney, Superior and Justice Court representatives, Public Defender, a Center inmate representative, Welfare Director, a member of the County Bar Association, Probation Office and representatives from local police in the service area will all be included on the Council.

Upon entering the facility, all offenders will be given a medical examination (and treatment if necessary) followed by an orientation session designed to acquaint the individual with the programs available through the Center. Educational, vocational and psychological testing, together with confidential interviews, will be used to obtain a profile of the offender. This profile may be subsequently used to recommend the individual for various rehabilitation programs. Also, the information may be of help to the courts in evaluating the benefit to an offender of alternatives to trial and sentence -- such as drug or alcoholic programs.

THREE PHASES

The pivotal concept of the Center is the custody/release concept. Custody/release is divided into three phases. The offender is afforded a specialized rehabilitation program, depending on the degree of custody/release in which he might be. The Phase I degree ("full custody") occurs upon entering the facility, as described above. Phase II and III involve different degrees of release and supervision. Under Phase II, "partial custody release," a person may be given hourly or day-to-day release in conjunction with a particular rehabilitation program. Phase III steps toward full 24 hour release, but still necessitates participation in a rehabilitation program until the full 24 hour freedom is earned.

Specific rehabilitation programs fall into six general categories: education, employment, group therapy, counseling, prevention, and other special programs. All programs work in harmony with the custody/release concept. For example, an inmate in Phase I (full custody), participating in an education program, may be restricted to in-house classes, tutoring, and correspondence courses. Library facilities will be available to him within the Center. Persons in Phase II or III may attend local adult school facilities. Vocational education will also encompass both training related to jobs within the Center, as well as training in the outside community itself.

CAMPUS PATTERN

The building plans have also been devised with an eye toward creating a flexible, cooperative atmosphere. An informal, open campus pattern, extensive use of wood for walkways and interiors, will dispel any hint of a sterile "correction" institution. The site selected for the Center is on thirteen acres, located west of the County Hospital and Juvenile Hall. Provision has been made for a County Motor Pool and Garage complex (which will provide automotive training for inmates) and a one acre truck garden. The Community Center will function as the focal point for inmate activity: a library, lounge, barbershop, and store are planned for this area. The dining hall will also house a portable stage to be used for movies, lectures, religious services, or live entertainment.

Clearly, Sheriff Bartolomie, the Board of Supervisors, and all others involved with MC/RCRC deserve the applause and commendation of the entire community. They have had the courage to look critically and unflinchingly at one of society's most pressing problems, criminal rehabilitation. People of lesser vision might have sought to justify poor prison conditions, or bowed to public fear of innovation and experiment. Their efforts on the behalf of both the offender and the law abiding public are classic examples of the Judeo-Christian ethic at work: for we must "visit those in prison" (Matthew 25:36) and strive to guide offenders into being responsible, tax-paying citizens.

FREEDOM OF THE PRESS

(Continued from Front Page)

would win out in its grapple with falsehood in the open marketplace of ideas. As libertarian John Milton stated in his famous Aeropagitica:

"... whoever knew Truth [to be] put to the worse in a free and open encounter."

In his work, ON LIBERTY, John Stuart Mill discussed the dangers that are made in the name of silencing probable falsehood: "If the opinion is right, (we) are depriving error for truth; if wrong, (we) lose, what is almost as great a benefit, the clearer perception and livelier impression of truth, produced by its collision with error."

Today, it is evident that this "self-righting" process in which truth is supposed to emerge, functions much less than perfectly, due primarily to the concentration of media ownership which has endangered the free flow of information.

THE ONLY SAFEGUARD

No one denies that the press is not perfect, that -- because of its freedom and its tendency often to publish that which sells best -- a goodly amount of error finds its way into print, sometimes causing an imbalance. But as Thomas Jefferson forthrightly stated in opposing the Alien and Sedition Acts of 1798, "To punish these errors too severely would be to suppress the only safeguard of the public liberty. The way to prevent the irregular interpositions of the people is to give them full information of their affairs through the channel of the public papers..."

Thus, it is the exchange of ideas or freedom to communicate that presumably allows a democratic citizenry to correct itself. The problem of presenting to readers, listeners and viewers adequate information as the basis for the intelligent decisions required of them as citizens, can only be compounded by the present threat to newsmen's sources. The threat is so real and dangerous that it prompted Supreme Court Justice Hugo Black to write in his opinion on the Pentagon Papers,

"... without deviation, without exception ... freedom of speech means that you do not do something to people either for the views they express or the words they speak or write ... The press must be left free to publish news, whatever the source, without censorship, injunctions, or prior restraints."

Support for at least one important aspect of Justice Black's views is apparently widespread. About 20 states have "shield laws" which protect newspersons who refuse to reveal their sources. Such laws are supported by both sides of the political spectrum. California's own conservative Governor Ronald Reagan signed an amendment to strengthen this state's shield law with the comment, "The right to protect his sources is fundamental to a newsman in meeting his full responsibilities to the public he serves."

MINISTERIAL NEWS:

For The Future... A COMMUNITY OF NEIGHBORS

116 years ago the first church in Ukiah was built by the Christian Church, Disciples of Christ denomination, which shared their building with the Methodists and the Baptists. But even though the Methodists and the Baptists have long since had their own church buildings, the First Christian Church still seems to possess the same strong spirit of brotherhood and sharing as it did over a century ago.

The very articulate pastor of First Christian Church, REV. ROBERT LEWIS, believes the church must be open to all and made available for use by whatever community groups or individuals have need of a facility. Thus, Ukiah's First Christian Church is being utilized by a nursery school, a community service club, and for the planning of local cultural programs.

Rev. Lewis feels the role of the contemporary church should be to give people models and alternatives for becoming total human beings, for living life to its fullest. He takes his example from the lives of Jesus and Paul. "There's a 'real you' somewhere, and when you're living it, you know it," says the Reverend Lewis. His desire is that the church help individuals become aware of their respective gifts so that each may express his "true self" in authentic living.

Rev. Lewis would like to see some of his ideas along these lines put to practice within the Ukiah Ministerial Association, to which he was recently elected President. "Preachers do have problems, contrary to the image most often seen, and they need to help each other out," the Reverend asserts. Most ministers in the local area belong to the Association, and Rev. Lewis would like to see its meetings involve more communication on a personal level. "After all," says the Reverend Lewis, "the ecumenical movement is not really to get churches together, but people together." And, if the labels are dropped off, it's easier for people to unite in the way that Rev. Lewis has visualized. He would like to see the various church families become a community of neighbors; he thinks more informal and personal discussions can help bring it about.

The Ministerial Association is involved in the community in such activities as assisting local convalescent facilities and providing emergency shelter, food and gasoline on an emergency basis to travelers passing through the area. Rev. Lewis would also like to develop some form of specialization committees within the association to give each minister the opportunity to "...take up something he is impassioned about and run with it."

Rev. Lewis views today's church as, "the safety net under the tight rope," and his ideas would seem to strengthen it as a place of security for those who might fall.

FIRST CHRISTIAN CHURCH, UKIAH

COMPULSION WON'T WORK

Compulsion simply will not put an end to the present inadequacies of the press and will do much more harm than good in attempting to ensure that truth overcomes error. Government coercion or censorship of the press is a cure many time worse than the disease. Coercion is a means by which the powers that be can stifle their critics. The more encroachment there is upon the press, the less freedom it will have to adequately fulfill its main role as a check upon the government.

The more control government has over the press, the less sure we will be that we're getting a fair and accurate report about those who determine the laws which govern our lives. The press cannot be coerced into becoming more responsible. If the attempt at coercion continues to be made, any demonstration of responsibility would lack conviction, because it would appear contrived. We would be left without the noble motives necessary to make free expression serve its righteous purpose.

FEWER NEWSPAPERS

The problem today is that the public's information needs are being supplied by fewer sources, so the press cannot afford to be as fallible as in the past. The legal right of the press to be private and free will stand if the moral duty to be balanced and fair is realized or tolerably approximated.

The government and the courts in any case, must keep hands off the press unless there is a clear and present danger to society or its members. (There is no such danger at this time.) Freedom of the press from official control is indispensable if an informed citizenry is to make democratic self-government work.

Unless we are willing to admit that this democratic system is unworkable, then it must be assumed that our country's citizens are capable of receiving, and eventually dismissing, wrong arguments and false information without being seriously hurt.

A free press lies at the very roots of a free society for as Alexander Meikeljohn states in his treatise, "Free Speech, and its Relation to Self-Government", "...as interests, the integrity of public discussion and the care for the public safety are identical..."

SUPPORTING THE PRESS

One of the most alarming things about the threat to the media is that so few individuals, groups, and organizations across the country are attempting to combat this repression. A notable exception, however, has been the Peoples Temple Christian Church of Redwood Valley, California, which has sent $5,000 to various media organizations throughout the United States. The church is widely known and respected for its humanitarian services which reach out to poor, suffering, and oppressed people in many areas.

A spokesman for the Peoples Temple stated, "As a church, we feel a responsibility to defend the free speech clause of the First Amendment, for without it America will have lost freedom of conscience and the climate will become ripe for totalitarianism."

The present threat against newsmen and their press freedom is indeed a giant step away from self-government toward totalitarianism. This shift towards repression must be resisted by the press and by the people of the nation with every ounce of their collective energies.

MASONITE'S CONCERN:
Quality, Jobs & Ecology

It sounds enormously difficult for a corporation which manufactures over a million square feet of hardboard paneling a day to keep from polluting air and water. But that's what the Masonite Corporation of Ukiah has accomplished following the expenditure of millions of dollars in an expansive effort to avoid pollution of any kind.

Masonite's 47 basic types of paneling are made primarily for interiors and exteriors of homes and buildings. Finished products number into the thousands. As one drives along Highway 101 and looks down at the huge Masonite mill, which has 11 acres under roof, the eye is caught by gigantic piles of wood chips, the primary raw material used. All the chips used in the hardboard-making process are retrieved from saw mills where they used to be burned as waste wood.

RECYCLING

Sawdust is another waste product that Masonite puts to use and that otherwise would have been burned. These materials go through a recycling process in which they are broken down into wood fibers and washed before they are made into hardboard. Most of the water from the wash is evaporated, leaving a thick molasses-type substance of liquid carbohydrates.

Years ago, fuel was mixed in with this residue and burned, causing a definite pollution problem. Now it is ingeniously refined into a substance called Masonex, which is used as a cattle feed supplement. Even buffalo have been fed with it successfully. Masonite sells about 3,000 tons of Masonex a month.

Some water is always left over after evaporation. This excess used to be chlorinated and poured into the river during the rainy season -- with state approval. When it was discovered that certain irrigation field grasses thrive on the liquid excess, Masonite found large fields where it could dispose of the impure water. Such disposal is harmless, because bacteria in the ground eat up any residue in the water and it is almost pure by the time it filters through into the earth-- far removed from any rivers or wells.

STEAM NOT SMOKE

Another pollution problem for Masonite involved damaged wood fiber mats, which had to be burned. In this age of recycling, however, when imaginative technologists are finding ways to break down and make over just about anything you can see, taste, or touch, damaged wood mats are no exception. They are simply broken back down into wood chips and wood fibers to become suitable raw material once again.

Trash presents another problem, and any corporation that employs almost 400 people and operates seven days a week around the clock has to grapple with its disposal. Fortunately, most of the trash can be burned, and this is done by permit, at high temperature to avoid smoke. It is important to realize that the vaporous matter that can be seen rising from the Masonite mill into the clean Ukiah air is steam, not smoke. Air pollution officials, as well as the Northern California Regional Water Quality Control Board, have given Masonite clean air and water bills of health.

So, in a time when many corporations are accused of maximizing at public expense - a local corporation has gone to great expense of its own to see that it does not cheat its community. It is enlightening to the public, and certainly to Masonite's credit, that the corporation voluntarily complied with environmental protection laws.

MASONITE CORPORATION, UKIAH

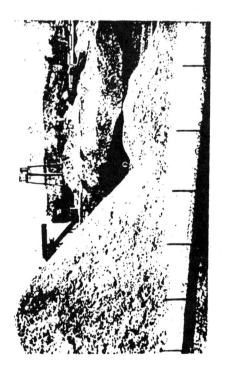

A Message From The Editor

If some are threatened by the size of Pastor Jones' congregation, such fears should be allayed, because our large number is never used as a political force. We are totally non-partisan as a church. Nor do we try to get special consideration from businesses even though we have hundreds of people patronizing the business and professional people of this area. Neither Is Peoples Temple interested in acquiring property so as to avoid taxes. We pay taxes on every one of the geriatric homes and other few such properties which have been acquired to serve people. Nor do we send to the County Welfare Department everyone who comes to us without a penny, for our church provides the total support of many, many persons, including some who came to us from other denominations and are perfectly eligible for County Welfare.

The typical church member does not deduct from his income tax the total charitable deductions to which he is legally entitled. Temple members, it is important to note, voluntarily pay more federal and state income taxes than are required because as church members they want to support the government -- particularly the health, education and welfare of this country, and its defense against all common enemies. This amounts to a savings of thousands and thousands of dollars in taxes to the federal government each year. This is done simply out of the spirit to help our government. All of this is documented.

There are many other points to show that our size should console our community and not constitute a threat to it. In addition to its direct monetary support of government, Peoples Temple provides extensive care for both people and animals as part of its human service ministry. For years the church has taken care of abandoned animals. The animal shelter Pastor Jones has inspired cares for every animal that is brought or dropped off, even every wounded little bird.

Pastor Jones has recently embarked on a project to help members of our church who have taken in pets and animals. He has now arranged for a crew to begin building proper shelter, housing, and fencing, so that these pets will not be a nuisance to neighbors and will not damage their property.

(Cont'd p. 7, col. 1)

COUNTY WELFARE DEPARTMENTS:

A STEP TOWARD HELP

An apparently successful effort is being made by the Mendocino County Welfare Department to help solve one of the major problems facing all welfare departments: that of communicating the availability of services to those in need of them. The local department in Ukiah has published a pamphlet, entitled "A Step Toward Help," which lists the many kinds of aid and assistance that can be provided through the welfare agency. They include areas of help for virtually all problems faced in daily living. The Welfare Department itself is not designed to help with every problem, but if it is not able to meet a particular need, welfare workers will seek out some person, group or agency who can give the needed assistance.

Besides financial aid and social services, workers also provide information and counsel in a wide range of areas. Some of them described include personal and confidential problems, dangerous situations for one's family or oneself, keeping a home and family together, overcoming a handicap, getting an education, solving legal problems, budgeting finances, repairing a home, job training, obtaining clothing and materials for school or work, family planning, and emergency care.

The "Step Toward Help" pamphlet was developed by Mendocino County Welfare Director Dennis Denny. Denny's concern is that many people needlessly live in terrible states of deprivation only because they aren't aware that help indeed exists. He cites as an example, poor elderly persons who live alone with no telephone and no regular visits from anyone. Many senior citizens find themselves in dire straits when they suddenly take ill or have some emergency need, but don't know what service is available or where they can turn for help. Now they can more readily find out by reading "A Step Toward Help," or by calling the welfare department in Ukiah at 462-1461.

The State Department of Social Welfare says the orange and black brochure, illustrated by Mrs. Patricia Denny, is the best effort they have received which attempts to meet the communications need between local communities and county welfare agencies. State welfare officials say the pamphlet may be made a requirement throughout California.

Editorial:
WHAT WAS THE REAL STORY?

Many people who are aware of the reasons why the San Francisco Chronicle (January 17, 1973) refers to Peoples Temple Christian Church as "highly regarded" have asked us to explain the motivations behind the one local bad story the church was previously subnique of "defaming" through a quote," he refused to talk to anyone about the many effective human service projects of the church (for example, its professionally-praised drug rehabilitation program, which at that time had already brought more than 150 young persons

Food For Thought
Walter Heady's Concern

Walter Heady of 1380 Road "A", Redwood Valley, former owner of Heady Wholesale Tire & Rubber Company, Ukiah, now semi-retired, has been noted for his helpfulness to people in all walks of life, and of all races, creeds and colors. Those who are raw and some are cooked.

According to Mr. Heady, there are two basic methods of economical "drying" of foods: 1) dehydration or regular drying such as with dried fruits, beans, rice, sugar -- the staple foods. While Mr. Heady feels that the cooking. This food is generally packaged in No. 10 cans, does not require freezing and there are 6 cans to the case.

Walter Heady has learned some "home" methods of food preservation, also -- no flavor or nutritional loss, he says. Wheat

Food Storage Article

...for a complete meal without

1) dry foods category of preservation offers many advantages, it also has some disadvantages. The quality of reconstruction (when water is added) is below the par of fresh cooked foods and the flavor and nutritional content is lowered considerably. Also, there is a variable storage life. Some dehydrated foods begin to deteriorate after only six months. Mr. Heady does not recommend the use of dehydrated foods because the disadvantages are greater than the advantages.

2) the FREEZE-DRY method removes the water, makes storage space much less, the quality and flavor of the food is superb, shelf storage life is indefinite (storage for as long as 10 years is possible) and a larger volume of food can be prepared and stored in a relatively small space -- much smaller than would be required for the same amount of dehydrated, frozen or canned food. Vitamin and mineral content and flavor are of the highest quality because no heat is used in preservation, preparation or reconstitution of the freeze dried foods. Return to their original state is generally accomplished by adding only water. Some of the freeze-dried foods can be prepared for serving by simply adding hot water for a complete meal without

and grain can be placed in 5 gallon cans or buckets and add a little bit of dry ice... as it evaporates, it eliminates all of the oxygen from the container. Give it about 20 minutes and then place the lid on, but not tightly so that any pressure that builds up from inside will let oxygen out. Then, take a mallet and tighten the lid so that it becomes airtight. In this way no bacteria or life in egg form will be present to cause any damage. Mr. Heady has some grains that he preserved in this way five years and more ago -- they are enjoying these on their table today with no loss of flavor whatsoever! The germ of the grain is not injured and they also use them for sprouts - giving a 600 to 700 percent increase in value from the natural grains to its sprouted, more nutritional form.

Mr. Heady points out to his friends and neighbors that a little investment now will bring a very high rate of return later should real food crises eventually come. And many scientists are predicting just such crises.

As a public service only, information as to where you may obtain freeze-dried foods will be made available upon request by writing: Freeze-Dried Foods, P. O. Box 192, Redwood Valley, California 95470.

know him personally are acquainted with the sincere and active interest he has always taken in his community.

Concerned with the "statistics" offered by so many scientists that food could become scarce under future conditions - due to wars, spoilage of the land, radiation and other unknowns of this century -- this far sighted citizen has conducted a continuing investigation on the subject of food storage.

Mr. Heady is presently concerned with both spiraling food costs and the unstable world situation, and joins many of his neighbors in an effort to alleviate conditions. As prices rise, and the pocket books of so many are affected, people like Mr. Heady become as beacons in the night. We as neighbors look to such responsible people to help set guidelines that all can follow.

As Mr. Heady puts it, food costs can be lowered by use of "freeze dried" and dehydrated foods... that even now, freeze dried foods are available through several companies at lower than market shelf prices: meats, vegetables, soups, fruits, combinations that include everything from chop suey to scrambled eggs, Spanish rice, meat dishes, fruit dishes, pastas, vegetable combinations and complete dinners. . .some foods

Church Defense Article

jected to - a story filled with fabrications and false and cruel innuendos. Although we cannot say we know all the motivations, three things are obvious.

First, no church or minister should ever assume they will always be spoken well of. Notwithstanding Peoples Temple having received much positive news coverage, if it were always spoken well of, one would want to avoid the church with a passion because True Scripture says: "Woe unto you when all men shall speak well of you!" (Luke 6:26) and also that "The time cometh, that whosoever killeth you will think that he doeth God a service." (John 16:2) Indeed, this suggests that persecution will have to come from people with "religious" intentions, not just materialistic, worldly elements, or carnal minds; rather, the revilers will be those who are convinced of, worship, and believe in God themselves.

completely off drugs). After looking quite hard, he was able to find only one negative source who he showed to have ever actually attended services.

Although he had never been a member, that one source was highly resentful at having years ago been the first and only person who was ever asked to leave our church. This was because he had refused to seek psychiatric help after it was discovered he had molested his daughter, a child. We are reluctant to cause that person any more pain than necessary by naming him, even though his daughter has asked us to name him so as to show the malice behind his motivation to lie, and also to show that the article in question was in fact based on total fabrications. Unfortunately, this serious charge is true, the man in question confessed to it in writing, and the local authorities were duly notified as a safeguard to the community.

DEMOTION

Second, appropriately enough that part of the article was written by a "religious" reporter who took up reporting after being asked to leave a church and who, apparently, resented having to confront a successful church, particularly one made up of all races and backgrounds. This same reporter during the past few weeks attacked the Christian Science Church and the Mormon Church, and wrote extremely unkind articles on Episcopalian and Presbyterian officials, several other large churches, Kathryn Kuhlman, and Billy Graham. Ironically enough, that reporter, our one critic, has been demoted from being religious editor of a big city newspaper to representing some newspapers in Idaho and Wyoming. Known for his rather questionable tech-

RESPECT OF PERSONS

Third, the "hearsay" sources for the most part revealed themselves racially bigoted in the worst sense. It is what God warned us to never allow to creep into our Christian experience when He declared: "For there is no respect of persons with God," and, "If ye have respect to persons, ye commit sin," (Romans 2:11; James 2:9). In First Corinthians 13 it is written, "Charity is not easily provoked," Rev. Jones, therefore, refused to be easily provoked into prosecuting these offenders, notwithstanding the evil consequences of their lies, including the brutalization of little animals. Instead, he asked us to follow Matthew 5:44, which admonishes people to "love your enemies" and "pray for them which despitefully use you."

OPEN FORUM

We solicit your ideas, questions or advice on topics of general and community interest. Please write to us at P. O. Box 214, Redwood Valley, California 95470. We'll be glad to answer any questions you may have concerning Peoples Temple Christian Church of the Disciples of Christ denomination, and welcome suggestions for future articles or columns. We would like to know what you would like to see in this newspaper. Maybe we can be of service by researching a knotty problem or running a column on a subject that is of interest to you. Perhaps you'd like to see some of your children's art work or short stories in print? Please let us know. We wish to be of service to the community. Thank you,

The Staff

YOUR SECURITY: THE BILL OF RIGHTS

First Of A Series

The American people have been blessed with a Bill of Rights since 1791, when ratification of the first ten amendments to the Constitution was completed. Perhaps it is overworked and over-worn -- even trite -- to cite our Bill of Rights as a cornerstone of freedom. Too many of us recall these fundamental rights only in the context of elementary or high school civics classes, a dusty list to be memorized for a final exam. And yet, despite our sophistication, our cynicism, or our sheer indifference, the Bill of Rights, together with our Constitution, remain stunning pledges of human rights and freedoms: monuments to truly great moments in our national history.

At times, however, our indifference can be appalling. Over the years many samplings of popular knowledge and opinion have been taken, and the results have been disturbingly constant from year to year and place to place. In 1951, two Wisconsin news reporters approached people at random, asking them to sign a petition saying that they believed in the Declaration of Independence. Out of 112 persons interviewed, all but one refused to sign. Similar experiments have been conducted in recent years in both urban and rural centers, and the results have been equally disappointing. The common response is fear, suspicion, or apathy.

It is more than ironic that while Americans justifiably reject any Communist ideology, nevertheless an overwhelming percentage of citizens not only are ignorant of the guarantees of American freedom, but often view these safeguards as "subversive!" This state of affairs might be humorous if it were not so frightening. After all, Hitler came to power on a platform that promised to rid Germany of the threat of communists, and his alternative proved to be just as bad, if not worse, than Communism itself. It is important, therefore, that we become aware of the strength and beauty of our Bill of Rights; in doing so we will stand alert to any threat to our liberty -- from the far left or the far right. This series of articles hopefully will provide some background on the origins and meaning of this Bill of Rights, and help underline the importance of defending the freedoms outlined within it.

MAGNA CARTA

The first and most crucial element in the American Bill of Rights is that we have a written Constitution, "enforceable as it stands, and unchangeable by ordinary acts of legislation." The significance of this aspect is more readily understandable when we compare our Bill of Rights to the English Magna Carta. King John originally made the charter law by his acceptance of it in 1215. Subsequent rulers found it necessary to reassert its legality by reaffirming it as law of the land: Henry III in 1217; Edward I in 1297; committed, but which subsequently were declared crimes); the freedom from any religious test as qualification for holding office; and the assurance that punishment for treason will not extend beyond the person of the traitor himself. This is only a partial list. Other provisions, for example the guarantee that titles of nobility will not be established in the United States, seem unimportant today, but were of very real concern to the men and women in 18th Century America.

THE FIRST TEN AMENDMENTS

The original ten amendments to the Constitution are what come more readily to mind when Americans are asked: what is our Bill of Rights? Since future articles will discuss some of the forces influencing their formation and adoption, perhaps it is best to review them now, the liberties, privileges, and immunities.

"I. Congress shall make no law respecting an establishment of religion, or prohibiting the free exercise thereof: or abridging the freedom of speech or of the press; or the right of the people peaceably to assemble and to petition the government for a redress of grievances.

"II. A well regulated militia, being necessary to the security of a free state, the right of the people to keep and bear arms, shall not be infringed.

"III. No soldier shall, in time of peace, be quartered in any house, without the consent of the owner, nor in time of war, but in a manner to be prescribed by law.

"IV. The right of the people to be secure in their persons, houses, papers, and effects against unreasonable searches and seizures, shall not be violated, and no warrants shall issue, but upon probable cause, supported by oath or affirmation, and particularly describing the place to be searched, and the persons or things to be seized.

"V. No person shall be held to answer for a capital, or other-wise infamous crime, unless on the presentment or indictment of a grand jury...nor shall any person be subject for the same offence to be twice put in jeopardy of life or limb; nor shall be compelled in any criminal case to be a witness against himself; nor be deprived of life, liberty, or property, without due process of law, nor shall private property be taken for public use, without just compensation.

"VI. In all criminal prosecutions, the accused shall enjoy the right to a speedy and public trial, by an impartial jury...and to be informed of the nature and cause of the accusation; to be confronted with the witnesses against him...and to have the assistance of counsel for his defence.

These animals are treated and brought to good health, fed immunized, and neutered so as to cut down the number of animals who suffer because of improper care and in some cases, outright starvation. This care for abandoned animals made it even more poignant to witness the despicable acts of a very small number of people who, perhaps promoted by the one false news article, intentionally harmed a few animals as well as some property. These were indeed, very few.

Total strangers call Pastor Jones at all hours of the night asking him to take someone in, to give someone a home, or to help people stranded out on a lonely road. Or, they may be calling for one of the many professional people to give them a helping hand or for crews to come in and help some older person with yard work or a leaky roof they cannot afford to repair. One could go on and on, discussing examples of this kind of "good neighbor" help.

This last minute message was prompted by what a local professional person reportedly said recently to some of his clients:

"I was out there and worshiped with them. Peoples Temple was nice when it was smaller, but now it is getting too big."

Although we are not as big as that person told his clients, one might ask, can anything that is good be too big? We have explained why Peoples Temple should be a consolation to our community. In referring to the person who made the foregoing statement, Rev. Jones said, "He's competent in his professional work, and thus his opinion about the church will have no bearing on us. I will continue going to him when I

"VII. In suits at common law, when the value in controversy shall exceed twenty dollars, the right of trial by jury shall be preserved, and no fact tried by a jury shall be otherwise re-examined in any Court of the United States, than according to the rule of the common law.

"VIII. Excessive bail shall not be required, nor excessive fines imposed, nor cruel and unusual punishments inflicted.

"IX. The enumeration in this Constitution, of certain rights, shall not be construed to deny or disparage others retained by the people.

"X. The powers not delegated to the United States by the Constitution, nor prohibited to it by the States, are reserved to the States respectively, or to the people."

Edward III in 1351. Parliament also added its weight. In all, the Magna Carta was enacted into law thirty-two times. Thus it seems that with relative ease, this central guarantee of English rights was able to drift in and out of an unwritten British Constitution.

In England, all acts of parliament are the validly enforceable law of the country, binding on the courts. Even if the law conflicts with or creates a hopeless tangle of complication and confusion in the Constitution, in England it is still law. Eventually, a body of similar law becomes laced with the sanction of antiquity, and is incorporated into the Constitution.

FIXED MEANINGS

On the other hand, the wording of the United States Constitution is fixed, definite. Conflict over the meaning of certain phrases may arise, but, especially in the case of the Bill of Rights, this is not the area of dispute. Here the problem is whether or not one chooses to accept or disregard the clear meaning of the words. The ignoring of this plain written code of American liberties will threaten our freedom and security.

There are other principles of government beyond the existence of a written Constitution, which form a part of the American Bill of Rights, although they are not specifically listed in the first ten amendments. They include: the existence of an independent judiciary; the separation and balance of powers; and the right of the people to elect their President, Congress, governors, and state legislators.

It is on the broad foundation of these Constitutional principles that we may enumerate the detailed provisions of the Bill of Rights. Although it is commonly believed that the Constitution itself does not contain specific guarantees, an examination of the document proves this is not so. Within the original Constitution, Americans are promised, among other things: the right to trial by jury; the privilege of the writ of habeas corpus (which can be used to obtain the release of a person illegally detained or confined in prison); the safety from any ex post facto law (a law which would make a person liable for past actions that were not illegal at the time they were

PRESIDENT NIXON

These, then, are the original ten amendments, the body of law we commonly call the Bill of Rights. The Civil War would add three more amendments, assuring our black and brown citizens the legal rights of Americans. Women gained the right to vote through the Nineteenth Amendment, and in 1964, the poll tax was eliminated as a weapon for restricting suffrage by the Twenty-Fourth Amendment. Contemporary news events constantly underscore the continued vitality of these freedoms, and the challenge to their operation is the foremost domestic issue of the day. Indeed, even our President is embroiled in the controversy. Irrespective of what one's feelings may be about this horrendous Watergate situation, Senate hearings seem to raise the question of whether or not President Nixon is being condemned without the exercise of due process of law. Seen as a connected whole, the rights spelled out in both the original Constitution and the additional amendments are all in the same spirit -- the spirit of unqualified devotion to human rights, human dignity, the liberty and equality of free men. Future articles will explore some of the currents that shaped this body of liberties. Our first task will be to glance back to 13th Century England, and the adoption of the historic Magna Carta.

---

need his services, and would recommend (speaking to the congregation) that you do so also."

In addition to the human service work for those outside, the church does all it can to maintain the needs of its own people, educating them as well as others in their own church dormitories into every kind of worthy profession, skill and trade. This has been instrumental in bringing hundreds of youngsters off of all habit-forming drugs and into such good citizenship that not one of them (according to a law enforcement agency to which we spoke) who has been active and stayed with the church has ever been arrested.

On their annual vacation each year Peoples Temple receives enthusiastic praise from people across the nation into Canada and Mexico for the way the members clean up the litter of others. They pick up the litter of others. The members receive letters throughout the year from all over the country expressing appreciation for assistance given on the roads and highways by Peoples Temple members.

This year Pastor Jones took several hundreds of people of all walks of life and professions several hundreds of people of all walks of life and profes-sions with him. They went to Washington, D. C. to see the national monuments and visit our representatives in Congress and the Senate. Pastor Jones goes on no vacation without giving every person in his congregation the chance to go with him whether or not they can afford it.

If Pastor Jones and his congregation were gone from our community one could not imagine the economic and moral loss that it would represent to everyone. The church gives to every kind of worthy cause, both church and non-sectarian. It has supported the charities of the leading denominations and the churches of all faiths throughout the United States to the tune of many, many thousands of dollars per year. This has been done in addition to the thousands of dollars it channeled through its own "Christian Church of the Disciples of Christ" denomination of 1.4 million in the United States. This money is freely given to serve the needs of all people irrespective of creed or color. Pastor Jones has praised and helped the work of many churches in this area as well as throughout the United States.

As you, the reader, may know, there is no effort by Peoples Temple to proselytize in the community. No one has gone door to door seeking membership or passing out literature, because the church members feel that they wish to serve those already unchurched and not take from other groups. People interested in affiliating with Peoples Temple Christian Church will make the overture themselves.

The response of Pastor Jones to the professional person who reportedly commented to several clients that Peoples Temple might be "too large" is typical of his consistent, kindly attitude toward people generally. We whose lives have been brought from despair to hope by the personal example of Jim Jones wish to say that he stands ready to be the friend of all who need him. He is the most loyal friend you might imagine and his word is better than gold. You, yourself, may well want such a friend one day.

One of our bus supervisors who works diligently on the church buses once did a terrible thing to Pastor Jones, seeking to bring every hurt that he could. Later when this same man needed help, Pastor Jones gave it without a second thought – help which was actually instrumental in the restoration of this man's health. There are several cases like this one, yet this writer has never seen anything like the forgiveness, the compassion and understanding that Jim Jones demonstrates. Try his spirit and you cannot help but see that he is a Godly person.

Peoples Temple, Los Angeles was founded a year ago to meet the needs of our thousands of Southern California members.

Members gather in Peoples Temple, Redwood Valley for Pastor Jones' lessons in Christian Living and Apostolic Sharing.

Pastor Jim Jones and his dedicated wife, Marceline, are seen here with their beautiful adopted rainbow family, "homemade" child and grandchildren.

Pastor Jim Jones is very busy with the many duties of Peoples Temple's vast human service ministry, yet he always finds time to extend his love to the many hundreds of children in our churches. The smallest child is never turned away, and he always takes time to respond to their questions and needs.

Pastor Jim Jones with Dr. Kleineibst, one of our Elders, visiting some of the senior citizens who live in Redwood Valley.

"For I was an hungered
and ye gave me meat;
I was thirsty
and ye gave me drink;
I was a stranger
and ye took me in;
Naked, and ye clothed me;
I was sick and ye visited me;
I was in prison,
and ye came unto me.

"Then shall the righteous
Answer him, saying,

When saw we thee an hungered
And fed thee?
Or thirsty,
And gave thee drink?
When saw we thee a stranger
And took thee in?
Or naked, and clothed thee?
Or when saw we thee sick
Or in prison,
And came unto thee?

"Verily I say unto you,
Inasmuch as ye have done it
Unto one of the least of these...
...Ye have done it unto me."

Matthew 25:35-40

PROFILE OF JIM JONES

PASTOR JAMES W. JONES

Rumors often surround the man or woman who chooses to do good. Timothy 3:12 warns that, "all who live godly in Christ Jesus shall suffer persecution." Such is the case for Jim Jones, pastor of Peoples Temple, the largest Protestant congregation in Northern California.

Officially ordained by the 1.4 million member Christian Church (Disciples of Christ), Rev. Jones has been pastor of his church for over 21 years. Described by the Ukiah Daily Journal as a "humble servant of humanity, an erudite wit, and a loving family man," Jim Jones has nevertheless been the subject of misunderstanding and falsely based suspicion. For the most part, this can be attributed to an unfamiliarity with the man, his character, and his work as a dedicated servant of the people.

"HE WAS SUPERB"

Prior to moving to Mendocino County in 1965 in order to provide an agricultural envi-

ronment for the many children (of 5 ethnic backgrounds), he and his dedicated wife, Marceline had adopted, Jim Jones had been an extremely successful businessmen and civic leader. So highly thought of was he as a businessman, public school teacher, and minister (he set up a free restaurant for the poor), he was appointed the first Executive Director of the Mayor's Commission on Human Rights "after long search."

Contrary to false rumors, Rev. Jones came to Mendocino County highly acclaimed for a distinguished performance in that powerful metropolitan post. Mayor Boswell himself wrote to the press:

"As a result of his efforts, many second-class citizens for the first time in the history of this city have become first-class citizens ... I have the greatest confidence in (his) integrity, ability, and true affection for his fellow man."

In an editorial, the Scripps-Howard newspaper called him "superb:"

"The Rev. James Jones will be sorely missed as executive secretary of the Mayor's Commission on Human Rights. He was hired after long search ... He was superb. He went about his job diplomatically but thoroughly and produced results."

Jim Jones had not been in Mendocino County two years before his abilities led him to being appointed Foreman of the Mendocino County Grand Jury. He was also appointed to the Juvenile Justice Commission and was elected President of the Legal Services Foundation of Mendocino County, on whose board of trustees he still serves.

For many years, Rev. Jones taught school, including daily making the long trek across the mountains to Boonville, as well as teaching adult education in Ukiah. His continuing concern for education is reflected by the fact that he has established a five hundred dollar humanitarian scholarship for the new Mendocino College.

Rev. Jones puts the needs of others before his own personal gain. This was shown most recently when he was scheduled to speak at the local junior high school graduation ceremony, but felt compelled to cancel the appearance so that he could attend to the needs of a prominent Baptist minister who was near the point of death.

An unwavering and unqualified defender of American liberties, Jim Jones has taken a firm stand in support of the Constitution and our Bill of Rights. Indeed, he has consistently spoken out in defense of the First Amendment and against current threats to the freedom of the press. Because of this determined stand, he and his church have recently been praised in the halls of Congress

and written up in the Congressional Record. The other 79 churches of the Disciples of Christ denomination for Northern California a few weeks ago commended by name the example of Peoples Temple in adopting a resolution in favor of supporting freedom of the press by an overwhelming margin.

SELFLESSNESS

The media itself has taken notice. Impressed with his practical concern for brotherhood and freedom, and his life of compassion and justice, network radio and television programs have invited Rev. Jones to appear as a guest speaker. A television News Bureau Chief and Correspondent for CBS News noted for his objectivity came to do a feature film story on the Peoples Temple Ministry of Human Service, Mike Prokes was so impressed with the integrity and selflessness of Jim Jones and the works of his church, that the young newsman immediately quit his position to work full time in the ministry of the Temple. Prokes states:

"In Jim Jones I have discovered the most dedicated person to the cause of humanity that I have ever met. I found his motives and humanitarian principles to be unquestionably honorable. He exemplifies the Life of Christ by working day and night to relieve suffering and establish true brotherhood wherever he can."

But the best testimony to his character is the Peoples Temple itself. Its far reaching program of human service includes: senior citizens' homes and convalescent centers; an animal shelter; a drug abuse prevention and rehabilitation service where 200 young people have become completely rehabilitated from drug use; college scholarships by which over 100 young people are receiving an education, sponsored either partially or in full by the church; a counseling service for troubled adolescents; a vacation program for inner-city youngsters, and a host of emergency services that involve food, clothing, nursing care, and legal counsel. Jim Jones takes the air of rumor in stride. Doing good for good's sake alone, is a full time job.

Peoples Temple
P.O. Box 214
Redwood Valley, CA 95470

Non-Profit Organization
U.S. Postage
PAID 1.7¢
Ukiah, Ca
Permit No. 149

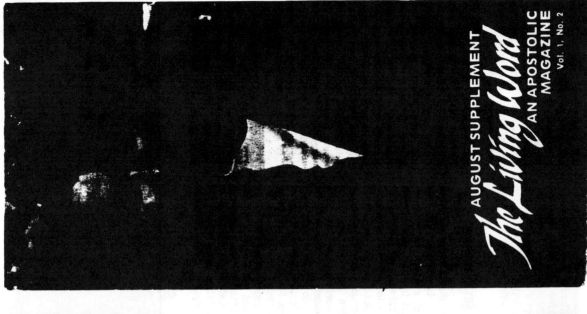

AUGUST SUPPLEMENT

The Living Word

AN APOSTOLIC MAGAZINE

Vol. 1, No. 2

PEOPLE'S TEMPLE RADIO BROADCAST SCHEDULE

Don't miss the Living Word spoken on the air!

Bring the Divinely Inspired words of Pastor Jim Jones in to your home. Let the Voice of People's Temple bring blessings to you as it has to so many!

San Francisco	KFAX	1100 KC	Mon-Fri 5:30am
			Saturday 11:00am
Seattle, WA	KBLE	1050 KC	Saturday 10:30am
	KBLE-FM93.3 MC		Mon-Fri 5:45pm
Blaine, WA	KARI	550 KC	Saturday 7:30am
Middletown, OH	WPFB	910 KC	Sunday 7:30am
Nationwide	XPRS	1090 KC	Sunday 10:30pm

People's Temple
P. O. Box 214
Redwood Valley, CA 95470

Nonprofit Organization
U.S. Postage
1.7¢ PAID
San Francisco, CA
Permit No. 9729

JIM JONES IN PERSON!
HEALING SERVICES

August 5-6	**LOS ANGELES**	Embassy Auditorium 9th and Grand St.	Sat. 2pm & 7pm Sun. 11am
August 12-13	**REDWOOD VALLEY**	Peoples Temple Christian Church East Road (7 miles north of Ukiah)	Sat. 7pm Sun. 11am
August 19-20	**SAN FRANCISCO**	Benjamin Franklin Jr High Scott and Geary St.	Sat. 7pm Sun. 11am
August 26-27	**SEATTLE**	MASONIC TEMPLE 801 E. PINE (at Harvard)	Sat. 2pm & 7pm Sun. 11am
Sept. 2-3	**LOS ANGELES**	Embassy Auditorium 9th and Grand St.	Sat. 2pm & 7pm Sun. 11am

PEOPLE'S TEMPLE CHRISTIAN CHURCH has extensions in many cities, and provides transportation to and from all its meetings. Call your local secretaries for information about meetings and transportation. They are:

REDWOOD VALLEY	Mrs. Edith Bogue	(707) 485-7469
BAY AREA	Mrs. Leona Collier	(415) 626-3365
SAN FRANCISCO	Miss Jane Mutschman	(415) 863-3290
OAKLAND	Mrs. Mattie Wimberly	(415) 654-3829
RICHMOND	Mrs. Mary Green	(415) 235-3209
SAN RAFAEL	Mrs. Bea Morton	(415) 457-3540
SAN MATEO	Mrs. Margaret Elsey	(415) 343-0722
PALO ALTO	Mrs. Mary Lendo	(415) 325-2589
SAN JOSE	Rev. Mabel Davis	(415) 272-0871
FRESNO	Mrs. Melvina Green	(209) 266-7854
SACRAMENTO	Mr. & Mrs. Louis Tennerson	(916) 383-8735
LOS ANGELES	Mrs. Irene White	(213) 234-1143
	Mrs. Corine Liggins	(213) 232-1749
	Mrs. Wilma McCloud	(213) 232-0397
SEATTLE, WA.	Mr. & Mrs. Harold Flowers	(206) 323-5836
	Sister Davis	(206) 325-4661
	Mrs. Frank Darnell	(206) 323-8222
RENTON, WA.	Mrs. Bessie Wroten	(206) 228-6092

This same spiritual healing ministry in no way opposes medical science, for "all good things come down from above." Many people have sought medical attention for the first time because they were encouraged to do so by this Divine Prophet of God, often with the result that they were spared from illnesses and potentially fatal conditions.

I suffered from a serious stroke which left me completely paralyzed on one side of my body. When I was in great dispair, Pastor Jim Jones, in whom Christ dwells, came to me and healed me instantly! Hallelujah!

ROSE SHELTON
Redwood Valley, CA

A fire broke out in our home when everyone was asleep. I awoke to find flames engulfing the entire house. My infant son was sleeping next to the wall near the stove from where the fire had started. Terrified for my son's life, I looked to the picture of Pastor Jim Jones that hung on the wall beside my son's bed, and called on the name of Christ who works through him. At that moment the flames died down, and the wall remained unburned, protecting my child until I could get him to safety. The Fire Marshall was amazed, and totally unable to explain this, as he said the wall near the stove should have been the first to be destroyed. Thanks to that anointed picture, my son is alive today.

WANDA SWINNEY
Ukiah, CA

Miracles Through Pictures

Since May, over 3000 such testimonies of miraculous healings and deliverances wrought through these pictures have been reported. Since these letters of gratitude were all unsolicited, we have every reason to believe they are true, even though we do not have the ability to investigate each one.

To get your picture, personally blessed by Pastor Jones, send a check or money order for $5, specifying by number which picture or pictures you desire, to PICTURE, P.O. Box 163, Redwood Valley, CA 95470. All proceeds from the sales of these anointed pictures which have brought blessings to so many go to help the 61 college students sponsored by People's Temple in our Guaranteed Education program.

Pastor Jim Jones baptizes one of his many members in the Temple Baptistry. In the last two months 2,083 have received Christ in these healing waters. Several hundred have emerged praising God and testifying to the miraculous healings wrought as they were being baptized. Glory to God!

The Holy Spirit Admonishes

that henceforth anyone wishing the health, well-being, and success that follows those who support this wonderful ministry must give honestly as they have prospered. NO ONE WHO HAS FOLLOWED THE TEACHINGS AND CONSCIENTIOUSLY SUPPORTED THIS WORK HAS DIED SINCE 1959. Keep in contact with God's work on earth today! Send your name, address, and freewill donation, together with a statement of how much you will be giving weekly or monthly, and any special pledges to: People's Temple, P.O. Box 214, Redwood Valley, CA 95470.

* * *

I was walking out the door after a Sunday service in Redwood Valley, when Jim's voice stopped me cold. He called my name and told me to be careful of vehicles that coming Friday morning between 8:00 and 8:30. He told me he saw me being struck by a car, but that he would protect me.

Friday morning came and I was making my first delivery at the Big John Market in San Francisco. I got out of the van. Just then I heard the sound of a racing engine. Jim's warning flashed through my mind, and without taking time to look or to think, I sprang to the sidewalk. A split second later, a speeding car crashed into the truck, shattering and splashing everything in it across the street. Had I doubted Jim's prophecy for a second, I would have been killed!

DON JACKSON
Ukiah, CA

"Thy Will Be Done In Earth..."

Pastor Jones ministers to a congregation of over 4000 active members. Facilities at the mother Temple on 60 beautiful acres in Redwood Valley, California include senior citizens' homes, a children's home, a community center with a large indoor heated swimming pool, a drug rehabilitation center where over 100 youths have been rescued from the drug scene, and an animal refuge. This semester the Temple is sponsoring 61 young people attending college, most of whom are living in the four college dormitories sponsored by the church. Pastor Jones also has congregations totalling several thousands in San Francisco, Oakland, Berkeley, Richmond, San Rafael, San Mateo, Palo Alto, San Jose, Sacramento, Stockton, Fresno, and Los Angeles, Calif.; Philadelphia, Pa.; Seattle, Tacoma, Wash. and Missionary outposts in Mexico and Africa.

THE LIVING WORD AN APOSTOLIC MAGAZINE, is published on a regular basis by People's Temple Christian Church (Disciples of Christ), a nonprofit religious corporation. All healings referred to depend exclusively on prayer. Mailing address is: Post Office Box 214, Redwood Valley, California 95470. Introductory copies are available free of charge. Persons wishing to receive this magazine regularly should write to the above address requesting to be added to the mailing list and, if possible, include a free-will donation. All rights reserved. Manuscripts: Unsolicited manuscripts sent to THE LIVING WORD must be sent with a stamped, self-addressed envelope; no responsibility is assumed for unsolicited manuscripts. Subscription correspondence: Send both new and old address. Third class postage paid at San Francisco, California, and at additional offices as required. Postmaster: Send form 3579 to THE LIVING WORD at the above address.

YOUR NAME _____ TELEPHONE NO. _____

ADDRESS _____

CITY _____ STATE _____ ZIP CODE _____

Date _____

Dear Pastor Jones,

    I will be able to take guests into my home while the PEOPLES TEMPLE Miracle Ministry is in my area.

    So that you can best suit your travelers to my accomodations, here is some information that will be helpful.

I can take _____ men, _____ women, and/or _____ children.
               number   number   number

The age groups I would best be able to house are   1-10 __ 11-17 __ 18-30 __
                                                    31-60 __ 61-100 __ 100-150 __

I Do __   Do Not __   have a Registered Nurse or an L.V.N. in my home.

There are _____ steps that a person would have to climb to get into my house.
             number

I Can __   Can Not __   provide my own transportation to and from service.

- -

Dear Friend,

    Pastor Jones deeply appreciates your cooperation in this matter. It helps us bring this healing and miracle ministry to your area.

    Christian generosity is rewarded with many abundant blessings, and your generosity will not go unnoticed. "You reap what you sow" are words that have deep significance for all Christians. We are looking forward to hearing from you soon.

When this form is completed, please send it in the enclosed specially marked envelope to:

PEOPLES TEMPLE
Housing Secretary
P.O. Box 214
Redwood Valley, California 95470

Thank you very much for your Christian Hospitality!

72

PEOPLES TEMPLE
OF THE
DISCIPLES OF CHRIST
Jim V. Jones,
Pastor

Dear Friend of Peoples Temple,

Tidings of good news come with this letter. It appears that Pastor Jim Jones and the miracle ministry that is touching the lives of thousands here in California is coming to your area this summer. Along with Pastor Jones and the miracle caravan comes a message of deliverance such as you've never heard before. Many of you have written to Pastor Jones and you may know something of the power of the Holy Spirit working through him. Perhaps you are one of the thousands who have written testimonies telling of deliverance – one of those who recognize Peoples Temple Christian Church as the most spectacular healing, miracle, and deliverance ministry in our time. This is a hope in a time of hopelessness!

There will be at least 10 buses full of workers travelling with Pastor Jim when he comes to your city. Many of those travelling with him were leading lives of misery and despair before they met Jim Jones. But then the love of the Christ working through him gave them new life and a purpose for living. Pastor Jim and these workers will need your help. Many will need housing the night we will stay in your area. Because you have shown some interest in this ministry in the past, we are asking if you could open your doors to one or more of these faithful workers. Even if you are able to take only one person, it would be a tremendous help. We are enclosing a special housing questionnaire and envelope for your use. We would greatly appreciate your taking the time to fill out this form and return it to us as soon as possible.

You should let nothing stop you from coming to these miracle healing and deliverance rallies. Meet this man sent from God, Jim V. Jones. The <u>hope</u> that is given to all who come to meetings <u>can lift your life also</u>. The <u>security</u> one finds with faith in Christ <u>will be imparted to you</u> through the loving inspiration of the Holy Spirit working through Pastor Jones. The <u>fulfillment</u> that comes in witnessing Christian equality <u>is yours</u> while in the atmosphere of this great Anointing. And the <u>peace of mind</u> that is so hard to find in these troubled days <u>is yours</u> with faith in the undeniable truth that God truly loves and cares for you.

Joy, hope, fulfillment, and peace can all be yours when you witness the 9 gifts of the Holy Spirit working through Pastor Jim Jones. Come and see if it is not true.

May Peace, Love, and Blessings be yours.

Sincerely,

Timothy J. Carter, Secretary

Post Office Box 214 Redwood Valley, California 95470   Telephone: (707) 485-7219

73

Your Choice of Anointed Gifts

Gift 50 Set of CUFF-LINKS, each with an Anointed Picture of Jim Jones in it.

Gift 20 Bottle of ANOINTED OIL.

Gift 60 Small PICTURE of PASTOR JONES blessed for "Safety from Attack."

Gift 25 LOCKET, blessed for "Safety from Evil." Comes with your birthstone on it, if you will indicate the month of your birth.

Gift 22 Heart-shaped LOCKET with an anointed picture in it.

Gift 21 Diamond-shaped LOCKET with Pastor Jones' picture.

Gift 26 KEYCHAIN anointed for "Safety on the Road."

Gift 30 LOCKET, anointed for "Safety for Children."

Gift 33 TWO-MINUTE TIMER for your car. Pastor Jones has urged that each person should take two minutes before each trip to think about their blessings.

Gift 27 Small PIN to wear on your clothes, with an anointed picture in it.

Gift 28 PHOTO-BUTTON with a picture of Jim Jones on it.

Gift 40 DISPLAY PLATE with a picture of the Los Angeles Peoples Temple on it.

Gift 41 DISPLAY PLATE with a picture of San Francisco Peoples Temple as it was before the fire. These Anointed Plates have been blessed.

The Christ Spirit has wonderfully used Pastor Jones. Through these gifts anointed by Pastor Jones, the Spirit works miracles of healing and deliverance as a demonstration that God is real and mighty to save. These anointed gifts have no curative power but serve as a contact with the Christ Spirit working through Pastor Jones to bring forth the faith that delivers.

PEOPLES TEMPLE   P.O. Box 214
          Redwood Valley, Calif. 95470

Dear Pastor Jones, I understand that these blessed gifts work only by faith, as it was in the days of Scripture. I also understand that there is no charge for the blessed gift, and since there is a limited supply I should order soon.

PLEASE SEND ME GIFT NO.____ for my blessing. Here is my offering of love.

$50____ $25____ $10____ $5____ Other $____

Name _____

Address _____

City _____ State _____ Zip _____

Send Your Loved Ones Anointed Gifts... Show You Really Care

75

Memories From The Past

When Pastor Jim Jones was just a young child, about 5 years old, his mother recalls that he was a very unusual child. Even at that age he showed concern and love for those he came in contact with. He took in the homeless animals and brought home those who were hungry so that they could enjoy a good meal.

One of the incidents that she remembers is when Little Jim had taken some prize flowers from the neighbor's yard during the day. That night the neighbor came over to his house and reprimanded him severely for "stealing" his flowers. Little Jim looked up at him perplexed, because it didn't seem reasonable for this man to condemn him without hearing his reasons.

He told the man that he had taken the flowers to an elderly woman who lived up the road. The man asked why he hadn't waited to ask him when he got home, and Little Jim replied, "That would have been too late, because she was going to be dead by that time."

The man went to the home that Little Jim directed him to, and found his flowers sitting in a vase next to the woman, and she was dead . . . just as he had said she would be.

The man was so impressed at this that he told Little Jim that he was welcome to take flowers from his yard any time he needed to, and that he could go into his basement and have any of the canned fruits or vegetables he needed, because he knew that Little Jim would only use these things for good purposes.

— —

His mother also recalls that when Little Jim would come into the church on Sunday, he was always followed by the many hungry dogs in the neighborhood that he had fed on the way. He and his dogs would usually take up a whole pew in the back of the church.

He showed love and compassion to all that he found suffering, people and animals alike. He was sensitive to all life.

OCT. 22- THIS DAY . . . I will do the work that is mine to do, and I will put my heart into it. I will not be lazy because I know that as I do my job with a willing heart, the tasks of those around me will be made easier.

OCT. 23- THIS DAY . . . I will strive to spend a little more time with the members of our family so that they will know that I am interested in each one of them.

OCT. 24- THIS DAY . . . I will follow through with what I know to be right. I will not give up because the going gets hard. I will be strong to live up to the convictions that I believe in. This will encourage the other members of our family to be stronger.

OCT. 25- THIS DAY . . . I will stand up for the truth, because I know the truth will bind a family together. I will not live a lie, because that can only cause pain.

OCT. 26- THIS DAY . . . I will encourage those with whom I come in contact to share with and care for those in need. This way our family will become more loving and will learn to care even more for one another.

OCT. 27- THIS DAY . . . I will become more frugal and watch carefully the expenditures, knowing that there are many who are hungry. Our family should not live in luxury while others do not have many necessities. I will encourage the members of our family to be wise in their spending.

OCT. 28- THIS DAY . . . I will make restitution where I have done wrong, because if I let these wrongs go uncorrected, I know it will hurt our family.

OCT. 29- THIS DAY . . . I will number my blessings and express my gratitude for the blessings that have come my way, and I will encourage others to do the same.

OCT. 30- THIS DAY . . . I will be happy because I know my spirit will be reflected in the attitudes of the rest of our family. I will keep a cheerful spirit and not allow my negative emotions to show to others.

OCT. 31- THIS DAY . . . Although my ability may not be great, I will not use this as an excuse for my failures. I will use the best of my abilities today, to help those who rely on me for strength.

Thoughts for October

PEACE IN THE FAMILY - AT CHURCH AND AT HOME

OCT. 1 - THIS DAY . . . I will attempt to do something that I have considered to be too difficult in the past. If I use courage and face the tasks that I find difficult, I can better help our family.

OCT. 2 - THIS DAY . . . I will become more practical. I will think my decisions and actions through carefully to be sure they are in the best interests of our family, and not place my own interests first.

OCT. 3 - THIS DAY . . . I will express my care and concern for the members of our family by my words and actions.

OCT. 4 - THIS DAY . . . I will control myself in an area that I am weak. I will use self-control, and as my character becomes stronger I will be better able to serve the members of our family.

OCT. 5 - THIS DAY . . . I will sacrifice something that I have been holding on to for my own selfish interests. I will put the interests of our family above my own interests.

OCT. 6 - THIS DAY . . . I will encourage the members of our family to tell me where I have failed. I will listen to their criticism and try to change in areas that I am weak.

OCT. 7 - THIS DAY . . . In all I do, I want to act for the best welfare of our family, and not for my own self-interest. I will give up something that I wanted to do for myself alone, and do something that will help our family instead.

OCT. 8 - THIS DAY . . . As situations come up that I find unpleasant, I will not consider my own emotional feelings, but I will consider the feelings of others.

OCT. 9 - THIS DAY . . . I will say a kind word about those I have criticised in the past. By doing this I will help to teach our family that we should look for the best in others.

OCT. 10- THIS DAY . . . I will not be domineering to those I feel are less qualified than I am. I will stop praising myself where I think I am strong, and I will give the praise to those who need encouragement.

OCT. 11- THIS DAY . . . I will be willing to learn from even the smallest, shyest member of our family. I will not think that I have all the answers, but I will begin asking questions.

OCT. 12- THIS DAY . . . No matter how important I may think I am, I will always be quick to serve and help. I must be willing to give up my own selfish interests.

OCT. 13- THIS DAY . . . I will learn to listen to the opinions of others and pay attention to their feelings, no matter how young or inexperienced they seem to be. If their thoughts seem to be right, I will pay attention to the lesson and apply it to my own life. If they seem to be wrong I will take time to discuss both sides of the issue.

OCT. 14- THIS DAY . . . I will become a friend to someone in our family I do not know well, and will listen to their ideas without imposing my own ideas upon them.

OCT. 15- THIS DAY . . . I will become more selfless in an area of my life so that I can be of greater help to our family.

OCT. 16- THIS DAY . . . Where members of our family have made mistakes I will learn to be patient. I will try, in a non-judgmental way, to help them to right the wrong things they have done. I won't just ignore them because I disagree or feel they are wrong.

OCT. 17- THIS DAY . . . I will consider my motivations to be sure that my concern is for the whole family, and that I do not show more love for those who I feel a special attachment to. I will learn to treat all with equal measure, and have no special loves.

OCT. 18- THIS DAY . . . I want to become responsible to the members of our family. Everything I do will be for the best welfare of the entire family.

OCT. 19- THIS DAY . . . If members of our family seem to be slow or inexperienced I will not ignore them. I will be a friend and give them the courage to keep trying.

OCT. 20- THIS DAY . . . I will show that I am a committed member of our family. I will not behave as though I think I deserve special attention.

OCT. 21- THIS DAY . . . I will unite myself in my mind with our family so that I can realize that it is my own family.

SAN FRANCISCO PEOPLES TEMPLE DESTROYED BY FIRE - AUGUST 23, 1973

PLEASE RUSH TO HELP OUR SAN FRANCISCO MINISTRY!

We need your immediate help. On August 23, 1973 the San Francisco Peoples Temple was burned and nearly destroyed by an arsonist, who will reap the whirlwind for touching God's anointed. San Francisco needs to keep the ministry of Pastor Jones in their area, and we know that you also will want to see this work continued in the highest order.

Before the fire, Pastor Jim had a Revelation of danger by fire. In the meeting in Redwood Valley the evening of the fire, he made several references, before the congregation of 1000 members to the church being burned, and stated that it would not hinder our work. There were 40 students scheduled to spend the night in the San Francisco Temple that night, but due to his prophesy of trouble, the Pastor changed the schedule before the entire assembly. Because of this no one was in the Temple but the custodian when the fire started. The custodian was not in her room - which was burned up - but in another room from which she was able to escape unharmed. This was only due to Pastor Jones leading her out through a window which had a thick grill over it - although he was in a bus travelling at the time. MIRACULOUSLY, not one person, animal or plant received even the slightest injury!

In several of the rooms there were Anointed Pictures, and although the frames were burnt on the large pictures, and the plastic around the small pictures was completely melted, the ANOINTED PICTURES THEMSELVES WERE NOT DESTROYED!! nor were they hurt in any way.

The musical instruments were literally melted by the heat. The microphone and public address systems, along with the chairs and other equipment were also melted. The whole interior of the building was destroyed, nothing is left with which to begin to rebuild - we need to replace everything. Your help is needed, and we know that you will help.

The robes which Pastor Jim wears, were hanging in one of the rooms that was destroyed by the fire. Although everything else in the room was demolished by the blaze, these robes were left <u>totally intact.</u> Pastor Jim has had a Revelation that these robes should be used to make Prayer Cloths which would be a special blessing to those who care enough about this work to help to rebuild or replace the San Francisco Temple and the furnishings.

Surely you will want to show your interest in helping this church to be reconstructed. Do so by sending your donation to PEOPLES TEMPLE, P.O. Box 214, Redwood Valley, Calif. 95470. Send it in the special envelope which is enclosed for your convenience. You will receive one of the prayer cloths which has been taken from the Blessed Robes which survived the inferno!

SAN FRANCISCO PEOPLES TEMPLE FIRE FUND
P.O. Box 214
Redwood Valley, Calif. 95470

Dear Pastor Jim Jones,

Here is my love gift to be put into the SAN FRANCISCO FIRE FUND. I would appreciate receiving the PRAYER CLOTH which has been taken from the Blessed Robes that survived the fire. I want to help the San Francisco Ministry to continue to grow.

MY LOVE OFFERING IS $5____ $10____ $15____ $20____ $25____ $50____ $100____

OTHER AMOUNT $_____

NAME_____ PHONE_____

ADDRESS_____

CITY & STATE_____ ZIP_____

Pastor Jim Jones and over 700 members of Peoples Temple traveled cross-country on our August 1973 vacation. A highlight of the trip was meeting on the steps of the nation's Capitol with congressmen. Temple buses prepare to tour Washington D.C.

The Living Word
October '73 Bulletin

PASTOR JIM JONES
SPIRITUAL HEALING &
HUMAN SERVICE MINISTRY

SCHEDULE OF MEETINGS

Wednesday	October 10	REDWOOD VALLEY	7:30 PM	COMBINED CONGREGATIONS Business (Membership) Meeting MIRACLE Healing and Deliverance Service
Thursday	October 11	LOS ANGELES	7:30 PM	
Friday	October 12	SAN FRANCISCO	8:00 PM	Singspiration Worship & Healing
Saturday	October 13	LOS ANGELES	2 & 4 PM	Dynamic Healing and Worship
Sunday	October 14	LOS ANGELES	11:00 AM & 2:00 PM	Spiritual Worship and Healing
Wednesday	October 17	REDWOOD VALLEY	7:30 PM	COMBINED CONGREGATIONS Business (Membership) Meeting MIRACLE Healing and Deliverance Service
Thursday	October 18	LOS ANGELES	7:30 PM	
Friday	October 19	SAN FRANCISCO	8:00 PM	Singspiration Worship & Healing
Saturday	October 20	SAN FRANCISCO	7:30 PM	Dynamic Healing and Worship
Sunday	October 21	SAN FRANCISCO	11:00 AM	Spiritual Healing and Worship
		REDWOOD VALLEY	8:00 PM	Apostolic Worship and Healing
Wednesday	October 24	REDWOOD VALLEY	7:30 PM	COMBINED CONGREGATIONS Business (Membership) Meeting MIRACLE Healing and Deliverance Service
Thursday	October 25	LOS ANGELES	7:30 PM	
Friday	October 26	SAN FRANCISCO	8:00 PM	Singspiration Worship & Healing
Saturday	October 27	LOS ANGELES	2 & 4 PM	Dynamic Healing and Worship
Sunday	October 28	LOS ANGELES	11:00 AM & 2:00 PM	Spiritual Worship and Healing
Wednesday	October 31	REDWOOD VALLEY	7:30 PM	COMBINED CONGREGATIONS Business (Membership) Meeting MIRACLE Healing and Deliverance Service
Thursday	November 1	LOS ANGELES	7:30 PM	
Friday	November 2	SAN FRANCISCO	8:00 PM	Singspiration Worship & Healing
Saturday	November 3	SAN FRANCISCO	7:30 PM	Dynamic Healing and Worship
Sunday	November 4	SAN FRANCISCO	11:00 AM	Spiritual Healing and Worship
		REDWOOD VALLEY	8:00 PM	Apostolic Worship and Healing

Peoples Temple
Radio Broadcast Schedule

Bring the Divinely Inspired words of Pastor Jim Jones in to your home. Let the **Voice of People's Temple** bring blessings to you as it has to so many!

San Francisco CA	KFAX	1100 KC	Monday-Friday	5:30 AM
			Saturday	11:00 AM
Seattle WA	KBLE-FM	93.3 MC	Monday-Friday	5:45 PM
Middletown OH	WPFB	910 KC	Sunday	8:00 AM
Philadelphia PA	WHAT	1340 KC	Monday-Friday	10:45 PM
Mexico to Canada	XPRS	1090 KC	Sunday	10:30 PM

Peoples Temple is a church that believes that THE GREATEST SERVICE TO GOD IS IN SERVICE TO MANKIND. Because of this belief, they sponsor a vast humanitarian ministry that gives aid and assistance to hundreds of people each week.

They sponsor four college dormitories in which many of their more than 100 students are living while they attend the college of their choice. There are young people in law School, Medical School, and following many other professions with the ultimate goal of using their knowledge to help others.

This church also has a Drug Rehabilitation Program that has brought hundreds of people out of the enslavement of the drug world. They also have several Senior Citizens homes, a Childrens Home, a Teaching Program for the younger children and many other service-oriented facilities. Each of the three churches also provides extensive help to those in need in the community.

If you would like to help in any of these undertakings, your love offering will be most welcome. Send your offering to PEOPLES TEMPLE, P.O. Box 214, Redwood Valley, Calif. 95470. We know that as you share what you have, your heart will be made happy - knowing that you are fulfilling the commission of Jesus when He said, "INASMUCH as ye have done it unto one of the least of these . . ., ye have done it unto me."

PEOPLES TEMPLE CHRISTIAN CHURCH
P. O. Box 214
Redwood Valley, Calif. 95470

The Blessings
Are Flowing

We were passing through the Arizona Desert on the Vacation Trip with the Church. As we approached a turn the busses were stopped to change drivers. As Bus 6 pulled over Bus 8 smashed into the back of Bus 6. Glass was all over the place, but no glass cut anyone or got in anyone's eyes. Everyone on the busses felt the crash, but no one was touched or hurt.

People on the bus were afraid that bugs and all sorts of flying objects or rain would come in. Jim Jones said that we did not need to worry, that he would provide an invisible windshield through which no rain or any other objects would come in.

Bus 8- Nothing came through the open window for a 1,500 mile stretch.

All the rest of the busses in front of and behind Bus 6 were bombarded by insects of all sizes on the windshields. Although we went through several storms, Jim's promise was fulfilled. Not one drop of rain or one insect came through, although we traveled 1,500 miles before we were able to get a new windshield. Over and over again throughout the two week trip we witnessed miracles such as this. When it was too hot, Pastor Jim said that it would rain to cool off the weather, and true to his word, IT DID RAIN!

Everywhere we went, where first we were faced with bigotry and hostility because we were an inter-racial group, we touched the hearts of the people, and their attitudes were changed before we left each location. At one stop a man who was a member of the Ku Klux Klan came by. When he saw all races getting along so well, taking care of the grounds and caring for each other, he gained a new understanding and said that he was going to stop being a member of that racist organization.

At a certain point in the South, our caravan was stopped by some racists. We got out and they commented "an integrated group, huh," and were quite hostile. Jim Jones got out of the bus and walked toward them. They immediately got into their cars and left. How blessed we are to be in this MINISTRY OF LOVE, where miracles of mercy happen every day!

Scripture Fulfilled in Redwood Valley

"For I was an hungered,
And ye gave me meat:
I was thristy, and ye gave me drink:
I was a stranger, and ye took me in:
Naked, and ye clothed me:
I was sick, and ye visited me:
In prison,
And ye came unto me."

The Most Unusual Healing & Prophetic Ministry You Will Ever See!

MIRACULOUS
Healing & Blessing Services
Pastor James W. Jones
Peoples Temple Christian Church

Pastor Jones' concern for every living thing is manifested by the number of stray and abandoned animals he has taken into the animal shelter maintained behind the modest cinder block house in which he and his family live. He is shown here with Auraurk, a colorful parrot rescued from an unhappy home.

Hilltop Haven Convalescent Home is managed by Peoples Temple members who love and care for the senior citizens residing there. This lovely home was recently commended by state officials for its outstanding level of geriatric care.

INVITE ALL OF YOUR RELATIVES AND FRIENDS TO JOIN IN THE MOST BEAUTIFUL AND INSPIRING FELLOWSHIP HAPPENING IN THESE TIMES! PEOPLES TEMPLE WILL BE HOLDING SERVICES IN:

CHICAGO:

Paul Dunbar Vocational High School
3000 S. Martin Luther King Dr.

Tuesday, August 14th
Wednesday, August 15th
Thursday, August 16th
7:30pm

Pastor Jones Cares Very Much About the Needs and Safety of Those Who Attend His Services. He Has Instructed That Our Modern, Air-Conditioned Greyhound-type Busses Provide Rides Home for Those Who Need Transportation at the End of the Meetings.

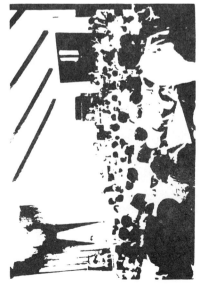

Members gather in the beautiful Mother Church in Redwood Valley for Pastor Jones' teaching in Christian Living and Apostolic Sharing.

81

Peoples Temple On Tour

Peoples Temple members will travel to Washington D.C. on Monday, August 13, 1973, to spend the day visiting the Nation's Capital where some of our Congressmen are giving us public interviews. Jim Jones' Human Service Ministry was recently praised in the Halls of Congress and written up in the Congressional Record.

BUSSES TO INDIANA AND OHIO: Temple Busses will leave Chicago for Indianapolis, Cincinnati, Dayton, Columbus, and return to Chicago for the meeting there on Wednesday, August 15. Housing will be available for anyone needing it. Write to P.O. Box 214, Redwood Valley, California 95470 for your reservations right away.

Bus Shuttle from Chicago
Schedule for Wednesday, August 15

City/Address	Arrive	Leave
INDIANAPOLIS		
10th & Delaware	7:00 AM	7:30 AM
CINCINNATI		
Vine & Elmwood	9:30 AM	10:00 AM
DAYTON		
5th & High Streets	11:00 AM	11:30 AM
COLUMBUS		
5th & High Streets	12:30 PM	1:00 PM

Arrive in Chicago 4:00 or 5:00 PM. Housing will be arranged for that night. Busses will leave the next morning for the return trip.

MOVING TO REDWOOD VALLEY: All persons wishing to join this Miracle Ministry of God are offered transportation with us back to Redwood Valley, California, where you will be able to live and make a new home.

There will be a blessing for those who call at least 20 persons a day inviting them to our services. . .

If you have any questions about the Peoples Temple Ministry or wish to receive any of the Anointed Materials, please write: Peoples Temple, P.O. Box 214, Redwood Valley, California 95470, Ph. No. (707) 485-7607.

The Power And Character Of The Prophet, Jim Jones as others see him:

REV. N. C. CRAIN, formerly of the Texas Baptist churches: "My friends, God has wonderfully blessed me. When I came here for the first time, I was brought in in a wheelchair. But thanks to Christ in Jim Jones, I can walk! Now, I've seen by Pastor Jones' example that I should become my brother's keeper. So I am giving away my fine clothes and I'm going out into the 'highways and hedges,' into the ghettos, where I can do God's work after the pattern of Jim Jones.''

LOVIE DE PINA of Los Angeles testifies of being saved from death: "For fifty-two years I suffered with such afflictions as Diverticulitis, Rheumatoid Arthritis, and Bowel Obstruction. After five operations I was given up to die. I was walking with death every minute. Then I met Pastor Jones and he told me during a service that I had suffered long enough. I was healed in a moment, and now my pain is all gone! Jim Jones has done so much for me -- I just cannot tell it all.''

DR. S. D. PETER was a former President of the largest churches in the East, located in Philadelphia. "I have known Pastor Jim Jones for twenty years and have found in him the same principled character as that of the man Jesus. Jim Jones' love and compassion for suffering humanity is overwhelming. I so much admire his great desire to see that the underprivileged be blessed and have the opportunity to work and support themselves as decent, respectable citizens. His great healing power prompted me to send sick and afflicted members of my former faith to him for help and they came back healed. I, too, was completely healed -- of glaucoma. Since the death of my former pastor, I have been looking for someone sent from God, and in Jim Jones I found the highest manifestation of God on Earth. After we met, he told me the thoughts of my mind and intimate details of my life that only I knew about. He also told me things that would happen in the future that came about exactly as he prophesied. I believe Jim Jones is the Essence of Love. He works day and night serving others and I have never seen him do a selfish act. He is truly the Word Made Flesh and, thank God, I have found him.''

ABOVE: Pastor Jones with his lovely wife, beautiful adopted rainbow family, "homemade" child, and grandchildren.

Pastor Jim Jones...

...from Redwood Valley, California, with an Active Pastorate of Over 10,000 Members in His California Churches. This Pastorate Supports Senior Citizens' Homes, Service Centers, Children's Homes and a Christian College Crusade. Pastor Jones is Bringing His MIRACLE HEALING & HUMAN SERVICE MINISTRY to Houston, Philadelphia, and Chicago During an August Tour of the United States. Thousands of People Across the Land Have Experienced INCREDIBLE MIRACLES and BLESSINGS Through Pictures and Oil Anointed by Pastor Jones. Scores of Others are HEALED EVERY WEEK by the Christ Spirit in This AMAZING PROPHET.

Pastor Jones is shown here exchanging a joyful greeting with a member.

A REVELATION FROM PASTOR JIM!

I feel that you have a genuine need, and although you have asked for help, you are still waiting for an answer. You have felt that you have faith – but still the answer to your prayer has not come. The *SPIRIT OF CHRIST* has instructed me to ask you to send me a photograph of yourself (if you have one) or a piece of cloth or handkerchief that you have worn. These items will not be returned to you

This unique request is presented as a challenge to you to exercise all the faith you have; for you to believe that as it was in the days of Scripture, when miracles were achieved in strange but gloriously effective ways, so it can be in this day for you.

You will remember when the rich man was instructed to bathe in the dirty waters of the Jordan River seven times. This took a great deal of faith!! The first six times he went down into the water he came up still plagued with Leprosy, but the seventh time he came up completely healed. Truly the SPIRIT OF LOVE that has worked through me for so many years, and that has healed so many thousands of people can work for you - if you will reach out in faith. I feel certain that your faith will not be disappointed, that the need you feel you have will be met and your prayers will be answered.

glue

DEAR PASTOR JIM,

_____ HERE IS MY PHOTOGRAPH OR
_____ A PIECE OF CLOTH WORN BY ME,
WHICH YOU ASKED ME TO SEND TO YOU.

I FEEL SO GOOD ABOUT WHAT GOD IS DOING FOR
ME THAT I WANT EVERYONE TO KNOW ABOUT IT!

You have my permission to use this photograph in the publications or other communications sponsored by Peoples Temple Christian Church or Jim Jones, Its Pastor, for whatever purpose they see fit. I sign this freely and without duress, because I believe in the Human Service Works of Peoples Temple Christian Church. I understand that these items will not be returned.

IN FAITH I AM SENDING YOU MY LOVE OFFERING.

$50____ $25____ $20____ $15____ $10____ $5____ Other $ _____

Signed _____

Address _____

City & State _____ Zip _____

As you send your letter, if you are able to send a GIFT OF LOVE: to help the work financially God will honor your faith. This offering of support will show that you DO have the faith to believe that this needed miracle can be performed in your life.

Your measure of faith should be the measure of your GIFT OF LOVE: God knows how much you can give, and as you prepare your gift, remember the story of the Widow's Mite - it was all she had. Jesus said that she would be blessed for her sacrifice more than the rich man would, even though he had given a large offering. It was the sacrificial offering that received the blessing.

It is vital that you heed this REVELATION OF THE HOLY SPIRIT and send your letter before another week passes. Write your special need and send it with your offering in the envelope provided.

My Strength, Love, and Peace
I Give To You

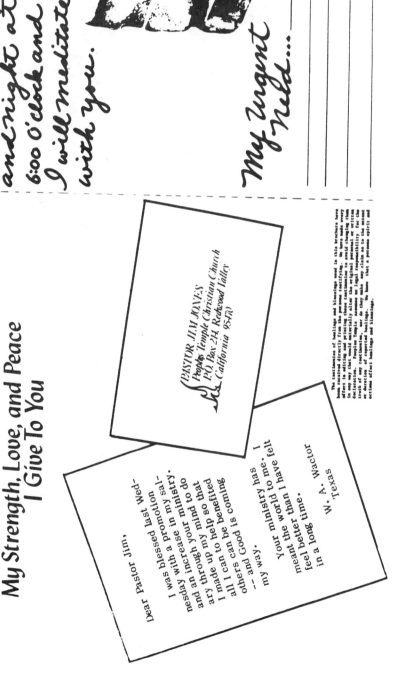

Pastor Jim,

Please meditate for my special need each morning and night at 6:00 o'clock and I will meditate with you.

My urgent need...

PASTOR JIM MAYES
Peoples Temple Christian Church
P.O. Box 214 Redwood Valley
California 95470

Dear Pastor Jim,

I was blessed last Wednesday with a promotion - an increase in my salary. I made up my mind to do all I can to be benefited and through my ministry. others can be coming -- and God is coming my way.

Your ministry has meant the world to me. I feel better than I have felt in a long time.

W. A. Wactor
Texas

Pastor Jim needs you!

Pastor Jim can't bear to see any child disappointed. Hundreds of children who would have been left out will be able to share in the fullness of Christmas this year...

IF YOU WILL HELP! PASTOR JIM IS COUNTING ON YOU!

✂- - - - - - - - - -

YES, PASTOR JIM, you can count on me! Here is my love offering:

$5 ___ $10 ___ $20 ___
$50 ___ $100 ___ Other ___

I want to share my blessings with the needy.

NAME _____
ADDRESS _____

MARY, Age 3. Her parents stayed "high" on drugs and dragged her from place to place.

JULIE, Age 7. Had to take care of her blind mother all by herself. Now both she and her mother have someone to take care of them because of our Pastor.

PAUL, Age 4. Born in jail to a drug addict and separated from her for his first nine months. Now he and his mother are reunited. She is rehabilitated and going to college. Paul is a very happy little boy.

MICHELLE. Age 6. Your love offerings have enabled us to care for her and her sister, so that their mother can finish a nursing course.

TAKASHI, Age 9. Sent from one foster home to another in his native land. Pastor Jim gave him a real home.

PATTY, Age 18 months. Her mother spent most of her time in jail. Your offerings have enabled a Christian family to give her a loving home.

Children are our Most Precious Gift

"SHAY-SHAY" and two of his friends were living on the streets of a big city in the East from what they could beg or find in the garbage cans. Haunted by hunger and by the city tough guys, they lived in daily fear for their lives. When Jim Jones came through their city with his 11 busses full of vacationers from Peoples Temple he saw these three little waifs.

His heart was touched by their pleas for help, so he asked his attorneys to make legal arrangements. Now the little boys are living in Redwood Valley where they have all the things they ever dreamed about. Where Christmas was only a dream to them before, now through the help of your generous offerings, these three little boys will know the thrill of a giant Christmas tree with presents for all the children.

YOU have paid for "Shay-Shay" to have extensive dental work on teeth that were rotting. All three boys have nice clothes, and three good meals a day - - luxuries they seldom knew before - - because you care enough to help.

So many thoughtful people have given clothes (they wear sizes 8, 10 and 12) that the boys never again will have to know what it is to have freezing fingers and toes. We know you will continue to help us take care of these little boys, as well as the needs of the scores of other children who have been taken in through your support of Pastor Jim.

Peoples Temple Records in Stereo.....

A long held dream is at last COME TRUE! Peoples Temple is able to bring to your home its full 200 voice interracial choir, orchestra and soloists, in full stereo.

BRING THE SERVICE INTO YOUR OWN HOME!

Each song is selected by Pastor Jones. Through them he sends his love. You will be blessed by the understanding of his teachings that comes to you through this ministry of song. Music carries a message and lifts the spirits of all into a glorious union with God ... which delivers us into His great humanitarian service.

You will close your eyes and imagine yourself right in the services of Peoples Temple with your Pastor, Jim Jones.

Get your record immediately. Do not forget to have them sent to your friends and relatives. Add the great blessings of His love through this great and beautiful music to enrich their lives.

The cost PER RECORD is $6.50 each, when you come in person to meetings, or if you wish it sent by mail, $7.00 includes postage, for each record.

(Side 1)

WELCOME..........Peoples Temple Junior Choir
WALKING WITH YOU FATHER............Shirley Smith and
                         Deanna Wilkinson
SET THEM FREE.................Joyce Parks
WALK A MILE IN MY SHOES............Melvin Johnson
HOLD ON BROTHER............Deanna Wilkinson
DOWN FROM HIS GLORY............**Pastor Jim Jones**
(Side 2)
HE'S ABLE........ ....Shirley Smith
SOMETHIN' GOT A HOLD OF ME............Ruth Coleman
BECAUSE OF HIM............Deanna Wilkinson
SIMPLE SONG OF FREEDOM........ ....Norman Ijames
BLACK BABY ....**Marceline Jones**
WILL YOU?............Peoples Temple full choir

Directors:

Anita Kelly and Norman Ijames

Arranger & Producer:

Jack Arnold Beam

Writers:

**Deanna Wilkinson, Jack Arnold Beam
and Loretta Cordell . . .**

Dear Pastor Jones:

Please send my record immediately. I enclose $7.00 which includes postage costs.

Name: _____

Address _____ Phone _____

PASTOR JIM JONES
People's Temple
P. O. Box 214
Redwood Valley, Calif. 95470

_____

At $7.00 PER RECORD, Please mail records to the following of my friends and relatives:

Name _____ Name _____
Address _____ Address _____
_____ _____

Just as our beloved Pastor, Jim Jones, has always selflessly helped us in our time of need, we also should make every effort to sacrifice and give of ourselves.

This is your opportunity to do so. The People's Temple ministry is in urgent need of another bus. There has been REVELATION given to our Pastor that it is essential to have this new bus for the PEOPLES PROTECTION -- as soon as possible. It will be specially equipped to meet the needs of the people on the road. The amount of missionary work we do and the number of workers has also been increased, further making another bus necessary.

OUR BUSSES HAVE TRAVELED OVER ONE MILLION MILES... WITHOUT ONE SERIOUS INJURY. You can be assured this bus will be put to the same Divine and holy work.

We all know that our Pastor does not waste or spend the people's money improperly. Recently he did not spend even a quarter for a parking lot space next to where he was going for an appointment. Instead, he looked many minutes for a free space until he found one several blocks away, thus living up to his pledge not to waste one penny of the people's money.

Those who contribute to the needs of this ministry of God have been blessed in thousands of ways. This is according to written testimonies sent to us. You too can be greatly blessed by helping to finance this expensive, but vitally necessary transportation vehicle. It is so true that when we give honestly and from our heart that we are REWARDED MOST ABUNDANTLY, for it is written...

"For as you soweth, so shall ye also reap..."

This universal law has been proven to us time and time again -- in meetings, in testimonies, and in our day-to-day existence. See for yourself the blessings that can be reaped through this holy and high calling.

PEACE AND LOVE BE WITH YOU AND YOURS.

- -

PEOPLE'S TEMPLE, P. O. Box 214, Redwood Valley CA 95470

Dear Pastor Jim Jones:

I want to be a part of the group buying this bus. I realize that it is so very vital to this work you do in carrying on your Divine Healing and Teaching Ministry. I wish to make a stand for freedom and God knowing that this alone will bring the true blessings I have prayed for in my own life.

Here is my love offering:

$5____ $10____ $15____ $20____ $25____ $50____ $100____ $1000 ____   Other $_____

Name _____   Address _____

_____

City _____ State _____ Zip_____ Phone _____

PEOPLES TEMPLE CHRISTIAN CHURCH

P.O. Box 163, Redwood Valley, Calif. 95470

A group of teachers and teacher-aids are finalizing their plans to move into this complex, where they will be better able to carry on the education program they now provide for the children of Peoples Temple Christian Church.

This program includes all the children in the church, up through the age of 13, in an active program of sports, tutoring, swimming instruction, and special classes teaching foreign languages, home making, first-aid and other important subjects.

Each age group chooses the type of activities it wants to participate in throughout the quarter, and then they meet throughout the week for classes and tutoring.

Although this seems like a busy schedule for these children, the amazing thing is that their grades in public school actually improve, and so does their general health, as they participate in this active program.

Several of the teachers and teacher-aides have children of their own; however, they are also bringing in children to live in these homes who need special guidance and love to redirect their lives.

This complex is adjacent to our Children's Home, so the children will have access to over 40 acres of country living where they will enjoy horses, cattle and many other animals and pets.

Peoples Temple is a nationally known and appreciated organization which takes in children from all walks of live, many of whom have been labelled incorrigible by the courts. Because of this, our expenses have become so great that we are forced to ask for assistance from our members and friends who may be unable to take children into their own homes, but who would like to be a part of this rewarding ministry which God is using.

If you too want to experience the blessing that comes from helping those who are too young to help themselves, we know you will want to give a generous offering to this program.

- -

Dear Pastor Jim Jones,

YES! I want to receive the special blessing that comes through helping children. My special donation for these children is

$5___ $10___ $15___ $20___ $25___ $50___ $100___ OTHER $_____

NAME_____

ADDRESS_____

CITY_____STATE_____

ZIP CODE_____ TELEPHONE_____

Return to:
PEOPLES TEMPLE
P.O. Box 163
Redwood Valley, Calif. 95470

The selfish man will say "God helps those who help themselves",
but God has said "It is more blessed to give than to receive".

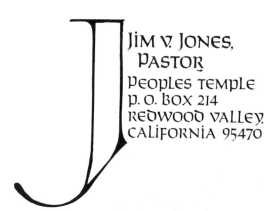

JIM V. JONES,
    PASTOR
Peoples Temple
P. O. Box 214
Redwood Valley,
California 95470

Dear One,

   Pastor Jim Jones has asked me to write to you to tell you that he cares very much for you and meditates often for your problems. He desires that your life be blessed and that your body be free from pain. In these past few weeks your needs and problems have been very much on his mind and he wants to help you RIGHT NOW in your time of need.

   The ANOINTED PRAYER CLOTH in the small envelope enclosed has been blessed for you. To receive the greatest blessings from this Prayer Cloth follow these instructions:
   1. Pin your Prayer Cloth to your clothing today.
   2. Wear it for two days and two nights.
   3. Send it in with your Prayer Sheet which is on the next page.

   Pastor Jones will meditate for your needs using your Prayer Sheet and Prayer Cloth for seven days. You can help him by carefully filling in each part of the Prayer Sheet and sending it back quickly. If you would like Prayer Cloths to be sent to your loved ones and friends include their names and addresses with your letter, and they will be sent out immediately, as soon as they have been anointed.

   Special blessings come to those who honor this work of God with their offerings. In recent meetings there has been a revelation about OBEDIENCE OFFERINGS of certain amounts. There are many who have been blessed when they gave as much as $700.00 or $999.00, and hundreds of others who received their miracles when they gave obediently as they were led by the Spirit. To know what your OBEDIENCE OFFERING should be, close your eyes and ask God to show you. When you ask with an honest heart you will be shown just how much you should give.

   God will also reveal to Pastor Jones what your obedience offering should be. It is important that you be honest with God! Remember, "His affection is more abundant toward you, while he remembereth the obedience of you." (II Cor. 7:15) Through your faithful obedience blessings can begin to flow your way — as you have always hoped and dreamed that they would.

   With many blessings,

   Karen Layton

   Karen Layton,
   Personal Secretary to Jim V. Jones

91

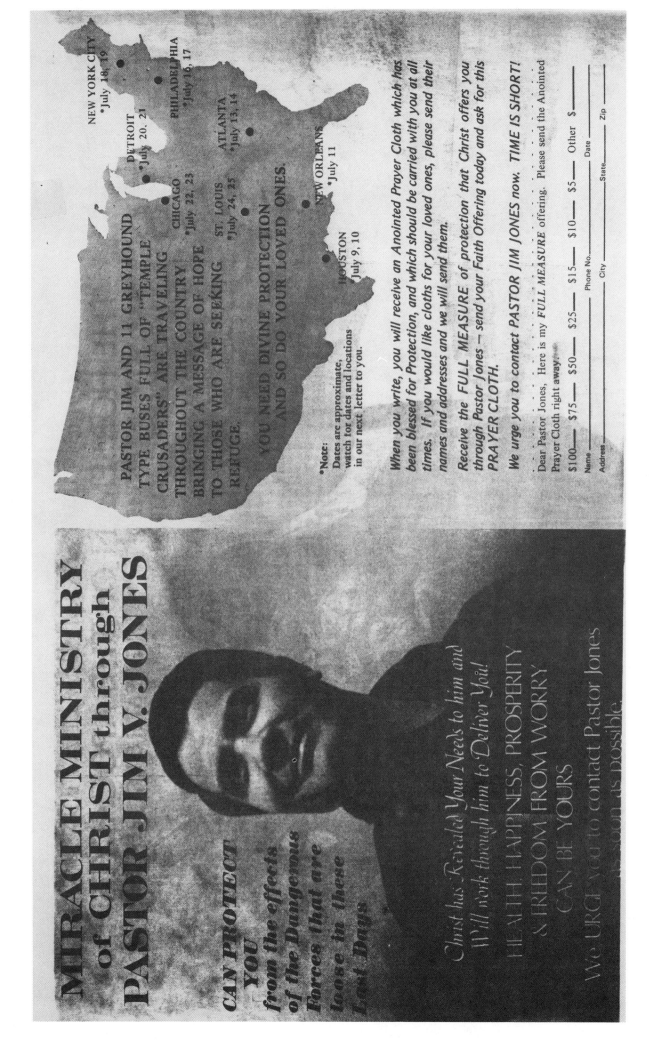

MIRACLE MINISTRY
of CHRIST through
PASTOR JIM V. JONES

CAN PROTECT YOU from the effects of the Dangerous Forces that are loose in these Last Days

Christ has Revealed Your Needs to him and Will work through him to Deliver You!

HEALTH, HAPPINESS, PROSPERITY & FREEDOM FROM WORRY CAN BE YOURS

We URGE you to contact Pastor Jones as soon as possible.

NEW YORK CITY *July 18, 19

DETROIT *July 20, 21

PHILADELPHIA *July 16, 17

CHICAGO *July 22, 23

ATLANTA *July 13, 14

ST. LOUIS *July 24, 25

NEW ORLEANS *July 11

HOUSTON July 9, 10

PASTOR JIM AND 11 GREYHOUND TYPE BUSES FULL OF "TEMPLE CRUSADERS" ARE TRAVELING THROUGHOUT THE COUNTRY BRINGING A MESSAGE OF HOPE TO THOSE WHO ARE SEEKING REFUGE.

YOU NEED DIVINE PROTECTION AND SO DO YOUR LOVED ONES.

*Note:
Dates are approximate, watch for dates and locations in our next letter to you.

When you write, you will receive an Anointed Prayer Cloth which has been blessed for Protection, and which should be carried with you at all times. If you would like cloths for your loved ones, please send their names and addresses and we will send them.

Receive the FULL MEASURE of protection that Christ offers you through Pastor Jones — send your Faith Offering today and ask for this PRAYER CLOTH.

We urge you to contact PASTOR JIM JONES now. TIME IS SHORT!

Dear Pastor Jones, Here is my FULL MEASURE offering. Please send the Anointed Prayer Cloth right away.

$100 ___ $75 ___ $50 ___ $25 ___ $15 ___ $10 ___ $5 ___ Other $ ___

Name _____
Address _____ Phone No. _____
City _____ Date _____
State _____ Zip _____

"OH! THANK YOU FOR SAVING MY LIFE!"

EXPRESS YOUR GRATITUDE - to receive the Greatest Miracles!! These letters from
and Johnson show dynamically how this works. Each time she said "Thank You" and
expressed appreciation for God working through Pastor Jones, she was blessed again.

January

Dear Pastor Jones,

I am a new member in your church and I want to say THANK YOU. This might seem like a small miracle to some, but to me it means a great deal. When you asked for questions in the service I held up my Anointed Picture of you and asked if you would autograph it for me. Very lovingly you explained that since thousands of pictures were in circulation, that if you would do this for me you would be obligated to autograph all the other pictures, because of your equalitarian beliefs. I know that you felt my disappointment, because when I got home that night something told me to turn my picture around. Although it had never left my hand throughout the evening, YOUR SIGNATURE APPEARED on the back side of my precious picture. I will treasure this all the rest of my life. Thank you so much.

February

Well, my Miracle Picture caused an even greater miracle in my life. Someone was trying to break into my house. I heard him tampering with the door, and I made up my mind to find out what was going on. I went to open the door to try to scare the person away, then I thought about my Anointed Picture of you. I placed it near the door and said, "I am in your care." The prowler left and never returned. Later you told me of your protection, and that had I gone out the door that night I would surely have been killed. You saved my life!

April

Miracles seem to be coming my way so fast that I can hardly believe it. Where I had a sick, broken body before, now my problems have vanished. I was going blind and you healed me of glaucoma. You healed me of a deteriorated vertebra and disc. Now my back brace is sitting in the closet — a constant reminder of the mighty Power of God that works through you. I had had three heart attacks before I met you, and the main aorta was twisted like you twist a piece of paper. Now the heart murmur that I had is completely gone and my heart is like new again. The crippling arthritis I was suffering with is gone. How can I say thank you for giving me a new life? I am trying to show my gratitude by working hard to help others, by practicing brotherhood and equality, following your example.

July

Never before have I known such love! Not only have you lifted all my burdens, but you have reached out to my loved ones who are not even members of your church. My son had just received a new car for graduation and he took two of his friends for a ride. A swarm of yellow jackets came in the car and he became so frightened that his car veered off the road. It hit a steel pipe which was the only thing that kept the car from falling hundreds of feet down to certain death. He was wearing the Anointed Prayer Cloth that you had sent to him through me just a short time before! You also saved my granddaughter in an accident when she was about to be crushed to death. When my daughter was very ill she said she had faith that her healing would come through you, and you did not disappoint her. She was completely healed. What manner of love is this that will reach to people you only know through knowing me?

September

I am so glad I was in the meeting the day you said that if we would give $7.00 our money could multiply. I gave my last $7.00 and went home knowing that more would come from somewhere. Shortly after that I received a check I didn't expect for $500.00. Now that's real multiplication! It came just at a time that I needed it most. THANK YOU for knowing my needs and granting my desires before I even need to ask!

Love, Mabel

EXPRESS YOUR GRATITUDE
to receive the Greatest Miracles!!
"We have a Kingdom nothing can destroy
Let us please God... with thankful hearts."

Hebrews 12:28

Dear Pastor Jones;

YES, I AM GRATEFUL for the blessings I continue to receive, and I want to obey the Voice of God by expressing my thanks. I know that gratitude for past blessings will open the channel for more and more wonderful things to happen. Please remember my special needs in your meditations. I want to tell you about the wonderful things that have happened to me through this ministry:

_____
_____
_____
_____
_____
_____
_____
_____
_____
_____
_____
_____
_____
_____
_____
_____
_____
_____
_____
_____
_____
_____
_____
_____
_____
_____
_____

HERE IS MY GRATITUDE OFFERING - SENT IN APPRECIATION FOR THE MIRACLES THAT HAVE BLESSED MY LIFE. $ _____

I hereby agree and consent to the use of this testimony and my photograph in the publications and other communications sponsored or otherwise influenced by Peoples Temple Christian Church, or Jim Jones, its pastor, for whatever purpose said church or pastor sees fit. I sign this freely and without duress and because I believe in the Human Service Work of Peoples Temple Christian Church.

Signed _____ Phone _____ Date _____

Address _____
               Street   City   State   Zip

Send your message to: Pastor Jim Jones, P.O. Box 214, Redwood Valley, California 95470

A SPECIAL EASTER BLESSING
To Your Loved Ones
From Pastor Jim

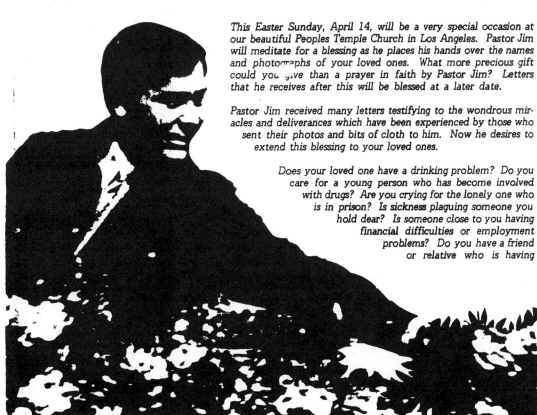

This Easter Sunday, April 14, will be a very special occasion at our beautiful Peoples Temple Church in Los Angeles. Pastor Jim will meditate for a blessing as he places his hands over the names and photographs of your loved ones. What more precious gift could you give than a prayer in faith by Pastor Jim? Letters that he receives after this will be blessed at a later date.

Pastor Jim received many letters testifying to the wondrous miracles and deliverances which have been experienced by those who sent their photos and bits of cloth to him. Now he desires to extend this blessing to your loved ones.

Does your loved one have a drinking problem? Do you care for a young person who has become involved with drugs? Are you crying for the lonely one who is in prison? Is sickness plaguing someone you hold dear? Is someone close to you having financial difficulties or employment problems? Do you have a friend or relative who is having

A SPECIAL EASTER BLESSING

Pastor Jim, Please Meditate for my Loved One

Loved One's Name _____

Address _____ Telephone _____

City _____ State _____ Zip _____

Church Affiliation _____

My Loved One's Special Need is; _____

_____

_____

_____

_____

Here is a Cloth or a Photograph of my Loved One.

GLUE

Pastor Jim, Please Meditate for my Loved One

Loved One's Name _____

Address _____ Telephone _____

City _____ State _____ Zip _____

Church Affiliation _____

My Loved One's Special Need is; _____

_____

_____

_____

Here is a Cloth or a Photograph of my Loved One.

GLUE

Pastor Jim, The names of my loved ones are being given to you in faith!

I enclose $ _____ for each person I listed. My total offering is $ _____

My Name _____

Address _____ Telephone _____

City _____ State _____ Zip _____

Church Affiliation _____

My Own Special Need is; _____

_____

_____

Here is a Cloth or a Photograph of mine.

GLUE

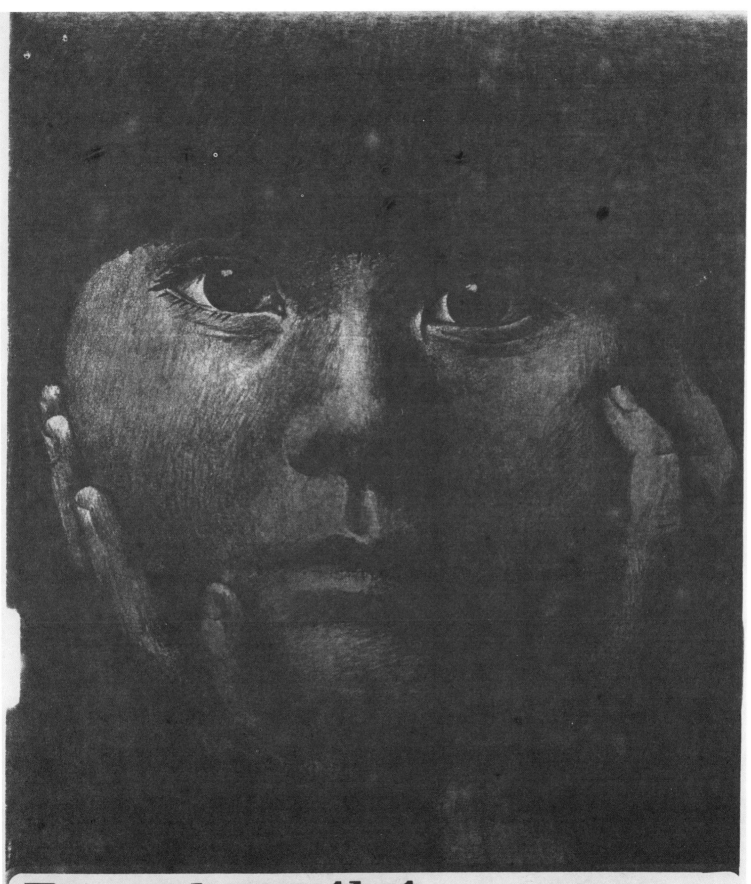

Do you know that
100,000,000 PEOPLE WILL
DIE OF STARVATION IN 1975?

"For I was an hungered
   and ye gave me meat;
      I was thirsty
         and ye gave me drink;
   I was a stranger
      and ye took me in;
         Naked, and ye clothed me;
   I was sick and ye visited me;
      I was in prison,
         and ye came unto me.

"Then shall the righteous
      Answer him, saying,

When saw we thee an hungered
      And fed thee?
         Or thirsty,
            And gave thee drink?
When saw we thee a stranger
      And took thee in?
         Or naked, and clothed thee?
   Or when saw we thee sick
      Or in prison,
         And came unto thee?

"Verily I say unto you,
   Inasmuch as ye have done it
      Unto one of the least of these
      ..Ye have done it unto me."

Matthew 25:35-40

A starving mother in Ethiopia sadly watches her children die.

The bountiful first harvest of corn, towering 8 feet into the air, is surveyed by Pastor Jim Jones.

Dear Christian Friend,

Did you know that some 400,000,000 people will suffer from malnutrition and 100,000,000 people are expected to die from starvation in 1975? It's time now for true Christians to unite to meet this universal challenge. Christians are being tested for the Judgment Day when they will be asked, "When I was hungry did you feed me? When I was thirsty did you give me drink? When I was naked did you clothe me?" So many people today are homeless and hungry, lacking the vision of salvation that only the Love of Christ can bring. We must be our brother's keeper in the true sense of the word — by our deeds and actions.

You ask, "What can I do to help?" There is so much to do! Because of the increasing shortage of food around the world, the congregation of Peoples Temple Christian Church of Redwood Valley, California, has initiated a program of direct action which will make food available in the time of need. The congregation has stepped out in faith to begin a Christian Agricultural Mission in South America. By means of sacrificial devotion from many hard-working members, the congregation has raised and expended more than $100,000. At this very moment acres of jungle are being cleared by church volunteers. Farm equipment has been sent, fields have been planted, and plans are being formulated to plant soybean and other protein crops which can be used to feed the hungry.

Throughout the years Peoples Temple has sent food and supplies to help those who face disease and starvation, to places both at home and abroad — including Biafra, Bangladesh, Appalachia, the Sub-Sahara region of Africa, and Indian reservations. The church has felt very deeply that wherever there is a need, dedicated Christians must be around to help! This human service ministry of Peoples Temple is so highly regarded throughout the world that the government of this South American country has made available to us 26,000 acres of fertile land to begin our Agricultural Missionary Program. This great miracle shows how God is working with us! We are so grateful for this sign of His approval. "What can we ever say to such wonderful things as these? If God is on our side, who can ever be against us?" (Rom. 8:31)

As our efforts to help those in need increase, we witness the mighty and abundant blessings of God's love. His love is causing this work to grow in effectiveness. If you are able to help us, we are sure you will experience the wonderful feeling that comes from sharing. Service to suffering humanity is indeed the highest form of worship of our God.

Remember that "Whatever measure you use to give — large or small — will be used to measure what is given back to you." (Luke 6:30) Your tax-deductible donation can mean the difference.

Your donation may be made payable to "Agricultural Mission, Peoples Temple," P.O. Box 214, Redwood Valley, California 95470.

Thank you so very much for whatever you are led to do!

G. Donald Beck,
for the Board of Trustees

Children from the mission field wave a fond good-bye to Pastor Jones as he leaves to come back to California.

THROUGH THIS UNIFIED CHRISTIAN EFFORT YOU ARE HELPING TO SPREAD THE GOSPEL BY WORD AND DEED.

YOUR GIFT WILL MAKE THE LOVE OF JESUS CHRIST REAL TO THOSE WHO ARE SUFFERING TODAY.

Yes! I want to help!   Here is my LOVE GIFT $_____

Name _____ *Date* _____

Address _____

City _____ *State* _____ *Zip* _____

___ *Please send me a receipt for tax purposes.*

Make your check payable to:

"AGRICULTURAL MISSION, PEOPLES TEMPLE CHRISTIAN CHURCH"
Post Office Box 214, Redwood Valley, California 95470

Report of My Visit to a Hungry or Lonely Person

Date_____

Dear Pastor Jones,

Today as you instructed I visited

_____
(name of person visited)

_____
(address of person visited)

_____
city   state   zip code

The food I took with me was_____

My personal message to the Pastor _____

_____

_____

_____

Here is my THANKSGIVING OFFERING. I am so grateful for my blessings! $_____

My Name_____ Phone Number _____

Address _____

City, State, Zip _____

It is important for you to fill out this sheet after you have made the visit requested by Pastor Jones. Send the completed sheet to:
    Pastor Jim Jones, P.O. Box 214, Redwood Valley, California 95470.

101

Personal
PRAYER SHEET
for:_____
Place your name here

_____
Address

_____
City   Zip Code

_____
Telephone   Birthdate

HERE IS MY OBEDIENCE OFFERING $_____

Pray for Me:_____
_____
_____
_____
_____

Here is the Prayer Cloth you sent to me. I have worn it for 2 days and 2 nights. Now I am asking you to meditate upon it as you pray for my needs.

Pray for My Healing Needs:_____
_____
_____
_____

Pray for My Financial Needs:_____
_____
_____
_____

Pray for My Spiritual Needs:_____
_____
_____
_____

Pray for My Loved Ones:_____
_____
_____

When your PRAYER SHEET is completed, send it along with your ANOINTED CLOTH to: PASTOR JIM JONES, P.O. Box 214, Redwood Valley, Calif. 95470

$328

Dorothy Hendrith

"I was in the service when the offering was being taken, and I emptied out my little billfold with all I had. It was only 20 cents and I didn't know where I would get any more money. But I thank God, when the mailman came I looked and there were two unexpected checks - $328.00 - to my surprise! I know it was you. I thank God and I thank you from the depths of my heart."

$177

"When my pastor said that $7.77 could cause financial blessings I gave that amount. The very next week I received a check in the mail that I did not expect or have any reason to receive for $177.00. I believe in miracles because I see them happening every day in my life."

Lucille Taylor

$800

Alberta Lindsay

"After I received your encouraging letter, Pastor Jones, a man who had owed us $700 repaid me. When I got home my husband and I counted out the $700 and I thought that was all. Then something made me look again into my purse. To my surprise there were five more $20 bills. I could hardly believe it! Thank God and thank you, Pastor Jones."

$13.77

"I gave $13.77, the amount that Pastor Jones has called the 'Miracle Obedience Offering.' That night on my way home I was glad I did. A stranger stepped up to my car at a stop sign. He had a long knife and tried to attack me through my open window, but I felt as if a 'protective shield' was around my car. The stranger couldn't get his knife close to my body, and he suddenly turned around and fled in terror."

Edith Bogue

$69

"I was in the service and gave $7.00 when Pastor Jones said this amount could bring special blessings. When I got my mail the next Monday morning I found an unexpected check there for $69.00. Shortly after that my last car payment was due, but before I could pay it, my pink slip came in the mail with a note from the bank thanking me for completing payment of my car."

Velma Darnes

$77

"I had money multiply in a beautiful meeting in Peoples Temple. During the offering when Pastor Jones asked if anyone had $7.00 I put this amount in. I looked again and $77.00 had miraculously materialized in my wallet. Praise God!"

Annie Moore

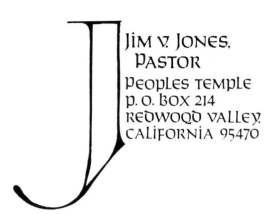

JiM V. JONES,
PASTOR
PEOPLES TEMPLE
P. O. bOX 214
REDWOOD VALLEY,
CALIFORNIA 95470

November, 1974

"Try to show
as much compassion
as your Father does
. . . for if you give,
you will get!

Your gift
will return to you
in full and
overflowing measure,
pressed down,
shaken together
to make room
for more,
and running over.

Whatever measure
you use to give —
large or small —
will be used
to measure
what is given
back to you."

Luke 6:30
The Living Bible

Dear One,

As Thanksgiving draws closer, our beloved Pastor takes this opportunity to personally extend his love to you. You have shown your love by your deeds and actions. Through your faith in the Power of God you have received many blessings. But his message to you is that the greatest blessings will only come when you show your concern for others. The rewards that come from giving to those in need will be great — for this is the highest form of worship. Pastor Jones reminds you that you can have as much of God as you are willing to pay for with the dedication and sacrifice of your life in service to others.

In the Bible we read that "Though you have faith . . . and have not charity, you are as nothing." Pastor Jones feels strongly that during the month of November you should demonstrate your charity by taking at least one item of food from your grocery shelf and giving it to someone who is hungry or lonely. Witness to them about his love. And most important of all, write and tell Pastor Jones whom you visited. As you reach out and respond to their need you will find that your own needs will be met in great measure.

Sincerely,

Karen Layton, Sec.

Karen Layton,
Personal Secretary to Jim Jones

SPECIAL NOTE FROM PASTOR JONES:

Oppression and famine draw close to home, and daily we read of new victims of injustice. There are a few who do not understand the love and compassion that this ministry has demonstrated, that holds our church family together. We regret to say that a small, foolish band of terrorists are seeking to hurt our peaceful group through vicious letters and lying phone calls that are not from our church. Possibly one of these people might try to contact you, although this seems very unlikely at this time. They might represent themselves as a member of this church. If you do receive such a letter or phone call, please let us know. The letters should be sent in, so that we can take appropriate action. The promise in the Bible is that our enemies will fall back and perish in the presence of the Holy Spirit of Love that is manifested in the world today.

" ...a feeling of freedom... "

collection of photographs & comments about the community of Jonestown

"...You know, people are so free here and they look so different. People's faces glow with freedom in their eyes. No more drugs, no more racism, no more rapes, no more prisons or jails..."

—Rosie Ruggiero

"...This is a dream come true. This is a whole new world—clean, fresh, pure..."

—Mary Wotherspoon

"...There is a place for everyone here and something for them to do. No one has special privileges and everyone feels worthwhile and a part. I am so happy, and that terrible feeling of insecurity is gone..."

—Penny Kerns

"...Jonestown is pure democracy in action..."

—Johnny Brown

"...When we first arrived on October 3rd, it was about 6:00 p.m. and everyone was eating dinner. Then they all came running towards the vehicle to greet three people—all of them came up to embrace us, saying, 'Welcome to your new home, Jonestown!' It made me want to cry..."

—Connie Fitch

"...I was afraid of facing retirement in that one-room apartment, but now I have my own cottage. I have all the free time I want and still plenty to do if I want. I am so happy to be here..."

—Lucious Bryant

"...You know, we had good jobs and a nice home—but we wanted to retire in a place of beauty. Well, we came to the right place!"

—Mr. & Mrs. E. Jones

"...I'm teaching a class in the Continuing Education Sessions and I've never felt so useful in all my 76 years..."

—Henry Mercer

"...Jonestown is truly a milestone. Nestled in the most exquisite forest surroundings, we have every convenience—plus more: the best in social services any community anywhere can offer!"

—Dorothy Worley

"...Everything grows well in Jonestown—especially the children..."
—Pat Grunnet (teacher)

107

...a feeling of freedom..."

—statements of Rev. and Mrs. John Moore, who had just returned from a week's visit at the Project, and Atty. Charles Garry, during a press conference held at Peoples Temple, May 28, 1978.

REV. MOORE:

"I'm John Moore. We have two daughters who are members of the Temple. One, the older girl, is a teacher, and the younger one is a nurse...The two words that come to my mind immediately, as I was there and as I tried to reflect upon my experiences were: 'impressive' and 'amazing'. It almost boggles my mind to see that great clearing and to understand how so much could have been done in the relatively short period of time.

"We wore ourselves out, walking around the facility. I think about 800 to a thousand acres have been cleared, and it's in the midst of a jungle, and that's part of what's impressive; and all except a part of the land that's not finally been cleared, has been planted with various crops.

"We went to the piggery, the chickery, to the dairy, to the mill, where the refining of flour from the tubers of the cassava [is done]. We were first impressed—certainly I was—with seeing the older people at the time we arrived ...about noon, engaged in calisthenics with an instructor, keeping their limbs and joints and muscles limber. And then we went to the nursery, the child care center.

"They have probably 35 preschoolers. I don't know how many they have in school. They have newborn babies; several babies have been born there. They have a day care nursery for parents who work, and there are those who are caring for them; and then they have the older people. That's really a part of the beauty of it, we felt.

"We talked about what they were doing, and what they were interested in, and all of them were engaged in some activity or work that was particularly important for them, they were about business which they regarded as important.

"I had a feeling of freedom...The food is provided for everyone, there's medical care for everyone, education-al opportunities for everyone; there are work needs and opportunities for the members of the community. I think obviously people with certain skills and experience move into those fields. If it's a tool and die maker in a machine shop, or a man in agronomy, they work in those parti-cular fields. On the other hand, some people have not had the experience in specific fields. One of the great things, I think, is the opportunity for some of the younger people, particularly, to be learning skills when that oppor-tunity is not present here."

In regard to the relationship of the project to the citizens and government of Guyana, Rev. Moore said, "The school is accredited by the government of Guyana... They've had people from the Department of Agriculture and their agricultural stations there working with the people at the project. The health services are provided for the Amerindians or people who live in the community as well as for members of the project itself."

BARBARA MOORE:

"My impressions are, having just experienced our visit there, that this is a beautiful, heroic, creative project! It is absolutely miraculous. There are excellent medical services, excellent educational services, and...it's a com-munity of caring and sharing with an added dimension, and this dimension I would say, is Love—if you want to use that term. In a sense it reminds me of...a New Testa-ment community, in the purest sense of the word, in the love and concern for all, that we observed. And with complete freedom for creativity! Those who want to farm, are farming; those who wish to teach, teach; those who like to cook, cook. They have an excellent nutri-tionist who is working scientifically all the time to dis-cover new uses for the indigenous plants and growths there, and is in contact with the Guyanese experts to discover new and useful uses for these various crops... That was very impressive to me.

"It was most impressive to see the elderly people, the older folks, who had their neat little yards, their little

(Cont'd. on page 12)

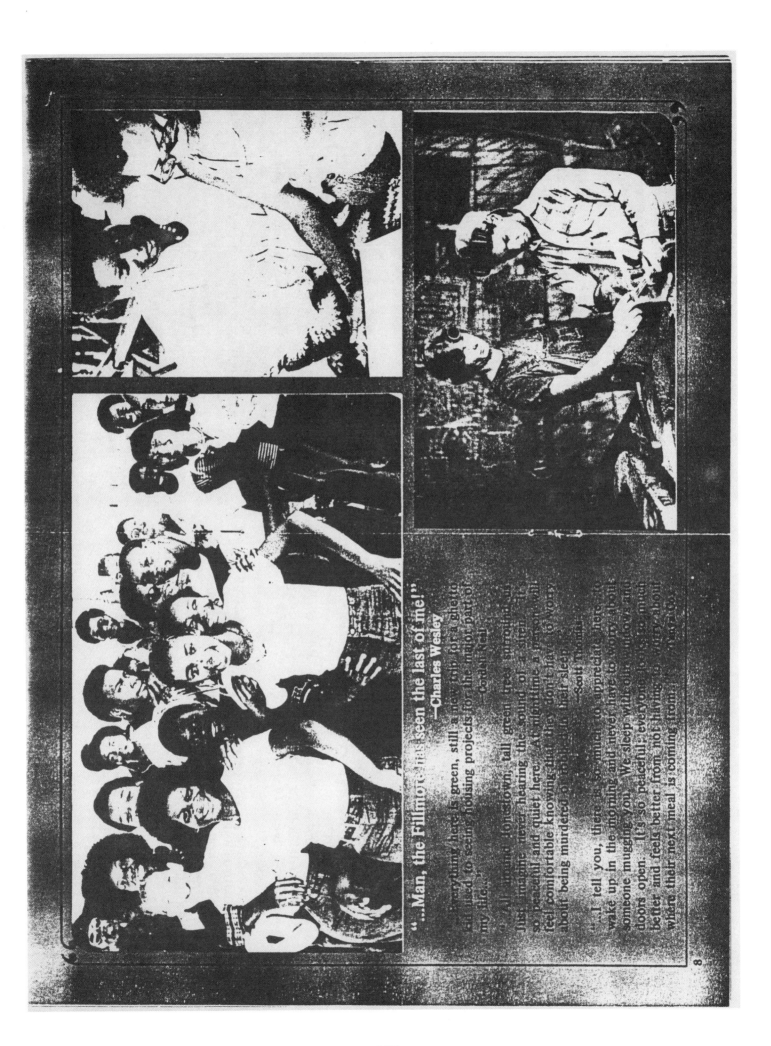

"...Man, the Fillmore has seen the last of me!"
—Charles Wesley

Everything here is green, still a new trip for a ghetto kid used to seeing housing projects for the mind, out of my direction.
—Corduroy

Just imagine never hearing the sound of a siren all around Jonestown, tall green trees sprouting up so peaceful and quiet here. At nighttime a person will feel comfortable knowing that they don't have to worry about being murdered or robbed in their sleep.
—Scott Norris

I tell you, there is so much to appreciate here. You wake up in the morning and never have to worry about someone mugging you. We sleep with our windows and doors open. It's so peaceful; everyone feels so much better and feels better from not having to worry about where their next meal is coming from.

8

109

Jonestown Guest Book

"IMPRESSIVE WORK"
Officer in charge of Guyana, Jamaica, Trinidad and Tobago, U. S. State Department

"I AM IMPRESSED"
Charge d'Affairs to U.S. Ambassador Andrew Young

"IMPRESSIVE" *Chief Medical Officer of the Ministry of Health, Guyana*

"PEACE AND LOVE IN ACTION"
Minister of Foreign Affairs, Guyana

"VERY IMPRESSIVE" *Minister of Education, Guyana*

"VERY PROGRESSIVE" *Regional Development Officer, North West Region, Guyana*

"VERY IMPRESSIVE, KEEP IT UP"
Representative, Ministry of Agriculture, Guyana

"A VERY PLEASANT DAY IN A VERY PLEASANT ATMOSPHERE"
Chief Official in the Ministry of Education, Guyana

"A MOST IMPRESSIVE START AND I WISH YOU ALL SUCCESS" *British High Commissioner in Guyana*

"IMPRESSIVE" *Chancellor of the University of Guyana*

"A WONDERFUL EXPERIENCE, A MODEL VILLAGE COMMUNITY TO BE EMULATED"
Permanent Secretary of the Ministry of Works and Transportation

"EXCELLENT" *Assistant Director-General of National Service, Guyana*

"IT'S VERY, VERY IMPRESSIVE. THANK YOU FOR THE OPPORTUNITY AND BEST WISHES"
Delegates from one of the world's largest news agencies.

"KEEP UP THE GOOD WORK"
Regional Minister, North West Region, Guyana

"FANTASTIC, BEYOND ONE'S IMAGINATION, MIRACULOUS, BEAUTIFUL, A TRUE EXAMPLE OF SOCIALIST LIVING" *Thirty-five teachers from the MacKenzie District, Guyana*

"THE HEALTH CARE IN THE COMMUNITY IS FANTASTIC. JONESTOWN IS A LITTLE BIT OF HEAVEN." After examining the teeth of 67 children he found only two cavities. "THIS," he said, "IS UNHEARD OF."
A dentist from India and founder of a dental school in Georgetown, Guyana

"IT'S MIND-BOGGLING TO SEE HOW YOU HAVE CARVED OUT OF THE JUNGLE A COMMUNITY THAT LOOKS JUST LIKE A TOWN IN THE UNITED STATES—AND WITH ALL THE PUBLIC UTILITIES."
In a letter following his visit, he wrote: "The training program of the youths and young adults at the Project is highly successful. I have met many and they have told me that they are so happy to be there, as it has made a great change in their life, and given them a chance to prove themselves."
Head of nearly a thousand physicians of a Medical Network of Amateur Radio Operators

"I also wish to give praise and credit to you and the other members of the Peoples Temple Church for the magnificent and humanitarian efforts that you are making. I feel certain that if there were more such organizations with devoted and sincere people such as Larry Schacht and yourself and the members of your church throughout the world that this planet would indeed be a better place upon which to spend one's life."

"Dr. Schacht is, in my opinion, a modern-day Dr. Schweitzer. I was truly impressed with..his activities in Mission Village regarding the comprehensive medical program that he is running there."
excerpts of letters from Dr. Albert Greenfield

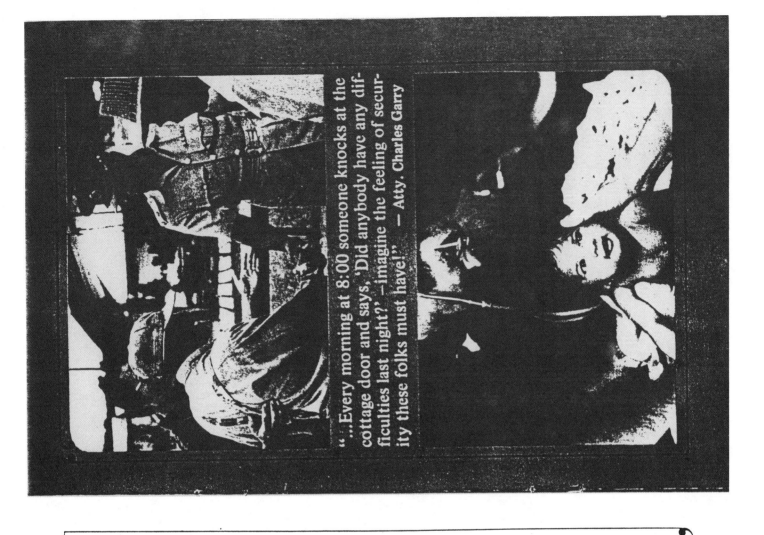

"...Every morning at 8:00 someone knocks at the cottage door and says, 'Did anybody have any difficulties last night?' —imagine the feeling of security these folks must have!"
— Atty. Charles Garry

(Cont'd from page 7)

white picket-type fences, and their opportunity to take classes if they wished to, or to garden, or to just sit. They also have a lovely library of over eight thousand volumes, from poetry to 'how-to-do-it'...and this was most impressive, that one could sit and read...

"It's a complete city, and one thing they do encourage is the nuclear family. There are families there with children. You can have your own home, or if you're a single person, you may live in a dormitory, whichever you prefer. They have a lovely nursery for infants; they have a nursery for toddlers, and of course a fine educational set-up."

One of the reporters in attendance at the conference stated that he thought she sounded impressed. He asked, "would you think it's rather Utopian there?" Her reply was, "Oh yes, a lovely Utopia."

CHARLES GARRY:

"I was impressed by the medical center particularly. All of the older citizens live right around the medical compound. The medical compound is something that you have never seen and you probably won't see unless you go there. It's almost a miracle. This young doctor, who was trained by the Temple, graduated with high honors from the University of California at Irvine, has performed miracles...Every morning at eight o'clock, someone knocks on the cottage door, and says, 'did anybody have any difficulties last night?' Can you imagine the feeling of security that these folks have, to feel that somebody cares for them, is interested in them, and will do things for them?"

A FIRST-CLASS EXAMPLE OF COMMUNITY LIFE

"It was a very rewarding experience," he said. "I have never before seen so many people of varying races working happily side-by-side without a single spark of friction. With its own school, sawmill, electricity, roads, houses, and so on, all being scrupulously clean, I could not help but be impressed." *Dr. Ng-a-Fook, Dental Surgeon [from a news article which appeared in the Guyana Chronicle following his visit to Jonestown]*

12

111

" "...Right now I'm sitting in our Pavillion. I can hear our saws going in the background, people are writing letters, playing in Spanish class, or in our Agriculture meeting. I work with Tom out in the housing area...I build closets in the cottages, and do some . the finish work on them. Then Charlie gives me various jobs, too, like building cabinets for the Nurse's Offices, and Radio Room. I feel like I'm really doing something worthwhile, especially when I walk around the houses and see the things I did on them, or go to the nurse and she reaches for my file in the cabinets I built..."

—Kim Brewster

"...I have changed my last name. I am now Tobi Mtendaji. My middle name is Chekevu. Put together these two names mean Happy Worker in Swahili...I am now on the construction crew building these beautiful cottages the family lives in. I guess I am just now bringing out my talents here..."

—Tobi Mtendaji

"...Greg and I live in our own cottage. We fixed it up really nice. I've planted eggplant along the sides. On the left side of the porch is a bread and butter tree, flowers, and some beans growing up the house. On the right side of the porch are cucumbers. I'm thinking of planting a papaya tree in the back of the house..."

—Erin Watkins

"...This place is growing by leaps and bounds. New and wider sidewalks are going up all the time; more cottages to accomodate more arrivals; electric wiring, fencing, planting, painting, gardening, everything you can think of. There is plenty to do and everyone enjoys working..."

—Loretta Coomer

"...We make all our own clothes now, and we get just the style, color, and material of something that you want and you don't have to shop for it!"

—Rheaviana Beam

"...There are experimentations going on in many phases, such as making our own clay bricks, our own smokehouse, experimental herbs, and all different kinds of woods to build some innovative carpentry items with also..."

—Ron Sines

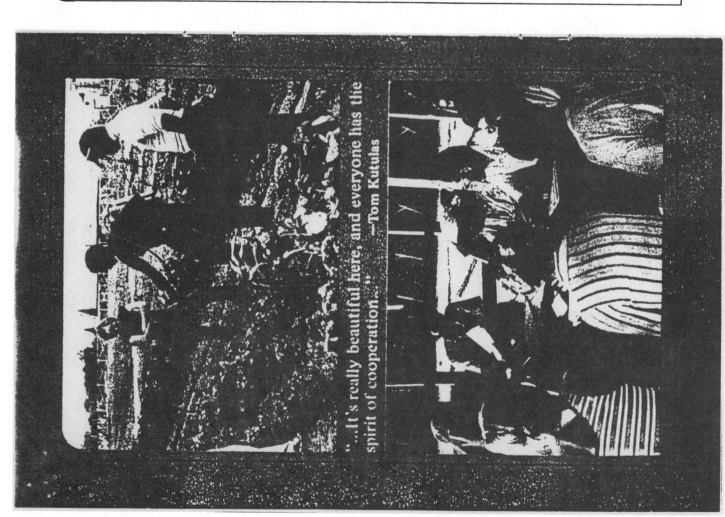

"...It's really beautiful here, and everyone has the spirit of cooperation."

—Tom Kutulas

"...Tell everybody they just don't know what they're missing..."
—Lena Benton

"...Talk about delicious food...you can't beat the menu at Jonestown..."
—Maria McCann

"...Your eyes will pop out of their sockets when you take a look at the beautiful piece of land called Jonestown. Words can't describe the beauty of this place..."
—Gary Tyler

"...The tropical rain showers are just like you read about. It is sunny and bright one minute, then all of a sudden the rain comes up quick—a gentle, steady rain. Just as suddenly, in 15 or 20 minutes, it clears up and the sun is shining again! It is absolutely refreshing..."
—Magnolia Harris

"...You should see our horses, especially the stallion—he is fine! I would never have been able to own a horse, but now I do..."
—Ronnie James

"...Maybe you've heard of the Ice Cream Tree—well, we really have it! It's called a sour-sop tree and it produces a fruit which weighs up to 4 kilograms. It is green outside with soft spines and a slightly fibrous green pulp inside. When ripe—split open and eat it with a spoon. It's like eating sherbet ice cream!"
—Mike Rozynko

"...There is a beautiful little waterfall located 1½ miles south of Jonestown past some of our crops. It is a breathtaking hike down a jungle path, and when you get there it is a long, smooth, sloping series of rocks and two pools of water (after a rain you can swim) and even a vine to swing over the water (or in if you fall). A large felled tree lays over the water so you can sit on it in the comfortable shade. It is one of my favorite places here..."
—Barbara Walker

"...It is a beautiful tropical night. There is a cool breeze blowing. I can look out the window at the full moon, hearing people laughing, and I can see Jonestown lit up in the moonlight. All else is quiet—it is just a perfect experience."
—Laura Johnston

16

113

" ...a feeling of freedom... "

—a collection of photographs & comments about the community of Jonestown by residents and visitors at the Peoples Temple Agricultural/Medical Project in Guyana, South America.

"...Jonestown grows dearer to me each day. There is so much beauty, so much joy in the faces of our children and seniors..."
—Mary Lou Clancey

PEOPLES TEMPLE
AGRICULTURAL PROJECT
Progress Report - Summer 1977

Introduction

The Peoples Temple Agricultural Project was initiated by Rev. Jim Jones in December of 1973. He conceived of the project in order to assist the Guyanese Government in a small measure, to feed, clothe, and house its people, and at the same time to further the human service goals that have characterized Peoples Temple for many years. The government allotted 3,824 acres in the North West District near Port Kaituma to the project. In October of 1974 the first ground was cleared — a 30 acre plot that fell by hand and by machine, near the spot where 11 were housed in a bark cottage.

Hundreds of acres are now cleared and under cultivation, and housing for nearly a thousand people has been constructed, the last of the housing being constructed with our own pre-fabricated siding. The sawmill operates 24 hours a day. Other innovations include a cassava processor, a planter, and a hammer-mill temporarily in operation until the government mill in Port Kaituma starts into operation. We've acquired 9 vehicles, including 2 caterpillar tractors, a dump truck, a crane, 3 large farm tractors, a small garden tractor and a pickup truck.

The agricultural experimenters are learning by trial and error how to produce nutritious crops that, in some cases, have never been tried on jungle soil, and the settlers are learning the art of cooperative living in a wholesome, satisfying and challenging environment. Realistically, we can now expect that the farm will become self-sufficient within three to five years. In the meantime, Peoples Temple members in the U. S. A. are contributing to keep the settlement going through these initial years. We are cooperating fully with the government's plan to buy local products, and we have begun manufacturing our own clothing in accordance with this plan.

The agricultural results are especially heartening to those who have put their "labor of love" into the project during these first few years. Other programs now under way are equally exciting. An educational program provides a balanced curriculum for 135 children, ages 3 to 18. Some youngsters who were said to have learning disabilities in their former setting are quick and willing learners in this cooperative environment. Many of the most extensive projects are supervised by young people whose talents never had the the opportunity to develop before. Seniors who were wanting for something to do are now engaged in satisfying programs that enhance their sense of accomplishment in their later years. The cooperative kitchen, which serves three meals a day, produces nutritious and delicious recipes using homegrown foods. It also provides two snacks a day for several hundred people.

Guyana's healthy and pleasant climate (the temperature stays between 65° and 85°F. and the trade winds have a tempering effect), the wholesome atmosphere, and the constructive life style offered by this pioneering project have impressed us deeply with the role Guyana has to play in the future of the Caribbean and the rest of the developing third world. We are deeply pleased to be able to participate. The expectations of Rev. Jones and this government are stimulating our project to be a success of many dimensions.

116

Page 2

Guyana: a brief note

Guyana, formerly the colony of British Guiana, achieved its independence in 1966. Though it is part of the South American mainland, Guyana has Caribbean cultural roots. The English-speaking population of nearly one million is mostly black and East Indian, in addition to native Amerindians, along with Chinese and Portugese inhabitants. Free from an oppressive heritage of slavery and colonialism, Guyana is undertaking to manage, develop, and control its own abundant resources. The nation is especially rich in bauxite. Though the majority of the population lives on the coastal plain, efforts have been underway to develop Guyana's rich interior. Peoples Temple's agricultural mission is part of that effort. It is the goal of the Guyanese government to insure that all of its population is adequately fed, clothed, and housed in the very near future. Though a young and relatively small nation, Guyana has taken a leadership role in the community of non-aligned nations pursuing a socialistic course.

117

Agriculture

MAJOR CROPS

Major crops include the bitter and sweet cassava, sweet potatoes, eddoes, papaya and dasheen. Here are brief descriptions of our experiences with some of these:

Eddoes: This has been one of our major crops from the start. We eat both the tubers and the greens. We had to clear the original planting site, which was thick jungle. The felled trees were left for a burn, and the first eddoes were planted between the burnt logs. We are now planting in well-prepared beds, 900 feet long, 2 feet apart, with good drainage ditches. Shells, TSP, and potash are applied for fertilizer. We are weeding frequently, and expect a very good crop this season.

Sweet potatoes: Sweet potatoes, planted last May, are currently under cultivation. Based on our previous experience, we are planting in beds, using drainage ditches, and fertilizing with TSP, potash, and urea. We are dipping the slips in aldrin before planting for worm control. Our last yield was 2 tons per acre, and we're hoping to top that with the current planting. Our second planting, in 1975, produced potatoes weighing 11 and 12 pounds. Since our crop of "better potatoes" was very fibrous, we are growing only sweet potatoes and yams at this time.

Bell yams: The first and second yam crops did not do very well. The third planting was therefore done in very rich soil, built up, and the current vines look very healthy.

Cassava processing: We are temporarily milling cassava in a mill designed by our workers, using materials we had around the project site. Once it is set up we will take our cassava to the government mill at Port Kaituma. We can grate 100 pounds of cassava in about three minutes using this homemade mill.

We collect bitter cassava from the field in open, 50 gallon drums, and wash them in the trailer wagon through the jostling action on the way to the mill. The grater is a heavy table, 3' x 8½', with a hole 12" x 14" in the middle. Two iron pulleys welded together work the grater. The grater blade is made with a small three-cornered file, sharpened to make a small hole at half-inch intervals, with each row off-set to the last. We use a 5hp electric motor to turn the grater. One person puts the cassava in the grater, and another uses a cassava root to push the cassava against the grater.

Grated cassava comes through the bottom of the mill into a tub lined with a plastic feed bag. This is then lifted to the press, which consists of two heavy truck wheel rims, 21" in diameter, with a solid bottom, except for a 2″ hole for the juice to escape. Cassava is pressed against the sides of a cylinder which has slits cut about 4″ apart and 6″ in length. In the bottom is a set of 5 ribs, made of crab wood, 2″ square with spacing to match. On these ribs is placed a lead cylinder to give better pressing effect.

The pressing plate is applied using a 10-ton hydraulic jack. It is set against a press frame made of wood timber. The cassava water drains into buckets and sits for about 30 minutes to let the starch settle to the bottom. The water is poured off into cooking vats and then boiled slowly for a few hours. It is strained through cheesecloth, then slowly boiled again until cooked down to a heavy syrup called *cassareep*. This is used in cooking as flavoring. The starch is also used in cooking, and to starch clothes.

The pressed cassava is put back through the grater and ground again, then dried on the floor. It is now about 40% of its original weight, and is mixed into pig feed. About 1,000 pounds of cassava produces 170oz. of cassareep; 100 pounds of cassava will make 50 cassava breads, 18″ in diameter.

We have grated and pressed sweet potatoes by the same process as the cassava, producing a substance slightly sweeter than cassareep. We dried the processed potato. Some of the Guyanese have used it for porridge, which they said was very good. We have also produced a sweet potato flour which, mixed with eggs and fried in small cakes, has a meat-like flavor. It could easily be used as a meat stretcher. It can also be stored for periods of time in this flour state.

GARDEN CROPS

In addition to the major crops, we grow all the vegetables we need for the settlers, including cucumbers, bora beans, cabbage, lettuce, and others. They are all doing well.

FRUIT ORCHARD

We are developing a fruit orchard including many fruit trees native to Guyana. The trees are healthy and bearing well, though the fruits are still small because the trees are young. Our citrus orchard includes about 3,500 to 4,000 trees. We are also growing extremely healthy, fast-growing cashew trees.

Pineapples: Pineapples are thriving alongside the road leading into Jonestown. Because suckers were not available at the time of our first planting, we planted tops which we collected wherever we could find them. From our first crop we planted 600 suckers. Being large in size, these suckers quickly produced, but the fruit was small. We are now planting only small suckers or tops, which will delay the fruit for a year or two, but should produce larger sized pineapples. A third crop of 1,000 suckers was planted, and another crop of 1,000 is ready. We expect to produce beyond our own need in the near future.

Bananas: We are harvesting an average of 2,000 pounds of bananas each month. We first planted approximately 3,500 banana suckers in a mile stretch alongside the road into Jonestown. We discovered that plantings done in the rainy season did not come up, and only those planted in windrows would last. We have not used an insecticide to date, relying instead on ash from the burning and rotting wood to reduce the incidence of insects. This combination has also served to fertilize, so we have added fertilizer only once in nearly three years. Three delicious varieties of banana are bearing: apple, cayanne, and fig, plus plantain. A propagation field has been developed for rapid growth of suckers. We have started a few dwarf cayanne trees and five black banana suckers.

EXPERIMENTING

Experiments with garden crops are conducted to test non-commercial fertilizers, utilizing ingredients "produced" at the project site. Onions, and some legumes such as mung beans, are examples of crops under experimental cultivation. We are also growing coffee. Sea shell, manure, and compost are distributed on one acre plots in 2 ton, 4 ton, and 6 ton quantities. Results show how much fertilizer is needed for best growing conditions. Long garden rows are measured for best proportion to the acre.

Generally, experience has shown that cultivars are acclimating, growing stronger with each crop. For example, the star-leaf sweet potato took seven months to harvest the first time it was planted. The last crop was ready for harvest in only 3–4 months, and some, the size of medium-sized grapefruit, were ready in 2 months.

Cutlass beans: In the face of warnings from some local people that the cutlass bean would make people sick, we have successfully cultivated it and turned it into delicious foodstuffs. The government analysis station in Georgetown reported it was a good source of protein. We also use it for stock and animal feed and green manure. If we have enough seeds, we roast them for excellent snacks. The vine, which is also high in protein, is used for animals only at this time, but we expect to develop recipes using it for the settlers as well. Its excellent qualities were discovered when someone "took a chance" and ate it. It is a particularly valuable crop because it will grow anywhere, any time, and in any weather, requiring only one weeding and little fertilizer.

A HOME MADE PLANTER

Using odds and ends from around the project site, like bicycle sprockets and chain, we created a mechanical planter that enabled us to plant 5 acres in an 8-hour day. We have since then converted our spring-tooth cultivator into a planter that covered the 5 acres in $3\frac{1}{2}$ hours, using one driver and four other people. This job previously took 20–60 workers 3 to 5 days to complete.

Here's how we did it: We reset the cultivator tines to match the furrows made by the wheel. Then we made a seat of boards that sits on top of the cultivator, large enough to hold four people at one time. Three-foot hoses are connected to the tines at one end, and to funnels made with cut-off plastic bleach bottles at the other end. The seeds are dropped through the funnels and the hoses to a pan set on the tines, from which they are dropped to the furrows. Another tine then follows to cover the furrows. The planter addition can be removed in one piece when the cultivator is needed for its usual purpose.

We similarly fashioned a homemade corn shaker, using wooden frames with mesh screens to shake the corn so we can clean out broken pieces of cob.

Experiments in Planting

<u>BUSH TEA</u>

We have been introduced to many bush teas by the Amerindians. The list consists of Sarsaparilla, Cupa, Locust Bark, Rose of the Mountain Bark, and Copadula. We started out making it as time permitted. Now, we substitute it for regular iced tea at supper. We add sugar and mint to taste, and we've found that it is good for the back and also as a diuretic.

<u>WINDROW PLANTING</u>

We have found that many things grow well in windrows. The only drawback is the control of weeds. As suggested by Guyanese, we grow watermelons, tomatoes, squash, hot peppers, cucumbers and papayas. All do well when properly weeded.

Papaya planting: To date, we have had the best results with papayas when they are planted in windrows. We will continue to plant in the windrows, but we are presently experimenting by interplanting with the eddoes. (These are eddoes without germination.) We will try orchard planting soon. We have found that manure helps to bring more and bigger fruit.

Asparagus: Our asparagus has been growing here for over two years. We got one seed to grow from a package and then the roots multiplied up to 36. We finally got some of our own seeds to grow and we now have 140 new plants started. The adult asparagus is growing the size of an ordinary man's middle finger.

Celery: We have been getting some medium-sized stalks so far. We are now preparing a seven-row flat area, with heavy organic matter. We will flood this area with water most of the time. This should give us normal-sized stalks.

Egg-plants, or Boulangers: Boulangers have been a good supply of food. The plant has to be fertilized every two weeks with potash and urea. We are also trying to breed our own type of boulanger because we have a more difficult time getting seed to reproduce in kind. We prefer the local variety.

Experiments with beans: We have a bean program aimed at finding out which kinds grow well here, and which type grow well in wet or dry seasons. Bora beans do very well in either wet or dry seasons. The exception is the hard bora bean, which still grows well in wet or dry seasons, but doesn't produce during the wet season.

We have found a black bean which is both a snap bean and a dry bean, which grows very well during the rainy season. We are now experimenting with the Winged bean. The Pinto bean grows well here, in the normal growing seasons. It is a very good eating bean. The Blackeye and Kidney beans are handled by the main farm crew. We are developing the Soybean seed from a type that has been growing for six generations.

Tomatoes: Although we have grown some in the windrows, we have had a raised earth section supported by aluminum roofing and a plastic canopy. This cover has been effective in keeping out the rain. The tomatoes grown here have been very high quality.

Carrots: These have also been grown in with the tomatoes, with varied success.

Cucumbers: These grow well with plenty of water, but they have to be planted before the rainy season starts for them to grow. They require plenty of potash and urea.

Onions and Shallots: The only way that we have had success in growing onions is to plant the adult onion, and have it multiply just like a shallot. Shallots grow well here with adequate fertilization. We add TSP after 21 days.

<u>SEEDLINGS</u>

We have used both seed boxes and seed beds to start seedlings. Both have worked well. The drawback is that, in the rainy season, there is too much damping off. The lack of sun is the worst problem. We intend to build a hot house in order to grow seedlings during the rainy season.

Soil Preparation

We have started a long range program to improve the soil. We are digging a pit the length of a row four feet wide and three feet deep. In this way, we bury off the fall from the food processing pavillion. This improves the soil at a deeper level than is possible with other methods.

FERTILIZATION

Soil testing in corroboration with the government's soil survey has shown the need for shell, manure, and TSP as the most effective combination for planting most crops here at Jonestown.

Shell as fertilizer: Dr. Teijens, who has done a large amount of work with various state agricultural experiment stations all over the U. S., has prescribed the use of unburnt limestone at the rate of 4 tons to the acre as a minimum for clay loams. The many benefits include ion-exchange which makes use of the clay, and the humus, to hold back minerals which were being dissolved and washed away with the heavy rains. Shell dissolves slowly and has the additional quality of soil conditioning by helping to form small granules of earth for good tilth.

COMPOST

We used a fast method for making compost, which was devised by Dr. Clarence G. Golueke, in his graduate studies at the University of California. There is a paperback booklet which has been our reference. Our procedure has been as follows:

1. Materials
   a) carbonaceous; fallen dead leaves from the jungle.
   b) nitrogenous wastes; banana stalks chopped fine with a cutlass.
2. Material proportion in pile
   a) two parts carbonaceous waste — 8" layer.
   b) one part nitrogenous wastes — 4" layer.
3. Moisture content
   a) the ideal moisture content of the compost pile is to range from 70° to 80° when leaves are used as the absorbent.
4. Preparing the compost (the pile should be at least 5" high to begin to heat up.)
   a) We used a combination of three bins, each adjacent to the others. On the first day, we loaded the first bin. We turned this bin into the second bin 48 hours later, and started the first bin. From this point on, we turned the bins each 48 hours, four turns for each pile. Then we let them sit for 14 days.
   b) If all the conditions are right, the temperature reaches 120°F in two or three days and 150°F in five or six days.
   c) At the end of 14 days, the temperature drops to 100°.
   d) A drop in the ph (acidity) takes place at the start, and the pile soon becomes alkaline; a ph of 7 (neutral) is desirable. Lime should not be used as it promotes the loss of nitrogen to the air.
   e) We covered the bins with a roof at least 6' beyond the bins to control the moisture content and the temperature of the pile.
   f) The compost is now ready to be put into the ground.

122

Nursery

The nursery was started by gathering all the seeds, seedlings, small trees and plants that we could obtain in the North West region. Some of the seeds for fruits were started from purchased fruits. At our first opportunity, in Georgetown, we collected many more varieties, both small trees and cuttings. We have gradually added new types of fruit trees to the list. We built a nursery building to cut down on the amount of sun on young trees. We built waist-high tables to keep the young trees in an organized manner.

POTTING SOIL PREPARATION

We used pen manure mixed with shell and the rotted wood. We also added any other organic matter we could find, plus a little TSP plus some topsoil. This was the mix we used for the pots. Just before the trees became rootbound, we planted them out in the ground. (We had cleared the land previously, in preparation for the young plantings.) The area around the nursery which has been used for an orchard, was planted in five different sections as clearing proceeded and as plants came of age for transplanting. We still use sections of the nursery to propagate sugar cane, bananas, and citrus fruits, as well as pineapples.

The total area covers five acres, and many of the trees are now bearing fruit. Here are the trees and flowers now growing in our nursery:

sugar cane	¼ acre	almond	19
grenadilla — vines all over the area		guava	10
breadfruit	47	pineapple	45
calabash	12	coconut	7
sugar apple	37	mango	17
soursop	28	pomegranate	22
five fingers	17	rose plum	4
souree	10	mammee apple	14
gooseberry	19	Bouganvilla — all colors	
French cashew	20	avocado	32
cashew nut	14	flamboyant — all over Jonestown	
jamoon	5	red leaf bush	10
Barbados Cherry	42	bamboo — many starters	
annattoo	2	tamarind	5

There are other fruit trees of lesser value. Aside from these plants, there is a large section for citrus only, and there are more trees in the citrus variety, including Shaddock, which is a large grapefruit with red flesh.

Livestock

CHICKEN PROJECT

Two years ago we attempted to raise chickens in the tropics. We were unsuccessful due to our lack of experience, and incorrect housing construction. Over these last few years, we have gathered information on on the raising of poultry, and we received important information from local veterinarians and the local Agricultural officers.

With the information at hand on building the homes, we chose land that was on a slope, with well drained ground, about 1½ miles from the main house.

For buildings, we have built eight gable-type chicken houses, 24′ x 18′. These are constructed out of raw material from the bush. They are round pole construction, with gutters along the roof to provide water, with drains which flow to tanks of from 50 gal. to 20 gal. The 20 gal. tank has a loose connection construction. Each building has a front door made from aluminum and wood framing, with hasping padlocks set up on the doors. The floors are clay, and are packed with a home made tamper, which is made of wood 14″ square, with a handle.

We have installed electricity, which is supplied by a generator. It provides lights and plugs for electrical appliances.

For litter, we use wood chips that are produced from our own planer, as well as the chips from the Government wood shops in Matthews Ridge, which are donated to us as no cost. The composted litter is used in the garden as fertilizer.

Each building has eight "tube-type" feeders. Four houses have roost-type perches, with drop tables 4′ off the ground.

All our chicks are purchased in Georgetown, from poultry hatcheries at $.65 per broiler. Their eggs are flown in from Florida, by Guyana Airways. The feed is purchased in Georgetown. We rent a truck to transport the feed from the store to the dock, where it is unloaded by us.

The feed for the broiler varies according to the age of the chicks. The first week, the feed averages 100 lbs. for 1000 broilers. We used 150 lbs. of feed the first week, 500 lbs. the second week, 800 lbs. the third week, 1250 lbs. the fourth week, 1400 lbs. the fifth week, and 1950 lbs. the sixth week. Chick starter is used for layers, and is given to them for seven weeks. They are gradually switched to growing rations, and then to egg rations at about 22 weeks.

PIGGERY

We received our first pigs in August, 1975, from the Ministry of Agriculture. They were: 1 Duroc boar, 12 weeks old; and 5 small pigs, 14 weeks. The pig family has grown to 130 pigs of all ages, and we can now raise our own breeding stock. We have, on our own, manufactured various feed mixtures using, in different combinations, cassava, coconut, rice, sweet potatoes, corn and cutlass beans, along with the hay of sweet potatoes. Equal parts of cutlass bean and bitter cassava have been selected as the primary feed, supplemented with bitter cassava tops and urea for additional protein. Putting the pigs to pasture on cleared land has helped their growth.

Our farrowing house, 100' x 25', is pole-constructed, with aluminum roofing. We are putting in crabwood floors which allow for adequate disinfecting for virus control. The feed building is 60' x 120', also pole-constructed, with a 20' drive-through so the dump truck can unload the feed.

Sawmill

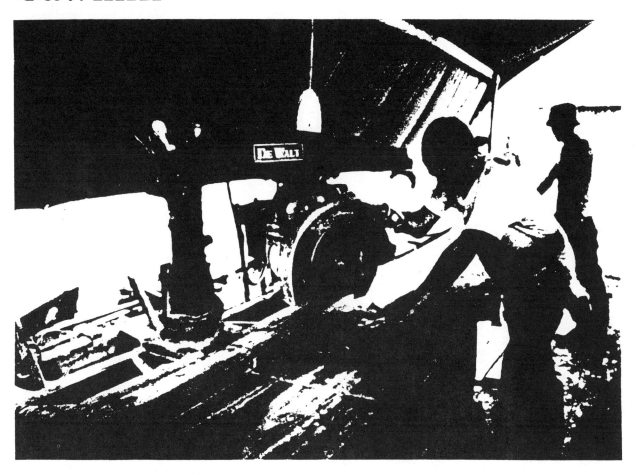

The sawmill, in general, first codes what materials are needed from the construction sites and the pre-fab house and construction crews. From the picking up and unloading of the wood for our sawmill until the finished product is delivered to the construction or prefab house site, each piece must go through the process of the chain saw, the edger, the planer, and the radial arm saw.

One of our sources of wood is the Wiani saw mill. We also obtain wood from various pitsawyers who saw the trees into 2" and 3" thicknesses. We get crabwood, an open-grain hardwood (also called South American mahogany) and use it for furniture and building. Our choice in utilizing wood over the native *troulie* is based on cost. Troulie (palm thatching) is becoming hard to find without going deep into the bush and for the same cost wood can be used, wood being preferable in that it endures longer than the troulie, and is more bug-resistant. We do have several of the troulies built in the local style which are very attractive, but we are not using it much currently.

Our fishing trawler often picks up 15,000 board feet of wood from the Wiani and then the tractors and dumptrucks unload these boats. All this wood is collected and brought back to our sawmill.

At the sawmill, wood is cut into boards, and some is fashioned into trim—frames, shutters, etc. All finished materials are delivered to the construction site. Also between all this the sawmill does finish work using silver bally and cedar, and keeps all construction sites supplied with appropriate materials (trim, siding, framing) at all times.

All cabinets are made and designed in our cabinet and furniture department. There is no end to what teamwork has produced in their department—fabulous furniture, doors, stools, shelves, cabinets, baby cribs, benches, rebuilt and modernized kitchen cupboards, etc.

Our competent machinist keeps up the edger and planer, radial arm saw and numerous power tools. All this is carefully gone over by the coordinating supervisors of the sawmill who also collect the designs, drafts, plans and material orders to prepare the sawmill's schedule for the next day's or week's work. All scraps are burned for cooking purposes and the charcoal is used for fertilizer. The wood chips and sawdust are used as mulch on the farm.

PREFAB CONSTRUCTION DEPARTMENT

The lumber is edged, sorted, planed and cut to correct length and angle before it is carried to the prefab building site. Here it is stacked on the appropriate pallet, which specifies its dimensions and purpose.

The prefab center is ingenious. In the 13' x 22' building is a platform 10' x 20' raised 3' above the ground level, to avoid stooping to work. This platform at first glance appears to be a bewildering maze of differently colored blocks. Each block is secured to the platform by screws and each is precisely placed. The colored blocks are color-coded channels in which the studs, plates, and rafters can be put into exact position to be secured to the adjacent parts.

This system is so efficient that a 8' x 20' wall frame complete with windows and door can be completed in 15 minutes; A 12' x 8" wall frame complete with windows and door can be completed in 10 minutes, rafters can be completed in 5 minutes. An entire 12' x 20' house, rafters included, can be framed in 12 hours by a crew of 3!

Jonestown School

In Jonestown education is a way of life which affects all aspects of life. It is our intent to make education relevant to the growth and maturity of the child physically, morally, socially, intellectually, artistically, and finally with the goal of guiding the child in the acquisition of habits, attitudes and skills such as will enable the child to participate in collective thought, values and activities.

PRE-SCHOOL

Nursery school children receive guidance, supervision of activities, and instruction. Most activities are group activities. Children are encouraged to participate. Curriculum includes learning the use of table utensils, cleanliness and health habits, number concepts, naming quantities, alphabet recognition, and dance routines with educational themes. Learning tools include manipulative toys, puzzles, individual chalkboards, and motor and perceptual motor facilities in the play yard to be described later.

ELEMENTARY EDUCATION

At present the Jonestown School includes grades 1 through 7. Classes are not organized by grade or age, but rather by ability. The child can progress as rapidly as he/she desires and is advanced to a higher ability grouping when the teacher determines that the child is able to perform with the next ability grouping. For example, we now have an eight-year-old child working on a level equivalent to that of two thirteen-year-old students.

The groupings currently in use are: pre-reading, elementary reading skills and moderate competency, and those with moderate to well-developed reading skills. However, reading skills are not exclusive. A basic phonetic approach is started, accompanied by auditory training. The goal initially is to shift emphasis from phonetic analysis to sight reading as soon as phonetic analysis competency is achieved. Also, structural analysis, configuration and content skills are taught. At less advanced levels perceptual skills are stressed: visual, audio, tactile, motor and perceptual-motor skills which are fundamental to academic skills.

The school curriculum presently includes: language arts, receptive and expressive language which includes reading, writing, spelling and composition skills, mathematics, physical and earth science, social science (with emphasis on Guyanese history and culture), political science, and arts, crafts and music.

An emphasis is placed on development of educational games, activities, and materials utilizing materials indigenous to this area and parts of discarded objects. For example, many games, puzzles, and activities have been developed using local woods. Many individual chalkboards are used in place of paper and pencils.

Chalkboards are usually made from steel plate with chalkboard paint covering. They are handy because pre-developed lessons can be secured to the chalkboard with the use of small magnets. Miniature chalkboards are also used for structural analysis, syllabication, prefix, root and suffix study and math fact drill cards, as everything can be wiped off and the boards re-used. Workbooks and paper lessons are done with the use of a plastic sheet cover and a wax lead marker. In this way the paper supplies and lessons can be re-used many times.

THE PLAY AREA

The children's playground at Jonestown is considered a vital educational tool as well as serving its traditional role as recreation. The playground includes many facilities designed to enhance basic body movement and balance skills as well as strength. The play items (which incidentally were designed by the Jonestown teacher and built by the children) include: a rolling barrel with an axle on pillow blocks, a great balance-developing device which rolls as the child "walks it"; a twenty foot stationary balance beam; a fifteen foot swinging balance beam; a bucking barrel designed to buck like a horse when the attached ropes are pulled from the sides; a twenty foot overhead ladder; double rings and trapeze bar; an acrobat bar (chinning bar) and two tether ball set-ups. Supplies also include basketballs, volleyballs, and nets, kickballs, soccer balls, baseball bats and accessories, badminton, and football. Central to the use of all equipment is the emphasis on cooperation rather than competitive values on the playground. Children are encouraged to help each other in performing various tasks on the playground.

THE WORK–STUDY CONCEPT

Students are involved in more than just "school" work in Jonestown. They are actively involved in the development and maintenance of Jonestown. Each child is required with help to care for his/her clothing, bedding, and living space and to participate in cleaning activities including domestic and yard and grounds care. Children even take some responsibility for maintenance of flower and plant beds and lawn care.

Also, on a merit basis, good workers are allowed to participate in the numerous work projects underway. Those who become conscientious, productive workers are frequently given the privilege of assisting with special projects. Indeed, the playground was one such project. Students helped collect, carry, debark the logs and poles and assisted with the construction.

(Note: This synopsis of the Jonestown School does not include a description of the vocational and technical training provided for young men and women beyond the seventh grade. In the fall, other academic training for older youth will begin.)

128

Medical Facility

In Jonestown we are in the process of developing an efficient medical clinic. We presently have a doctor and two licensed medical practitioners, one in neuro-surgical specialty and the other in pediatrics. We also have six registered nurses and a doctor of pharmacology with experience in teaching.

Preventive medical care is emphasized. Physical examinations are given each 6 months to everyone in Jonestown with special attention to bimonthly well-baby checkups, pre-natal care and follow-up for those with chronic diseases such as diabetes mellitus and epilepsy. A dietician supervises the kitchen aided by one of the registered nurses who prepares therapeutic diets and maintains a high nutritional standard in the meals served.

Therapeutic vitamins are provided for all of the local children who were malnourished before coming to Jonestown. Those with anemic disorders have been treated with supplemental iron preparation. Such treatment has been effective in treating many of the children of this area.

Our clinic is becoming well-stocked and we are prepared at all times to give first aid.

Communal Kitchen

One of the first buildings one sees when traveling up the road to Jonestown is the all-purpose kitchen where meals and treats are provided to workers and residents there.

THE KITCHEN

Three complete wood-paneled walls are designed to make the best use of space, working materials and comfort, including large shelved and divided cabinets and drawers above and below the glassy-varnished spacious counters. Commercial refrigeration and freezer units are used to store perishable items (when other means of feed preservation cannot be used). Food is stocked to the maximum with edibles from all the basic food groups including meats and proteins, starches and all varieties of succulent fruits and vegetables. Our kitchen has an ice-making unit, two cooking stoves (gas and kerosene) and a large, triple sectioned sink. Water comes from a hand-dug well that never runs dry all year long. It provides water for cooking, drinking, cleaning, laundry, and bathing for all Jonestown facilities.

The front wall of the kitchen is a full length serving counter having large removable partitions which can be raised or lowered at the servers' convenience to allow food to be served while reducing the entrance of insects to the kitchen itself. Such screening allows for the entrance of bright and healthy sunlight, while maintaining sanitation standards.

A large work table is secured in the middle of the floor under which airtight, water-resistant drums contain sugar, oil, various grains, and flour. Heavy duty pots of all sizes hang from the center ceiling. A large variety of kitchen utensils are stocked in the kitchen (including knives made in our metal workshop, providing all types of useful cutting edges).

A large, Guyanese-style wood oven is used for our massive bread-baking during the drier season. Cassava flour is one of the basic ingredients used in our bread.

Menus: Menus are planned in advance to allow for food supplying areas to be filled and for the medical staff to check for maximum nutritional health and vitamin standards to be maintained. Almost all foods are home-grown and home-prepared. The kitchen is an organized center of activity almost 24 hours a day as work teams prepare for the next day's meals, or bag lunches for workers further removed from the central dining area in their day's work. Working in shifts on a team basis has been found to be the most efficient method and also allows for ample rest for all participants and maximum use of all materials.

Meals: Meals are always promptly served. Breakfast is served in three shifts. First, the outdoor workers eat from 5:40 to 6:30 am, then the senior citizens eat from 7:00 to 7:30 and finally the children eat from 7:30 to 8:00 am. Naturally allowances are made for seniors or for any ill persons to have their meals served to them in their residences. Breakfast menus include such foods as eggs from Jonestown chickens, cooked cereals, pancakes and homemade syrup and verying fruits seasonally available.   Biscuits, rolls, and breads are baked daily by the cooking staff.

Many lunches are pre-made for workers and are distributed at breakfast time. The bulk of lunches utilize sandwiches made of cutlass bean patty, fish patty, peanut butter, egg salad, fried egg, eggplant, or pork meat products. Nuts, fruits, pastries or cookies are added as desserts. These are eaten at sheltered spots right on the work site. Seniors and children are served a hot meal in the communal dining room.

The kitchen also works closely with the nursing department to prepare calorie-rich, nourishing snacks and drinks in the mid-morning and mid-afternoon for children and underweight individuals. Those who are overweight are encouraged to take advantage of low-calorie meals, especially dished up by our medical staff.

Our cooking staff is comprised of an RN (who once managed an Italian restaurant), and a number of experienced individuals of all ages and the menu planning reflects their various cultural and ethnic backgrounds, as well as incorporating all local foods and products they have absorbed from the Amerindian adaptation of local products.

Kitchen cleanup crews work on a rotating schedule. Each person carries out his/her specific duties in a quiet, efficient manner. The dishes are cold-water rinsed, washed and stacked, then washed in a soapy detergent with bleach and boiling water, and put away. The cleaning process is carried on during and after kitchen activities. All surfaces are continually scrubbed and sanitized from ceiling to floor to provide the most healthful environment.

Afterword

The agricultural project has been financed entirely by members of Peoples Temple. Valuable in-kind services have been provided by the Guyana government on a number of occasions. We could never have progressed so far so fast were it not for the total cooperation given by the Guyanese at every step of the way.

We look forward to a relationship of friendship and mutual support between our mission settlers and Guyanese from every walk of life. We can only express our appreciation by trying to make our experiences useful for others engaged in similar efforts to expand and improve cultivation and development of the rich interior of Guyana, with the goal of benefiting her people.

Rev. Jim Jones, founder of the Peoples Temple Church and Prime Minister Forbes Burnham of Guyana.

131

You who have given to help the starving are blessed with the Love of Christ — bringing warmth and fulfillment to you during this Christmas Season.

Let this starving Ethiopian mother and her two children remind all that the Christian role is to be our BROTHERS KEEPER.

Display this card and remind others to care . . .
AS YOU DO!

"For I was an hungered
   and ye gave me meat:
   I was thirsty
      and ye gave me drink:
I was a stranger
   and ye took me in:
      Naked, and ye clothed me:
I was sick and ye visited me:
   I was in prison,
      and ye came unto me.

"Then shall the righteous
   Answer him, saying,

When saw we thee an hungered
   And fed thee?
      Or thirsty,
         And gave thee drink?
When saw we thee a stranger
   And took thee in?
      Or naked, and clothed thee?
Or when saw we thee sick
   Or in prison,
      And came unto thee?

"Verily I say unto you,
Inasmuch as ye have done it
   Unto one of the least of these...
      ...Ye have done it unto me."

Matthew 25: 35-40

PEOPLES TEMPLE AGRICULTURAL MISSION
Post Office Box 214, Redwood Valley, Calif. 95470

133

OPERA-TION BREAD BASKET

Peoples Temple is beginning a Mission Program to help provide food in an underdeveloped country. A beautiful potential site has been found across the sea in a jungle where the land is rich and fertile. In times ahead Pastor Jones will be able to help keep people from going hungry.

Pastor Jim Jones personally toured the jungle to find the perfect site for OPERATION BREAD BASKET. He needs your help to make this building and agriculture program a success. He asks that you seriously consider the commission of Jesus in Matthew 25 where He tells us to . . .

"...FEED THE HUNGRY"

If you would like to help support this project send your Love Offering today to help us aquire equipment and land. We will tell you more about this program in the weeks to come. Tell us what YOU want to help provide for this Missionary Endeavor. Your help will be appreciated!

HERE IS WHAT YOUR OFFERING CAN BUY

__	$ 2.00	Drill Bit	__	$ 50.00	Router
__	$ 5.00	Saw Blade	__	$ 75.00	Skil Saw
__	$ 7.00	Shovel	__	$ 100.00	3 Boxes Electric Wire
__	$ 10.00	Machete	__	$ 200.00	1 Acre Jungle Land
__	$ 15.00	Carbite Blade	__	$ 500.00	Table Saw
__	$ 20.00	5 Rakes	__	$1000.00	Garden Tractor
__	$ 35.00	Com-Saber Saw	__	$2000.00	Home for 13 People
			__	$5000.00	Used Electric Generator

- -

Pastor Jim, I am interested in helping the hungry people of the world. Here is my OFFERING OF LOVE to use in this Mission Work.

I enclose my offering in the amount of $ _____

Name _____ Address _____

City _____ State _____ Zip _____

_____ Please add my name to your LIST OF PEOPLE INTERESTED IN THIS MISSION FIELD. I know Pastor Jim will meditate on my name as it is added to the blessed list.

Return this card to: **OPERATION BREAD BASKET**
Peoples Temple Christian Church
P.O. Box 214
Redwood Valley, Calif.   95470

TIMOTHY OLIVER STOEN
Attorney at Law
POST OFFICE BOX 126
UKIAH, CALIFORNIA 95482
October 24, 1971

Letters-to-the-Editor Section
The Indianapolis Star
307 North Pennsylvania Avenue
Indianapolis, Indiana

Re: Pastor James W. Jones

Dear Editor:

Silence when truth is called for is hypocrisy, and therefore I
must speak out in protest against the distortions in your October
14th "news" article on Pastor James Jones. Furthermore, I request
that you forthwith publish a retraction attesting to the facts
which upon fair investigation will show beyond all doubt the gran-
ite-like integrity and honesty which characterize Pastor James
Jones in his total Christ-centered ministry to mankind. Jim Jones,
as he prefers to be called, does not need or expect accolades or
other praise. He and all other Americans, however, expect fair-
ness from the press. So does the First Amendment and a civilized
sense of decency. I know you, too, will have the grace to acknowledge this.

Your reporter was like the blind man who felt only the elephant's
tail and then argued to everyone that an elephant is a piece of
rope. He went to two meetings conducted by Jim Jones as part of
this Christ-centered ministry of sane spiritual healing. He then
felt himself qualified to make the following silly remark: "The
people who were called upon in the evening had a striking resemblance to some who were called upon earlier in the day." Striking
resemblance! Maybe all people look the same to him. At any rate,
my wife happened to have interviewed the people called out that
same day. No two persons were the same, and each one attested to
having been healed exactly as Pastor Jones had said had happened
as the result of Christ working through him. Exactly.

The strange thing, really, is this: Why did your reporter refuse
to ask the persons called out any questions? Was this slight
breach of professional competence due to his being afraid that
the truth might discredit his narrow-minded preconceptions? He
was the first reporter of the many who have covered such meetings
of Jim Jones through these many years who did not write fairly
and positively. Jim Jones does not, of course, expect everyone
who comes to his meetings to automatically believe in the para-
psychological. But the other reporters have shown themselves able
to recognize joy when it touches the lives and faces of people.
Even when they did not understand what the Bible says about the

gift of spiritual healing, they had the unpretentious ability to understand what Shakespeare meant when Hamlet said:
"There are more things in heaven and earth, Horatio,
Than are dreamt of in your philosophy."

Besides failing to ask any questions, your reporter twisted his perceptions in significant ways. He correctly states attendance was "standing room only" and erroneously concludes this to be "about 500" when it was probably 3 times that number. He conveniently neglects to mention that Jim Jones was spending his nights in a sleeping bag on the floor of the church with "the people", not aloof in some posh hotel. He conveniently neglects to mention the offer by Pastor Jones to take back with him to California the 15 drug users for rehabilitation free of charge. If your reporter were truly interested in whether Jim Jones is authentic, he could have asked burly Christopher Lewis how he kicked his $200 a day heroin addiction without any pain of withdrawal simply upon a word from Pastor Jim Jones. Why did he not ask professional social worker Linda Amos why she no longer has cancer after a word from Pastor Jim Jones?

I recognize that the editors of a metropolitan newspaper meeting deadlines in a crisis-charged world cannot be held accountable, at least directly, for the bias or distortions of a reporter. I am sure that Jim Jones gives you the benefit of the doubt as to your motivation. Since there are people by the hundreds in Indianapolis who have asked him to return, and since Pastor Jones goes where he is wanted and needed (notwithstanding the arderous responsibilities of ministering to his own church, People's Temple Christian Church, which has well over 4,000 participating members), he will continue to purchase advertising space from you. You would, to my mind, however, do well to discover the incredible quality of this Christ-centered minister when he comes back.

In addition to the praise bestowed on the healing ministry of Jim Jones by the press heretofore, there is the high esteem in which he is held by sensitive and kindly souls throughout the ecclesiastical community. For example, as I write I have before me a letter addressed to Jim Jones and just received from a professor at a leading theological seminary in Indianapolis who attended the same series of meetings as did your "reporter". The professor states: "I attended several of your recent meetings in Indianapolis and was very much impressed with your splendid ministry. God bless you (Although it seems perfectly evident that you are blessed by God)." I am a member of the Board of Directors of the Christian Church of the Disciples of Christ for Northern California and can bear witness to the extraordinary regard accorded Jim Jones by many other ministers, even those who do not claim an understanding of the gift of spiritual healing.

The crucial point here is the integrity of Pastor Jim Jones. Therefore a personal word from me is in order, for I am in a far better position than was your reporter to evaluate the invincible Christian character and integrity of Jim Jones. I am an attorney and a former skeptic. I first met Jim Jones four years ago when I was a prosecuting attorney and he was Foreman of the Grand Jury. For three years I scrutinized his life from outside of his church, gradually coming to the astounding conclusion that Jim Jones is the first person I had ever met (including at Wheaton College and Stanford University) who actually lives by the hard words of Jesus in Matthew 25 and the spirit of the Sermon on the Mount. I came also to another astounding conclusion: the power that works through Pastor Jim Jones to heal people in the name of Christ is real, authentic, efficacious, witnessed by me first hand in hundreds of instances, attested to by the persons healed for years thereafter, and documented as to completeness of healing by many first-rate physicians. To whom truth is given, action is required. My action consisted of giving up political ambitions to join People's Temple and assist Jim Jones serve Jesus Christ by significantly helping to bring about God's kingdom right here "on earth".

Now, I think there is an even more compelling reason to conclude Jim Jones is a man of utter integrity who does what he says he does. In court one finds this to be a realistic principle: If a person is honest in small matters he is honest in large matters; if dishonest in small, dishonest in large. I would like our truth-seeking reporter to consider the following empirically-verifiable facts about this fantastically dedicated man by the humble name "Jim Jones", and then apply the aforesaid principle:

Fact One: He wears only used clothes (the shoes he wore in Indianapolis were left by a man now dead) for the stated reason of saving money to help the poor and the oppressed.

Fact Two: He refuses to permit any new furniture at all in his house, his stated reason being this position is for him morally necessary while two-thirds of the world's children are so poor they go to bed hungry each night.

Fact Three: He takes in abandoned animals, and has established an animal shelter to take care of them.

Fact Four: He fearlessly preaches unpopular truths about war and social injustice, and he simply never flinches notwithstanding periodic attempts having been made on his life (one which I witnessed personally).

Fact Five: He loves children to such an extent that he literally has adopted seven (7) of all major races. He also has taken under his roof for extended periods of time many more.

Fact Six: He cares for, and takes time to listen to, the aged and the old. He has established a senior citizens center for them. (He has been praised by leading "conservatives" in the community for helping take the load off welfare services.)

Fact Seven: Although he has an I.Q. generally classified
as that of a genius, he does not hobnob with the rich nor seek
wealth or power for himself, but rather spends his time helping
human beings in need.

Fact Eight: He accepts the "misfits" of society, including
drug addicts and parolees, patiently counsels with them, stands
behind them, and is not afraid to accept them into his church and
to risk being "embarrassed" by them.

Fact Nine: By voluntary choice he lived for thirteen (13)
years, with his family, in an urban ghetto.

Fact Ten: He consistently preaches and practices the highest standards of Christian love and service to his fellow man.
His congregation provides free medical and dental care to poor
people. He constantly strives to meet the needs of people in
distress (for example, providing groceries and housekeeping free
of charge to anyone in the community he learns suffers a tragedy
in the family and needs help). I remember him once paying all
the living expense for a family of five for nine months until
the father found a job--he never asked for a dime of it back.
He preaches that the best way to stop big government is for the
churches to actually practice Christian love and look after the
people, and then government would not have to.

Fact Eleven: He has worked five of the past six years full
time as a public school teacher notwithstanding the well-nigh
crushing burdens of administering and pastoring his church (he
gets less than two hours sleep per night).

Fact Twelve: He has been honored by appointment to positions
of public trust, including Chairman of the Indianapolis Human
Rights Commission and Foreman of the Grand Jury of Mendocino
County, California.

Fact Thirteen: He has rehabilitated in the name of Christ
more than 100 young persons from dependency on drugs, including
some on heroin, and these young people now are active in the
evangelical and social outreach work of People's Temple.

Fact Fourteen: He has established a program which guarantees
a college education for every young person in the church who needs
financial help. People's Temple is helping support approximately
58 college students, most of whom live in church-owned dormitories.
He makes sure every child in the congregation who cannot afford it
get free music lessons.

Fact Fifteen: He constantly attends to people who are sick
and to those in prison. He has established a free poverty law
program which intercedes for persons throughout the United States
who are in legal difficulty but cannot afford a lawyer.

Fact Sixteen: He views his spiritual healing ministry as
complementary to medical science and as strictly subordinate to
his message. He views it mainly as the Divine stamp of approval
upon his message of consecrated Christian Living.

Fact Seventeen: He has been the pastor of his church and kept faith with his congregation not simply for one or two years, but for more than twenty (20) years.

In conclusion, therefore, I would like to thank you for publishing this letter and I would ask each reader who is interested in truth to linger on each of the 17 preceding points, and then to ask himself this question: If Pastor Jim Jones has this kind of integrity and honesty in these matters, would he not have the same kind of integrity and honesty in the matter of healing people through Jesus Christ?

Sincerely,

Timothy O. Stoen
Attorney at Law
400 Oak Park Avenue
Ukiah, California 95482

cc: Dr. Karl Irvin, Jr., President of the Christian Church of
        the Disciples of Christ for Northern California
cc: Honorable Vance Hartke, United States Senator
cc: Honorable Birch Bayh, United States Senator

PEOPLES TEMPLE

OF THE
DISCIPLES OF CHRIST

Jim V. Jones, Pastor

Post Office Box 214
Redwood Valley,
California 95470
Pb. (707) 485-7219

1859 Geary Blvd.
San Francisco, Calif.

1366 So. Alvarado
Los Angeles, Calif.

"For I was an hungered
    and ye gave me meat;
I was thirsty
    and ye gave me drink;

"I was a stranger
    and ye took me in;
Naked,
    and ye clothed me;

"I was sick
    and ye visited me;
I was in prison,
    and ye came unto me.

"Verily I say unto you,
Inasmuch as ye
    have done it
Unto one of the least
    of these . . .
Ye have done it unto me."

Matt. 25:35-40

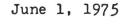

June 1, 1975

Mr. Edward Plowman
CHRISTIANITY TODAY
1014 Washington Bldg.
Washington, D.C. 20005

Dear Mr. Plowman:

Following our long distance phone conversation, I felt I should write to you and clarify a few things that I perhaps did not make clear. It's not that we mind publicity. As I mentioned, we have had a deluge of articles on this ministry-- all very positive-- in recent months, a very few of which I am enclosing. Our purpose, however, is not to gain recognition for the good things we've accomplished for Christ, but to communicate with other churches, of all denominations, who follow the belief that Jesus Christ is Lord and Saviour; that He is the only answer to totalitarianism as manifested in Communism and Fascism, or anarchy and hedonism that also threaten free societies today.

We wish to share with others the type of ministry we carry on, in the hopes that they will respond in like manner, because we want this to be a two-way street. This aim is being achieved more, it seems, through personal letters to various churches, as we are getting a great deal of positive feedback through this means; and it doesn't cause the resentment of our success that the media could create. Our Board of Elders and Deacons discussed this whole issue and it was generally agreed that, unfortunately, there is still too much competition among some churches today, and that our considerable favorable media coverage might be threatening to a number of them. It was felt that publicity extoling our program might cause some churches to rationalize away our practical humanitarian works that help greatly to lift up Christ to a needy world. Hence, came the decision to communicate through letters.

We only accepted good publicity in the first place really to offset the misunderstanding and harassment caused to our people and work by a few but fanatically misguided racial bigots. You see Mr. Plowman, just as your ecumenical magazine, we would like to see all people working together in the unity of the Spirit of Christ, thus we have members of every race and ethnic background. Gerald McHarg, one of the Southern California regional pastors of our own denomination, the Disciples of Christ, said after visiting Peoples Temple, "One gets the impression of being in the midst of the human race at its best; a community of people whose primary concern is to love and to serve." (This was in a written report to the region.) But when it was told by

that former priest in his sensational articles that lied upon us,
that our church is fully integrated, there was a negative reaction
on the part of a small but vociferous racist element. This has
been the root of any opposition we've had, as one of the prominent
ministers of a large church in Ukiah said, who headed the ministerial federation.

So when we heard through several of our many minister friends,
whom I mentioned to you, that this so-called reporter had "bent
your ear" and "got your head on straight about Peoples Temple"
that's when we decided to send you some materials about us and how
we are regarded by others. It is evident that this man has an ax
to grind stemming, no doubt, from being dismissed from his former
newspaper employer. If you will peruse his attacks on Dr. Billy
Graham, Dr. Peale, and the Bay Area's most prominent evangelical
Baptist Church (First Church), just to mention only a few of his
irresponsible and cruel articles, you will clearly see why they
deemed his dismissal necessary. He is opposed to Evangelical
Christianity and makes fun of the great Bible traditions, as his
own newspaper columns clearly show (also see Letter to Ed. enclosed).
He was sharply rebuked in a Presidential Press Conference, according
to the Associated Press, by the President's Press Secretary and the
press corp for his behaviour. (One respected reporter, I believe
with the Washington Post, called him a "braying jackass" publicly.)

In his articles on Peoples Temple, which, incidentally, represent the only negative publicity we've ever gotten, that reporter told
one lie after another. For example, he wrote that a young lady who
died was counseled by one of the Assistant District Attorneys, who is
a faithful member of our church. The truth is that she had never
even met the man and, in fact, was a Baptist who attended Peoples
Temple only a few times, and had never once counselled with our pastor or any representative of our large parish. The Asst. D.A. was
accused of marrying a minor when, in fact, she was 21. The article
stated the Asst. D.A. was not ordained when, in fact, he is fully
ordained with our Disciples of Christ denomination. It reported that
we require that marriage be across racial lines when our Temple pastors have stated repeatedly that marriage is difficult enough without
adding this problem to it. Not that we prohibit interracial marriages,
but we have only three such couples, who fortunately do have successful relationships. In one of these instances, the couple joined our
communion because of the prejudice and terrible discrimination they
had encountered in other churches.

In one of its fabrications the article said people were raised
from the dead, when it was never expressed that they were clinically
dead. It was only stated in the service that Christ's love had a
remarkable effect in reaching people whose vital signs appeared to be
gone. In most services we don't even emphasize spiritual healing, and
we require consultation with medical doctors following prayers for
Divine healing. (See enclosed statement run this month in Bay Area
newspaper re: spiritual healing and medical science.) The article also
reported the ludicrous statement that we call our pastor "God" when
they heard him say that he preferred being called "pastor" or just
simply "Jim"; and in no way was he "God" to his people, much less the

Creator and Heavenly Father. He speaks Christ in us as our hope of glory and being Temples of the Holy Spirit on occasion, but vehemently affirms again and again that Jim Jones is nothing and Christ is All! He flatly told that so-called journalist that he was no Diety of any kind-- merely a servant of God to His people.

It is unfortunate that Pastor Jim Jones must be defended when his life is so tremendously self-sacrificial in serving Christ. He lives modestly in a cinder-block house with his wife, Marceline, who is a Registered Nurse and professional medical research investigator and evaluator of hospitals for the state. They have adopted eight of all different races. The pastor is so unpretentious that he wears only used clothing and has only one pair of shoes. He doesn't even own a car, but chooses to ride one of our buses with the rest of the members. His schedule allows him only a few hours sleep each night.

But apparently the truth had no effect on this man, because we have many friendly witnesses in government agencies and a cross-section of civic and denominational leaders who heard him say he would do anything to get us! We seriously considered suing him for all the lies he wrote until we received subsequent coverage that gave a very fair representation of our ministry, followed by a letter from the owner of the entire chain which praised us for sharing common ideals and for being a front-line defense against all forms of totalitarianism.

Hundreds of our members read or subscribe to your magazine, Mr. Plowman, and we appreciate your clear witness for Christ. (One of your past articles on a Black Baptist church, I believe, located on the Southeast coast, is presently pinned up on our bullentin board.) Our pastor referred publicly to the fine article you did, I think it was entitled "Friendship--The Way of Life", and read excerpts to our congregation, as he has done on other occasions. "Christianity Today" is a most remarkable tool in helping us convert people to Christ and bring a revival, as well as a practical witness, to the Body of Christ.

If you would like, we can provide you with material from church people all across the United States who would testify to the character of our witness and what we do for Christ's Kingdom through our extensive ministry. Just this month, a denominational official, Mr. Dennis Short, who heads the Urban Life program in our Disciples of Christ, said in referring to our pastor and our church, "The ministry of this man and his congregation is surpassed by none in our denomination." (We have a copy of the letter that carries the statement, which Mr. Short sent us.) And the general counsel of our entire denomination stated of our congregation in a written review of the Peoples Temple congregation, "I can say that they are the most committed and dedicated group of people I have known in any church anywhere." (Attorney Wade Rubick)

Yet, Mr. Plowman, we know that we can never do enough for the cause of God in these trying times. Again, thank you for your own meaningful and significant witness, and if we can ever accomodate you or your staff, in your travels, please let us know.

Very respectfully in Him,

Michael J. Prokes

Michael J. Prokes
Associate Minister

P.S.   I'm also including some of the many supportive statements
from various officials outside of the religious community
which I thought might be of some interest to you.

I didn't understand too clearly on the phone something you
said about a man, unfamiliar to me, who did not believe in,
I think you said, the Diety of Christ. I was fatigued from
having been up most of the night traveling back from a
speaking engagement at a church conference, and thus I can't
recall whether I answered your question clearly about Jesus
being God. I was taken back by the statement that a purported
Evangelical could even believe otherwise. In our humble and
never quite adequate witness, considering the needs in these
dark days, Peoples Temple, to the last congregant, believes
Jesus Christ was Immanuel Almighty, God with us, and is now at
the Right Hand of God making intervention for His church.

A final item I should call your attention to is the recent
Richmond Palladium article (enclosed), whose editor made the
request to write the article on Pastor Jones and published it
on the midsection front page. Before it came out, the "reporter", referred to earlier, acted so despicably as to try to
antagonize certain residents and officials of Pastor Jones'
home state, where he and his family had served for years and
were highly esteemed. The situation was reconciled, as you
can see, when the Palladium published the fine article last
month, which shows that Jim Jones is still remembered and well-
regarded, despite the attempts at vilification by our one critic.

It just occurred to me that newspapers do not seem to refer to
our basic beliefs. They often delete portions about our belief
in fundamentalist Christianity, particularly in reference to
souls being born again and converted to Christ. Thus, if you
are interested and upon your request, we can send you one of
our own news bulletins, which I didn't have with me in our San
Francisco office. (I'll bet this is the longest P.S. you've
ever read.)

Statement of the
GENERAL MINISTER AND PRESIDENT
Administrative Committee of the General Board
March 12, 1979

I want to report to you on the tragedy of Jonestown relative to our structure and relationships, and offer you my recommendations.

Some 48 hours after the tragedy -- even before the scope of it was fully known -- I issued a statement of concern for the families of the victims and for survivors, and acknowledged the relationship of both the congregation and its pastor-to the Disciples of Christ.

At the same time, I took what I felt to be an appropriate step of getting the question of denominational followup action out of the hands of staff and into the hands of those who initiate and make policy. Because of the questions being raised as to what the Disciples were planning to do about People's Temple, I indicated that I would make an inquiry with the legislative bodies of the church whether there ought to be a procedure for disavowing congregations, a procedure which we have never had.

The recent dissolving of People's Temple makes the specific question moot. But the issue remains. Does this church have an obligation to itself, to other Christians, and to society to institute a procedure of disassociation from congregations that run amuck?

If fanatical fringe groups can enhance their credibility by aligning themselves with major denominations, the ministry and mission and witness of all mainstream Protestantism suffers. The anti-religionists tried more than once on national television following Jonestown to make the point that People's Temple was not a cult but a part of the Christian mainstream.

There is the church-state issue involved as well. The government would like to close the tax loopholes which cults and pseudo-religious bodies can take advantage of. We have come to the point where government is beginning to define what constitutes a church, and what appropriate church activities are. We believe this to be an infringement on the First Amendment protection of religion.

So, I bring to you, as I indicated I would, the matter of whether we have a weakness in structure that endangers Christian witness and mission. Let me share with you my own observations and recommendations.

First, whatever we do, <u>let us act with the good of humanity in mind, and not the reputation of the church.</u> We are concerned with people and ministry. We are concerned with love and compassion. We are here to save the world, and not the institution, even when the institution is the church. As great a tragedy as Jonestown was, we should not act precipitantly with our self-protection as the motivation.

Second, having a policy to disavow congregations probably could not have foretold or averted Jonestown. People's Temple, until at some point near the end, behaved much like many other congregations with a strong devotion to their pastors. In any case, it is unlikely that the church would have used a disavowal procedure against an entire congregation, having no comprehension that strange behavior by a pastor and complaints of mistreatment by members was the prelude to mass murder and suicide. We have developed responsible policies and criteria for the order of ministry in the Christian Church (Disciples of Christ) and those policies were operative concerning the standing of Jones at the time of the tragedy.

Third, just as we ask the individual prospective member only if she or he believes in Jesus Christ, we offer relationship to congregations on the same basis, and accept on faith the reply in each case. Recognition is achieved by action of the congregation and the endorsement of the region. The covenantal relationship thus formed with the whole church is one of mutual support and accountability. Let God be the judge of deviation from the gospel. And society judge violations of the civil law.

Fourth, it is not so much a body of common beliefs that binds us together as Disciples of Christ but an understanding of the church as one. Historically we have said the church of Jesus Christ on earth is essentially, intentionally and constitutionally one. In tolerating and welcoming difference of opinion, we leave ourselves no measuring rod by which errancy can be determined. A congregation can be a part of us because it believes the church is one.

Fifth, the social witness, which got Jim Jones interested in the Disciples in the first place, should not be lost by the church because opponents tie it to the aberrations of Jones. Let me share with you part of a letter that appeared in the Indianapolis Star: "As one who is not a member of the Disciples of Christ, but who has observed for a long time their deep concern for the minorities in our land, I would like to express my sympathy to their leaders and members over the recent painful events in Guyana. It is my hope that the tragic events over which we all agonize will not discourage that denomination in continuing to be sensitive to the needs of the spiritually and socially disinherited among us. By affirming ecumenical vision the Disciples of Christ have won the admiration of us all."

And last, if we have shortcomings in connection with our congregations and ministry, it is at the point of shepherding, not policing. Perhaps the most significant decision we Disciples made in the restructure period of the sixties was to recognize ourselves as a covenant church. We are still learning what that means. The covenant concept takes seriously the New Testament image of the church as "the body of Christ." It recognizes the organic unity of the body. By God's design the parts of the body are dependent on one another. They "care for one another. If one member suffers, all suffer together; if one member is honored, all rejoice together." To say that we are in a covenantal relationship is to say that, in Christ, we are responsible for one another as members of any living body are. In practical terms, this means that in the Christian Church, we sense the interdependence of various structural manifestations of the body -- congregation, region and general organization.--These parts not only serve and support one another but also rely on one another. This relationship is described in part in paragraph 83 of The Design:

2

146

As part of the Christian Church (Disciples of Christ) congregations share creatively in its total mission of witness and service. Equally, the Christian Church (Disciples of Christ) in its general and regional manifestations sustains its congregations through its commitment to their welfare and needs. Thus, concern for the integrity of each manifestation is shared and witness is given to the interrelatedness of the whole church.

We need to amplify the meaning of this covenantal relationship through a closer relationship among our congregations, all of them, not just those that ask for denominational services. We have a responsibility to visit and nurture them, just as congregations have a responsibility to visit and nurture their members. I have recently proposed to the Conference of Regional Ministers and Moderators that the Conference be responsible for encouraging all regions to develop consistent procedures in applying the policies and criteria we have adopted for the order of ministry in matters of candidacy, licensing, ordination and ministerial standing. The regions will be encouraged to establish ways and means for at least annual visits to every congregation regardless of its size and degree of participation. The regions will be asked to encourage all persons who hold ministerial standing to report annually on the ministry in which they are involved. This will enable the regions to be faithful to their responsibility for maintaining standards; assist in maintaining accountability and contact; help in the development of a comprehensive and accurate picture of the region's total ministry and provide a basis for support. The General Board committee on ministerial standing which is responsible for certifying the standing of persons engaged in non-regional ministries will be asked to develop specific procedures to apply when persons assume positions outside the boundaries of our regularly constituted regions and are not related to any of our denominational organizations or ecumenical bodies with which we have official relationships. Our aim as a church is and ought to be to accept responsibility for, and accountability to, one another as we seek to carry out God's mission.

Therefore, it is my recommendation to this Administrative Committee of the General Board that the Christian Church (Disciples of Christ) reaffirm its commitment to the covenantal relationship which binds us together as a church, and to congregational freedom, taking no action that would involve passing judgment on a congregation's ministry, and that we continue to develop new and creative ways for shepherding congregations and encouraging them to accept and live in a relationship of mutual support with other congregations in their region and in the whole church. I would further recommend that we reaffirm our commitment to the two priorities established by the Kansas City General Assembly -- to extend human rights and to renew congregational life and witness. It is my hope that all of the tragedies of the human family will be seen in the context of God's ultimate triumph.

3

AN UPDATE ON QUESTIONS
THAT MAY BE TROUBLING SOME CHURCH MEMBERS

(This is a redraft of the background information on Jonestown, World
Council grants to liberation groups, and the homosexual ordination
issue, following the discussion in the Sharing in Mission training
event February 12. The material is not designed for general dis-
tribution but to assist you in answering questions if they arise
during educational conferences.)

Jonestown

1. Did any of our money go to the People's Temple?

   ANSWER - No. Instead, People's Temple gave some money to our
   outreach. During 1978 the Temple gave $4,000 to outreach, of which
   $3,000 went into the general outreach distribution and $1,000 to
   Reconciliation. In 1977 the total was $6,150, only $750 of which
   was for basic mission finance, the rest about evenly divided between
   Reconciliation and the Southern California region. (If questioners
   quote enormous outreach figures of $100,000 or more, it is due to
   People's Temple Year Book reports in which the congregation claimed
   credit for outreach apparently not related to the program of the
   Disciples of Christ, since it was not identified.)

2. What was the relationship of People's Temple to All Peoples Christian
   Center?

   ANSWER - None. Only an unfortunate similarity of name and a location
   in California.

3. As a denomination, are we financially liable in the People's Temple
   tragedy?

   ANSWER - Not that we are aware. Like any congregation, People's
   Temple managed its own financial affairs. It would be difficult to
   assume responsibility for that over which we had no control. Under
   paragraph 84 of the Design for the Christian Church (Disciples of Christ)
   the congregations are guaranteed their right to " manage their affairs,"
   to " own, control and encumber" their property, and to establish their
   own financial policies.

4. Is People's Temple still listed as one of our churches?

   ANSWER - The 1979 Year Book and Directory, which will be out about
   mid-year, will not include People's Temple. The regional ministers of
   Northern and Southern California have verified that People's Temple
   operations in both regions have been disbanded. That is the only way a
   congregation can be removed from the Year Book without a notarized statement of withdrawal from the congregation itself.

5. Is there a push at the general level to develop a procedure for removal
   of errant congregations?

   ANSWER - No. Dr. Kenneth L. Teegarden, general minister and president,
   in light of the upset by some members over our inability to disassociate

ourselves from an existing congregation, agreed to take the matter to
the legislative processes of the church, which he still intends to do.
He personally does not favor any disavowal procedure and there is no
move afoot by anyone else of which we are aware.

World Council grants to revolutionaries

1. Did any of our money to the World Council go to revolutionaries in
    Africa?

    ANSWER - No. The only money available for grants by the Program to
    Combat Racism of the World Council of Churches is money that is
    designated specifically for that purpose. No Disciples of Christ
    money was so designated, unless by individuals or congregations who
    chose to do so with their own funds. By design, no World Council
    general support money goes into the liberation fund. And no Disciples
    general units earmarked any of their funds for the grants.

2. Isn't it true that we support those liberation movements indirectly?

    ANSWER - More than indirectly. The General Assembly of the Christian
    Church in Kansas City in 1977, with several thousand Disciples present--
    the majority of them lay persons--voted"unequivocal" support of majority
    rule in southern Africa. Our Division of Overseas Ministries has had
    contact for years with Africans, many of whom are mission school products,
    who are in the thick of the liberation struggle. As part of our human
    rights effort, one of two denominational priorities, we have helped
    political prisoners and refugees, have opposed publicly the investments
    of American companies in white-dominated African countries, and have
    assisted poor people the world over in organizing to pursue self-reliance
    and self-determination. Further, World Council staff do administer the
    Program to Combat Racism and Disciples do help underwrite World Council
    administrative costs.

3. How does World Council justify the liberation grants?

    ANSWER -The World Council Central Committee reaffirmed its support of the
    Program to Combat Racism at its January meeting in Jamaica. The grants
    are intended to show that the Council cares about food, health, shelter
    and education for refugees among people who feel they are fighting for free-
    dom. There are said to be 162,000 refugees in the care of the Rhodesia
    revolutionary groups and the money is committed to humanitarian purposes.

4. Can't the money be diverted to the purchase of guns?

    ANSWER - The money is given on the basis of trust that it will be used
    for the stated humanitarian purposes, the same guarantee required of
    Rhodesian government-approved relief organizations, which have received
    more than $2 million from the World Council. Removing some of the temp-
    tation is the free flow of arms from the Big Power rivals vying for in-
    fluence in southern Africa.

II

Magazine Coverage of the Peoples Temple

RAPE OF THE INNOCENTS

NO. 1 • PDC • 56503-7

THE UNTOLD STORY

$1.50

OF THE Jonestown

MASSACRE

a **LOPEZ** publication

**CONGRESSMAN
LEO RYAN**
. . . The do-gooder who
came to a tragic end

JIM "DAD" JONES
. . . The speed freak
who played god. . . .

LARRY LAYTON
. . . Charged in 8 counts of
murder and attempted murder

THE JONESTOWN DEAD
. . . Horror that defies belief

JACQUELINE SPEIER
. . . Congressman Ryan's aide
who survived her gun wounds

JONES IN DEATH
. . . Shot to death
by whose hand?

Huge American helicopter arrives at Jonestown to assist in ferrying suicide victims to airport for flight to Dover, Delaware.

154

THE UNTOLD STORY
OF THE Jonestown
MASSACRE

Volume 1   Issue 1

CONTENTS

ADRIAN B. LOPEZ
Publisher

HERBERT McLEAN
Editor

LEN KABATSKY
Art Director

JERRY HERNANDEZ
Production Director

THE UNTOLD STORY OF THE JONESTOWN MASSACRE. Published by Histrionics Publications, 21 Wet 26th Street, New York, N.Y. 10010. Single copy price $1.50. Copyright 1979 by Histrionics Publications, Inc. For additional copies please send $1.50 plus 50¢ for mailing charges.

3

The Jonestown Massacre:

Death Strikes Swiftly in the Guyanese Jungle

Death reigns in Peoples Temple Meeting Hall at Jonestown, jungle home of Jim Jones's cult. More than 900 bodies were found by U.S. Army graves registration soldiers who returned all to States.

THE first reports out of Guyana made Sunday morning front page headlines across the U.S. They told the world that a U.S. congressman, 53-year-old Leo J. Ryan, a California Democrat, had been reported shot in a jungle airport as he sought to bring a number of defectors from the Peoples Temple, a religious colony in the Guyana jungle back home to the U.S. Those headlines were startling enough but, as so often happens, the first reports were only the tip of the iceberg. Next came the word that Ryan and some reporters were dead. On Monday came the reports that also dead was the founder of the cult, the Rev. Jimmy Jones, and, as it turned out 911 of his followers, who had joined him in mass suicide.

Rep. Ryan had gone to Guyana to look into reports that Americans, many of them from his San Francisco constituency, were being held against their will at the Peoples Temple, a controversial religious settlement in Jonestown, Guyana, in an isolated area about 150 miles northwest of the Guyana capital of Georgetown.

Before leaving San Francisco five days before on what was to be his last fact-finding mission, Ryan announced, "I am going to investigate the conditions of Americans (in the settlement) who, I have been told, are working from dawn to nightfall, with terrible mental and physical punishment if they don't work hard enough."

4

156

Picking flowers was one of Reverend Jim Jones's more affable hobbies as this picture would indicate. It was found in an album at Jonestown after the massive suicide-massacre that shocked world.

Before leaving for Guyana, one of Ryan's aides, Jackie Speier wrote out her will, checked Ryan's, and left them in his office where his staff was to find them on Sunday, Nov. 19, when word of his death reached them. Miss Speier was wounded in the airport attack but airlifted safely back to Baltimore. Ryan, a veteran of submarine service in World War II, was brought home in a flag-draped coffin.

Police in Port Kaituma, site of the jungle airport, estimated that bloody Saturday night that "about 20 people" were involved in the attack. They had no way of knowing, then, that another 900 were also "involved"—in a final involvement at the Peoples Temple, not far away.

Ryan had decided as far back as last summer to look into Jonestown, first hand, and, on Nov. 1, he wired Jones: "I am most interested in a visit to Jonestown and would appreciate whatever courtesies you can extend." The reply came, Nov. 6, from Mark Lane, the lawyer who had made so much noise about the officially-accepted versions of the assassination of President Kennedy. His reply to Ryan was in the form of a threat, a suggestion that Jones might move his whole colony to "two anonymous countries" (Cuba? Russia?) to show the U.S. up if Ryan should indulge in what Lane called "a witch hunt" in Guyana, where Lane was protecting Jones from CIA "infiltration and harrassment."

5

Only a few hours before his murder in Guyana, congressman Leo
Ryan of California (left) talks to Brian Bouquette, a member of
the Peoples Temple from Burlingame, Calif. Bouquette was told
that his mother was in Georgetown and wanted to see him—and he
refused. He died at Jonestown. (copyright 1978 Chicago Tribune)

6

Though not unaware that there was some risk involved, Ryan went ahead with his trip, gladly taking along any reporters who might be interested in joining him. Said an aide later, "He felt the press was his best protection." Three newsmen and one dropout from the cult were to die with Ryan at the jungle-edge airport, as it turned out. On the other hand, the reporters felt safe enough because, after all, nobody would kill a congressman. Or so they thought.

The group arrived in Georgetown on Nov. 14, and there the mission seemed to bog down before it even could really begin. Word came from Jones that he was sick and unable to meet press or congressman. A public relations aide, Sharon Amos, met Ryan in Georgetown with petitions from Jonestowners for Ryan and his band to stay away.

For instance, "Many of us have been visited by friends and relatives. However, we have not invited, nor do we care to see, Congressman Ryan." There followed hundreds of signatures from within the compound. But Ryan decided to press on anyway, with or without the invitation of the cultists or the permission of their leader.

Lane and Charles Garry, another attorney employed by Jones, came to Ryan and interceded with the leader. Garry, it has been reported, told Jones "You have two alternatives. You can tell the Congress of the United States, the press and the relatives to go—themselves. If you do that, it's the end of the ballgame. The other alternative is to let them in, and prove to the world that these people criticizing you are crazy." Logic like that, and assurances that Gary and Lane would keep an eye on the congressional party, finally swayed Jones and the barriers were raised.

And so the party of 19, including nine newsmen and four relatives of cultists, hopped a Twin Otter aircraft and flew into Port Kaituma, the nearest airstript to Jonestown, a fishing village six miles from the compound. An armed man was one of the angry delegation from Jonestown who met them at the airport. Finally, the party piled into a dump truck for the hour-long ride over a twisting dirt road through the thick jungle to the tropical Eden.

The first glimpse of the Peoples Temple was serene. Many of the communards presented a friendly welcome, including Jones' wife, Marceline, who led them to her husband after solicitous words that any polite hostess might offer, words like "You must be hungry. The food is waiting at the pavilion."

Jones was waiting there, and not looking very happy. But he sat down with the visitors for a dinner, and unusual one for the commune, as later reports would have it, of smoked pork, eddoes, (something like potatoes) and coffee. The congressional visitors and press were serenaded by an eight-man band, the Guyanese national anthem, "America the Beautiful," soul music, the blues . . . and a series of conversations with a number of commune members—carefully picked?—that moved Ryan to tell the congregation over the loudspeakers that were directed at the entire 900-acre enclave, "I can tell you right now by the few conversations I've had with some of the folks here already this evening that there are some people who believe that this is the best thing that ever happened in their lives."

Ryan went to sleep in Jonestown that night favorably impressed and a big breakfast awaited him in the morning . . . pancakes and bacon . . . not, it was to develop later, necessarily the standard fare for most of the people of the commune. And the less-than-best face soon appeared. Ryan and newsmen were turned away as they tried to enter one building. When newsmen persisted, Garry and Lane convinced the authorities to let them in. They found about 60 old folks crowded in a small dormitory which, Lane admitted later, loked "like a slave ship."

There followed an interview, gruelling for Jones, with NBC News' Don Harris. It was an adversary interview. Harris had all these hard questions, tough ones to field about drugs in the compound, and corporal punishment for the followers. Guns around here? "Lies," Jones claimed. Did some people want to leave the cult? "People play games, friend," he replied. "They lie. What can I do with liars? Are you people going to leave us? I just beg you, please leave us. Anybody that wants to go can get out of here. They come and go all the time." Harris and Bob Brown, who held the minicam for him during the interview that was so rugged for Jones, died with Ryan at the airport.

Tropical rains beat on the tin roof of the pavilion as Jones saw his empire dissolving before his very eyes. "I feel sorry that we are being destroyed from within," he said as a list of those who wanted to leave with the Ryan party began to grow. It started with a note from two members begging Harris "Please help us to get out of Jonestown." And before long, there was a report of a family of six that wanted out . . . and soon, the total was 16. At least one family was divided. A woman and her husband fought openly over their child. "Don't take my baby," screamed the woman, who wanted to stay, to her husband, who wanted to go.

Finally, the dump truck was loaded for one more trip over the jungle road, to the airport. It was crammed with baggage and was slick with mud, so people had to hold onto sideboards for dear life.

Just as the truck was about to leave, as Ryan was saying good-bye to Jones, and Jones was seeing more of his onetime followers defect, one of the leader's aides, Don Sly, grabbed the congressman by the throat and held a six-inch fishing knife to his throat. The screaming aide was restrained by Garry and Lane, but when Ryan boarded the truck, he was stained with the blood of Sly.

As the truck made its way to the tiny airport, Jones called for Lane, frightened. Not all of the com- ⁷

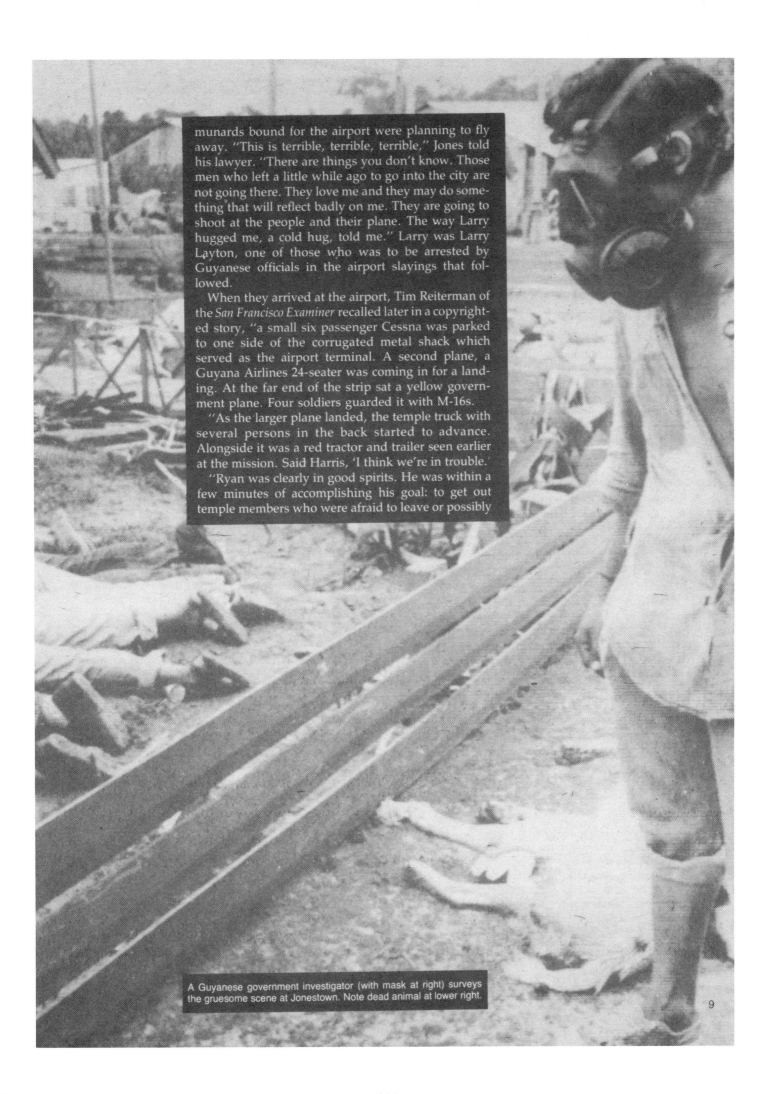

munards bound for the airport were planning to fly away. "This is terrible, terrible, terrible," Jones told his lawyer. "There are things you don't know. Those men who left a little while ago to go into the city are not going there. They love me and they may do something that will reflect badly on me. They are going to shoot at the people and their plane. The way Larry hugged me, a cold hug, told me." Larry was Larry Layton, one of those who was to be arrested by Guyanese officials in the airport slayings that followed.

When they arrived at the airport, Tim Reiterman of the *San Francisco Examiner* recalled later in a copyrighted story, "a small six passenger Cessna was parked to one side of the corrugated metal shack which served as the airport terminal. A second plane, a Guyana Airlines 24-seater was coming in for a landing. At the far end of the strip sat a yellow government plane. Four soldiers guarded it with M-16s.

"As the larger plane landed, the temple truck with several persons in the back started to advance. Alongside it was a red tractor and trailer seen earlier at the mission. Said Harris, 'I think we're in trouble.'

"Ryan was clearly in good spirits. He was within a few minutes of accomplishing his goal: to get out temple members who were afraid to leave or possibly

A Guyanese government investigator (with mask at right) surveys the gruesome scene at Jonestown. Note dead animal at lower right.

9

161

had been held against their will.

"First the Cessna was filled, with Ryan frisking each boarder, looking for guns and knives. Meanwhile, the tractor, with several men in the trailer, rilled toward the terminal shack and halted a short distance away. Quietly, the men with the tractor motioned aside a curious group of Guyanese children and other bystanders.

"Speier was signing on passengers, while a reporter helped her check for weapons. The closest thing to a law-enforcement officer, a pleasant young policeman with a pink shirt and 16-gauge shotgun, was disarmed by temple members."

Then came the first shot. Other gunmen opened fire from the tractor. When they were through, Ryan, Harris, Brown, photographer Gregory Robinson and Patricia Parks, a defector, were dead. In a few days Temple aide Larry Layton was accused of the slayings which touched off the mass suicide six long miles away at the compound Saturday night, and the most memorable chapter in what might be the closing days of the history of the Peoples Temple.

Back at the compound, the final stages were being set for the ending of more than 900 more lives.

"They will never reach the United States, and we will all commit suicide," Jones told those around his throne at the pavillion that Saturday afternoon as the carnage went on at the airport. And so he ordered the potion prepared. That was the job of Dr. Lawrence Schact, a 30-year-old Houston native, who had joined the sect in 1977 after a brief internship in San Francisco. Those who remember Schact remember "a very intense young man with a tremendous concern for people." He was described as dedicated, empathetic with the poor and "a very solid performer."

Schact, who had married into the cult, taking as his bride a follower named Becky and adopting four children, had long nourished a dream of doing medical missionary work in South America, so, when he left the intern program in San Francisco, and "just disappeared into the jungle," it might have been no huge surprise. Nor was the intensity he brought with his work, and the pride he took once in saving the life of a child bitten by a snake. Nor might you be surprised at the care with which he prepared his final brew. But the ingredients that went into that 50-gallon washtub were, to put it mildly, a little different.

For flavor, there was grape Kool-Aid, which kids love. There were, also, the tranquilizer Valium; sedatives thorazine and largactil; pain killer demerol; a very strong sedative often used to settle down people who are violent, haloperidol; an antihistamine that hastens absorption of substances into the bloodstream, phaerengen, and enough half-gallon jugs of cynanid to kill more than 900 people.

Jones had at least one act of kindness left in him. He called attorneys Lane and Garry to him. "Feeling is running very high against you two," he told them. "I can't say what might happen at the meeting," the

one he was about to call. The two lawyers were put in a guest house, where stood two guards, armed with rifles. They were, the attorneys said later, one Jim Johnson and one Pnacho. "It's a great moment, we all die," said one, a huge communal suicide in protest against racism and fascism.

Lane suggested he and Garry might write about it to the world, and that seemed a good idea to the guards, who let the two elderly lawyers slip into the jungle, where they hid through what was to ensue.

It has been surmised that Jones had a plan, that Layton was to board the plane, allow it to take off, then kill the pilot. Congressmen, newsmen, defectors and, presumably, at least one martyr, would die in the crash that followed. The mopup on the ground would be done on the cultists who followed the dump truck to the airport. But, as Jones may have feared, there was a slipup. Layton wasn't able to get onto the plane. It never got off the ground. But there was a massacre, and the congressmen, the reporters and one defector were assassinated.

Now it was time for the last White Night.

"Alert! Alert! Alert! Everyone to the pavilion," Jones shouted into the microphone that fed his loudspeakers. And many realized why they were being called. Cook Stanley Clayton, 25, for instance, was quick to surmise that this was the real thing. Usually, cooks were excused from the drill because they had to prepare food for all when it was over. But now, bodyguards ordered the cooks to the pavilion.

Now Jones, a sometime worker of dubious miracles, promised one more. The congressman's plane would tumble out of the sky, he told his followers. It didn't. And then the dump truck rumbled back from the airstrip. Aides conferred with Jones in hurried whispers.

"The congressman is dead, and the journalists. The Guyana government army will be here within 45 minutes. We must die with dignity," the voice blared out over the public address.

Then Schact and Joyce Touchette, one of the commune leaders, set up the tub of the deadly brew at the edge of the pavilion and now came the chilling words: "Bring the babies first."

Jones watched from his elevated throne as babies and then older children were taken to a table at the tin-roofed assembly hall where a nurse waited. She squirted the poison down their throats with a syringe and gave them a grape drink. After the children had been given the poison, eyewitness Odell Rhodes said later, it came the turn of the adults to line up for the lethal doses from the nurse. He said that people stood around in small groups and family gatherings talking as they waited for the poison to do its work. It took about four or five minutes.

Later, an extraordinary tape recording was found at the Jonestown Temple. It was recorded during the first 45 minutes of "white night" and provides a harrowing collection of sounds. It is filled with church

The Vat of Death. Positioned where it would be made available to all, this vat was filled with a grape drink mixed with cyanide.

11

organ music, the screams of children, and shouted arguments among his followers as Jones exhorted his suicide instructions over the loud-speaker. If the tape reveals anything at all, it shows that many of those present weren't altogether in favor of drinking poison and dying.

But Jones insisted that anyone in Congressman Ryan's party who survives the ambush at the nearby airstrip would get back to the United States and criticize Jonestown. "They'll make our lives like hell—we're sitting on a powder keg," Jones shouted over the amplifier. "If we can't live in peace, let's die in peace"

The initial calm was replaced with panic, according to Rhodes, when the survivors saw the convulsive agonies of the dying. Many died weeping, he said.

12

He added that he had no idea how many had escaped, but that he had heard only one shot as he hid in the jungle. The next day, at the Port Kaituma airport, he said, he saw the body of Jimmy Jones with a bullet wound in the right temple. It was the same man who Rhodes said, he had heard telling his people the night before that they should "tell their children that it was not painful."

Other reports had it that security force men armed with guns coerced many of the people to kill their children and themselves. Lane and Garry said they heard shooting from their jungle hideout. And, it seems, Maria Katsaris, Jones' mistress, and 11 other disciples put their poison cups in a bread pan and small pail to carry them to Jones' house. Five died in one bedroom, and seven in another. Katsaris was shot.

In Georgetown, capital of Guyana, a government guide leads U.S. military personnel across Timerhri Airport as preparations get underway for removal of nearly a thousand bodies from Jonestown.

13

San Francisco Examiner photographer Greg Robinson was with the group ambushed and slain while returning from Jonestown visit.

And so was Jones, with his own hand, when the dying of the others was nearly over.

The camp's water supply was poisoned, investigators were to find, and they presumed that the intent was to kill what was left of the communal livestock. Even the camp's mascot, a monkey named Mr. Muggs, was shot.

First reports had it that many of the communards had taken flight, and escaped the last horrors in the jungle. For one thing, nobody could believe tht hundreds would so docilely take their own lives. For another, 803 U.S. passports and, everybody thought, 405 bodies were found. Where were the bodies that belonged with the 400 passports? The answer came soon enough, when U.S. army graves registration people arrived at Jonestown, they found some 500 more bodies, for a grand total usually but at 909. And for a third, it seemed that millions of dollars were missing. For a time, there were those who thought that Jones, too, missed the terrible last appointment.

But one of the coffins flown back to the U.S. in the ensuing grim airlift was marked "Rev. Jimmie Jones, 13B," and fingerprints were to establish that this was, indeed, all that was mortal that remained of a man powerful enough to lure almost everyone in a crowd of nearly 1,000 to follow him to death. And, though U.S. Air Force pilots searched the nearby jungle for survivors later there were no sightings.

Instead of the 45 minutes that Jones had estimated it would take for Guyana authorities to reach the scene, it took them more than 12 hours from the first reports of the deadly incident at the airport to reach the survivors there. They were delayed in part because Port Kaituma strip has no light for night landings. The Guyana army arrived at 6 a.m. Sunday, and the survivors of the airport massacre were flown to Georgetown, leaving behind on the ground the bodies of the congressman and the others.

There were, finally, more than 70 survivors. Some, like Lane and Garry and Clayton and Rhodes, escaped by fleeing, One, Hyancinth Thrush, 76, slept through it, and lived. Two-hundred sixty children did not survive

Among those who survived also was Larry Layton, a 32-year-old Californian who styled himself as an X-ray technician at Jonestown. Four days after the slayings at the Port Kaituma airstrip, Layton issued a statement, which later was read in court at Georgetown. In this statement, he accepted the "responsibility" for the deaths of Congressman Ryan and the other four persons who died at the airstrip. Even though Layton was the only person actually charged in the Ryan murders, witnesses have testified that he did not himself shoot the Congressman but that he tried to shoot the others. (Survivors of

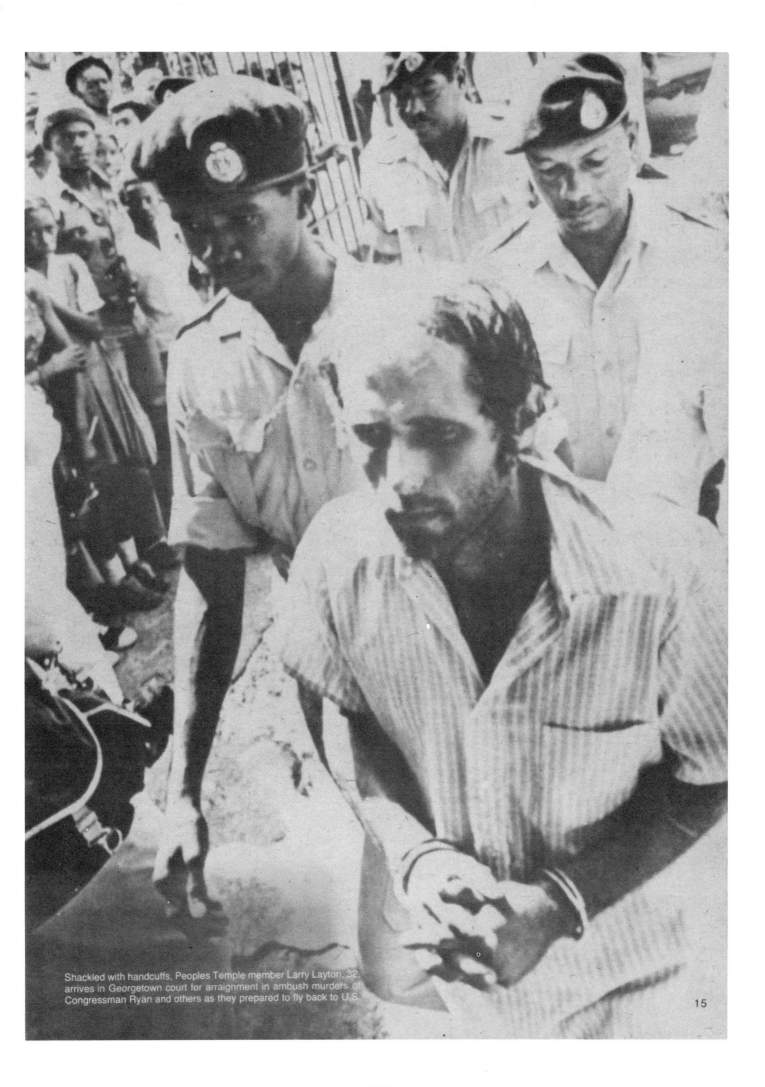

Shackled with handcuffs, Peoples Temple member Larry Layton, 32, arrives in Georgetown court for arraignment in ambush murders of Congressman Ryan and others as they prepared to fly back to U.S.

15

167

A wide variety of drugs was found scattered along table inside the Peoples Temple. Drugs were prescribed for certain cultists.

16

168

Jonestown say that those who actually shot and killed Ryan, died there).

In still another confession, this one coming a full month after the Jonestown debacle, Stephan Jones, 19-year-old son of the Rev. Jim Jones, told a magistrate's hearing in Georgetown that he had killed cult public relations aide Sharon Amos, 42, and her three young children. The victims had been found with their throats slashed in the bathroom of the Temple's headquarters in Georgetown. Stephan's confession came during an inquest to determine whether Charles Beikman, a Temple member, would actually stand trial for the Amos murders. Beikman was charged with the slayings but denied committing them, even though he admitted being present when they occurred. Despite Stephan's statement, the prosecutor at Georgetown did not immediately dismiss the charges against Beikman but he did add Stephan Jones as a defendant in the case.

Tim Jones, 19, and Jim Jones, adopted sons of the leader, were away from the camp at the time of the mass suicide, with 15 other members of the Peoples Temple basketball team. It was thought by many that they and a third adopted brother, Louis, who died with the others, were the ruling triumvirate of Jones' notorious security forces. They denied that they were part of a hit squad directed to kill U.S. officials, or that they had anything to do with beatings at the camp. "I don't even remember a fist fight," said Tim. He also pish-toshed reports of an aggressive, armed security force. It was only there to protect the family against theft and threat of kidnaping against his father. Guns? They were to shoot "rats and opossums that were helping themselves to the crops," Jim said.

Jim added that "I never beat anybody," and Tim went so far as to say he had "never seen anyone beaten," and, in fact, wasn't even part of a security force. "No, man," he said. "I just helped my dad." Guyana saw no reason to charge the young men with anything, and in fact, released them from protective custody within two weeks of the mass suicide. But a Pan American Airlines pilot refused to fly them back to the U.S. without an FBI agent or two on board his plane to keep an eye on things.

There were other survivors, people who had never seen Guyana or, perhaps, ever heard of it. But they were members of the Peoples Temple in San Francisco, and their loyalty to the ideal remained firm, even in the shocks of the first days of the ghastly revelations.

Meeting reporters in San Francisco, members said they could not understand "this terrible tragedy," but when a reporter called out "Who will replace Jim Jones," one Hugh Fortsua replied, shouting, "We all are." Indeed, the surviving members seemed intent on having the good works of the Temple go on. "I'm proud to be a member of the Temple and will continue to be," said Jean Brown, a young white woman.

"What has happened is terrible," she said, "We have all lost relatives and friends but there has been 30 years of total and selfless dedication Jones has given to bring us together and that record stands. Nothing can change it."

Fortsua backed her up. "I'm not making excuses. My wife is missing in Guyana, but what Jones stood for was good and we at the temple would like to make restitution to the families of those who died." Such as, whatever assets of the Temple "could legally be used" might be shared among surviving family members of those lost in Guyana.

Garry recalls hearing the last words of Jones from his hiding spot, "Mother! Mother! Mother!" and wonder whether he was calling for his own mother, who was buried in Jonestown a year ago, or to his wife, Marcie, who died with him.

When the Guyana army troops arrived at Jonestown that Sunday morning, they found those who had not survived. "Most of them," said eyewitness Chris J. Harper, "were lying face down on the lawns near the banana bushes outside the pavilion. One man clutched his dead dog to his chest. Children, who only hours before they died, were playing on the nearby swings, cuddled next to their parents. Some of the victims wore their best clothes . . . a few showed the awful suffering of their last few moments of life, the five minutes or so while the cyanide was taking its effect. Their faces were twisted into violent contortions, and matted blood was smeared over them after it had streamed from their noses, and mouths," Harper, writing in Newsweek, recalled. They were those who, in their last moments on earth, had passed the "loyalty test" of Jim Jones, who built a dream of altruism, of brotherly love and love-thy-neighbor, a utopian ideal, a dream, that in its bitter end, was to become a nightmare for the world to share.

Fully a month after the mass suicide, all kinds of reports circulated concerning the type of activity that actually went on at Jonestown. One such report said Jim Jones had been engaged in the training of guerrilla troops in the handling of Soviet-made automatic weapons, handguns and high explosives. This was given as one of the main reasons why Jim Jones dreaded the arrival of Congressman Ryan and his party—the fear that they would find out and tell the world about the guerrilla training program, as well as all the other repulsive aspects of life at Jonestown.

Jones was known to have cultivated contacts with the Soviet Embassy in Georgetown, and that some of the Embassy's officials had visited Jonestown. Survivors of the mass suicide-murder say that shortly after the Soviet contacts were made, Jones began teaching Temple members to speak Russian, sometimes refusing them food unless they could ask for it in the Russian language. He also talked about moving the entire communal settlement, lock, stock and barrel, to the Soviet Union—that move, of course, to be

17

169

contingent upon whether the Russians would have them.

It was also subsequently reported by the Guyanese police that letters, bequeathing more than seven million dollars to Russia's Communist Party, had been carried out of Jonestown on November 18th, the day of the mass murder-suicide. The letters were reported inside a suitcase which also contained cash from the Temple treasury. The letter, and four others, detailed plans to transfer of the money to the Russians from accounts in the Banco Union de Venezuela in Caracas and branches of Swiss banks located in Panama. But when approached in Georgetown for a statement on the matter, a Soviet Embassy official told newsmen the Russians wanted "no part of the cult's bequest."

More than three weeks after the Jonestown tragedy, the Guyanese government's chief medical examiner, Dr. C. Leslie Mootoo, startled the world public by stating in Georgetown: "I do not believe there were ever more than 200 persons who died voluntarily at Jonestown." He based his belief on a series of autopsies, performed on some of the victims, and close examination of other bodies at the scene. Dr. Mootoo said dozens of adult victims had died of cyanide poison injected into their *upper* arms—and, according to the doctor, it's virtually impossible for a person to inject himself or herself in the upper arm. Also, of the 911 victims, 260 were children and the doctor asked: "Could a child take his or her life voluntarily in that way (by injection)?"

Eventually, just before Christmas Day, a Guyanese coroner's inquest ruled that Jim Jones and others were "criminally responsible" for the deaths of 911 persons at the Peoples Temple. And that Jones himself was slain by "some persons or persons unknown." It was pointed out that the gun that killed

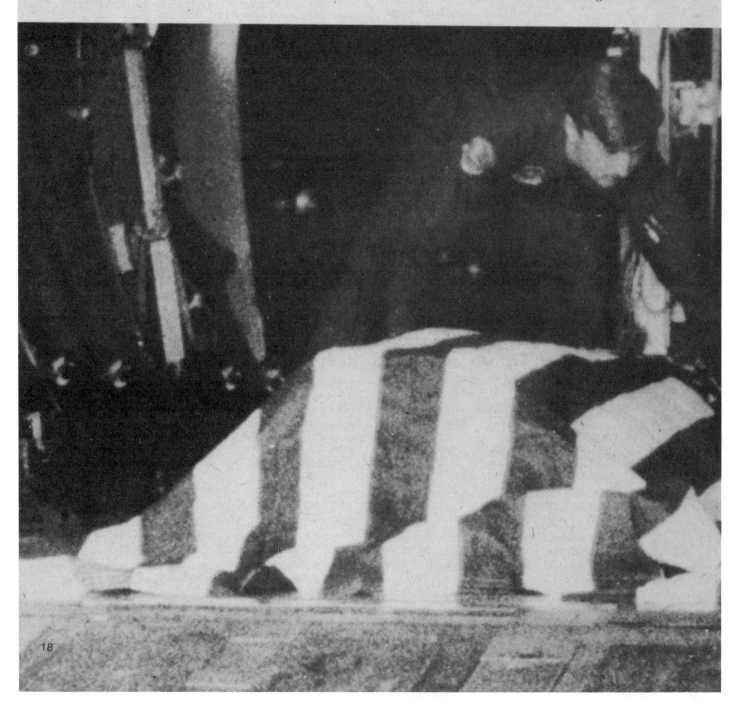

18

170

Jones was found some 20 yards away from his body—a distance he could hardly throw it after shooting himself, even though someone could have moved the weapon after Jones dropped it. It left open also the possibility that Jones instructed someone to shoot him, or perhaps he was actually murdered. By making Jones and others "responsible" for the 911 deaths, whether by murder or suicide, the coroner's inquest made it legally possible to issue the death certificates required for burial of the bodies in the United States.

As the bodies were being flown back to the U.S. mainland at Dover Air Force Base in Delaware, a controversy arose when many angry taxpaying Americans and some members of Congress demanded that the State Department make clear just who would pay the bill. An estimated four million dollars was involved in the embalming, transport and perhaps eventual burial or cremation of the bodies, not to mention more than $45,000 for a telephone hotline to Guyana. Complained one congressman: "I had a letter from a man whose mother died in Spain, and he said, 'Nobody paid to bring her back.' "

The question of "who would pay" arose, of course, after the Guyanese government refused to allow burial of the bodies in Guyana. At last reports, however, the U.S. Justice Department had located more than ten million dollars deposited by the Peoples Temple in banks in Panama, and steps were taken to "freeze" the money. First order of business would probably be the recovery American funds spent on airlifting the Jonestown victims' bodies back to the States. That would be one way of making certain the Russians didn't fall heir to all of the Peoples Temple treasury.

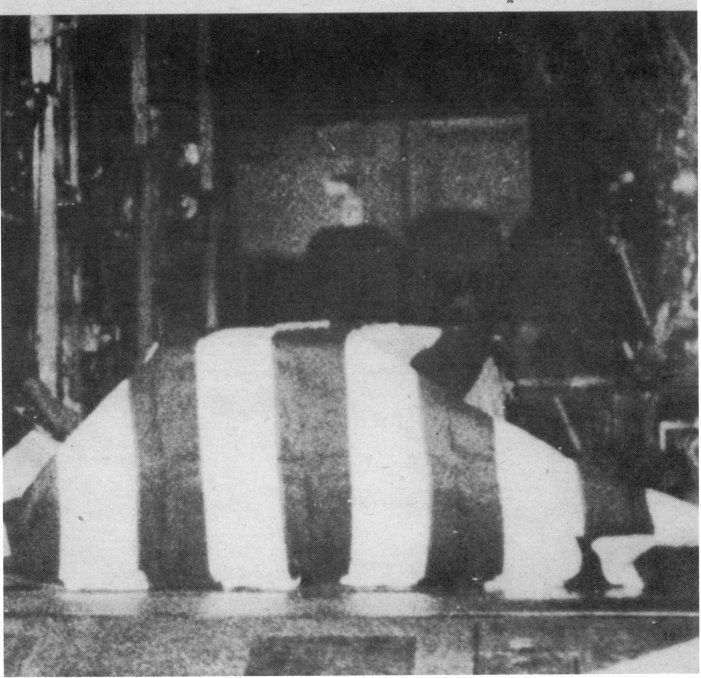

Among the coffins of these victims of Jonestown horror, is one numbered "13-B" which contains the remains of the cult's charismatic leader, Jim Jones, who was reported killed by gunshot wound.

20

172

*Master of Coercion
and Perversion:*

Jim "Dad" Jones— Both God and Devil to His Followers

The Rev. Jim Jones, or James Warren Jones as he was named when he was born in Lynn, Ind., then a whistle-stop town of some 70 miles east of Indianapolis on May 11, 1931, was not unknown at the time of his death. But his name was not exactly a household word, either. It was his sudden death that catapulted him into widespread notoriety.

Wire services had prepared canned obituaries of the man who, as much as a year before his personal Gotterdammerung, was perceived as a spiritual leader to some and as a charlatan to others. He told the world that "service to my fellow man is the highest service to God." —

But others told of coercion—and even perversion—in his jungle Fiefdom. More than a year before the fearful ending of Jones and those pitiful hundreds of his followers, it was alleged that his people were victims who had been bilked out of their property, conned out of their religious beliefs, physically abused, and used as pawns in political power games.

It became apparent that the Peoples Temple ran on a double standard—one set of rules for the leader, and another for the flock. For instance, as early reports from Georgtown pointed out, Jones surrounded himself and his wife, Marceline, 50, with the comfortable trappings of the so-called good life of our times—closed circuit television and the latest radio and electronic equipment. Nothing like that for his people. And, it was whispered, he permitted himself male lovers—but would not permit any thing of that sort among his followers.

"Jones used to say that only perfect heterosexual around was himself. All of us had to admit that we were homosexuals," one male survivor told Pete Carey in a copyrighted interview for the Knight-Ridder Newspapers. "Then we found out that it was him. He was having sex with guys. The guys, they'd brag about it right up front."

But, another survivor, 27-year-old Chris O'Neal, said at least one homosexual offender was beaten on stage in Jonestown before an audience of believers. "It was nothing bad, what the guy did, but Jones took the law into his own hands," in O'Neal's opinion. "They beat him up on a stage in the compound. The blood was running off his face and they sent him down the aisles. The people were asked to beat him some more.

"So they hit him, and Jones said: 'Kick him where he deserves it,' and they did. He just swelled up," O'Neal told the world, "That poor guy. I couldn't believe it. Nobody ever told me this stuff was going on."

Author Jeannie Jones, 39, who, with her husband and five children, left the sect in 1975, says Jones talked openly of bisexuality, and once asked everyone in a room who had had sex with him to stand up. When 20 men and women rose, Jones said one person had not been honest, and another man then stood up.

Long before Rep. Ryan made his fateful investigation of the Peoples Temple, district attorneys in the San Francisco area were looking into reports of shady property transfers to Jones and his sect.

Marceline Jones described her husband as a Marxist "who holds religion's trappings to be used chiefly for

social and economic uplift." A minister of the United Church of Christ for a quarter-century, Jones' views veered from the orthodox in recent years. "Jim has used religion to try to get some people out of the opiate of religion," Marcie once said while recalling a telling incident: "Marcie, I've got to destroy this paper idol," she says Jones once blurted out as he slammed down a bible he held in his hand.

People who knew Jones from his earliest days recall "a mean little 6-year-old kid, the Dennis the Menace of Lynn., Ind." Make of it what you will, but even before his birth, his mother, Lynetta Jones, was convinced that her son would be a messiah. As a young anthropologist working with primitive tribes in Africa, Mrs. Jones felt she was in a deadly crossfire between her career and marriage. In a dream, Lynetta thought she heard her mother calling to her from the far side of a river. The vision told Lynetta that she would bear a son who would right the wrongs of the world.

Then along came James Thurmon Jones, a railroad section hand...and a member of the Ku Klux Klan. A man of 47, he proposed. She accepted. And then along came James Warren Jones, the promised messiah—in the loving eyes of his mother, who was delighted that the boy Jones "had a way" with animals. She saw it as a gift from St. Francis. Their son was to die at 47—the age of his father when Lynetta accepted him.

"Jim always had several animals," says his cousin, Barbara Shaffer. "He befrieded everyone—animals and people." That was encouraging to Lynetta, who had to often leave young Jimmy in the care of neighbors whenever she worked in a factory 20 miles away to keep the bodies and souls of the needy Jones family together.

They had parted, the man and wife, in 1945. Jim, the father, died when Jimmy was 14. He had carried, to the end, the effects of gassing received in World War I. Lynetta died in 1977. She was 17 years younger than the husband she had chosen to domineer.

Young Jim was to recall his heritage with some pride. He claimed Lynetta was part Cherokee. In his adult years, Jones occasionally described himself cheerfully as "an All-American mongrel." But cousin Barbara was, in later years, to suggest that "He made that up (his mother's Indian ancestry) to impress somebody."

Despite the deviltry that neighbors remember, Jones spent thousands of boyhood hours in the Methodist Church. "We used to play pretend-church," recalls childhood playmate Vera Price. "He'd always be the preacher, standing up and making sermons."

And there were hints as to what sort of calling he had. When only 7, he exhorted his playmate congregations to strict discipline. "He would have ten or twelve youngsters and put them through their paces," recalls a neighbor. "He'd hit them with a

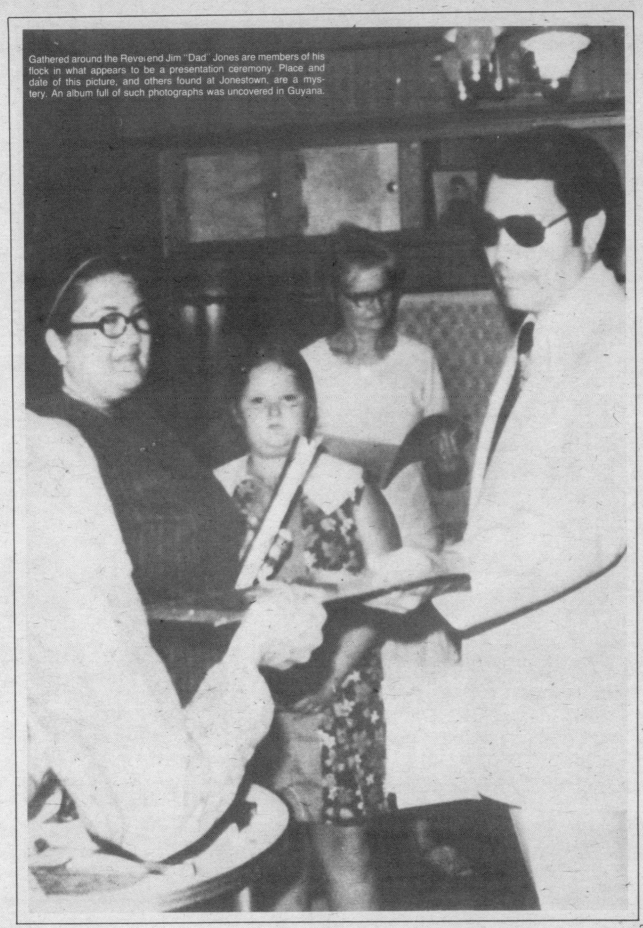

Gathered around the Reverend Jim "Dad" Jones are members of his flock in what appears to be a presentation ceremony. Place and date of this picture, and others found at Jonestown, are a mystery. An album full of such photographs was uncovered in Guyana.

23

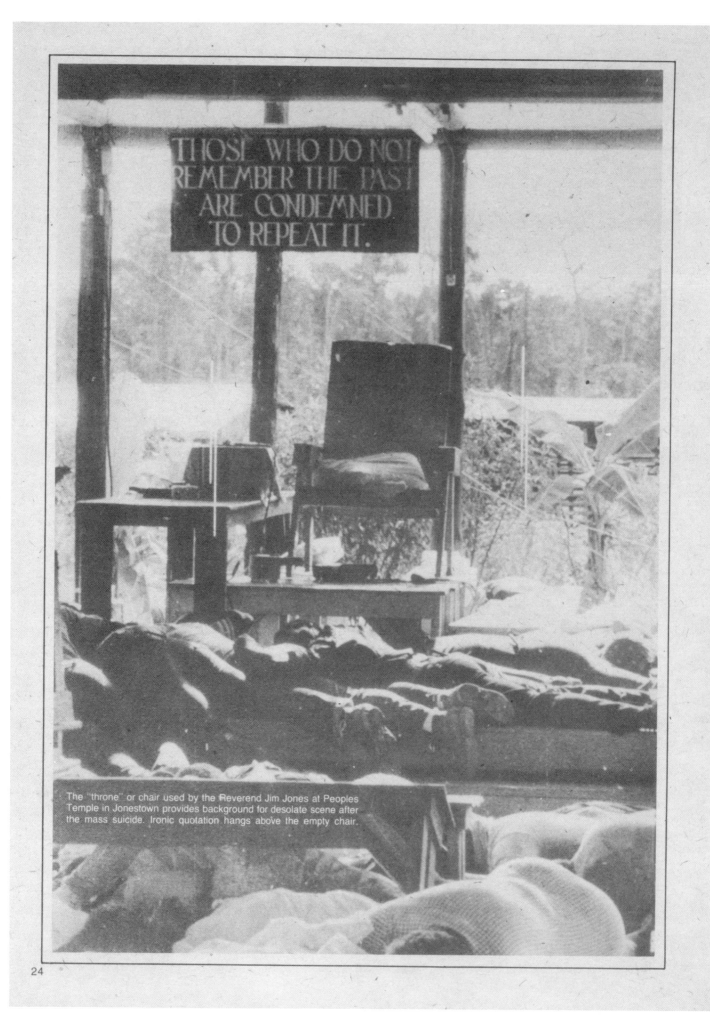

THOSE WHO DO NOT
REMEMBER THE PAST
ARE CONDEMNED
TO REPEAT IT.

The "throne" or chair used by the Reverend Jim Jones at Peoples Temple in Jonestown provides background for desolate scene after the mass suicide. Ironic quotation hangs above the empty chair.

24

stick and make them cry. He had a power that most boys don't have." And that neighbor, now 73, has seen a lot of young boys grow up . . . and cry.

But perhaps there was another side to that attachment to animals—and the pretend church. Harlan Swift, a Chicago insurance executive at the time of the final religious experience in Guyana remembers. Like many other smalltown children, "Jonesie" conducted funerals for small animals and birds found dead in the neighborhood. Swift recalls fairly extravagant productions that included burning candles. And a matchbox. In the matchbox, Swift reported, might be a dead mouse. "He had a service all organized," Swift told Time "very, very intense dramatic service for that dead mouse." Precocious?

Precocious, indeed? What of the recollection of another former classmate, Tootie Morton. "Some of the neighbors had cats missing, and we always thought he was using them for sacrifices."

Not too mind-boggling when you consider that the major industry in Lynn, which has now exploded to a population of 1,360, is casket making. Is it too grim to speculate that Jones may have considered the economy of his old hometown at the end, when caskets for more than 900 were needed?

The church-pretending continued. He took to carrying a Bible—that book he was later to reject so violently—and he showed an early inclination to boss his contemporaries around. No playmates argued back much. Jimmy was pretty big and strong for his age. In the make-believe sermons, he might harangue his playmates. By age 14, he had first mounted a real pulpit as guest of some young black friends who invited him to speak at their church. But, remembers Swift, "You could see there was something haywire even then." Others remember warmly that "He had a little white shaggy-haired dog. They were inseparable. I want people to know Jim Jones had a good side," said one old friend.

In Richmond High School, 20 miles from Lynn, James Warren Jones showed some potential for a medical calling. "His six-syllable medical vocabulary astounds us all," says his senior class yearbook. But classmates who were reached after Jones' death catapulted him into some sort of "media immortality," don't remember an overpowering personality. He was remembered as a popular member of the Hi-y, a young man with a growing interest in religion but not as a fanatic, and certainly not as a messiah.

And yet, one middle-aged man who stayed in Lynn recalls another premonition of the macabre. "I had a hunch that something bad was going to happen to him," recollects one man. "He was smart as a whip. But he had some strange ideas. He never fit in with the town. He was different." They notice who's "different" in mid-America.

And so the time came for the "prophet" to leave his home town, to go on to college. He started at Indiana, in Bloomington, then chose Butler University, not so terribly far away at that, in Indianapolis. Jones went through that institution the hard way, doggedly, struggling to support himself and a wife. He eventually earned a Bachelor of Arts degree, but it took him ten years. His studies were off-and-on, partly because he had to work. At one time, he was a hospital orderly. That was when he met, and married, Marceline. Others say he first met her when he was 14 and she 20. Hmm?

It was also when he began his career in the pulpit for real. For a time, he professed that most unusual faith of Unitarianism. Then, he became pastor of a Methodist church in Indianapolis, but he did not achieve 100% backing from this congregation, particularly when he preached integration. Indianapolis wasn't quite ready for that in the 1950's—and he was jeered. People were so upset enough with his views, so heretical for those placid days of the fifties, that they cast dead cats into his church.

Things like that made Jones begin to think, "there was no love" in the Methodist Church. And so he founded his own, the Community National Church, with a brief sabbatical as associate pastor of the Laurel Street Tabernacle. Again, his belief in equality of all, yes, even black people, got him in trouble with his flock. He went so far as to suggest that blacks should be admitted into the Laurel Tabernacle, and that seems to have upset members of the church board. What was needed for all, Jones decided, was a more liberal church—his own.

But the dedicated lover of animals, man, and God needed money on which to found his church. If you bought a pet monkey from a door-to-door salesman in Indianapolis back in 1954, you probably bought your pet from Jones himself. He sold them at $29 apiece. Pedaling a bike from door to door, he made his way around the town and bigots noticed. At one point, he was knocked off his bike by northern "rednecks" but he got up and went on. And by 1956, he was able to open the doors of his new church, the first Peoples Temple, on North New Jersey St., Indianapolis. It had cost him some $50,000 to buy that old Synagogue structure.

The first Peoples Temple, and the second on North Delaware St., nourished the spirits and flesh of its members. Volunteers manned an employment desk, one that actualy helped people find work. There was a nursing home, and a soup kitchen. Jones and Marcie became the parents of a boy of their own, Steven, now 19, and there was apparently room in the hearts of the Joneses for eight more—children of varying racial backgrounds whom they adopted. What must it have done to Jones, and Marcie, when she was spat upon for walking with one of their black adopted children? Six of them, and Marcie, were to die in the jungle with Dad—as followers fondly called the Rev. Jones.

But he seemed to be making a gigantic contribution in the world where it was needed when his Peoples Temples first got underway in Indianapolis, and, before long, (1961), he was appointed director of the 25

26

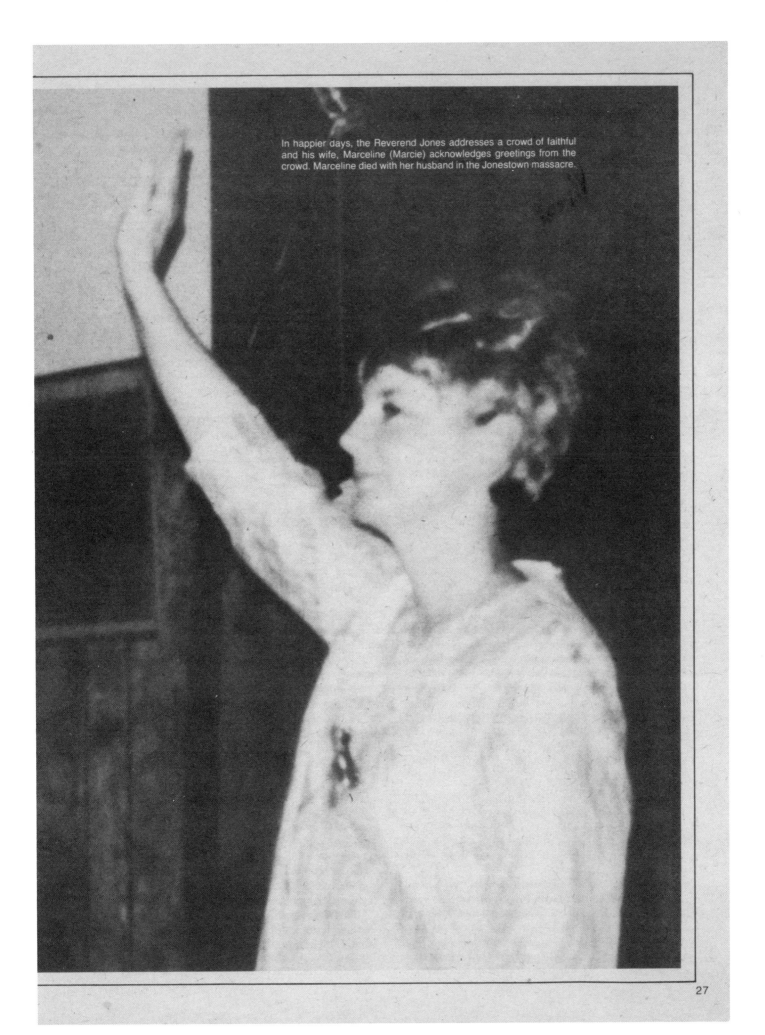

In happier days, the Reverend Jones addresses a crowd of faithful and his wife, Marceline (Marcie) acknowledges greetings from the crowd. Marceline died with her husband in the Jonestown massacre.

Indianapolis Human Rights Commission by Mayor Charles H. Boswell.

Barton Hunter, executive director of the 16,000 member Fellowship of Reconciliation, a 65-year-old pacifist organization, recalled the early days of Jones' church, describing the young clergyman as "an obviously intelligent, eager, concerned person of great initiative." But that was in the 50s. In ten short years, the leader of the Peoples Temple was "healing" the ill instead of merely caring for them, Hunter added. And he was recruiting minority members to his church rather than simply welcoming them.

But Indianapolis was becoming too small for Jones, his churches, and the rest of the people. As though bringing his mother's dream to life, Jones saw himself in a messianic role, leading 70 families who gave up their homes and jobs in Indiana to move to California, because of what Jones considered "harrassment." And all this foreshadowed the even more drastic move of a decade later from California to the jungles of Guyana.

Meanwhile, Jones was being influenced himself, by Father Divine, leader of a black cult in Philadelphia. Jones and some young followers visited Divine and came back with much that would stay with the Peoples Temple, like gospel songs—and demands for fierce personal loyalty to the leader. Before long, the Peoples Temple had an interrogation committee, created at Jones' behest. Its purpose was seemingly to root out those who might speak against the leader. "He said, everybody ought to love him," former associate minister Thomas Dickson, "If they didn't, he'd get awfully violent—not physically, but verbally." And sometimes disciple Judy McNaulty foresaw the worst. "I knew that when he got his idea to play God. Not too long after that, I got out."

And jolting changes came into his church, little things like major efforts not to render unto Caesar. Jones, who professed Marxist leanings, who claimed to be a man of the poor people, was suddenly into big business. One by one, he was establishing a string of corporations. He was making a not-inconsiderable force felt in real estate. One corporation the Jim-Lu-Mar Corp., was an accountant's delight. At least one accountant chuckled as he considered what might happen if what he saw could become available to the Internal Revenue Service.

Showing those millionaire's instincts, Jones once told an associate (as they went about the purchase of a building for one of his two "nonprofit" corporations), "We'd better put this one under Christian Assemblies because Wings of Deliverance won't stand investigation."

Jones' faith began to erode in the early 1960s, and perhaps it was replaced with a new cynicism. Edward Mueller, of Indianapolis, remembers Jones' attempts to recruit him into the ministry. "He said there was no easier way to make money. Once he told me, "Just look at my hands. They're not dirty." And suddeny, Muller found himself becoming a victim. His mother,

at 73 was persuaded to kick in $25,000 in cash and property. And, before he knew it, son Mueller was disinherited.

It wasn't long before Jones' denunciations of the Bible became public, along with his denial of the Virgin Birth. It was in 1961 that he challenged his congregation to say which of them saw it his way. Only one hand was raised against the ancient belief. And guess what? That loyal follower, almost immediately, was made a trusted aide. Others broke from the church when provoked by things like Jones hurling a Bible onto the floor and proclaiming: "Too many people are looking at this instead of me."

And something else was happening in the windmills of Jones mind, manifesting itself in a certain restlessness. Not only bigots were bothering him now, but also bombs. Like his mother, he had a vision. This one was of a nuclear holocaust. Others of his time built bomb fallout-shelters. Jones sought to escape altogether. It was in April, 1962, that he moved his family to Belo Horizonte, a Brazilian industrial city about 250 miles north of Rio de Janerio, a city of two million but one which, according to a magazine article Jones had read, was among the world's nine safest spots should the unthinkable—atomic war—come to pass.

The visit to Brazil foreshadowed Jonestown. In South America Jones and another American, Jack Beam, established a refuge for indigents. For two years, he gave food, clothing and advice to all, including those who answered ads he had printed in newspapers. In Brazil, he found a new influence, perhaps even stronger than Father divine—faith healer David Martins de Miranda, who was considered "Envoy of the Messiah" by his followers, and whose flaming oratory kindled strong responses in those who felt they just had to believe.

What Jones himself seemed to believe in more and more was doom. His fear of atomic annihilation was so intense that, it was said, "There were times when just the sound of an airplane flying overhead would start him crying." And, if the doom came not from a faceless enemy, it might come from within. He told a neighbor that "he had some sort of skin disease that had turned into cancer. He also talked a lot about having been operated on for removal of some warts and moles on his neck. His big fear was cancer." (And, indeed, the world was allowed to know that, at the end, that fear was upon Jones when he told attorney Mark Lane that he had terminal cancer. But when graves registration soldiers at Dover, Delaware, peeled away Jones' skin to find the fingerprints that were to positively identify the body before them, and others completed an autopsy, they found no sign of cancer, terminal or otherwise.)

Back home again in Indiana, new stresses were observed. Former disciple Wanda Johnson remembered that "You weren't even welcome if you didn't have money."...to donate to his church. And, said Johnson,"He stretched everything. If he brought ten

28

180

The Rev. Jim Jones found time to give this German shepherd a pat.

29

181

30

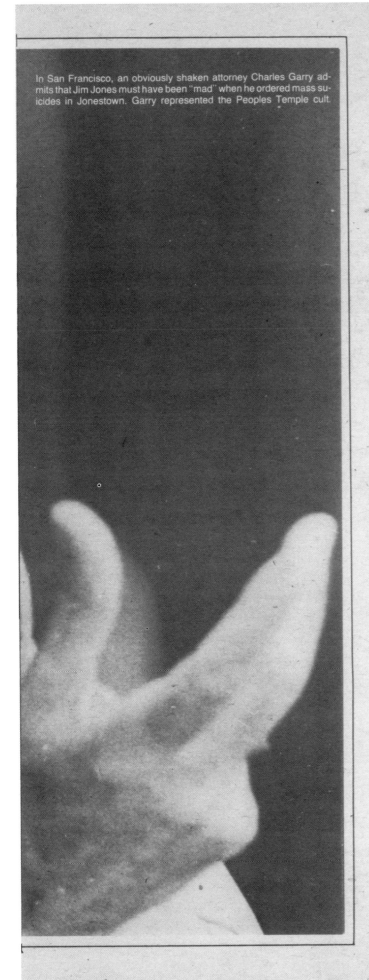

In San Francisco, an obviously shaken attorney Charles Garry admits that Jim Jones must have been "mad" when he ordered mass suicides in Jonestown. Garry represented the Peoples Temple cult.

people to the altar, he would say there were twenty."

And then he began to provide the world with miracles, of a sort. Could he feed multitudes? Maybe. Although one aide reports that "Jim wasn't even a Christian," Jones told an assistant: "You go out and preach, and I'll back it up with miracles."

Now it's 1965, three years after the confrontation between the U.S. and the USSR over missiles in Cuba, and Jones sought out new hiding place from bombers and missiles and all the other things that disconcerted so many more-or-less rational people in those early days of Vietnam. he took 100 or so from Indianapolis to a Hamlet near Ukiah, far in the north of California in Redwood Valley, named after the giants of the forest.

Several hundred of the faithful eventually followed the first trek to Redwood Valley where the predominantly white population viewed the whole thing with suspicion—and, as it turned out, with good reason. Jones was confronted with a tremendous task if he was to succeed in establishing the Temple on California soil. Employment had to be fund for those physically able to work. Nursing homes were needed for the elderly. Money was necessary for recruiting. And it was Jones who had to make all the decisions.

Looking back on his weird career, it's not surprising that he turned to amphetamines, those mind-distorting drugs of high potency, as means of keeping himself working at a furious, little-or-no-sleep, pace. When he made the trip to California from Indiana, two registered nurses accompanied him, supplying amphetamines in pill form and injections. After taking up residence in California, helpful doctors provided him with drugs by prescription and it's said he never left the Temple without a nurse who carried a handbag full of medicines and drugs.

Eventually, the entire work of the Peoples Temple and its congregation became the victims of Jones' drug-induced psychosis. And Jones himself became a speed freak who played god.

Now Jones began to assume a Godlike stance to his worshippers—as must they have been. Many remained in Indianapolis, but those who stayed with him might be rewarded with "miracles." A just society, he told the multitudes who would listen, needs a living God. Guess who that might be.

He affected outlandish garb and attempted healings that an earlier generation might think were made by snake oil. One cure that another acquaintance remembered "had people go to a house and use the bathroom. They would look into the medicine cabinet", she told *Newsweek* "and find medicine for, say, heart disease. Then they'd get this person to come to the church, and Jim would pick the guy out, scare him to death and say, 'you got heart trouble.' Other times, he would tell a person he or she had cancer. Then they would send the person to the bathroom. Usually Marcie would go, too. And his wife would carry back a towel with bloody meat in it. Jim would holler, 'Don't get too close, that's cancer.' But I would look at it and you know, it was the same

31

183

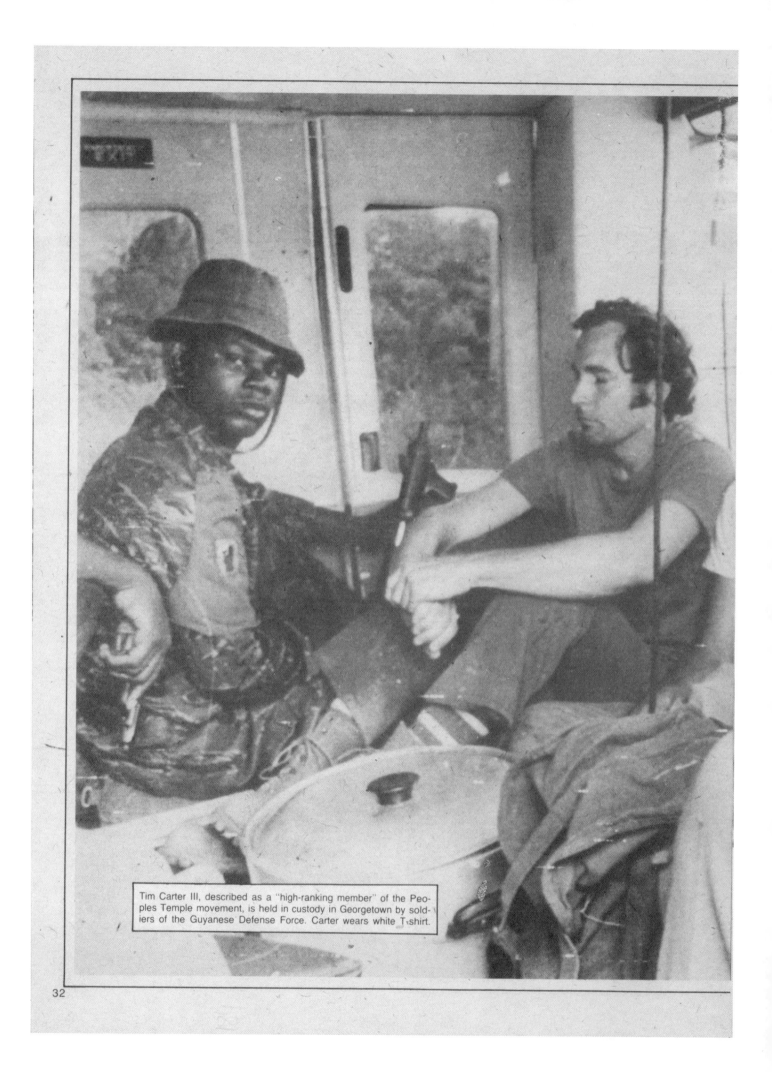

Tim Carter III, described as a "high-ranking member" of the Peoples Temple movement, is held in custody in Georgetown by soldiers of the Guyanese Defense Force. Carter wears white T-shirt.

piece of meat every week. I think they kept it refrigerated."

Later, there were mixtures of chicken entrails and the very blood of Jones' aides. It could, as was reported, be left in a room until the mess congealed into something rancid—and convincing.

Convincing? In those days, Jones was fully able to heal himself of an apparent gunshot wound. Possibly with the aid of "spirits" with which he was in contact. Of course, he had the ability to address an audience that was not entirely hostile. Might he have been able to pack it?

"Dad" had, he said, "the curse" of a huge penis. Of course, that made women beg for his attention. Of course. *Newsweek* claims, no woman in the flock should be denied. A former member of the cult claims that "Once Jim handed out a questionnaire that asked, "Do you fantasize about 'Father' sexually?" Well, the former cultist, Sandy Rozynko Mills, now 19 remembers that she was then 14 and was wondering "What......?"

"But," she remembered, "we were all supposed to say yes, so I said 'yes'."

Fantasy or reality, as is well known, Jones could make great claims. Despite his public beatings of putative homosexuals in Guyana, he did tell attorney, Charley Garry that he had managed sex 16 times in one day. But in a generous fashion. He had enjoyed the favors—and, presumably, vice versa—with 14 women and two men. And it's also whispered that he made at least one error that might be kept in somebody's closet. Five years ago, he was arrested for making an advance to a man in a Los Angeles adult theater. Bad luck, he had approached an undercover cop. Of course, the charges were dropped, for insufficient evidence.

Some idea concerning Jones' bizarre attitude toward sex has been supplied by a former member of his "Inner Staff"—a secret committee of women who served as Jones' personal aides, helpers, couriers and, whenever the situation demanded, his spies. For five years from 1968 to 1973, Ms. Linda Dunn was in this role and told about her experiences and impressions of the Rev. Jim Jones in a recent interview with the *Los Angeles Times*.

Ms. Dunn, who is 35, was among those who "defected" from the Peoples Temple before the move to Guyana, but she says she isn't bitter. Still, she agrees that "there was never really anything good about Jim. Everything he did was unreal. He lived a lie. He told everyone that sexual relations were merely a need for ego fulfillment. But he was using a young woman when I got to Ukiah (where the Temple was located in 1966) and I didn't find out till years later that he really screwed her head around."

In recounting some Temple activities, Ms. Dunn said she was the subject of several of Jones' healings, all of which were phony. She also was among those who would see Jones, claiming to be the reincarnation of Jesus Christ, preach with plastic bags of blood

4

hidden in his hands, then burst them to show his Christ-like hand wounds. Ms. Dunn also said she renounced sexual relations with her husband and, at Jones' bidding, placed her children in the homes of other Temple families.

On occasion, also, she saw Jones collapse from a self-proclaimed "physical attack" of some kind, then call upon his female aides to arouse him sexually as a means of making him well again. Moreover, even while telling his followers they should have no sexual relations at all, he constantly sought relations with his female members and aides (and even males, as mentioned before). As Ms. Dunn described it—"He'd get one of the women to sleep with him, and then he'd put her down in front of the others when she wasn't present."

Despite everything, Ms. Dunn believes she has extracted whatever "positive" there was to be gained from the Temple. "There are things Jim Jones instilled in me that I still carry, and I was never interested in getting back at him. But if my children had been down there in Guyana (which they weren't), I would have been fighting tooth and nail."

Even some two weeks after the events at Jonestown, those who were close to Jim Jones speculated as to what, actually, motivated his mad decision to order the mass suicide, and massacre, of his cult membership as well as those who were investigating its activities. Peoples Temple attorney Charles Garry, interviewed on the CBS morning News, joined others in saying that a custody fight over a six-year-old boy may have unhinged Jones, at least in part.

Little John Victor Stoen, whose body was believed to have been that of a six-year-old boy found near Jones' body at the Jonestown Temple, was the center of a custody fight brought on by his mother, Grace Stoen who was trying to get him back from Guyana. Jones had resisted her efforts, claiming the boy was legally in his custody.

In the twisted last years at Guyana, it is said, young women with posters of movie stars were forced to replace them with blow-up pictures of Jim Jones. And to keep this aspect of his vanity in working order, we learn that his aides would obtain for him such items as mascara to darken his hair and eyelashes, and apply make-believe sideburns and chest hair.

As we have seen, the trail from Lynn., Indiana, to Jonestown, Guyana, was long, bloody and incredible. And the lessons for all mankind are numerous, Jim Jones, for instance, had that magic personal quality called, charisma. It's the quality in a person that appeals to the masses of people—whether for good or evil. Jesus of Nazareth had charisma. So did John F. Kennedy, Richard Nixon, Franklin D. Roosevelt and Adolf Hitler. Billy Graham has it, George Wallace of Alabama has it too, only he calls it "cherisma."

But the point to be made here is: While there's nothing wrong with admiring charisma in a person who professes leadership, just make certain the charisma isn't used for evil.

Eyewitnesses to the Horror:

"HURRY! IT'S YOUR TIME TO GO!"

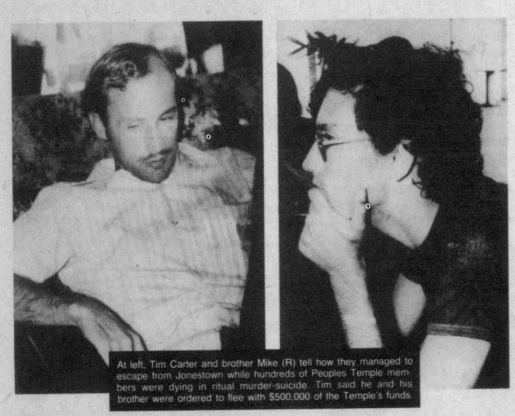

At left, Tim Carter and brother Mike (R) tell how they managed to escape from Jonestown while hundreds of Peoples Temple members were dying in ritual murder-suicide. Tim said he and his brother were ordered to flee with $500,000 of the Temple's funds.

OF course, there were some left to tell the tale.

One survived by sleeping through the last days of Jonestown. Others survived by slipping into the jungle, or by escaping on an airplane meant for the Ryan party. Or by more sinister means. Some of those who did not die were detained by Guyanese authorities who thought these particular survivors might have had something to do with the execution of Jones' last wishes.

Here is what some of the survivors had to say in the first days following the day that shook the world:

STANLEY CLAYTON, 25, a cook who escaped by diving under a tent, crawling through to the other side, slipping under another tent, and dashing into the jungle where he hid for several hours under a log until he no longer heard shots from the camp, told the Chicago Tribune that the finale of Jonestown

was, in reality, mass murder. He said inhabitants were forced by armed guards to take poison as Jones screamed "Be quiet and die with dignity. Hurry up." Guards, he said, wandered through the thongs force-feeding the poison and telling people "Hurry up, it's your time to go." He told Michael Sneed and Timothy McNulty that he saw the dying convulse, with their eyes rolling and bugging out. Some lurched from the supine positions—directed by "nurses" into sitting positions and vomitted. Though some docilely took the poisonous batch of Kool-Aid, others had to be forced. Some of the poison was given intervenously by the "nurses" and "doctor".

Clayton says with a shudder that he remembers Jones pressing his cult to hurry, calling their potion "the last and only drink."

There were debates whether to go through with the mass suicides after the murder of Ryan, Clayton in-

35

187

sists. He says he heard Jones demand: "Who is against taking their own life." And a woman replied: "I have a right to do with my life what I want and you have no right to take my life away from me." She was Christine Miller, says Clayton. Jones' reply was "I can't leave you behind. The GDF (Guyanese Defense Force) will torture you. They will castrate you. They will shoot you after they question you. I can't leave any member of my family behind."

Then, Clayton told the Trib, some residents began to scream: "You don't have any sense. Even if you don't want to die, you're going to die anyway. We will make her die."

(Clayton said the group was surrounded then by guards—dozens of them—armed with guns and crossbows.)

The eyewitnesses reported that Jones ordered the nurses to "prepare a potion," as he called the lethal drink. It took no more than five minutes to produce two tubs from the schoolyard—and a half-gallon jug of poison.

Then Jones uttered the awful words: "Bring the babies first." They did.

Only about 100 were left alive, Clayton says, when he decided to choose life. He snuck through a large tent. Stopped by a guard, Clayton says he told him: "I'm counting the living, but I'm getting ready to go." That meant to the guard, "I'm getting ready to die." The guard embraced him, and turned away and then, Clayton says, he made his stealthy break to life.

LARRY LAYTON, 32, also survived. The Guyanese courts have charged him with the slaying of U.S. Rep. Ryan and four others. Fearing that he, himself, might be an assassin's target, Layton told Sneed and McNulty how it was from his close point of view:

"I remember being there. I remember the sound, something going off—and then, I just wanted to turn myself in to the police." Layton, son of a Quaker and a registered conscientious objector to the war in Vietnam, was behind a double steel screen as he told the Trib team, "I'm so confused. I'm so confused. It was awful. I'm so confused."

Authorities think that he had feigned a desire to defect from the Peoples Temple to go with the Ryan party and back to the U.S. . . . at Jones' direction. Some Guyanese officials believed: "He is terrified for his life, and so are the rest of the survivors. They don't want to go back to the U.S. They fear they will be killed. Some even fear they will be assassinated by a member of the cult send here from San Francisco to carry out the job."

TIM REITERMAN, a reporter from the *San Francisco Examiner*, was wounded in the airport attack in which Ryan and others of his party died.

He remembers glowering faces of those who stayed behind as he and the Ryan party boarded a six-wheel-drive dump truck to the Port Kaituma Airport. He recalls angry shouts and the slime of mud in the truck. And the first threat on the congressman. And a

Two American consular officials are halted at a road barrier as they attempt to enter Jonestown area to pick up survivors. Such security action by Guyanese soldiers delayed flights by hours.

U.S. Army Major Richard Helmling (center) directed task force that evacuated bodies from Jonestown. At left is task force public relations officer, John Moscatelli. At right, U.S. Embassy's Stephane Kibble. They are conferring at Embassy in Georgetown.

reporter saying, as the tension grew at the airport, "I think we're in trouble." And then, the certain knowledge of trouble.

The shooting had begun. "As I dropped to my belly, Reiterman wrote in a copyrighted AP dispatch, "a bullet ripped through my left forearm . . . and another hit my wrist and knocked off my watch.

"They were shooting to kill.

"Springing to my feet, I ran 40 yards across the runway as shotgun, rifle and pistol fire rang out.

"I dove headlong into the tall grass, then crawled until I came to taller bushes and brambles, clawing my way into a pocket in the brush.

"I stopped and listened. The shots still were sounding. I could hear the groaning and crying of the wounded. Although I couldn't see over the tall brush, I could hear the shots become less frequent. Then there were just a few.

"My arm was gushing blood, so I stripped off my belt and pinched down the biggest wounds.

"After a shot or two more, the tractor pulled away. After they had been gone a few minutes, I crept up and saw five bodies around the plane, and a few injured.

"Near the boarding steps was the body of Robinson, with his camera bag and cameras scattered around him. There was a gaping wound in his shoulder and possibly his rib cage.

"Ryan, his thick hair bloodied, was near the front of the plane. Harris, 42, a Los Angeles-based NBC

James Cobb, one of those who went to Jonestown to check on relatives who were there, tells reporters in San Francisco about the murder of Congressman Leo Ryan at the Port Kaituma airport. Behind Cobb is Grace Stoen, former Temple member who tried to regain custody of her six-year-old son from Jim Jones and the cult.

37

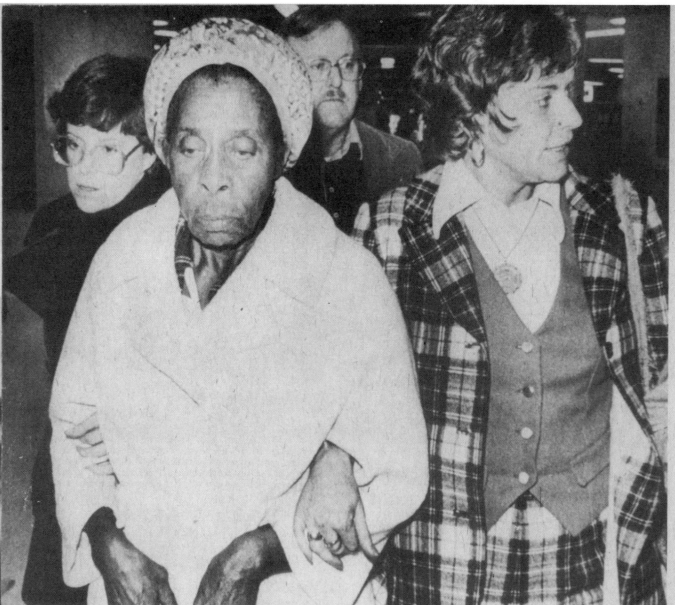

Two elderly survivors of death ceremony come home to San Francisco but they said little, no doubt fearing vengance from members of a "hit squad" reported still active in Peoples Temple.

reporter, had also been killed.

"Also dead was Bob Brown, 35, an NBC cameraman and the sort who relished action stories. Patricia Parks' head was shattered in the doorway of the plane before her husband's eyes.

"Speier's right leg had a gaping wound, and her arm was injured. Steve Sung, NBC sound man, had chunks of one arm blown away. Anthony Katsaris, brother of Jim Jones' aide, Maria Katsaris, suffered chest wounds that caused doctors to remove him from a medical evacuation flight in Puerto Rico.

"By nightfall, the seriously wounded, some of them on litters provided by the community, were sheltered in Army tents. The rest were accommodated in a private home. Every loud sound put the Americans on edge, with some wondering aloud, "will they come back to finish us off?" But during the night, the only thing that arrived was more rumors about the imminent arrival of Guyanese troops and medical evacuation planes."

38

GROVER DAVIS, 79, was a cultist who escaped by hiding in a ditch. Coming home to Los Angeles from Guyana, he said: "Jones didn't force anybody as far as my knowledge, and I didn't see him shooting nobody with no needles and I didn't hear nobody say they wasn't ready to take suicide shots. They were willing to do it."

ODELL RHODES, 36, escaped death. He has described himself as a cured drug addict from Detroit who had lived at the commune since September, 1977. He was widely quoted as saying "They started with the babies."

He said that while he was hiding, he heard only one shot. He said that he slipped out as Jones urged his followers to follow him—to eternity.

Leaning against a fence near the assembly hall, surrounded by guards, he said he had been "thinking about trying to get out of there." His chance came, he told the UPI, when a nurse asked him to find a

stethoscope. He slipped away, and hid, but he said it seemed to him that the cultists lined up for poison without too much need of persuasion, gentle or otherwise.

Rhodes said that Jones had urged parents to tell their children that "it was not painful," and "the children were not crying." Why was everyone so willing to go along with the mind-boggling mass suicide? "Some of these people were with Jimmy Jones for ten or 20 years. They wouldn't know what to do with themselves without him."

"The first adult to die," he said, "was a young woman who went up with a baby in her arms, had the poison shot down her throat, walked into field and sat down and died."

And why was the carnage necessary? When Ryan

Ron Javers, a staff reporter for the San Francisco Chronicle, was at Port Kaituma airport when cultists opened fire on Congressman Ryan and his party. Wrote Javers: "Jonestown is every evil thing that everybody thought. We knew that before the shooting started. The slaughter began at 4:20 pm Saturday at airstrip."

Three survivors who had harrowing escape from Jonestown. Tracy Parks (left), 12, and her sister, Brenda, and Brenda's boyfriend, Chris O'Neal, lived to tell about the airport attack that killed Congressman Ryan and others, including girls' mother, Patricia.

39

191

Hugging each other goodbye, survivors of the massacre prepare to leave Peoples Temple in Georgetown. This group was among first to fly back to States. Others followed on later commercial flights.

Two Guyanese children, who said a 17-year-old relative of theirs had joined the Peoples Temple at Jonestown, sit on a coffin made by their uncle as they await word of recovery of relative's body.

left, Rhodes said, Jones declared, "They will never reach the United States, and we will all commit suicide . . ." If the defectors were allowed to get away with getting away, he said, "others would come from the U.S. and take away their family members. Jones couldn't stand to see his organization break up," Barnes thought. "He had a tremendous ego."

Though he heard Jones demand "You must die with dignity," Barnes added, it wasn't a very dignified death. Many of the dying wept and then, of course, there were the convulsions.

JAMES COBB JR., saw much. From a Jonestown street . . . and later, from the top of a tree in the jungle that lined the airport where Ryan and his party were attacked and so many of them slain.

He saw his two sisters pulled away from him in Jonestown. Mournfully, he recollected almost immediately after the slaughter, "I thought I'd never see them again. They and his mother were members of the Peoples Temple.

Cobb, who opposed the Temple and what it stood for in his eyes, had accompanied Ryan to Guyana. He wasn't a welcome visitor. He had dropped out of the sect in 1973, and filed suit against it last spring.

Almost as soon as the truck rolled out of the compound, Cobb said, those on board were saying, "we

40

192

Seventy-six-year-old survivor Hyacinth Thrush is being carried up stairs by U.S. consular official to begin flight back to United States. Other survivors await their turn to climb steps to safety.

won't get out alive." When Layton got into the truck, apparently posing as a defector at Jones' instructions, "He looked like a crazy man." In Cobb's eyes, "When he got in, I knew there would be big trouble. I told them to keep an eye on Layton." But, he said, Ryan and Jacqueline Speier made the fatal error, despite warnings, of letting Layton onto the plane.

The shooting broke out on the plane as Layton let fly a flurry of death. Cobb says he escaped by ducking behind a plane and dashing for the jungle. He spent that Saturday night in a tree 50 yards into the bush.

"I had a premonition there would be a gunfight," he said. "But I was absolutely incredulous at what was happening because here I am. Last week I was in dental school and here I am, in the jungle, hiding out in a tree where they will shoot me or I'll be eaten by a jungle cat."

He told newsmen that he felt the attack on Ryan et al "meant the end of Jim Jones." But, as he shuddered through the night in that treetop, hearing shots from Jonestown, he really didn't realize they were the accompaniment to the final chorale, the mass suicide.

STEVEN SUNG, 44, an NBC soundman was connected by a cable to one of the newsmen who was slain. Sung fell two feet from his reporter and, cover-

ing his head with his arm, played possum. It saved him.

"The next thing I heard, they were walking toward us," he was to recall later. "Someone shot Bob Brown in the leg. He screamed 'Ouch,' or 'Sh—,' and the next thing I know the guy came close and blew his brain off . . . the next thing I know, I have tremendous pressure, explosion right next to my head and my arm feel like falling apart." That was when the assassins at the airport "finished off" Ryan and two others by firing into their heads at point-blank range.

CHARLES KRAUSE, Washington Post South American correspondent, records some of the last impressions of Jones. He remembered Grace Stoen's observation that Jones was vain and power hungry even though he was always claiming humility. In fact, Stoen had said, he even filled out his sideburns with eye pencil. "It was true," Krause noticed. As the hours ticked away on the final day, Jones exploded at the reporters, Krause says. "Threat of extinction! I wish I wasn't born at times. I understand love and hate. They are very close." He denied reports of physical abuse in the cult. "I do not believe in violence. I hate power. I hate money. All I want is peace. I'm not worried about my image. If we could just stop

41

193

Alvaray Satterwhite (second from left), 61-year-old survivor, arrives in Los Angeles and is tearfully greeted by family members.

Hyacinth Thrush, elderly Jonestown survivor, arrives in Georgetown where she was taken to a local hospital before flying to U.S.

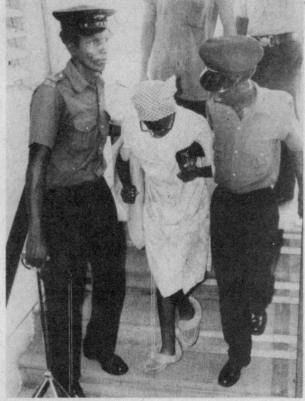

it, stop this fighting. But if we don't, I don't know what's going to happen to 1,200 lives here."

CHARLES GARRY, San Francisco-based attorney, often described as a "radical," who had defended Huey Newton and Angela Davis, among others, says he was able to save Ryan from the first attack. Garry, who made it to safety, had some kind words for the Peoples Temple experience. He called it "a jewel that the whole world should see." But he also recalls the first attack on Ryan, when Don Sly ran up on the congressman from behind, grabbed him around the neck, and brandished a knife, shouting "I'm going to kill you." Garry and Mark Lane, it is reported, wrestled the knife away from Sly.

Then Garry and Lane saw the disaster build further. "When 14 of his people decided to go out with Ryan, Jim Jones went mad. He thought it was a repudiation of his work. I tried to tell him that 14 out of 1,200 was damn good. But Jones was desolate."

The Ryan party left for the airport. Ryan and Lane thought this was a good time to take a walk. When they came back to the center of the village, there were all its residents meeting at what was to be their place of death.

"You and Mark better not attend, because tension is running pretty high against you," Garry says Jones told him. That was good enough advice to the lawyers and they sought out high ground in a guest house several hundred feet from the pavilion.

It wasn't a bad idea to retreat to that previously unprepared position. Lane and Garry became concerned, to say the least, when they saw eight men hurry to a nearby building and arm themselves, with rifles and boxes of ammo. Garry remembers, "These two young men whom I knew very well came to us with rifles at the semi-ready. They were smiling, very happy. 'We're going to die in revolutionary suicide—with dignity and honor.' They were both black. I got the impression that they were sent down to get rid of us."

MARK LANE, attorney, was with Garry still. He was quick, as always, on the feet, when the two young men came at them, according to TIME. Said Lane, "Charles and I will write the history of what you guys believed in." That stopped the gunman for a moment, "Fine," said one. Then, apparently, there were hugs all around. Said Lane, "Is there another way out?" The armed men pointed into the bush, telling the lawyers that it was the way to Port Kaituma. As they struggled to safety, the men heard the last words from Jones: "Mother, mother, mother . . ."

Life at the Peoples Temple:

BE SURE TO LEAVE POISON WITHIN REACH OF CHILDREN

Man's best friend, a lonely dog, wanders through the Peoples Temple auditorium at Jonestown which is strewn with victims' bodies.

WHILE Jimmy Jones had lent his suport to the Carter campaign, had appeared in the hustings with Rosalynn, and had received a polite note of thanks; while his Peoples Temples were endorsed by no less personnages than Sen. Henry Jackson, the late Sen. Hubert Humphrey, HEW Secretary Joseph Califano, Vice President Mondale, Roy Wilkins, the late Mayor George Moscone, and even Bella Abzug—shortly after the first reports of the mass suicide, the State Department admitted it really didn't know much about the Guyana community, and really nothing about its relations with the Guyanese government.

But twice in the preceding year, the Social Security Administration had asked the State Department to find out whether residents of the Peoples Temple were being made to turn over their Social Security checks to the community.

And a $25-a-plate dinner had been planned for San Francisco on Dec. 2—two weeks after the searing events—to benefit the medical program at the mis-

43

sion in Guyana. Entitled "A Struggle Against Oppression," its principal speaker was to have been Dick Gregory, along with the cult's lawyers, Mark Lane and Charles Garry. Plans were made by supervisor Harvey Milk who, it turned out, had a previous rendezvous with fate—and a gunman—in his City Hall office nine days after the jungle calamity.

Besides the suspicious death of Robert Houston, an apparent suicide who stepped in front of a train in San Francisco, the incident that first pricked the curiousity of Rep. Ryan, the curiousity that turned out to be so fateful—and fatal—there were reports from the jungle that the cultists were behaving peculiarly, as cultists will. "A counsular officer might come away from a Jonestown visit somewhat uneasy at the fervor of the Peoples Temple members," an official said later, "But fervor of itself was not his responsibility and certainly not contrary to the laws of Guyana."

In fact, the world was largely blissful in its ignorance of what was going on at Jonestown. And just what was this noble experiment all about? Well, the communards weren't too anxious to tell the outside world. As the clock raced toward the end of Ryan, Jones, Jonestown and the others, Ryan first became uneasy as he noticed the behavior of all the elderly white communards. They were mechanically clapping as they swayed to the beat of throbbing soul music in the last hours of the community. "Look at that man's face, just look at his face," Ryan said at one point as he spotted a middle-aged white, Tom Kice Sr., a man with a gray crew cut who was bouncing around with glazed eyes. But when reporters approached him, he bounced away and melted into the multitude.

Back in San Francisco and Redwood Valley before the 'big move" to the South American jungle, Jones had his own physical and psychological methods for attaining control of those who cast their lot with him—body and soul. He had his legal methods too, such as having his followers sign away their finances, property and even their children. Most of all, Jones was a master at the art of playing on the fears and insecurities of the poor blacks and middle-class whites who came under his influence.

Some of Jones' methods were described by a California woman—Mrs. Jeannie Mills—who has written a book on the subject. Mrs. Mills and her husband had been Temple members for six years after joining in 1969 and leaving its membership in 1975, two years before the move to Guyana. The book describes Jones as a strange figure who puritanically forbid drinking, smoking and sex among his members, then humiliated them by making them participate in public sex acts—with public floggings for those who desisted.

Mrs. Mills says her 16-year-old daughter, Linda, was observed "hugging" another girl whom Jones

44

196

Struggling with two body bags, U.S. military recovery team pushes ahead with task of placing Jonestown victims aboard transports.

45

197

considered a "traitor". For this, Linda was forcibly held by two men and struck 75 times with a long wooden paddle. The girl's screams were amplified to the congregation with a microphone held to her mouth.

Other Jones methods were described as:

Members who couldn't swim were sometimes thrown into a swimming pool with their hands tied behind them—but no one was left to drown.

Although Jones reportedly banned sexual intercourse, even between married couples, he once distributed a questionnaire which asked, 'Do you find your leader sexually attractive?" and "Do you want to have sex with your pastor?" Those who answered in the affirmative were given the opportunity to arrange an appointment.

It was when these methods and others began to fail that, apparently, the Rev. Jones became concerned over losing his hold on his flock—and the prospect of moving to Guyana beckoned:

"I'll be able to keep them in line," he reportedly told the Mills, "when they're in the jungle without any place to go."

It wasn't hard to sell the idea of Jonestown to those who were most vulnerable. They were presented with the notion of a tropical idyll through color movies and expensive full-color brochures. They were presented with a higher ideal: love, racial harmony, good works in a commune where all members were dedicated to the happiness and well-being of all the others.

It was described as a fertile valley, 900 acres of good land wrestled from the jungle. Brochures depicted healthy, tanned women doing laundry, baking bread. Compelling photos of comfortable accommodations were alluring—you would live in well-furnished cottages with rugs and drapes. A school, a clinic, blooming fields and event rudimentary industry beckoned from "an interracial, sharing community." And the final irony: "the laughter of children rings through the air. Our children are our greatest treasure."

It wasn't necessarily so.

The commune seems to have gotten off to an auspicious beginning when Jones and his followers made their way into the back country of Guyana in 1974 and, indeed, succeeded in hacking fields out of the jungle. Houses were built—not the Jonestown Hilton, you understand, but livable. The medical facilities they established were at least superior to most of what was available in most of Guyana. Something like brotherhood of black and white man did exist and there wasn't much bickering or worse on racial bases. Reports back home tended to glow. Maury Janaro, 16, wrote her mother back in San Francisco: "I just picked up a hurt monkey out of the jungle and he's going to be all mine. I love it here."

When some 800 Temple members immigrated to Guyana in 1977, there seems to have been some question as to whether it was in violation of the agreement Jones had reached with the Guyanese government. Also, as Jonestown gradually became an armed camp during the settlement's final year, there are indications that Guyanese officials looked the other way, ignoring numerous warnings as to what was actually going on at the Rev. Jones' domain.

Some on-the-scene observers believe that Jones managed to keep official interference at a minimum with a public relations approach, including charitable and political contributions and even sexual favors extended to influential politicans. It was when these methods, or some of these methods failed, the threats of mass suicide were issued.

Racial harmony was not the norm in Guyana, a former British colony and neighbor of Venezuela. Most of the residents of Jonestown were black American or Caribbean expatriates. Most of the residents of Guyana are East Indian or Dutch laborers. But descendents of African slaves, who are in the minority, control the government and civil service. One of them, Forbes Burnham, the prime minister, is a Marxist and Jonestown, he thought, would be a model community. Furthermore, the commune opened new acres of the nation to farming and that could only help eliminate the food shortages the nation was suffering.

Right up to the end, the commune put great stress on the value of the education of its children. In the rubble, reporters found the school, a 12-by-40-foot shelter of a tin roof supported by posts of wood, not far from the Sojourner Truth Apartments, across from Mary McCloud Bethune Terrace, just off Cussy Lane. It was landscaped with baby plantain trees, many of which have been uprooted and are dead. In the litter, there were textbooks, a blackboard, phonograph records. Music was played and, as in classrooms around the world, there were drawings. The artists worked in pastels and crayons. Jennifer liked yellow. She drew a huge sun rising over a mountain, mostly in yellow. Sonya drew a small dog, entitled "Puppy Love." Nicky drew a fish tank. There were, written in childish hands, slogans like "Jonestown is a place of peace.," and "Be good to those around you," and "Soviet Foreign Minister Gromyko spoke of the problems of strengthening peace in the world over Soviet TV," "Black is beautiful" and "Forbes Burnham, PNC—We Must Have Unity."

But all was not heaven here below, as was to be shown so thunderingly by the visit and assassination of Rep. Ryan and then the mind-boggling end of the whole experiment. About a year ago, the community had to tighten its belt. Though once meat was served twice a day, it was suddenly cut to once a day—and finally, not at all. The working day was changed from eight hours to 11. The guards got tougher. Those close to Jones himself said they saw signs of decay, as though he were as ill as he seems to have imagined. He started to put on weight. His speech came out slurred. His eyes no longer seemed alert—they were glazed. It all became too much for one former close

46

198

The gruesome job continued as even more bodies were discovered, bringing the initial total of about 400 up to nearly a thousand.

aide, Deborah Blakey, last spring. She had the audacity to break out. It drove Jones berserk. He is said to have shouted over and over into the camp loudspeakers, "I am the alpha and omega" and indeed he was. From then on, Jonestown became a prison, a virtual concentration camp in the words of a Newsweek man.

Jones claimed that his Temples had grown to 20,000 members. He began to "heal," by producing "cancers" that were really the gizzards of chickens. It is said that Jones ordered his flock to buy small pictures of himself and sell them to the public as a nemesis against evil. The leader who had, for some time, been calling himself Jesus, assumed the identity of God, the one who made the heavens and the earth.

And now began the beatings. Fear was in control.

Al Mills, 50, a carpenter, said he had witnessed a thousand beatings in five years with the Peoples Temple, including, about 75 times, the punishment of his teenaged daughter. He said he had watched without emotion as the girl was beated with a wooden plank for not obeying the rules of the Temple. "They held down her arms and legs and took out a two-inch thick board," he said. "When it was over, my daughter's butt looked like hamburger meat. Can you imagine sitting there and watching your own daughter get beaten? That's the kind of hold this man had over us."

Mills had signed over 20 houses that he owned to the Peoples Temple when he joined. Now he runs a

Stephan Jones (C), young son of cult leader Jim Jones, tells newsmen in Georgetown that he would continue his father's work if other Temple members wish him to do so. With him are cult members, left to right, Deborah Touchette, Marva Adams and Lee Ingram.

48

17-room center in Berkeley as a haven for former cultists.

That 11-hour working day began, former members recount, with the loudspeakers. It was 6 a.m. when they began with the order to rise and shine. The communards' first business was to hurry to a tent where they lined up for the Jonestown standard meal, the speciality of the day every day, every meal, the only menu: boiled rice, which might occasionally include a soupcon of pig offal or what disenchanted cultists called "pig weed," a bitter green vegetable.

Not exactly lollygagging over their meals, the communards set directly after breakfast off for the day's work: laboring in the fields of the lord—Lord Jim Jones. It was a bitter struggle now with the environment, and the environment, as it always must, seemed to be winning. "We had agronomists, botanists and chemists out there," Harold Cordell, 42, remembered. "But you couldn't make anything grow. The weeds would come back and choke the plants within 24 hours."

Not everybody had to work the fields. There were some privileged characters, and the children. And the workers weren't alone in the fields. Security forces went with them, to keep an eye on them . . . to spy on them. Juanita Bogue, a 21-year-old girl who es-

49

201

caped hours before the mass suicide claimed "We'd work in temperatures as high as 120 degrees all day with only a ten-minute break," she remembered. "If you stopped to rest, and leaned on your hoe, the security forces would write down the time you wasted."

While part of the idea of the commune was to help feed the people of Guyana, by the time of the total collapse of the Peoples Temple, it wasn't even pro-ducing enough to feed itself. Juanita's father, Jim, who also escaped, told Newsweek, "We weren't getting enough protein. They just popped out, boils and blisters." Most of the survivors were covered with half-healed sores all over their bodies. While there were pigs, cattle and chickens on the farm, meat, say survivors, was sold or given to "selected people," like Jones, his family and his favorites.

In the evening came education hour. They seemed

202

endless. The meetings went on and on and on, and the lectures were blared forth from the loudspeakers with so much volume that only the sleep of total exhaustion was possible. And the commodious living quarters? They were well-filled, with maybe 30 people to a unit. On special occasions came the new-celebrated suicide rehearsals, the preview of White Night. Eleven days before the end, one woman wrote to "Dad"-"A few months back, the time we drank the

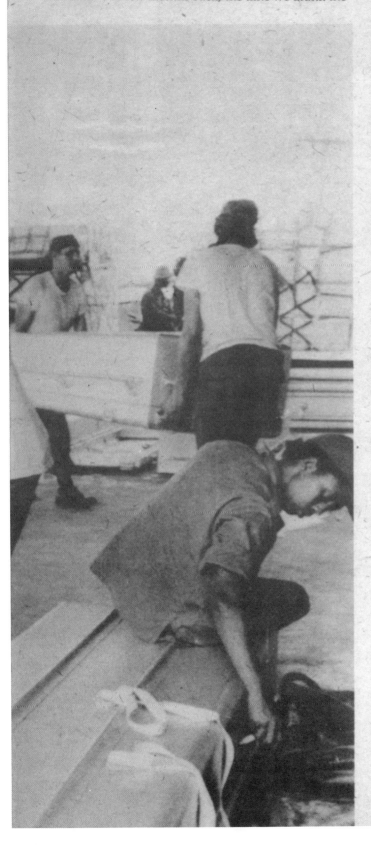

Kool-Aid, I thought it was real. (Her son) stood very close to me squeezing my hand tight and never saying anything. I never said anything to him about my being scared to fight. But he probably knows. What can I say? I'm sorry." The woman, one of those who was finally to play the role for which she had rehearsed, went on, "I used to think about the States all the time. I wanted to go back . . . Now I see how important the structure is and I'm dealing with it. I don't want to go back now or ever."

She wasn't the only one to criticize herself, as Jones had directed. Many such letters were found inside Jones' cottage after the deaths. One of them read, "I have a desire to speak out about the injustice of the oppressed people around the world, but if I had to go anyplace it would be back to the States to fight in the streets if necessary for the freedom of black people, and would gladly die. Dad, I do not want my living to be in vain."

The children of Jonestown, who were to be a part of just about all of its activities, including the punishments and finally its ghastly end, were also encouraged to criticize themselves. One letter was found to Dad from Larry Jones. It read: "Self analist to DAD: 1. I'm guilty because in the states I would always steal pamphlet money and go buy ice cream, candy bars. And stuff like that. And another guilt is I always would fight and get in trouble. And waist Dad and the peoples time on the floor. I'm guilty because I do not show enough time with seniors."

Where there was guilt there was, of course, punishment. It seemed to be the high point of the day for Dad at times. Snitching of food was grounds for public beatings, like those given to Mills' daughter. Mischievious children might be tied up and left in the jungle at night, surrounded by the fearsome jungle cats and other predators that might molest anything, particularly a helpless small human. Or they could be dunked into the well of the commune. That was the visit to Bigfoot, as it was styled on the onetime manganese mine now transformed to a hell on earth. Thrown into the dark well, the child would be pulled underwater by an adult who would also be sure that the child could come up for air. "If he doesn't scream loud enough," an escapee said, "Jones would send the child back down."

"You could hear the child screaming all the way there and all the way back."

Other children , those who forgot to call Jones "Dad," or even those who didn't smile at him, were blindfolded and tied to a stake in the jungle where, they were told, poisonous snakes would bite them. Children might also be tortured by being put in darkened rooms with electrons attached to their bodies. Electric shocks were then applied. Next time, most of them remembered to smile.

Teenagers might qualify for Jonestown's "extended care unit." Those who had erred—by that universal teenage sin of noncomformity—were sent to isolation cells. There they were shot up with drugs, and there

51

203

they stayed for, maybe, a week. "When they came out," Cordell reported, "They were changed. They couldn't talk to you and they walked around with empty faces."

Minor transgressions, like those picked up by the spies in the fields, such as goofing off in the fields, could get you "the floor." That was a performance at those nightly meetings that could run from 7:30 p.m. until 3 a.m. There the transgressor was made to stand before the "throne" Jones established in one of those tin pavillions, the one where were inscribed that paraphrase of Santayana: "Those who do not remember the past are condemned to repeat it." There they would be beaten by guards and otherwise abused in public, of course, until the person being punished, perhaps weeping, would beg forgiveness.

Those who really goofed, by being caught trying to escape, refusing or even showing reluctance to give up personal belongings to Jones, might really get it—severe beatings, by guards or others. Eyewitnesses said that Jones once urged some elderly followers to beat a woman with their canes. "It will be good for your hypertension," he told them.

Once Tommy Bogue, 17, tried to flee. Caught, he was beaten into insensibility by guards and other communards screamed, as ordered, "Kill the little bastard." When it was over, he was shackled in red hot metal handcuffs and put on extra hard labor. Another woman, caught nipping wine, and turned in by her loving husband, was lashed 100 times with a leather belt. Or you could be made to box members of the security forces who were wearing special weighted gloves.

And finally came the rehearsals for White Night, the code name for the mass suicide. One of them lasted three days. That was when the benevolent Dad would call on the people from his throne and demand, "Would you kill one of your children? You would if you loved them enough." And he would ask, "How would you kill your child?" Some might suggest shooting, or something similar. The benevolent Dad would then reply, "Well, I wouldn't kill them that way. I would do it gently with a sedative. Just put them to sleep." That's not quite how it turned out. The five minutes it took the faithful to die finally were agonizing.

The last rehearsal for White Night was indeed a preview. Summoning his people to his tent with his screamed "Alert, alert, alert" over the public address, he told them that their dream of paradise on earth was about to be shattered. He called for a 50-gallon vat, filled with orange drink. It was brought to the pavillion. He commanded his followers to drink, telling them they must, that they had to sacrifice themselves for the "movement." They were told they would begin to feel dizzy, that when they did, they should go out and lie down. All drank. Two women began to moan, and toppled over. Were they plants? The power of suggestion was so strong that many who drank the potion they thought lethal, rushed outside and began to keel over.

52

Like many other cultists, Jones had a need to control the sex lives of his people. A couple who wished to live together had to apply to the camp Relationships Committee for permission. Then came a three-month "dating period," a time of enforced chastity, before they were allowed to have sexual relations. And it wasn't exactly a honeymoon cottage they got even then.

Couples, and single people, slept on a narrow mattress, separated from others in their living cottages only by a sheet hanging from a cord. A witness remembers, "People could hear your every noise, cough and whisper." Interracial "partnerships" were definitely approved. And there was a curious puritanical approach to the affairs. A woman who had been with a man without permission of the Relationships Committee was forced to have relations with another man—before the eyes of all other members of the cult.

Those lengthy "business meetings" by night were meant to be attended by loyal cultists who paid attention. Those who did not pay attention received none-too-gentle reminders from the security people, who would "hit your shoulder and tell you, 'Wake

53

up,' if you started to nod, 'Stand up if you have to. Stay awake.' "

But the image the Peoples Temple attempted to convey to the world, right to the end, was of a viable, going concern. It was really, not much more than a year before the grim end of the commune that Manhattan ham radio operator Paul Miller had contacted—WB6MID/8R3, the Peoples Temple Agricultural Mission in Guyana. He first heard from the mission just after midnight on July 12, 1977.

"We are members of the Peoples Temple in Guyana. We are trying to make contact with someone in Los Angeles to get us medical assistance. Can you help us?"

It was no problem for an old pro among amateurs, like Miller, who quickly reached another ham in L.A. Soon he was to receive a long letter of thanks from President Carter and from the Temple. The letter from the Temple did include some special pleading. It fairly glowed with zeal and optimism. "We now

have a thousand residents, here in the community," it read. "And we have been able to help many people in surrounding communities as well as our own with a variety of needs. Our medical facilities have expanded and we are planning to even do more in the near future to help as many as possible. Agriculture, livestock, construction and all kinds of projects that have been developed are proving that, even in the jungle, people who work together can accomplish much. We are inspired by what has been accomplished through combined efforts and a spirit of good will and service to our fellow man."

But meanwhile, Rep. Ryan was beginning to have his doubts, the doubts that were to kill him. It was only as recently as 1976 that Mayor Moscone appointed Jones director of the San Francisco Housing Authority—but that was what seemed to have triggered the first published reports of excesses within the Temple in Guyana—reports that had, until

54

206

A small arsenal of weapons was found in the Temple at Jonestown after Guyanese soldiers moved into the area to conduct search.

207

The job of removing more than 900 bodies from the Jonestown jungle village is finally over. Here, a member of the U.S. military recovery team leans against empty, unused caskets at Temple site.

then, only been whispered rumors. When Moscone said, in 1977, that "From everything I've seen, he's been a good chairman," his remarks were countered by comments from former Temple members. The *Daily News'* Theo Wilson reported that since Temple members had begun to talk more freely, they had begun to tell tales of a "slavemaster" who conducted fake faith healings, and mass torture sessions. There were charges of beatings, death threats, exhausting work schedules, with members being forced to contribute a fourth of their income if they lived outside the Temple and to donate all of it if they lived within it.

The words that perked the curiosity of the congressman came from Sam Houston, son of apparent suicide Bob Houston, who died in 1976 after dropping out of the Temple. The father, a photographer for the Associated Press, insists that his son was driven to self-destruction because of brainwashing by Jones. "Jim Jones is an animal," the elder Houston said. "He is insane. All of the Temple members are insane. They no longer have minds of their own, they are zombies."

Ryan, who had taught young Houston in high school, began to look into the reports he had heard, and that was the beginning of the end for him and most of the cult. But not for all of it. It continues in San Francisco, and there are survivors of the mass suicide, some free on the West Coast, and some incarcerated in Guyana.

56

Can It Really Happen Again?

Asked by newmen if he were insane, Charles Manson replied, "It all depends on your point of view." Exchange took place outside Los Angeles courtroom in 1970 in Manson's trial for murder.

CULTS ARE THRIVING ON THE AMERICAN SCENE

THE devastating news from Guyana shocked the world but few found it unbelievable. The world had been prepared to an increasing extent in recent years to believe that masses of little people, seeking something to cling to in an uncertain world, might attach themselves to one strong personality. A Charles Manson. An Adolf Hitler. A Chairman Mao. An Elvis Presley. A Jimmy Jones.

Though many of the more popular cult figures, like Presley or Shaun Cassidy, might do little harm, others had proven a sinister bent, an ability to cause others to work wickedness.

Manson, be it remembered, was able to persuade his "family," that poor assortment of souls who clung to him on the Spaun Ranch in the California wilderness, to slash actress Sharon Tate and others to death in his name. And not only in the name of the wizened little murderer—also to bring down "Helter Skelter," a code name, interestingly enough, taken from the name of a Beatles song—and it meant what Manson considered to be the inevitable war between blacks and whites, one that Manson seems fervently to have hoped the whites would win—overwhelmingly. And the waifs of society—young divorcees, children of the middle class whose dreams had shattered—were in his thrall not only when each joined him in sexual orgies, but for months later as they underwent their trials for the blood-stained slaughter they worked. They were willing to hack innocent strangers to death and assume blacks would be blamed. They were willing to try to silence one of their own by feeding them hamburgers laced with L.S.D.

Manson's commune wasn't the only one around in those early days of this decade, but it was to become a household word, unlike most. What was it that made the leader able to inspire those zombies to such evil? Some thought it was simply a look from his piercing black eyes. Hard to believe. But reporters who attended the Manson trial said that you felt the eyes were hypnotic as he stared at you—thinking who knows what?—in the courtroom. Many of the reporters who felt that cold stare may have been quite relieved to know that Manson's sentence was for life—and they may not have been overwhelmed with disappointment when they learned that his plea for parole had been denied last fall—right around the time of the end of the Peoples Temple, Jonestown branch.

While the excesses of the Manson family were surely the most spectacular workings of wickedness fostered in recent year by just one man, the public had also become accustomed to many other cults and cult-like organizations that could awe you simply by the iron hold they took on loyal throngs of imposing size and devotion.

The Moonies. The Rev. Sun Myung Moon was quick to denounce those who made comparisons of his Unification Church with the Peoples Temple and other cults. "The tragedy in Guyana was in all our minds (this week)," he said one point when it was, indeed, Topic A in all the papers and electronic media reports. "One reason is that we all realized that we could be destroyed by a mad man in power. But today at the push of a button, we could be destroyed by nuclear warfare. This is why we must restore sanity to our world—to save the world from moral and physical destruction." And, of course, one very good way to do that is to renounce this world and embrace the Unification Church to one's bosom.

Whether or not that Unification Church provides the answers most of us seek, it certainly has provided New Yorkers and residents of other cities with un-nerving sights—the beautiful, flower children selling candy for the reverend, singing pretty songs in sa-loons to raise that money—clean youths with short haircuts, clean clothes and the faces of automatons. They are dedicated. The sort of personal sway Moon holds over his followers is enough to overpower any attachments to home or other familiar surroundings, enough to forsake all to work without question for the reverend and his various activities.

Many people think that the recruiting techniques of Moon and his aides have reached the highest level of sophistication of any of the cults. They begin with the assumption that all people are vulnerable. For college

Devil worshippers perform a ritual before a black-shrouded altar in basement of a suburban Louisville, Ky., home. This couple organized a local chapter of satan worshippers. The parent organization was based in San Francisco and claimed 15,000 members.

59

211

Escorted by a dozen New York City policemen, Father Divine leaves courtroom after being arraigned on charges of assault. . . .

students, the time might be ripest at examination time, a time of tension and insecurity for all but the most intellectually gifted—and self-confident.

Exam time is a time when many a backpacker is born, a time of dropping-out—to "find" oneself, as so many of today's youth have done.

Richard Delgado, a professor of law at UCLA, told *Newsweek* that "These kids are looking for a sense of significance and belonging. Everybody is vulnerable. You and I could be Hare Krishnas if they approached us at the right time."

When they find someone who seems susceptible, the Moonies launch their "love bombs." Lonely students might find themselves casually brought into conversation and then, apparent quick friendship. Maybe a young person will find himself invited to dinner on the spur of this sudden, and very welcome, relationship. And it deepens, or so it seems. Soon there are bunches of smiling strangers, bombing away with that love. New people want to hold their hands and then come the compliments, the flattery . . . the invitation to a weekend retreat.

It starts out with continuous games and songs and

endless bull sessions which might make a glancing shot at religious discussions. What there is not a lot of is sleep. And what there is also not a whole lot of—but few realize it at the time—is truly frank discussion or genuine closeness. Probing questions are not encouraged and attempts at true personal relationships may be met with the old brush.

"As instructors, we didn't tell them the truth," Erica Heftmann was to relate in retrospect. "If we had told them that we believed Moon was the Messiah or that we stayed up all night praying in the snow, they'd never join."

Instead of genuine friendship, the recruits find themselves provided with escorts—monitors who stick to them like flies to flypaper—old Moonies who go everywhere with them, even to the lavatory. The washing stage of the mind of potential cultists requires isolation from former friends, family—all the trappings of the familiar world. On the Sunday of the weekend retreat comes a big step, and one that is nearly always as good as final. The recruit is cajoled to stay for one last party.

"Once they called their family or employers and

60

Unification Church faithful hold a giant rally at the Washington Monument. They heard an address by Korean evangelist Sun Myung Moon, head of the Unification Church's membership.

told them they weren't comng in on Monday," Heftmann has said, "we knew we had them for seven full days. And if they stayed seven days, they almost always became a member."

But more time yet is needed to make a full-fledged member. You've got to be carefully taught to love Charles Manson, or Sun Myung Moon, or Jimmy Jones. Some of the time-honored means, as used by the Moonies and the Hare Krishna and the Children of God provide new names, or private members of time, known only to the initiated, to develop mind control. Members can probe the minds of the new people to find where they feel the deepest guilt about their "former" lives. The guilt may be assuaged if the newcomers renounce their past and prepare themselves to be reborn, like "me, your new brother, or sister," in their new family, the cult. As captured GIs may remember from the brainwashing days in Korean prisoner of war camps in the early 50s, other techniques help in the building of new minds and personalities. Like forms of sense deprivation, through loss of sleep, or low-protein diets. Cultists may add to these exhausting rounds of praying,

chanting and study of the dogma of the new father figure.

Sex is at the core of many cults and it can be usd as a way of keeping the members in order. In the order, that is, that might be preferred by a Jones or a Manson or, in his own way, by a Moon. Manson and Jones, of course, used followers—both ladies and gentlemen—for their own sexual gratification. Other cults keep the sexes apart and some even preach that sex is naughty. All Moonie marriages are the business of Moon himself, who arranges all of them. Life in his community is so monastic, so laced with guilt trips about sex, so repressive of natural urges that, we are asked to believe, the beautiful children may revert to the innocence they enjoyed before the charming age of puberty. One Moonie dropout, 24-year-old Christopher Edwards, told *Newsweek* that "Women stop having their periods sometimes and men may find that they do not shave as often." So that's why they seem so clean-cut. "People begin to look younger," Edwards has claimed. "I was 22 when I came out and people told me I looked 15."

The general public readily accepts weird goings-on,

61

213

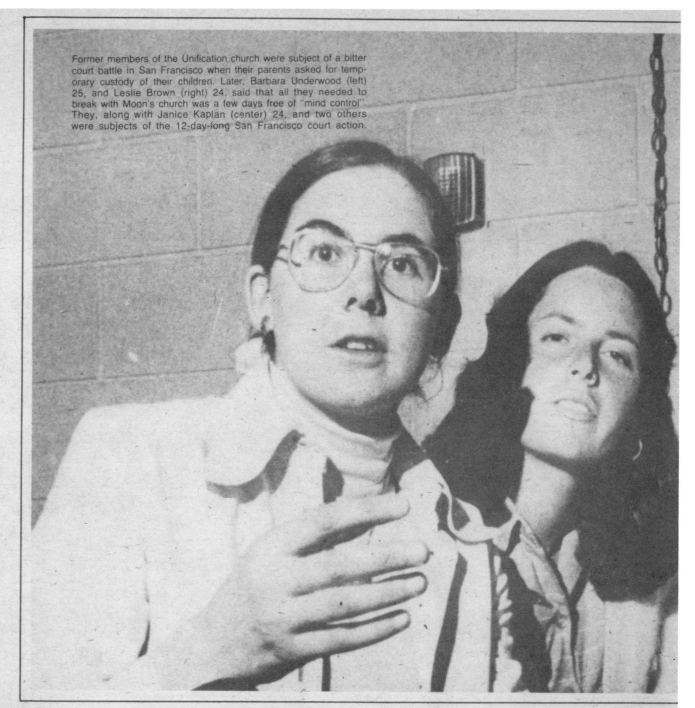

Former members of the Unification church were subject of a bitter court battle in San Francisco when their parents asked for temporary custody of their children. Later, Barbara Underwood (left) 25, and Leslie Brown (right) 24, said that all they needed to break with Moon's church was a few days free of "mind control". They, along with Janice Kaplan (center) 24, and two others were subjects of the 12-day-long San Francisco court action.

like voodoo, that are associated with cults. When that presumed enemy of Synanon found a rattlesnake waiting for him in his mailbox, people in the 'pubs said, "Gee whiz, we wouldn't put it past them," even though they had little if any first-hand knowledge of those involved. You just expect the off-beat. There may be something in the California air, however, that helps cults take root. Of course, most of the Guyana lemmings were from San Francisco or thereabouts. And both Mayor George Moscone and city supervisor Harvey Milk were mentioned in the first newspaper accounts of the background of Jones. And they, of course, were dead almost within a week of his finale, murdered, it is asserted, by Dan White, a former city supervisor himself who had resigned his appointment, reconsidered, and now was being rejected in

his bid to return. No one has, by the way, made an allegation of any further connection between the tragedy in Guyana and the slaughter in San Francisco that followed.

But it was unsettling to San Franciscans, who, on the one hand, live in one of the most civilized cities of the world and who, on the other hand, are able to say things like "California is going nuts. Everyone's killing everyone." Herb Caen, a steadfast defender of that bay city where so many have lost their hearts, stoutly spoke for his city in his column. "The kook capital . . . we who have lived here a long time resist that description. What others call 'kook,' we look upon as characters in a charade we smile at. We think we understand that show, having played our own roles for so many years. Maybe we are wrong."

62

Quick to put things into perspective was Dale Hess, assistant general manager of the Convention and Visitors' Bureau. "This could have taken place in any city," he pointed out. "It shouldn't affect tourism." He meant to say it shouldn't reduce tourism, it shouldn't frighten people away. The scary thought is that it might attract some people. And those are the sorts of people who might be attracted to a cult.

Cults are, by definition, religious in nature, although the religion may not be one that you prefer. But religion it is. Are you sure that those who worshiped Elvis, the man and the legend, weren't seeing something of a deity? Perhaps a lesser one than some of the traditional ones, but nevertheless a deity.

Those who followed Father Divine believed indeed that he was God. He attained that plateau in 1932 and, by 1939, had been promoted . . . to Dean of the Universe, which, in the eyes of his followers, was an even bigger job. Father Divine enters this narrative at this point because it was he who inspired the young Jim Jones. Father Divine, born as George Baker and as the son of a slave, died fabulously wealthy—at perhaps 100—in 1965. He had been for most of the 20th century the leader of an international religious cult whose central article of faith was that the Father was God. It appealed to legions of black people—and attracted the notice of Jimmy Jones, who learned much at the feet of this master during a visit to Philadelphia in the declining years of the Father and in the ascendancy of the preacher who was to become "Dad." Father Divine's legacy to the Peoples Temple

63

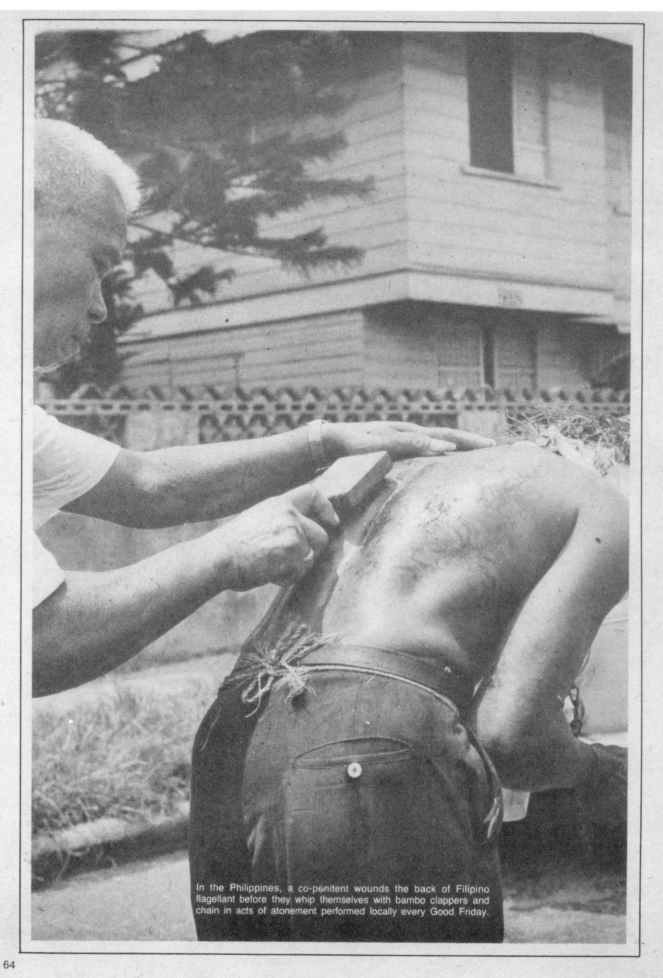

In the Philippines, a co-penitent wounds the back of Filipino flagellant before they whip themselves with bambo clappers and chain in acts of atonement performed locally every Good Friday.

64

Cult bomber and victims. Peter Kamenoff (second from left), also known as Brother Elzibah, was identified as one of the two men who killed themselves and eight others by dynamiting the main buildings of a religious cult near Chatsworth, Calif., in 1958. Cult was known as "Fountain of the World." (Wide World Photo)

included a fistful of gospel songs—and the sure knowledge by the leader that complete dependence on him by his followers was absolutely necessary.

At the end, Father Divine died in bed on his vast estate, Woodmont, in Gladwyne, a suburb of Philadelphia. At his bedside were his white "spotless virgin bride" and 18 "secretaries." The pudgy five-foot-two "messiah," as contemporary accounts named him—in quotes—was worth anywhere from six to $200 million.

His church seems to have gotten off the ground in the depths of the depression, in 1932, when a New York judge sentenced him to a year in prison for maintaining a nuisance by giving elaborate and noisy feasts. Four days later, there went the judge . . . dead suddenly. He had, to all outward appearances, been in good health. The word swept Harlem: "Our Lord done struck down the judge," and "Thank you Father. It's wonderful!" Whether or not Father Divine really had anything to do with the departure to greener pastures of Justice Lewis J. Smith, the Appellate Division for sure granted an appeal a few months later from Smith's verdict in the Suffolk County police raid on Father Divine's "heaven," where they picked up 80 noisy practitioners, including the Father himself.

Harlem was ready for miracles. Before long, mil-

lions became converts. The converts, Father Divine's "angels," forsook earthly possessions, giving them to Father, who, in turn, welcomed them into his "heavens," where they could eat at 15¢ a meal and live, at $2 a week. The Divine enterprises included cooperative businesses, like groceries, coalyards, bakeries and dressmaking shops. In time, he had millions of followers, thousands of them white.

Divine had come up from slavery to surround himself with a sort of beauty and a very practical way for desperate people to survive a depression. His angels took gorgeous names, like Virtue Bloom, Glory Heart, St. Luke Faith, Holiness Love, Light Child. When not turning a tidy profit for the collctive good, they attended to their devotions. The services were productions of vast sweep, featuring, of course, inspirational oratory: "It is personifiable and repersonifiably metaphyzcalzationally reproducible. . ." It wowed 'em. Against pollution (they had it way back then, too, you know): "Do they want those things filled with the contagious germs of diseases that will destroy the people or do they want God on earth in a body that is bringing peace out of confusion, joy and happiness."

Can you guess the answer? You can? Did you guess:

"It's wonderful to be in love with Father. It's won-

65

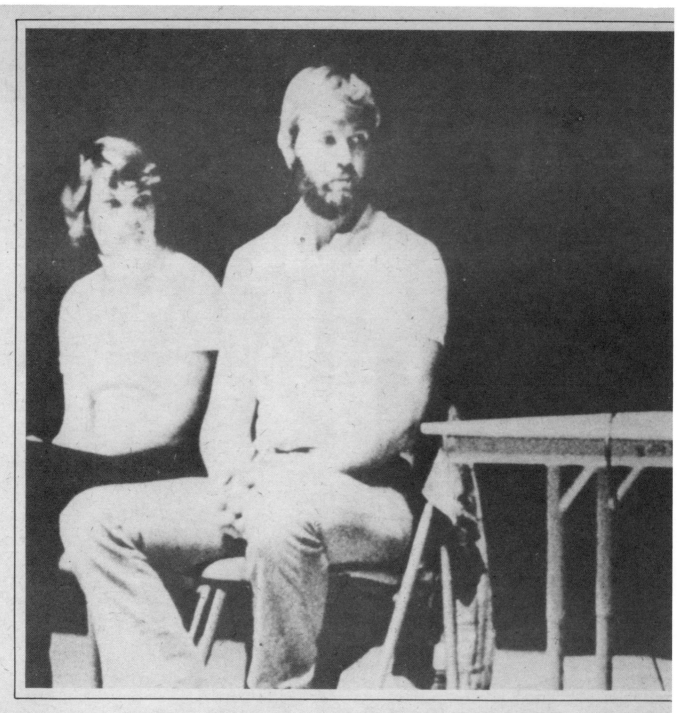

derful to be in love with you, dear sweet Father Divine. You're in this heart of mine. It's wonderful to be in love with you."

Besides this rare incantation, the services included singing, dancing and feasting to prepare the mind and body for ectasies—or mass emotionalism, as cynics called it—testimony by angels to help correct the thinking of those who had slipped or failed to see the light year—pictures, signs and symbols to remind believers of their leader, if he were not corporally present.

Divine knew his roots. He came from a long line of religious leaders. The slaves owned by Benjamin and Samuel Baker, who settled near Savannah, Ga., in about 1760, came from the Ivory Coast, in west Africa. They descended from the Galas, whose chiefs

were semigods and doctors of magic.

After the Emancipation Proclamation, some of the former slaves—who had by now adopted the name of their owner, Baker, moved toward Savannah, where George Baker was to be born. Those who raised him imbued him with the best of Christian and the best of pagan virtues to help him survive in a hostile world. Before long, Baker began to realize he could work miracles—very convincing ones—and he went from a 50¢-a-week gardener to a millionaire cult leader, genuinely beloved by the multitudes who greeted each other with "Peace, brother," and what's bad about that?

He was surely convincing, so much so that he put a taboo on sexual relations, even between man and wife, and made it stick. Meanwhile, he found work

66

218

Him and Her (right), as they termed themselves in Oregon when a number of persons gave up their "worldly possessions" and agreed to take a trip on a spacecraft to "a plane higher than Earth."

for the neediest angels, and persuaded many who had given up all hope of improving themselves to educate themselves as well as they could. Would he rip off good angels like Understanding Wisdom, Joy Love, Perserverance Star, Peace Harmony, Faithful Heart, Living Rest? Maybe a little. Maybe a lot. But, in the last analysis, life in his heavens was probably much better than life on this earth for most of his devout followers.

Though his heaven—and his demands on the total faithfulness of his people—served as a model for Jimmy Jones' utopia, it is not reminiscent of some other cults that live today. Cults that menace. Are you sure that the Peoples' Temple has not sent emissaries of survivors out into the world to bring more to join Jones and the others in death?

And what other cults may lurk in shadowy worlds, awaiting the chance to break out and work who knows what evil on who knows what people for who knows what twisted purpose?

Cults, appealing to the lonely, the nurses of deep formless angers directed against who knows whom, are everywhere. While many, even most, have innocent enough beginnings, even highly admirable ones, they can be contorted to tragic ends, like the Peoples Temple and the Manson family. The discipline, the blind allegiance demanded of those who would be admitted to the holy presence of the leader, can be directed to evil ends. Another Guyana is by no means impossible.

People who feel no direction in their life, no firm commitment to religion, no dedication to their work

As one woman handles a curled snake, others participate in services at the First Strait Creek Holiness Church in Rainsville, Ala. Some states have passed laws against snake-handling cults.

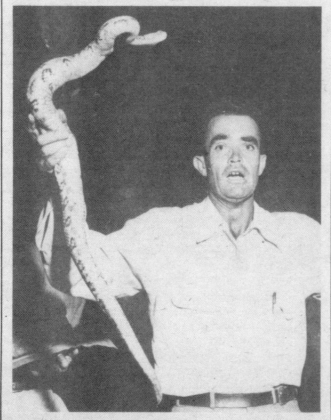

Because of adverse publicity, many snake-handling cults have gone underground and allow only members to witness services, such as the one shown above. Handler has in tow two writhing rattlesnakes.

68

At Manchester, Ky., in remote hills, a Holiness Church congregation member demonstrates his faith by handling four rattlers.

or their family or any guiding philosophy can be lured into cults.

One of the tragedies of the Symbionese Liberation Army, kidnapers of Patricia Hearst, was that they had ideals of a better world—but they thought in their misguided innocence that they could make it a better world with guns and bombs and fire. Instead, their world ended in a flaming, suicidal shootout with Los Angeles police. Similar misfits made up the Manson family, who saw little Charley as Jesus Christ. While Manson preached of love, he demanded gory violence and that finally spelled the end of his band. Jones followers looked on "Dad" as God. He preached love, but led the devout to mass murder and suicide.

"The cult leaders may not start out evil," says Margaret Singer, a clinical psychologist at the University of California at Berkeley (not so very far from San Francisco), "But it's almost the age-old motto: 'power corrupts.' When the group gets to a certain size, the leader starts telling the group that the outside world is against them. A kind of paranoia grows up. It's when they feel they have to defend themselves against the outside world that the potential violence develops."

(And it wasn't long after the last body was flown to Dover, Del., from Guyana when reports were begun to be received of the convoluted codes with which the Peoples Temple was able to slip an arsenal past Guyana customs, and how Jones may have secretly banked upwards of $10,000,000 for himself.)

If the cult leader suddenly begins to believe what may have started out as the big lie—that of his own divinity—the problem compounds, and the potential for disaster quickens.

New York City police psychiatrist Dr. Martin Symonds reminded Alton Slagle of the *New York News* that in religious or patriotic fervor, ordinarily decent people have done horrendous deeds of violence. Says Dr. Symonds, director of the "victimol-

Flashing his "promised land" smile, Father Devine rides head car in a parade of some 2,000 of his "angels" on their way to their "heaven" in Ulster County, N.Y. Year of this movement was 1936.

70

program at the Karen Horney Clinic; "Individuals devoted to a cause will conduct acts based on a higher order. It depends on what the leader of the cult pulls. It can be brainwashing, involving terror or love. True religions don't teach this," he says, "True love gives freedom. But someone who feels hopelessness is always searching for a leader. He reaches out for someone to lead him from the wilderness. Most of us maintain reasonable loyalties but still have reason to question. But this is almost like selling your soul to someone for promises he offers. If you're that emotionally hungry, you'll do it. It's a delusion of belief based on the need for safety. If you're frightened enough, you'll follow any leader. Violence is the quickest solution to any conflict."

One man who was saying "I told you so," is Gifford Cappellin, a Pennsylvania lawyer who works with a deprogramming group called Freedom of Mind Inc. The group has restored hundreds of onetime cultists to this world, including quite a few who had been directly connected with the Peoples Temple.

Cappellin talking to Slagle of the *Daily News*. "We've been telling the government for years that this would happen," he said. "It is highly probable," he adds, "that the Moonies and others could be involved in suicide and terrorism. Many Freedom of Mind staffers are former followers of Moon."

Bizarre things happen. In Rochester, N.Y., the Sudan Muslems carved a man up, sticking him with a knife near the heart, cleaving his breastbone, tearing open his stomach. The leader said the man had asked for the ritual of "a cleansing ceremony."

Two leaders of the Body of Christ Church in Maine were hauled before a court and charged with beating a waitress until she spat blood. That was to exorcise the devil from her body.

Synanon, which began as a widely-admired society of those dedicated to kicking the drug habit, all of a sudden showed members on the streets with shaved heads. Two of its members were charged with conspiracy to commit murder by placing that rattlesnake in the mailbox of a lawyer they considered an enemy. And sex reared its sometimes ugly head. Tales began to slip out of organized wife swapping among the membership—and the forming of an armed guard, for self-defense, of course, with the fancy name of the Imperial Marines.

The Circle of Friends took root in Morristown, N.J. It was the dream of a wartime Nazi collaborator, now a middle aged suburbanite. It was reported that he was buying up expensive estates, and that he was developing a cure for cancer. He let it be known that he was developing a cure for cancer, and that he sat at the head of a band of young people—the friends. Such good friends. They were such good friends that they gladly worked 16 hours a day and willingly turned over their paychecks to the leader.

A chapter of the Church of Satan was doing well enough in Germany that a private firm found it worthwhile to donate $30,000 to teach military chaplains what to do about that satanic church.

The farthest out? Maybe it was Him and Her, the unisex him and her from Oregon, who dressed alike and thought alike and were able to get across their message: that they were awaiting a space ship that would pick up a deserving few and rocket them to a better world. To show themselves deserving, of course, potential passengers would have to prove themselves to be scornful of the material possessions of this world. Enough so to sacrifice them. To donate them to Him and Her. All of them, of course.

When the youth movement of the sixties failed to bring paradise to earth, RIGHT NOW, it may have had something to do with the surging popularity of cults. That's what Katherine Kemp told *Daily News* Washington reporter Judith Randal. "When the riots and demonstrations failed to eradicate strife and human suffering," she said, "people, young people especially, turned for answers to a religious, seemingly peaceful solution."

And so, suddenly, there appeared on the street corners of America unknown numbers of bald-headed, saffron-robed young Americans chanting, "Hare Krishna, Hare Rama," a prayer reputed to have its origins in the earliest days out of the caves and trees. And it succeeded in an equally ancient art. As soon as mankind wore pockets, they needed to be lined. Who knows what the Hare Krishna movement was worth to A.C. Bhaktivedanta Swami Prabhupada, scholar of Sanskrit and Calcutta chemist, founder of the sect, before his death last year at 81?

And who knows what will be the outcome of the trials to be faced by 11 officials of the Church of Scientology, who are to be tried on charges of conspiracy to burglarize government offices, steal documents and plant spies and bugging devices in federal agencies. Nonsense, say the Scientologists. Government persecution. It all grew out of a continuing war between the Church of Scientology and a foe worthy of respect, the Internal Revenue Service. Seems the feds are having the devil's own time with a legal battle to end Scientology's tax exemption as a nonprofit church.

And what will come of a House subcommittee's finding that Moon's Unification Church has been constantly braking federal laws in a campaign to build a worldwide government based on the church. The committee, in an 18-month investigation, found that the church had used thousands of members and millions of "Moonbucks" to conduct business and political activities here and abroad. Many of the enterprises, the subcommittee felt, dodge immigration statutes, financial laws and tax codes, meant to keep a check on churches with federal tax exemptions. That, says the church, is a good example of hounding by a government.

And who knows when will come another incident like the killing that accompanied the 1977 seizure of buildings in Washington, D.C., by Hanafi Muslims.

Or when will come another scene to rival the one in Jonestown?

Of intense interest to millions around the world are

71

With a scratched cross visible on his forehead, Charles Manson is led into court at Los Angeles for trial on murder charges in the death of actress Sharon Tate and six others at Tate mansion.

the comments of evangelist Billy Graham. His thoughts on the subject of Rev. Jim Jones and the Jonestown tragedy appeared recently in a statement in the *New York Times* and are quoted here in part:

"As the nations of the world reach for new levels of affluence, social and economic prosperity, they are bewildered when these things do not bring personal peace or fulfillment. People are confused, but true inner peace never comes through possessions or 'the better life.' Perhaps this is why we are living in a time of such tremendous spiritual experimentation. Thousands are turning to gurus and cults of various sorts. Voodooism, satanism, witchcraft and other demonic forms have emerged from their closets to haunt us in our generation...

"An individual's life can only be transformed by a personal experience with God that gives to each one moral guidelines and a new value system. Unfortunately, in that search for God it is all to easy to blun-

der into the arms of Satan instead.

"This is what happened in Guyana.

"One may speak of the Jones situation as that of a cult, but it would be a sad mistake to identify it in any way with Christianity. It is true that he came from a religious background but what he did and how he thought, have no relationship to the views and teachings of any legitimate form of historic Christianity.

"We have witnessed a false messiah who used the cloak of religion to cover a confused mind filled with a mixture of pseudo-religion, political ambition, sensual lust, financial dishonesty and, apparently, even murder. None of this has anything to do with true faith in God......

"Apparently, Mr. Jones was a slave of a diabolical supernatural power from which he refused to be set free. He was like a drug addict or an alcoholic who refuses to admit need, or to seek help from the only one who could have set him free—God!"

72

224

Andrea Robinson, sister of slain news photographer Greg Robinson, expresses her grief in arms of a relative at church services.

COULD JONESTOWN HAVE BEEN PREVENTED?

HISTORIANS were quick to recall other times when huge numbers of people had voluntarily ended their lives, as it became more and more clear that practically all of those who died in Jonestown had been suicides.

For the Jewish Zealots of Masada, threatened in 73 A.D. with slavery under the swords of Rome, death was preferable to subjugation. The Zealots, organized at the time of Herod the Great, were a Jewish sect that revolted not only against Rome but also against Jews who conformed with the ways of Rome. In the end, at the fortress of Masada, they were besieged by Roman legions. When it became apparent that they faced slaughter or slavery, 960 men, women and children chose death.

Of course, the ending of their lives seemed to them

73

Mrs. Connie Brown (right), wife of slain NBC cameraman Bob Brown; their adopted daughter, Kim 15, (center); and his sister-in-law, Eileen Kelty, await arrival of transport plane at Los Angeles.

to be the choice of highest honor available to them. And so must it have seemed to many of Jones' loyal followers. "The time has come to meet in another place," he told them as he announced that now was White Night, the final fruition of the suicides they had rehearsed. Survivors said that many of those who took the poison, certainly at first, did it voluntarily.

So did the hundreds of Japanese civilians who leaped to their deaths off the cliffs of Saipan as U.S. forces drew inexorably nearer and the handwriting appeared on the wall for the imperial Japanese forces in World War II. How was their vision of the end of civilization—as they saw it—to be compared with the destruction of the dream of an agrarian jungle commune, a place of peace and plenty, that was shattered in the view of Jones and his followers with the slayings of Rep. Ryan and the newsmen?

Found on the body of the cult leader was a note, which the FBI said might have been written to Jones or by him. It read:

"Dad: I see no way out. I agree with your decision.

I feel only that without you the world may not make it to communism. For the most part I am more than tired of this wretched merciless planet and the hell it holds for so many masses of beautiful people. Thank you for the only life I've known."

A dream shattered. Many of the survivors of the mass suicide, such as elderly people with not the slightest hint of association with security forces, said that they still believed deeply in Jones when they returned to civilization. A younger man, Tim Carter—who at one point was held in protective custody after the deaths of the multitudes by Guyana authorities, had this to say:

"It may sound funny, but I never once thought he (Jones) was crazy until I saw my wife and 15-month-old son dying of convulsions last Saturday." (Cyanide kills by paralyzing the lungs.)

And so, when the people of the commune said "Dad knows best," that was what they meant. And there are those among us who see that mass suicide or murder might come again. The rigid conformity demanded by leaders of cults from their dedicated

Mrs. Autumn Ryan, mother of Congressman Ryan, is escorted as she leaves service at All Souls Catholic Church, South San Francisco

following makes violence, generalized violence against enemies of the group, possible. Observers think that we are now in one of those approximate 50-year cycles in the United States when cults flourish. Looking around, they point to Synanon, whose leader, Charles Dederich was recently found unfit to stand trial for whatever role he may have had in the attempt to murder a lawyer who had beaten Synanon for $300,000. Onetime alcoholic Dederich, 65, was found to be too drunk to be arrested early in December. But he leads a cult of 900, which he would like to see incorporated as a religion.

Although the members of the Hare Krishna cult seem to be seen in more conventional clothes than the saffron robes they once effected, they remain firmly dedicated, even after the death of their leader, Swami Prabhupada. And Unification Church leader the Rev. Sun Myung Moon, 58, wields enough authority over his Moonies that they seem ready to accept his mass marriage of some thousands of Americans who remain Moonstruck. And the Children of God, who began appearing on street corners in the late sixties, now number a worldwide membership of some 10,000 in 120 communes. All of these, as has been noted elsewhere, are fertile breeding grounds for the sort of violence that came down in Guyana—if something goes really wrong.

One of the first, and most nagging, questions that came out of that steaming jungle was: what could the outside world have done to prevent things like the squirting of poison into the throat of 6-year-old John Stoen as his mother, Grace Stoen, waged a legal battle to have him restored to her from the Peoples Temple. The mother, once a highly-trusted aide to Jones, had no recourse with the courts of Guyana. According to U.S. courts, she had won the battle for his custody. According to Guyana courts, possession remained all points of the law, and little John was in Jonestown, and that is where he stayed until the bitter end. The U.S. was powerless to help.

In fact, the most powerful government in the world was unable to prevent any of the 900-some deaths.

Since the U.S. has no power to prosecute crimes committed overseas, except in some military cases,

In San Bruno, Calif., at graveside ceremonies for Congressman Leo Ryan were, left to right: Ryan's sister, Dierdirie; his mother, Autumn; his son, Kevin; Congressional Sgt-at-Arms Ken Harding; Chip Carter, the President's son, representing the White house.

and the Constitution seems to prevent the FBI and others from doing the job of looking into cults that they would like to do, incidents like the mass suicide can not even be prosecuted by the U.S.

Many defectors from the Peoples Temple remind all who will listen that they had issued warnings long ago that there was something rotten in Jonestown. Why, they would like to know, didn't the State Department put some heat on the government of Guyana to do something in the interest of those who were held there against their will?

Deborah Layton Blakey, who fled the commune last spring, but whose brother, Larry Layton, stayed long enough to be charged in the slaying of Rep. Ryan, is one of them more outspoken critics of the U.S. role in the tragedy.

(Layton, by the way, is accused of something that can be prosecuted in U.S. courts, the assassination of a congressman. That law went into the federal books after the assassination of John F. Kennedy.)

Mrs. Blakey said she forecast the possibility of mass suicide last June. She says that the State Department did nothing about it, and that the Guyana authorities might not have been entirely enthusiastic about cooperating, not as long as Jimmy Jones kept the ladies coming their way—enough to build up a fine little case of blackmail on many of those leaders of the emerging nation.

State was quick to reply that it had, indeed, faced up to all its responsibilities in Guyana, within the limits imposed by law and constitutional guarantees of the right of privacy. But others acknowledge that, when you come right down to it, federal agencies really do not have the power to do much about the actions of a madman, or anybody else, just a few short miles off the U.S. coast, never mind far away in some remote jungle.

Or, to put it another way, before the mass suicide, was there anything Jones had done that he could be prosecuted for? In fact, supposing he had survived the bizarre tragedy himself, could he be charged with

Former wife of Congressman Ryan, Margaret Ryan Wiliams (left), and his two daughters, Patricia (center) and Shannon, attend the graveside services at Golden Gate National Cemetery, November 22.

anything serious for ordering 900 people to kill themselves?

There had been requests to the Justice Dept. by many congressmen, including Ryan, to look into the charges of brainwashing, and physical abuse in religious cults. Freedom of religion holds investigators back on that one. The Federal Communications Commission has said the Peoples Temple had broken some of its rules for ham radio operators. The Social Security Administration had been curious about what was happening to, say, $60,000 worth of cultists' checks. These questions were enough to send Ryan to the jungle, but not enough, as the *New York Times* pointed out, to send the marines.

And, if Jones had a fistful of secret banks in Switzerland, holding millions, what business was that of even the Internal Revenue Service. And what might it do to make it its business that it wasn't able to do with any other wheeler-dealer?

From the time Jones took his Peoples Temple from Indianapolis to Ukiah, Calif., in 1965, and on to San Francisco in 1971, he impressed many as *fanatical*, but just about nobody as *crazy*, and he was appointed to many a public office. He had letters of praise from a number of noteworthy figures, though some of the commendatory notes seem to have been faked. But, as the *Times* pointed out, they were the sort of letters that just about any preacher "with even minimum rspectability—and a large congregation—could obtain from almost any politician."

When Jones' son, Stephan, denounced his father as a racist, a paranoid, and a fascist, it was too late—for the Rev. Jimmy, for the congressman, and for all the others.

And governments also don't step in because they assume, almost always correctly, that cult A, B or C is composed of generally harmless folks of the sort some call kooks, kindly-souled, well-meaning people who wouldn't harm a hair on the head of a Hare Krishna. Others may see the cultists as misguided, perhaps psychotic, but, still harmless. While that is almost always so, it isn't 100% so.

77

Father Charles Durkin (extreme right) officiates at Ryan funeral services at All Souls Catholic Church in South San Francisco. At center, Ryan's aide, Joe Holsinger, strides toward the altar.

In the days after the mass suicide at Jonestown, other cults with missions of death were recalled. Well-meaning Christian missionaries arrived in the South Sea islands and sold the islanders on the idea that they were living in dark ages, far inferior to the life they did not know in Europe. Then along came World War II, and the GIs who replaced the missionaries. God, the cultists came to believe, was sending crates of cargo to the islanders, but the Americans were picking them off. So the Melanesian groups built their own airstrips and warehouses to be ready for the great day when the Westerners would be forced out.

The Ghost Dances of the American Indians a century ago swept the message through the plains tribes that the buffalo would return, the white man would go, and the bullets of the white man would not hurt the Indians. It didn't work out that way, any more than did the belief among the Mafi-Mafi of East Africa just before World War I that the bullets of the Germans would turn to water if the natives would only stand up. Those who did were slaughtered.

Contemporary observers see similarities between the Peoples Temple and many other American institutions, like those who followed Aimee Semple McPherson and her Church of the Foursquare Gospel, the Jehovah's Witnesses, the Amish, the Shakers, the Mennonites. There's nothing too unAmerican about going off into the wilderness to find a colony where religious or political freedom may live and the benefits of grinding a living from the environment may be obtained.

Look at the Mormons, those Latter-Day saints who, like the Israelites of a century later, wrestled an

earthly paradise out of the desert. (The Mormons, who are now regarded as having the very soul of conservative values, were considerd sort of outlandish in their day because of all those wives. People raised in Salt Lake City might remind you that it was for the economic benefit of all that the Mormons had all those wives, but eyebrows were surely raised from Batavia, N.Y., to, even, San Francisco.) There was more than polygamy in the Mormon experience for pagans to consider, however. In September 1857, 60 Mormons, disguised as Indians, joined 300 Indians in the massacre of 120 men, women and children in the Fancher Party, which, after all, was simply passing through Utah on the way to California. One historian throws the book at those 60 individuals thus: "It was the logical and culminating act of a society whose leaders believed themselves superior to the rest of mankind and who maintained that their own ecclesiastical laws took precedence over the laws of their country."

When Jones told the devout that "Everyone must die. If you love me as much as I love you, we must all die or be destroyed from the outside," the hundreds seemed to believe him. Some of those who did not, did escape, now convinced that the man was crazy. But it is clear that most of those who died, went along with Dad.

"Can people do this?" Dr. Ari Kiev, a Cornell University psychiatrist who specializes in suicide asked rhetorically. And the answer he gave was, "Yes, of course they can. We can't appreciate these people from our perspective. They see the world as a hostile one in which they are rejected. The group gives them a sense of belonging, a sense of purpose in the world.

79

When the group is threatened, as they apparently thought they were, the only thing they have in life appears to be caving in."

And Charlotte P. Ross, executive secretary of the International Association for the Prevention of Suicide adds: "Just as the body can stand only so much injury before dying, so the psyche can take only so much. If what is closest to you is lost, there is a feeling that you are psychologically dead already."

And so, the unthinkable, the events at the Peoples Temple seem to prove, is not altogether impossible. But, it also seems, such events may be impossible to prevent.

THE LIST

In mid-December, one month after the tragic events in Guyana, the State Department released a list of those who were either murdered or had committed suicide at Jonestown. The list, when issued in Washington on December 17th, consisted of two parts—first, victims whose kin had not been notified (at that time); and second, those victims whose kin had been notified.

With regard to the first list, the State Department requested that anyone with information about next of kin, or friends, to please call 202-632-3712 between the hours of 8 A.M. and 6 P.M., Eastern Standard Time.

The two lists include whatever information that was then available on ages, states where born, and last known town or city of residence before Jonestown.

KIN WERE NOT NOTIFIED

ARMSTRONG, Oreen 74, Texas (San Francisco)
BEAL, Geneva M 38, Miss. (San Francisco)
BECK, Daniel 12, Calif. (Redwood Valley, Calif.)
BELL, Alfred 69, Ark. (San Francisco)
BELL, Beatrice 23, Ark. (San Francisco)
BELL, Elsie I. 60, Ark. (San Francisco)
BOWER, Donald R 51, Calif. (Oakland, Calif.)
BOWIE, Kenneth B 18, La. (Redwood Valley, Calif.)
BOWMAN, Anthony 14, Calif. (Los Angeles)
BOWMAN, Delores 29, La. (Calif.)
BROWN, Luella 59, La. (Redwood Valley, Calif.)
BUCKLEY, Loreatha 21, Ind. (Ukiah, Calif.)
CAIN, Ruthie M 38, Miss. (Los Angeles)
CANADA, Mary Francis 77, La. (Pittsburgh, Calif.)
CHAIKIN, David Lee 15, Calif. (Redwood Valley, Calif.)
CHAMBLISS, Jose E 76, Va.,(San Francisco)
COBB, Sandra Yvette 22, Ind. (San Francisco)
COLE, Arvelle 66, Miss. (San Francisco)
COLEMAN, Mary 84, Texas (San Francisco)
COLEY, Alma (also known as Coachman) 54, La. (San Francisco)
CONLEY, Corlis D 19, Calif.
DAVIS, Cynthia 29, Texas (San Francisco)
DAVIS, Frances B 60, Oakland, Calif.
DAVIS, Margaret V 28, Pa. (San Francisco)
FARRIS, Lore B
FITCH, Thomas R 29, Mass. (San Francisco)
GARDENER, John L 18, Calif. (Ukiah, Calif.)
GERNANDT, Eugenia 55, N.M. (San Francisco)
GODSHALK, Viola May 67, Calif. (Redwood Valley, Calif.)
HARRIS, Dorothy L 17, Ga. (Ukiah, Calif.)
HARRIS, Josephine 71, Miss. (Los Angeles)
JACKSON, David B 86, La. (Los Angeles)
JACKSON, Karen
JACKSON, Luvenia 81, La. (Los Angeles)
JACKSON, Ralph 26, Calif. (San Francisco)
JACKSON, Thelma 42, La. (San Francisco)
JAMES, Margaret 60, Miss. (San Francisco)
JANERO, Daren Richard 14, Calif. (Redwood Valley, Calif.)
JAY, Love or Lave
JOHNSON, Denise 17, Calif. (San Francisco)
JOHNSON, Helen 51, Miss. (Los Angeles)
JOHNSON, Karl
JOHNSON, Rosa
JOHNSON, Verna L 20, Calif. (San Francisco)
JONES, Ava 27, Ind. (San Francisco)
JONES, Lew E 22, Korea (Redwood Valley, Calif.)
JONES, Mary 24, Mont. (San Francisco)
JONES, Valerie Y 20, Texas (San Francisco)
KAY, Marie
KEELER, Elaine R 34, N.Y. (San Francisco)
KENDALL, Elfrieda 69, Texas (Los Angeles)
LANG, Lossie M 74, Texas (San Francisco)
LANGSTON, Carrie O 55, La. (Redwood Valley, Calif.)
LOGAN, Henry L
LOOMAN, Carolyn S 35, Ohio (San Francisco)
LOWE, Love L 90, Mo (Redwood Valley, Calif.)
MALLOY, Lillian 73, N.C. (San Francisco)
MASON, Irene 86, Ala. (Los Angeles)
MIDDLETON, Virginia 63, N.Y. (San Francisco)
MILLER, Lucy S
MITCHELL, Beverly D 16, Calif. (Los Angeles)
MITCHELL, Tony L 13, Calif. (Los Angeles)
MOORE, Betty K 28, Va. (Los Angeles)
MOREHEAD, Leola K 52, Ark. (Oakland, Calif.)
MORGAN, Lydia 30, Calif. (San Diego, Calif.)

MORRISON, Lugenia 51, Texas (Los Angeles)
MORRISON, Yvonne 19, Calif. (Los Angeles)
McINTYRE, Joyce F 21, Miss. (San Francisco)
McKINIS, Levatus V 72, Miss. (Berkeley, Calif.)
McKNIGHT, Earl 83, Miss. (San Francisco)
McMURRAY, Theodore D 20, Wash. (Oakland, Calif.)
NELSON, Enola M 58, Texas (Los Angeles)
O'BRYANT, Winnieann Z 79, Okla. (Redwood Valley, Calif.)
OLLIE, Marie
OMAN, Edna M
PARKER, Victoria G 8, Calif. (Pittsburgh, Calif.)
PAYNEY, Lucille E 78, Ill. (Ukiah, Calif.)
PERKINS, Lenora 65, Ark. (Los Angeles)
POINDEXTER, Amanda 97, Va. (Redwood Valley, Calif.)
PUGH, James R 71, Iowa (Redwood Valley, Calif.)
ROBINSON, Benjamin O 25, Ga. (Los Angeles)
ROCHELLE, Anthony E 6, Calif. (Los Angeles)
ROSAS, Kay 38, Calif. (Redwood Valley, Calif.)
RUSSELL, D'Andrea Moton 30
SANTIAGO, Alida 30, N.Y. (San Francisco)
SCOTT, Karen L 19, Okla. (San Francisco)
SHARON, Rose O 71, Va. (San Francisco)
SMITH, Kivin 30, New Jersey (Oakland, Calif.)
SOLOMON, Dorrus H 22, Ga. (Redwood Valley, Calif.)
STEWART, Aurora M 11, Calif. (Santa Barbara, Calif.)
STRIDER, Adeline M 74, Colo. (Ukiah, Calif.)
THOMAS, Evelyn 34, Calif. (San Pablo, Calif.)
THOMPSON, Etta 74, Texas (Ukiah, Calif.)
TUPPER, Larry H 14, Calif. (Redwood Valley, Calif.)
TURNER, Bruce E 24, Texas (Redwood Valley, Calif.)
WILKINSON, Deanna K 28, Ill. (Los Angeles)
WINTER, Curtis L 53, Ind. (Redwood Valley, Calif.)

KIN WERE NOTIFIED

ADDISON, Stephen Michael 34, Mo. (Santa Rosa, Calif.)
ALBUNDY, Ia Maria 73, Miss. (San Francisco)
ANDERSON, Jerome Dwayne 18, Calif. (San Francisco)
ANDERSON, Marice 16, Calif. (San Francisco)
ANDERSON, Orelia 68, La. (Los Angeles)
ANDERSON, Samuel M 67, Miss. (Oakland, Calif.)
ANDERSON, Tommy Lee 19, Calif. (San Francisco)
ARNOLD, Luberta 71, Texas (Los Angeles)
ARTERBERRY, Linda T 30, Calif. (San Francisco)
ATKINS, Ruth 74, Texas (San Francisco)
BACKMAN, Viola E 28, S.C. (San Francisco)
BAILEY, Geraldin H 66, Okla. (San Francisco)
BAILEY, Mary J 63, Ark. (Los Angeles)
BAKER, Tarik P 17, Calif. (Pomona, Calif.)
BALDWIN, Mary B 52
BARGEMAN, Rory L 17
BARRETT, Cathy A 25, Ind. (Ukiah, Calif.)
BARROW, Jack D 57, Del. (Redwood Valley, Calif.)
BATES, Christine 73, Texas (Ukiah, Calif.)
BEAM, Eleanor M 17, Ind. (San Francisco)
BEAM, Rheaviana W 54, Ky. (San Francisco)
BEAM, Jack A 55, Ky. (Ukiah, Calif.)
BEIKMAN, Rebecca M 38, Ind. (Redwood Valley, Calif.)
BENTON, Lean C 68, Texas (Los Angeles)
BERRYMAN, Ronnie D 26, Calif. (Los Angeles)
BIRKLEY, Julia 69, Ala. (Los Angeles)
BLACKWELL, Odell 68, N.C. (Los Angeles)
BLAIR, Ernestine H 61, Ark. (Los Angeles)
BOGUE, Marilee F 19, Calif.
BORDENAVE, Selika G 60, Miss.
BOOQUET, Brian 25, Calif. (Burlingame, Calif.)
BOUQUET, Claudia 22, Calif.
BOUTTE, Mark A 21, Calif. (San Francisco)
BOWERS, Christine S 21, Calif.
BOWMAN, Patricia A 21, La. (Los Angeles)
BRADSHAW, Pamela G 22, N.Y.
BRADY, Michaeleen P 35, Calif. (San Francisco)
BREIDENBACH, Lois F 50, Okla. (Redwood Valley, Calif.)
BREIDENBACH, Melanie L 18, Calif. (Redwood Valley, Calif.)
BREIDENBACH, Wesley K 19, Calif.
BREWSTER, Kimerly L 23, Calif. (San Francisco)
BREWER, Dorothy A 40, Texas (San Francisco)
BRIDGEWATER, Miller 70, Texas (Palo Alto, Calif.)
BRIGHT, Ruby 31, Mo. (San Francisco)
BROWN, Jocelyn 20, Calif.
BROWN, Johnny Moss, Jr. 28, Texas
BROWN, Joyce M 18, Ind. (San Francisco)
BROWN, Rulette 25, Calif.
BRYANT, Lucioes 53, Ark. (Los Angeles)
BRYAN, Princeola 66, Ark. (Los Angeles)
BUCKLEY, Dorothy H 17, Miss. (San Francisco)
BUCKLEY, Minnie L 37, Miss. (Ukiah, Calif.)
BURGINES, Rosy L 25, Ark. (Los Angeles)
BUSH, William P 14, Ark. (Los Angeles)
CANNON, Thelma M 48, Texas (San Francisco)
CAREY, Jeffrey J 28, Mich. (Redwood Valley, Calif.)
CARR, Karen Y 15, Calif. (Los Angeles)
CARROLL, Ruby J 41, Texas
CARROLL, Mildred A 79, Va. (San Francisco)
CARTMELL, Patricia A 49, Ohio (San Francisco)
CARTMELL, Patricia P 24, Ohio (San Francisco)

CARTMELL, Walter C 50, Ky. (Redwood Valley, Calif.)
CASTILLO, Mary F 58, Md. (Los Angeles)
CASTILLO, William R 34, Texas (Los Angeles)
CAINEY, Georgia M 61, Ark (Redwood Valley, Calif.)
CHACON, Stephanie K 18, Calif. (Berkeley, Calif.)
CHAIKIN, Gail S 17, Calif.
CHAIKIN, Phyllis 39, Calif. (Redwood Valley, Calif.)
CHAIKIN, Eugene B 46, Calif.
CHAVIS, Loretta D 23, Calif. (Los Angeles)
CHRISTIAN, Vernetta C 34, Texas, (San Francisco)
CLANCY, Mary L 24, Calif.
CLARK, Joicy E 67, Texas (San Francisco)
CLAY, Nancy 69, Texas (San Francisco)
CLIPPS, Ida M 61, Texas (San Francisco)
COBB, Sharon B 30, Ohio (Redwood Valley, Calif.)
COLE, Arvella 72, Miss.
COLE, Arlander 72, Miss.
COLE, Clarence 15, Calif. (Ukiah, Calif.)
COLEMAN, Ruth V 58, Miss. (Los Angeles)
COLLINS, Susy L 78, Texas (San Francisco)
CONEDY, Inez 69, Ark. (Palo Alto, Calif.)
COOK, Bertha P 66, Ala. (Los Angeles)
COOK, Mary E 64, Mo. (Los Angeles)
CORDELL, Barbara J 40, Mich. (Redwood Valley, Calif.)
CORDELL, Candace K 18, Ind. (Redwood Valley, Calif.)
CORDELL, Chris M 21, Ind. (Redwood Valley, Calif.)
CORDELL, Cindy L 19, Ind. (Redwood Valley, Calif.)
CORDELL, Edith E 76, Ind. (Redwood Valley, Calif.)
CORDELL, James J 18, Ind. (Redwood Valley, Calif.)
CORDELL, Loretta M 41, Ind. (Redwood Valley, Calif.)
CORDELL, Teresa L 20, Ga. (San Francisco)
CORDELL, Julie R 17, Ind. (Redwood Valley, Calif.)
COREY, Carrie L 44, N.C. (San Francisco)
COTTINGHAM, Mary M 79, S.C.
CRENSHAW, Lucy 53, Miss. (San Francisco)
CUNNINGHAM, Millie S 74
DANIEL, Betty L. 27, Texas (San Francisco)
DARNES, Velma L 52, La. (Santa Rosa, Calif.)
DARNES, Searcy L 16, Calif. (Santa Rosa, Calif.)
DASHIELL, Hazel F 79, R.I. (San Francisco)
DAVIS, Barbara M 53, Texas (Los Angeles)
DAVIS, Isabel 53, Miss.
DAVIS, Lexie S 69, Texas (Los Angeles)
DAVIS, Minnie (Isabel?)
DAVIS, Robert E 42, Washington, (Ukiah, Calif.)
DAWKINS, Beatrice 60, Miss.(Los Angeles)
DEAN, BURGER L 72, Ark. (Los Angeles)
DELANEY, Edith F 65, Kans. (Ukiah, Calif.)
DENNIS, Eddie L 50, La. (Los Angeles)
DENNIS, Ellihue 46, La. (San Francisco)
DENNIS, Orde 46, La. (Los Angeles)
DE PINA, Lovie H 78, S.C. (Ukiah, Calif.)
DEVERS, Darrell A 23, Ill. (Los Angeles)
DICKERSON, Roseane E 71, La. (Richmond, Calif.)
DICKSON, Bessie L 64, Texas (Los Angeles)
DILLARD, Violatt E 51, Texas (San Francisco)
DOMINICK, Katherine M 84, Texas (San Francisco)
DOUGLAS, Ferene 68, Texas (Los Angeles)
DOVER, Vicky, L 20, Ind. (Redwood Valley, Calif.)
DOWNS, Nean B 50, Texas (Los Angeles)
DUNCAN, Corrie 72, Texas (San Francisco)
DUNCAN, Verdella 54, Texas (San Francisco)
DUPONT, Ellen L 48, Ariz. (Los Angeles)
DYSON, Florine 88, Va. (San Francisco)
EDDINS, Irene 76, Ark. (San Francisco)
EDWARD, Aipporah 73, Ala. (San Francisco)
EDWARDS, James 58, Miss.
EDWARDS, Shirley 27, Miss. (San Francisco)
EICHLER, Erin J 18, Calif. (Redwood Valley, Calif.)
EICHLER, Evelyn M 23, Calif. (Redwood Valley, Calif.)
FAIN, Tinetra L 20, Calif. (San Francisco)
FAIR, Amanda 70, Okla (San Francisco)
FAIR, Sylvester C 70, (San Francisco)
FARRIS, Marshall 71, Ark (San Francisco)
FARRELL, Barbara L 45, Ind. (San Francisco)
FIELDS, James D 46, N.Y. (Northridge, Calif.)
FIELDS, Lori B 13, Calif. (Northridge, Calif.)
FIELDS, Shirley A 41, Miss. (Northridge, Calif.)
FINNEY, Casey N 13, Calif. (Los Angeles)
FITCH, Betty J 23, Calif. (San Francisco)
FITCH, Donald K 32, N.H.
FITCH, Maureen C 29, Calif. (Ukiah, Calif.)
FLOWERS, Rebecca A 25, Ind. (San Francisco)
FONZELLE, Toi 23, Calif. (Los Angeles)
FORD, Viola D 44, Miss. (Los Angeles)
FORKS, Fannie 44, Texas (Berkeley, Calif.)
FORTSON, Rhonda D 24, Colo. (Los Angeles)
FOSTER, Beulah 75, Miss. (Los Angeles)
FOUNTAIN, Betty J. 29, Washington (Los Angeles)
FRANKLIN, Robert E 20, Mo. (Oakland, Calif.)
FROHM, Constance B 23, Texas (Redwood Valley, Calif.)
FRY, Kim A 14, Washington (Ukiah, Calif.)
GARCIA, Cleveland D (Los Angeles)
GARCIA, Mary H (Los Angeles)
GEE, Herman W 81, Texas (Oakland, Calif.)
GIBSON, Mattie 73, Ark. (San Francisco)
GIEG, Renee E 23, Calif. (San Francisco)

GIEG, Stanley Brian 19, Calif. (San Francisco)
GIEG, Robert W 27, Calif. (San Francisco)
GILL, Betty Jean
GOODSPEED, Claude 73, Texas (Los Angeles)
GOODSPEED, Lue D 71, Texas (Los Angeles)
GRADY, Willie James 24, Ark. (Los Angeles)
GRAHAM, Willie Lee 71, La. (Los Angeles)
GREENE, Juanita 62, Okla. (Oakland, Calif.)
GREENE, Anitra R 17, Calif. (Los Angeles)
GRIFFITH, Amanda 18, Calif. (San Francisco)
GRIFFITH, Emmett 20, Calif. (San Francisco)
GRIFFITH, Mae K 37, Texas (Los Angeles)
GRIFFITH, Mary M 52 (San Francisco)
GRIMM, Ronald 41, Calif. (San Rafael, Calif.)
GRIMM, Sue L 37, Calif. (San Rafael, Calif.)
GRIMM, Tina L 18, Calif. (San Rosa, Calif.)
GROOT, Pauline 28, Wash. (Santa Rosa, Calif.)
GRUBBS, Gerald E 33, Washington (Los Angeles)
GRUBBS, Lemuel T 37, Washington (Los Angeles)
GRUBBS, Sylvia Elaine 40, Calif.
GRUNNET, Patricia L 37, Calif. (Redwood Valley, Calif.)
GUIDRY, Mercedese M 70, La. (Los Angeles)
GURVICH, Jann E 25, La. (Berkeley, Calif.)
GUY, Brian 12, Ill. (San Francisco)
GUY, Keith L 11, Ill. (San Francisco)
GUY, Kimberly D 7, Ill. (San Francisco)
GUY, Ottie J 34, Miss. (San Francisco)
HALKMAN, Rochelle D 26, Mo. (San Francisco)
HALL, Heloise J 67, Kan. (Los Angeles)
HALLMON, Eddie J 23, Ind. (San Francisco)
HARMS, Karen M 20, N.C. (Ukiah, Calif.)
HARPER, Artee 68, La. (Los Angeles)
HARRINGTON, Ollie B 38, Miss. (Los Angeles)
HARRIS, Annie M 74, Ark. (Los Angeles)
HARRIS, Annie M 74, Ark. (Los Angeles)
HARRIS, Lian 22, Calif. (Redwood Valley, Calif.)
HARRIS, Linda 42, Calif. (Redwood Valley, Calif.)
HARRIS, Magnolia 62, Ark. (San Francisco)
HARRIS, Nevada 68, Texas (Los Angeles)
HARRIS, Willie M 56, Ga. (Ukiah, Calif.)
HAYDEN, Eyvonne P 79, Calif. (San Francisco)
HEALTH, Florence 50, S.C. (Pittsburgh, Calif.)
HEALTH, Michael 14, Calif. (Pittsburgh, Calif.)
HELLE, Joseph L 28, Calif. (San Francisco)
HERRING, Nena D 72, La. (San Francisco)
HICKS, Marthea A 43, Mich. (San Francisco)
HILL, Emma M 63, Texas (Los Angeles)
HINES, Mable 65, Okla.
HINES, Rosa M 70, Texas (Los Angeles)
HILTON, Osialee 84, Ark. (Los Angeles)
HOLLEY, Patricia A 31, Wash. (San Francisco)
HOLMES, Peter Jr. 46, Tenn.
HORNES, Hazel 63, La. (Los Angeles)
HOUSTON, Judy L 14, Calif. (San Francisco)
HOUSTON, Phyllis D 34, Calif. (Oakland, Calif.)
HOWARD, Doris H 56, La.
HOYER, Barbara F 30, Md. (San Francisco)
IJAMES, Judith K 29, Ind. (Capella, Calif.)
IJAMES, Maya L 9, Calif.
INGHRAM, Alice L 42, Texas (Redwood Valley, Calif.)
INGHRAM, Ava J 15, Calif (Redwood Valley, Calif.)
JACKSON, Beatrice 82, Texas (San Francisco)
JACKSON, Corinne M 33, Ind. (Redwood Valley, Calif.)
JACKSON, Donald 34, La. (San Francisco)
JACKSON, Eileen 13, Calif. (Redwood Valley, Calif.)
JACKSON, Gladys M 59, Texas, (Los Angeles)
JACKSON, Kathryn D 26, Calif. (San Francisco)
JACKSON, Lourence 37, La. (San Francisco)
JACKSON, Paulette 27, Ala. (San Francisco)
JACKSON, Rosa L 39, Tenn. (San Francisco)
JAMES, Lavana 74, Texas (Los Angeles)
JAMES, Ronald D 23, Calif. (San Francisco)
JAMES, Toni D 19, Calif. (Los Angeles)
JANERO, Mauri L 16, Calif. (Redwood Valley, Calif.)
JEFFERY, Eartis 65, Texas (Los Angeles)
JEFFERY, Margrette 65, Texas (Los Angeles)
JERRAM, Susan J 33, Ind. (San Francisco)
JOHNSON, Berda T 86, Miss. (Los Angeles)
JOHNSON, Clara L 46, Texas (Los Angeles)
JOHNSON, Gerald D 17, Calif. (Los Angeles)
JOHNSON, Irra J 26, La. (San Francisco)
JOHNSON, Janice A 18, Texas (Los Angeles)
JOHNSON, Jessie A 78, Ark. (Los Angeles)
JOHNSON, Joe Jr 21, Mo. (San Francisco)
JOHNSON, Mahaley 68, Texas (Los Angeles)
JOHNSON, Mary 51, W. Va.
JOHNSON, Naomi 50, Ill. (San Francisco)
JOHNSON, Richard L 20, W. Va. (Daly City, Calif.)
JOHNSON, Robert 75, Miss. (Ukiah, Calif.)
JOHNSON, Ruby L 57, Texas, (San Francisco)
JOHNSON, Samuel L 26, Calif.
JOHNSON, Willa J 19, Texas, (Los Angeles)
JONES, Agnes P 25, Ind. (San Francisco)
JONES, Annette T 52, Ill. (Los Angeles)
JONES, Brenda Y 30, Texas
JONES, Earnest 56, Miss.
JONES, Eliza 68, Ala. (Ukiah, Calif.)
JONES, Forrest R 52, Ky.
JONES, James (Rev) 47, Ind. (Redwood Valley, Calif.)
JONES, Jessie W 54, La. (Los Angeles)
JONES, Larry D 25, Texas (San Francisco)
JONES, Marceline M 51, Ind. (Redwood Valley, Calif.)
JONES, Nancy M 77, Ark. (Pittsburgh, Calif.)
JONES, Timothy B 19, Calif.
JORDAN, Dessie J 70, Ark. (San Francisco)
JORDAN, Fannie A 65, La. (Los Angeles)
JORDAN, Lula E 71, Texas
JURADO, Emma J 70, Miss. (San Francisco)
KATSARIS, Maria 25, Pa. (Redwood Valley, Calif.)
KEATON, Rosa L 71, Ark. (Los Angeles)
KEATON, Tommie S 64, Texas (Los Angeles)
KELLER, Darrell E 29, Montana (Oakland, Calif.)
KELLEY, Viola 72, La. (Redwood Valley, Calif.)
KELLY, Anita C 28, Ind. (Ukiah, Calif.)
KEMP, Barbara A 38, Ala. (Ukiah, Calif.)
KENNEDY, Emma A 67, Ga. (Los Angeles)
KERNS, Carol A 20
KICE, Robert E 30, Calif. (Redwood Valley, Calif.)
KICE, Thomas D 43, Mo. (Redwood Valley, Calif.)
KING, Charlotte 81, Ala. (San Francisco)
KING, Teresa L 31, Texas (San Francisco)
KING, Leona 65, La. (San Francisco)
KING, Wanda B 39 Ind. (Ukiah, Calif.)
KISLINGBURY, Sharon J 22, Calif. (San Francisco)
KLINGMAN, Martha E 32, Calif. (Ukiah, Calif.)
KUTULAS, Demosthenis 51, Calif. (Redwood Valley, Calif.)
KUTULAS, Edith 49, Calif. (Redwood Valley, Calif.)
LACY, Georgia L 68, Texas (Redwood Valley, Calif.)
LAND, Pearl 76, Texas (San Francisco)
LANGSTON, Marianita 23, Calif. (Richmond, Calif.)
LANGSTON, Zuretti J 19, Calif. (Richmond, Calif.)
LAYTON, Carolyn M 33, Calif. (San Francisco)
LAYTON, Karen L 31, Calif. (Ukiah, Calif.)
LEE, DAISY 22, Calif. (San Francisco)
LENDO, Karen M 18, Calif. (San Francisco)
LEROY, Laetitia M 48, Washington (San Francisco)
LEWIS, Dorsey J 39, Okla. (San Francisco)
LEWIS, Lisa 16, Calif. (San Francisco)
LEWIS, Lue E 48, La. (Los Angeles)
LIVINGSTON, Beverly M 46, Calif. (Ukiah, Calif.)
LIVINGSTON, Jerry D 37, Calif. (Ukiah, Calif.)
LOCKETT, Gordon E 60, Okla. (Oakland, Calif.)
LOWERY, Ruth W 57, Tenn. (Los Angeles)
LUCAS, Lovie J 75, Tenn.
LUCIENTES, Christine R 26, Calif. (Ukiah, Calif.)
LUNDQUIST, Diane 32, Calif. (San Francisco)
LYLES, Minnie M 50, Texas (San Francisco)
MACON, Dorothy 33, Texas (Redwood Valley, Calif.)
MARCH, Earnestine 48, Texas (San Francisco)
MARSHALL, Charles 21, Texas (San Francisco)
MARSHALL, Danny L 24, Texas (San Francisco)
MARSHALL, Diana L 19, (San Francisco)
MASON, Francine R 24, Calif. (San Francisco)
McCALL, Cheryle D 31, Texas
McCALL, Estelle 48, Texas
McCANN, Maria 26, N.Y. (San Francisco)
McCAN, Eileen K 18, Calif. (San Francisco)
McCLAIN, Allie 88, (Los Angeles)
McCOY, Carol A 33, Ind. (Redwood Valley, Calif.)
McELVANIE, James N 46, Texas (Ukiah, Calif.)
McGOWAN, Alluvine 90, Texas (San Francisco)
McGOWAN, Annie 70, Miss. (Redwood Valley, Calif.)
McKENZIE, Clara 49
McKNIGHT, Diana 22, Calif. (Oakland, Calif.)
McKNIGHT, Raymond A 3, Calif.
McKNIGHT, Rose M 25, Calif. (Oakland, Calif.)
McMURRAY, Deidre R 17, Germany (Berkeley, Calif.)
McMURRAY, Sebastian R 23, Texas (Berkeley, Calif.)
McNEAL, Jessie B 68, Okla. (Los Angeles)
MERCER, Henry 76, Ga. (San Francisco)
MILLER, Christine 61, Texas (Los Angeles)
MILLER, Lucy J 65, Ala. (San Francisco)
MINOR, Cassandra Y 22, Calif. (Redwood Valley, Calif.)
MITCHELL, Annie L 48, Ala. (Los Angeles)
MITCHELL, Lee Charles 47, Ala.(Los Angeles)
MITCHELL, Shirley 21, Calif. (San Francisco)
MOORE, Anne E 24, Calif.
MOORE, Edward 63, La. (Los Angeles)
MORGAN, Oliver Jr 29, Calif. (La Palma, Calif.)
MOTON, Glen 68, S.C. (Philadelphia, Pa.)
MORTON, Mary N 36, S.C., (Pittsburgh, Calif.)
MOSES, Eura L 79, Texas (Los Angeles)
MOTEN, Danny M 22, Calif.
MOTON, Viola M 58, Fla. (Pomona, Calif.)
MUELLER, Esther L 76, Ind. (Redwood Valley, Calif.)
MULDROW, Yvette L 20, Calif. (San Francisco)
MUTSCHMANN, Jane E 31, Wis.
NAILOR, Gertrude 68, Miss. (Pasadena, Calif.)
NEAL, Cardell 24, (Calif.)
NEWELL, Christopher 17, Miss. (Los Angeles)
NEWELL, Hazel M 51, Miss (Los Angeles)
NEWMAN, Darlene R 30, Texas (San Francisco)
NICHOLS, Ida M 78, Okla. (San Francisco)
NORWOOD, Fairy L 48, Okla. (San Francisco)
OLIVER, Bruce H 20, Calif. (San Francisco)
OLIVER, Shanda M 19, Calif. (San Francisco)
OLIVER, William S 19, Calif. (San Francisco)
OWENS, Janie E 58, Ark. (San Francisco)
PAGE, Rhonda E 24, Calif. (Oakland, Calif.)
PARKER, Beatrice L 84, N.C. (San Francisco)
PARKS, Patty L 44, Ohio (Ukiah, Calif.)
PARTAK, Thomas J 32, Ill. (San Francisco)
PATTERSON, Carol A 30, Texas (Los Angeles)
PERKINS, Maud E 29, Texas (Redwood Valley, Calif.)
PERKINS, Richardell E 36, Calif. (San Francisco)
PERRY, Leon 71, Texas (San Francisco)
PETERSON, Rosa L 78, Ark. (Pasadena, Calif.)
POLITE, Glenda B 21, Ark. (San Francisco)
PONTS, Donna L 16, Calif. (Ukiah, Calif.)
PONTS, Lois A 21, Calif. (Ukiah, Calif.)
PROBY, Bessie M 63, La. (Los Angeles)
PURIFOY, Denise E 26, Calif. (Ukiah, Calif.)
PURIFOY, Kathy J 19, Ind. (San Francisco)
PURSLEY, Cynthia 22, Calif. (Berkeley, Calif.)
RAILBACK, Estella M 74, Texas, (Los Angeles)
RAMEY, Darlene 19, Calif. (Los Angeles)
RANKIN, Robert L 39, Tenn. (Redwood Valley, Calif.)
REED, Willie B 65, Ala. (Los Angeles)
REESE, Bertha 69, Texas (Los Angeles)
RHEA, Jerome 26, Md. (Ukiah, Calif.)
ROBERSON, Odenia A 73, La. (Los Angeles)
ROBERTSON, Acquinetta E 24, Texas (Los Angeles)
ROBINSON, Leo O 59, La. (San Francisco)
ROBINSON, Shirley A 23, Ga. (Los Angeles)
ROCHELLE, Jackie 22, Mo. (San Francisco)
ROCHELLE, Tommie C 28, Ark. (San Francisco)
RODGERS, Mary F 86, La. (Los Angeles)
RODGERS, Mary J 52, La. (San Francisco)
RODGERS, Ophelia 58, Ala. (Los Angeles)
RODRIGUEZ, Gloria M 26, Calif. (Santa Barbara)
ROLLER, Edith F 63, Conn. (San Francisco)
ROLLINS, Dorothy J 22, Calif. (Richmond, Calif.)
ROSA, Santiago A 24, Honduras
ROSS, Elsie Z 89, La. (San Francisco)
ROZYNKO, Annie J 54, N.J. (San Francisco)
ROZYNKO, Christian L 24, Wash. (San Francisco)
ROZYNKO, Michael T 22, Wash. (Redwood Valley, Calif.)
RUBEN, Lula 71, La. (Los Angeles)
RUGGIERO, Elizabeth 24, N.Y. (Eagle Rock, Calif.)
RUGGERIO, Roseann 19, Calif. (Eagle Rock, Calif.)
RUNNEL, Judy A 12, Texas (San Francisco)
SADLER, Linda 21, Tenn. (San Francisco)
SANDERS, Dorsey J 31, Calif. (Bakersfield, Calif.)
SANDERS, Douglas 29, Calif. (Bakersfield, Calif.)
SHACT, Lawrence 30, Texas (Redwood Valley, Calif.)
SCHEID, Don E 17, Calif. (San Francisco)
SCHROEDER, Deborah F 29, Calif. (San Francisco)
SCOTT, Pauline 57, W. Va. (Los Angeles)
SHAVERS, Mary L 53, La. (Ukiah, Calif.)
SHELTON, Rose J 76, Mo. (Redwood Valley, Calif.)
SIMON, Alvin 33, Calif. (Cotati, Calif.)
SIMON, Bonnie J 29, Calif. (Cotati, Calif.)
SIMON, Anthony 24, Calif. (Los Angeles)
SIMON, Barbara 23, Calif. (Los Angeles)
SIMON, Jerome 20, Calif. (San Francisco)
SIMON, Jose 62, Calif. (Middletown, Calif.)
SIMON, Marcia A 23, Calif. (San Francisco)
SIMON, Melanie W 23, La. (San Francisco)
SIMON, Pauline L 46, La. (San Francisco)
SIMPSON, Dorothy 56, Mont. (Bakersfield, Calif.)
SIMPSON, Jewell J 57, Okla. (Bakersfield, Calif.)
SINES, Nancy V 29, Calif. (Redwood Valley, Calif.)
SINES, Ronald B 30, Calif. (Redwood Valley, Calif.)
SLY, Donald E 42, Calif. (Redwood Valley, Calif.)
SLY, Mark 17, Calif. (Los Angeles)
SMART, Alfred L 18, Calif. (Los Angeles)
SMITH, Barbara A 34, Calif. (Ukiah, Calif.)
SMITH, Bertha C 76, La. (Los Angeles)
SMITH, David E 52, Colo. (Los Angeles)
SMITH, Edrena D 20, Calif. (San Francisco)
SMITH, Gladys 32, Texas (Redwood Valley, Calif.)
SMITH, James A 19, Calif. (San Francisco)
SMITH, Jerry G 27, Calif. (San Francisco)
SMITH, Kevan D 17, Calif. (Ukiah, Calif.)
SMITH, Ollie 19, Texas, (San Francisco)
SMITH, Shirley 30, Texas (Redwood Valley, Calif.)
SMITH, Vernon 55, La. (Los Angeles)
SNEED, Clevyee L 58, Tenn. (Pasadena, Calif.)
SNEED, Eloise 71, Texas (Los Angeles)
SNEED, Novella N 71, Texas (Redwood Valley, Calif.)
SNEED, Willie D 59, Ill. (Pasadena, Calif.)
SNELL, Helen 76, Texas (San Francisco)
SOLOMON, Dorothy P 38, Ga. (Redwood Valley, Calif.)
SOLOMON, Syria L 19, N.J. (Ukiah, Calif.)
SOUDER, Martha M 62, Ark. (Los Angeles)
SOUDER, Wanda K 25, Calif. (San Francisco)
STAHL, Alfred R 67, Ky. (Ukiah, Calif.)
STAHL, Bonnie L 8, Calif. (Ukiah, Calif.)
STAHL, Carol A 40, Calif. (Ukiah, Calif.)
STALLING, Lula M 54, Okla. (Los Angeles)
STATEN, Abraham L 66, Va. (Los Angeles)
STEWART, Terry F Jr 19, Calif.
STEVENSON, Francis L 62, Ind. (San Francisco)
STONE, Sharon L 36, Calif. (San Francisco)
SWANEY, Nathaniel B 56, Ohio (Redwood Valley, Calif.)
SWINNEY, Cleave L 67, Mo. (Redwood Valley, Calif.)
SWINNEY, Timothy M 40, Ind. (Redwood Valley, Calif.)
SWINNEY, Wanda S 31, Wyo. (Redwood Valley, Calif.)
TALLEY, Ronald W 33, Calif. (Ukiah, Calif.)
TALLEY, Vera M 75, Texas (Ukiah, Calif.)
TARDY, Armella 32, Miss. (San Francisco)
TARDY, Bernell M 64, Ark. (San Bruno, Calif.)
TAYLOR, Lucille 80, Tenn. (Redwood Valley, Calif.)
TAYLOR, Virginia V 84, Ohio, (San Francisco)
THOMAS, Bernice 68, La. (San Francisco)
THOMAS, Caroline A 29, Texas (San Francisco)
THOMAS, Ernest 59, La. (Los Angeles)
THOMAS, Gabriel 59, Ark. (San Francisco)
THOMAS, Scott Jr 21, La. (San Francisco)
THOMAS, Willie A 18, Calif. (San Francisco)
THOMPSON, Vennie 76, La. (San Francisco)
TOUCHETTE, Albert A 24, Ind. (Redwood Valley, Calif.)
TOUCHETTE, Carol J 45, Ind. (Redwood Valley, Calif.)
TOUCHETTE, Michelle E 20, Ind. (Redwood Valley, Calif.)
TOWNS, Essie M 75, Okla. (Los Angeles)
TROPP, Harriet 28, N.Y. (San Francisco)
TROPP, Richard D 36, N.Y. (Redwood Valley, Calif.)
TRUSS, Carnelius L Jr 18, Calif. (Oakland, Calif.)
TSCHETTER, Alfred W 57, S.D. (Ukiah, Calif.)
TSCHETTER, Betty J 19, Korea (Ukiah, Calif.)
TSCHETTER, Mary A 50, Ind. (Ukiah, Calif.)
TUCKER, Alleane 49, Tenn. (Ukiah, Calif.)
TUPPER, Mary E 18, Calif. (Redwood Valley, Calif.)
TUPPER Ruth A 22, Iowa (Redwood Valley, Calif.)
TURNER, James E 19, Calif. (Los Angeles)
TURNER, Roosevelt 52, Okla. (Long Beach, Calif.)
TURNER, Syola W 66, Texas (Los Angeles)
TYLER, Gary 20, Calif. (San Francisco)
VICTOR, Lillie M 20, Calif. (San Francisco)
WADE, Roberta L 68, Texas (Richmond, Calif.)
WAGNER, Inez J 51, Okla. (San Francisco)
WAGNER, Michelle 24, Calif.
WALKER, Barbara 25
WALKER, Gloria 41, Kan. (Inglewood, Calif.)
WALKER, Mary N 74, Ark.
WALKER, Newhaunda R 19, Calif.
WALKER, Tony G 21, Calif. (Inglewood, Calif.)
WARREN, Brenda A 17, Miss. (San Francisco)
WARREN Gloria F 19, Miss. (San Francisco)
WARREN, Janice M 18, Miss.(San Francisco)
WASHINGTON, Annie B 66, Ala. (Los Angeles)
WASHINGTON, Grover 51, S.C. (Pittsburg, Calif.)
WASHINGTON, Huldah E 77, Texas (Los Angeles)
WATKINS, Gregory L 23, Miss. (San Francisco)
WESLEY, Bessie M 63, Ala. (Richmond, Calif.)
WHEELER, Marlene D 36, Calif. (Redwood Valley, Calif.)
WHITMIRE, Lisa 12, Calif. (Santa Barbara, Calif.)
WILHITE, Cheryl G 23, Calif. (San Francisco)
WILLIAMS, Charles W 36, Texas (San Francisco)
WILLIAMS, Louise T 65, Texas (San Francisco)
WILLIS, Mary P 38, La. (Los Angeles)
WILSEY, Janice L 29, Calif. (San Francisco)
WILSON, Jerry 17, Calif. (San Francisco)
WILSON, Jewell 49, Ark. (San Francisco)
WILSON, Joseph L 24, Ga (Redwood Valley, Calif.)
WILSON, Shirley M 33, Ark. (San Francisco)
WOTHERSPOON, Mary B 29, Mich. (Ukiah, Calif.)
WOTHERSPOON, Mary M 8, Calif. (Ukiah, Calif.)
WOTHERSPOON, Peter A 31, Chile (Ukiah, Calif.)
WRIGHT, Arlisa L 17, Calif. (Los Angeles)
WRIGHT, Leomy 57, Texas (Los Angeles)
WRIGHT, Stanley G 18, (Los Angeles)
YOUNG, Elois C 50, Ind. (San Francisco)

Married housing

Pavilion

Jones' house

We

Dormitories for single girls, senior citizens, problem children

Eating area, kitchen

Road to Port Kaituma

The village of Jonestown appears peaceful and deserted after departure of U.S. transport planes carrying last of some 911 bodies back to the United States. These huts were looted by neighboring Guyanese residents after the suicide-massacre took place.

December 4, 1978 / $1.25

Special Report
The Cult Of Death

Alert! Alert! Alert! Everyone to the pavilion!" The Rev. Jim Jones was on the loudspeaker, summoning the members of his Peoples Temple to their last communion. Dutifully, they gathered round; some of them, without a doubt, knew what was in store. "Everyone has to die," said Jones. "If you love me as much as I love you, we must all die or be destroyed from the outside." Mothers grasped their children to their breasts. "What have they done?"

one screamed. Jones ordered his medical team to bring out "the potion," a battered tub of strawberry Flavour-aide, laced with tranquilizers and cyanide. "Bring the babies first," he commanded.

At the fringes of the huge crowd, armed guards fingered guns and bows and arrows. Some families edged forward voluntarily. Others held their ground. The guards moved in, grabbing babies from recalcitrant mothers and holding them up to let "nurses" spray the poison down their throats with hypodermics. A

Drinking the poisoned Flavour-aide: 'Bring the babies first'

man shoved a gun into the ribs of Rauletter Paul, who was clutching her year-old son, Robert Jr. "You dumb bitch," he shouted. "You better do it or we're going to shoot your ass off." Tears streaming down her face, she shot the poison into the baby's mouth, and he immediately began to scream and go into convulsions.

Many walked willingly up to the poison vat and took away their cups of Flavour-aide. "We'll all fall tonight," said one, "but he'll raise us tomorrow." One old man resisted violently; he was thrown to the ground, his jaws were pulled open, and a cupful of poison was poured down his throat. "It is time to die with dignity," said Jones on the loudspeaker.

'MOTHER! MOTHER!'

After they had drunk their potions, members of the Peoples Temple were led away by the armed guards and told to lie in rows, face down. Family groups often held hands or embraced. Within minutes, they began to gasp and retch. Blood flowed from their mouths and noses. On his raised chair on the pavilion stage, Jones kept saying, "I tried. I tried. I tried." Then he cried "Mother! Mother!" Finally, there was a shot. Jones toppled over backward, a bullet hole in his head. And a terrible silence began to settle over the camp deep in the South American jungles of Guyana.

The apocalyptic end of Reverend Jones and his Peoples Temple last week was a tragedy that strained all comprehension. The carnage in Jonestown conjured up comparisons with the Zealots of Masada, who killed each other rather than surrender to Rome in A.D. 73, and the 1,000 Japanese civilians who hurled themselves from a cliff in Saipan as American troops took control of the island during World War II. But in this case it was not the passions of war that had prompted the self-slaughter, but rather the paranoid fantasies of a single leader. Somehow, in Jones's twisted reason, a fact-finding mission by U.S. Congressman Leo Ryan became a mortal collision that left more than 900 people—Jones's followers, newsmen, Ryan and Jones himself—dead.

Explanations for the disaster could be drawn only from the murky pathology of madness and mass indoctrination. Jim Jones, 47, was a self-appointed messiah with a vision of a socialist paradise on earth and a lust for dominion over his fellow man (page 54). He attracted hundreds of fanatic followers, whose fierce loyalty and slavish work on his behalf smacked of the psychological disintegration that accompanies brainwashing (page 72). His success, and its awful consequences, posed disturbing questions about the flourishing of cults that has given the U.S. everything from saffron-robed devotees of Lord Krishna to the weird regimen and ugly threats of Synanon (page 78). It was as if all the zany strains of do-it-yourself religion and personality-cult salvation that have built up in America had suddenly erupted with ghastly force. And to add a touch of the macabre to the tragic, the scene was a faraway jungle outpost where corpses bloated under the tropical sun and the pile of bodies was so thick that the original count turned out to be too low by half.

The heart-of-darkness tragedy at Jonestown actually began in San Francisco eighteen months ago when Ryan received some bad news from an old friend named Sam Houston, an AP photographer. Houston's son Bob, 31, had been found dead, his body mangled, in the railroad yard where he worked. The day before, Houston told Ryan, Bob said he planned to quit the Peoples Temple. The police didn't know whether they were dealing with an accident or a murder.

40   Illustrations for NEWSWEEK by Stan Hunter   **Newsweek**

Shaken, Ryan vowed to keep an eye on the Peoples Temple and he hired a special staff investigator. Over the next several months, parents and friends of Jonestown commune members told him that Jones was keeping his followers prisoners in Guyana. A former Jones bodyguard said Jones practiced physical and psychological torture regularly. Tim and Grace Stoen, two dissident communards, claimed Jones was holding their 6-year-old son hostage in Jonestown. And last spring, Debbie Blakey, the colony's financial secretary, fled Guyana with the most chilling report of all: Jones was collecting $65,000 a month in social-security checks due elderly communards—and running regular mass-suicide drills.

STAFF WARNINGS

Other sources, however, said Jonestown was a counter-culture paradise. Jones's attorney, Charles Garry, a San Francisco radical who had numbered Huey Newton and Angela Davis among his clients, called the colony "a jewel that the whole world should see." Last summer, Ryan resolved to see it for himself, despite warnings from his staff. "He knew it was relatively dangerous," Ryan's daughter, Pat, 25, said last week.

On Nov. 1, Ryan sent Jones a telegram. "I am most interested in a visit to Jonestown and would appreciate whatever courtesies you can extend," he wired. On Nov. 6, a reply arrived from lawyer Mark Lane, best known for challenging the Warren Commission's report on the John F. Kennedy assassination. Jones had hired Lane to collect evidence proving that intelligence agents were infiltrating and harassing Jonestown. Lane wrote Ryan that if the congressman staged a "witch hunt" in Guyana, Jones might embarrass the U.S. by fleeing to "two anonymous countries" (apparently the Soviet Union and Cuba) that were willing to offer him refuge.

Ryan decided to go ahead with his trip, and he welcomed reporters who asked to go along. "He felt the press was his best protection," said Joe Holsinger, a Ryan aide. The Washington Post assigned its South America correspondent Charles Krause, The San Francisco Examiner sent reporter Tim Reiterman and photographer Greg Robinson and The San Francisco Chronicle sent reporter Ron Javers. NBC News assigned reporter Don Harris and cameraman Bob Brown—both news veterans of Vietnam. "We all assumed they would be pretty safe—since no one would kill a congressman," said West Coast producer Steve Friedman of NBC's "Today" show.

Not all the members of Ryan's party shared the same comfortable assumption. In Washington, Ryan's legislative aide Jackie Speier, who was also making the trip, wrote out a will addressed to her parents. Speier, 28, also made sure that Ryan's own will was in order. The day before the trip, she tucked the two wills into envelopes and left them in her desk. Then she packed her bags. In Los Angeles, Bob Brown told his wife, Connie, and adopted Vietnamese daughter, Kim, that he was having frightening premonitions. The day he set off, he had breakfast with a friend. "Goodbye," he said. "I won't see you again."

On Nov. 14, the entire group flew to Georgetown (pop-

WHAT I SAW

By Chris J. Harper

Most of them were lying face down on the lawns near the banana bushes outside the pavilion. Husbands and wives were arm in arm. One man clutched his dead dog to his chest. Children, who only hours before they died were playing on the nearby swings, cuddled next to their parents. Some of the victims wore their best clothes, probably because of Rep. Leo Ryan's visit. A few showed the awful suffering of their last few moments of life, the five minutes or so while the cyanide was taking its effect. Their faces were twisted into violent contortions, and matted blood was smeared over them after it had streamed from their noses and mouths. It was the most gruesome sight I have ever seen.

I had flown out of Guyana's capital of Georgetown, heading to Jim Jones's commune, in the same single-engine Cessna that members of Ryan's party had taken. The bullet holes in the front passenger door had not yet been repaired, and the back of one seat was still smeared with the blood of one of the victims. We landed at Port Kaituma, where the second plane caught in the shoot-out, a Guyana Airways green and yellow twin-engine Otter, had not been moved; its left tire was still flat, punctured by bullets.

We made the final stage of the trip by helicopter. From the air, Jonestown looked like a patchwork quilt: scattered blotches of brilliant reds and yellows and blues, slivers of green and silver, a border of brown. The chopper began its descent, and the scene changed. It now resembled something like the midway at a county fair, with colorfully dressed revelers apparently shoving their way forward to see the attractions in the main tent. Even up close, it seemed surrealistic, perhaps the set of a Hollywood movie after a fierce battle scene.

I spent nearly two hours in Jonestown. It was a steamy, muggy tropical day. The shimmering heat and the stench from about 900 decaying corpses almost overcame me. I devised a makeshift face mask out of a scrap of chamois, then began to walk toward the pavilion where most of the bodies lay. Many were not recognizable as human corpses; they had ballooned to nearly twice their size and resembled some sort of grotesque dolls.

A POISONED FIELD

Amid all the death, I saw occasional, pathetic signs of life. But it was not human life. Two parrots gazed at the bodies from atop a fence. In the classroom of the commune's school, I came across a bowl of tropical fish. And in a nearby field, a scrawny golden-brown mongrel dog was sniffing, obviously searching for food. There was a sign in the field that read: "Danger. Insecticide. Poison." I have had a dog for eight years, and I ran up to this mutt and shooed him out of the field. There was no reason, I thought, that anything else should die at Jonestown. But I knew that once I left, the dog would be back in the poisoned field—and that it too would probably die.

The day that I was in Jonestown—last Tuesday—the American soldiers who would later remove the bodies for shipment back to the U.S. had not yet arrived. A towering, 6-foot 3-inch man with a bandolier strapped across his chest, Pancho Villa style, greeted me cordially as I jumped out of the helicopter. But he and the other 200 Guyanese soldiers sent to guard the camp kept away from the sights and smells of the corpses. They sat on the porches of the cottages farthest from the pavilion. One of them had picked up a crossbow and a pack of arrows—part of the arsenal maintained by Jonestown's security forces—and was idly shooting arrows into the distance. It was one way to pass the time. One soldier patiently walked with me through the field, explaining that these plants were banana trees, those were "eddoes."

"What are eddoes?" I asked. "Something like potatoes," he answered.

A PERVASIVE STENCH

The soldier was polite, helpful, eager to tell me what he knew. But he would not go near the bodies, and neither would a third soldier I tried to talk to. He concentrated on ignoring everything around him. He had wrapped a

ulation: 164,000), the sleepy, tin-roofed capital of Guyana. For a time, it looked as if Ryan might get no further. On Wednesday, he began to dicker for permission to enter Jonestown, a 900-acre enclave carved out of thick jungles 150 miles northwest of Georgetown. His contact was Sharon Amos, one of the commune's public-relations people who presented her unwelcome guest with long scrolls bearing the signatures of hundreds of Jonestowners. They read coldly, "Many of us have been visited by friends and relatives. However, we have not invited, nor do we care to see, Congressman Ryan." Word came that Jones was ill and wouldn't talk. But Ryan decided he would go to Jonestown whether Jones gave permission or not.

Then, Lane and Garry flew in to break up the impasse. The two lawyers, who openly spoke of the commune's commitment to integration and egalitarian values, radioed Jones. "You have two alternatives," Garry told Jones. "You can tell the Congress of the United States, the press and the relatives to go ---- themselves. If you do that, it's the end of the ball game. The other alternative is to let them in—and prove to the world that these people criticizing you are crazy."

When Garry and Lane promised to escort the party and make sure that things ran smoothly, Jones finally gave in. The

fragrant nut in a handkerchief, and stared sullenly ahead, breathing the aroma deeply as if it could eliminate the stench that pervaded the camp.

I walked back to the pavilion, and went inside. About 50 corpses lay facing the stage where Jim Jones had transfixed his congregation with his messianic mix of religion and hatred. It was as if the dead were still worshiping Jones. The cult leader's body lay where it had fallen. He was dressed in a red dashiki and light-colored pants. He had tumbled off the dais on which his "throne" sat and he lay sprawled on his back, the fatal gunshot wound plainly visible in his head. I saw the woefully inapt quotations from Santayana and the Bible: "Those who cannot remember the past are condemned to repeat it." "Where the spirit of the Lord is, there is liberty." "All that believed

were together, and had all things common." For the believers who flocked to the Jonestown commune, what they had in common was death.

A BAG OF DRUGS

Finally, I went into Jonestown's inner sanctum, the cottage where Jim Jones had lived. An array of boots, adults' and children's, was meticulously lined up on a rack, but the rest of the cottage was a shambles. The porch was littered with heaps of letters written by the communards, letters in which they spoke glowingly of Jones and of the Peoples Temple—and admitted their own shortcomings. There was a pitiable quality to them: the handwriting was infantile, the words misspelled as often as not, the phrasing banal. Amid the rubble, there was a large plastic bag. I poked into it. It was filled with

drugs: Thorazine, Darvon, Pentothal, Valium.

There were more corpses in the Jones cottage. Twelve commune members—including several of the camp's privileged elite—had carried their doses of poison in a bread pan and a small metal pail into the house. They drank it there and died there. Jones's mistress, Maria Katsaris, lay on a bed, her once attractive face discolored and stained with blood. A family—a man, a woman, a baby—clung to each other on a second bed, and four more victims lay on the floor. A pail of poison was next to the corpses, and a small black and white kitten was crawling among the bodies, whining. And on walls of the bedroom were a smattering of crayon drawings—simple stick figures—done by several of the commune's children. I turned and walked away.

two lawyers made a dash for the airport and caught up with Ryan. His party had ballooned to nineteen members including nine newsmen and four relatives of commune members. At 3 p.m., their Twin Otter took off for Port Kaituma, a small fishing village with a landing strip nestled in thick jungles 6 miles north of Jonestown. When they landed one hour later, they were greeted by an angry group of Jonestowners, including one man with a gun. After some more bargaining, Ryan's group finally boarded a dump truck for the hour drive to Jonestown on a twisting dirt road bordered with dense jungle brush.

The scene at Jonestown was surprisingly pleasant. They found children on swings in a small playground and cheery communards baking bread and doing laundry. Commune members trotted alongside the guests, smiling and asking polite questions. Jones's wife, Marceline, led the welcoming delegation. "You must be hungry," she said. "The food is waiting at the pavilion." She led the party to a building with a corrugated-tin roof and open walls, where Jones, perspiring and looking ill, was waiting. He sat down with Ryan and the others to a dinner of smoked pork, eddoes (a root vegetable), coffee and tarts. The commune's small band broke into the

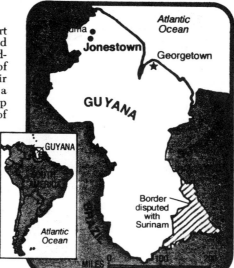

Susan Johnston

Guyanese national anthem—and a chorus of "America the Beautiful."

Jones then threw a two-hour soul review for his guests. There was an eight-man band—made up of electric guitars, drums and saxophones. Old women sang old-fashioned blues. Younger communards wailed modern soul and rock songs. Ryan interviewed 40 commune members as the show went on. Finally, Ryan stood up, took a mike and said, "I can tell you right now that by the few conversations I've had with some of the folks here already this evening that . . . there are some people who believe this is the best thing that ever happened in their whole lives." The crowd cheered for nearly twenty minutes.

BAD VIBES

If the good vibes were thunderous, they soon began to appear a bit suspect to Ryan and the newsmen. At one point, the congressman noticed that all of the commune's elderly white members were mechanically clapping and swaying to the beat of the throbbing soul music. "Look at that man's face, just look at his face," Ryan said to the Post's Krause, pointing out Tom Kice Sr., a middle-aged white in a gray crew cut who was bobbing about with glazed eyes. But when reporters edged out into the crowd to ask a few questions, most

Ib Ohlsson—Newsweek

ATTACK AT THE AIRSTRIP

GUYANESE SOLDIERS GUARDING OLD AIRPLANE WRECK

BAR WHERE SOME WOUNDED SPENT NIGHT

JUNGLE

RYAN HARRIS ROBINSON PARKS BROWN SHED

TENT WHERE SOME WOUNDED SPENT NIGHT

TWO PASSENGERS IN CESSNA WOUNDED BY GUNMAN FROM COMMUNE

PORT KAITUMA LANDING STRIP

GUNMEN OPEN FIRE ON AMERICANS BOARDING AIRPLANE

of the communards gingerly moved away.

Krause had been sitting next to Jones. He recalled that Grace Stoen had told him that Jones was vain and power hungry despite all his protestations of humility—and that he filled out his sideburns with eye liner. Krause looked closely. "It was true," he reported to the Post later. Jones suddenly exploded in rage at one of the newsmen's questions: "Threat of extinction! I wish I wasn't born at times. I understand love and hate. They are very close." And when newsmen pressed him on the reports of physical punishments in the camp, he shouted, "I do not believe in violence . . . I hate power. I hate money . . . All I want is peace. I'm not worried about my image. If we could just stop it, stop this fighting. But if we don't, I don't know what's going to happen to 1,200 lives here."

OVERNIGHTING AT THE BAR

At 10 p.m., the entertainment ended. One of Jones's lieutenants told Jones that the reporters had secured lodgings in Port Kaituma and would be driven there for the night. The reporters had made no such arrangement; some argued that they wanted to stay overnight to get a better fix on living conditions in the commune. "Get them out of here. I will not have them staying here overnight," Jones whispered to his wife. The newsmen and the relatives were driven to the Weekend Bar, a tiny nightspot in Port Kaituma. They persuaded the owner to let them sleep on the living-room floor of his house nearby. A local cop told the newsmen that the Jonestowners had at least one gun, an automatic rifle, registered with the Guyanese authorities.

Ryan, Speier, Lane, Garry and two others were allowed to spend the night in Jonestown. Lane went to bed early. Garry stayed up into the night, discussing the day's events with Jones, who was in good spirits. His 103-degree fever had vanished and he seemed in control. A red-letter day, Garry told him. Ryan had been impressed—things were going well.

Jones also seemed cheerful the next morning. Ryan and the other overnight guests were given a hearty breakfast of pancakes and bacon. The dump truck went into Port Kaituma to bring back the newsmen. Then the atmosphere began to sour. Krause discovered four barnlike buildings that turned out to be dormitories. When he attempted to get into one of them—Jane Pittman Place—he was turned away. The newsmen protested. After Garry and Lane prevailed on the commune's leaders to let the reporters in, they discovered about five dozen elderly communards jammed into a small room with

Sly pulling a knife on Ryan: 'Does this change everything?'

long lines of bunk beds. "It was like a slave ship," said Lane.

Things took a turn for the worse when Jones agreed to sit for an interview with Harris. For 45 minutes, he sat stonily under the eye of Bob Brown's mini-camera while Harris peppered him with hard questions about weapons, drugs and corporal punishment. Finally Harris asked about the gun the newsmen had heard about the night before. "A boldfaced lie," said Jones. Then Harris showed him a crumpled note from a communard who had asked Harris for help in leaving Jonestown. Jones's eyes narrowed slightly and his voice tightened. "People play games, friend," he said icily. "They lie. What can I do with liars? Are you people going to leave us? I just beg you, please leave us . . . Anybody that wants to can get out of here . . . They come and go all the time."

The possibility of real defections seemed to have rattled Jones badly. After the interview, Ryan told him, "Jim, there's a family of six here that wants to leave." Jones grew furious. "I feel betrayed," he shouted. "It never stops." "He

Gunmen jump from the tractor-trailer at the airport: A point-blank fusillade at Ryan, Harris and Robinson

245

just freaked out," said Garry. "It was as if all hell broke loose." When Jones began to rant about liars and traitors, Garry stepped in quickly to calm him. "Let them go," he told Jones. "Who gives a shit if six leave or 60? It won't change what you've done here." Jones mumbled that he had been stabbed in the back. Garry grew more and more worried. "I just wanted to get out of there," he recalled.

At 3 p.m. Saturday, Ryan was summoned to the pavilion. An American Indian named Al Simon wanted to leave with his three children; Simon's wife refused to let the children go. Garry and Lane persuaded the parents to let a court decide the matter. Ryan then assured Jones that he would not call a Congressional investigation when he returned home. He had just thanked Lane and Garry for making the trip possible. With no warning, a Jones lieutenant named Don Sly grabbed him around the throat and put a 6-inch fishing knife to his chest. "Congressman Ryan, you are a mother----er," Sly yelled. Garry and Lane grappled with Sly; Ryan fell free; Sly's hand was cut; blood splattered on Ryan's shirt. Jones stood watching. "Does this change everything?" he asked. "It doesn't change everything," said Ryan. "But it changes things."

'THIS IS HELL'

With Ryan finally aboard, the commune dump truck set off for Port Kaituma at 3:15. Near the airstrip, the entire family of Gerry Parks caught up with the truck and begged to be taken along. Parks, his wife, Patty, his brother, Dale, their mother and two children had arrived in Jonestown last spring. Parks had buttonholed the congressman earlier and whispered, "We gotta get outta here, this is hell." But his wife had refused to leave—until she saw the commune's security forces hauling out a stash of automatic weapons. "They started getting out the big stuff and she finally knew it was coming down on us," said Parks.

Another, more sinister latecomer also joined Ryan's party: Larry Layton, 32, a thin, blond, white man who had been one of Jones's close followers. "He's not really going," objected Dale Parks. "This is a plot—something is going to happen." The plea was dismissed, but it was prophetic. After the dump truck left the commune, Jones summoned Lane. He told him that other communards were also bound for the airstrip. "This is terrible, terrible, terrible," he said. "There are things you don't know. Those men who left a little while ago to go into the city are not going there. They love me and they may do something that will reflect badly on me. They're going to shoot at the people and their plane. The way Larry hugged me, a cold hug, told me."

At about 4:30 p.m., the Ryan entourage arrived at the Port Kaituma dirt airstrip. At about the same time, a white Cessna six-seater touched down and ten minutes later, a nineteen-seat, twin-engine Otter landed. The planes did not have enough seats for all the members of Ryan's party. He had promised to take all the defectors out first and they crowded nervously forward. "The congressman said I could go on the first plane," grumped Layton as the Otter began to load. He discreetly made for the Cessna when Ryan personally started frisking the passengers boarding the Otter.

The two planes began to warm up their engines. Aboard the Cessna, Layton suddenly whipped out a pistol and fired three shots, wounding two of the other commune defectors aboard the plane. Then his gun jammed. Dale Parks and Vernon

Suspects: Cult members Mike Prokes and Tim Carter while in custody

Gosney wrestled the gun from his hands. Layton jumped from the plane and fled.

At the same moment, Harold Cordell, another of the commune defectors, looked out of the window of the Otter and saw a Jonestown tractor pulling a trailer onto the runway. Men armed with automatic pistols, semi-automatic rifles and shotguns suddenly stood up in the trailer. Gerry Parks also saw the trailer. "Now we're going to get it," Parks thought. His wife, Patty, stood in the Otter's doorway. Shots snapped out, her head shattered and blood and brain tissue splashed into Cordell's lap. Tom and Tina Bogue, children of dissident Jonestowners, sprinted to the Otter's door. Both were wounded in a new hail of gunfire but they managed to slam the door shut. "If those children hadn't shut that door," said their mother, Edith, "those gunmen might have gotten on the plane—and we'd all be dead now."

Ryan and the newsmen on the ground outside the Otter were not so fortunate. Waving aside Guyanese civilians on the airstrip, the assassins in the tractor-trailer bore down on the two planes, firing as they came. Reiterman took a slug in his left arm; another fractured his wrist and blew off his watch. Javers was wounded in the shoulder. Krause was wounded slightly in the hip. All three sprinted for cover and survived. But the gunmen cut down cameraman Brown at the tail of the Otter. Photographer Greg Robinson fell near the port engine, his body riddled by bullets. Harris and Ryan dived behind the plane's starboard wheel. The tractor-trailer pulled around the right side of the plane—and the gunmen killed both men.

Steven Sung, 44, an NBC soundman connected to Brown

by a cable, fell 2 feet from the cameraman. He put his arm over his head and feigned death. "The next thing I heard, they were walking toward us," he said. "Someone shot Bob Brown in the leg . . . He screamed 'ouch' or 'shit' . . . and next thing I know, the guy came close and blow his brain off . . . the next thing I know I have tremendous pressure, explosion right next to my head and my arm feel like falling apart." The gunmen walked up to Ryan, Harris and Robinson and fired point-blank at their heads.

As the shooting erupted, a squad of Guyanese soldiers armed with rifles stood guarding a crippled Guyanese plane at the end of the airstrip. "We need guns," shouted NBC field producer Bob Flick, who rushed up seeking help. The guards turned away. Oddly enough, the gunmen also withdrew, leaving behind eight wounded. The terrified survivors dragged themselves from the planes. Some fled into the jungle at the edge of the airstrip. Embassy official Richard Dwyer, wounded in the thigh, took charge of the others. Night fell. The survivors huddled miserably, still fearing that the assassins would return to finish the job. A Guyanese nurse refused to come to the field to treat the victims and the local medical dispensary declined to send bandages and medication. Some residents even demanded tips when the survivors asked them to bring water to the airfield. Finally, the most seriously wounded were placed in an army tent at the end of the airstrip, and the others holed up in a nearby saloon called the Rum House.

Back at the commune, Reverend Jones had a very different plan in mind. At about 5 p.m., the camp loudspeaker summoned everyone in Jonestown to the pavilion. Garry and Lane walked over, stopping to talk to Jones. He seemed calm and controlled. "Some of those people who left had no intention of leaving," he said. "They went to kill somebody . . . and they've taken every gun in the place."

'WE ALL DIE'

Jones told the two stunned lawyers to wait at a guest cottage. "Feeling is running very high against you two," he said. "I can't say what might happen at the meeting." At the guest house, two young communards named Pancho and Jim Johnson stood by the door, rifles at the ready. "We all going to die," Pancho said. "It's a great moment—we all die." The two guards explained that Jones was ordering a revolutionary suicide to protest racism and Fascism. "Isn't there any alternative?" asked Lane. When the two said there was none, Lane popped up hopefully: "And Charles and I will write about what you do?" The notion seemed to please the guards. They turned to leave. "How do we get out of here?" asked Lane. Pancho waved some directions, and Garry and Lane ran into the jungle.

In retrospect, Jones's plan seemed clear: Layton was to kill the pilot of the Otter as it was flying over the jungle, causing a crash that would wipe out Ryan, the newsmen and the defectors. Anyone left behind at the airstrip would be finished off by the gunmen in the tractor-trailer.

Afraid that the plan might fail, Jones prepared his followers for death. First he sounded the alarm for a White Night, the sect's suicide plan. With a shock, Stanley Clayton, 25, a cook, realized that this was no drill. Ordinarily, Jones allowed the cooks to skip White Nights because they had to prepare food for the commune when a drill was over. This time, a grim bodyguard came to the camp kitchen and ordered the cooks to the pavilion.

Standing at his throne, a wooden chair on a raised dais inside the pavilion, Jones told the crowded assemblage that Ryan's plane would fall from the sky. Time passed. Nothing happened. Finally the camp's dump truck returned from the airstrip. Two of Jones's lieutenants rushed up and whispered to him. He grabbed a microphone. "The congressman is dead ... and the journalists," he said. "The GDF [Guyanese Defense Forces] will be here in 45 minutes ... We must die with dignity."

A JUG OF CYANIDE

In a tent next to the pavilion, Larry Schact, a medical-school graduate who acted as camp doctor, prepared a vat of strawberry Flavour-aide. He dumped a quantity of painkillers and tranquilizers into the pinkish-purple brew. Finally, Jones ordered Schact and Joyce Touchette, one of the leaders of the commune, to bring forth "the potion." Half-gallon jugs of cyanide was then poured into it. The tub was placed at the edge of the pavilion. Jones ordered the mothers of Jonestown to bring their children forward, and the killing began.

For a while, Jones sat calmly on his "throne" and watched the carnage unfold. More and more members began to balk. The resistance angered Jones. He finally stepped down from the throne. With guards at his side, he waded among his followers, whipping them on to finish the ghastly rite. "Hurry, hurry, hurry," he shouted. "The man was crazy," said Clayton. "He was out of his mind."

In the swirling confusion, a few of Jones's followers managed to escape. Clayton, a street-wise kid from San Francisco, told guards he had been assigned to count the living; he made his way to the camp's library tent, hid, then fled into the jungle when a guard at the tent door turned aside. Odell Rhodes, 36, leaned against a fence, waiting for his turn at the poison tub and thinking "about a chance to get out of there." When a nurse asked him to go to the camp's nursing station for a stethoscope, he eagerly volunteered; he hid under the building until the enforced suicide ceremony was nearly over. Then he managed to sneak off into the jungle. He made it to Port Kaituma—and sounded the first alarm on the Jonestown apocalypse.

Before Guyanese authorities could reach the camp, Jones and his inner circle completed the suicide pact. A death squad poisoned the commune's water supply in an attempt to kill cattle, chickens and pigs. Mr. Muggs, the camp's mascot monkey, was shot. Two brightly colored parrots, a tankful of fish in the commune's school aquarium and one yellow dog survived, not much more. Jones's mistress, Maria Katsaris, and eleven disciples put their poison cups in a bread pan and small pail and carried them down to Jones's house. Five died in one bedroom, seven in another. Katsaris was shot. When the death trip was nearly complete, Jones finished it: he put a gun to his head and pulled the trigger.

Lane, 51, and Garry, 69, heard the shots as they plunged into the jungle beyond Jonestown. They struck out for the road to Port Kaituma. Emerging on a trail lined with cassava plants, and catching sight of two strange men hauling boxes on their shoulders, they ducked back into the bush and stayed there for 26 hours. Lane ripped strips from some extra sets of underwear to mark a trail, and the two lawyers eventually reached Port Kaituma, considerably on the outs with one another. "It was utter madness to go in there," Garry said in anguish last week. "Mark Lane knew about everything; the guns, the drugs, the suicide pact—and he never told anyone."

It took Guyanese authorities more than twelve hours to reach the stranded survivors of the Ryan party, in part because the Port Kaituma airstrip had no lights for night landings. At about 6 a.m., the first Guyanese Army units arrived. The survivors were flown to Georgetown that afternoon. As the evacuation planes lifted off, the dazed survivors could still see the bodies of Ryan, Harris, Robinson, Brown and Parks lying where they fell. The U.S. Air Force dispatched a C-141 medical plane to Georgetown, and the badly wounded were ferried back to Andrews Air Force Base near Washington, where they were recovering last week.

The sight that met the Guyanese troops when they entered Jonestown was as horrifying as anything out of a Hitlerian death camp. Bodies lay everywhere. The troops also found a trunk crammed with 803 U.S. passports and scores of social-security checks that the older members had turned over to Jones. More than $1 million in cash also turned up.

ANXIOUS RELATIVES

For a time, how many people had died in Jonestown was very much a mystery. After making a preliminary count of the victims, Guyanese officials set the figure first at 373, then at 409. The discrepancy between that number and the total cache of passports sparked rumors that hundreds of communards had fled Jonestown for the jungle. Anxious relatives in Georgetown and the United States cautiously hoped that Jones might not have taken all his flock with him.

Their hopes were dashed. The U.S. Government dispatched a team of graves-registration and body-identification experts to Jonestown to help the Guyanese measure the toll and to return the bodies of the Jonestown victims. In a terse news conference, Air Force Capt. John Moscatelli, spokesman for the body-removal task force, said the initial count of the Guyanese had been "seriously in error." He set a revised figure of 780 "with more to come." The problem, he explained, was that the bodies had fallen in stacks. Adults lay on top of children, big people on small people, making it easy to miss many of the victims. As the body detail worked its way inward from the perimeter of the dying ground to the center, the stacks grew deeper—and the count rose to more than 900.

Air Force pilots made a last sweep over the jungle beyond the commune looking for survivors. Choppers flew low, announcing over loudspeakers that it was safe to come out of hiding. "There were absolutely no sightings," said one U.S. official. "They must be dead, they must be dead," wept Claire Janaro, who sat sobbing in the Georgetown Hotel as the search went on. She had hoped that her two children, Maury and Daren, had somehow escaped death.

Not all of the communards died in Jones's holocaust. In Washington, the State Department and FBI warned police in San Francisco and Los Angeles to look out for more suicides in the Temple's surviving enclaves. None occurred last week. In Port Kaituma, police arrested Layton and charged him with Ryan's murder. They also took into custody—and later released—three of Jones's lieutenants, Mike Prokes, Tim Carter and Mike Carter, who turned up in Port Kaituma after the deaths. And they arrested Charles Beikman, charging him with the murder of Sharon Amos and her three children.

'AN INSANE ELEMENT'

In Georgetown, the cult's office was sealed off, and 46 followers, including the basketball team, were put under house arrest. Steven Jones, 19, leader of the Georgetown Temple followers, disavowed his father. "There was an insane element in the leadership," he said. Despite the disclaimer, some Jonestown survivors said they feared the younger Jones as much as his father.

A C-141 military air transport brought the bodies of Ryan and the newsmen back to the United States. The congressman's body was in a metal casket. The newsmen were in plain, wooden coffins. Harris was buried in Vidalia, Ga., where he had started out as a local radio broadcaster and where local people still knew him by his original name: Darwin Humphrey. Ryan was buried on a gloomy, rain-washed afternoon in South San Francisco. Dozens of congressmen, and California's Gov. Jerry Brown attended the ceremonies in Golden Gate National Cemetery. In the will that aide Jackie Speier had attended to before the trip, Ryan had asked to be buried in that place so his "ghost will be looking out over the bay he loved so much."

Had Ryan and the newsmen really understood what they were getting into when they set off for Jonestown? Some of Ryan's aides charged angrily last week that the State Department should have been more alert to the dangers of the Peoples Temple. State Department officials said that they had warned Ryan of flying in a small plane over uncharted jungle into a dirt airstrip that was remote, far from local police protection and beyond easy reach of the two-man United States mission in Georgetown. They also maintained that they had warned Ryan that the Peoples Temple had become "increasingly hostile" to outsiders. "But at no time did any of us think that there was any physical danger to his person," said one unhappy department officer.

'JONES BECAME A DEVIL'

The future of the Peoples Temple was another intriguing question. Less than three dozen of Jones's followers were left in the Temple's buff, brick church in San Francisco last week. Eleven adherents turned up there alongside lawyers Lane and Garry for a post-mortem press conference. "Jones became a devil," said Lane. "If you cannot be God, you don't just fall back to the rank and file . . . If you win, you're Moses, if you lose, you're Charles Manson." The remaining communards denied reports that Jones had organized a team of trained assassins. They said they would try to keep up the Temple's anti-racist, humanitarian good works. But from the beginning the Peoples Temple was very much a one-man show and without leader Jones, it seemed unlikely that it could survive.

As for Jones, there was some worry for a time that he wasn't really dead. In the Bay Area last week, worried defectors from the Peoples Temple kept bodyguards posted against the possibility that he still had hit men in place to carry out vengeance against those who had left him. But a metal coffin with the name "Rev Jimmie Jones" scrawled upon it arrived at Dover Air Force Base in Dover, Del., when the Air Force began ferrying the Jonestown victims back home last week. When they opened the coffin, the body inside was unrecognizable. A technician had to peel the skin from one hand to make a set of fingerprints. It was Jones.

—TOM MATHEWS with CHRIS J. HARPER, TONY FULLER and TIMOTHY NATER in Guyana, GERALD C. LUBENOW in San Francisco and bureau reports

December 4, 1978

53

THE EMPEROR JONES

He was a self-proclaimed messiah in a polyester suit, a man who played God from behind mysterious dark glasses that gave his followers the impression that he was omniscient. With Gantryesque oratory and "miracles" of healing that were pure medicine-show hokum, he mesmerized his flock and demanded fanatical loyalty and adoration. His appeal to the poor, the black and the troubled—and his ability to deliver their votes and their support—made him a friend of public figures. But behind locked temple doors, he flaunted his power over people and forced them to fulfill his consuming needs for financial, egotistical and sexual gratification.

PARANOID ILLUSIONS

Jim Jones wanted to be many things: a con man and a cult hero, a political force in California and a dictator in his own Utopia. But as his public and private lives began to tear him apart and his foulest paranoid illusions loomed as realities, Jones reached out for the one dream that probably dominated all his actions. Godlike, he dealt out death.

Among grieving relatives of the dead, embarrassed friends of Jones's in high places and millions of horrified onlookers, the search for answers will go on long after the last bloated body has been counted. This was no firebrand revolutionary, but a man who preached a nonviolent socialist brand of love and racial equality. This was not a Manson, transforming the wounded birds of society into deadly weapons, but a leader who told young people who felt like "nothing going nowhere" that they

could "be someone" and do good. "He had this soft, beautiful voice," says a former member of his Peoples Temple. In and out of the Temple, it was difficult for many people to recognize the monster that was growing within the man who could always smile and reassure them: "Just call me Jim."

Perhaps the story should begin with the dream. Lynetta Jones was once a young anthropologist, working with primitive tribes in Africa and trying to decide between her career and marriage. Torn, she dreamed repeatedly of her dead mother. Finally, from the far side of a river, Lynetta's mother called to her that she would bear a son who would right the wrongs of the world. Lynetta accepted a proposal of marriage. Her first child was a boy. And she was convinced that James Warren Jones was a messiah.

Jim was born in 1931 in Lynn, Ind., a hamlet of 900 about 70 miles east of Indianapolis. His parents were white and his father, James Thurmond Jones, was a member of the Ku Klux Klan. Young Jim claimed that Lynetta was part Cherokee, and would later refer to himself with pride as "an All-American mongrel." Jim's father was in poor health and

died when he was young. The family was poor, and Lynetta worked occasionally in a factory 20 miles away, leaving her son in the care of a neighbor. But Jim was close enough to his mother to give her reason to keep believing in the dream.

"Jim always had several animals," recalls his cousin Barbara Shaffer. "He took in strays all over town. He befriended everyone, animals and people." Lynetta Jones was thrilled by her son's way with animals. She saw it as a gift from Saint Francis.

SEEDS OF HORROR

Raised as a Methodist, Jim was fascinated by pulpit oratory. "We used to play pretend-church," says Vera Price, who played with him as a child. "He'd always be the preacher, standing up making sermons." Another neighbor says that even when he was only 7, the boy would lace his speeches with calls for strict discipline. "He would have ten or twelve youngsters and put them through their paces," recalls the neighbor, now 73. "He'd hit them with a stick and make them cry. He had a power that most boys don't have."

High-school classmates don't recall any such displays of power. They say that Jones was popular but not a leader. They noticed his growing interest in religion, but never thought of him as a fanatic. Only in retrospect does anyone claim to have spotted seeds of the horror to come. "I had a hunch something bad was going to happen to him," says a middle-aged man in Lynn. "He was smart as a whip. But he had some strange ideas. He never fit in with the town. He was different."

After graduating from Richmond High School, 20 miles from Lynn, Jones required ten years of on-and-off studies before receiving his Bachelor of Arts degree from Butler University. During that decade, he worked part-time as a hospital orderly and met and married nurse Marceline Baldwin. He also became pastor of a Methodist church in Indianapolis, where his strong integrationist views made him a target of bigots who jeered him and even tossed dead cats into his church.

Soon Jones decided that "there was no love" in the Methodist Church. Disenchanted, he carried his message into a church of his own, the Community National Church. He also served briefly as associate pastor of the Laurel Street Tabernacle. But his belief that blacks should be admitted there stirred up a furor on the church board, and he became committed to the idea of his own liberal-minded church. To raise the money, he sold pet monkeys door to door, at $29 each. When bigots knocked him off his bicycle during his selling rounds, he only grew more determined. By 1956, he opened the doors of his new place of worship on North New Jersey Street in Indianapolis: the first Peoples Temple.

At that site and then at a former synagogue on North Delaware Street, the Temple seemed to flourish as a model of integration and liberalism. A soup kitchen fed anyone who was hungry. An employment desk was staffed with volunteers who helped people to find jobs. A

nursing home provided health care. Jones and Marceline, parents of one boy of their own, eventually adopted eight children of varying racial backgrounds; they encouraged members of the racially mixed congregation to follow their example. In 1961, Indianapolis Mayor Charles H. Boswell appointed Jones as director of the city's Human Rights Commission. As his mother's dream had promised, Jones seemed to be making at least a dent in the wrongs of the world.

A STRANGE POWER

But while he remained unshaken by local bigots, Jones appeared vulnerable to forces within his own mind. "I think perhaps he started out to do something good," says the Rev. Raymond Bosler, a retired Roman Catholic priest who served with Jones on the Human Rights Commission. "But he had a strange power over people, and that kind of power tends to go to the head."

Ross Case, a Disciple of Christ minister who worked with Jones for several years, echoes that theme: "I've never seen anyone relate to people the way he could. He would build them up, convince them that anyone as intelligent and sensitive as they were ought to do whatever it was that he wanted them to do."

At about that time, Jones's sense of his own powers drove him toward Father Divine, the famous black cult leader in Philadelphia. He took a group of young people to visit Divine and returned with some of Divine's gospel songs, as well as

the evangelist's insistence on fierce personal loyalty. Soon Jones instituted an interrogation committee in the church to question anyone who dared to speak against him. "He said everybody ought to love him," says his former associate minister, Thomas Dickson. "If they didn't, he'd get awfully violent—not physically, but verbally." Adds former disciple Judy McNaulty: "I knew that was when he got his idea to play God. Not too long after that, I got out."

Those who remained witnessed some startling changes. The poor people's socialist set up several corporations and began flexing his capitalist muscle in the real-estate market. Going over the ledgers of Jones's profitmaking Jim-Lu-Mar Corp., one accountant chuckled that he was glad the Internal Revenue Service couldn't see the books. Later, when purchasing a building for one of his two nonprofit corporations, Jones coolly told his friend Case: "We'd better put this one under Christian Assemblies, because Wings of Deliverance won't stand investigation."

Cynicism was also eroding the religious beliefs of the young man who had once loved to play "pretend-church." "He tried to get me to be a minister once," recalls Edward Mueller of Indianapolis. "He said there was no easier way to make it. Once he told me, 'Just look at my hands. They're not dirty'." If Mueller was put off by that approach, he was even more distraught when his 73-year-old mother turned over $25,000 in cash and property to Jones—and then disinherited her son.

By 1961, Jones was going public with his doubts. He confessed to his congregation that he no longer believed in the Virgin Birth—and demanded to know who agreed with him. Only one hand was raised—and that single ally was immediately made a trusted aide to the minister. During other sermons, Jones began to rant against the Bible. His associate Dickson recalls breaking away from Jones after the pastor threw a Bible to the floor and complained, "Too many people are looking at this instead of me." To the consternation of his fundamentalist-style flock, the man who had walked with dignity past segregationists who spat on his adopted black child was now seen spitting at the Bible.

As some followers became uneasy about him, Jones himself grew restless. He said that he had a vision of a nuclear holocaust, and he wanted to find a place that would be safe from bombs as well as bigots. He had read a magazine article about the nine safest spots in the event of nuclear war, and in April of 1962 he moved his family to one of them—Belo Horizonte, a Brazilian industrial city of nearly 2 million people, about 250 miles north of Rio de Janeiro.

MESSIANIC IMPULSES

In Brazil the dream seemed rekindled. Jones and another American, Jack Beam, threw open the doors of their large house to the poor and the desperate. Jones took out newspaper ads offering help to the populace, and spent almost two years doling out food, clothing and counseling. He also used that period to study the work of the fire-and-brimstone Brazilian faith healer David Martins de Miranda, who is known to his followers as the "Envoy of the Messiah." But Jones's own messianic impulses were never apparent to neighbors. "He told us he was a pastor," said one. "But he mainly preached racial harmony and integration. I wouldn't say he had followers."

Amid all the good works, however, there were hints that Jones was being pursued by darker forces. He was so paranoid about nuclear war, one neighbor says, "There were times when just the sound of an airplane flying overhead would start him crying." He also spoke frequently of health problems. "He told me that he had some sort of skin disease that had turned into cancer," recalls attorney Elza Reis Rocha. "He also talked a lot about having been operated on for some warts and moles on his neck. His big fear was cancer."

In 1963, Jones visited Guyana, where he apparently had his first fleeting vision of a remote utopian settlement. Then his mingled fears and dreams drove him north toward home and Indiana.

There his followers sensed still another change. While his earlier gestures of power grabbing and apostasy had been mercurial and sporadic, he returned in a purposeful mood—a man in a hurry. "If you had money to donate to the church, he would still grab you and hug you," says former disciple Wanda Johnson. "But if you didn't, he would shun you. You weren't welcome if you didn't have any money." His stay in Brazil also seemed to have heightened Jones's gift for exaggeration. "He stretched everything," says Johnson. "If he brought ten people to the altar, he would say there were twenty."

LUSTFUL GIANT

Among intimates, his hyperbole soared even higher. "You go out and preach me," he told black assistant minister Archie James, "and I'll back it up with miracles." Ross Case says that when Jones returned from Brazil, "Jim wasn't even a Christian." But the concept of Christianity was very much with him. Jim Jones began telling friends that he himself was Jesus Christ.

In 1965, the messiah rushed onward to Redwood Valley, a hamlet near Ukiah in far northern California—an area Jones also deemed safe from nuclear holocaust. Only about 100 of the Indianapolis faithful followed him, and many left as the services focused increasingly on Jones as God. But California proved fertile ground for the Peoples Temple. Gradually Jones built a new flock that probably grew to several thousand—about one-fifth of his own inflated estimates.

Among the redwoods, God as played by Jim Jones emerged as an awesome caricature of the Biblical force he scorned—a wrathful, lustful giant who doled out unspeakable punishments

Jones exhorting his flock: An awesome caricature of a Biblical God

along with his "miracles" and appeared before various audiences in whatever shining guise would serve his purpose. To build a just society, he told his listeners, people needed a living God rather than a scriptural one. And Jones was willing to resort to almost anything to seize that role.

The "healings" were strictly carnival stuff. Whitie Freestone, who claims to have been skeptical even while his wife was following Jones west from Indiana, offers an outline of a typical cure: "Jim had people go to a house and use the bathroom. They would look into the medicine cabinet and find medicine for, say, heart disease. Then they'd get this person to come to the church, and Jim would pick the guy out, scare him to death, and say 'You've got heart trouble.' Other times he would tell a person he had cancer. Then they would send the person to the bathroom—usually Jim's wife would go, too—and his wife would carry back a towel with bloody meat in it. Jim would holler, 'Don't get too close, that's cancer.' But I would look right at it and you know, it was the same piece of meat every week. I think they kept it refrigerated."

Eventually Jones refined the cancer act, commanding his top aides to find a better prop. They devised a mixture of chicken entrails and their own blood. Then they left it in a warm room until it congealed into a rancid and apparently convincing mess. Jones also allowed congregations to eavesdrop on his conversations with "spirits"—aides who hid in crawl spaces in the ceiling. Once he even healed himself of a mysterious gunshot wound from an unseen sniper—and he displayed his bloody shirt in a glass case like an icon. The stunts were often orchestrated to suit the audiences. The elderly blacks who formed a majority of his followers usually witnessed old-fashioned tent-revival-style cures, for example, and visiting radical celebrities might be treated to a seance with the soul of sainted labor leader Joe Hill.

INTRAMURAL TERROR

Jones was just as meticulous in structuring his congregation. The paranoia that was his constant companion was also his weapon; he forged loyalty by convincing many members that without him they would be killed or imprisoned by the Ku Klux Klan, the CIA or any number of free-floating forces of evil. But as an extra safeguard, he encouraged intramural terror. Members were encouraged to inform on spouses or children who trans-

gressed, and his supposedly classless society was set up according to a rigid and unforgiving hierarchy.

Closest to Jones were a dozen or more "Angels," who handled Temple finances, acted as advance men when he approached public officials and meted out vengeance and punishment—perhaps including the ambush of Rep. Leo Ryan and his party. The second echelon, the Temple Planning Commission, was assigned many day-to-day chores such as organizing bus pilgrimages to San Francisco and Los Angeles and enforcing petty rules. But when Jones called for acquisitions of members' property, severe public paddlings or the serving of fake poison in suicide-practice rituals, he usually called on the Angels.

He also called on them for sex. Jones's sexual self-image was as tormented and exaggerated as his religious one. Night after night he would harangue his followers about the "curse" of his huge penis, which he said made women plead constantly for his attentions. To make that particular gospel come true, Jones required every woman who was close to him to have sex with him regularly. Often that idea was instilled early in church training. "Once Jim handed out a questionnaire that asked, 'Do you fantasize about "Father" sexually'," says former member Sandy Rozynko Mills, 19, who left the Temple three years ago. "Here I was 14 years old and I was thinking, 'What . . . ?' But we all knew we were supposed to say yes, so I said yes."

Jones was also intrigued by homosexuality. "He'd say that everybody else in the Temple was gay and he was the only heterosexual," says Mills. "And we didn't question it. If Father said we were homosexual, then we must have been

homosexual." Straight or not, Jones also had several male lovers. But sex with males was used as a tactic to control, humiliate or blackmail them. Often he would require a male follower to engage in sex with him and call in some female member to observe or photograph the act. "He'd explain," says Mills, "that the only reason he went to bed with anyone was to help the cause."

SEXUAL BOASTS

The contradictions in Jones's sex life were as blatant as those in his theology. On his organizational charts he was listed as the "main body," and he took the term literally. Everyone in the cult was expected to recognize "Father" as the only meaningful source of guidance, discipline—and sex. Jones also took pleasure in rising above his own rules. While underlings were beaten for homosexual acts, Jones would arrogantly flaunt his own such behavior.

Like his crowd estimates at services, however, his sexual boasts may have been exaggerated: he once told his attorney Charles Garry that he had had sex sixteen times in one day—with fourteen women and two men. For all his posturing Jones had a scared and secret side. Five years ago, he was arrested for making a lewd advance to an undercover cop in a Los Angeles adult theater. Charges were dropped because of insufficient evidence.

The sexual theme was central to the survival of the Temple. Young women with posters of movie stars were forced to replace them with huge portraits of Jones. Parents were required to prove their love for their leader by signing away not only their possessions but their children; some signed bogus confessions claiming that they had hideously molested their kids. In the Temple, no love counted but love of Jim Jones. Those who experienced such twisted love would not leave and expose his secrets. The rest, Jones hoped, could not leave—out of shame and terror of the photographs and documents they would have to leave behind.

While old members hesitated to depart, new members kept joining. In 1971, Jones purchased new temples in San Francisco's Fillmore district and in Los Angeles. To create the impression of vast local followings, he required hundreds of members to ride a fleet of eleven buses to his sermons at the distant temples. The groups traveled in the overcrowded vehicles—with children often sleeping on overhead racks and some members riding for hours in airless luggage compartments—while Jones alone enjoyed a private compartment at the rear of his bus. Perhaps the enormity of Jones's public mirage can best be shown by the juxtaposition of those nightmarish all-night rides against a state assemblyman's gushing tribute: "Anytime you wanted a crowd, you called Jim."

But the public acclaim of Jones was all too genuine. His people earned much of it by establishing effective drug-rehabilitation programs, clinics and nursing homes—although much of the state funding for the latter appears to have supported Jones rather than elderly patients. Jones also had a keen sense of public relations. He contributed money to local police forces and to newspapers in "defense of the free press"—and received kid-glove treatment in return from both sources. Above all, when a solid liberal politician needed telephone volunteers, enthusiastic crowds or a few hundred crucial votes, Jim Jones was the man who could deliver.

CELEBRITY STATUS

Jones's clout was strikingly illustrated in 1975, when he delivered a bloc of votes that helped liberal Democrat George Moscone to edge a conservative rival in a tough San Francisco mayoralty race. The grateful Moscone offered Jones a seat on his city's Human Rights Commission. Jones thought the reward wasn't good enough, or so it's said, and turned it down. Then he was made chairman of the Housing Authority. He soon turned that fairly routine position into his kind of podium, packing meetings with his supporters and basking in their adulation when he solved what he described as crises.

Such bizarre scenes failed to trouble many politicians. In addition to Mayor Moscone, Temple visitors included San Francisco District Attorney Joe Freitas, Assemblyman Willie Brown and Gov. Jerry Brown. When Walter Mondale campaigned for the Vice Presidency in 1976, Jones was invited aboard his plane. When Rosalynn Carter appeared, Jones helped gather one of her largest campaign crowds—and dined with her later at the Stanford Court Hotel.

Ironically, it was his sudden celebrity status that led to Jones's ruin. Apart from an occasional appreciative feature about one of his community projects, the press had largely ignored him until he began to wield political power. But in late 1976, a San Francisco Chronicle reporter, Marshall Kilduff, proposed a probe behind the locked doors of the Temple. His city editor, who had been befriended and frequently praised by Jones, vetoed the idea. So Kilduff took the story to New West. A few months later, Kilduff and magazine staffer Phil Tracy were ready with a piece quoting ten Temple defectors about the beatings and misuse of funds under Jones. As publication neared, New West editors learned even more about Jones's influence: they received protest letters from advertisers, politicians and even the American Civil Liberties Union. "Can you believe it?" says Kilduff. "He had the ACLU trying to kill a news story."

When his pressure tactics failed to squelch what he knew would be a devastating piece, Jim Jones prepared to move on again, this time to his leased tract of 27,000 acres in Guyana. As usual, he built his travel plans on paranoia. Black followers were warned that if they stayed behind they would be put in American concentration camps. Whites were told they were on a CIA "enemies" list. And always, there was the threat of blackmail and violent reprisal against defectors. Finally, with the New West piece due on the stands within weeks, Jones slipped out of California and went to Guyana. "I'm not running away," he told a friend. "I'll be back." But he never intended to return. And when the Aug. 1, 1977, edition of New West appeared, it was clear why.

In the aftermath of that article, more defectors appeared. One, Gwen Johnson, told The Indianapolis Star of beatings of children as young as four months old. In California, others recalled that Jones had watched such punishments with a bemused smile. He was discredited, and his temples became little more than supply depots for those who wanted to follow him to his Guyana settlement. And, incredibly, 800-odd souls were ready to do just that. The ultimately tragic exodus began shortly after the article was published, as busloads of believers crossed the country to Miami and flew on to their promised land. They found a hothouse where the evils of the California temples grew like jungle weeds. At the same time, Jones's own health was unraveling. His lungs were racked with a fungus infection. A prostate condition rendered him unable to urinate, and he had to be catheterized. His blood pressure soared and his temperature ranged between 101 and 105, as aides tried desperately to hold it down by packing their leader in ice. Jones was sometimes rambling and incoherent; at other times he was sullen and almost comatose. The "Living God" was subsisting on rising dosages of drugs—and staring wild-eyed at the specter of death.

PARADISE LOST

It arrived in the form of Ryan and his media entourage. Jones sat helplessly through the visit. Then came the airstrip assassinations. Now Jones's most grotesque fears had come true, and the world would know of his secrets. He felt surrounded by real and imagined inquisitors—the media, the CIA, the defectors in his midst. His $10 million fortune was useless to him now. So were his former friends in high places and his powers over his flock. Paradise was a hideous trap. There was only one exit.

Lynetta Jones had died a year earlier, but perhaps in his last moments her son believed that he could speak to a spirit who wasn't secreted in a ceiling. Just before he put a bullet through his head, Jim Jones cried out to his mother. It could have been the final hopeless shriek of the dream messiah who had long ago lost his way.

—PETE AXTHELM with GERALD C. LUBENOW, MICHAEL REESE and LINDA WALTERS in San Francisco, SYLVESTER MONROE in Indianapolis and bureau reports

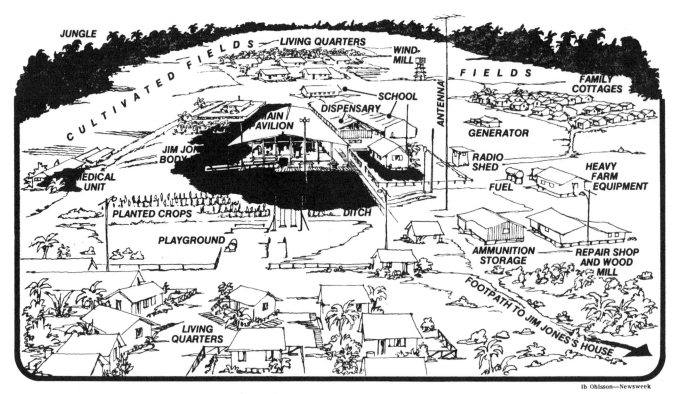

Jones's jungle outpost: A tropical socialist commune that turned into a fear-ridden concentration camp

Ib Ohlsson—Newsweek

LIFE IN JONESTOWN

The color movies and glossy promotional brochures painted the picture of an idyllic tropical paradise, a love-filled commune dedicated to good works and racial harmony. They showed smiling, suntanned women cheerfully making bread and doing laundry. They showed comfortable, well-furnished cottages, complete with drapes and carpeting. As the leaders of the Peoples Temple told it, their devout and dedicated members had conquered 900 acres of hostile jungle and in its place they built Jonestown—"an interracial, sharing community" with lush fields, a school, a clinic and even the beginnings of industry. And every day at Jonestown, the brochures said, "the laughter of children rings through the air. Our children are our greatest treasure."

There may have been a day when some, perhaps much, of that was true. In 1974, the followers of Jim Jones heeded his call to build a Christian, socialist commune in the wilds of Guyana. They planted their crops and built substantial, if plain, housing. They established medical facilities that were advanced by Guyanese standards. There was little racial friction. Children seemed especially happy. "I just picked up a hurt monkey out of the jungle and he's going to be all mine," Maury Janaro, 16, wrote to her mother in San Francisco. "I love it here."

Then, about a year ago, life at Jonestown began to change. Meat, served twice a day at first, was served once, then

not at all. The workday increased from eight hours to eleven. The commune's security forces began to impose harsher discipline. Jones himself seemed to deteriorate physically; he began gaining weight, he started to slur his words, he looked dazed—and the rumors began to spread that he was on hard drugs, or seriously ill. Last spring, Deborah Blakey, once a trusted aide, escaped from Jonestown and Jones went into a frenzy. He shouted endlessly over the loudspeakers, "I am the alpha and the omega." From then on, well before its grisly end, Jonestown turned into a virtual concentration camp.

RICE AND GRAVY

By day, all but a select handful of Jonestown's residents labored under the broiling sun; by night, they endured endless re-education meetings and sleep-destroying harangues that boomed out over the camp's public-address system. Their living quarters—the pleasant cottages of the film—were crammed with as many as 30 people. Their food was rice and gravy. Their sins—drinking a glass of wine or snitching a packet of powdered fruit-drink mix—were punished by public beatings. Not even the children were exempt. When they misbehaved, they were tied up and left in the jungle at night, or dropped into the waters of a well, to be pulled out only when they screamed for forgiveness. In every sense, says Edith Bogue, who escaped

from the camp hours before the mass suicide, Jonestown was "a nightmare."

Jonestown's day began at 6 a.m. The public-address system blared out the wake-up call, and the communards lined up in a tent for the food they were given at every meal: boiled rice, occasionally flavored with bits of pig offal or a bitter, green vegetable that the cult members called "pig weed." Then they set off for the fields, for what was often a futile day's work. "We had agronomists, botanists and chemists out there," recalled Harold Cordell, 42. "But you couldn't make anything grow. The weeds would come back and choke the plants within 24 hours." Each day, Jones's security forces followed the workers to the fields, lurking in the shade of the surrounding jungle to spy on them. "We'd work in temperatures as high as 120 degrees all day with only a ten-minute break," says Bogue's daughter, Juanita, 21. "If you stopped to rest and leaned on your hoe, the security forces would write down the time you wasted."

The commune was billed as an agricultural experiment designed to help the Guyanese people. But there was not even enough food to feed Jonestown's settlers, and the few who escaped last week's mass suicide were undernourished, with half-healed sores covering their bodies. "They just popped out, boils and blisters," says Jim Bogue. "We weren't getting enough protein." There were cattle, pigs and chickens at Jonestown, but meat was either sold or reserved for "selected people"—namely Jones, his family and his favorites. The community's elite enjoyed imported coffee and soft drinks, canned ham and tuna fish. When Jones wanted to reward a cult member, he occasionally did so by passing that person a few leftovers from his second heaping plate of food.

Jones and his handpicked lieutenants regulated every aspect of life at the commune, even the sexual lives of the cult members. A couple who wished to live together applied to the camp's Relationships Committee for approval, and had to spend a three-month trial "dating period" before they could have sexual relations. Even then, they received no special living arrangements. Like single members of the commune, couples slept on a narrow mattress, separated from others in their living cottages only by a sheet hanging from a cord. "There was no privacy," says Harold Cordell. "People could hear your every noise, cough and whisper. We were packed in like cattle."

PUBLIC HUMILIATION

Interracial "partnerships" were encouraged in Jonestown. Promiscuity was not, and commune members who violated Jones's moral code were subject to beatings and public humiliation. One woman who had had sex with a male cult member without the permission of the Relationships Committee was forced to have sex with a second man—while all other members of the cult watched. At the evening meetings, Jones often ordered women and men to tell of their sexual relations with him. "I've been ------ by Jim Jones and believe me, sisters, it's the best ---- I've ever had," women would say.

In the early years of the commune, the "business meetings," as Jones called them, were held only once or twice a week. In Jonestown's final months, they became a nightly ritual that often lasted from 7:30 until 3 a.m. Jones would

ramble on for hours, railing against everything from the white man's sins in Africa to the venality of some communards who balked at giving him their wristwatches. "If you started to nod off, the security people would come up behind you," recalls Cordell. "They would hit your shoulder and tell you, 'Wake up. Stand up if you have to. Stay awake'." After the exhausted cult members finally went to sleep, Jones would often flick on the public-address system, screaming "Alert, alert, alert!" He would then order all of Jonestown's residents to gather in the commune's pavilion to listen to his warnings about impending attacks by the U.S. Army, the Central Intelligence Agency or other "enemies" of the settlement.

To Jones, almost everyone—including the cult members themselves—was a potential enemy. The inhabitants of Jonestown were unable to communicate with their families, and letters from relatives in the U.S. were never delivered to those in the commune. When Edith Bogue tried to speak to her husband by shortwave radio before she moved to Jonestown from San Francisco, she was invariably told, "Sorry, too much atmospheric static. Maybe next time." Only carefully selected members were allowed outside the camp, and even then their children were kept at Jonestown as hostages to ensure their return.

The strict isolation of the communards was only part of Jones's rule. In the commune's final weeks, rebellious teenagers were put in Jonestown's "extended-care unit"—isolation cells where they were pumped full of sedatives and other drugs. "When they came out a week later, they were changed," says Cordell. "They couldn't talk to you and they walked around with empty faces." Cult members considered to be guilty of minor infractions, such as taking an extra rest period during the workday, were called on "the floor" at the nightly meetings. Forced to stand in front of the chair

that Jones called his "throne," they were harassed and threatened by the armed security forces until they broke down, wept and pleaded to be forgiven.

More severe "crimes"—attempts to run away, unwillingness to give personal possessions to Jones, direct criticism of Jones—were punished with severe beatings. The beatings were usually administered by the security forces as the other commune members watched. On one occasion, Jones ordered a group of elderly communards to beat a woman with their canes, explaining, as one witness recalls, that "it will be good for your hypertension."

WEIGHTED GLOVES

At other times, transgressors were forced into boxing matches with husky members of the security forces wearing weighted gloves. One woman, whose husband turned her in to the authorities when he caught her drinking wine, was lashed 100 times with a leather belt. When another communard, Tommy Bogue, 17, tried to escape, he was called on the floor and beaten unconscious by a security guard while his fellow commune members were ordered to shout, "Kill the little bastard." After the beating, Bogue was dragged out, shackled in red-hot metal cuffs and put in a hard-labor work detail clearing away a section of the jungle.

There were special tortures reserved for errant children. Sometimes they were taken into a darkened room where electrodes were attached to their bodies; after the electric shocks, they were told that was what happened to children who failed to smile at Jim Jones or forgot to call him "Dad." At other times, they were blindfolded, tied to a stake in the jungle and told they would be left there until poisonous snakes bit them.

When Jones wanted to punish children especially harshly, he threatened them with a mythical creature that the communards called Big Foot. After dark, a child would be tied up and taken to a well in which two commune disciplinarians were hiding. The youngster would be lowered into the well where the cultists would grab his feet, pull him under the water and then let him be pulled out—only to be dragged in again and again. As one commune member recalls:

"You could hear the child screaming all the way there and all the way back, 'I'm sorry. I'm sorry, Father. I'm sorry, Father.' And if he didn't scream loud enough how sorry he was, then [Jones] would send the child back down."

'WOULD YOU KILL?'

Toward the end, Jones called the cultists together for one of his White Nights, this one a three-day period of brainwashing and intimidation. "Would you kill one of your children?" he asked. "You would if you loved them enough." He pointed to people in his captive audience and asked, "How would you kill your child?" When some suggested a violent method, Jones said, "Well, I wouldn't kill them that way.

I would do it gently with a sedative. Just put them to sleep."

Announcing that the commune was on the verge of being destroyed, Jones then ordered a 50-gallon vat filled with orange drink brought into the pavilion. He told the commune members that all must drink, and sacrifice themselves for the Peoples Temple. They would begin to feel dizzy, Jones told them, and when they did, they were to move outside to a grassy area and lie down. The commune members drank. Two women among them, apparently shills, began to moan and toppled over, and suddenly dozens rushed outside and began to keel over. There was no poison in the orange drink—they had been felled by the power of suggestion. That White Night was just a rehearsal for the deadly performance that was to come.

—RICHARD STEELE with TONY FULLER and TIMOTHY NATER in Georgetown

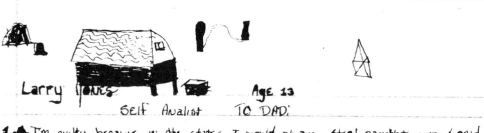

Larry Jones   Age 13
SELF Analist   TO DAD:

1. I'm guilty because in the states I would always steal pamphlet money and go by icecream, candybars, And stuff like that.
And another guilt is I always would fight and get in trouble And put Waist DAD and the peoples time on the floor.
I'm guilty because I do not show enough time with seniors.

True confessions: An exercise in self-analysis by a Jonestown youth

LETTERS TO 'DAD'

NEWSWEEK'S *Chris Harper examined a number of letters that members of the Jonestown commune wrote to Jim Jones. Excerpts:*

From Rosa Keaton, 71:
Thanks for all the wonderful opportunities which you have provided for us all who are members of this beautiful Socialist family . . . You, Dad, have bought six months food for us here in Jonestown, at the cost of $675,000. No one else would do that. You practice the highest principle of Socialism-Communism than anyone else in the entire universe. We should emulate you and Mother because you are the best Father anyone can have. Mother is the best Mother that we can have . . . I have given material things, money and time to the cause, but I will not betray my trust to the cause knowingly. I do not have a commitment to anything but the cause . . . I know that

one is due to obey authority and respect authority. I try daily to be obedient and respectful . . . I have no hostility towards Dad for anything and I do not regret being in the cause. I only am sorry that I did not know about it 20 years ago . . . Up until 1959, I was afraid of death and dying, but since then I have thought of death and dying as just going to sleep . . .

From Larry Jones, 13:
. . . I'm guilty because in the states I would always steal pamphlet money and go by ice cream, candybars. And stuff like that . . . I'm guilty because I do not show enough time with seniors. I tear down structure in class. I take advantage of people kindness. I talk about the states. I gossip about people, specially sisters. I don't like to stop my games and listen to the news, I sleep in service because I like to act bad and tough in front of my friends, I talk

back to my teacher when he or she confronts me in class . . .

From Osislee Hilton, 84:
. . . I am so glad to be in Jonestown. This is the happy time of my life. Started August 18, 1977 when I got here . . . Dad, you no the first white night we had here before then I was afried to die, I stood in the rain that night. I saw divided time between life and death, I have not ben aferid cience. I have something to die for now and something to live for. I love the little childrens, see them grow here, them crying, see them smiling. Watching the elders, hoping they are glad as I am because they are here . . . I brought four blankets here. Have not got one now, someone els have them. I love to have one nice blanket. Thank you . . .

From Stephanie Jones, age unknown:
. . . Sometimes I'm over hard on the children I teach which Im sure studds their groth. Im lazy in my work and I dont put your examples you show me into action . . . I think that when people say oh I want to dies its selfish as hell and I hate the fact that people say it. It pisses me off because they arn't thinking of the children that hafe to try to understand it . . . I also think its selfish because they want to die so bad and they can take so much pain but they cant take the pain to work . . .

LEO RYAN'S LAST MISSION

To some of his wary colleagues, Rep. Leo Ryan looked like one of those moral grandstanders not unfamiliar to their ranks—a reformer who liked causes, and liked his publicity, too. Whether donning jailhouse denims for an inmate's-eye view of California prison conditions or wrapping himself in an arctic windbreaker to witness the slaughter of baby seals in Newfoundland, the 53-year-old Democrat seldom failed to get his picture taken in the process. This fall, when he tried to enlist fellow lawmakers for an on-scene investigation of the Peoples Temple colony in Guyana, he didn't get a single taker. Said one Californian who declined the invitation: "I just thought, 'There goes Leo on another one of his things'."

But to constituents and staffers, Ryan's commitment to oppressed citizens—or seals—seemed genuine. Outrage at the witch hunting of the McCarthy years propelled him into politics, they said. As the son of a crusading Nebraska journalist, he displayed an affinity for press people, and as a Shakespeare buff, he had an admitted instinct for the theatrical. Yet he withheld announcing the Guyana trip until after his landslide re-election last month to avoid any implication of a vote-grabbing ploy, and aides claim that reporters, scenting a good story, joined the journey largely on their own initiative. Ironically, they speculate now, Ryan might have survived the chancy venture had he gone without the newsmen and TV cameras.

EYE-CATCHING SORTIES

Lanky, silver-haired Leo Ryan was a congenital activist. Born in Lincoln, Neb., he emerged from a World War II Navy stint to earn a master's degree in Elizabethan drama and teach English in Nebraska. Moving to California, he embarked on a political career that carried him from the city council of South San Francisco to the state legislature and on to Congress in 1972.

As the first Democrat from San Mateo County in 39 years, he attracted notice with some of his eye-catching investigative sorties: having already taught school in Watts and served eight days in Folsom prison, he rushed off to Newfoundland to denounce the annual seal-pup "harvest." Yet, he was not so much flamboyant as headstrong. "On issues," says California Rep. John Burton, "he would take on anybody, sometimes just for the sake of taking them on."

Even though the Peoples Temple stood outside his district, he took it on at the behest of an old friend whose son had mysteriously died after proposing to quit the cult. San Francisco Examiner reporter Tim Reiterman, who had been following the story closely, got permission to accompany Ryan, together with photographer Greg Robinson. The San Francisco Chronicle asked him to make room for reporter Ron Javers. Meanwhile, West Coast free-lancer Gordon Lindsay, who had been pursuing the story on his own, contacted NBC and The Washington Post. NBC's "Today" show decided to send him as a consultant along with investigative reporter Don Harris and cameraman Robert Brown, and the Post dispatched South America correspondent Charles Krause.

There was a mutual convenience in the suddenly swollen Ryan contingent. For the reporters, the congressman's mission gave them entree to Jonestown. For Ryan, his aides say, the presence of reporters and TV cameras seemed to provide insurance against possible violence. But inevitably the expedition hit Jonestown like a blunderbuss. Reporters began wandering around on their own, asking hard questions. When tough-minded fact-finder Don Harris handed Jones a letter from cult members seeking to leave, it was plainly provocative to a man who seemed explosively primed for provocation. In the violence that followed, Ryan, Harris, 42, Brown, 36, and Robinson, 27, were fatally shot; Krause, Reiterman, Javers, NBC producer Robert Flick and sound man Steve Sung survived (Lindsay had been barred from entry into Jonestown).

After last week's funerals for Ryan and the slain newsmen, there was some agonized reflection in San Francisco city rooms and network studios. Said one NBC staffer: "We had long talks about our fault in sending Harris and Brown. We believe we did the right thing. But the toughest thing to face is the question, would it have happened without a TV camera?" Others argued that violence was implicit in the Jonestown situation and would have burst forth anyway. "Any guy who's going to hold suicide drills and pull a trigger is going to do it whether there are cameras rolling or not," said ABC news producer Av Westin.

'ACTION PEOPLE'

Ryan himself was not insensitive to the dangers, but he followed his usual penchant for investigating things firsthand. "You have to put fear aside and do what you think is right," he told Holsinger on the eve of the trip. Holsinger recalls that when Ryan met Harris and his camera crew, an immediate rapport developed. "They were action people," he said. "You could see the camaraderie forming." Harris, too, had been troubled by the "gray area" of conflicting reports out of Jonestown. According to co-workers, he was determined to get the answers. But in sad retrospect, it was as if the adventurous group had been drawn together inexorably, for an appointment in Samarra.

—DAVID GELMAN with GERALD
C. LUBENOW in San Francisco,
BETSY CARTER in New York
and bureau reports

HOW THEY BEND MINDS

How could more than 900 people be twisted to the point of swallowing fatal doses of poison? Clearly, the immolation at Jonestown wasn't entirely voluntary. But the orderly rows and heaps of dead and the linked arms of family groups were powerful testimony that Jim Jones's disciples hadn't enough will to resist his orders, backed up by a few armed guards. And perhaps the greatest horror in the scene lay in the realization that more or less ordinary people had been so indoctrinated—and in the seed of fear that nearly anybody might be manipulated the same way.

In a sense, such mind-bending is only an extreme form of familiar human experience. In military training, soldiers are taught to take appalling risks in the name of discipline and love of country; extending that process, Japan's kamikaze pilots in World War II accepted certain death. Jailers can be permitted to abuse and even torture their prisoners, and citizens easily shut their eyes. At the extreme, Adolf Hitler engineered the Holocaust that massacred 6 million Jews. Powerful personalities often gather groups of dependent admirers: the demonic charisma of Charles Manson mesmerized his ghoulish groupies to murder total strangers with sadistic pleasure. Jones was only the latest extreme in the wave of cult leaders of the past decade.

To many scholars who have studied the new American cults—and to many ex-cultists themselves—the behavior of Jones's following was shocking but not surprising. "As a Moonie, I would have done exactly what they did," maintains Erica Heftmann, 26, who left the Unification Church of self-styled Korean messiah Sun Myung Moon more than two years ago. "I was drilled and instructed to kill." Isolated from the real world and pressured by their peers, converts become wholly accepting of the leader's power—and his paranoia—and they put their welfare and their will totally in his hands. Jones's people even practiced suicide drills, in which they swallowed a drink of bitter liquid he said was poison. "I would think, before being told it wasn't poison, that soon I would be dead," recalls Wanda Johnson, 42, who spent eight years in the Peoples Temple and lost her youngest child at Jonestown. "I would think, 'It doesn't matter if I'm dead.' I felt relief."

Almost any passionate enthusiasm can generate cultic behavior if there is a charismatic figure to beguile disciples. In recent decades, cults have coalesced around crusading politicians, rock stars, visionary intellectuals and gurus of the human-potential movement.

CHARISMATIC LEADERSHIP

In religion, sociologists typically distinguish cults from mainline churches, which serve as custodians of normative values, and from sects, which partially withdraw from society in order to purify established doctrine. Cults emerge when groups wholly withdraw from prevailing religious practices and members commit themselves completely to the leadership of charismatic and highly authoritarian figures. Although today's cults vary widely in their ideologies, the most successful use much the same methods of indoctrinating converts.

Most cults know exactly which kind of recruits they are looking for. Synanon guru Charles Dederich prefers drug addicts, whom he can rehabilitate and then bind to his community for life. Jones sought out the oppressed—especially poor blacks, prostitutes and other outcasts—who would welcome his message of egalitarianism and his offer of a communal home. But religious groups such as the Moonies, the Children of God and the Hare Krishnas prefer college students of above-average intelligence and idealism who will be a credit to the cult. In her own interviews with more than 300 former cult members, University of California psychologist Margaret Singer found that no more than a third were suffering from marked psychological distress at the time of their induction.

'A SENSE OF BELONGING'

Timing is the key factor in seeking converts. Religious recruiters like to hit the college campuses at exam time, sit in libraries, waiting to make "eye contact" with students who are having difficulty deciding on a course of major study or recovering from a broken romance. In cities and resort areas, proselytizers seek out footloose backpackers who have taken time off from school to "find" themselves. "These kids are looking for a sense of significance and belonging," says UCLA law professor Richard Delgado, who has been studying cults for years. "Everybody is vulnerable. You and I could be Hare Krishnas if they approached us at the right time."

Studies indicate that the Moonies have devised the most sophisticated methods of luring converts. They call the first phase "love bombing." Once recruiters spot lonely students, they draw them into friendly conversation that typically ends with an invitation to dinner. Surrounded by smiling strangers who hold their hands and shower them with compliments, the students are then invited to a weekend retreat. "As instructors, we didn't tell them the truth," recalls Erica Heftmann. "If we had told them that we believed Moon was the Messiah or that we stayed up all night praying in the snow, they'd never join."

During the retreat, guests are subjected to an endless round of games, singing, exercise and vague religious discussions, with little time for sleep. Only the most discerning recruits realize that they are not being allowed to ask probing questions or make close friends. Yet ev-

explains Stanford University psychiatrist Donald T. Lunde. "It's a very tricky mental defense mechanism exploited to the hilt by the charismatic leader."

Cults may also exploit members by sending them into the streets to solicit funds or sell things like flowers, usually on behalf of pseudonymous organizations. "The leader tells you to go out and get $250," says Sherry Dietrich, 28, who joined the Children of God after a divorce in 1974. "Believe me, you beat your brains out to get that $250, and you don't come home until you get it."

In virtually all cults, sex is a central means of controlling members' lives. Some cult leaders, like Manson and Jones, use some of their followers—both male and female—for their own pleasure. But most religious cults rigidly segregate males and females and teach them that sexuality itself is evil. "Father" Moon not only arranges all marriages but also demands such powerful repression of sexual feelings that many members revert to pre-puberty innocence. "Women stop having their periods sometimes, and men may find that they do not shave as often," reports ex-Moonie Christopher Edwards, 24. "People begin to look younger. I was 22 when I came out and people told me I looked 15."

OUTLET FOR AGGRESSION

To bind members tighter to the cult, its leaders create the image of an evil outgroup that is supposedly trying to destroy them. For Hitler, it was the Jews. For Manson, it was blacks. For Jones, it was the FBI, the CIA and the Ku Klux Klan. For Synanon's Dederich, it is the government and the news

ery recruit is assigned a monitor who accompanies him everywhere, even to the bathroom. On Sunday, the potential converts are pressured to stay on for one last party. "Once they called their family or employer and told them they weren't coming in on Monday, we knew we had them for seven full days," says Heftmann. "And if they stayed seven days, they almost always became a member."

Isolation—from family, friends and all contact with the outside world—is the first step in what Los Angeles psychiatrist Frederick Hacker calls "the washing stage" of cultic mind control. Next, recruits are made to feel guilty about their past lives and recognize their need to be reborn like their all-knowing "brothers and sisters" in the new family of the cult. Several cults, such as the Children of God and Hare Krishna, even give recruits new names or devise private measurements of time to underscore the cult's new reality. But the development of a new personality is gradual. It requires various forms of sense deprivation, inculcated through loss of sleep, low-protein diets and exhausting rounds of chanting, praying and indoctrination in the thought of the new father figure.

TOOL OF SATAN

"It's all so simple," observes Tufts University psychiatrist Stanley Cath, who has studied the conversion techniques used by cults. "Converts have to believe only what they are told. They don't have to think, and this relieves tremendous tensions." Indeed, at Synanon, members tell recruits, "We will do your thinking for you," and inside Moon's camps independent thought is labeled a tool of Satan.

A critical point in the conversion process occurs when recruits are forced to make a major commitment to the cult. This may mean signing over one's property, bank account or children to the group, as in some religious cults, or even joining in drug or sex orgies, as demanded by Charles Manson in his "family." "Once you've done something that major, it's very hard to admit even to yourself that you've made a mistake, and subconsciously you will go to great lengths to rationalize what you did,"

media. And for most of the militant religious cults, the enemy is the members' natural parents. "Cults allow people to hate without feeling guilty and provide a safe, group-sanctioned outlet for aggression against the enemy," observes psychiatrist Hacker. Cult leaders also persuade members that they will die, either at the hands of enemies or cult loyalists, if they defect. The Children of God tell defectors that either God or Satan will strike them dead, and perform exorcisms on those who persist in leaving. Ex-Scientologists recall warnings of the "2-45" solution—anyone who drops out should get two .45-caliber slugs.

BASIC NEEDS

What transforms some cult leaders from spirited humanitarians into frenzied despots? Jones, for one, began his career by providing a humane haven for society's outcasts, yet ended up crushing those in his care. In such cases, a charismatic leader, who may be slightly disturbed, discovers that he is fulfilling a basic human need for increasing numbers of people. "Pretty soon, he is believing more and more in his own power, and it grows so that he begins to be burdened by it and a little paranoid," reasons psychiatrist Ari Kiev of the Cornell University Medical College. So he develops new, more punitive measures for binding his followers to him. "And if there comes a threat, a terminal illness or exposure, the leader resents the idea of anyone surviving him," adds New York psychiatrist Herbert Hendin. "He doesn't want any part of whatever is left to survive."

Jim Jones's Peoples Temple differs from other cults because of its emphasis on suicidal imagery, says Yale psychiatrist Robert J. Lifton, a specialist on death and thought control. Last week's atrocity, Lifton believes, "was a mixture of submitting to mass suicide and submitting to murder." As his own mind deteriorated into paranoia, Jones prepared his people for collective death by running them through suicide rehearsals. This enforced group commitment and the illusion that death for them would merely be a transition to an eternal community. "When Jones asked them to die for him, some may have gone willingly with him, but a large number probably just didn't know how to resist," Hendin argues. "You're dealing with a suicide, not of the mass group, but of the leader, who is taking the group with him."

Thus the tragedy at Jonestown was only superficially like past cases of mass suicide—the Jewish Zealots at Masada who killed themselves rather than be captured by the Romans, for example, or the Japanese who died on Saipan rather than surrender to the Americans in World War II. Instead of patriotism, religious faith or a cause larger than themselves, Jones's followers were ensnared by Jones himself. And like most charismatic figures, he left no one who could replace him as the personal embodiment of the cult. Although survivors in San Francisco insist that the Peoples Temple will go on, ex-members say it cannot survive without Jones.

Inevitably, the Jonestown atrocity has triggered national debate over cults and whether they can—and should—be curbed. Church scholars caution that the religions of Jesus, Muhammad and Buddha all began as cults, and civil libertarians warn that religious practices, no matter how odious, are protected by the First Amendment. The only legal way to attack them would be to prove that the psychological techniques practiced by some cults amount to coercive mind control, leaving their victims legally impaired. But the theory is tenuous. Dr. Stephen P. Hersh, assistant director of the National Institute of Mental Health, believes that the brainwashing attributed to cults is, in most cases, "high-pressure salesmanship." "Just because converts adopt beliefs that seem bizarre to their families, it does not follow that their choices are dictated by cult leaders," he says.

Historians say cults emerge whenever there is a serious break in the structure of society. The Industrial Revolution in England, the French Revolution and the westward movement in the U.S. all spawned new religious sects. Some scholars believe that the traumas of the '60s attracted young Americans to charismatic politicians and then, after the war in Vietnam, to equally charismatic religious figures. Although some experts think the current interest in cults has peaked, most insist that the better-financed groups, such as Moon's, will be around as long as the basic institutions of society—the family, schools and established churches—continue to turn out emotional orphans susceptible to a cult leader's blandishments.

A HEAVY PRICE

Even critics concede that many of today's cults work for social good and individual need by drawing recruits away from drugs and anomie into a steady life of service. But at best, the price is a heavy one in a free society: in joining a cult, the recruit surrenders a large measure of personal responsibility and potential growth in exchange for spiritual security. The mass deaths at Jonestown may yet do some good if they make searching young people think twice before seeking a family among the cultists.

—KENNETH L. WOODWARD with MARY HAGER in Washington, JANET HUCK in Los Angeles, MICHAEL REESE in San Francisco, RACHEL MARK and WILLIAM D. MARBACH in New York and bureau reports

Newsweek, December 4, 1978

77

THE WORLD OF CULTS

They crouch in dark basements in New York and San Francisco, worshiping the Devil. They wait patiently for the Second Coming or scan the skies for the spaceship that will bring the New Age. A few practice polygamy in isolated mountain communes. Tens of thousands have abandoned their families, friends, educations and careers to follow the teachings of a leader they will never meet.

By one estimate, 3 million Americans espouse the teachings of 3,000 religious and nonreligious cults. The groups run the gamut from the Bible-toting pacifists of The Way in Ohio to the marijuana-smoking Rastafarians from the Caribbean, who revere the late, deposed Ethiopian Emperor Haile Selassie as the Messiah. Some cults condemn all forms of violence and serve as unquestioned forces for good in the world: The Farm, for example, a 1,200-member commune in Tennessee, has donated more than $1 million to build homes and hospitals for earthquake victims in Guatemala. The Bible of the Church of Satan, on the other hand, declares: "If a man smite you on the cheek, smash him on the other."

DEFENSIVE ALLIANCES

Cults have ebbed and flowed through American history almost from its beginning, and there are signs that the latest wave may have peaked in the mid-1970s. But after the horror of Jonestown, warns sociology Prof. Jim Richardson of the University of Nevada, "there's a possibility of a backlash. There is already an anti-cult movement that has tried to get investigations and tax rules against cults." In reaction, some cults are exploring defensive alliances; last April, the Church of Scientology, the Unification Church and the Children of God formed APRL, the Alliance for the Preservation of Religious Liberty. Synanon donated at least some supplies and equipment to the Peoples Temple, and links have

been reported between Synanon and the Hare Krishnas.

Among the more conspicuous—and controversial—cults now active:

SYNANON: When Charles Dederich, a former alcoholic, founded Synanon in 1958, it was considered a revolutionary therapeutic community. Hundreds of alcoholics, drug addicts and down-at-the-mouth toughs moved into the California drug- and alcohol-rehabilitation center and, through a rigorous self-help pro-

gram, emerged healthy and happy. Aided by its skillful PR and contributions from wealthy liberals, Synanon became a $20 million business.

But as the community grew and prospered, it changed. Dederich, a powerful, hypnotic leader, came to see Synanon as an alternative to the outside world. He ordered his followers to shave their heads and swap spouses. When he decided there were too many children at Synanon, he mandated vasectomies for men (himself excluded) and abortions for women. Dederich, 65, began a campaign of intimidation against the media and anyone else who criticized the community. One lawyer who won a $300,000 judgment against Synanon was bitten by a rattlesnake left in his mailbox—allegedly by two members of Synanon. Today, the 900-member community resembles a cult far more than it does a drug center, and Dederich is trying to have it formally incorporated as a religion.

HARE KRISHNA: "We don't consider ourselves something that's sprung up in the '60s, founded by some man, but followers of an ancient tradition stemming from Krishna himself," says Laxmi Nath, president of the Berkeley, Calif., temple of the International Society for Krishna Consciousness. The Hare Krishnas began in the sixteenth century in India, where they were just one of many sects worshiping a reincarnation of the Hindu god of creation. A. C. Bhaktivedanta Swami Prabhupada brought one version of Krishna worship that was never very popular in India to the U.S. in 1965 and it turned into an easily identifiable cult. Young Hare Krishnas shaved their heads, put on saffron robes and took to the streets with their Hindu chants. They studied the ancient Vedic texts and promised their followers inner peace as an alternative to political chaos.

The Krishnas can be aggressive in their repeated requests for money, and some members have had serious run-ins with the law. But for the most part, they live quietly on several large farms they own, or in the houses they rent in metropolitan areas. Since Prabhupada died earlier this year, the group has not had a charismatic leader and may now be becoming more sect than cult. Most members now dress conventionally in public, and have stopped their street-corner chanting. Stillson Judah, who has studied the Krishnas at the Graduate Theological Union in Berkeley, believes the group wants to find a "way of accommodating itself with society."

UNIFICATION CHURCH: South Korean evangelist Sun Myung Moon, 58, controls the lives of 37,000 U.S. followers. When they join the Unification Church, young Moonies (their average age is 24) are encouraged to break all ties with their families and work as long as eighteen hours a day soliciting donations. As is typical of many cult leaders, Moon lives in comfort on a $625,000 New York estate while his followers reside in communal centers and are encouraged to give all their possessions to the church.

Moon preaches a contorted blend of Christianity, Puritan morality and Oriental philosophy. His followers hardly seem to notice that his spiritual message—that all the world's religions should be merged into a single movement headed by Moon himself—sounds secondary to his financial and political motives. He controls an empire of at least $75 million that ranges from a Wyoming delicatessen to a Tokyo trading company, and the U.S. Congress has investigated his ties to the authoritarian government of South Korea. Moon, who came to the U.S. in 1972, does not seem worried. "God has been very good to me," he says.

CHILDREN OF GOD: They began standing on street corners in the late 1960s, exhorting passers-by to give up their worldly ways and follow God. At first it was hard to tell them from the other Jesus freaks of the time. But the Children of God were clearly different. Their leader, David (Moses) Berg, now 58, taught that doomsday was just around the corner—and that he was God's messenger for the final days. He communicated with his followers through rambling "Mo letters."

Many of these epistles show a preoccupation with sex. In recruiting, Berg urged his female disciples to use their charms: "You roll those big eyes at them and peck them with that pretty little mouth and you flirt all around them," advised one Mo letter. By at least one report, things didn't stop there: on the island of Tenerife, COG women were accused of taking prospective recruits to bed. When local prostitutes complained of the competition, Berg reportedly put a curse on the island—and shortly after that, the worst accident in airline history took 583 lives on the runway at Tenerife.

Life with Berg isn't easy. Former COG members tell how they had to memorize Bible verses before they could sleep or eat, and pick through garbage for food and clothes. Berg fled the country in 1974, just before the New York attorney general published a highly critical report on the COG. But the cult still claims 10,000 members in 120 communes around the world, and Berg still keeps in touch with periodic Mo letters.

Some organizations can come to resemble cults even though their members do not live communally or share religious beliefs. Werner Erhard, for example, has impressive power over thousands of Americans who have taken his est courses. He promises them spiritual and emotional fulfillment in 60-hour seminars in which the chief techniques are attacking the ego, restricting food and drink and inducing mental strain.

Growing numbers of parents of cult members are worried enough about losing their children to take the extreme, and costly, step of kidnapping and "deprograming" them. Ever since deprogrammer Ted Patrick was sentenced to a year in prison in 1976 for such a kidnapping, many have first sought legal sanction through "conservatorships" to temporarily gain court-ordered custody of their adult children. The process is clearly working. Hundreds of devotees of various cults have been deprogramed in the last few years. But some cults are fighting back with lawsuits to bar deprograming as an infringement on religious freedom, and sometimes the faith of the young believer is not shaken. Several have successfully sued their deprogrammers for invasion of privacy.

In desperation, some parents have asked the Federal government for help. But government spokesmen say their hands are tied by the Constitution's guarantee of religious freedom, lack of hard evidence that specific cults are committing crimes, and by agency guidelines. The Justice Department must have information that a "kidnap" victim is being held against his will, for ransom and has been taken across state lines before it can prosecute a case. (Before last week's tragedy in Guyana, the FBI had only one complaint against the Peoples Temple: a letter from the worried mother of a cult member alleging kidnapping, but there was no evidence that he was being held against his will.) The Federal Bureau of Investigation can monitor a group only when there is evidence that it has broken Federal law or poses a security risk. Many government officials say they would not change the present laws, even if they could. "We can't have it both ways," said Homer Boynton, bureau spokesman. "In a democracy, in order to have freedom and liberty, there has to be a certain amount of risk-taking."

'ATTRITION IS VERY HIGH'

But cults—even the most religious—are not above the law. The government can prosecute a group when it appears to have committed a crime. Last summer, for example, eleven Scientologists—members of the quasi-scientific, self-help cult founded by former science-fiction writer L. Ron Hubbard—were accused of breaking into a government office and were indicted on 28 counts of conspiracy, stealing government property, obstruction of justice and perjury. Six states outlaw use of marijuana and other drugs in cult religious ceremonies.

In the end, the best hope for those concerned about the power of cults may be that many members are dropping out of their own accord. "A lot more people leave these groups voluntarily than they or the deprogrammers would like to admit," says sociologist Richardson. "Attrition is very high." Even within the mind-bending anthills of the cults, Americans seem to retain at least some of their native wit—and their stubborn independence.

—MELINDA BECK and SUSAN FRAKER with ELAINE SHANNON in Washington, JEFF B. COPELAND in San Francisco and bureau reports

ONE DOLLAR · DECEMBER 18, 1978

New West

The Making of a
Madman

By Phil Tracy

THE MIND rebels. Too much death; too much madness; too many grotesque details. The punditry mills grind on. Some quick and dirty analysts have tried to blame the various tragedies on some specifically California malaise, some disease of permissiveness, some half-formed notion that tolerance destroys other values and reaps its own ghastly, inevitable rewards. This is media foolishness, of course, the slick and slippery generalization. California is no more a breeding ground of insanity than Uganda or Bangladesh or Wounded Knee, South Dakota; the human capacity for villainy is not geographically determined. And yet...we do seem to have more than our share of paranoid personality cults. As more and more people seem willing to cede their identities to loony authority figures and participate in obscure rites with masochistic fervor, the other issues of human life, the questions directed outside the simplistic universe of the cult, become obscured. The motivating questions of journalism— what does it mean? how does it work?— get lost in the shuffle of rhetoric and ritual. It therefore becomes all the more necessary to examine the nature of reality, to explore the outside world, to attempt to grasp fragments of the truth, in the belief, ironically emblazoned over the throne of Jim Jones, that those who do not remember the past are condemned to repeat it. In uncovering and printing the facts about our investigation of Jim Jones, we have done some violence to the memory of the late George Moscone. That is regrettable, but it seemed that we had little choice. Assassination inevitably makes heroes of its victims, Leo Ryan no less than George Moscone, and that emotional reality is true but irrelevant. We are searching for reasons, for the lessons of death and madness. That's the point of Phil Tracy's revealing look at the mental and emotional pressures that motivated Jim Jones, and Jeanie Kasindorf's examination of how Jones manipulated power in San Francisco. We wish to remember the past as it really happened; we do not wish to be condemned to insane repetition.—The Editors

JIM JONES
THE MAKING OF A MADMAN
By Phil Tracy

IT DOESN'T matter now. Nothing can change what has happened. But just for the record, there was a time when James Warren Jones preached the social gospel of Jesus Christ and preached it well.

In the late 1950s, the state of Indiana was every bit as bigoted toward blacks as any town in Mississippi. Rest facilities were segregated, and the textbooks used in the black school system taught its half-illiterate students that Negroes were mentally inferior to whites. The Ku Klux Klan was active, and people protesting for their civil rights were openly beaten on the streets of Indianapolis. It was here that Jim Jones, Indiana born, the son of a Klan member, chose to establish a racially integrated congregation.

The first Peoples Temple was located in downtown Indianapolis. Services were held on Sundays and two nights during the week; free meals and clothing were provided for the neighborhood's destitute. Inside, Jones would exhort his followers to hark back to the spirit of the early Christians, preaching that the struggle for black equality was no different from the persecutions suffered by Christians at the hands of the Roman Empire. Just as the early martyrs had been slaughtered for their faith, so too must modern Christians risk persecution for their belief in equality for everyone.

It would be useful if we could pinpoint the exact moment when Jones first stepped over the line that separates the saint from the psychotic. But we can't. The line is so thin, and surely he overreached it before anything showed in his behavior. For convenience, let us say Jones crossed the threshold of sanity the first time he declared himself God before his congregation. That was sometime in 1964.

But Jones had been building toward that announcement for some years. Starting around 1960, he dropped the references to the social gospel and began preaching something else: an odd mixture of Malcolm X and Father Divine. He would spend four or five hours in the pulpit each Sunday telling his mostly black audience that they were like the children of Israel, set upon by enemies. Persecuted for their love of Jesus and their black skins, they must arm themselves with the strength of the Almighty. He would plunge the congregation into the depths of despair, exaggerating the bitterness and hatred that always confronted them beyond the doors of the church and embellishing the portrait of their bleak condition with predictions of far greater sorrows to come.

45

Then, gradually, Jones would begin to reverse their anguish. He described their ultimate triumph over all who surrounded them—if only they would follow the path of the Lord and his chosen minister, Jim Jones. Now he would build them up to fever pitch with his picture of the promised land they would create for themselves, a land where everyone would be as equal in life as they were in the eyes of the Lord.

Jones became so adept at oratory that his followers developed reverence for the man. They called him "Father," asking him to heal their ills, both real and imagined. Jones obliged, practicing a fairly common form of faith healing by laying his hands upon the sufferer's head. Soon they called him prophet.

Jones's apocalyptic visions became bolder. A nuclear holocaust was coming. The anointed would have to obey him unflinchingly if they were to survive immolation.

Step by step Jones and his faithful flock kept upping their dependence on each other. The more his followers praised him, the greater were Jones's claims of power: a deadly two-step dance. By the time Jones "revealed" himself, they were primed to accept him as their messiah, the one who would lead them out of the treacherous, blindly evil world he had created inside their heads. Within his tiny Indiana congregation, at its height no more than 500 strong, Jones achieved a degree of power rarely felt by mortal men. No one dared question his word. In the eyes of his flock, he was omnipotent.

JONES'S FIRST MOVE

was to relocate his followers to the Northern California community of Redwood Valley, located a

few miles from the county seat, Ukiah. Some hundred persons eventually made the journey. Houses had to be rented for them. Jobs had to be found for those who could work. Jones wanted to open half a dozen nursing homes like the two he had operated in his and his wife's name back in Indianapolis. The homes could be staffed by members unable to hold down outside jobs, and elderly members who qualified for Medicare would act as patients. But first they needed money and a base from which to recruit new members. Redwood Valley's somewhat suspicious white population was out of the question. There was so much work to do, and Jones was the only man capable of making the properly in-

A man with a congregation convinced he was God addicted himself to one of the deadliest mind-distorting drugs available

spired decisions.

So Jones reached out for help. Always given to working extraordinary hours, sometime shortly after reaching Northern California Jones began taking amphetamine to help himself keep up the pace. A man with a congregation convinced he was God addicted himself to one of the deadliest mind-distorting drugs available.

There were two registered nurses who made the trip with Jones from Indiana. They kept him supplied with the drug in tablet form and an occasional injection. One of them was eventually caught in the act of stealing and was let go, but nobody pressed the matter in court. Later, it was rumored, friendly doctors in the Mendocino area provided the drug by prescription. During his San Francisco years, Jones was said never to leave the temple without a nurse who traveled with him and carried a satchel of medicines.

It is written in the medical books and known on every street corner where junkies collect: After a while, speed drives you mad. It also drives you sky-high and provides the kind of synthetic adrenalin that lets you work 30, even 40 hours in a row, at peak efficiency. The perfect kind of drug for a messiah about to engage in a monumental undertaking.

The exact nature of that undertaking was slow to emerge. The threat of nuclear holocaust was beginning to wear a little thin, and even though Jones occasionally mentioned some secret caves where the temple was stockpiling food supplies and equipment, the war in Vietnam made the possibility seem somehow remote.

Jones began to visit the San Francisco Bay area without his congregation, attending various civic and protest rallies, gradually picking up on the latest New Left theories—everything from radical feminist beliefs to the oft-predicted fascist counterrevolution. He learned about ego-denial, confrontational consciousness raising, communal living and revolutionary discipline.

Jones came to believe that his mission was to emulate not Christ, but Lenin or

Mao Tse-tung. He was going to create a brand-new social order based on racial equality, revolutionary communalism and sexual liberation. All races would live together. All goods would be held in common. All bourgeois family patterns would be broken down. To help him accomplish this massive transformation, Jones determined he would have to recruit and train a highly skilled, elite corps to carry out his orders.

For the first time Jones began to go out and actively recruit whites to his church. He chose them carefully, with an eye toward the services each could provide. Attorneys, social workers, young single women with office backgrounds—all were sought out and given the Jones treatment. Some came by chance, others after a carefully laid-out plan of introduction. What Jones was always looking for was the unfulfilled, the incomplete and dissatisfied. He went after college dropouts, former drug users and those who hung out on the fringe of left-wing politics. To each he made elaborate overtures of love and concern. He would listen for hours to their theories on how to reconstruct the world and then throw his own version of their words back at them. In each case an all-fulfilling love was offered if only the individual would commit himself to Jones.

In late 1966 and continuing over the course of the next two years, some 100 to 150 new church members, mostly white and mostly young, were induced to join Jones's older, mostly black congregation. They were quickly given positions of responsibility within the temple. In addition to bringing some order to temple financial records, these new recruits helped to increase the community's income through the use of mass mailings and selected mailing lists. Where Jones had relied on car pools to bring Sunday worshipers up from San Francisco and Oakland, his lieutenants leased Greyhound buses. Attendance at the Redwood Valley temple shot up from 500 to 2,000 and, later, double that. Jones began to hold massive rallies in cities as far away as Portland and Seattle. The church income kept doubling, and doubling again.

One day Jones announced that he was appointing a twenty-person "planning commission" that would thereafter be responsible for the running of the temple. When in a matter of months the planning commission had grown both in size and stature in the eyes of the rest of the temple members, Jones called the commission together in secret and revealed his daring conception for a new social order and the role he expected its members to play in bringing it about. Both the older members who still saw Jones as God and the younger ones who considered him their personal leader accepted the challenge immediately.

THE MADNESS wasn't so much in the social order Jones intended to create. Perhaps his ideas were more idealistic than most, but they contained nothing that hadn't been preached in one form or another somewhere in California for at least 40 years. The madness was in the methods Jones employed to bring his transformation about. The methods of a paranoid, whose mind was under assault by the constant use of speed.

Sometimes, late at night when the speed made him ramble, he would tell commission members exactly what he was doing. Every revolutionary movement had been run by a highly trained, dedicated cadre. Great suffering and sacrifice always accompanied such upheavals. He had to break down their inbred defenses in order to recondition them for his new social order. Discipline was everything. Swept up in his speed-laced euphoria, Jones thought he was remaking his planning commission into a programmed, revolutionary vanguard. Actually, he was making its members over in his own defective image. He was driving them stark, raving mad.

Demonstrations of loyalty were required continually. Jones introduced all-night sessions during which commission members were ordered to stand in the middle of a circle while their friends and loved ones barraged them with personal criticism. Next, they were informed that their marriages and sexual partnerships were corrupt vestiges of the bourgeois order. Husbands and wives were forced to sleep with different partners. Jones had a special habit of arranging for a husband or wife to walk into the room as

Illustrated by James Grashow

he was seducing the person's spouse. Jones required confessions on a regular basis, statements describing sexual perversions or acts of violence that had supposedly been committed.

Spying was systematized. Jones announced that government agents were trying to penetrate the planning commission, and that thereafter each member should be prepared to inform him as to the actions and statements of any other member. Within a matter of months it was part of the daily routine for the constantly increasing number of planning commission members to report on the conversations, attitudes, behavior and personal life of all the other members with whom they had contact.

Only someone ensnared in the paranoiac throes of amphetamine would dare set up such a system. A saner person would have folded under such an information overload. Jones methodically campaigned to undermine and destroy every vestige of ego and self-respect remaining in his already bewildered lieutenants. He would catch them off guard, repeating conversations they'd had with others and pretending he had received the information through a vision. During "self-criticism sessions" Jones would have commission members reveal intimacies they had shared with each other. Mockingly, he would then describe his own sexual encounters with them. Any personality quirk—a fear of mice, a dislike for housework—was used to ridicule, humiliate or punish whoever had displayed it. Casual sentences, little vanities, a flirtatious smile could provide grounds for group discipline.

But the worm at the heart of Jones's covenant with his brainwashed elite was the constantly increasing seizures of madness that were overtaking him. Some joy-riding teenagers fired a couple of .22s at the Redwood Valley Temple one beer-drinking Saturday night. Jones responded by building a 40-foot guard tower manned day and night by lookouts with high-powered rifles. Armed patrols dressed in military attire protected the entrance.

Jones's behavior during Sunday services became more erratic. Although temple ads in Bay Area papers prominently mentioned the church's longstanding affiliation with the Disciples of Christ and announced sermons on the gospel of Jesus, Jones periodically startled his congregation by denouncing the Bible as a pack of lies and calling Christ "just another prophet."

The healing services grew bizarre. Old black women, gripped by momentary, self-induced hysteria, were deluded into thinking they had "passed" cancerous tissue. The "cancers" were actually marinated chicken livers prepared in advance. Aides would parade up and down the aisles of the church holding the foul-smelling tissue above their heads.

Shortly after Martin Luther King was killed, Jones faked his own assassination with the help of an aide who fired blank cartridges and a Baggie full of chicken blood to stain his shirt. Jones reappeared an hour later, claiming he had raised himself from the dead. After that, planning commission members dressed in costume and makeup would collapse "dead" at a prearranged signal, and be brought back to life by Jones. These antics eventually attracted the attention of the *San Francisco Examiner*'s then religion editor; in September of 1972 he wrote a series of articles on Jones's healing powers. But Jones was able to squelch any follow-up investigation by organizing a massive letter-writing and picket-line campaign against the paper.

Within the temple, though, the *Examiner* series did have immediate impact. Jones decreed that thereafter no temple member could go anywhere, except to work, unaccompanied by a guardian. Temple members were not to speak to strangers unless the conversation had been prearranged for some specific purpose. Two temple services would be held on Sunday, one for the masses who had yet to see the light and another for the hard-core members who had made a complete commitment to Father.

The second service rapidly evolved into an all-night discipline session. The same brainwashing mechanisms that had worked so well with his planning commission were unleashed by Jones upon a congregation of more than 1,000 people. In one sense it was audacious. At any moment, had 50 people stood up and said they were leaving, the whole enterprise might have collapsed. But they didn't. Many of the blacks still believed Jones was God, even when he started telling them there was no God and that he was the reincarnation of Lenin.

Jones told them that the United States was about to be taken over by a fascist dictatorship. Once in power, the new rulers, including the Ku Klux Klan, would practice racial genocide on all blacks in America. They, the members of Peoples Temple, were going to escape to a new promised land, the Marxist republic of Guyana, South America.

BUT FIRST an enormous amount of material and money would have to be collected. Throughout the five-year "preparation

period" that followed, Peoples Temple became a huge vacuum, swallowing property, inheritances, gifts, whatever

valuables its members were able to get their hands on. And they worked at it. Children confronted their non-temple parents and demanded that they make donations to the church. Single people were instructed to apply to the state as foster parents so the monthly income provided by the government could be turned over to the temple. Working members were required to turn over at least one fourth of their salaries. The elderly were expected to sign over their Social Security checks. Temple youngsters were sent out to beg.

Jones told his rapt and overwhelmed congregation how the government, the CIA and the FBI were dedicated to thwarting their escape to Guyana. Even as he spoke, spies existed within their midst. For that reason and to prove their love for Jones and the revolution he was leading, church members would have to report to "counselors," members of the planning commission who were each made responsible for ten to twenty ordinary church members. They were to report any conversation they had with other church members that might seem out of the ordinary. If anyone expressed any kind of doubt about Jones, a report would be made to a counselor immediately. The counselors, in turn, reported back to the planning commission, which would make a recommendation as to the appropriate discipline to be meted out. Jones always made the final decision.

As the months went on the closed services grew to three a week. Often they were ugly. Whereas in the beginning discipline had been limited to a handful of swats with a large leather whip, now people were being beaten 50, 100, 150 times with a four-foot wooden paddle. The PC, as planning commission members came to be known, patrolled the aisles, reaching in and grabbing anyone who might have fallen asleep or didn't seem to be paying attention. They'd be beaten, humiliated and made to say thank you. Almost anything could get a person singled out for a beating: talking to strangers, eating too much at dinner, making an unauthorized visit.

In time, such mind-bending cruelty and constant harassment had the desired effect. The entire temple congregation was made over into Jim Jones's psychotic vision of the world that was to be. A clockwork model of self-induced, self-sustaining terror, the Peoples Temple became a sprawling, monstrous manifestation of the madness attacking Jones.

It took close to five years before Jones's insane artifice finally unraveled itself in the jungles of Guyana. Along the way a couple of hundred deserted, snapped back into reality by the horrors befalling them. But nearly 1,000 stayed, unswerving, right up to the very end. Their revolutionary suicide was the ultimate commitment to Father, in whom they had trust. ▄▄

JIM JONES

THE SEDUCTION OF SAN FRANCISCO

By Jeanie Kasindorf

"We could make it to the big time in San Francisco."

—The Reverend Jim Jones

JIM JONES came to San Francisco and he made it to the big time. Jim Jones came to San Francisco with his devoted followers and he sold their votes for political power. Then, when the first stories of the horror that was Peoples Temple were revealed, he used that power to buy political protection.

From 1971 to 1977 Jim Jones answered the age-old political question: Who can you buy with the right number of people? In San Francisco last week the answer was clear: the Mayor. The District Attorney. The city's most powerful black politician, Assemblyman Willie Brown. And along with Brown, the voice of the *San Francisco Chronicle* columnist Herb Caen.

SAN FRANCISCO was the perfect city for Jim Jones. For the politics of San Francisco are a unique blend of old-fashioned ward politics, where black ministers are the men politicians count on to deliver votes, combined with power-to-the-people slogans left over from the sixties. Jim Jones had the slogans. And Jim Jones had the people.

In 1971 he started to move his Peoples Temple followers from Mendocino County to the city and bought a temple building on Geary Street in the heart of the Fillmore District. He immediately began to search for political allies in San Francisco's black community.

Terry Francois, then the one black member of the Board of Supervisors, remembers it well. "All of a sudden I began to get these very flattering letters saying that Pastor Jim had told them what an outstanding job I was doing and what a fine leader I was and inviting me to attend their services. Well, I became suspicious. It was obvious to me what he was trying to do. And I didn't want to become a captive of Jim Jones. I never did respond. But others, obviously, did."

Assemblyman Willie Brown, a folk hero in his Fillmore District, became one of Jones's strongest political supporters. "Willie didn't need his votes," Francois says, "but what people like Willie Brown have to worry about is that a guy like Jim Jones could field a candidate and beat them. When politics is your career, that's a very legitimate fear, so you try to join them. If you can't beat 'em, you join 'em."

Jones also formed a political and personal alliance with Dr. Carlton Goodlett, the publisher of the *Sun Reporter*, the black newspaper in San Francisco. Goodlett became Jones's personal physician and professional publicist in the pages of the *Sun Reporter*.

Jones was setting a pattern that he would repeat successfully in the white community: forming an alliance with the major politicians and major media voices at the same time. "You know," Terry Francois said, when it was all over, "I must confess that I didn't take him on publicly. How could I? Goodlett would have editorialized against me."

Jones also went after control of the major black power bases in San Francisco: the NAACP, the Black Leadership Forum and the black churches. When he sent the Black Leadership Forum, the major black political endorsing body, a check for $750 for annual dues for 30 Peoples Temple members, the officers saw what was coming. "Those 30 persons all would have been eligible to vote, and we saw Jim Jones or one of his lieutenants becoming the president," says H. Welton Flynn. "So we rewrote the bylaws."

When Jones made a similar effort to take over the San Francisco NAACP, he did much better. One NAACP board member says that Jones paid the $10 annual dues for an estimated 300 Peoples Temple followers. Jones was then elected to the NAACP's board of directors.

The Reverend Hannibal Williams, a black preacher-politician and longtime foe of Jim Jones, remembers the day one NAACP worker called him to complain about Jones. "They had to go and leave their offices and get in a public phone booth," he says, "because the switchboard girl at the NAACP belonged to Peoples Temple and they were afraid she was reporting everything that went in and out of that office."

Williams, who was president of the San Francisco Inter-denominational Ministerial Alliance, tried to stop Jim Jones from taking over other churches' congregations. His story was a forewarning of what was to come.

"Almost every minister who had a large church got stacks of letters," Williams recalls. "He thought he was going to lock up his ownership of the territory. So another minister said to me: 'Somebody's got to do something about this guy.' So I set up a meeting at the Third Baptist Church. What happened was there were a couple of black ministers in there who Jones already owned, and they went back and reported everything to him. It was after that that I started receiving threats. I received at least a dozen telephone calls threatening me with everything, including death.

"I took this to the chief of police and to our so-called district attorney, Freitas.

Jim Jones had made it to the big time by buying the silence of San Francisco. Last week, San Francisco began taking stock and laying blame.

THE LATE MAYOR, George Moscone, said that his office would not conduct an investigation into Jones or his temple.

And the chief of police goofed me off, and Joe Freitas goofed me off. At the district attorney's office, they said fill out a form and that's the end of it. Chief Gain sent me over to somebody who practically told me complaining was a waste of time."

SOMETHING had happened in San Francisco. In the intervening years between the time Peoples Temple sent Hannibal

Williams friendly letters and the time Peoples Temple sent him threats of death, there had been a city election in San Francisco.

The city election of 1975 could not have been better suited to Jim Jones's goals. Mayoral candidate George Moscone and district attorney candidate Joe Freitas were both in tough races. They needed every vote they could get, and Jim Jones was there to deliver them. For Jim Jones was the only political leader in San Francisco who could completely control the way his followers would vote.

The Reverend Jones could turn out a crowd for any politician's speech and did it so often that Peoples Temple members became known among the mayor's and district attorneys staff as "the troops." If you gave Jim Jones six hours' notice, he could deliver 2,000 people. "They were made to order," one Democratic county chairman's staff member raved. "You should have seen it—old ladies on crutches, whole families, little kids, blacks, whites."

The Reverend Jones could also turn out a crowd for election day. Temple members had to write letters for candidates, register others to vote and ring doorbells on election day. Every Wednesday night was letter-writing night, when members would spend six hours writing hundreds of letters. "They told us to use different pens, types of paper, different envelopes, to write small here and large there," former Peoples Temple member Jim Cobb said. "We would look at telephone books and get a first name here and a last name there, to make up the false names."

The night before the election, Jones had secretaries call each Peoples Temple member. "Father loves you very much and there's a danger out tonight," they said. "Get a pencil and paper and take down these names." The next day church members had to turn in their ballot stub to Jones to prove that they had voted.

In the December, 1975, run-off elections, Jim Jones turned out 150 precinct workers, plus an estimated 2,500 voters for the mayor. Willie Brown would later claim that Jones won the election for Moscone (who won by only 4,000 votes) and for Freitas (who won by only 9,000). "In a tight race like the ones that George or Freitas had," he said, "forget it without Jones."

The mayor returned the favor when his screening committee named Jim Jones as one of 43 candidates for appointment to the city boards and commissions. The mayor first asked Jones to serve on the city's Human Rights Commission, but Jones said no. The mayor's office said Jones turned down the appointment "because he had intensive travel ahead of him." Former Peoples Temple member Grace Stoen said Jones turned it down because the Human Rights Commission "wasn't big enough fish."

In October, the mayor came through with what Jones considered a better appointment. It was to the San Francisco Housing Authority Commission, where Moscone could guarantee that Jones would be chairman.

As soon as Jones became Housing Authority chairman, the mayor's office called the Housing Authority staff to say that three members of Peoples Temple would be coming over to apply for jobs. The message was clear: Give jobs to them. Jones got a $15,496-a-year job running employee-training programs for one of his closest aides, Jean Brown; a $9,256-a-year secretary's job for temple member Vera Young; and a $14,420-a-year job as Jean Brown's assistant for yet another temple member, Caroline Layton.

Jones played no major role at the Housing Authority other than chairing the twice-monthly meetings. A Housing Authority employee remembers those meetings well. "It was always very creepy," he says. "It was weird because he kept one guard in his car all the time. And he showed up with three or four bodyguards and a busful of supporters. They sat in the auditorium and they clapped at everything he did. Even if he sneezed, they clapped."

The mayor's office was not the only one where Jim Jones developed political muscle. Jones had his chief legal adviser, Tim Stoen, sitting in an assistant district attorney's office. It was a tactic that Jones had developed back in his Mendocino County days. When Stoen, then a young Alameda County lawyer, joined the temple, he got a job as assistant district attorney for Mendocino County. When Jones moved his power base to San Francisco, Tim Stoen got a job with the San Francisco district attorney.

Mendocino County Supervisor Al Barbero, who had worked with Stoen, remembers it well. "The day Mr. Freitas

was sworn into office," he says, "I was watching TV and I look at the first guy in the front row, on the TV show at eleven, and there's our Tim Stoen sitting down there. So I run into him back here and I said: 'Tim, you take a good picture on TV.' 'Oh,' he says, 'I just happened to be there, Mr. Barbero.'" Barbero chuckles. "And I said: 'Isn't that funny.'"

Five months after that swearing-in ceremony, Tim Stoen became head of the voter-fraud unit for Joe Freitas. Jones ordered Stoen to get an office right next to District Attorney Freitas's. This time Stoen didn't succeed.

Tim Stoen was assistant district attorney for San Francisco and chief legal adviser to Jim Jones from May, 1976, to April, 1977. It is not known whether Stoen used his job to help Jim Jones avoid investigation, or whether Stoen used his job to spy for Jim Jones. What is known is that Stoen's presence made people afraid to file official complaints against Jim Jones in San Francisco as his presence had also done in Mendocino County.

ONCE JIM JONES had helped get city politicians elected, he began to devise ways to keep them under his control. With his

temple members, it was threats of death or beating that maintained loyalty. With San Francisco's leading politicians, it may very well have been the threat of blackmail.

Jones was prepared to smear politicians as right-wing fascists or left-wing radicals if they didn't go along. "Jones used racism," explains Leo Ryan aide Joe Holsinger. "Here he was bringing all races together, and if you didn't go along with the game, you were a racist in the San Francisco community. It's political blackmail."

Al Mills was the official temple photographer until he left the group in 1975. "If it was a politician Jones wanted to compromise," he says, "he would have someone standing behind the podium, and on cue they would raise clenched fists and I would take a picture. They would look like revolutionaries. He just wanted these pictures on file if some politician ever turned against him."

Jones may have used sexual blackmail as well. For two years rumors have circulated in San Francisco that two of the city's leading politicians were provided with women by the Reverend Jones. They were only rumors until the week of

COLUMNIST Herb Caen attacked New West's first reports of beatings in the temple and extortion of property.

the Guyana massacre, when Wayne Pietila, a former Jones bodyguard, told Oakland's KTVU that Jones had ordered women to try to sexually compromise local politicians. "I was there with him when he made assignments," Pietila said. "Part of their job was to compromise politicians sexually."

POLITICIANS were not the only people Jim Jones tried to compromise. Jones also tried to compromise the city's press. He started by courting *San Francisco Chronicle* city editor Abe Mellinkoff and *Chronicle* columnist Herb Caen. Mellinkoff didn't buy Jones's story. Herb Caen did. As Caen's longtime friend Willie Brown tells the story, "Peoples Temple provided $500 to a needy child, and somebody, I assume now it was from Peoples Temple, wrote Caen about it." Caen set up a luncheon meeting with Jim Jones and Willie Brown. It was the first of two long lunches with Jim Jones and several admiring Herb Caen columns.

When city editor Mellinkoff left that job in 1975, Jones contacted the new city editor, Steve Gavin. This time it worked. "He liked me, I guess," Gavin says today. "I sort of liked him. He was a very exciting, very impressive person who said all the right things. He was a fascinating man, absolutely fascinating, possibly the most fascinating person I've ever met. He invited me to the service and it was a real high, this joyous kind of feeling of love and caring for each other."

Gavin was susceptible. Gavin's reporters were not. When Gavin asked *Chronicle* reporter Julie Smith to do a Peoples Temple story in March, 1976, she started asking more questions than Jim Jones had bargained for. Smith became the target of a massive letter campaign. Jones had Peoples Temple members tape-record her calls to study her voice, and District Attorney Joe Freitas, on Jones's behalf, called a friend of Smith's to ask if she "could be trusted."

"It was so distressing," Smith said. "Just this vast thing coming at you. All the letters, all the phone calls, all this murmuring from people in high places. What happened, in my case, was that I ended up being completely ineffectual. The article ended up being a goddamn valentine."

Jones had won. But not for long. Smith's story piqued the interest of another *Chronicle* reporter, Marshall

Kilduff. "I went to Gavin," Kilduff recalls, "and I said: 'You know, Steve, this guy seems sort of political. Gee, he gives me the creeps—the security, the refusal to be interviewed. I don't think we've really taken a good look at this guy.'" But by now Gavin had gotten to know Jones and Peoples Temple even better. Gavin wouldn't let Kilduff investigate the story.

It was then that Kilduff took the Peoples Temple story to *New West*. On February 7, 1977, senior editor Kevin Starr gave Kilduff an assignment to go ahead with the story. On February 14, 1977, a delegation of Peoples Temple members, consisting of a group one editor later called "the lawyers and the bouncers," marched into *New West*'s San Francisco office to talk to Starr. It took just one conversation.

On February 15, 1977, Starr killed the story. "A large delegation from the Peoples Temple called upon me yesterday and convinced me that further publicity at this time would have a bad effect upon the church's ministry," Starr wrote Marshall Kilduff. *"New West* Magazine has no wish to interfere with the most important work of the Peoples Temple at this time. *New West* Magazine is very interested in maintaining good community relations. I am therefore asking you not to do the Peoples Temple story...." Starr sent a carbon copy of the letter to the Reverend Jim Jones.

Two weeks after writing that letter, Starr, who was a protégé of *New West* founder Clay Felker, resigned from the magazine in the wake of the *New West* take-over by publisher Rupert Murdoch. Starr was replaced by Rosalie Muller Wright, an editor at the *San Francisco Examiner*. Soon after Wright took over, Kilduff (who had had the piece assigned and then rejected by *San Francisco* magazine after another visit from a Peoples Temple delegation) brought the story back to *New West*.

"I REMEMBER it so well," Wright says today. "Marshall sort of put the manuscript down and said: 'I don't know whether I'm crazy or not. I just can't get anybody to print this story.'" Wright assigned Kilduff and *New West* contributing editor Phil Tracy to continue work on the story.

Throughout that spring and into the summer, *New West* was the target of a high-pressure campaign organized by Reverend Jim Jones and the San Fran-

cisco mayor's office to keep *New West* from running the Peoples Temple story.

Telephone calls came in at the rate of 50 a day. Advertisers received calls asking them to pull their ads. Publisher Rupert Murdoch received 600 pleading letters and phone calls in three weeks.

This time the letters were not sent from fake names that Peoples Temple members took out of the telephone book. Jim Jones and the mayor's office successfully used the San Francisco city fathers for this campaign. "It was as if they turned out the entire old-boy network of San Francisco," Wright recalls. "Cyril Magnin called me and told me: 'I got a call from the mayor's office. I hear you're doing a story that will reflect badly on San Francisco.' "

THE SECOND week in July, 1977, as the *New West* story was going to press, Jim Jones left San Francisco for Jonestown, Guyana, on a trip from which he would never return. In the mayor's and the district attorney's offices, staff members laughed, "Well, there go the troops."

On July 18, 1977, *New West* hit the newsstands with the first story of the horror inside Peoples Temple. Kilduff and Tracy reported eyewitness accounts of how Jim Jones forced members to turn over their life savings to him, stole funds that the Alameda County Probation Department paid him to care for wards of the court, staged fake cancer cures with plastic bags of chicken livers, beat Peoples Temple members and threatened to kill a young man who wanted to leave the temple.

On Sunday, July 24, Assemblyman Willie Brown, who had been in touch with the temple by phone the week after the *New West* story broke, attended the service at Peoples Temple to speak about the good work of the Reverend Jones.

"The *New West* article didn't disturb me," Brown says today. "*New West* had tried to get me, so I could not feel it was a friendly organ. I think the efforts of people in *New West* should be taken with a grain of salt. When people [like those interviewed in the story] leave good friends and get into a pissing contest, it certainly would not be an objective appraisal."

On July 26, the mayor's office issued a statement. "I have read the recent well-publicized article concerning the Reverend Jim Jones and the Peoples Temple," the statement said, "and find it to be a series of allegations with absolutely no hard evidence that the Reverend Jones has violated any laws, either local, state or federal. The mayor's office does not and will not conduct any investigation into the Reverend Jones or the Peoples Temple."

On August 3 the mayor's office announced that the Reverend Jones, dictating his message by short-wave radio from Jonestown, Guyana, had resigned from the San Francisco Housing Authority. Jones could not continue in the post, the statement said, because of "lack of time."

On August 8, Herb Caen began sniping at *New West* and defending the Reverend Jones. On August 18, Herb Caen ran the following item: "The Reverend Jim Jones, target of a ceaseless media barrage these days, wants to come home and answer the charges being leveled against him and his Peoples Temple, but his lawyer, Charles Garry, is advising against it. 'Garry thinks Jim would be chewed up by the media,' says Jones's aide, Mike Prokes. 'Jim is dying to come back,' from the South American country of Guyana, where he is running a church-backed mission. 'This campaign against Jim,' suggests Prokes, 'is orchestrated at the highest level, perhaps FBI or CIA.' "

Willie Brown insists that he has no influence over Herb Caen. "I do not attempt to pimp Herb Caen, period," he says. Still, it was not the first time Caen had come to the defense of Willie Brown and his friends. Several months before, when *Chronicle* reporters broke a story that Willie Brown had received a free six-foot television screen from a massage-parlor owner, there was a bitter in-house fight at the newspaper between the reporters and Caen, who sniped at the news story in his column.

The only public figure in San Francisco who did not continue to defend Jim Jones was district attorney Joe Freitas. The morning the *New West* story hit the newsstands, Freitas announced that his special prosecutor, Robert Graham, would conduct an investigation into the allegations against Jim Jones. Eight weeks later, Freitas announced that a staff of five attorneys had found no evidence that could be used to prosecute anyone at Peoples Temple.

Freitas and Graham emphatically defend that investigation. "The people we talked to," Graham says, "could give you all the hearsay in the world, but they didn't actually witness anything. The people who did witness something wouldn't talk to anyone because they were getting advice from Charles Garry to keep their mouths shut."

Peoples Temple defectors are skeptical. "They simply feel," one said, "that Jim Jones helped get Freitas elected and that Joe Freitas was not too eager to press forward and so didn't give it his full energy or commitment." Supervisor

Quentin Kopp, who called for an investigation, is equally skeptical. "All he did was build a file," Kopp says. "I mean, how the hell could he miss? How could he miss?"

Phil Tracy remembers that period well. He remembers how, despite continuing articles in the San Francisco papers, the issues he and Marshall Kilduff had raised were forgotten in San Francisco. "Once Jones and his people left for Guyana," Tracy says, "San Francisco simply wanted to wash their hands of it. They figured they were in Guyana. And whatever happened from then on in, forget it. Don't investigate it. And look what they have on their hands right now."

JIM JONES had made it to the big time by buying the silence of San Francisco. Last week San Francisco began taking stock and

laying blame.

George Moscone, who would be the victim of another tragedy just one week later, wanted none of it. "I am not going to take responsibility for what happened there," he said. "It's just not mine to shoulder. It's not fair to connect the mayor of San Francisco with a slaughter on another continent."

Willie Brown wanted none of it. "I have no responsibility in any fashion for that person's existence. None at all, are you kidding me? Oh my god, do you think that's a legitimate question? That's outrageous, I'm serious, that is very outrageous. I'm not going to get into a position where you're going to run me up a tree because I'm a Jones person."

There were many in San Francisco who thought they deserved a lot of it. "There's all this talk about how he was doing a lot of good and then he became berserk in the jungle," Hannibal Williams said. "You know, that's not so. People begged at politicians for months and months to rescue their relatives. I helped some young men from my church get away. It was known throughout the community. All these things were happening in the community and they didn't hear about it? I can't believe it."

Williams looked at the pictures of the dead, the pictures of the people from the Fillmore, the district's young men, the district's babies, the district's old women. "They are dead because their leaders betrayed them," he said. "Jim Jones must have laughed at the way he was able to come in and take over here."

THE CHILDREN

WHY DID juvenile authorities fail to check on how Jones was treating the juveniles that the court released to him? The temple newspaper, the *Peoples Forum,* said that 130 youths in Guyana—presumably all now dead—were wards of the juvenile court.

VOTER FRAUD

TWO FORMER Peoples Temple members have reported that 750 members from Los Angeles voted in one San Francisco election, and that 1,700 members were illegally registered to vote in another election. Did this voter fraud occur, and if so, did Tim Stoen, who was in charge of the voter fraud unit in the San Francisco district attorney's office, play any role in it?

STOLEN DOCUMENTS

FORMER PEOPLES TEMPLE member Al Mills says he has been told that a letter complaining about Jim Jones was take from the district attorney's office in San Francisco and given to Jones. Were there thefts from that office, and if so, why did no one report them?

POLITICAL SPYING

THERE ARE numerous reports of Peoples Temple members gaining employment in public offices and suggestions that they were used as spies by Jim Jones. Was San Francisco government a target of such spying?

POLITICAL BLACKMAIL

DID SAN FRANCISCO politicians allow themselves to be set up for blackmail by Jim Jones by having sexual relations with women from the temple?

INVESTIGATION

WILL THE San Francisco D.A. reopen his investigation into Jim Jones's chief aides Michael Prokes and Tim Carter, who will return from Guyana if the Guyanese authorities do not press charges against them? ■

THOMAS SZASZ

The freedom abusers

SINCE THE DEATH OF the Reverend Jim Jones, the diagnosis of paranoia has been falling on his memory like snowflakes in a winter storm in Syracuse. I suggest that we take another look at some of the facts reported about this Marxist-Christian minister before the sordid truths about his behavior and that of his followers are completely buried beneath a blanket of psychiatric speculations and diagnoses.

Virtually everyone who knew Jones —among them some prominent and presumably perceptive and intelligent men and women—regarded him as perfectly healthy mentally. For instance, during the 1976 Carter presidential campaign, Rosalynn Carter and Jim Jones dined together in San Francisco. Mrs. Carter, who is, as we know, one of America's foremost experts on mental health, found no sign of mental illness in Jones—on the contrary: In March 1977, she wrote him a letter praising his proposal to give medical aid to Cuba, and after the election she invited him to attend the inauguration, which he did.

That Jones was accepted as at least "normal" in California liberal political circles has by now become notorious. That he was still widely regarded as both mentally healthy and morally admirable during the weeks and days immediately preceding the massacre is evident from the fact that a gala, $25-a-plate dinner benefit for the Peoples Temple was planned in San Francisco for December 2, 1978. Called "A Struggle Against Oppression," the affair was to feature Dick Gregory and

THOMAS SZASZ, a contributing editor, writes a monthly column for INQUIRY. His most recent book is The Myth of Psychotherapy.

the Temple's two lawyers, Mark Lane and Charles Garry, as speakers. It was endorsed by 75 prominent city leaders and politicians. It was cancelled after the massacre.

Actually, in view of Jones's impressive record of good "psychotherapeutic" works, the enthusiasm of evangelistic mental healthers for him should come as no surprise. Jones "cured drug addicts." He "rehabilitated" aimless Americans and put them on the road to a communitarian salvation. He was, officially at least, even against suicide —when it was a course chosen on one's own. On Memorial Day in 1977 (only 18 months before the Jonestown massacre), Jones led a delegation of Peoples Temple members on a march onto the Golden Gate Bridge in San Francisco, demanding that the city build a suicide barrier on the bridge.

In addition to these testimonials to Jones's good mental health and commendable character, we also have the word of Jones's personal physician that the minister was both psychiatrically normal and morally admirable.

Dr. Carlton Goodlett, identified as a "prominent black doctor" in San Francisco who had also attended Jones in Guyana, told the *New York Times*: "I was convinced that Jones was involved in a brilliant experiment in Guyana that actually put people in better shape down there than they had been in San Francisco." Even after the massacre Dr. Goodlett offered this psychiatric opinion—not about Jones, but about his disenchanted followers: "The deserters from the church had come to me, but they were just a neurotic fringe."

To say that Jim Jones was widely regarded as mentally healthy, is indeed an understatement: He was regarded as a brilliant healer of minds, a great "therapist." Many of his followers were former drug users. Two survived the massacre. One of them, Tim Carter, told the *Times* he had been "heavily involved in drugs in California" and was cured by Jones. Tim's father, Francis Carter (both of whose sons were "on drugs"), praised Jones's treatment of drug abuse to a *Times* reporter: After joining the temple "they gave up drugs, became rehabilitated, and got better." Odell Rhodes, another survivor, "had been a heroin addict from the Detroit ghetto. [W]ith the help of Jim Jones's power he had beat heroin, he said. He felt he needed his mentor to keep him straight."

*A*FTER THE BUTCHERY in Guyana, Jones's followers and friends were eager to dismiss him as "paranoid." Steven Jones lost no time diagnosing his father as psychotic, an opinion he kept carefully to himself until "dad" was dead. Why did Steven Jones think his father was mad? Because he destroyed the concentration camp that young Jones evidently loved dearly. "He has destroyed everything I've worked for," said Steven Jones.

One of Jones's lawyers, Charles Garry, characterized the commune as "a beautiful jewel. There is no racism, no sexism, no ageism, no elitism, [sic] no hunger." After the massacre, Garry declared: "I am convinced this guy was stark raving mad." If Garry believed this before November 18, 1978, he violated his professional responsibilities as a lawyer and his moral responsibilities as a human being; and if he concluded it only because Jones finally carried out his oft-repeated threat of mass murder and suicide, then Garry is asserting a platitude in declaring his

safely-deceased client "mad."

Mark Lane, Jones's other lawyer and a renowned expert on conspiracy and paranoia, described his former client to the *Times* as "a paranoid murderer who, after four weeks of drug injections, gave the orders that resulted last weekend in the deaths of Representative Leo J. Ryan. . . ." The great conspiracy-hunter thus sought to exonerate Jones by attributing the mass murder and suicide not only to "paranoia" but also to "drugs." But the fact is that Lane accepted Jones as a client and continued to represent him, up to the very moment of the debacle.

I cite all this as presumptive evidence that, before the final moment, those closest to Jones did not believe that he was psychotic. Their subsequent conclusion that Jones was paranoid is intellectually empty and patently self-serving. (Today everyone who reads newspapers and watches television has been taught that mass murderers are mad.) While Jones was alive his friends and followers did not regard him as paranoid, quite simply because they liked what he was doing. For the bottom line is a moral judgment: Jones's supporters think that he was a good man who suddenly became mad; I think he was an evil man—and not just on the day of the massacre.

Whether or not Jones had been "crazy" long before the massacre, depends on the meaning one wishes to attach to that word. However, it is now clear that for a long time Jones's behavior had been sordid and evil. It is also clear that when his followers were faced with certain facts, they deliberately looked the other way. Consider the following reports of Jones's behavior during the period when his followers and those "outside" regarded Jones as not merely "normal" but "superior":

—Jones insisted that everyone call him "dad" or "father." When there was a disagreement in the commune, the members would tranquilize one another and themselves by repeating the incantation, "Dad knows best. Just do as dad tells you."

—Jones had a wife, several mistresses, and "had sex" with many of the women and several of the men in the commune. "He told their husbands [according to Tim Carter, an aide] that he only did it to help the woman."

—Jones claimed that he was Jesus and could cure cancer.

—According to Jerry Parks, another cult member, "Everyone had to admit

that they were homosexual, even the women. He was the only heterosexual."

—Several times before the final butchery, Jones conducted rehearsals of the communal carnage.

—Members of the commune had to turn their possessions over to Jones, had to work like slaves, were starved and were kept from sleeping, and could not leave the commune.

*D*ESPITE THESE UNSAvory facts (and many others not catalogued here), I cannot recall, in the thousands of words I read about the Jonestown affair, a single commentator—journalist, politician, psychiatrist, anyone—characterizing the Reverend Jim Jones as an evil man. Mad, insane, crazy, paranoid, and variations on that theme— that is the consensus. James Reston's judgment of Jones was sadly typical. After quoting the opinion of "one of the most prominent members of the Carter Administration," according to whom the Jonestown massacre was a symptom of "mass lunacy in an age of emptiness," Reston delivered the craven diagnosis that liberal intellectuals, when faced with evil, instinctively issue. The Reverend Jones, declared Reston, was an "obviously demented man."

The most imaginative diagnosis was offered, not surprisingly, by a psychiatrist. Explained Dr. Thomas Ungerleider, professor of psychiatry at the University of California at Los Angeles: "I believe it was the jungle. The members got no feedback from the outside world. They did not read *Time* magazine or watch the news at night. . . ." Dr. Alvin Poussaint, professor of psychiatry at Harvard and one of the leading black psychiatrists in America, offered this shameful and revealing diagnosis: "We cannot in good conscience fault the mission of the rank-and-file because of the acute psychosis of their leader. . . . The humanitarian experiment itself was not a failure, the Reverend Jones was."

I think we can do better than that. The evidence—despite Reston and the anonymous high Carter administration official—suggests that Jones was depraved, not "demented," and that what his congregation displayed was mass cruelty and cowardliness, not "mass lunacy." I believe that plain English words such as "evil," "depraved," "cruel," and "cowardly" furnish a better description of what

5

happened at Jonestown than does the lexicon of lunacy in which those despicable and pathetic deeds have been couched.

This instant metamorphosis of Jones from prophet to psychotic now conceals—as did previously the deliberate denial of the significance of his everyday behavior by those who knew him —the self-evident evil that animated this bestial tyrant long before his supposed "degeneration into paranoia." That is the phrase used by *Time* magazine, where Jones is described as an "Indiana-born humanitarian who degenerated into egomania and paranoia." *Newsweek* confirms the diagnosis: Jones's "mind," we are informed, "deteriorated into paranoia."

I object. It is fundamentally false and distorting to view every gesture to help the poor—regardless of motives, methods, and consequences—as "humanitarian." What tyrant has not claimed to be motivated by a desire to help the helpless? We know only too well that to those hungry for power, the prospect of "helping" life's victims presents a great temptation; one that complements the temptation that the prospect of oblivion through alcohol or drugs presents to those hungry for a simple solution to life's problems. That is why these two types of persons are drawn to each other so powerfully, and why each regards the competent, self-reliant person as his enemy. So much for Jones's "humanitarianism."

AS FOR JONES'S "PARA-noia," we accept the proverbial wisdom that one man's meat is another man's poison. Similarly, we should accept that one man's prophet is another man's paranoid. It is simply not true that Jones "degenerated into paranoia." Jones was the same person on November 18, 1978 (the date of the mass murder and suicide), that he was the day before, the month before, the year before. Jones did not suddenly change. What did change suddenly was the opinion certain people entertained and expressed about him.

What we need, then, is not so much an explanation of what happened in Jonestown, which is clear enough, but rather an explanation of the explanations of the carnage that the purveyors of conventional wisdom have offered us. Briefly put, such a metaexplanation might state that paranoia in a dead and dishonored "cult" leader is caused by the sudden realization of his followers and others that they have been duped, which instantly transforms them from sycophants (and sympathizers) into psychodiagnosticians.

Much could be, and should be, made of the carnage at Jonestown. What I want to make out of it here is, briefly, this: Access to drugs entails what is now smugly called "drug abuse." How, indeed, could it be otherwise? Why, then, the shocked surprise that access to freedom entails "freedom abuse"? Assuredly the abuse of freedom—like the abuse of alcohol, drugs, food, or any other good that nature or human ingenuity provides us—is a small price to pay for the boundless benefits of freedom. That the abuse of freedom entails risks to innocent persons is one of the tragic facts of life. The children murdered at Jonestown are a somber reminder of the awesome power parents have over their children —a power that, as Jonestown and other communal experiments have shown, the collectivization of the family can only amplify.

The ultimate ugly and undeniable facts are that of the 909 bodies at Jonestown, 260 were those of children, butchered by the peaceloving, "humanitarian" followers of the Reverend Jones; and that, like their leader, these butchers hated the open society and "fled" their homeland to settle in a socialist country. The men and women of Jonestown rejected liberty; it is as if they had turned Patrick Henry's maxim, "Give me liberty or give me death!" on its head, and had sworn allegiance to the maxim, "Give me death rather than liberty!"

As for Congressman Ryan and his party, they paid a heavy price for their naiveté and miscalculation, but, after being warned repeatedly about Jonestown and after being emphatically disinvited by the inhabitants, their attempt to "liberate" would-be defectors without adequate arms was as illadvised as would be an attempt to scale the Alps without proper shoes or clothing. When Congressman Ryan insisted on staging his inspection-invasion to foist on them the liberty they loathed, the Jonestown patriots proved that they had the courage of their convictions. The point is not merely that actions speak louder than words, which is obvious enough; it is rather that in the base rhetoric of butchers—regardless of whether they come garbed as priests, politicians, or physicians— "love" means "hate"; "I will take care of you" means "I will kill you."

Cult Wars on Capitol Hill

Dire warnings, and First Amendment pleas

The Moonies were out in force on Capitol Hill last week. Outside the Russell Building the Rev. Sun Myung Moon's disciples had a band oom-pahing in protest; inside, they packed the gallery, unleashing standing ovations, boos and shouts of "Liar!" as they thought the testimony warranted. The occasion was an unofficial hearing on "cults," presided over by Republican Senator Robert Dole.

The cults issue was thrust into harsh focus by last November's carnage at the Peoples Temple commune in Jonestown, Guyana. The most dramatic moments of the four-hour hearing came from Jackie Speier, a legislative counsel who accompanied the late Congressman Leo Ryan on his fatal visit to the Rev. Jim Jones' headquarters and survived gunshot wounds. Speier stated that there are 10 million cult members in the U.S. and warned: "The most important fact about Jonestown is, it can happen again!"

As an afterthought, Dole included several witnesses who held, in line with First Amendment principles, that Government should not crack down on religious organizations unless they break the law. The bulk of the witnesses were anti-cult, however, and though they were openly, and understandably, hostile to the Moonies and other groups under discussion, they were unable to offer hard evidence of criminality, much less Jonestype mass murder. Nor did they define precisely what distinguishes a "cult" from an acceptable religion.

The main academics in the anti-cult lineup were Harvard Psychiatry Professor John Clark and University of Washington Law Professor Richard Delgado. Clark raised frightening specters of suicide, "uncontrolled violence," trances and total loss of memory, even distorted sense of smell (unexplained), among cultists. He made it clear that he saw the cultists as mindless zombies who pose a clear threat to democratic societies. "There are armies of willing, perfectly controlled soldiers," he told the assorted Senators and Representatives. "The level of public nuisance is so high that Government must act before it is too late."

But act how? Delgado offered five proposals: 1) laws forcing proselytizers always to identify their organizations; 2) a required "cooling-off period" before deciding whether to convert; 3) spiritual "living wills" to forestall future conversion; 4) licensing of high-pressure recruiters; and 5) as a last resort, court-ordered psychiatry for converts.

Jeremiah Gutman of the American Civil Liberties Union called this "impossible constitutionally." In his view the Government simply cannot monitor voluntary private conversations aimed at persuading people to change their beliefs, or attempt to control what religions people adopt. He said that "forced psychotherapy" to attack unwanted belief is "precisely what is going on in the Soviet Union today and precisely what Ted Patrick does on a smaller scale. It is already against the law."

Patrick, of course, is the creator of "deprogramming" for cult converts, and he was on hand also. He works with family members to abduct converts and subject them to nonstop ranting by teams of operatives until they renounce their new faith. Warning that "there is a conspiracy to turn [the U.S.] into a totalitarian state," he stated that he has personally deprogrammed 1,600 people, ranging in age from 13 to 81. In a forthcoming *Playboy* interview, Patrick includes First Sister Ruth Carter Stapleton, a neo-Pentecostal "memory healer," on his list of cult leaders who bear watching. Another witness, Author Flo Conway, stated that deprogramming should be "recognized as a new and valuable form of mental health therapy."

In the S.R.O. audience was Paul Pasquarosa, a devotee of "The Way," a zealous anti-Trinitarian group, who says that Patrick slashed at him repeatedly with a straight-edged razor at a December deprogramming in Massachusetts. As a result, Patrick, who has served time elsewhere, has been charged with assault with a dangerous weapon.

Another listener was Cynthia Slaughter, 27, a star witness at a similar hearing on cults held by Dole in 1976, who asked if she could testify again but was turned down. Slaughter, baptized into the Disciples of Christ as a youth, became a Moonie in 1975 and was deprogrammed by Patrick, then joined him and others in deprogramming work and giving dozens of anti-Moon speeches across the nation. She also wrote a first-person 1976 article in TIME. Now Slaughter, who would seem to be a highly suggestible sort, has reconverted.

Slaughter contends that the anti-cult network in which she was so active is itself a kind of "cult" and that Patrick's technique is psychologically "destructive." She said that it "scarred me," stirred up resentment and violent dreams, and that an anti-cult psychiatrist told her she came close to a psychotic break during her deprogramming. She freely admits that Moonies use high-pressure indoctrination methods, but she compares them to Zen-like spiritual disciplines. She also denies Patrick's theory that converts are "brainwashed."

It is unclear whether Senator Dole will pursue his cult hearings any further. Nor has Congress given any clue as to whether it will consider legislation to attack either the questionable religious groups, or the strong-arm tactics being used against them. There is always that little problem of squaring any such attacks with the First Amendment. ∎

Communities

THE TWISTED ROOTS OF JONESTOWN

by Reggie Major

OVER 900 PEOPLE dead. A year after the nightmare at Jonestown, they are remembered, but not memorialized. We don't know much more about the followers of the Rev. Jim Jones or why they died than we did in November of 1978. The label "mass suicide" doesn't tell us anything.

Peoples Temple was an organization that had been variously described by outsiders as a social service ministry, a progressive Christian church and an example of apostolic Christianity. With the deaths, it suddenly became a cult, an extension of the devil, an example of religious chicanery gone wild. That also explains nothing.

Nine hundred dead is an appalling body count. Airplane crashes with far fewer deaths merit detailed investigations that scrutinize all elements of the tragedy in search of an explanation. After the deaths in Guyana, however, there was little or no investigation that provided information for people—especially black people—in the United States to digest.

There was little digging despite the fact that, according to a Guyanese medical examiner, a minimum of 700 of the dead did not commit suicide at all, but were the victims ot cyanide injections; and despite the fact that Jim Jones died with a bullet in his head, while top officials of the church beat it into the jungle with suitcases full of money—only a tiny fraction of the incredible sums involved in this operation.

For all its contradictions, Peoples Temple was the "black church" that had been singled out for approval by the white power structure, from San Francisco's then mayor, the late George Moscone, to Jerry Brown and Rosalynn Carter. But when Jonestown exploded, the

EDITOR'S NOTE: *It has now been one year since the horrifying events at Jonestown, Guyana. Yet, except for an initial flurry of articles and overnight paperback books, remarkably little has been written about it. Few people, even at the time, paid much attention to the fact that the Rev. Jim Jones was white and that almost all his dead followers were black. Fewer still looked at the politics of Jonestown from the point of view of the black community of San Francisco. Mother Jones has asked Reggie Major, a veteran black journalist in San Francisco to do so in this retrospective on Jonestown.*

white officials who had blessed and, in many cases, benefited from the church were in such a hurry to disentangle themseives from the remains that they wanted nothing less than to find out more about Jonestown.

From the black community, too, there was no national outcry, no demand for a public hearing. There is no memorial because there is unfinished business here. The people who died in Jonestown have not been well represented by the living.

Why was there no force in the black community capable of counteracting so obvious an operator as Jim Jones? Why is it that most of Jones' parishioners came to him directly from the pews of other religious organizations—primarily black churches? And what have the black church and black leadership done since Jonestown to protect the community? Until these questions are answered by and among blacks, the horror of Jonestown will not have been ended.

Even at a time when Jim Jones was at his peak of political prestige, the true nature of the church was far from undetectable. Jones was a charlatan with a style that was authoritarian, manipulative and militaristic. Elizabeth Jamerson, an old-time Baptist and a devout churchgoer, saw through Jones and did her part to unmask him.

Her story is interesting because it comes from the grassroots. No top-down investigations, no articles in white newspapers could do what Betty Jamerson did—expose Jones at the level at which people believed in him.

Jamerson, who runs a small grocery store, says the Holy Ghost visited her one night and challenged her to prove that Jim Jones was a fraud. Jamerson had been having a series of arguments with her sister over Jim Jones. "He's nothing but a crook," was one of her milder remarks, and she and her sister Mary would stop speaking to each other for a time. The Holy Ghost ordered Jamerson to stop fighting with her sister and to instead expose Jones.

To do so, she joined his church. "From that point on, I sold more Jim Jones than groceries," said Jamerson, "and I tithed to Peoples Temple, not Third Baptist."

Jones, unaware of her mission, decided that Jamerson could help produce miracles for the edification of others. He would "cure" her of cancer. During a gathering at Benjamin Franklin junior high school, Jones called Jamerson to the lectern and told her to put two fingers down her throat.

"I knew what the game was," she said. "When you start to gag, you close your eyes. But I kept mine open. I wanted to watch the man's every move."

A nurse (Jones' wife) held a basket under Jamerson's chin, which Jones had grabbed with one hand. His other hand, while heading toward her mouth, was hidden from the audience by Jamerson's bulk. "I saw he had something in his hand. I waited until he got his thumb in my mouth. Then I bit down—hard.

"Jones jumped and dropped the piece of chicken liver he was trying to claim came out of my mouth. Now, I might be big, but I can move when I have to. I pushed both Jones and the nurse away, picked up the chicken liver and held it high over my head. I explained to everybody that Jones was trying to put that dirty liver in my mouth and then pretend that he had taken out a cancer.

"Jones kept on saying that I was mistaken and started to talk to me. They must have kept me up there for an hour, trying to convince me that I was mistaken. But I knew I was right and I knew I had done the job I was sent to do. When I proved he was a crook, I pulled out some of my relatives and a lot of my friends, but not before they gave Jim Jones about $300,000."

Today, Jamerson knows where she, at least, lays the blame for Jonestown: "Jim Jones came to the community because Uncle Tom preachers let Jim Jones in. They ought to whip Carlton Goodlett. He was a doctor and he used his medical license and his newspaper to help Jim Jones take advantage of black people."

Jamerson has a point. Goodlett, a respected San Francisco political figure, knew very well that whatever lip service Jim Jones gave to the wonders of faith healing, he called upon Goodlett whenever there was something wrong with himself or his family. But far from exposing Jones, Goodlett's paper, the *Sun-Reporter* (a widely read black paper in the Bay Area), acted almost as an arm of Jones' church, printing stories that gave credence to Jones' success as a faith healer.

As for the Rev. George Bedford—pastor of one of the largest black churches in San Francisco—whom Jamerson urged to oppose Jones, it was not his nature to condemn. Bedford had provided the route by which Jones had entered the black community. After the assassination of Martin Luther King, Bedford believed that black and white should pray together. The two ministers exchanged pulpits and sermons beginning in 1968. By 1969 Bedford was beginning to feel uneasy about Jones, but consoled himself with the thought: "If it is of God, it will last. If it is of man, it will perish."

Bedford's relationship with Jones proved to be very perishable a few months later, when he watched Jim Jones "extract a cancer" from a young black Baptist minister whom Bedford had ordained. But Bedford's subsequent break with Jones only underscored the vulnerability of black people toward Jones' manipulations. An estimated 30 percent of Bedford's con-

gregation remained with Jones after the split, creating a situation that Bedford preferred not to discuss.

By this time there was hardly a black church in the Western Addition—one of San Francisco's largest black communities—that had not been hard hit by Peoples Temple. Ministers were in a quandary. Substantial numbers of their parishioners had left to follow a white man who sounded stronger than they did about racism.

These preachers certainly weren't going to begin sounding like radicals in order to attract their former parishioners. Yet, in the face of the urban decay around them, they couldn't attack Jones' social ministry and sound particularly rational.

Jones had come into a disheartened community, which had been rocked by outside attempts to destroy it. The block on which Peoples Temple stood had all of the solidity of a movie set. Behind those brick structures was a vacant lot that stretched for close to half a mile. One half-block away from Peoples Temple was an open-air drug market where junkies and their suppliers transacted business.

Urban renewal, a process that began in San Francisco in the 1950s, had succeeded in

reaching into the Western Addition and totally disrupting a stable and progressive black community. The redevelopers used meat-ax techniques to dislodge small shopkeepers, black families, renters and storefront churches.

The disruption in the black church wasn't immediately apparent; parishioners who were forced out of the neighborhood commuted, for a while, to their former churches. But a process had begun of physically separating black churchgoers from the churches in what had been their neighborhoods.

Coupled with this was a kind of arch-conservatism in the church itself, a reactionary vision of what was appropriate in social action, which alienated young people. There was minimal church support of the agitation and civil rights fervor that gripped San Francisco from the late 1950s to the middle 1960s.

When there was direct church support for social action relating to black people, it came from white churches. The Black Panther Party Breakfast for Children program, for instance, was located at the Sacred Heart Catholic Church because no black church would support the Panthers. White churches established street ministries in and around the Western

Addition, where white ministers, invoking the spirit of Martin Luther King, established a kind of social-work-oriented ecumenicalism that spoke to understanding the pressure for change from the black community.

The withdrawal of young politically minded blacks from church-oriented activities was gradual, but it was significant insofar as the churches lost, in large numbers, the very people who could give them meaningful direction.

When Jim Jones showed up, the established black churches began to suffer attrition again, this time from the centers of the congregations. He captured many of the solid churchgoers and he even began to pull back the disenchanted youth.

Jones declared from the authority of the pulpit that struggle—political struggle—was the essence of caring Christianity, the flesh and blood of a living ministry.

There were no images of Christ in the church; he had banished the blue-eyed deity that young blacks refused to worship. Jones took the position that racism—all racism—was evil, diseased, corrupt and invalid, and that he, in combination with human-kind, should be judged according to his practice, not condemned as a result of his skin color.

And then he fudged on the question of his own paternity, implying to some that the darkish complexion that accompanied his black, straight hair resulted from American Indian ancestry and intimating to others that he was at least as black as those straight-haired, white-skinned Creoles in Louisiana, who have long been accepted as part of the American black population.

His stationery had a quote from Matt. 25, exhorting the faithful to feed the hungry and clothe the naked. Jones did that. But, as the Rev. Hannibal Williams observed, "You can feed a lot of poor people on the money you make from selling their homes." Because Williams has operated since the mid-'60s among and with various city agencies, he could see how Jones was using his position as the minister of a West-ern Addition church to become a power in city politics.

As a white man, Jones found it easy to convince white officials to turn to him as the leader of the black community, while the power he gained through them was used to advance his status even further. One small story indicates how Jones was able to do this.

It begins with Mayor George Moscone, who had forgotten a scheduled appointment with some black community women. When they arrived at city hall to see him, he rudely dismissed them and they returned to their neighborhood in tears.

Jones was called and told of the insult. He, in turn, called Moscone and demanded that the mayor send his official limousine into the Western Addition to pick up the black women, that they be driven back to city hall, that Moscone apologize publicly for the insult and that he then hold the previously scheduled meeting. Moscone complied, a gesture that few black ministers could have extracted from him.

Politicians want and need the black vote, but prefer it to be directed by what they call "responsible leadership." Jones controlled a large and fast-growing group of hard-working, pious, politically conscious blacks—almost all of them registered voters.

That was Jim Jones' political appeal, and it was also his hold on the black community. "Jones tried to steal our thunder," remarked Williams. He knew how to play both the demanding radical and the cooperative moderate.

Black leadership remained doubtful about Jones, and never totally accepted him. When he applied for membership in the Black Leadership Forum, a somewhat conservative organization that represents black political power in San Francisco, he was refused after a bitter split. Jones managed to elect himself to the NAACP board, however, by first providing several hundred of his members with NAACP memberships and then running for office.

Meanwhile, white leaders poured glory on Jones' efforts. Moscone appointed Jones to the San Francisco Housing Authority, and he soon became its president. He was featured on a television program as a miracle man who had a drug rehabilitation clinic that did everything but convert the pusher to Christianity. He was an honored guest, along with then Vice President Nelson Rockefeller, at the annual awards dinner given by Religion in American Life, which named Jones one of the nation's 100 outstanding clergymen.

Few public figures were aware of the lonely protesters within the black community, like Hannibal Williams, who led the effort to block Jones' membership in the Black Leadership Forum. Much less would they have heeded a parishioner like Betty Jamerson, who was one of the first to try to expose Jones.

The religious people who traveled with the Rev. Jim Jones to Guyana did not go seeking death. They were seeking, more than anything else, a combination of spiritual experience and social revolution. To them, the trip was meant to be a modern version of the middle passage—the historic journey out of slavery and into the promised land of freedom. That they had no one better to turn to for a guide than Jim Jones was and is the Jonestown tragedy.

Reggie Major is the author of A Panther is a Black Cat *(Wm. Morrow, 1971) and* Justice in the Round *(Third Press, 1973), about the trial of Angela Davis. He is a free-lance reporter who writes regularly for San Francisco's* Sun-Reporter.

Jim Jones: The Deadly Hypnotist

Behavioral scientists perform a "psychological autopsy" of last year's mass suicide in Guyana

BY JOEL GREENBERG

For Dad's Eyes Only: If you were to die tonight of a natural death and your wishes were to follow the leader who you appoint, I would give my life as I would for you at any moment for the cause... I would proceed on my own to subdue as many enemies I could get hold of... also killing myself.

— Cliff G.

As the world was to learn in the fall of 1978, the sentiments expressed by People's Temple member Cliff G. in his letter to "dad" —leader Jim Jones—were not those of just one isolated, radical devotee of Jones's cult in Guyana. Indeed, it is now clear that many of the more than 900 mass suicide victims at Jonestown participated willingly, with a common bond of fanatical devotion that was incomprehensible to outsiders. One temple member recently was quoted as saying: "Had I been in Jonestown on Nov. 18, 1978, I would have been the first in line to take the poison, if I had been so honored."

In the year since that grisly slaughter in the forest-shrouded commune, behavioral scientists have been conducting their own "psychological autopsies" on the forces that would ultimately drive members of an entire community to knowingly drink grape punch laced with lethal amounts of cyanide. If the results of such studies have not yet produced definitive explanations, they have begun to shed light on Jones's awesome power and control over his "flock." And in the end, it was this very twisted and primitive idea of power that dictated the downfall of Jonestown and its "father."

The cloistered, no-escape world of the Guyana compound was but the final phase of a calculated series of steps designed by Jones to achieve what University of Miami psychologist José I. Lasaga describes as "mass hypnosis at a social level...a unique process of group regression that led to a full acceptance of the leader's delusional system."

That process, analyzed in a symposium earlier this year at the annual meeting of the American Psychological Association, began with careful selection of Jones's followers. "They were people who were highly dissatisfied with the American way of life," says Lasaga, "either because of personal and family frustrations, or because of social frustrations — like racial discrimination — or because of political idealism—people longing for a more just form of social organization."

But it is one thing to identify unhappy and dissatisfied persons, and another to convince them that the solutions to their worries lie in one man: Jim Jones. According to some psychologists, Jones often began this task by creating an air of deception that might have been envied even by the CIA (which, coincidentally, Jones frequently singled out to his followers as a potent enemy of the People's Temple). "The recruitment was very sophisticated ...Jones was a modern master of deception," says Margaret Thaler Singer, a clinical psychologist at the University of California in San Francisco.

378

From interviews with Jonestown survivors and temple defectors, Singer detailed various recruitment scenarios: A potential recruit who seemed "impressionable" was investigated first by Jones's emissaries, who would rummage through the person's garbage can and report on discarded letters, food preferences and other clues. In some instances, two temple members would visit the home of a prospective recruit. While one member initiated conversation, the other would ask to use the bathroom, where he or she would copy names of doctors and types of medications off pill bottles. Temple members also would phone a recruit's relatives and, under the pretense of conducting a survey, gather vital information such as date and place of birth and years of residence in California, where the church was located.

Armed with such information (it was frequently taped to the inside of his lectern), Jones would demonstrate his "magical powers" at the next lecture attended by the recruit. In a typical lecture, Jones might preach that he "sensed the presence" of a woman about 45 years of age who had diabetes and was under the care of a Dr. Johnson. The listening woman, of course, would be "deeply impressed," according to Singer.

Convinced of their leader's "divine" powers, new members usually would faithfully submit to what Lasaga describes as the "basic techniques of political control" employed by Jones:

• Control of his followers' property and income. As mandated by the temple, all personal property and social security checks were to be turned over to Jones — rendering the followers fully dependent on him as a provider..."like a child in relation to his father," Lasaga says. Indeed, many referred to Jones as "Dad."

• Weakening of family ties. "Jones tried to weaken the relationship between husband and wife, and he was personally involved in a large number of extramarital affairs," Lasaga notes. But Jones's quest to "become the most important love object in the whole community" went beyond that. His sexual partners — both women and men — were often forced to stand before the community and testify to Jones's sexual prowess. In one instance, Jones forced Larry Layton (who was later to be charged with the murder of Congressman Leo Ryan and four others) to submit to a homosexual act in the presence of a women with whom Layton was romantically involved; Jones also broke up another of Layton's romances by simply taking the woman away from him. "Larry's sister, Deborah, remembers how she watched her brother's mental condition deteriorate as he became more and more caught up in the almost hypnotic-like spell cast over him by the charismatic Jim Jones," reports Richard Barrett Ulman, assistant professor of psychiatry at the New York Medical College.

• Institution of a sociopolitical caste system. A strict power pyramid consisted of Jones at the top, from where he oversaw a planning commission, and enforcement guards, or "angels." "The common people were absolutely powerless," Lasaga says.

• The no-escape society. Most members came to believe that leaving Jonestown was out of the question. The reasons were both geographic (isolation in a dense jungle) and political — escape was equated with treason and subject to severe punishment. According to Ulman, Jones warned black temple members that if they ventured into the outside world, they would be herded into concentration camps. "He convinced white members that they were under CIA investigation and would be tracked down, tortured, imprisoned and killed if they did not go along with his dictates," reports Ulman.

• Control over verbal expression.

"Overt criticism was harshly punished, and a zealous spy network reported all expressions of dissent to Jones," Lasaga says. "In this type of society most people behave like little children who do not dare express their feelings because of their fear of a terribly punitive father, and this means there is no room for external dissent."

• Cognitive and emotional control of the mind. This aspect of Jones's character permeated the entire community of Jonestown. Ultimately it set the stage for one of the most astonishing instances of mass suicide in history. "There was a process of continuous indoctrination carried out by Jones," notes Lasaga. "On the other hand ...no outside sources of information were available to the community except those which had received his explicit approval. Let us emphasize the tremendous psychological power of these techniques."

Such indoctrinations took place for hours each day both through powerful loudspeakers and lengthy, exhausting speeches by Jones. Members were frequently interrogated in front of the others about their political ideas — which invariably led to expressions of identification with their leader. "This caused in many cases a problem of cognitive dissonance [a state of tension caused by conflict between one's attitudes and behaviors]," Lasaga says, "and it is highly probable that

sooner or later those who internally disagreed tried to persuade themselves that what they were forced to say was not completely false."

Lasaga and others have compared Jones's methods with those of a hypnotist. Several researchers have conceptualized hypnosis "as an interpersonal process in which the hypnotist requires the subject to close all his channels of communication with the external world except one: the voice of the hypnotist," according to Lasaga. "Since there are no other channels available to check the truth of the hypnotist's statements, his or her voice becomes a substitute for reality....It is mass hypnosis at a social level."

The group meetings at Jonestown, he says, were "a frightful emotional experience" that went far beyond the mass contagion of most evangelistic services.

Jones's nonstop diatribes were always woven around "the Truth." But his speeches were frequently punctuated with the public humiliation of individuals; sometimes, according to investigators, he would have certain members remove their clothes in front of the group and participate in bizarre boxing matches — often pitting an elderly person against a strong, young man. Paddle-beatings were used on breakers of the strict rules.

But the most haunting of rituals, reflecting Jones's preoccupation with death, were the suicide rehearsals. During so-called "white nights," about 50 rifle-toting members would go from cabin to cabin to round up members as sirens blared. As described by Deborah Layton (according to Ulman): "A mass meeting would ensue. Frequently ... we would be told that the jungle was swarming with mercenaries and that death could be expected at any minute...we were informed that our situation had become hopeless and that the only course of action open to us was a mass suicide for the glory of socialism. We were told that we would be tortured by mercenaries if we were taken alive. Everyone, including the children, was told to line up. As we passed through the lines, we were given a small glass of red liquid to drink. We were told that the liquid con-

Continued on page 382

...Jonestown

tained poison and that we would die within 45 minutes. We all did as we were told."

As well as the group's vulnerability, what Jones played upon — and what finally turned such rehearsals into the real thing — was the "self-hatred" of not only his followers but of himself. As one member wrote, "Dear Dad and Savior—I have many times been so disgusted with myself ... I hate being old I hate it...I know you are the truth and the way ... I hope I die before I ever betray you." Such letters, says Ulman, "suggest that whatever agony was in these people's lives before they joined the People's Temple was not merely mirrored in Jonestown but rather shaped by Jones so as to give their pain and anguish the seeming virtue of self-sacrifice and ennoblement."

As for their leader himself, Jones's own self-hatred was evident in his constant need for omnipotence, to be loved by everyone and to be everyone's "best" lover. "Everyone had to say he [Jones] was the only true heterosexual man in the world ... to compensate for his feelings of inferiority," Lasaga says. "He was bisexual, but he 'hated' homosexuals — as he demonstrated by punishing them. Therefore, he hated himself...there was tremendous cognitive dissonance."

To help cope with his own internal struggles — and those of his followers — Jones turned to drugs. "He was a very heavy user of amphetamines," says Singer. And to temple members, Jones dispensed vast amounts of Quaaludes, Demerol, Valium, morphine and Thorazine to control behavior, according to the researchers. These all appeared to contribute to the community's steady withdrawal from reality and to the final tragedy.

In such an atmosphere, says Ulman, "a pathological, collective regression may take place whereby the leader and followers become partners in a form of group decompensation. In a sense they are victims of each other. ... [Jones] stripped the group of the ability to fight for their lives, [and] their acquiescence and adulation probably contributed to his weakening hold on reality."

What most group members sought, Ulman says, was "to magically merge with their idealized omnipotent leader in hopes of overcoming their lack of a positive self-image and correspondingly healthy self-esteem. Unfortunately, the price they paid was total masochistic surrender to Jim Jones."

To Lasaga, "Jonestown was a mini-totalitarian state ruled by the primitive mind of a paranoiac." Jones had to be "reassured every day that people would die for him." The mass suicide, he adds, was the ultimate "orgasm of power." □

285

III

Reaction of the Black Community to Jonestown

Black Panther Party Statement On Jonestown Massacre

WE CHARGE GENOCIDE!

The Black Panther Party charges the United States government, specifically the Central Intelligence Agency and the U.S. Department of Defense, with the murders of over 900 innocent men, women and children at the Peoples Temple settlement in Jonestown.

The Party demands an immediate citizens' investigation into the Jonestown tragedy. In no way should this investigation be organized or controlled by the American government, which *alone* bears the responsibility for viciously slaughtering a group of Black and poor people who left the oppression of this country to build a society where there would be none.

We must not be tricked by the CIA-created mass hysteria and confusion that is sweeping through the country about the Jonestown massacre. If there were freedom and justice for all in America, there would have been no need for Jonestown in the first place. If Black and poor people could live in peace and dignity in this country, those 900 people who told the world they had found perfect happiness in Jonestown and, under no circumstances, would give it up, would not be in their graves today.

The Black Panther Party does not believe one single word of the "official" explanation of the Guyana massacre. The government has told lie after bold-faced lie about Peoples Temple, Jim Jones and Jonestown.

•The State Department has admitted its "investigation" into Jonestown produced absolutely no evidence that Peoples Temple was a "dangerous" or "violent cult."

•Before he left Jonestown, Leo Ryan told Jim Jones that he liked what he had seen at the settlement and was going to make a favorable report upon returning to America.

Shortly afterwards, Leo Ryan was killed...

•(Ryan was the source of information for a CBS reporter who uncovered a secret CIA operation in Angola in 1975. The CIA does not hesitate to kill those who stand in its way.)

•In October of this year, Peoples Temple held a press conference to announce that it had exposed a government conspiracy to destroy the Temple, Jonestown and Jim Jones. Within 90 days, the Temple said it would file a multimillion dollar lawsuit against the CIA and other government agencies responsible for the plot.

Six weeks later, Jonestown was destroyed...

"THOSE WHO DO NOT REMEMBER THE PAST ARE CONDEMNED TO REPEAT IT."

•Many people who died at Jonestown were Black. Since Black people were brought to this country as slaves in 1619, we have done *whatever* was necessary to survive. It is not in our nature to commit suicide.

•Why, for three days, did the government say there were 400 bodies at Jonestown and then mysteriously, on the fourth day, there were 800? Do they take us for complete fools?

•The bodies of people who die from cyanide poisoning are generally in a twisted and contorted state. This is not at all how the bodies shown by the news media at Jonestown looked. The pictures of the Jonestown victims, in fact, looked almost exactly like those of the people who were murdered at Dachau, Auschwitz and My-lai.

•There were allegedly several dozen bottles of drugs found at Jonestown. Some of these drugs are known to have been used by the CIA for experimentation with mind control of human beings.

•The Jonestown settlement was mysteriously attacked several months ago by a band of armed men, allegedly concerned relatives of Jonestown residents...

The government's explanation is that over 900 people living in a paradise on earth committed mass suicide by drinking grape Kool-Aid "laced with cyanide." Because this is the story being promoted by the government, we must assume it is a lie.

It is quite possible that the neutron bomb was used at Jonestown. The neutron bomb contains radioactive molecules, which, when released into the atmosphere, kill human beings — but do not destroy property.

Mass genocide, not mass suicide, took place at Jonestown. Peoples Temple is a socialist organization that sent over 1,000 people to a socialist Latin American country to build a new society. Jonestown had to be wiped out. It was too much of a success, too much of an embarrassment to the American government.

All of us have a responsibility to the families who lost loved ones at Jonestown and to the remaining members of Peoples Temple who must carry on their work in the face of relentless government attacks. We must demand that the truth about Jonestown be told *now*, not in 15 or 20 years by some Senate "intelligence committee."

Jonestown is not an isolated incident that took place in a faraway country. The dead were our mothers, our fathers, grandmothers and grandfathers, our brothers and sisters, our children.

We must not allow this government to get away with the genocide at Jonestown. Tomorrow it could be Hunters Point, East Oakland, Watts or Harlem. □

The Black Panther

PUBLISHED BIWEEKLY BY THE BLACK PANTHER PARTY, 8501 EAST14th STREET, OAKLAND, CALIFORNIA 94621, TELEPHONE: (415) 638-0195.
YEARLY DOMESTIC SUBSCRIPTION RATES: $6.50
SECOND CLASS POSTAGE PAID AT OAKLAND, CALIFORNIA

RESEARCHER CHARGES NEWS REPORTERS IN GUYANA C.I.A. AGENTS

(Chicago, Ill.) - Sherman Skolnick, head of the Chicago-based Citizens Committee To Clean Up the Country, told THE BLACK PANTHER late last month that he had "liberated" CIA files showing that some correspondents of *United Press International* in Guyana are CIA agents.

Skolnick, whose 15-year-old group has exposed many corrupt politicians in Chicago, was the first researcher to expose the agency's MK-ULTRA program involving experiments with mind control drugs..

Skolnick noted that a vast majority of the articles concerning the Jonestown tragedy that have appeared in the U.S. press were written by *UPI* reporters. He said the documents he has give the names and addresses of the undercover CIA agents in Guyana. He indicated that the Agency has used the *UPI* as a means of discrediting Rev. Jim Jones and the Jonestown settlement.

Some of the most prominent figures in U.S. journalism have been exposed for conspiring with the CIA by award-winning investigative reporter Carl Bernstein.

Bernstein, co-author with Bob Woodward of the best-selling books on the Watergate cover-up conspiracy, *All The President's Men* and *The Final Days* said in a copyrighted story last year in *Rolling Stone* magazine that at least 25 U.S. news organizations provided "covers" for CIA employees disguised as journalists abroad.

Bernstein, a reporter for the *Washington Post*, charged, "Journalists provided a full range of clandestine services from simple intelligence collection to serving as go-betweens with spies in communist countries."

News publications and agen-

Peoples Temple founder and leader Rev. JIM JONES (left) with Guyana Prime Minister FORBES BURNHAM.

cies cited by Bernstein are ABC, NBC, *United Press International (UPI)*, *Associated Press (A.P.)*, *Newsweek*, Mutual Broadcasting, the *Miami Herald* and the now defunct *Saturday Evening Post* and *New York Herald-Tribune*.

Since the mass murders at Jonestown, Peoples Temple has been the subject of a nationwide media campaign calculated to discredit and destroy the organization and prevent further investigation into the highly suspicious circumstances surrounding the deaths of over 900 Temple members.

INDICATION

One indication of a U.S. establishment press conspiracy against Peoples Temple is the upcoming publication of a book on the Jonestown slaughter. Three days after the tragedy occurred, Dell Book Publishers announced it would have a book on sale about Jonestown on December 2 — only two weeks after the Guyana mass deaths.

How could a book be written in two weeks on Jonestown?

The media blitz against Peoples Temple is clearly meant to

complete the total destruction of the group by (1) giving the U.S. government grounds to confiscate all remaining Temple properties and assets; (2) causing members to be arrested and tried on trumped-up charges; and (3) isolating remaining Temple members and crushing their spirit.

In his autobiography, *Revolutionary Suicide*, Huey P. Newton states, "Power is the ability to define phenomena and make it act in a desired manner." In the past year, the U.S. establishment press has used its power to persuade the American public into believing that Peoples Temple is a lunatic religious cult.

Following the November 18 killings of Bay Area Congressman Leo Ryan, NBC reporter and cameraman, Don Harris and Bob Brown, respectively, *San Francisco Examiner* photographer Greg Robinson and Temple member Patricia Parks, the press failed to report on an important statement Ryan made to Jones.

One of the reasons Ryan went to Guyana was to investigate

CONTINUED ON PAGE 15

Researcher Charges

CONTINUED FROM PAGE 3

charges made by relatives of Jonestown residents that their families were allegedly being held against their will in the rich agricultural commune.

At a November 22 press conference in San Francisco, Temple attorney Charles Garry, who was with Ryan's party at Jonestown, said that the California congressman told Jones that it didn't matter if "400 people wanted to leave. You (Jones) are doing beautiful work, and I am going to tell everyone."

Ryan said this *after* he was attacked with a knife by a Temple member whom many people now believe was an undercover agent.

Minutes later Ryan was shot and killed on the Kaituma airstrip near Jonestown.

First word of the Jonestown tragedy received by the American people from the press was that there had been "mass suicide" at the Guyana settlement. Through such news sources as *UPI* and *A.P.*, the country was bombarded with stories that Jim Jones had gone crazy and, due to his fear that Jonestown would be destroyed because of Ryan's investigation, he had led Temple members into sipping Kool-Aid "laced with cyanide."

News "analysts" such as Patrick Buchanan described Peoples Temple as "a bunch of crazies," "hard core revolutionaries" and a "highly secretive cult."

The press reserved most of its venom for Jim Jones. He has been described as a "deranged dictator," "bisexual," a "suicidal fanatic" and a "devious Marxist." One newspaper article about the Temple founder had the headline, "Death, Sex, and Power."

Jones was found shot to death in the head, along with his wife Marceline. Two women who had responsibility for the organization's finances were also found shot to death. The fact that the other over 900 people allegedly died from poisoning has been of little concern to the media. Since there are no known living witnesses to the shootings, the press has promoted the belief that the four people committed suicide.

Given the growing widespread belief that the Jonestown massacre was carried out by the CIA, there is the strong possibility that some ex-Temple members and Jonestown survivors, with their tales of false healings performed by Jones, may be agents or may have been threatened into lying about what really happened.

Why alienated blacks are the easiest prey

By Earl Ofari

Los Angeles Times Special

In attempting to understand the horrible events at Jonestown, nearly every commentator has cited the tremendous attraction and power of cults. But is that a sufficient explanation?

Because the overwhelming number of victims of the Guyana tragedy were black, it is imperative that other factors be examined. One of these is black receptivity to messianic or "cult" groups, such as the People's Temple, which has deep roots in the fabric of American history.

At various times during the civil- and human-rights struggles of the last two centuries, black groups and individuals have engaged in escapist searches for the proverbial Promised Land. Before the Civil War, blacks organized at least three separate attempts to flee the racial persecution of American society.

THE FIRST MOVEMENT WAS initiated by a black seaman, Paul Cuffee, in 1815: the second by a black physician, Martin Delaney, in 1850, and the third by a black minister, the Rev. Henry Highland Garnet, in 1855. All were designed to lead blacks to a society of peace and freedom by inciting them to make a mass exodus either to Africa or to the West Indies.

Though all three attempts petered out, in each case a handful of proselytizers did manage to spark a great deal of discussion and debate among large numbers of blacks over the relative merits of emigrating or staying put.

In the decades following the Civil War and emancipation, a few black leaders, sensing a mood of despair among their people, once again raised the issue of emigration. Africa, Canada and the American West, still largely unsettled, were only a few of the places that these leaders named as potential havens.

Those appeals especially attracted the most dispossessed elements of the black lower class. In more instances than not, the proponents of separation sought to heighten its allure by cloaking their overtures in religious cloth; often claiming a spiritual mandate that translated into heavenly inspiration. Yet it was the bitter racism and socio-economic oppression experienced by the black masses in the post-Reconstruction South, rather than religious exhortation, that led so many blacks to support the cause of emigration.

THIS WAS ALSO TRUE of the largest mass black separation movement of this century, Marcus Garvey's "Back to Africa" movement of the 1920s. Garvey exploited the issues of unemployment, lynchings and segregation to draw hundreds of thousands of blacks to his separatist banner.

Calling his movement "Black Zionism," Garvey skillfully used symbols (flags, uniforms and other regalia) and highly emotional rhetoric to fire up his followers. In the end, as was the case in similar movements before "Black Zionism," thousands of enthusiasts lost money, suffered broken promises and became victims of outright fraud. The movements finally collapsed when the federal government imprisoned Garvey and then deported him to his native Jamaica.

But the success that Garvey had experienced in enlisting the black poor in his emigration scam was not lost on a small-town black minister who called himself Father Divine—the man whom Jim Jones was to claim as a major influence in founding the People's Temple.

Father Divine's "peace movement," as he called it, drew a huge number of disciples during the Great Depression. As his predecessors had, Father Divine built his following on the poverty and alienation blacks suffered.

FATHER DIVINE SAW his mission as the transformation of America into a color-blind society, with a government under one god—Father Divine himself. His program, the trappings of which were duplicated later by People's Temple, called for a collectivist economy and total submission to his own authority.

The willingness of a sizable segment of blacks to embrace movements that have run the gamut from "back to Africa" to People's Temple stands as a reflection of their utter desperation. The lesson, surely, is not that cults hold a particular fascination for blacks, but that the most deprived members of American society—those who see the least hope of making it within the system—are the easiest prey for charlatans preaching that paradise lies just over some falsely Technicolored rainbow.

Earl Ofari is public-affairs analyst and the author of "The Myth of Black Capitalism."

DICK GREGORY CHARGES CONSPIRACY AT JONESTOWN

(San Francisco, Calif.) - A major American military operation was underway in Dover, Delaware — the sprawling military base where the Jonestown genocide victims were brought — one week *prior* to the November 18 tragedy.

In a conversation with members of Peoples Temple here in late November, Black comedian-activist Dick Gregory said that he was in Dover, located 75 miles from Philadelphia, the week before the Guyana mass murders.

Gregory said a friend of his in Dover told him that something "heavy" was going on at the military base.

"Then I checked into a hotel," the renowned Black comedian said, "and I saw all these civilian pilots. I automatically thought their presence meant that something big was about to happen."

Gregory, long a target of government harassment and surveillance because of his outspoken views on conditions of Black and poor people in America, said he immediately left the Dover hotel because the presence of the large number of pilots made him uncomfortable.

The Black entertainer, who has vowed to remain on a hunger strike "until the truth about Jonestown comes out," said that Kool-Aid, with which the Jones-

CONTINUED ON PAGE 6

293

JONESTOWN CONSPIRACY

CONTINUED FROM COVER

town victims were allegedly poisoned to death, is made by General Foods, whose national headquarters is in Dover, Delaware.

Gregory raised several questions pointing to the blatant discrepancies in the government's story about what happened at Jonestown.

Discussing the television film shot by NBC cameraman Bob Brown minutes before he, Congressman Leo Ryan and three other people were killed by gunmen at the Kaituma airstrip near Jonestown, Gregory said, "Every time this government makes a hit, there's a film made."

"A film was made to show that Lee Harvey Oswald shot President Kennedy so that no one would think anything else about it," the comedian-activist said. He added, "When you know what this government is doing and you watch it closely, you can start to see things that don't make sense."

Gregory raised the question of why the NBC film made at the airstrip wasn't destroyed by the gunmen. "You're not going to tell me that they came and put a gun to their heads, blew their brains out and didn't destroy the camera and take the film," he said.

Gregory believes Brown did not shoot the film, but that it was created by the government "as an aide to convince us. They (gunmen) went there expressly to kill the people with the information about Jonestown," Gregory charged.

Concerning the government lie that the Jonestown victims committed mass suicide by drinking Kool-Aid "laced with cyanide," the Black entertainer maintained, "You cannot make 13- and 14-year-old children kill themselves."

DEAD DOG

Pictures taken of the mass murder scene in Guyana showed a picture of a dead dog. "Dogs do not drink Kool-Aid," Gregory said. "Some commandos came in, dropped some kind of gas on the people and then did what they wanted to their bodies."

"Something so big was going on in Jonestown that had it gotten out," Gregory said, "all hell would have broken loose. The government had no choice but to go in there and close it down and wipe out everybody."

Emphasizing his firm belief that the Guyanese settlement was destroyed as the result of a U.S. government conspiracy, Gregory said, "Jonestown is big. It's everybody. I don't know if it's going to take a week, 10 years or 20 years for the truth to come out. I don't know how or where it's going to come out, but it's going to come out."

GREGORY CHARGES CONSPIRACY

A major American military operation was underway in Dover, Delaware—the sprawling military base where the Jonestown, Guyana, genocide victims were brought—

one week *prior* to the November 18 tragedy, Black comedian-activist Dick Gregory charges.

Gregory said that he was in Dover the week before the Guyana mass murders, and that a friend of his in the city told him something "heavy" was going on at the military base.

"Then I checked into a hotel," the renowned Black entertainer said, "and I saw all these civilian pilots. I automatically thought their presence meant that something big was about to happen."

Gregory, who has vowed to remain on a hunger strike "until the truth about Jonestown comes out," said of the U.S. government's lie that over 900 people committed mass suicide by drinking Kool Aid "laced with cyanide," "You cannot make 13- and 14-year-old children kill themselves. Some commandos came in, dropped some kind of gas on the people and then did what they wanted to their bodies," Gregory declared.

Continuing, he added, "Something so big was going on in Jonestown that had it gotten out, all hell would have broken loose. The government had no choice but to go in there and close it down and wipe out everybody."

The current issue of THE BLACK PANTHER also features an article on Phillip Blakey, a former top aide to Rev. Jim Jones. The assassinated Peoples Temple leader sent Blakey to Guyana in 1974 to begin the Jonestown settlement, and a year later, Blakey—still a Peoples Temple member—served as a mercenary and mercenary recruiter for the CIA-backed Union for the Total Independence of Angola (UNITA).

295

monthly report

THE INSTITUTE OF THE BLACK WORLD
87 Chestnut Street, S.W.
Atlanta, Georgia 30314

February 1979

IN THIS ISSUE

On November 19, 1978, the U.S. State Department reported that Congressman Leo Ryan and members of his party had been killed during an investigative visit to Guyana, and that their deaths had triggered a mass suicide-murder in the South American Country. Hundreds of bodies were discovered at a religious commune established as Jonestown by its leader, Jim Jones, and settled by members of the People's Temple, a religious movement in California organized by Jones. Later reports of the Guyana incident revealed that an estimated 1,000 bodies had been discovered. A great percentage of them were black. IBW resumes publication of the MONTHLY REPORT *with a feature editorial pondering the significance of these events for black people and American society.*

BLACK REFLECTIONS ON THE JONESTOWN HOLOCAUST

by William Strickland

Most Americans, one feels, have been stunned by the tragedy at Jonestown and have been trying to sort out its meaning. The press has bombarded us with front page stories and numerous T.V. specials. All major news magazines have carried feature stories. Investigations, documents and confessions by members and former members abound. Indeed a mini-industry seems to have sprung up for the express purpose of explaining - and explaining away - the meaning of Jim Jones and People's Temple. Three books are already on the market (Guyana Massacre, The Suicide Cult and Hold Hands and Die) and more are on the way. Yet the more information that comes about Jonestown and Jim Jones, the more unsatisfying the explanations appear. One has a sense, an intuition even, that there is something about what happened in Jonestown that is of greatest significance to Americans and American society. Yet what that significance is remains obscure. And the official explanations, both sociological and lurid, remain, essentially, unconvincing.

The need for black people to make sense of Jonestown is especially crucial since black people and the black experience vitally influenced the life and theology of Jim Jones. And the fact that some seventy to eighty per cent of his followers were black raises provocative questions about the present and future of black America.

THIS PUBLICATION IS MADE POSSIBLE IN PART BY A GRANT
FROM THE CITY OF ATLANTA, BUREAU OF CULTURAL AFFAIRS

One such question is posed by the racial composition and leadership structure of People's Temple: white leader, black followers, for it seems part of a larger pattern now current in American life. On television it is "Different Strokes," and "The White Shadow;" in politics it is Jimmy Carter; in music it is K.C. and the Sunshine Band, among others. And, now in religion it is Jim Jones. All around us, in every walk of life, one observes the phenomenon of whites leading Blacks and there is something familiar yet novel about it. What is familiar is that whites have always asserted their right to be custodians of our welfare. What is new is our cheerful and apparently uncritical acquiescence to such a state of affairs, the erosion of our racial instinct for self-determination, self-direction, and self-preservation. And that is a commentary not upon Jim Jones, Carter and K.C. but upon ourselves and the vacuity of contemporary black leadership. It suggests that a need is being better met outside the race than within it. Why so many Blacks turned to Jones is a question for all of us to ponder.

Some friends insist that I am making too big a thing of the race relations of Jonestown. They believe that there is nothing basically different about black people following Jim Jones than black people following Father Divine or Prophet Jones* or Reverend Ike. Besides, they say, Jim Jones modeled his ministry after Father Divine and Prophet Jones and therefore it is understandable that some black people were responsive to it. Finally, they say it was California and all manner of strange things abide and flourish in California among white folk and black. One must admit to being partially persuaded by these arguments--but only partially. The nagging feeling persists that there is still more to People's Temple than an imitated black religious tradition or California kookiness; more than has been admitted.

For instance, anyone remotely conversant with black history or black struggle finds it exceedingly difficult to believe that a thousand people and a thousand passports, mostly black, simply left the country without arousing the interest of the government of the United States. One is even more skeptical of the FBI's disclaimer that it was unable to investigate People's Temple because doing so would have been "a violation of religious freedom." It is impossible to reconcile this position with the FBI's history of malfeasant surveillance of the Nation of Islam and the Southern Christian Leadership Conference, of Malcolm X and Martin Luther King, Jr. For it to suddenly embody such constitutional virtue, strains credulity.

Credulity, or at least logic, are similarly strained by some of the press stories about Jonestown. In the week following the Guyana holocaust, the public was rocked by "disclosure" after "disclosure" concerning People's Temple: millions of dollars were discovered and millions more were alleged to have been deposited in foreign banks. Jones was accused of being a womanizer on the one hand and a homosexual on the other. There were rumors of child-beating and kidnapping; collusion with the government of Guyana and the American embassy in Guyana; secret relations with the Soviet Union and mysterious links to Cuba. Jones himself was reputed to have been dying of an undisclosed illness; tortured in his last days by drug-induced, paranoid fantasies.

The problem with this press scenario is that it raises far more questions than it resolves; chief among them being how it was possible for the press to unearth this mass of scurrilous information so easily while a plethora of government agencies including the State Department, the FBI and the Treasury Department insisted that

* Father Divine and Prophet (James F.) Jones were leaders of two of the thousands of black cults which abounded in the major cities of the East and Midwest from the 1920's to the 1950's.

-2-

Jones was "harmless." In fact, the Treasury Department was notified by the San Francisco police more than a year and a half before the murder of Congressman Ryan and his party that the People's Temple was involved in illegal shipments of guns and money out of the country. Yet no investigation took place. We are left, then, with an interesting conjecture. Either the press is right and Jim Jones and Jonestown were inherently and palpably evil and the government of the United States was persistently and dogmatically inept or else the government was giving favored treatment to Jim Jones for some purpose of its own.

There is a smell of deeper political connivance about Jonestown which is buried amidst all the efforts to explain it away as simply a fanatical religious cult. In point of fact any reading of Jim Jones' career makes it abundantly clear that People's Temple was a politico-religious organization whose rise must be attributed as much to Jim Jones' shrewd manipulation of the political systems of the United States and Guyana as to any magical "charisma." From his earliest office in Indianapolis as Human Rights Commissioner to his post as head of the San Francisco Housing Authority, to his admiring letters from the First Lady, the Vice-President, the Secretary of HEW, etc., Jim Jones stroked the American political system into enthusiastic and friendly support of his interests.

At bottom then, as responsibility for Jonestown is being parceled out, it must be affirmed that there was nothing more or less corrupt about Jim Jones than there was about the system which gave him his power and his legitimacy. For up until the deaths in the jungle, Jim Jones was legitimate in the eyes of this system: lunching with the First Lady and being relied upon by important segments of California's political establishment.

This is the linkage that the commentators refuse to acknowledge. It is also the reason why Jonestown must be now disowned officially and why the deaths of Jonestown must be presented as more murder than suicide. For if a thousand people voluntarily chose death to repatriation, what a terrible repudiation of America that is. That is why they must be found either murdered or mad, or both. Jonestown simply cannot have been an act of free will without, at the same time, being the most damning judgement of the essential spiritual emptiness of American society.

What then, ultimately, is the difference between the people of Jonestown and ourselves?

They were followers of a doctrine and social philosophy and way of life that, in the end, led to their destruction. But so too are we. As Felix Rohatyn, the banker charged with the task of trying to save New York City from default, recently said: "Our economy is out of control, our currency is in danger, our institutions of government are unresponsive or inept...We are at war today: with inflation, with unemployment, with lack of education, with racial discrimination. We are futhermore not winning.... (emphasis mine)"

What distinguishes the people of Jonestown—the whites and the Blacks, the young and the old, the rich, the middle class and the poor, the exdrug addicts, former criminals and other "misfits" of America—from ourselves is that they apparently shared the banker's assessment of the crises in American society and accepted the challenge of creating an alternative, however flawed their efforts might have been. Most Americans—black as well as white—remain committed to the American way of life that has produced these crises. We "survivors" of Jonestown then are just as much followers of a failed religion as the disciples of the People's Temple. And our resistanceless followership may prove in the not-so-long run, to be every bit as deadly to us as the cyanide-spiked Kool-Aid consumed in the South American jungle.

-3-

Churchmen Hunt Clues on Cult's Lure for Blacks

Consultation on the Implications of Jonestown

The following special report was filed by Henry Soles, Jr., a black journalist minister, and television producer. He attended the conference described below (much of which was closed to outside news media) as a delegate and on assignment for CHRISTIANITY TODAY.

When cult leader Jim Jones's dream of carving a Marxist utopia from the Guyana jungles ended in a nightmare of suicide and murder last November, shock waves ripped through the world religious community. United States church leaders tried to disassociate themselves from Jones and his pseudo-Christianity.

Black church leaders, however, were particularly bothered by the implications of Jonestown. The People's Temple in San Francisco opened in 1971 in a rented building in a predominately black area. Jones's followers, who at one time numbered 20,000, were estimated to be 80 percent black. Though Jones and virtually all of his ruling hierarchy were white (he often used the phrase "we blacks" in speeches to predominately black audiences), most of the Jonestown victims were black.

Because of this disturbing affinity among some blacks for Jones, more than 200 of the nation's black leaders—mostly clergymen—attended a two-day conference last month, billed as "A Consultation on the Implications of Jonestown for the Black Church."

The Southern Christian Leadership Conference (SCLC) and the National Conference of Black Churchmen (NCBC), cosponsors of the conference, invited the delegates, who traveled at their own expense, to San Francisco's historic Third Baptist Church, reputedly the oldest black church west of the Mississippi. There the delegates explored the meanings of People's Temple, Jim Jones, and the catastrophic deaths of hundreds of black people in Guyana for the mission,

history, and self-understanding of the Black Church.

Keynote speaker for the conference was Kelly M. Smith, president of the NCBC—a group formed in the sixties by blacks mostly from mainline denominations who wanted a greater voice in church affairs. Smith made note of the fact that the People's Temple hierarchy was virtually all white, and he labeled Jonestown "a tragedy perpetrated upon the black masses by unscrupulous and unprincipled white leadership."

"This is not the first time," Smith stated, "that trusting blacks have been led down a path of deception to their own destruction by persons who stand outside the black experience."

Smith

Smith, assistant dean at Vanderbilt Divinity School, challenged the black church to "dress the wounds" caused by Jonestown, and to "address the issues . . . [to] pause and listen."

And listen the delegates did. The parade of speakers included Guyana Information Minister Shirley Field-Ridley, who defended her country's often-criticized handling of the tragedy. For the most part, however, speakers called attention to the "life-affirming nature" of the black church and the role it has played in addressing the concerns of blacks.

Scholars, primarily from the behavioral sciences, discussed the sociological, psychological, and theological context out of which cults grow. C. Eric Lincoln, Duke University sociology professor, analyzed the nature of cults, sects, and the institutional church. Interspersed between the major addresses and scholarly reports were inspirational sermons delivered in the traditional black preaching style.

During conference discussion, one question repeatedly surfaced: why did Jones exert such influence over black Americans and, in particular, blacks in

the Bay area? During his heyday, Jones had been endorsed by a number of black leaders, including California lieutenant governor Mervyn Dymally and state legislator Willie Brown. In 1977, California Governor Jerry Brown attended a celebration of the late Martin Luther King's birthday at People's Temple, selected as the meeting site by sponsoring black community leaders. (Not all black leaders were sympathetic; for example, San Francisco pastor Roosevelt Brown stood outside People's Temple every Sunday morning for six months pleading with members not to go in.)

Illusion of benificence

Hannibal Williams, pastor of San Francisco's New Liberation Presbyterian Church, explained that Jones "created the illusion that he was the benefactor of the poor," and thus attracted to his church the poor, the dispossessed, and the alienated—although a number of middle class blacks also followed Jones.

Williams, an early and fearless Jones critic, contended that he had been subjected to repeated threats of violence by Jones and Jones followers. He called Jones "the new plantation boss" who co-opted San Francisco civil rights groups by buying memberships for his followers in those groups, thereby creating his own power blocs. Williams believed Jones was "demon-possessed" and a "false prophet."

According to Amos Brown, pastor of the Third Baptist Church, Jones's attraction grew because "the black church in the Bay Area didn't have the economic and political clout that Jones amassed through chicanery and public relations." Indeed, Brown pointed out, Jones had staunch allies in the local press, among the white business establishment, and local politicians.

SCLC president Joseph Lowery supported Brown's argument. He noted that "whiteness still represents a symbol, a seat of power," and that "the resources available to white leadership are not available to black leadership."

Calling Jonestown "the ultimate manifestation of the depersonalization of black people," Pacific School of Religion psychologist Archie Smith said many blacks gravitated to People's Temple because they found group support and social involvement.

According to some observers, Jones had wanted to become the undisputed kingpin of San Francisco's black community. To accomplish this, he first needed to win the allegiance of pastors of the city's largest black churches. One of his tactics in wooing them was to send stacks of flattering letters to the pastors.

For the most part, this plan backfired. Only a handful of San Francisco black pastors fell in behind Jones. The vast majority warned their members to shun People's Temple. While many parishioners heeded their pastors' advice, others joined People's Temple anyway. Many blacks were attracted by Jones's much-reported "fake healings."

An elderly black woman gave the conference delegates an impassioned account of her experience with Jones and bogus healings. She met Jones shortly after he set up operations in San Francisco. Jones had informed her that she had cancer, though doctors found no such condition. He prayed for a cure, while holding one hand on her head and the other over her mouth. The woman said Jones pretended to pull from her mouth a cancerous tumor, but what she discovered was a "marinated chicken liver." Upset by this fake miracle, the woman said she began spreading the word that Jones was a false prophet.

Speakers' attacks on Jones prompted one complaint during a question and answer period. One conferee (who, it was later found, was a People's Temple member) said the speakers completely overlooked the good Jones did.

Affirming black symbols

But the black church, itself, also came in for criticism. San Francisco State University professor Raye Richardson, a sister of a Jonestown victim, blasted the black church as a "tool of whites." She accused it of "joining hands with the state, and of not validating black women." Richardson said that her sister once described "the peace and serenity" of Jonestown, and said that Jones used black symbols to affirm black values—something, Richardson said, many black churches don't do.

Her remarks sparked a ringing defense of the black church from H.H. Brookins, a bishop in the African Methodist Episcopal Church. He acknowledged that "black religion is sometimes misused and distorted," but said the church "has a life instinct . . . Jones had a death instinct."

Like conference organizers and many delegates, Brookins blamed government negligence for much of the Jonestown tragedy. "Did officials simply look the other way because most of the people involved were black people?"

A milder criticism of the black church was voiced by Kelly Smith. He said that too many times "when our community has needed a prophetic voice, we have provided a pathetic echo. Like our white counterparts, we, too, have often neglected to fight for our people. Jonestown challenges us to rise up to the fullness of our potential."

Bay area pastor Don Green described the two-day meeting as "educational and inspiring." Green, member of the Bay Area Black Pastors' Ecumenical Conference, the hosts, said local pastors had been spurred to aid the families of Jonestown survivors and to meet for discussion of the issues relevant to the poor and blacks in the Bay area. Conference organizers promised that a conference report would be distributed to the delegates' respective denominational headquarters. They hoped the conference proceedings would stimulate dialogue among local congregations regarding the implications of Jonestown.

Meanwhile, Bay area clergymen from various church groups filed a joint suit against People's Temple. They sought to free funds to pay burial expenses for Jonestown victims and to reimburse families of survivors, who have already paid large amounts for funeral expenses.

What, then, should be the mission of the black church in light of Jonestown? To enrich the life and fellowship of the church as the family of God, said Lowery and Smith, and "expand the churches' resources to deal with the poor and the helpless." Lowery urged the delegates to "put on the shoes of sensitivity to human need" and to preach one gospel that is "both spiritual and social, and both evangelical and prophetic."

Before his demise, Jones frequently predicted an impending fascist-inspired race war between blacks and whites. But at the close of the San Francisco conference, Lowery's message to black churches was one of healing: he called for a holistic gospel that would minister to the needs of all society. □

IV

Newspaper Coverage of the Peoples Temple

People's Temple colony 'harassed'

People's Temple, its leader the Rev. Jim Jones and its Jonestown colony in Guyana are under a heavily financed attack by the U.S. intelligence establishment, Mark Lane charged here.

Lane, a Washington lawyer, educator and author whose works include "Rush To Judgment," a book on the John Kennedy assassination, is a director of Citizens Commission Inquiry and was invited by its local chapter to look into temple affairs.

He appeared at a news conference at the temple in San Francisco yesterday after a trip to Guyana.

Attacks on the colony, both in Guyana and in Congress, have been financed with large sums of money "laundered through banks in neutral countries," and there is evidence of "a concerted effort by the U.S. intelligence establishment to destroy Jonestown," Lane said.

Included in the effort was a trans-jungle trek by a party of 20 men armed with rocket launchers and small arms, Lane said. He declined to name the leader of the group, whom he characterized as an employee of Interpol, the international police coordination agency.

He said the leader gave him a full statement because "he said he felt misused." The group had been sent to fire on the colony's generator building, darkening the compound, after cutting their way through the supposed barbed wire and minefields around the compound. After darkening the area, Lane said, they had planned to "free the children" from the supposed evil influences of the colony.

When they discovered there were no minefields nor barbed wire, Lane said, they contented themselves with sniping at the compound for six days. Lane related that the patrol leader told him he was amazed to be invited to visit the colony and stayed there several days.

"He told me he was satisfied that the 'concentration camp' charges against Jonestown were false and that he thought he had been misused," Lane said.

Lane declined to name the agent, but hinted that he might be named after the filing of a multi-million-dollar suit against the government, which Lane said could be expected "within 90 days."

The suit will charge, he said, that a host of federal agencies are doing all they can — much of it illegally — to scuttle the Jonestown colony.

To be named as defendants, he said, are the FBI, CIA, Department of State, Internal Revenue Service, Treasury Department, Postal Service and virtually everybody but the Coast and Geodetic Survey.

The motive for the alleged government conspiracy, he said, is that the colony of 1,200 American expatriates is an embarrassment to the government because of its success.

As to charges that people once in the colony are not free to leave, he said that the U.S. Embassy staff has on several occasions sent a car to the colony and offered anyone who wanted one a free ride to the airport and a free flight home.

On the other hand, at another point in his dissertation, he said there are no roads to the colony but that transportation is available by boat or a complicated series of train trips or flights.

Lane was backed up by four persons who had recently returned from the colony, and by Jones' wife, Marceline, also recently returned.

Mrs. Jones said that her husband had remained in Guyana because of the advice of his attorneys and because his presence is needed there.

303

Newsmen shot in Guyana
Congressman feared slain

From Sun-Times Wires

WASHINGTON—The State Department said Saturday night it has been told Rep. Leo J. Ryan (D-Calif.) and several reporters were shot and killed in an attack on Ryan's fact-finding mission at the airport in Port Kaituma, Guyana.

Ryan was leading a delegation investigating a report that Americans were being held prisoner at a controversial U.S. religious settlement at Jonestown in the South American country.

Police in Georgetown, Guyana, quoted Port Kaituma authorities as confirming "about 20 people" were killed in the attack.

State Department spokesman Tom Reston said the report reached Washington by a flash message from the U.S. Embassy in Guyana, formerly a British Colony. Reston said the attack and Ryan's death had not been confirmed.

Reston said the report was relayed by a pilot who was flying Ryan, the reporters and a Ryan staff worker to the People's Temple, a settlement of about 1,200 Americans established in Guyana a year ago by Jim Jones, a former San Francisco city official.

THE PILOT escaped by flying away in a plane on the landing strip near the settlement.

Before leaving San Francisco Monday, Ryan had said: "I am going to investigate the conditions of Americans [in the Jones settlement] who, I have been told, are working from dawn to nightfall, with terrible mental and physical punishments if they don't work hard enough."

The State Department said it was unclear when the shootings took place.

Jeff Dieterich, of the department's Latin American desk, said the pilot, who has not been identified by name or nationality, said it appeared an entire NBC-TV crew headed by correspondent Don Harris was shot with Ryan. The crew members' conditions were not known, Dieterich said.

Also left behind after the shooting was Mark Lane, the lawyer representing James Earl Ray, Dr. Martin Luther King Jr.'s convicted assassin. Lane was along as counsel for Jones.

DIETERICH SAID reports from the U.S. mission showed two planes had flown to Jonestown and were preparing to leave when the shooting began.

He said nine members of the controversial settlement were leaving with Ryan and had boarded one of the planes when one of the nine pulled a gun and began shooting.

The pilot and crew members that were to fly the departing sect members jumped from the plane, ran to a second plane and flew from the remote Port Kaituma strip, Dieterich said.

The pilot reported general panic, with Ryan and the NBC crew lying, as if dead, and others still moving but wounded and still others running for cover.

Dieterich said the Port Kaituma strip is not lighted and is blocked by the damaged plane. He said Guyana officials were flying soldiers and police to a nearby, lighted airport. He said confirmation of the shootings probably would not be available before first light Sunday morning.

ON THE FLIGHT WERE:

Jackie Speier, legislative counsel to Ryan; Lane; Charles Gary, a lawyer; Richard Dwyer, U.S. deputy chief of mission at Georgetown; Guyana; Harris; Bob Flick, Robert Brown and someone identified only as S. Long, of NBC; Ron Javers of the San Francisco Chronicle; Tim Rieterman and Gregory Robinson of the San Franciso Examiner, and Charles Krause of the Washington Post.

The controversial People's Temple was founded by Jones in northern California 15 years ago and claims a membership of 20,000.

Cult accused of terror tactics

SAN FRANCISCO (UPI)—The People's Temple religious cult has been at the center of controversy for years.

Reports of beatings, extortion and forced imprisonment of terrified parishioners have circulated around the activities of the organization's San Francisco headquarters since its South American mission was set up in Guyana in June, 1977.

That was when controversial, flamboyant temple leader Jim Jones departed with his flock, resigning his post as San Francisco Housing Authority chairman.

Aside from accounts by disgruntled former members or Jones loyalists, little was known about the Guyana settlement. Rep. Leo J. Ryan (D-Calif.) went to Guyana to investigate complaints by former cult members that the 1,200 settlers of the "Jonestown" colony were being held against their will.

Reports from Guyana over the months maintained that Jones used physical force to punish temple members and pressured them into donating homes and property.

Typical of accounts from inside the 27,000-acre settlement was that of former temple aide Deborah Layton, 25:

Layton told of public beatings, armed guards and threats of mass suicide at the Guyana outpost.

As examples of discipline, she said, an elderly woman has humiliated by being forced to strip. Fists were ground into the foreheads of younger members and others were forced into an underground "box" for a day at a time. But allegations of this kind were stoutly denied by Jones loyalists.

At the peak of People's Temple activities in California before the Guyana mission was opened, Jones claimed a following of 20,000. He had moved into his church leadership from a position of influence within San Francisco political circles.

Among the many signs that all was not well within his organization after the Guyana settlement opened was a suit filed in August, 1977, against Jones and the temple by two former members who claimed They were forced to surrender their property to the church.

A spokesman at temple headquarters refused to comment Saturday on the shooting reports, nor would she disclose the whereabouts of Jones.

304

U.S. MONITORED CULT BUT TOOK LITTLE ACTION

By ROBERT PEAR and SUSAN SCHMIDT

Washington Star

WASHINGTON — The State Department and the Federal Communications Commission had received numerous complaints about a religious cult known as the People's Temple, but neither took decisive action to curb alleged abuses by the strange sect that flourished in California and in a remote South American jungle.

FCC officials said they had been monitoring for more than a year coded radio transmissions between the San Francisco headquarters of the religious group and its sprawling agricultural commune in the former British colony of Guyana.

The Rev. Jim Jones, founder of the sect, led more than 400 of his devotees in mass suicide-murder rites over the weekend after members of the cult had ambushed and killed Rep. Leo J. Ryan, D-Calif., and four other U.S. citizens.

Ryan was on a fact-finding mission to investigate reports from his constituents who said friends and relatives were being cruelly mistreated at Jones' settlement, known as Jonestown.

The FCC has been monitoring a ham radio station operated by a People's Temple member in San Francisco. The investigation centers on alleged violations of FCC radio rules, including the use of ciphers and codes; transmission on frequencies outside the approved range; using transmissions to conduct business; and failure to give adequate station identification.

The commission, however, has cited only a single technical violation. One of the operators was fined $50 for failing to give adequate station identification.

The long night of fear at Guyana airstrip

By Tim Reiterman
Examiner Staff Writer
1978 San Francisco Examiner

ANDREWS AIR FORCE BASE, Md. — That terrible series of gunshots in Port Kaituma, Guyana, signaled only the beginning of an interminable night.

When the murderers drove away from the airport, some survivors cautiously climbed out of the disabled Guyana Airways twin-prop plane and others inched out of the dense jungle growth lining the strip.

The first task was counting the dead and moving the injured into the tall grass, away from the plane, in case the Peoples Temple assassination squad returned to

Examiner reporter Tim Reiterman, injured in the ambush that killed five, filed this report from Andrews Air Force Base Hospital in Maryland.

complete the job.

Anthony Katsaris, brother of temple leader Maria Katsaris, was carried just off the gravel runway, blood streaming from his nose. He had a wound in his chest.

Jackie Speier, legal aide to Rep. Leo Ryan, was flat on her back, an eight-inch slab of her right thigh blown away, one arm shattered and a bullet in her pelvis.

A few feet away, NBC technician Steve Sung was crying out in

pain, with the muscles of his right arm shot away in two places by a high-powered rifle.

Some of the uninjured were bent over the severely hurt, trying to stem the bleeding, while the less severely wounded bound their injuries with shirts and belts, their eyes wide in shock and amazement.

After a while, Sung was delirious with rum and pain, calling to his wife and daughter and to Speier.

"You're beautiful and brave,

Jackie," he cried. "We're going to make it."

"Hang on, Steve," she called back. "We may even laugh about this some day."

Almost two dozen townspeople milled around the five bodies near the plane. Some shook their heads in disbelief, then drifted over to the Americans. "Why?" implored a little man with great white teeth and a wide-brimmed straw hat. "Why did they do this to you?"

"We don't know," I said at the time.

While some Guyanese

—See Back Page, Col. 1

306

— From Page 1

brought us river water and rum. others looked at our injuries with pity and whispered among themselves about Peoples Temple and the Rev. Jim Jones.

"What happened?" they were asking.

When the entire sequence of increasingly tense and violent events was recounted — the congressional fact-finding mission of Rep. Ryan, the fine food and entertainment at the Temple's agricultural project, the subsequent defection of 16 temple members, the attempt to slit Ryan's throat, and finally, the massacre — these people of Port Kaituma reacted with fear and horror.

After all, their wives and children lived in modest houses around the airstrip, well within bullet range. It consoled them little to hear that the temple death squad had waved aside the Guyanese and did not attempt to kill the Guyanese in the party.

"We are with you," the outspoken little man said. "We will protect you. My God ... how can they do this? We are all human beings."

And these were wonderful human beings, these compassionate men with shoeless children.

"Anything we can do, anything, will be done," declared the spokesman, jabbing with his index finger.

Cigarettes and lights were passed around, and a bearded man named Patrick McDonald Duke said, "Please give me your address. We will correspond."

When the offer of help was made, it felt as though we had just signed an important treaty. We still were wounded and terrified in the middle of the South American jungle, but we had allies.

As night fell over the airfield. our only flashlight was pulled from a pack. Dick Dwyer, of the US. embassy, went over the passenger list on his clipboard, marking the five dead, five seriously injured. five less seriously injured, six missing and nine uninjured.

Dwyer, a tall, husky, middle-aged man in khaki, assumed the leadership early. His first announcement was that the pilot of the bullet-disabled airplane had radioed the airport tower in Georgetown and that help supposedly was on the way.

Georgetown was an hour's flight away. However, Dwyer was a realist who knew something about government in general and this poor country in particular.

"You all should know there is a strong possibility we will be spending the night here," he said.

That conjured up the nightmare of Peoples Temple farm vehicles bristling with weapons, or commando attacks from the curtain of jungle surrounding the airport.

Shortly after dark, our Guyanese friends appeared with three bedsprings and mattresses to use as litters.

Dwyer had negotiated with four Guyanese soldiers guarding a grounded military plane near the end of the runway so we were able to bring the severely wounded to their tent, where they would have armed protection.

The soldiers, Dwyer said, were not willing to stand between the rest of us and any attackers.

Some thought was given to simply camping in the tall grass. but it was felt that that would afford little protection from a night-time raid.

The villagers at first encouraged us each to hide with a different family, but under these conditions a house-to-house search by the temple would increase the possibility of encountering a resident sympathetic to the temple.

The Guyanese said the brutal shootings of unarmed people rinsed away virtually all their good relations with the temple.

It finally was decided that the ambulatory would walk to a nearby rum shop and disco. Toting our bags up the muddy main road. we straggled into Sam's Disco — the airport area counterpart of Mike's Disco. where the temple had arranged our lodging the previous night.

The dance floor was quite similar — with black walls. black lights and fluorescent hand-painted slogans and graffiti.

A bench ran along one wall to a bar with shelves of local rum and whiskey. Our hosts sat around rum and beer bottles as Dwyer explained that the able-bodied would work in shifts tending the sick at the tent.

The others would stay at the disco rum shop.

Our protectors arrived from their nearby homes with an assortment of weapons — a single shotgun, a machete and a long-bladed knife. We added a hunting knife — a Scout survival knife that Sung had bought for the trip.

These weren't exactly the Green Berets, but they were trustworthy and eager to help.

"I was in the army until two years ago," said one young man.

"When the army gets here, I may have to put on my old uniform again," joked another, a former colonel.

* * *

During the second tent shift, NBC field producer Bob Flick and I tended to the patients, borrowing a flashlight from the M16-armed soldiers.

Most of the time we sat on the damp ground, a little skeptical about whether the Guyanese troops would arrive before daybreak.

Periodically, a couple of times in response to moaning, we went into the tent. But all that could be done was to make our patients more comfortable with aspirin, rum and water or a re-arranging of bedclothes. We had no antibiotics, little sterile dressing and virtually no medical skills.

"Do you have anything for pain?" Jackie Speier said.

"There is one pill wrapped in a paper by your head."

"I'd better save it," she said. "I'll take rum instead."

Those in the tent should have been in a dry, well-staffed hospital hours ago, rather than alternately sweating and shivering in damp clothes on a non-sterile canvas floor.

* * *

Back at the disco, the owner's wife, Elaine, directed us to a back room. The rest of the group either were sleeping on floors and beds in two small rooms or sitting around a kitchen table drinking strong coffee Guyana style, with a healthy dose of cream and sugar. There were former temple members, relatives of temple members and reporters.

The day's tragedies raised several questions: Would the airport assassins come back to town? What was happening at the temple mission? And did Jones order the attack?

No one knew how safe we were, yet the consensus among former members was that Jones had indeed ordered, or at least approved, a massacre with such far-reaching consequences.

As for Jonestown, Harold Cordell, who joined Jones in Indianapolis 25 years ago, said: "You're going to see the worst carnage of your life. It's called revolutionary suicide."

Explained Dale Parks, who had made his break from the temple hours earlier: "The theory is that you can go down in history saying you chose your way to go. It is your commitment to die rather than accept capitalism."

The next step?

"Jim Jones said if mass suicide happened, he and his trusted aides would get back to the United States and kill everyone who ever left the church."

Sleeping was too risky for most of us. Every approaching truck was potentially from the temple. But the lady of the house, Elaine, could give us the owner's name by listening to the engine and transmission sounds.

How many trucks could there be in a town of several hundred persons?

Because time drags, Parks, who onced worked at the University of California Medical Center, changed our bandages and used gin to disinfect the wounds. Elaine tore down some of her curtains to make bandages.

Jerry Parks, a balding yet trim man in a tank top, spoke of the death of his wife, Patricia, that afternoonin the ambush. "Her brain was all over me," he said. "A high-powered rifle caught her. She was down to 111 pounds. When she came over here, she was 137. She wasn't getting enough to eat."

Suddenly everyone was startled by a loud boom that sounded like a gunshot. People squatted on the floor, simply froze, or tried to peek out the windows. Someone cursed our lack of arms.

After the guards assured us that the sound was only a limb falling on a roof, we went back to waiting. A short time later, Dwyer reported, "We're trying to get a U.S. med-evac plane into Mathews Ridge or Georgetown."

The report raised our hopes just like all the others, but not much. Everyone had learned to protect himself with pessimism. Finally, some temple refugees said they heard the whistle on the train from Mathews Ridge, an hour and a half away.

Dawn approached and passed.

Then, at about 8:30 a.m., Guyanese soldiers arrived to protect us and to take us to arriving airplanes.

We and some Guyanese celebrated with a traditional local breakfast drink — condensed milk laced with rum.

ones wasn't man they used to know

INDIANAPOLIS (UPI) — If Jim Jones beat people and promoted murders and suicides in his Peoples Temple in Guyana, he was radically changed from the man who founded the group in Indianapolis, say people who knew him.

The Rev. James W. Jones, 48, who later moved his ministry to the San Francisco Bay area, set up his Indianapolis church in the early 1950s as an interracial congregation with an active community program.

Jones, who served 18 months as director of the Indianapolis Human Rights Commission, headed to Ukiah, Calif., in 1965 with 140 of his faithful, saying he could no longer live in a state as racist as Indiana.

A dynamic but calm man, he was sincerely concerned for the poor and minorities, former acquaintances said. They were shocked that he would be involved with violence.

"I remember him as a very quiet, non-aggressive person," said former Mayor Charles H. Boswell, who appointed Jones director of his Human Rights Commission in 1961.

"He was just the opposite of the person I've heard described in the recent publicity. It seems there'd been a tremendous personality change, the symptoms of which never appeared here."

Jone, born at Lynn, Ind., began his Peoples Temple after leaving an all-white church where the board disagreed with his inviting black attendance.

In an old synagogue building, he built a large interracial congregation — a daring enterprise in a city known then for discrimination against blacks.

"His group was at least 50 percent black, and that led to some negative feeling in Indianapolis," said Barton Hunter, former executive secretary of the United Christian Missionary Society.

He met the problems of his church's ghetto neighborhood with a soup kitchen, a job placement staff and a clothing pantry for applicants.

He set an example, living in the neighborhood. He adopted eight children — some of them black.

Boswell said Jones ably led the Human Rights Commission, persuading several restaurants and a theater to open their doors to minorities.

After leaving the city post, he shuttled between Indianapolis and South America where his church was supporting a ministry in Brazil that included an orphanage.

Faith in the Extreme

By Richard L. Kenyon

Journal Religion Reporter

Mass suicide, like that of the more than 400 Peoples Temple members in Guyana, is not unprecedented in human history.

Japanese soldiers committed suicide in mass numbers during World II. In Europe during the Middle Ages, people chose suicide over death by plague and widespread pestilence. There are other examples throughout history.

Perhaps the best known instance of mass suicide was the death of 960 Jewish Zealots at the fortress at Masada in 73 A.D.

Dr. Basil Jackson, chairman of the department of psychiatry at Lutheran Hospital, said, however, that the incident at Masada and most other mass suicides were not the same as the bizarre deaths at Jonestown.

Jackson, who also holds a degree in theology, has studied the phenomenon of mass suicide.

Those at Masada, he said, faced almost certain death or enslavement by the Roman legions that were relentlessly attacking the towering fortress. Those at Jonestown were following blindly someone they considered an incarnation of God.

Jackson agreed that one of the elements similar in many suicides, including Masada, the Japanese soldiers and apparently Jonestown, is death for an ideal, albeit a misguided and misunderstood one.

"These people were basically sheep who, sadly, like so many people, would do anything under the right psychological conditions," Jackson said.

"This guy, (the Rev.) Jim Jones, had the right kind of charismatic, dictatorial appeal. And he successfully brainwashed them, using techniques like those used by Koreans on UN troops.

"The brilliance in it was that he isolated them. He took them to a remote part of the world, and they suffered from sensory deprivation and sensory isolation. Every contact they had with the outside world was mediated through him. His voice was broadcast 24 hours a day. Any time of day, that's who, that's what they heard."

The Rev. Gordon Melton, a Methodist minister in Evanston, Ill., who has studied small American religious groups, including the Peoples Temple, said Jones' followers, by all sorts of conditioning, felt an intense connection to him.

"There was a strong ego involvement at work here, within the group," he said, "and those in the group believed that when Jones spoke it was the truth with a capital T. It was, they were led to believe, the will of God. They were fanatics.

"It happened at Masada, during the Reformation, in the 1400s in Czechoslovakia. Fanatics who do weird things that for them is internally consistent. It doesn't happen overnight. It takes a long time of a certain sort of conditioning on a certain personality to produce this sort of behavior."

Jackson said that people who would join a cult like that of Jones and follow a man like him were the extreme case of the world's followers.

They died, he said, because they were told to.

"They were zombies at that point. They had been seduced into massive submission. Closest thing to that was the brainwashing of troops in Korea. They stood up when told to and sat down when told to. In psychiatry we call it automata — just automatic behavior.

"They were people who would let a leader make their decisions for them, people who don't want to go through the pain of decision making."

He said the people in Guyana who drank the poison believed they were "taking a trip to a better world."

The other element, beside the victim's personality, is the personality of the leader.

"This guy had a messianic complex and was on a power kick. He had become like Hitler. His followers let him become their alter egos, let him think for them."

The Pilot

Official Newspaper of the Archdiocese of Boston, Mass., Established 1829

Page 4   Friday, November 24, 1978

A Deadly Cult

The facts are there, frightening to see in print and photo, impossible to assess in terms of the savage attack on human and spiritual values. The messianic madness of the leader of the People's Temple came to a ghastly climax with the mass suicide-murder of some 400 camp followers. Cyanide was the death potion in the grisly sacrifice that the Rev. Jim Jones had rehearsed for the members of his sect. The strange mixture of Christian fundamentalism and a communal living allowed a zealot to lead his people first to the wilderness life of Guyana, then to a bizarre death ritual.

Traditionally, the sense of cult has been identified with things divine and religious. In our day we have witnessed cultic worship of much more mortal and fragile dimensions. The secular has replaced the sacred whenever personal cult is praised — the athlete, the politician, the performer, the psuedo-prophet — even though the adulation and the kingdom is short-lived. The transfer of power, reverence and obedience from God to creatures is fraught with danger that knows no bounds and the tragedy at Jonestown testifies to such an alienation. Yet, the horror that the enormity of this slaughter evokes in a society that has become hardened to value of life is no guarantee that it could not happen again.

What cannot be overlooked in the fanatical finale to this curious living experience is the realization that the setting may have been in a remote part of South America but the victims came out of urban America. Led by a man driven by an obsessive spirit — his son described him as 'paranoid' — more than a 1000 men, women and children, black and white, many of them with problems and unable to adjust to the American society, sought new beginnings in the chosen land of Guyana. In the end, Rev. Jones bid them to go 'to another place' by way of murder and suicide.

The wanton waste of life in Jonestown defies any reasonable explanation. However, this will not stop efforts to analyze how and why it should happen. Experts in the fields of religion, medicine and politics will try to sift through the sketchy details of the tragic events together with the background information available on the People's Temple to find the key to the strange hold that its frantic founder had on these troubled victims. Meanwhile, some of these who had lent various forms of support and encouragement to Rev. Jim Jones are seeking to put distance between themselves and the religious-political sect. If nothing else maybe this mass killing may make those in positions to write helpful recommendations and to endorse plans and projects of individuals and groups a little more hesitant about this practice in the future.

The shock of the news which began with the shooting of Congressman Ryan and members of his party, and concluded with the carnage at the commune altar of sacrifice has given way to a feeling of sympathy for all the victims and their families who must live with this nightmare. The true expression of religious concern must not be confused with the cruelty evidenced at Jonestown. Nor should religion be made the scapegoat for the horrible scene that took place there in the manner of agreeing with that old bromide that "religion is the opium of the people." For hundreds of Jones's devotees it was a deadly cult that exploited them, a perversion of religious instincts that culminated in the cyanide toast. The hunger of people for spiritual nourishment must be satisfied in the true worship of God and never false idols whatever form that may take. Jonestown just might point to the starvation that very much prevails in our society.

New Revelation of Jonestown Deaths Shocks Remnant of Peoples Temple

SAN FRANCISCO, Nov. 24 (UPI)—The faithful remnant of the Peoples Temple reeled under a new blow today as word came that hundreds more of their families and friends had been found dead in Guyana.

"I don't know what to say. It's a shock. It's terrible," said June Crym, one of dozens of persons secluded in the temple headquarters in fear of violence from people who lost relatives in the Guyana tragedy.

Crym, when told that many missing members of the Jonestown colony were now known to be dead, said she could only hope that this would dispel "rumors that there is a hit squad or plot" by surviving temple members to harm anyone.

The news of more bodies found at Jonesville stunned the temple faithful.

"We always hoped. You know, if you have children or loved ones and you haven't heard, you think there is always a chance they will come out of the jungle as others have," Crym said.

Crym said that while she did not have any relatives at Guyana, most of the people in the temple did, and that some have been waiting anxiously in the hope that their loved ones had somehow avoided the terrible death ritual.

If all are now accounted for, she said, it will end the anxiety, but also the hope.

"But we are still alarmed and disturbed by the rumors being thrown out on no basis whatsoever," she said. "People have been whipped up to such a frenzy by the reports of hit squads in the temple."

She said some enemies of the Rev. Jim Jones who had let their feelings spill out could incite "crazies" to attack the temple.

"The police have been very cooperative. They are protecting us. We have no way of knowing" whether the temple and its faithful might be actually be attacked, she said. "But over the past week we have received many death threats."

"We thought we should gather together here for safety," she said. "We are now a small number."

Crym said she does not know how many persons are still in the Peoples Temple congregation, which numbered 3,000 a few weeks ago. No Thanksgiving Day services were held. The faithful few in the temple had a quiet dinner by themselves.

Other churches have offered assistance, Crym said, and the local Council of Churches has asked the temple members if any help is needed.

"People have been calling expressing sympathy and understanding," she said. "We are encouraged about this and we are determined this is not going to end the temple."

Jones' Burial To Be in Indiana

RICHMOND, Ind., Nov. 24 (AP)—The bodies of the Rev. Jim Jones, his wife and son will be returned to this eastern Indiana city for burial, the mother-in-law of the cult leader said today.

Charlotte Baldwin said funeral plans are contingent on the release of the bodies from Dover Air Force Base, where corpses from the Peoples Temple settlement have been taken for identification. The FBI already has positively identified Jones' body.

Baldwin said she and her husband, Walter, wanted their daughter, Marceline, to be buried in her hometown of Richmond, near the Indiana-Ohio line. Her grandson, Steven, agreed that the bodies should be returned here, she said.

U.S., Fearing Rights Violations, Ruled Out Investigating Cults

Associated Press

The Justice Department ruled out investigations into alleged brainwashing and physical abuse in religious cults because of fears such inquiries would violate constitutional guarantees of freedom of religion, a department spokesman said.

Spokesman Robert Havel said Thursday night that Rep. Leo Ryan (D-Calif.), who was killed while leading a fact-finding mission to the Peoples Temple settlement in Guyana, had asked the department to investigate the religious group.

Ryan and Rep. Robert Giaimo (D-Conn.) in May 1977 told the department that several religious cults controlled their members through brainwashing and physical abuse.

The two congressmen said they had also received allegations that some religious organizations were illegally converting members' veterans benefits, welfare payments and food stamps for their own use.

Benjamin Civiletti, then chief of the department's criminal division told the congressmen that brainwashing and other thought-control tactics "would not support a prosecution under the federal kidnaping statute" and that an investigation could infringe on the freedom-of-religion guarantees in the Constitution.

Havel said, "Certainly there are constitutional problems involved. If the person is an adult and not being held against his will, there is not much we can do."

312

Day by day, a new stunning horror

A CHRONOLOGY of major events in the Jonestown, Guyana, murder-mass suicide tragedy:

Nov. 16, 1978—U.S. Rep. Leo J. Ryan [D., Cal.] and a 13-person delegation arrive in Guyana to inspect the People's Temple settlement after receiving continuing reports about the mistreatment of sect members. About 40 other Americans, worried about relatives living in Jonestown, accompany Ryan.

Nov. 17—Ryan, an aide, and a small group of relatives of sect members receive permission from People's Temple leaders to visit Jonestown. They fly to the sect's settlement.

Nov. 18—The People's Temple office in Georgetown issues a statement saying Ryan held a dozen private interviews in the settlement and then addressed a gathering of more than 1,000 residents. It says Ryan praised the "friendly" reception he got at Jonestown. But inside Jonestown, a sect member assaults Ryan and threatens to kill him with a knife held to Ryan's throat, before he is overpowered.

Nov. 18, 4:20 p.m. [Guyana time]—Ryan and other members of his party, including reporters and cameramen, and an American woman who had asked the group to help her escape from Jonestown, are at an airstrip seven miles outside Jonestown, waiting to board two airplanes. "Eight to a dozen" men from the Temple appear on a truck and trailer and begin firing rifles and shotguns at the group. Ryan and four others—newsmen Don Harris, Robert Brown, and Gregory Robinson, and Patricia Parks, the woman seeking to flee—are killed. Nine others are wounded. All the dead and wounded are Americans. The gunmen escape.

Nov. 19—In Washington, the U.S. State Department says it has received "alarming indications" that at least 200 of the settlers at Jonestown committed suicide after the ambush. Guyanese troops are sent to check out the reports.

Nov. 20—The information minister of Guyana says Guyanese troops found between 300 and 400 bodies at the Jonestown camp, in what appears to have been a mass-ritual suicide. Hundreds of cult members are said to be missing in the jungle.

Nov. 21—The Guyana government raises the Jonestown death toll to 383, including many children, and says most apparently died by drinking poison—cyanide mixed with Kool-Aid in a wash tub. Later, the toll is raised to

Tribune Map

409. Cult leader Jones is revealed to be among the dead—killed by a gunshot wound in the head. In San Francisco, former members of the People's Temple express fears they will be hunted down and murdered by the cult's "death squads."

Nov. 22—Stephen Jones, son of the cult leader, who was away from Jonestown when the massacre occurred, says he believes "murder, not suicide" left many of his father's followers dead. He calls his father "paranoid" and drug-addicted. American soldiers are flown into Guyana to help bring out the bodies of the victims.

Forty survivors of the mass suicide ritual are found in the jungle near Jonestown.

Nov. 23—Larry Layton, 32, a cult member at Jonestown arrested in connection with the murders of Ryan and four others at the airstrip, is "terrified for his life," Guyanese police say, and fears he himself will be assassinated.

In the United States, federal sources disclose that Jones reputedly left a cache of $10 million to $12 million, much of it in secret bank accounts in the U.S., Canada, Switzerland, and the African nation of Ghana.

Nov. 24—The acting chief of the U.S. mission in Guyana, Vic Dikeos, discloses that U.S. troops have found many more bodies at Jonestown than previously reported. Many of the bodies were found under previously counted bodies, another U.S. official says.

Nov. 25—State Department officers announce that the tentative death toll in the mass murder-suicide is 910, nearly 500 more than originally estimated.

Chicago Defender

JOHN H. SENGSTACKE

Editor & Publisher

 SENGSTACKE Newspapers

CHICAGO DAILY DEFENDER	PITTSBURGH COURIER
MICHIGAN CHRONICLE	OHIO COURIER
FLORIDA COURIER	DETROIT COURIER
TRI-STATE DEFENDER	NATIONAL COURIER
GEORGIA COURIER	PHILADELPHIA COURIER

Senseless orgy

Now that most of the discussion and analysis of the shocking Guyana affair has been finished, there remains one lingering lesson: We live — all of us — far closer to the jungle than we like to believe. •

There are times in life, especially when things are going well or our spirits are warmed, when we can become almost convinced that humankind is on a steadily ascending road. There are moments when we feel certain that our undeniable scientific and technological progress is being matched by almost equal moral progress. There are seasons when peace on earth, good will toward men doesn't appear to be an altogether impossible dream.

And then comes Guyana. Then we are forced to reassess. Despite occasional appearances to the contrary, we live in a world where the potential for terrible hatred and violence is lingering just below the surface. There is a certain irony in the fact that the followers of James Jones left their urban homes in an effort to escape from fear and loneliness and to build a genuine Utopia here on earth. But the awful things that occur so often in cities followed them to this far away land. They gave up the urban jungle for another, deadlier kind. They all died in a senseless orgy of murder and suicide.

It doesn't make any sense? Oh yes, it does — if you accept the premise that underneath our occasional good manners and the restraints of civilization rages an untamed beast. You can label it original sin, human weakness, genetic deficiency, chemical imbalance or plain lunacy. But the fact remains that it is far more pervasive than we want to admit, and it is horrible.

Social scientists will continue to wrestle with the unique human factors which led Jones to play God and thousands of his followers to obey him so blindly. Such studies are helpful up to a point. They cannot, however, tame or even explain the beast who roams the jungle of Guyana or the Jackson Park CTA train.

Meanwhile, we find ourselves talking in little groups about Guyana, trying to sort out what it means, struggling to put some sense in the senseless. And when all is said and done, we have to admit it's not Jones or his followers we are thinking about with so much fear and confusion; it's ourselves and our children.

Church Officials Ponder Lesson of Guyana Events

By Russell Chandler

Los Angeles Times Service

Los Angeles, Calif. — The Christian Church (Disciples of Christ), with which the Peoples Temples are affiliated, dislikes labels.

As America's oldest and largest indigenous religious movement, the Disciples of Christ gives each of its 4,416 local congregations complete autonomy in managing its affairs. The 1.3 million members tend to reject denominational titles, preferring to call themselves simply "Christians."

However, in the wake of the horror and killing at the Peoples Temple compound in Guyana, officials at the national headquarters of the Christian Church in Indianapolis are considering adopting procedures that would allow the ouster of erring congregations.

The Rev. Kenneth L. Teegarden, denomination president, said:

"The congregational autonomy of a denomination such as ours, and the resultant tenuous relationship with many local churches, left us with a bare knowledge that Peoples Temple of Redwood Valley, Calif., had a Guyana colony and no appreciation of a fanaticism that could have led to the human destruction that took place."

Limits on Freedoms

Noting that the denomination had "stood firmly for a variety of styles and approaches to Christian mission and ministry," Teegarden said steps would be taken immediately to see if limits should be set on the freedom of local congregations.

Until last weekend, the Peoples Temples in Redwood Valley and San Francisco — though untypical of Disciples' congregations — seemed to be no serious cause for alarm, according to a church official.

Scott Lathrop of Sacramento, Calif., chairman of an informal review committee set up early last year, said that although complaints had been heard about alleged abuses at the temples and in Guyana, no formal charges had been filed.

The Disciples' emphasis on individual liberty of opinion has been held dear since the founding of the movement in the early 19th century.

Frontier Preacher

Patriarch of the movement was a frontier preacher named Barton W. Stone, born in Maryland in 1772. An ordained Presbyterian clergyman, he began his career conducting frontier revival meetings but soon became convinced that denominationalism was the curse of Christianity.

He called upon believers in the Bible to unite in a new fellowship, based solely on the teachings of Scripture. Adherents called themselves "Christians" to make it clear that they were not part of any particular doctrinal group or denomination.

The movement grew rapidly, and in 1809 a remarkable father and son team, Thomas and Alexander Campbell, lent further impetus through their vision of an ultimately united Protestant Church. The Christian movement split after 1906, however, leading to the establishment of another branch now known as the Churches of Christ.

Logical Conclusion

The Christian movement carried to its logical conclusion the Protestant principle that each person is free to interpret the Scripture for himself.

Although there are evangelists, pastors, elders and

deacons, the church teaches that anyone may approach God through prayer for direct guidance for all problems arising in the conscience.

Disciples have no catechism and no prescribed rituals, although they baptize by immersion in the name of the Trinity. A distinctive event at most Christian Church congregations is the celebration each Sunday of the Lord's Supper.

It is difficult to generalize about the beliefs members have about heaven and hell, though most believe in the immortality of the soul.

Resembles Protestants

Disciples of Christ congregations are peopled by conservatives and liberals, theologically and politically. In many ways, typical Sunday morning services resemble those of most main line Protestant churches.

Just how the Rev. Jim Jones, the Peoples Temple founder who died in the Guyana massacre, became involved with the Disciples is not fully clear.

One former top Jones aide said Jones studied under Father Divine, the famed black minister, in the 1950s and patterned his Peoples Temple after Divine's Kingdom of Peace community in New York.

It is known that before 1960, Jones had founded the first Peoples Temple in Indianapolis and had been ordained as a minister.

The Rev. John W. Harms, who was executive minister for the Disciples in Indiana in 1962-'63, said Jones came out of a Pentecostal background but "was trying to find his way out of this."

"He was a mixture of orthodoxy and fundamentalism, while being very liberal on social issues and human rights . . . " Harms recalled.

Because Harms and other church officials believed Jones lacked theological understanding, they denied him ordination by the regional body of the church unless he completed added academic and theological study.

Jones apparently did not complete the recommended work, however, and moved to Northern California from Indianapolis in 1965 and founded the Peoples Temples there.

Persons attending services in the Peoples Temple near Ukiah, Calif., in the 1960s recalled that the singing involved social action, protest and brotherhood songs rather than traditional hymns of the church.

Jones often used the Sunday newspaper as a text for his sermons, according to Kenneth Compton, who in 1968 and 1969 was president of the Northern California region of Christian Churches.

"He would sit on a tall bar stool at the front of the church and identify people in the newspaper who should be praised for various social action enterprises," Compton said. "The services were long — an hour and a half to three hours. Kids often fell asleep on the floor."

By the mid-1970s, the controversial Peoples Temples (congregations had also opened in San Francisco and Los Angeles) had developed a reputation for social works.

These included housing and feeding senior citizens and medical convalescents, maintaining a home for retarded boys, rehabilitating youthful drug users and assisting both members and nonmembers of the church by providing legal assistance and college scholarships.

Jim Jones: Portrait of a madman

'...he plugged into us, sucked away our wills'

By Ray Moseley

HE TOLD HIS followers he was the reincarnation of Jesus Christ and called himself "the prophet of God."

At other times, he said he was the reincarnation of V. I. Lenin, the founder of the Russian revolution.

He claimed to have raised more than 40 persons from the dead. He said he had cured many of cancer and other diseases.

He ruled his flock with an iron hand. Once he ordered a woman beaten be-

cause her husband complained she had left a gas flame burning on their kitchen stove. He giggled as the woman was paddled on the buttocks.

ONCE HE LED an anti-suicide demonstration on San Francisco's Golden Gate Bridge.

At other times, looking out at his vast following from behind dark green sunglasses, he would incite them to prepare for the sacrifice of their lives.

"How many in here will lay down their lives for me?" he would ask.

"How many in here will lay down the lives of their children? How many in here will lay down the lives of their wives?"

As one follower recalled, "We would scream and jump up and down and yell: 'I will, father, I will.'"

On Nov. 18, in a remote settlement on the fringe of the Guyanan jungle, more than 900 followers of the Rev. Jim Jones made good on that pledge either willingly, or, as some maintain, at gunpoint.

THEY DRANK purple Kool-Aid laced

with cyanide and died in agony as their charismatic leader died by gunfire.

The mass killings came shortly after the murder of U. S. Rep. Leo Ryan [D., Cal.] and four other persons in his party at a nearby airstrip. Ryan had gone to Guyana to investigate conditions in the communal settlement that Jones founded.

Who was Jim Jones? Was he simply the consummate con man, a silver-tongued spieler who was somehow swept

Continued on page 18, col. 1

'Reincarnated Christ' turns out to be the devil

Continued from page one

over the precipice into megalomania and paranoia?

The evidence of his bizarre end in his jungle Gotterdammerung, and in his earlier ministry at the People's Temple in San Francisco, suggest a simple answer to those questions.

BUT THERE WERE facets of his personality and behavior in an earlier time that to many bespoke a different sort of man.

As a young minister in Indianapolis in the 1950s, Jones displayed a passionate commitment to the cause of racial equality and to the poor, according to those who knew him well.

He established a soup kitchen and opened it to anyone. He opened one nursing home and then a second. He started a clothes pantry and then a service to help young people in poor neighborhoods get jobs.

He persuaded some theaters and restaurants to change racially discriminatory practices.

EVEN AFTER he went to San Francisco, where his behavior became increasingly bizarre, he was involved in a drug-rehabilitation program, a free restaurant and the medical clinic, and a legal-aid service through his church.

His 19-year-old son Stephen, who now speaks of him with hatred, says, "I feel at one time he was a good man."

But perhaps the seeds of his self-destructive end had been there all along.

James Warren Jones was born in an old, run-down 1½-story house beside the railroad tracks in Lynn, Ind., population 1,360.

He is remembered in Lynn as "an ornery little devil."

"HE COULD CUSS the hat off your head," said Russell Pierson, 63. "One minute he would be cussing you and then he'd tell you he was going to be a preacher."

George Southworth, a childhood neighbor and now a professor of journalism at the University of Miami, said 6-year-old Jimmy Jones had "special words of endearment for me" whenever they met.

"Good morning, you son of a bitch," would be his greeting.

Southworth said Jones' father, James Thurman Jones, worked as a railroad section hand and was a member of the Ku Klux Klan. His mother, Lenetta, did housekeeping and factory work in Richmond, Ind., to help support the family. Jimmy was her only child.

During his early years, Jimmy became attached to an elderly neighbor woman who began taking him to church with her. Later he began to talk about becoming a preacher.

"ONE TIME HE started his own little church in a building out behind his house," said Bill Townsend, a childhood playmate and now a high school guidance counselor.

"Later I think he joined every church in town at least once."

Willard Fields, another Lynn resident, recalls Jones frequently carried a Bible

with him when he was in high school.

"You'd see him standing off from the rest of the kids in the schoolyard, reading his Bible and thinking," he said.

He was a B student in high school but a former teacher said he was "probably brighter than his grades showed."

DURING HIS junior year, he and his mother moved to Richmond, 30 miles to the south, leaving his father behind in Lynn. The reasons for the family separation are unclear.

The following year, he took a part-time job as an orderly in Reid Memorial Hospital in Richmond. There he met a nurse named Marceline Baldwin. She was four years older than Jones, but they married in 1949, the year he was graduated from high school.

They enrolled at Indiana University at Bloomington, where he studied education and his wife continued her nursing education. After two years there, they moved to the Indianapolis suburb of Beech Grove and became affiliated with the Sommerset Southside Church, a Methodist church.

JONES LATER SAID he left because the congregation would not welcome blacks into its fold.

He continued his studies at Butler University in Indianapolis, mostly through

night school, until he was awarded a degree in secondary education in 1961.

During the mid-1950s, Jones founded his own church, the People's Temple, and affiliated it with the Christian Church [Disciples of Christ, a mainline Protestant denomination].

He gave away monkeys to members who brought the most new people to Sunday School. To raise money for a new church building, he also sold monkeys for $29 each, sometimes riding his bicycle door-to-door to peddle them.

JONES AND HIS wife began adopting children at this time, including one black and one Korean. Eventually they adopted seven children and had one of their own, Stephen.

The People's Temple met resistance in conservative Indianapolis because of it attracted a large following. About half of the members were black.

In 1961, Jones was appointed executive director of the city's Human Rights Commission. As a pastor, he was thought to be able to reason with businessmen, "and he did," said former Mayor Charles H. Boswell.

"I remember him as a very quiet, not aggressive person," said Boswell. "It seems there's been a tremendous personality change, the symptoms of which never appeared in those days."

A RABBI WHO worked with him during this period, Maurice Davis, said, "There was no indication that this thing was going to turn into a cult and that he was going to get flaked out with power. He was an earnest, idealistic, rather intense young man."

In 1961, Jones said he had received a "vision" that Indianapolis would be destroyed in a holocaust. He left the city and spent two years in Belo Horizonte, Brazil, as a missionary, and visited Guyana briefly.

A former neighbor in Brazil, Maria Machado, recalled him last week as a friendly and helpful man but "not very normal." She said Jones told her the United States was "on the verge of a nuclear revolution in which all would die of hatred."

IN 1963 HE returned to Indianapolis but left again two years later, saying

Timothy O. Stoen, former assistant prosecuting attorney of Mendocino County and a Jones follower, once wrote to the San Francisco Examiner:

"Jim has been the means by which more than 40 persons have literally been brought back from the dead . . . I have seen Jim revive people stiff as a board, tongues hanging out, eyes set, skin graying, and all vital signs absent. Don't ask me how it happens. It just does."

OTHER FORMER followers said Jones would claim to cure members of cancer. He would have them spit into a handkerchief, then pull from the handkerchief chicken entrails which he had claimed was cancerous tissue he had miraculously removed from the sick persons.

A long-time associate, the Rev. Ross Case, said Jones began acquiring "some pretty grandiose ideas about himself" about the time he moved to California.

"Jim turned completely against the Bible," he said. "He was denouncing it, disproving it, calling it a paper idol . . . Jim stopped calling himself the reincarnation of Jesus and started calling himself God."

In the summer of 1977 trouble started for Jones when New West magazine published two articles quoting 30 former temple members as saying Jones had built his power through fear, fraud, physical beatings, the appropriation of members' property, and misuse of government funds.

SOME FORMER members said they were forced to sign false confessions of crimes ranging from plots to overthrow the government to immoral sex acts.

Others said they had been cajoled into deeding over their homes to the church and had been talked into giving the temple government funds they received for running foster-care homes.

Michael Cartmell, who was married to one of Jones' daughters until he left the church two years ago, said: "He was like a father to me and other members, but he could be horribly cruel. There was a kid who was paddled 150 times on his buttocks. The kid passed out from it. It made me sick."

Other former members said Jones would sometimes laugh or say "hit him

Full coverage of Guyana tragedy

As the first reports came from Guyana late in the evening a week ago Saturday, telling of the massacre and suicides, The Tribune's news staff went into action.

Correspondent Timothy McNulty was sent to Guyana from his office in Atlanta. From Chicago, reporter Michael Sneed and photographer Val Mazzenga were dispatched to the South American country.

Correspondents Ronald Yates and Michael Coakley flew from their base in Los Angeles to San Francisco, the home of Jim Jones' People's Temple. Investigative reporter Ronald Koziol also was sent to San Francisco from Chicago.

Reporter Robert Unger went to Indiana to provide background on Jones' early years there, and The Tribune's Washington Bureau provided additional coverage from the nation's capital.

This story was written from their reports.

The Rev. Jim Jones sent out this flier to promote a May, 1976, appearance in Chicago.

Key to cult: the man was paranoid

By Ronald Yates
Chicago Tribune Press Service

SAN FRANCISCO—Jim Jones preached a strange amalgam of political and religious philosophies. His sermons, which mesmerized audiences, were an improbable oplate of Leninism, Christianity, Buddhism, and faith healing.

And lurking beneath the surface of them all was the one mechanism that seemed to make Jim Jones tick—paranoia.

"A race war is coming, my friends," he would warn from the pulpit of the cavernous People's Temple here. "A terrible, fascist-inspired war between the black and white races, a war that will end with the destruction of the United States."

use of hyperbole and Jesus' teaching methods as an attempt to emphasize priorities and to show that no earthly relationship should be allowed to come before God in the life of believers. To say Christ was teaching parents to hate their children contradicts the Biblical commandment to "Honor Thy Father and Thy Mother."

Yet, like most cult leaders, Jones twisted the teachings of Christ to fit his own priorities. Literal interpretation "and misinterpretation" of the Bible have long been the favorite intoxicant used to stupefy and confuse masses of people who are looking for uncomplicated answers to complicated questions.

And Jim Jones had all the answers —even down to the use of sex, punishment, *and faith healing to keep his flock in line.*

the city was "too racist" for him. He led about 145 of his followers to Redwood Valley near Ukiah, Cal.

He acquired a new church there with a baptismal swimming pool, a new parsonage, 11 buses, and thousands of new followers. In 1974, he moved his church to San Francisco and began involving himself in politics and community affairs.

Jones became an important figure in the San Francisco political establishment because of the votes he controlled in the Western Addition, a pivotal black neighborhood where his temple is located.

IN 1975, HE endorsed George Moscone for mayor of San Francisco and provided 200 precinct workers on election day. The following year, Moscone as mayor appointed Jones chairman of the City Housing Authority.

By then, the People's Temple was attracting up to 5,000 people to Sunday services. They included poor blacks and middle-class whites.

The church had supported such controversial figures as Angela Davis and American Indian Movement leader Dennis Banks. But politicians, aware of Jones' power to turn out the vote, were attracted too.

California Gov. Jerry Brown was among those who visited the church. In 1976, Jones helped organize a San Francisco rally in support of Jimmy Carter's presidential bid.

MRS. ROSALYNN CARTER spoke at the rally and afterward Jones escorted her to her hotel. They had dinner together in the hotel restaurant.

Jones preached from a high wooden pulpit flanked not by Christian symbols or scriptural writings, but by a copy of the U.S. Constitution and a picture of the late Dr. Martin Luther King Jr.

When he mounted the pulpit, he became a man with all the answers. His soft baritone voice seemed to embrace the audience, mesmerizing them with visions of the glorious afterlife they would enter together; frightening them with prophecies of an impending race war that would destroy the United States; comforting them with his assertions of divine power.

BUT PRIVATELY Jones was a brooding sort of man who would spend long hours by himself, convinced that he was a target of some national conspiracy organized by the government.

After solitary reflection, Jones, like the late Howard Hughes, would pick up the phone at 1 or 2 a.m. and call associates to tell them he was frightened of being assassinated.

He would never venture out of the People's Temple without a phalanx of bodyguards.

"ONCE A WOMAN collapsed and was said by a man claiming to be a doctor to be dead," said Mrs. Lena McCown, 38, a former follower. "Jones jumped off the stage. He told others to stay away. He laid his hands on her, and she got up. Now I know it was an act. But then, I believed he had raised the dead."

harder" when beatings were being administered. Floggings were administered for smoking, drinking alcohol, or dancing.

"SOME TIMES he would forbid members from having sex," said one former member.

Even more than discipline, Jones seemed preoccupied with death.

"Jim told us all along that if anything ever happened to him, if the government closed in on us, that we would have to kill each other," recalled Birdie Marable, who once ran a rest home for the temple.

"Kill the children first,' he told us. We'd have to cut each other's throats, and those who couldn't cut throats would drink poison. We signed our names. We said we'd do it."

TOM FLEMING, city editor of the Sun-Reporter, San Francisco's major black-oriented newspaper, still calls Jones a "good friend, and still a good man in spite of all the things he did.

"He faced a lot of antagonism because he had blacks and whites in those pews worshiping together," Fleming said.

"He was trying real social experiments at that church. It was a real community center—he had a nursery school, lodging for senior citizens, medical care, a kitchen. He wasn't one of those who had a big car or anything. He wasn't in it for the money."

Jones achieved tremendous expertise as a speaker and was like a special effects man for a Cecil B. DeMille film. Soul and gospel singers poured forth music; dancers leaped and pirouetted; musicians played their golden trumpets; and there would be faith healings and fiery sermons.

FOLLOWING A People's Temple service, "you left drained of energy, yet somehow all charged up," said Robert Potts, a former member. "It was as if he plugged into us and sucked away our will. And the funny thing was that each Sunday we couldn't wait to go back for more. We were addicted. Religious junkies, and you know what happens to a junkie—he eventually O.D.'s [overdoses], like all those folks down there in Guyana."

IN MARCH, 1978, Jones sent a letter to Congress, warning that his flock in Guyana was committed to death. Complaining of bureaucratic harassment, he wrote: "I can say without hesitation that we are devoted to a decision that it is better even to die than to be constantly harassed from one continent to the next."

Guyanese officials say Jones and his followers were admitted to their country because he "presented references of the highest caliber."

One was a letter from Mrs. Carter, written April 12, 1977, in response to a

JONES WOULD then launch into lengthy discussions of Lenin and Marx and the communal way of life. He was particularly adept at reconciling the atheistic philosophy of Lenin with the teachings of Christ, combining them into a spurious philosophical piece of Swiss cheese.

"We must draw close, avoid old ties to our families, even avoid our wives, husbands, and children if they are nonbelievers," Jones, who claimed to be both Christ and Lenin incarnate, would say. "And you must be willing to die for me."

Then, borrowing from the King James Version of the Bible, Jones would reinforce his claim by quoting from Luke 14:26 in which Jesus tells his disciples:

"If any man come to me and hate not his father and mother, and wife and children, and brethren and sisters, yea, and his life also, he cannot be my disciple."

SOCIOLOGIST Ronald M. Enroth in his book "Youth, Brainwashing, and the Extremist Cults" explained this

letter to her from Jones.

"I don't remember anything about him. He was just a person," Mrs. Carter said last week.

ANOTHER WAS from Vice President Mondale, saying: "I am grateful for . . . the work of the People's Temple Christian Church in defending the First Amendment guarantees of freedom of the press, in managing the drug program, and in running the ranch for handicapped children."

There was a similar letter from Joseph Califano, U.S. secretary of Health, Education, and Welfare.

Mondale and Califano said they could find no record of having written such letters.

Surviving members who accompanied Jones to Guyana said their leader lived in a three-room house with his mistress, guarded by closed-circuit television.

GERALD PARKS, 45, said that all members were required to admit that they were homosexuals, but they found out that Jones was one himself.

"He was having sex with guys. The guys, they'd brag about it right up front," he said.

Jones told his followers that he was sexually desired by all the men and all the women in his church. On one occasion, he punished a black male and a white female for breaking the sexual rules at the camp by making them become intimate in front of the entire camp, including children.

His son Stephen said Jones was addicted to drugs in Guyana and complained of suffering from cancer and heart disease. His behavior became increasingly erratic and bizarre.

HE DEALT OUT minor punishments to people who were unable to answer properly when quizzed about events in the news. He forced people to stand and listen to his "teachings" and these sometimes went on half the night.

He did not permit families to live together. He promised skilled medical

ACCORDING TO former People's Temple followers, Jones would frequently bed young women members of the church in an effort to stire "new messiahs." On some occasions he would forbid women followers to have sex with their spouses so he could be sure it was his child that the woman would bear.

Elaborately-staged faith healings were frequently held in which followers would not only be "cured" of terminal illnesses, but on occasion, raised from the dead—thus propelling Jones light years past his contemporary religious flim-flammers.

Strict discipline was also a part of Jones' philosophy, and punishment, bordering on sheer sadism, was meted out to those who disobeyed.

In effect, Jones used religion to control sadistic tendencies in people by directing it inward and making his followers masochistic.

"Some people enjoyed being punished," recalled temple member Lena McCown. "And Jim Jones enjoyed punishing them."

care but staffed the camp with a single "doctor" who had not completed his internship and was described as a quack.

Over the months, reports filtered out that members were being mistreated, and were detained against their will.

Parents of some cult members sent notarized affidavits earlier this year stating that Jones had confiscated passports and money of people arriving at his commune, prohibited contact with outsiders, forbade telephone calls to relatives, and censored incoming and outgoing mail.

ONE AFFIDAVIT said children were forced to eat South American hot peppers as a means of punishment.

There also were reports that children were disciplined by being thrown into a deep well with ropes tied around their bodies.

Investigators in San Francisco said that drugs, weapons, and money were smuggled into Guyana last year in containers marked "relief clothing" or "agricultural machinery." The containers were not subject to customs inspection.

The weapons were carried by Jones' bodyguards and were used in the attack on Rep. Ryan and his party after Ryan had ended his visit to the settlement called Jonestown.

IN THE WAKE of the massacre that followed, the question of why so many seemingly reasonable people made such a commitment to one man remains unanswered.

Claire Janaro, 39, of Philadelphia, a dedicated follower of Jones, said: "We were outcasts of society, and the closeness and the caring at Jonestown held us together."

Janaro, who was on a flight [from] New York to Guyana when the massacre occurred, said she did not know why Jones did what he did.

"He was the kind of father you always wanted and never had, but in a way he was always isolated," she said.

By Death Possessed

A Prophet, a Cult And Mass Madness In Guyana Jungle

"The horror! The horror!"

That is what Mr. Kurtz, the civilized man dying in the jungle, tells the narrator of Joseph Conrad's "Heart of Darkness." Conrad's hero, dreading the truth about the human heart, avoids learning what the horror in the jungle had been. But that was in the 1900's, when news traveled slowly.

The news from the Guyanese jungle is still traveling under handicaps, some of them apparently imposed by Guyanese and American officials. But since Friday, Nov. 17, when Representative Leo J. Ryan and his party left Georgetown to visit the commune of the People's Temple in northeastern Guyana, a new horror emerged from the jungle almost daily.

Mr. Ryan and 17 other men and women, including members of the press, disaffected former cult members and Congressional staffers, went to Guyana to investigate complaints of brainwashing from his Northern California constituents. The group spent most of Saturday walking about the commune and talking to members, most of whom expressed enthusiasm for the temple and its works. But some cultists chose to leave with Mr. Ryan.

As the group prepared to board their planes and depart the following day, commune members started shooting. Mr. Ryan, three newsmen, and a defector were killed and others fled to the jungle, but one plane escaped.

The Rev. Jim Jones, the cult's creator and leader, apparently planned for all 18 visitors to be killed. When he learned of his failure, said a witness who escaped, he told his followers "The time has come to meet in another place," and set in motion a plan surviving cult members have declared Mr. Jones had repeatedly and carefully rehearsed with his congregation. A concoction of Kool-Aid and cyanide was made and nearly every man, woman and child of the commune partook or was forced to partake.

Rumors that "possibly as many as 200" of the commune's members were preparing to kill themselves reached the State Department, which passed them on to the press; in San Francisco, the cult's American home town, a spokesman for the People's Temple denounced the report as "sensational and patently untrue." In fact, its only untruth lay in its modesty.

On Monday, Guyanese officials issued the first body count: 405. Mr. Jones was said to have been shot to death. An American military team, sent to fly the dead out of the jungle and back to the United States, arrived at the suicide scene by Wednesday. The trickle of survivors — numbered only in the dozens — stopped after one day. Suspicion mounted: What had become of the hundreds that could account for the gap between some 400 bodies and the more than 800 American passports Guyanese searchers said they had found?

But on Friday, American officials in Guyana disclosed that the true number of bodies might be closer to 780, and yesterday in the United States the probable toll was raised to 900. They did not say why it took so long to find out, or why the Guyanese had miscounted so badly. Guyana's Minister of Information explained that bodies had been found under other bodies. If this is true, no one noticed for five days that bodies were stacked two deep.

Who was Jim Jones, and who were the people who quickly killed themselves just because he told them to? In San Francisco, only former members of the cult, and reporters who had spoken to them, seemed to have noticed anything strange. Mr. Jones had preached a blend of fundamentalist Christianity and social activism; he had appealed powerfully to the dispossessed; 80 to 90 percent of church members were reckoned to be black, and the elderly and middle-aged were disproportionately represented. But ex-members told, as they began to do last year, of fake miracles, of physical and mental coercion, of members required to turn over all their wealth to the church, of sexual abuse and intimidation. It was following such reports that in August, 1977, Mr. Jones left for Guyana, taking much of his congregation with him.

Mr. Jones first set up the People's Temple in Indianapolis, took it to Ukiah, Calif. in 1965, and to San Francisco in 1971. He struck some as fanatical, but none as crazy, and served in minor public offices. Local political leaders respected him because he had followers who were voters also. He collected, Guyanese authorities said, letters of commendation, in general terms, from such people as Vice President Mondale, Rosalynn Carter, Senator Henry M. Jackson. Some of the letters now appear to have been faked, but they are the sort any preacher with even minimum respectability — and a large congregation — could obtain from almost any politician. After the fact, Mr. Jones's own 19-year-old son described him to the press as a paranoid and a fanatic, but by that time everyone else knew the same.

Could anyone have prevented the murders and the suicides? It is far from clear that, before the massacre, Mr. Jones had ever done anything he could have been prosecuted for. The Justice Department has several times rebuffed Congressional requests, including one from Mr. Ryan, to look into allegations of brainwashing and physical abuse in religious cults, on the ground that such investigations would violate Constitutional guarantees. The Federal Communications Commission said the sect had been breaking the ham radio rules. The Social Security Administration had been curious about possible irregularities in the assignment of cult members' checks to the commune. Enough to recommend a Congressional factfinding trip, but nothing that would have justified a Marine landing in the heart of darkness.

Jonestown Has

Many Precedents

Had they died for a cause in which everyone could believe, they would have been called martyrs. But the members of the People's Temple shared a belief system that, though surely coherent and laudable to them, seems to others tragically misguided and even psychotic.

Yet, from what psychologists know of the human mind and from what anthropologists know of how peoples have behaved when their belief systems were threatened, it is clear that the rise of the California-based cult, its retreat to Guyana and its cataclysmic end have ample precedent.

Indeed, the birth and death of the People's Temple fits a pattern repeated many times in many cultures. An examination of these phenomena sheds light on the nature of the universal human need not only for an explanation of the unknown but of the personal need for acceptance by society.

The evidence is that whenever a group has been made to feel that its belief system is no longer generally shared or, at a minimum, respected, something radical happens.

A common pattern is for a small group to find that its traditional values are no longer respected in a changing larger culture. A new cult, typically messianic, emerges, often with a charismatic leader who promises his followers that the millennium is coming and that they will be prepared for it while the evil larger society will be cast into darkness.

Among the best known examples are the cargo cults of New Guinea and Melanesia. Christian missionaries arrived in the last century and persuaded the islanders that their religion and way of life were inferior to the ways of Europe and America. Rocked by such teachings and preaching that a blending Christian and native concepts and preaching that a return to fundamental values would usher in a utopian age in which Melanesians would dominate Europeans. The concept of the meek inheriting the earth — the strong made weak and the weak strong — has been a feature of messianic cults everywhere.

As the Western impact on the Pacific Islands continued, with military forces replacing missionaries in World War II, utopia-promising cults continued to emerge and fade.

To Western eyes, the most poignant instances involved the belief that God was labeling crates of cargo for delivery from the skies to the Melanesians but that Westerners were intercepting the shipments. To prepare for the millennium when the cargo would reach its rightful owners, Melanesian groups built elaborate airstrips and warehouses.

Many American Indians suffered a similar destruction of native culture with the westward migration of white settlers. In 1870 the Ghost Dance religion emerged in Nevada

and swept through several tribes of Indians. A Paiute medicine man had had a vision that a new era was coming in which the ungodly would be punished and the native Americans restored to a promised land. To prepare themselves they were to learn the rituals of the Ghost Dance.

Even in Western cultures messianic cults have been common. "It's easy for us to look on the People's Temple as aberrant, but they reflect a phenomenon that runs through many cultures, including our own," said Dr. Theodore Schwartz, an anthropologist. "America has had a long history of similar religious cults."

Among the better known of these are the Shakers, the Mennonites, the Amish, the Jehovah's Witnesses, Father Divine's Peace Mission and Aimee Semple McPherson's Church of the Foursquare Gospel.

The Millerites, whose predicted dates of apocalypse came and went, finally modified their beliefs to survive as today's Seventh Day Adventists. The Mormons, once viewed as bizarre, migrated to the Utah wilderness and became respectable. All the world's great religions, of course, began as tiny sects repudiating the beliefs of the majority.

As many sociologists have observed, the idea of going off into the wilderness to start a new way of life is a thoroughly American tradition. Over its two centuries this country has seen the founding and, usually, the foundering of scores of utopian communities and religious sects.

The United States was, after all, founded by minority religious groups seeking freedom from persecution. The pioneers who pushed the frontier westward were often driven by a need to find a place where their belief systems could be lived out without harassment from others.

California was, for most, the geographical end of the search for a Promised Land and, perhaps for that reason, the beginning of the psychological search. Dr. Charles Glock, a sociologist who has studied California cults, argues that the country has always spawned new cults but believes that the social turbulence of the 1960's increased the rate.

He suspects that the rise of new cults probably peaked about 1974. Prominent today are such groups as the Rev. Sun Myung Moon's Unification Church, Scientology, the Hare Krishna movement and Synanon.

What is common to nearly all the movements is that they began as small bands of people who suffered what anthropologists call "relative deprivation" — not necessarily in the material sense. The hypothesis deals with people who feel they are being deprived of influence in the mainstream even: though they adhere to the proper values and "live right." Such people feel a need to band together for the social approval society denies them.

"It's a feeling," said Dr. Mervyn Meggitt, an anthropologist who has studied the phenomenon, "that people are redefining the world in a way that excludes us even though we are doing the proper thing. We are abiding by the word of God but others have taken control of society."

Scorned belief systems, it appears, do not automatically wither. The believers seek reassurance and, if there is a leader prepared to unite them, a new cult emerges. It provides the social approval that individuals need and concentrates the momentum of individual dedication to a cause into a small religious counterculture. The almost universal expectation is that someday God will put it all right.

The success of a cult often depends on the presence of an effective, often charismatic, leader who knows how to deliver the approbation so needed by his followers.

Such leaders often accumulate and display great personal wealth, something outsiders believe ought to arouse resentment among followers. Examples include Father Divine, Rev. Ike, and Garner Ted Armstrong. In fact, it appears that followers often take pride in their leader's wealth, seeing in it evidence that God is indeed rewarding the godly.

In a way, so-called brainwashing procedures condense the historical process that spawns cults into a program of altering the belief systems of individuals. Victims are subjected to personal degradation and isolation from approval until they begin to question the rightness of their beliefs.

At this point a new set of beliefs, approved by the brainwashers, is introduced. As the victim demonstrates acceptance of the beliefs, both material rewards and social approbation are delivered. So powerful is the need for these, psychologists suggest, that belief systems that satisfy the needs are embraced more strongly

In the formation of cults, one other psychological mechanism is at play — the effect of power on the leader. As the leader becomes the embodiment of the group's hopes for a millennium, his ability to separate himself from his office can be severely tested.

Often enough the very qualities that push him to leadership impel him further. He identifies so closely with the prophets of his belief system — Jesus, Lenin, Mohammed, whomever — that his decisions as leader are regarded as infallible or divinely inspired and, therefore, quite capable of overriding the older tenets of belief.

The process is familiar to psychiatrists who have seen countless persons whose behavior develops almost imperceptibly over a period of years from unremarkable patterns into full-blown delusional psychoses. "In our mental hospitals," Dr. Schwartz said, "you'll find many people who are a cult of one. They don't all find followers."

Followers of such a leader, as were the settlers at Jonestown — most of them very much excluded from the mainstream of American life — may find the only source of social approbation for their belief system lies only in obeying the dictates of their leader.

Willingly going to one's death for a cause that transcends death is, of course, a proud and noble tradition in the history of religion.

Boyce Rensberger writes on science for The New York Times.

322

South Florida Cults

From Voodoo to Krishnas, Sects Fear Jonestown Backlash

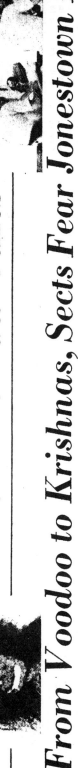

By ROBERT LISS
Herald Staff Writer

The rhythmic bongo drums of Santeria believers punctuate the Little Havana night.

From Haitian neighborhoods come voodoo chants and the occasional shrieks of a sacrificial animal.

In South Dade, shaven-headed men and saffron-robed women chant *Hare Krishna.*

White-robed Christian prophets occasionally wander the turnpikes, Seminoles and Miccosukees have their Green Corn Dances, and fundamentalist Jewish groups pray together three times a day on Miami Beach.

South Florida — a crossroads of African, Asian, European and New World thought — has dozens of identifiable cults, sects, and religious groups whose nature is unknown to outsiders.

"There are so many smaller groups that are almost invisible to people around this city," said Dr. James Huchingson, chairman of philosophy and religion at Florida International University. "There are at least a dozen secret groups of four

Body Count Reaches 900	*22A*
Radio Blared Joy	*22A*
Flock Punished	*22A*
The Herald's Story	*1B*
The 'Seduction Syndrome'	*1E*

or five people out there who live together and have a leader who tells them what to do ..."

All these groups, most of the time, have little in common. But last week, in the wake of the Jim Jones People's Temple mass suicide, many of the groups suddenly did have a common concern.

They were worried. They were suspicious. They feared a reaction.

"We would specifically object to being lumped with these other groups," said Robert Chulock, attorney for Dade's 55-member Krishna commune. "I think lumping them together at this time and in this situation can be inflammatory."

Universally, members of South Florida cults interviewed by The Herald de-nounced the Guyana event. Said Joy Mc-Clenathan, "sponsor" of the tiny, Depression-era "I Am" cult here:

"I think it's a horrible, terrible thing. It's a sign of the times. All the prophecies of the Bible have been fulfilled. I feel we're near the end of the world."

Members of the Eckankar cult had agreed, earlier in the week, to be photographed. Thursday, South Miami Eckankar representative Joy Winans called to say they weren't "too keen" about the

Turn to Page 23A Col. 1

323

Sects Flourish in 'Rootless' Florida

▶ FROM PAGE 1A

photograph with "everything that's going on." Representatives of the Sufi order canceled an appointment and Santería experts who were not even cult members asked to have their names left out.

One expert predicted the events in Guyana would lead to a closer look at all secretive religious groups.

"There is a negative side to religion, which in our liberal culture we have tended to pretend wasn't there," said Huchingson. "We are beginning to see that dark side now. Religion has a power that can go in either direction."

South Florida has been compared to California as a region of rootless people, but few South Floridians have attempted to root themselves in the soil of such California-style religions as the People's Temple, a Herald survey indicates.

Instead, South Florida has developed a unique assortment of fringe religions, the most popular of which look to the Caribbean rather than the West Coast.

Classified by their origins, South Florida's cults include:

● Afro-Catholic — Santería, voodoo and other variations of the blend that occurred between African and Iberian religions during and after the days of slavery.

● Jamaican cults — Rastafarianism and the Zion Coptic Church are the best known. They are also highly controversial because they advocate smoking marijuana.

● New Age cults — Eckankar, Scientology, the International Society of Krishna Consciousness, The Divine Light Mission, The Children of God, the Reverend Moon's Unification Church. Most are based in California, most claim or have ancient roots, but all experienced tremendous financial and numerical growth following the intellectual turmoil of the 1960s.

● Universalist cults — Bahai and Sufi both originate in the Middle East. They differ in many respects, but both advocate a unification of all religions; they retain many holidays and respect the prophets of the major religions.

● Entertainment Cults — The Royal Order of Warlocks and Witches, various astrology circles, and the Church of Satan are groups whose members combine an irresistable fascination for the occult with a rational skepticism and, frequently, a sense of humor. The degree of belief is impossible to determine, and faith is mingled with irony.

● Unclassifiable — The Jewish mystical groups of South Miami Beach, communes such as "Plenty House Farm," such small, wandering groups as the 18-person "Christ Family," or the "Rainbow Family of Living Light," and such minor Christian denominations as the "I Am" group, do not fall into any classification.

Generalizing about such a colorful and varied mosaic of religious expressions may be difficult and misleading: the most pronounced quality about them is their difference.

SOME GROUPS — the Krishnas, the Zion Coptics, the Lubavitcher Hassidim, the Children of God — have members living communally. In some cases, such as the Coptics and the Krishnas, parents have claimed their children were brainwashed, although the courts have not seen things that way. In other

cases, such as the Hassidic groups, the communal study quarters have caused no problems.

Some groups have raised vast sums of money, purchasing property for study centers and sometimes providing the leaders with lavish lifestyles. The Divine Light Mission, led by Guru Mahara Ji, is one such group. The young leader was denounced in 1975 by his mother as a playboy because of his fondness for flashy clothing, expensive jewelry, private airplanes and big cars.

Other sects, however, appear unconcerned with money. The wandering Christian cults, the Plenty House Farm, the Haitian voodoo groups, carry on with little money.

But these differences often vanish when outsiders talk of religious cults, or attempt to deal with one of them, members said.

"IN A ZONING case I tried to explain why they (the International

Society for Krishna Consciousness) needed their property set up as it is; so they can have a cow nearby, since they think it is holy," said attorney Chulock. "The judge said, 'Well, don't they kill chickens in ceremonies?' Of course they don't kill chickens. They don't kill anything. They are vegetarians. But they get lumped together with the other groups."

The most regionally unique and possibly the fastest-evolving fringe groups in South Florida are the Afro-Catholic cults. Santería and the various voodoo cults were almost unknown in Miami 25 years ago. But with the large influx of Cubans and the more recent immigrations from Haiti and other islands, the cults have mushroomed. Estimates of Santería devotees now run around 10,000 in Dade alone.

"Santería seems to be growing very significantly," said Huchingson. "But it's very secretive and hard to get a handle on."

Santería has 16 gods, according to a woman whose brother and sister are both priests (Santeros) in the religion. The gods, she said, are based on Catholic saints. Other authorities say they originally were gods of the Yoruba tribe, gods once worshiped by millions in the plains of Central Nigeria.

THE CULT IS picturesque, with its many herbs, its animal sacrifices, its musical rituals. It differs from voodoo in that it cannot place a hex. It also differs in that most of its devotees in Florida are whites. This was not always so, according to one Santería devotee.

"Santería is changing," she said. "The commercialism that has developed within it began with the massive interest of the white Cubans in the religion, searching for ways to solve the problems created by the revolution.

"People of higher economic means are coming into the religion. In Cuba, anyone could be initiated for $300 ... Here the same thing sometimes costs $5,000. You just can't explain where that money is going."

Initiates are expected to form rigid bonds with other initiates, as though they were all from one family. However, the devotee said these ties "could never produce something like what happened in Guyana. Santería preaches love to the saint and the gods ... the individual does not lose his personal identity."

VOODOO CULTS, much more difficult to penetrate, have been connected with three South Florida shooting deaths during the 1970s. In two of the incidents, those who did the shooting said in court they had done it to prevent a voodoo hex. In a third case, a Fort Lauderdale man claimed he shot his common-law wife while under a voodoo spell.

Murders and marijuana smuggling have been attributed by some police to devotees of the Rastafarian cult, which claims about 70,000 members in Jamaica. It originated there in the 1930s.

Rastafarians and some other police officers deny that a true "Rasta" would do anything violent. They say the religion attracts intel-

ligent, artistic people, and that drug smugglers are using the social status of the cult — which developed reggae music — as a mask.

There are, police say, 100 to 200 Rastafarians in Miami, with no central headquarters.

THE CULT WAS started by Marcus Garvey, a Jamaican who preached that blacks should return to Africa and that blacks eventually would have tremendous power. Reggae singer Bob Marley has helped spread the religion throughout the Caribbean.

"A lot of people have hidden behind their name to do unscrupulous things," said Donnie Dawson of the Jamaican Tourist Board. "They are not the true Rastafarians, I can assure you. Not everyone who wears his hair in dreadlocks (long, curly braids) is a Rastafarian."

A controversial Rastafarian offshoot is the Ethiopian Zion Coptic Church, with 33 Miami members living at 43 Star Island. There reportedly are about 2,000 members of the sect, all of them black, living in Jamaica. Those living in Miami are white.

The cult has had many troubles: Members of the cult, which advocates marijuana use, have been arrested on drug-smuggling charges (the cases have not yet come to trial). Miami Beach zoning officials say they will go to court against the Coptics on zoning violations. And one young inductee this week was returned to his family by police.

ACCORDING TO "Brother Louv," current leader of the Star Island group, Coptics treat marijuana as a eucharist. They oppose haircuts and shaving, follow a puritanical sexual code and obey Biblical dietary laws common to Orthodox Jews and Muslims.

Brother Louv blamed the Guyana incident on the immorality of American society.

"You have to start with Mr. Carter and go right down to the devil, and examine the fiber of American society," he said. "This is supposed to be such a moral, dignified, sane place. It's not. It has a climate that caused this kind of violence."

The New Age groups in Miami — with philosophies based on varying blends of Christianity, Buddhism, Western pragmatism and whatever else the leader may fancy — resemble those elsewhere in the country.

*   *   *

Herald staff writers who contributed to this story include Barry Bearak, Edna Buchanan, Ileana Oroza, Sylvia Thompson, E.A. Torriero, and Kate Wheeler.

324

THE CALIFORNIA-based Krishna cult, begun in 1966, claims about 10,000 members and more than 100 communes, or ashrams. The cult, which claims its origins are from 500 to 5,000 years old, sends its members to chant and to beg for money in airports.

The Miami branch has 55 members, who live at 10900 Coral Way, a 10-acre estate the group purchased for $300,000.

"They get quite a bit of harassment," said Chulock. "They have had situations where people have shot at them. They have people who drive by and yell obscenities at them."

Krishnas are obvious targets for harassment with their unusual mode of dress. A New Age religion that does not encounter such difficulties, and appears to be spreading more rapidly, is Eckankar, "The Path of Total Awareness."

ECKANKAR IS based in Menlo Park, Calif. and has 80 to 400 members here. The faithful follow a master named Sri Darwin Gross and study a literature based on Buddhist writings. The writings are said to have been revealed to Sri Paul Twichell, a master who came and died before Gross and whose wife Gross inherited. Followers purchase the writings doctrine by doctrine, generating considerable funds for the church.

No one knows how many "Eckists" there are nationally; they have claimed seven million, considered an exaggeration. Three thousand attended a convention last year on Miami Beach. The church, which has remained under the same leaders for its 13-year lifespan, recently purchased a large tract in New Mexico for nearly $1 million.

"We are not bothered by the 'community,'" said South Dade "Mahdis" Joy Winans. "We look like Baptists and Catholics. Who cares? We look just like everyone else . . . we don't walk around with sandals and beads."

The highly controversial "Children of God" movement, also California-based, established a com-mune in Fort Lauderdale in 1972. They were later evicted. In 1974, the sect was accused of sexually abusing young members, of rape, kidnaping, brainwashing and virtual enslavement, in a report released by New York State Attorney General Louis Lefkowitz.

KOREAN EVANGELIST Sun Myung Moon and his Unification Church have made little headway in South Florida, where they have no headquarters and reportedly only 12 followers. Those followers do beg for money in Broward County, but the Fort Lauderdale license review board resisted renewing the church's solicitation permit. They are now soliciting under a three-month permit, pending a review of the city's fund-raising ordinance.

The Divine Light Mission of Mahara Ji reportedly has about 200 members and a storefront headquarters at 4029 LeJeune Road. They also operate a restaurant next door and a health food store in South Miami.

Some cults — such as Bahai, Sufi and the little-known "I Am" group — seem to attract a peaceful, non-militant devotee, usually female.

The I Am group, with about 20 to 25 persons attending Sunday services, owns a well-kept building at 447 NE 22nd St. They are led by Joy McClenathan.

McClenathan said group members must be clean-cut, and frown on liquor, gambling, smoking, meat eating and drugs.

Finally, there are Miami's few witches. One of about 12 in Miami is Steven Poznansky, owner of the Mi-World Occult Bookstore, 511 W. 49th St., Hialeah.

Witches don't prance around naked, call up devils or use a cult name, says Poznansky. They hold quiet ceremonies indoors, where it's warm and there are no bugs. They do however, have psychic powers and study the preparation of potions.

"NINETY-NINE per cent of the people on this earth perform white magic," he said. "Take perfume. You wear it to attract a person. The ceremony of perfume is one of the oldest there is."

With all these different groups in South Florida, is there anything they have in common? Huchingson believes there is.

"Most of what you would call cults have a charismatic leader," he said. "This is a man who has some special power of persuasion . . . he is possessed by a sacred or a demonic power and you can sense this when you come in his presence."

Charisma, said Huchingson, also is found to a high degree in rock stars and to some degree in some political figures, but in religious leaders "the difference in degree is so great as to become a difference in kind."

Lawsuits Expected in Cult Deaths

UPI, AP, Washington Post

A medical expert in Pittsburgh and Delaware's deputy attorney general predict that there will be hundreds of lawsuits stemming from the mass deaths in Guyana because of failure by US authorities to perform autopsies on the victims.

"I predict many lawsuits will be filed," Allegheny County Coroner Cyril Wecht said Tuesday in a telephone interview. "They will be filed against the federal government, the state of California and the Peoples Temple."

Wecht said the suits probably would be brought by relatives of the victims who died in the jungles of Guyana earlier this month.

"The Rev. Jim Jones either had them murdered or made them commit suicide," Wecht said. "There will be a question of life insurance policies. Some insurers pay nothing for suicides. I'm not predicting the outcome, of these potential legal battles, but you bet that there will be lawsuits."

He said that as far as he knows, no autopsies have been done by medical authorities at Dover Air Force Base in Delaware, where the bodies were transported from Guyana.

Delaware's deputy attorney general, Edward F. Kafader, says the state will not perform autopsies on any of the 912 bodies, even though this could create legal problems.

Immediate Problem

"The immediate problem is the transportation of the bodies out of the state of Delaware," Kafader said Tuesday after meeting in Wilmington with state and federal officials.

"We just don't have the facilities to do autopsies on 900 bodies in a short period of time," he said.

The corpses were airlifted to Dover last week after rotting for several days under the tropical sun in Jonestown, Guyana. Most of the dead apparently died of cyanide poisoning Nov. 18 in a death ritual led by Jones. Others at Jonestown were shot.

About 150 military and civilian workers are trying to identify the badly decomposed bodies.

By Tuesday evening, hampered by a lack of medical and dental records, officials said they had positively identified only 44 of the 912 bodies. Officials had fingerprinted 886 bodies and embalmed 178. No body had left the base.

One of the bodies has been identified as that of Dr. Lawrence Schacht, who allegedly administered the cyanide to cult members.

Air Force officials had no plans Tuesday for disposing of any unidentified or unclaimed bodies.

Meanwhile, congressmen are saying that taxpayers shouldn't have to foot the bill for airlifting the dead and surviving members of the cult from Guyana.

Appeal to President

Rep. Edward Beard (D-R.I.) said Tuesday that he had written President Carter saying it was unfair to ask taxpayers to finance the Guyana operation.

Rep. Philip Crane (R-Ill.), an announced 1980 presidential candidate, said in Middletown, Ohio, that he didn't think "American taxpayers had any responsibility to absorb one cent of the burden of dealing with the problems in Guyana. ... Before it's over, I bet the cost will be over $20 million."

As of last Saturday, the State Department said it had spent $2 million to $3 million, not counting military salaries, to recover bodies from Jonestown. Unofficial estimates that apparently included fixed costs have placed the cost as high as $8 million.

The State Department said it would pay for the airlift because of the "backwardness" of Guyana and its inability to cope with the enormous number of dead.

The department said later Tuesday that it was looking into the possibility of recovering millions of dollars in cash and property found at Jonestown to pay the government expenses.

Seven elderly members of the cult, who missed the mass suicide rite, were scheduled to arrive in New York Wednesday evening. They apparently have agreed to be flown to South Carolina for questioning by federal authorities.

One other elderly member of the cult, who had fallen ill, was flown to San Francisco earlier this week.

The Guyanese cabinet, meanwhile, met Tuesday to discuss which of the 72 other cult survivors would be allowed to leave the nation.

Cultists Were Not Unusual

Some psychiatrists say that given the proper circumstances it could have been anyone who died in Jim Jones' commune in the jungles of Guyana.

The more than 900 who were led to drink cyanide in the bizarre suicide pact were not especially unusual individuals, according to several psychiatrists.

"I assume that all of us respond when somebody comes along who meets a basic need," said Dr. Ronald VanValkenburg, director of psychiatric services at the Indiana University Student Health Center, Bloomington.

"From the information I have, I infer that the people were less than well off. What Jones seemed to promise was a kind of redistribution that got them out of a situation in which they were not satisfied," he said.

Dr. Gordon Brown, an Indianapolis psychiatrist, said persons under the influence of a strong leader such as Jones will do things they ordinarily would not do.

"Many people are in search of a charismatic, heroic leader, someone who will give them rules to live by and rules to die by, like 'here's a roadmap to life,' " Dr. Brown said.

The followers then abdicate their independence and autonomy, suspending good sense and judgment to accomplish the leader's goals, he said.

Each of Jones' followers may have had a different reason for accepting him and his cult on blind faith, but it indicates an emptiness of life, according to Dr. Fred Coons, a Bloomington psychiatrist.

"Any of us, under a particular situation, may be swayed into not thinking and letting someone else make the decision. Those people were ready for someone like Jones," Dr. Coons said. "They met Jones at a time when they were vulnerable."

Most persons could be susceptible to a cult leader's magnetism during some insecure period of their lifetime, said Dr. Larry Davis, an Indianapolis psychiatrist.

Psychologically "normal" people could be seduced if they needed the protection, involvement or emotional support offered by the cult leader, he said. Why intelligent, reasoning persons remain in a cult is a complicated question for which he has no answer, Dr. Davis said.

"Jones must have had the quality of meeting a lot of different needs in people," Dr. VanValkenburg said. "Those people in California took what he had to give as their lifeblood."

Some dynamic leaders such as Jones are con artists who know they're conning people, Dr. Brown said. Others are wrapped up in their beliefs and think what they're saying is true.

He thinks Hitler believed what he said, in another case of persuasive leadership resulting in tragedy.

A leader who starts as a con artist, however, can slip into the sickness of believing in himself, "which I surmise is probably what happened to him (Jones)," Dr. Brown said.

Cult leaders typically feel somehow superior and think they are justified in directing others' behavior, often in extreme ways, Dr. Davis said.

Another Indianapolis psychiatrist suggested Jones was acutely paranoid and moved beyond the easily crossed, thin line separating madness and genius.

"One suspects he had genius and crossed the line. He must have been a charismatic person to get people to follow him like they did. It's a pity," he said.

Jonestown

By Franchot Pearson

Nine hundred and twelve members of the controversial People's Temple died as a result of drinking cyanide (poison) mixed with grape Kool Aid. This occured after Rep. Leo J. Ryan (D., Cal.) and several reporters were gunned down at the airport in Port Kaituma, Guyana on Saturday, November 18 by members of the People's Temple.

Not all of Ryan's party were killed by the ambush. Some escaped while others, like Ron Javers of the San Francisco Chronicle, and Rep. Ryan's aide, Jackie Speier were wounded.

Mr. Ryan was investigating a report that Americans were being held prisoner at the People's Temple headquarters at Jonestown (In the South American country) by the temple's leader "Rev." Jim Jones who commanded some of his members to kill all of Ryan's party.

The Chicago Tribune (November 21) states that "Jones apparently had hoped to kill all of the Ryan party. The planted gunman was suppose to shoot the pilot of a 24 seat Twin Otter when it was in the air and cause a fatal crash. But he got into the wrong plane." The article points out that "when Jones learned that some members of the Ryan party had survived the ambush, he assembled his flock, "said Carles Garry, a prominent San Francisco attorney, who was counsel for the cult.

"The cult had rehearsed mass suicide and signed suicide notes," stated Stephen Katsaris, the psychologist father of Jones' mistress.

According to the Suntimes (November 25) in an interview with Odell Rhodes, a survivor of the Guyana mass "suicide," Rhodes said, "Mr. Jones had called a general meeting at the camp assembly hall and told people the time had come for the ritual mass death." Mr. Jones told the crowd that "Mr. Ryan and party would never reach America." Rhodes states, "when the gunmen returned from the airstrip with reports that some in Ryan's party had escaped, Mr. Jones said it was too late for anything but suicide."

Rhodes was asked why Mr. Jones issued the order for mass death. Rhodes said, "the Charismatic leader had warned his followers that family members would come from the United States and take others away if some were allowed to leave."

Rhodes further states, "he (Jones) had a lot of ego and had to be in control. The decision (for suicide) was based on the fact that he felt he was losing control."

The Chicago Tribune (November 21) quotes Vickim Moore, a zealous disciple of Jones for 19 of her 38 years as saying "in the beginning the church was good. Jones represented himself as an advance prophet who had a more involved consciousness than the rest of them." She said, "I believed him."

According to another Suntimes report (November 25) Fannie Ford, 44 said (and believed) that Jim Jones was God because he had supposedly helped her overcome her physical and emotional problems. These are just two examples of hundreds of people who believed and trusted Jim Jones. But as years went on and the people's Temple grew, Jim Jones' operation changed.

The Chicago Tribune (November 25) explains that "real estate records on file in San Francisco show that a large number of people gave their homes to the temple free and clear, the sect then selling them whenever more cash was needed." They also stated that "more than $65,000 a month in social security checks never reached the intended recipients. Instead, they were intercepted by Jim Jones and his top aides—who had complete legal control over finances of most camp residents in the Temple's jungle camp in Guyana."

In reality, Jim Jones' absolute power, as the social scientists say, corrupted absolutely.

All this means is that Jones would have lost his power over the people. And with the absence of this power the people would begin to think for themselves and rely on themselves for guidance and direction. With this a clearer awareness of their situation and self identity would have grown. Like the change from Communism to a Democratic society.

In the book **Power and Society**, B.F. Skinner, a Behavioral psychologist states that "All behavior is determined by prior conditioning." He says, "brainwashing is an effective means of accomplishing behavioral modification. In this light it would not be an injustice to say that the Nine-hundred-and Nine people who died had been conditioned to obey Jones' wishes for them.

But not all were conditioned to the point of death. Some were forced to drink the poison. And regardless if one was forced or willfully drank, the facts are that they were deceived and mislead.

The members of the People's Temple were once a part of this society, your's and mine. They were your people, my people, our people; and God's creation.

They found themselves at the mercy of a man who to some was once thought of as a god, a redeemer, a guide towards freedom. Instead this "god" (Jim Jones) who was served and his message that was preached lead many, by the hundreds, to their grave.

In St. Matthew's gospel in the 24th chapter (eleventh verse) it says "and many false prophets shall rise, and shall deceive many."

Satan, the author of deception and false angel of light, who no doubt influenced the "Rev." Jim Jones' "ministry," is over-joyed with the results that People's Temple members were poisoned.

This tragedy puts a black-eye on true Christianity, for the "Rev." Jim Jones was also called a charismatic preacher. In other words some people might equate this to true Christianity; and others might justify their views by saying that the charismatic movements which are in progress could be equally deceptive.

US Probes New Tale of Cult Escapees

(c) New York Times Service

Washington, D.C. — The US government is investigating an unconfirmed report that 30 to 40 people were seen moving toward the Guyana-Venezuela border shortly after the mass suicide at Jonestown and may have entered Venezuela, authoritative government sources said Thursday.

If this report is accurate, it would be the largest unaccounted for group of escapees from the death scene at the Peoples Temple compound. These same sources discounted an earlier report that members of the cult had fled Guyana by means of a Peoples Temple boat.

The report under scrutiny is that a Venezuelan border patrol aircraft saw the group on the day after the mass suicide heading toward, or actually at, the border. The United States has asked the Venezuelan government to check into the matter. Venezuela reportedly stepped up its southern border surveillance to see if it could locate any persons who might have entered.

Earlier there were reports that at least one Peoples Temple boat was missing and might have been used by the Rev. Jim Jones' armed security guards to flee the country.

From a geographical standpoint, the suggestion that a group from the temple could walk to. Venezuela is not impossible. The Jonestown camp is approximately 25 miles from the border in an area of Guyana that has long been the source of a dispute with Venezuela.

What is unlikely, several sources said, is that a group that size could move through the rough jungle country of southeastern Venezuela without contacting settlements and attracting official attention. A spokesman for the Venezuelan Embassy here said he had no confirmation that there had been entries by Jonestown survivors.

In another development, correspondence made available to The New York Times showed that the State Department had received explicit warnings for more than a year that the lives of American citizens were in jeopardy at the Peoples Temple commune in Guyana and that the Guyanese government had been corrupted by Jones.

Two lawyers in San Francisco who represented defec-

Turn to Cult, page 10, col. 3

From Page 1

tors from the sect said they had made three visits to the State Department starting in August, 1977, and had written numerous letters warning of the situation.

According to the lawyers, Jeffrey Haas and Margaret Ryan, they sent an affidavit to the State Department last June signed by a former cult official, Deborah Layton Blakey. The affidavit asserted that Jones was "sick" and was plotting "mass suicide for socialism." Mrs. Blakey also said she was convinced that "Rev. Jones had sufficient control over the minds of the residents that it would be possible for him to effect a mass suicide."

Compromised by Jones

In an interview this week, Mrs. Blakey also asserted that high officials had been compromised by Jones, who had sent female members of the commune to seduce and blackmail them. She said one of the highest ranking officials of the Guyanese diplomatic corps had a mistress assigned to him by Jones.

Mrs. Blakey is the sister of Larry Layton, who has been charged in Guyana with the slayings of Rep. Leo Ryan (D-Calif.) and four other Americans.

She said that before she left the commune last May, she was part of a delegation that had been negotiating the transfer of the socialist commune to the Soviet Union. She said the Soviet intelligence agency, the KGB, had sent at least one agent to the commune.

After Jonestown—Six Family Portraits

By Jacqueline Trescott, Michael Kernan
and Lynn Darling

One of the families, in 1964, from left: George Brady, Michaeleen Talley Brady, Ronald Talley, Marlene Talley Wheeler, Maureen Talley Fitch and Christine Talley Bowers.

SAN FRANCISCO—It is always so much easier to deal with numbers. They don't die and rot so you have to wear gauze over your face and peel skin off fingers to get the prints to tell who they are.

It is comfortable to think about people as numbers when you don't really want to think about them. In World War I they spoke of "wastage." During World War II, for 6 million Jews, it was the Final Solution.

You can say "6 million" and not feel a thing. You can say "911" and study the photographs of the bodies piled up at Jonestown, and it is a horror, all right, but an abstract horror.

How do you find a human scale for the Jonestown tragedy?

The story of these buried and scattered lives and how they ended in that steamy compound at Jonestown compels many of us to seek out parallels, references, some anchor that will make it seem more real to us. Some people speak of the bridge of San Luis Rey. Some start talking about an appointment in Samarra. It doesn't help. We are still left with all those converging fates, those lives so neatly wound up at the same time and place. The impossible mystery of why things happen anyway.

The Talleys

There were Maureen and Marlene and Christine Shannon Talley, who came to live with Helen Evans, and went to school in Long Beach and went to Guyana.

"They were little Irish Dubliners," said Helen Evans, their aunt. "They had good report cards. They went to

church every Sunday—Our Lady of Victory. They always wanted to help the underprivileged. They talked about how they wanted to live in the country. But the main thing about these kids was that they wanted to act as a family."

Marlene was quiet and dark-haired, "she came back home every day and studied." Maureen had "fiery red hair with the disposition that went with it. She was always looking to do good." And Christine Shannon—she was her aunt's favorite. Chrisune who loved animals and wanted to be a veterinarian, joined the debate club and tutored the other students at the Catholic boarding school to which Helen Evans sent her.

"They were all beautiful girls," said their aunt. But their parents' deaths and the death of a much-loved grandfather seemed to mark them permanently. Their father had been a battalion chief in the Long Beach fire department, a man well-liked by his men. He died of cancer in 1960. Four years later their mother, Betty Tal-

ley, died as well, dropped dead in the street, the night before their eldest daughter's engagement party.

"They were hit every time they turned around," said Helen Evans. "And Christine simply refused to accept the fact that her parents were dead."

The fireman and his wife left five children. Maureen, Marlene and Christine went to live with their aunt in the small frame house in Compton, a lower-income suburb, predominantly black. The eldest girl, Michaeleen, was married within the week of her mother's funeral. The only son, Ron, got a job in a Long Beach liquor store.

In Helen Evans' home, there was a strict upbringing, a firm discipline, a planting of austere principles that were supposed to keep the girls from blowing away in those windy times.

"I believed you should do what you should do when you should do it," Helen Evans said. There was a 10 p.m. curfew on weekdays, 1 a.m. on Saturday nights.

See VICTIMS, G2, Col.3

VICTIMS, From G1

They were never late. "I was conservative, very conservative," Helen Evans said. "But I wanted them to have everything they needed, without too many of the fancies." Christine Shannon went to Europe with her classmates her sophomore year, came back glowing, the way young girls do when the wonder of the world first smiles at them.

"I tried," said Helen Evans. "I put 11 years into trying."

Marlene was the first to go. She had married the year she graduated from high school and was married for four or five years; it didn't work out. She had two young sons, she had no job, and she had very little money. She had always been very religious.

She was living in San Francisco in 1970, near the Peoples Temple. She told her aunt about the people there, and it may have been that they helped her with the food and support that living alone with two young children demanded. At the Temple they told her about the ranch in Ukiah, Calif., and she told her aunt how it seemed as if it might be a nice place to raise two young sons. She visited the ranch in the fall. In the spring, she moved there, working as a housekeeper in the compound there where retarded adults were cared for.

One by one, the others followed her, as quietly as leaves falling in a forest. Ron was next; he brought his ex-wife with him. And then Maureen and her former husband. Maureen went to work as a nurse in Ukiah, and Ron went to work for a large company there. Broken marriages and the hard scratch for money were buried, it seemed, among new dreams and duties in northern California.

Michaeleen had worked as a beautician after her own marriage broke up, until she fell ill and could no longer care for her two daughters. Her sisters came and took the children away. Michaeleen could not get them back. She too went to Ukiah.

"I was nervous all the time," Helen Evans said. "But back then, you remember those times, all the young ones were doing their own thing, they were joining all sorts of groups and religions, it seemed to be in the air."

Now there were eight of them together—three of the sisters, their brother, the four children. They were united now, except for Christine, and every other week they would come to Los Angeles on the big crowded buses filled with the faithful.

The family would visit their aunt. They said little about the cult, using only the brightest of paints and the broadest of brushes to describe their new lives. And they would call, to urge their aunt to let Christine come to Ukiah, calling often from the time Christine was 14 until the time she was 17.

Sometimes, some of the other members of the Temple would get on the line as well and urge Evans to let Christine come to Ukiah.

"I didn't want her to go," Helen Evans said. "I wanted her to wait until she was old enough to make up her own mind." Besides, there were other considerations. The children had been raised on their dead father's pension. As they grew up and left Evans' home, the money reverted to Christine. By the time she was 18, there was $57,000 saved.

When Christine came close to reaching her majority, Helen Evans consulted with the school psychologist, the counselors. "I wanted to do the right thing," she said, and so she sought their advice. They told her, and she agreed, that it would be useless to keep Christine from the Temple if she wanted to go, that the harvest would be bitterness and resentment. Christine went.

"I don't think it was ever political with her," Evans said. "I think she just wanted to be with her brothers and sisters." Christine spent her senior year at the high school in Ukiah. Her aunt asked that her report cards be sent to her, to make sure she stayed in school. The report cards said she was doing well.

Christine turned 18, old enough to assume control of the $57,000. She wrote her aunt, asking her to have the lawyer

See VICTIMS, G3, Col. 1

VICTIMS, From G2

transfer the money to the cult's lawyer in Ukiah. "I don't think she ever saw that money," Helen Evans said. "She didn't even buy a new car for herself."

Michaeleen was not very happy. "She didn't believe everything she was told," said her aunt. Michaeleen would leave the Temple and take her two daughters. At first, she would come to her aunt's house. After a while, she went elsewhere. "She knew," said Helen Evans, "that I would be the first one they'd call. They always found her." And brought her back.

Every year, on her birthday, Evans would receive a beautifully made card from Christine. She said she was well. She gave her aunt her love.

The nine didn't tell their aunt they were moving to Guyana. The first letter was from Michaeleen in August of 1977. "I'm doing well," it said. "We're growing all sorts of fruits and vegetables. I'm going to stay. I'm free and happy now and the girls are also with me and you know how important that is to me."

A few other letters followed, dry as the paper they were written on, sounding, Helen Evans later discovered, just like all the other letters that the relatives from other families received.

Last summer, there was a letter from Christine. "I'm the happiest I have ever been in my life," it said. "My family's close to me and I'm in a beautiful country where it's warm and green all the time. . .I have wonderful opportunities here. . .enough to keep a blossoming veterinarian busy. . .Our senior citizens seem to do so well. The sun gives them a healthy look. . .I wish you could picture the beautiful jungle."

It will cost $15,000 to bury the nine. Helen Evans does not think it fair. Now they have all been "officially" identified and the plans have been made to bring them back, to bury them in Long Beach.

Helen Evans remembered the day Maureen and Marlene came to the house in Compton—for Christine. The old aunt took her niece into the bedroom. "I told her it was up to her to make the decision," she said. "I asked her if she wanted to go. She said, 'I guess I'll go.' " Just then, just as the question had been asked and answered, the two sisters walked into the bedroom. The conversation was over.

"Now that I look back," said Helen Evans, "there was no excitement in Christine's voice, no enthusiasm. I often wonder what she would have done, if only the others hadn't walked in, at that moment." **—L.D.**

Florence Heath

The Peoples Temple is a broad beige brick building in a poor-looking part of the Fillmore district, in effect San Francisco's black ghetto. A fast-food place stands on one side and an auditorium on the other. At night, police cars park outside the Temple, and a floodlight turns the adjacent alley dead white.

Behind, in the big parking lot, stand several large buses and many cars. It looks like the backyard of any busy church that goes in for trips and picnics and outings.

The only thing wrong is that many of the cars are so thick with dust you can hardly tell what color they are.

"I believe this happened for a reason. They were chosen for this. It was meant as a warning to the whole world."

Nathaniel Alexander is 33. He and his brothers Steven and Robert own a plumbing business in Oakland. But Bobby isn't here at the moment because he has gone east to try and identify the bodies. There are six.

There is the grandmother, Mary Cottingham, 83. Their mother, Florence Heath, 53. Their uncle Grover Washington, 50. Their sister Mary Morton, 37, and her daughter Vicki, 10. And their 14-year-old brother Michael Heath.

Nate Alexander used to argue with his mother about the Temple. He went a couple of times himself, "to see what she was getting into"; but it didn't seem like a church to him. The first time he went, people wanted to know his address and other things about him. That wasn't so bad, but the second time there were red-hatted guards and Jim Jones, the man his mother thought so much of, was "preaching evil things, scaring people."

"At first the changes in her were good," he said. "She was active and happy, and I was glad to see her getting out and around. It gave her something to do. She was getting through a divorce at the time. It was '72."

Even though it meant commuting nearly 50 miles from Pittsburg, far on the other side of Oakland, Florence Heath still made the Peoples Temple the center of her life.

She was one of those who cooked for the others there; she drove people who needed rides; she visited the sick; she went on the Temple's famously uncomfortable bus trips to Los Angeles and other cities. Things were done for her too: medical attention, instructions about diet and healthy living.

"Nate," she would say, "I've been in churches all my days, and nobody's done anything like this man has done."

She said Jim Jones was her God. "At least I have a God I can see," she would say, and when her son brought out the Bible to dispute her, she would say the Bible was just a white man's tool.

"We talked about it every time she came over," Alexander said. "I told her Jones was a devil, and even though he was white he was telling them all this stuff about black genocide, things he thought they wanted to hear. Finally we agreed to stop arguing because she was afraid Jones would retaliate."

Florence Heath believed Jones could literally hear what they said there in Alexander's downtown Oakland apartment. And his sister Mary claimed Jones had cured her of cancer.

(Alexander's aunt Essie Mae Flynn had no such luck. Her sister brought her down from Pittsburg, where she still lives in a country housing project, to be treated by Jones for her bad heart, epilepsy, asthma and a nervous condition. She got so sick that she had to be put to bed upstairs at the Temple. Later she went on a trip to Los Angeles with the group and was taken desperately ill, spending three weeks in a hospital. Essie Flynn, 49, never went back to the Temple. It wasn't a church, she said, wasn't truly ordained, so she and her sister and her mother drew apart, though they remained on friendly terms.)

Florence Heath was born in Florence County, but soon moved to Queens, N.Y., to a house behind Kennedy Airport. Her husband was a construction worker.

She divorced him and married Alexander's father, a master sergeant in the Army, and for some years the family moved around the country: Takoma, Wash.; Seaside, Calif.; Georgia; South Carolina. Twenty years ago they moved to Pittsburg.

Her brother, Timothy Washington, told reporters he believed she had sold the Pittsburg house for $25,000, giving half to her husband and half to Jim Jones, along with her car; but Nate Alexander says he knows nothing of all this and doesn't care to speculate about it.

In any case, she did sell the house and came to San Francisco. Alexander thought she would buy a place here, but instead she simply lived at the Temple, and then suddenly was off for Guyana.

"She was a very helpful person," he said. "She was always concerned for her relatives and family and involved in other people. She was a housewife most of her life, but she did start some kind of nursing program to learn to take care of patients. She made some income from that, and then there was the alimony."

He got his last letter from her in March. Like all the others and like the letters from his sister, it was full of happiness. She wrote about the good fresh food they had at Jonestown, and how they had doctors and dentists and no crime.

Even Grover, whom she had brought along because he needed someone to care for him, had learned to work and for the first time in his life to do something for himself, she wrote to another family member.

Nate Alexander didn't want his mother's last letter quoted. "I'd like to keep that private," he said. Most of the family snapshots have been taken to the State Department to help with identification, but he did have one small picture of Vicki Morton when she was even younger than her 10 years. He didn't want to part with that, either.

"It was a sign of the times, this thing. People are confused and perplexed, and the morality, the economic system, are deteriorating. The monetary system is breaking down. Everything is corrupt."

"You can't get wrapped up in an individual like Jones. You have to listen to what's being said. I can see his appeal—they've been hearing stuff all their lives and nothing happens, and then he comes along and he produces, he gets action. That town wasn't just some dream, it was really there. But you've got to be aware of what's happening, and not put your faith in a man. Those you thought might do something for you turn out to be just as corrupt as the rest. You're on your own, and you have to realize that." **—M.K.**

Michael Rozynko

Ten years ago, when Michael Rozynko was 11, his parents divorced. He had liked both his parents and had adjusted easily to the moves they made up and down the West Coast as their medical jobs changed. Then when the marriage disintegrated, he withdrew.

"The breakup had a shattering effect on him. Mike was really a genius, but he fell apart," said his younger sister, Sandy. The three Rozynko children, Chris, Mike and Sandy, stayed with their mother Annie, a registered nurse, in Ukiah, Calif.

At school Rozynko was teased because he was short and fat. He seemed to find companionship only in food and books. His mother, a native of New Jersey who had moved out west at an early age and married a psychologist, shared his loneliness. She didn't have many friends, but she found Marceline Jones, wife of local minister Jim Jones, very sympathetic.

Out of curiosity, and loneliness, she attended a meeting at Jones' church at Redwood Valley. "My mother dragged us, forced us to go. I was scared because everyone was singing these religious church songs," recalled Sandy Rozynko Mills, who joined the Peoples Temple with the rest of her family but left in 1975.

Mike Rozynko, who had been raised a nominal Presbyterian like his brother and sister, seemed to find himself. His scholastic record shot up to straight A's, he took up photography as a hobby and began to talk of medical school.

His mother found the emotional support she needed, though she questioned every statement of Jim Jones. "My mother was a very intelligent woman who lacked confidence. With the church she found support, just the feeling someone she knew was there," said Mills. At the church meetings, said her daughter, she would probe Jones' possessive philosophy. Her outspokenness embarrassed her children. "She wasn't a person to join the crowd, but she was afraid to be alone." Mills left home when she was 13 because of what she described as her mother's strictness, but she didn't immediately leave the church. Chris Rozynko stayed home until he finished high school. Mike moved to a commune before he finished high school.

The two Rozynko boys had their own dreams. But, then, as Jim Jones began to think more and more of his followers as possessions, he dictated his own dreams for his young followers. Chris was forbidden to go to a law school where had been accepted. Mike was told the Temple was more important than medical school.

"Mike had really looked forward to college, he really wanted to be a doctor. But Jones said that professional schools for the younger people kept them from being involved in the cause. The cause turned out to be him."

Sandy Mills, now 19, her ruddy complexion pale from her personal loss of her brothers and mother in Guyana, bent her long, blond, frizzed hair over her coffee cup. For awhile she turned the white cup round and round and didn't speak.

In his own way, while retaining his loyalty to the Temple, Mike Rozynko fulfilled his goal. He became a registered ambulance driver. At the Temple he became the photographer for the publishing center and would spend hours discussing different methods of photography.

Once, before her family moved to Guyana, Mills tried to talk to Mike. "I told him that I loved him and that he would always have a place to come to if he left the Temple. His responses were very mechanical, unreal."

Just last summer Mills talked to Mike on a ham radio. "I said the people are not being hung from the Golden Gate Bridge, like you are being told. The Ku Klux Klan is not marching through the streets." Mills said she tried to keep her voice matter of fact, but her hope that her brother was really listening plummeted when he replied: "We know what you are doing. Why are you hurting my friend?" Mills answered, "What am I doing?" And the last thing she ever heard her brother say was: "You know what you are doing."

—*J.T.*

Leon Perry

Leon Perry, 61, never went in for frills. He loved his family, his church and his machines. Around the Protestant church he had supported for many years and around his low-income San Francisco neighborhood he was known as Brother Perry. And that's what his family called him, with firm admiration for a man who never drank, gambled, cussed or danced. That's what they called him at the Peoples Temple.

"No one is saying he was a saint because he did move up to Ukiah with a woman when he got involved with Jim Jones," said the oldest of Perry's two daughters, Veronica, 30. "But he was a good man, a man with his own means. He wasn't a lazy person who hid behind welfare."

It seems Brother Perry did work his own way. When World War II broke out, Perry left his childhood home of Beaumont, Tex., joined the Army and settled in San Francisco. An eighth-grade graduate, he drove a bus for the city, worked as a mechanic for the city and 12 years ago bought two Peter-Built trucks and did independent long-distance hauling.

When he wasn't working on his trucks, he doted on his two daughters and his wife, Ruby, a cosmetologist. When Ruby, a practicing Roman Catholic, went to a dance, Perry stayed at home, waited for her call and then picked her up. Once he gave his daughters a red table, two red chairs and a pile of transfers from the bus company. They played bus.

Seven years ago, right after a mild heart attack, Perry seemed to change. "I think it was because no one from his church ever came by with any food or good wishes," said Veronica Perry. Sitting in a soul-food luncheonette in San Francisco's Fillmore district, she angrily pushed aside a plate of fried chicken, and flipped through a family photo album. Brother Perry was a well-built man, appearing taller than his 5 feet 9 inches, with close-cropped hair, a thumbnail mustache and bright, friendly eyes. "There's not much that's negative about him. He did have a temper and once stopped the bus he was driving and yelled at some people fooling around in the back."

His daughter said this quickly, even though she does admit their differences, over her alliance with black nationalist organizations in the 1960s and over Jim Jones' purposes. He told her "all white people aren't bad," she said, laughing a laugh of distress and bitterness. "Now what can I say? He had a strong belief in brotherhood."

In 1972 Perry moved to Ukiah, shared a house with a woman and operated his trucks for the Peoples Temple. "The trucks kept his name on them, but I am sure he gave Jones the money," said his daughter. "But he would be happy anywhere as long as he thought he would be doing something with his trucks."

In the summer of 1977, he came by his former home to tell his family he was going to Guyana. By this time his wife had divorced him. His daughters overheard him say he was going to haul dirt and lumber so Jim Jones could build a village in the jungle. Three months after his departure, his former wife had a massive stroke and remained in a coma for two months. Veronica Perry's $8 telegram went unanswered and, she said, her request to use the ham radio at the Peoples Temple headquarters was denied. Once she was told by Temple members, she recalled emotionally, "What do you want with him?" When her father finally wrote, all he said was, "How is everything?" and spoke of how the climate was helping his hypertension and his weight control.

The last time Veronica saw him, Leon Perry seemed to get extreme pleasure from the cup of tea he was drinking at her mother's kitchen table. "And all it was was Lipton's, but I have been thinking about how he really enjoyed it."

—*J.T.*

Laurence Schacht

The other doctors at San Francisco General Hospital, especially the experienced ones, liked Laurence E. Schacht. He was quiet, intent, slightly more dedicated and anxious to please than the other interns who joined the staff in the summer of 1977.

Schacht, a soft-spoken man of medium build with thinning light-brown hair, wore a tie and didn't espouse the nontraditional forms of medicine, like a natural food diet and acupuncture, that some of his young co-workers did. "He was plain, not very vocal. It was your effort to get to know him," remembered Brent Blue, the chief resident of family practice at the hospital. Schacht was assigned to the pediatrics out-patient clinic.

Schacht, who grew up in Houston and left no legacy there except a restless annoyance with those who criticized his family's anti-Vietnam war views, arrived at the hospital with the highest recommendations. He had left Houston after finishing high school in 1967, joined the antiwar effort in California and then went to Guadalajara University. At some point he joined the Peoples Temple and they paid for his tuition. He finished medical school at the University of California at Irvine, 16th in his class.

Back home in Houston, Schacht is remembered as a quiet youngster. His father, Ezra, is a self-employed electrical worker and his brother Danny, 33, works with the family firm. "Right now all I can remember is that he was interested in art. He liked to draw. Ambitious? I can't recall. He was a typical teen-ager," said his father. Recalled Duke Lane, one of his high school teachers, "Evidently he was just an ordinary student. I really can't recall him." In the Lamar High School Annual for 1966, Schacht's junior year, he is pictured with a group of fellow students who judged the bulletin board contest. In his graduating year, 1967, he is listed with the students who didn't have their pictures taken.

Wherever he worked, Schacht is remembered for his unobtrusive, steady presence. One former member of the Peoples Temple recalled, "He hardly ever said anything. I never saw him smile or crack a joke."

At the hospital one child-health worker spoke of his reliabilty and reticence. "He was very conscientious and particularly interested in nutrition, asking how to prepare diet and mix formulas," said Doris Wong, 24.

A few weeks into his internship, Schacht took a vacation, unexplained and hurried. Then, one of his professors received a call from a woman claiming to be Shacht's sister. "His father," she explained, was in South America suffering from meningitis. "He wanted you to know that only something of that magnitude would take him away," the woman told the professor.

In the Guyana complex Schacht trained paramedics, had his own medical cabin and delivered twins by ham radio. The last person who saw Schacht, a Jonestown teacher who escaped, reported that he was brewing cyanide and Kool-Aid and spooning the liquid into the mouths of babies.

—*J.T.*

See VICTIMS, G5, Col. 3

VICTIMS, From G4

Karen Tow Layton

She could have skipped through life, just being beautiful, gifted and comfortable in the affluent surroundings of her home, Paradise, Calif. But Karen Tow Layton, 31, was not cut from the conservative mold of her community and friends. She wanted to walk through the trenches.

So Karen Tow, the petite blond Miss Paradise of 1965, went to a nearby migrant labor camp and fought the bosses until they tore down the tar-paper shacks. It was a lonely battle. "But she was vocal about injustices, more outspoken than her friends," said her mother, Lea Tow. An old boyfriend, Carl Stackey, now a rice farmer, concurred: "She was concerned about the underprivileged and minorities. She was the most politically oriented person in our class." Besides her own efforts, Tow was an ally of Virginia Franklin, who was the focus of a celebrated case in which she was accused of teaching communism in the classroom.

That case put Paradise on the national map. Paradise is a small community with pine trees and clear air in the foothills of the Sierra Mountains. It was not too slow for Karen Tow but too stodgy politically. "She was affected greatly by the terrible times of the 1960s, by the racism, by the killing of the children in Alabama," recalled her mother, Lea Layton. "She accused her father of being a racist. There was a rift and I was torn between the two. But she was the radiance in our lives and she stayed at home until her second year in college."

After two years at Chico State College, where she studied social work, Tow went to Hawaii to live with a man. The romance soured very quickly and she returned to take a job as a secretary in Ukiah. It was 1968. She was disillusioned about society at large, remembered her mother, but content with her own life. No one thought of her as a joiner. "She had a very positive attitude about life. You never had the feeling she could be swayed," said Thomas Dimas, a former teacher.

Suddenly, however, Tow joined the Peoples Temple and became uncommunicative. "When I asked to go, she said I wouldn't understand. It was eight years before I got into the church," said her mother. Tow married Larry Layton, now accused of murder by the Guyanese, but she told her mother and her older sister that it was "a friendship, not a marriage."

One of Karen Tow Layton's stories about those years stands out. She went to an orthopedic surgeon to check a pain in her arm, and he diagnosed cancer. He told her she might have to have the arm amputated. The minute Karen got home, her mother recalled, the phone rang and the Rev. Jim Jones told Karen she had been to the doctor and that she had cancer. He suggested she ride to San Francisco with him. Along the way he occasionally touched her arm, Karen's mother recalled her saying, and when she got to San Francisco she realized the pain was gone. "You've cured me," she told Jones.

"Now when you hear a story like this from your own daughter, you begin to take a second look," Lea Tow said. Eventually she attended a healing session herself and "received a message from Jones during the service that she would suffer." Six months later she had a massive heart attack. "I was taken in for a year. Then I began to see that his message was socialism. I couldn't buy that," said Lea Tow.

At the Temple, Karen did secretarial work, always appeared attentive to Jones' sermons and lived in the San Francisco headquarters in a small, neat but sparse bedroom. One former member remembered Karen being chastised for being vain, but said she was steadfast in her loyalty.

When Lea Tow told her daughter Jones was "psychotic," she didn't listen. Then in July 1977 Karen wrote her mother and asked her to take care of her dog. Again and again Lea Tow wrote her letters saying Jones' teachings and justice were frauds. Now, sitting by the phone in her home in Paradise, with the dog barking in the background, Lea Tow says, "I tried and I didn't make it."

—*J.T.*

Church Leaders Come to Defense of Fringe Groups

By GEORGE VECSEY

Fear of a backlash against all religions has spurred some leaders of major denominations to come to the defense of smaller, fringe groups in the aftermath of the Jonestown tragedy.

Some officials say that a wave of investigations, new laws, financial restrictions and public hostility against the small groups could expand into widespread reaction against all sects. A few incidents have already been reported.

"One man's faith is another man's fraud," said the Rev. Dr. Dean Kelley, an official in the National Council of the Churches of Christ, who added, "I'm afraid it's going to be open season on the so-called cults."

New Form of Paganism

Elder Neal A. Maxwell of the Church of Jesus Christ of Latter-day Saints recently said that a new form of paganism — which he called "irreligion" — might soon become the state religion. He added, "This new irreligious imperialism seeks to disallow certain people's opinions simply because those opinions grow out of religious convictions."

The main concern of a backlash seems to be from local reaction, not from a coordinated government effort, some note. Since the Guyana tragedy, the White House, the Justice Department and the Federal Bureau of Investigation have cautioned against witch hunts and spoken in favor of tolerance.

In the past, groups like the Mormons or Mennonites or Jehovah's Witnesses might have been the suspect "cults" while Jews, Roman Catholics, Quakers, Lutherans, Huguenots, Puritans and other groups had their turn in the past. Now new groups have taken their place.

Dr. Kelly says that the "most inviting target" of public antipathy toward charismatic leaders would be the Rev. Sun Myung Moon, founder of the Unification Church. At the moment, Mr. Moon has a strange combination of religious leaders backing his right to be a religious figure.

"I consider it absolutely essential that Moon's people be allowed to speak," said Rabbi Balfour Brickner, director of interreligious activities for the Union of American Hebrew Congregations. "I consider the man a little dangerous, but the way to get him is when he crosses the financial line, not when his people exercise their freedom of speech."

At a science conference held by the Unification Church in Boston last week, a handful of protesters raised the usual charges of "brainwashing" and financial exploitation against the Moon empire. The protesters also charged the group's followers, often called Moonies, with incipient violence.

Rejection of Violence

"They said we tell people to kill their parents," said Robert Sullivan, an official of the Unification Church. "My question is, when did you ever hear of somebody from our church doing anything violent?"

Other groups have heard themselves stereotyped as "cults" by the public and by the media. Within hours of the news from Guyana, a television newscaster went to the Hare Krishna Temple in Manhattan and asked Romapada Das, the president of the temple: "Do you hold suicide drills?" The follow-up question was: "Well, if you did, how often would you practice them?"

Romapada Das said later: "We have a theology. We are a religion. We do not believe in violence against the human body. The people from Jonestown were a cult under the whammy of a charismatic leader."

Another noticeable religious group, the Jehovah's Witnesses — once considered a "cult" — still encounters its share of hostility for preaching door-to-door. However, a spokesman said there had been no increase in hostility since the deaths in Guyana and he added: "If anything, people are more interested in talking, and that gives us a chance to preach the Scripture."

A few people contend that there are signs of increased incidents against small groups. Jeremiah Gutman, a lawyer who works with the American Civil Liberties Union, says he has heard of more attempted "deprogrammings" than usual in the past two weeks.

"I'm afraid the deprogrammers will think it's more acceptable now," Mr. Gutman said. "Parents will think they're saving their children's lives. I represent a group in New Jersey called the Circle of Friends, which is not even a religious group, but a communal group. They're suing somebody for kidnapping one of their members. At a break in the trial, people kept asking them, 'If you lose this case are you going to commit suicide?' It's ridiculous."

An assault on an unpopular fringe group can become an assault on all religions, and strange combinations have come about from religion trying to protect their flanks.

Everett Parker, the director of communications for the United Church of Christ, recalled his denomination filing a brief in support of the controversial preacher, Billy Joe Hargis, in a court case trying to force Mr. Hargis to disclose financial figures.

"He said he didn't want our help," recalled Mr. Parker with a chuckle. "But this was important to us. We're all concerned that every D.A. in the country is going to roll up his sleeves and investigate religion. It's easy to turn the pressure on some of these small guys, but anytime your civil rights are threatened, mine are next to go."

38 MORE SURVIVORS RELEASED IN GUYANA

Officials Give No Information on When 34 Others of People's Temple May Start Home

By JOSEPH B. TREASTER
Special to The New York Times

GEORGETOWN, Guyana, Dec. 2 — The Government announced today that 38 more members of the People's Temple were free to leave the country, and within a few hours six of them were aboard a Pan American Airways flight to New York.

The others, who were freed shortly before the plane left this afternoon, were expected to leave Guyana tomorrow. Neither American nor Guyanese officials would indicate when the 34 other survivors of the cult might be allowed to depart.

"We went over to the embassy yesterday and they told us they didn't think we would be free for some time," said Harold Cordell, an accountant who had left Jonestown with the assistance of Representative Leo J. Ryan and was at the airfield where Mr. Ryan and four others were shot to death.

"We're asking for specifics about our situation, whether we're witnesses or there's some other problem, but we're just left hanging. We don't know whether we'll be released tomorrow or held for weeks," Mr. Cordell said in his room at the colonial-style Park Hotel, where he and about 20 others are in protective custody.

Consular Office Reply

In response, Douglas Ellice, the senior American consular officer here, said: "I've given them all the information I have. When I know something they know it."

Mr. Cordell spoke in a low monotone just above a whisper, his face expressionless. Two plates of food, hardly touched, rested on the dresser next to him. His former wife and five children had refused to leave Jonestown with him and his present wife, and they are believed to have died with the more than 900 others.

Mr. Cordell looked around the bare hotel room. "A place like this almost drives you stir crazy," he said. "There's no radio, we've got no magazines or books to read.

"After a tragedy like this," he continued, "I think the best thing a person can do is keep active. We can't. All we can do is sit here and twiddle our thumbs and think about what we've been through. It's no fun."

Dr. Hardat Sukhdeo, a New Jersey psychiatrist who has been interviewing the survivors at the Park Hotel, said that several had been showing signs of increased depression and that he had asked the Guyanese Government for antidepressant medication.

334

Medical Examiners Criticize Actions on Cult Bodies

By LAWRENCE K. ALTMAN

Special to The New York Times

DOVER AIR FORCE BASE, Del., Dec. 2 — The Government's actions concerning the bodies of 911 People's Temple members who died in Guyana two weeks ago was illogical and based on dubious legal principles, according to several medical examiners not connected with the investigation of the deaths.

Six leading medical examiners said in interviews that they recognized the logistical and other difficulties involved in the gruesome task of identifying the bodies. But they said it was clear from developments that the Government had no established procedure for medical investigation of such situations, and that similar mishandling would occur if another catastrophe, such as a plane crash, occurred today.

"Of the several ways the situation could have been handled, certainly the one chosen was the most unsatisfactory," said Dr. Sidney B. Weinberg, Medical Examiner for Suffolk County, N.Y.

The medical examiners described as "inept," "incompetent," "embarrassing" and "doing it backwards" what they contended was the Government's failure to meet a basic social and legal responsibility to determine the manner and cause of deaths of the cult members.

They criticized, among other things, the failure thus far to perform autopsies and the embalming of bodies before collection of samples for toxicological tests. They also criticized the awkward steps by which the Government, in a reversal of an earlier policy, now plans to do autopsies on seven of the 911 bodies.

Dr. Weinberg and other medical examiners said the Government should have sent a team of specialists in forensic medicine to Guyana immediately to collect samples for toxicological tests, to do autopsies, and to conduct as orderly an investigation as possible under the circumstances. Such a step would have greatly facilitated later medical investigations, Dr. Weinberg said.

The medical experts also criticized, on medical and humanitarian grounds, the Government's decision to fly the bodies here instead of to an Army mortuary in Oakland, Calif., that would have been nearer to most relatives. Proximity to relatives would aid in a medical investigation, they said.

State Department officials said Dover was chosen because the shorter distance from Guyana allowed a quicker" turnaround time for the flights removing the bodies. But the medical examiners contended that months of investigational time might have been lost for the sake of saving a few hours of flying time.

Dr. Leslie I. Lukash, Medical Examiner for Nassau County, N.Y., said that autopsies would be the most important step in determining how many of the People's Temple group were shot or poisoned. Such information is crucial in determining whether an individual committed suicide or was murdered, an important question in insurance settlements.

Without autopsies, Dr. Lukash said, "Everything is presumptive about the cause and manner of death."

Dr. Lukash criticized the Justice Department's plan to do autopsies on four randomly selected bodies to confirm cyanide poisoning as the cause of death for the group, saying "no court will accept that," as evidence of how all members of the group died.

The medical examiners were particularly disturbed by the Government's steps in seeking to do autopsies on the four bodies as well as on those of the cult's leader, the Rev. Jim Jones, his mistress, Maria Katsaris, and Dr. Larry Schacht, the physician who purportedly mixed the cyanide potion drunk by cult members.

Legal Problem Cited

Justice Department officials have said that no Federal legislation authorizes autopsies on the bodies of people who are murdered or die in foreign countries or on Federal property in this country. Exceptions are made for a President and other Government officials.

Department officials have said that if permission from relatives is not granted for the seven autopsies, they will ask Delaware officials to order them under state law.

Dr. Cyril Wecht, Medical Examiner for Allegheny County (Pittsburgh), said, "This is the worst possible way because it puts a club to a family's head and it could create legal problems if court approval becomes necessary."

The medical examiners said that when circumstances make it necessary to do an autopsy for medical-legal reasons, it is standard policy to proceed without asking permission from relatives.

Dr. Wecht, who is a lawyer and a doctor specializing in forensic pathology, contended that even in the absence of a specific Federal law, the United States could have proceeded with the autopsies.

"When you come across 900 bodies that didn't die naturally, that's a medical-legal situation," he said.

"It would be just as illegal to do four autopsies as to do 900 under these circumstances. If you rob a bank of $10 or $10 million, you're still a bank robber," he said.

Dr. Lukash, addressing himself to the same point, said: "If they wanted to do the autopsies, they'd do them."

335

Cult Funds Put at $10 Million

New York Times, AP

San Francisco, Calif. — The Rev. Jim Jones, who died with 910 followers in Guyana Nov. 18, left a network of secret bank accounts around the world totaling more than $10 million, according to former aides. With his death, a mysterious international battle has begun for the fortune amassed by the Peoples Temple.

According to his former associates, Jones had established at least six and possibly a dozen or more accounts in Switzerland, Panama and Romania using anonymous numbered accounts and dummy corporations to conceal their ownership. One former official of the cult said the total might be as much as $15 million.

Timothy Stoen, a San Francisco lawyer who was once a Jones aide and legal adviser, developed the plan for the international network of secret bank accounts before he left the Peoples Temple.

Cash Was Abandoned

Stoen said Jones had spoken of channeling the money to the Palestine Liberation Organization. Another former aide said Jones, a Marxist, had once mentioned giving the money as a gift to the Soviet Union if he should die.

Members of a group of survivors of the Guyana killings said that after the deaths they had been on their way to the Soviet Embassy in Georgetown, the Guyanese capital, with $500,000 in cash, but had abandoned the money in the jungle. It was too heavy to carry, they said, so they hid it where it was later recovered by Guyanan officials.

Two women — one of whom may be dead — appear to have the answers regarding the bank accounts. The women, Carolyn Layton and Terri Buford, both in their late 20s, were graduates of the University of California and close financial advisers to Jones.

Death Not Confirmed

Miss Layton was one of Jones's mistresses and financial administrator just prior to his death. Witnesses reported that they saw her shortly before the killings and suicides at Jonestown, the Guyanese jungle commune of the People's Temple, but her death has not been confirmed.

Mrs. Buford managed the People's Temple accounts until she defected from the cult last month. Although Mrs. Buford's exact whereabouts is not known, there are indications that she was residing recently in so-called safe houses selected by Mark Lane, the cult's attorney.

Charles Garry, a San Francisco lawyer for the Peoples Temple who was in Guyana with Lane at the time of the suicide-murders, said in an interview that Lane had told him that there was $3 million in Peoples Temple money in Guyana. Garry quoted Lane as saying that he had access to a woman who once controlled that money and other Peoples Temple assets.

Explosives Found

Meanwhile, there were these other developments:

The district attorney's office in Los Angeles said two raids of a real estate office linked to the Peoples Temple turned up nearly 200 rounds of ammunition, bomb making plans, a dummy time bomb and the secret address of two temple "defectors."

Investigators also confiscated what they said were documents reportedly showing that the temple expected to make $2 million on real estate obtained by "fraud and extortion ... from members of the temple."

The Associated Press reported that Jones and his senior aides had Guyana's top law enforcement official stop an impending police investigation of the Jonestown settlement earlier this year. The information was contained in 120 pages of Jones' personal papers obtained by the wire service.

The AP said Jones helped repay this and other favors from the Guyanese government by having his followers become deeply involved in local party politics. He even agreed to have his more than 1,000 followers vote illegally on the side of the ruling People's National Congress Party in an important referendum last July, according to the papers.

The Guyanese government permitted 38 more members of the People's Temple to leave the country Saturday. Six flew to New York Saturday and the rest were expected to leave Georgetown Sunday. There was no indication when the 34 other survivors of the cult might be allowed to depart.

Papers reveal role of cult in Guyana politics

JONESTOWN, Guyana (AP)—Suicide cult leader Jim Jones and his senior aides had Guyana's top law-enforcement official stop an impending police investigation of the Jonestown settlement earlier this year, according to material contained in 120 pages of Jones' personal papers acquired by the Associated Press.

Jones helped repay this and other favors from the Guyanese government by having his more than 1,000 People's Temple followers become deeply involved in local politics. He even agreed to have the cult members vote illegally on the side of the ruling People's National Congress Party in an important referendum in July, the papers show.

The wheeling and dealing by Jones' aides among senior government ministers and officials in Socialist, tightly controlled Guyana was an echo of his activities in San Francisco, where for a time he was a valued ally, able to bring disciplined forces to vote as a bloc in political campaigns.

BUT THE DOCUMENTS, discovered by one of the first persons to reach Jones' jungle settlement after the mass suicide-murder that took more than 900 lives, indicate that his ambitions grew until he attempted to manipulate national policy in Guyana.

As the documents came to light, six more survivors of the death rite arrived in New York from Georgetown, Guyana, Saturday night and were questioned by Federal Bureau of Investigation and Secret Service agents before continuing to their homes. Another 37 were scheduled to leave Sunday.

Police in Georgetown said some of the remaining survivors will be held as witnesses in their investigation.

The documents obtained by the AP cite one memo to Jones dated March 7 of this year. It said that at the request of the People's Temple, the Cuban Embassy asked.

Prime Minister Forbes Burnham to reinstate fired Foreign Minister Fred Wills, who was a cult confidant. Burnham turned down the request, but an official told Jones' aides that Burnham was not upset by their gesture.

The AP tried for a week without success to get comment from the Guyanese officials mentioned in the Jonestown papers.

The documents show that the major recurring concern of Jones' people was the possibility of a police investigation prompted by newspaper investigations in the United States.

WHEN THE DEMAND for an investigation first was taken up in Guyana by former cabinet minister Brindley Benn last Christmas, Jones' top aide in Georgetown, Sharon Amos, demanded that the request be withdrawn. When Benn stubbornly persevered in his demands in the pages of his party news-

paper, Amos spread the word that Benn had asked the U.S. Embassy "for CIA aid to overthrow the government of Guyana."

The official spearheading the investigation drive was Police Comr. Lloyd Barker. In April this year, Barker told Amos and other aides that he intended to go to the Jonestown settlement to investigate it.

Unable to dissuade Barker, People's Temple aides sought help from Wills, the fired foreign minister.

Jones' aide Deborah Touchette wrote in a memo that Wills "told us of a situation where Barker . . . and some others were trying to get this guy to make a statement, confess. They put an explosive up next to his scrotum and the explosive went off and blew his scrotum to hell. There was a bet_

Turn to Page 108

Continued from Page 107

that it wouldn't reach the courts."

JONES' AIDES took this information to another apparent confidant, Barker's superior, Home Affairs Minister Claude V. Mingo, responsible for police and national security. They told him of the explosive incident and, Touchette said, "we told him what Barker had said about coming up to investigate us. We were tired of investigations; could he do something about this?"

Mingo discounted the explosive incident, but promised to "talk with Barker and explain to him the official government position toward us."

The memo, dated Feb. 27, said that "the next time we saw Mingo 9-3-78 Barker came out of his office as we were waiting to go in. He was extremely nice, making a very pointed effort to say hello and smile . . . a much different attitude than I have seen before, so I think that Mingo did talk to him."

In the same memo, Jones' aides wrote about Mingo: "He said the PM [prime minister] has never expressed anything adverse against the People's Temple. He said it was not true that the opposition asked for an investigation of People's Temple.

The last reference found in the documents to Barker was in a memo dated June 26, 1978, from Amos, that concluded: "The monthly booze for Barker. I think he'll see through this (but I am sure I could be wrong about this and we'll do it if it will help with him)—maybe it should be staggered tho so it's not so regular."

THE PAPERS SAY it was Mingo who not only approved licenses for the cult to carry weapons and solicit for funds, but also encouraged members to participate in Guyanese politics.

In an April memo written by Touchette, Mingo is quoted as explaining the importance of a July referendum to give Parliament full powers to act and to end future

public referendums.

The People's Temple followers frequently marched around Georgetown during the referendum campaign with banners calling for the public to support the issue. It was declared approved by a large majority.

The six survivors who arrived at Kennedy Airport Saturday night were identified as Julius and Sandra Evans, both 30, and their children Sonya, 11, Sharia, 7, and Shirella, 6, all of San Francisco, and Edith Parks, 64, of Ukiah, Calif.

An FBI spokesman said the Evanses escaped the massacre because they were in Georgetown at the time. Mrs. Parks was in the Jonestown jungle commune, but it was not immediately known how she escaped.

JONES PERSUADED his followers to participate in the death ceremony after Rep. Leo J. Ryan (D-Calif.), three newsmen and a disaffected cultist were shot to death Nov. 18 while trying to leave from an airstrip near the religious commune.

Larry Layton, of San Francisco, has been accused in the airstrip attack, and Charles F. Beikman, of Indianapolis, is charged with killing a sect member and her three children.

Here is a list provided by Guyanese authorities of 31 members of the cult who are scheduled to fly to New York Sunday.

Maryan Cassanova; John Cobb; Nedra Yates; Vessie Lee Perkins Cassanova; Andrea Walker; Preston Wade; Laura Johnson; Guy Mitchelle; Thomas Beikman, 17, Indianapolis; Beatrice Orsot; James Jones, 12; Linda Mitchelle; Cleveland Newell; Leflora Tounes, and Paul McCann.

Also, Ruby Johnston; Mark Cordell; Bobby Stroud; Michael Simon; Chuck Kirkdehol; Aaron Hendricks; Timothy Jones; Clifford Gieg; Walter Williams; Dawn Mitchell; Burell Wilson; Johnny Franklin, 33, San Francisco; Leslie Wilson, 30, Sacramento; Diana Louiarozenko, 26, New York City; Richard Clarke, 42, New Iberia, La.

U.S. had no proof of cult danger

From Tribune Wire Services

WASHINGTON—The State Department, answering charges that it ignored warnings about the People's Temple, says that in 18 months of monitoring the commune in Guyana, it never found any proof it was violent or dangerous.

At a news briefing Friday, spokesman Tom Reston also dismissed a Jonestown defector's charge that cult leader Jim Jones had provided a mistress for a U.S. Embassy official in Georgetown. He said the charge was "without substance."

Reston said the State Department has "carefully examined the record of its actions with respect to the People's Temple community and the Jonestown community" since the Nov. 18 slayings of Rep. Leo Ryan [D., Cal.] and four others.

"IT IS ABSOLUTELY clear from the record," Reston said, "that the State Department and our embassy at Georgetown have discharged their responsibilities fully and conscientiously within the limits placed upon them by law and basic constitutional uarantees of the right to privacy.

"We believe it is safe to say that more attention has been devoted by the U.S. government to this particular group of Americans living overseas over the last 18 months than to any other group of Americans liging abroad."

Regarding the mistress charge, Reston said the embassy official involved has made a sworn statement "categorically denying any sexual misconduct in Georgetown." He refused to identify the official.

IN OTHER developments:

● Some 200 rounds of ammunition, bomb-making plans, a dummy time bomb, and the secret address of two "defectors" were found by Los Angeles investigators searching a real estate office linked to the People's Temple.

Also confiscated in two raids, eight days apart, were documents showing the temple expected to make $2 million on real estate obtained by "fraud and extortion from members" of the temple, the district attorney's office said Friday.

Deputy District Attorney Lee Cogan said searchers found ammunition of various calibers, from .22 to .45, in the office of the Enola M. Nelson Realty Co.

The company is owned by the sister of James McElvane, described as a top aide to Jones.

Rev. Jones promised utopia — delivered death

By JOHN D. LOFTON JR.

WASHINGTON — The Peoples Temple. The minute you heard the name of this outfit, you knew it had to be a fraud, a hoax, a con, a swindle.

Think about it.

The People's Democratic Republic of Algeria. The People's Democratic Republic of Yemen. The People's Republic of Angola. The People's Republic of Albania. The People's Republic of Bulgaria. The People's Republic of Mozambique.

And, of course, the People's Republic of China, in which there is the People's Liberation Army, the People's Daily newspaper and the People's National Congress.

And then there was the People's Party of the 1890s, which proposed helping the working man by having the government print unlimited amounts of silver coinage and paper notes.

There was the People's Bicentennial Commission, a group of radical leftists who sought to convince us that our Founding Fathers were really nothing more than the ideological ancestors of Mao Tse-tung and Lenin.

And there was the People's Peace Treaty, a document drawn up in the early 1970s by a clique of so-called "anti-war activists," the implementation of which would have brought not peace to South Vietnam, but a Communist victory, which was the object of these Trojan-horse tacticians all along.

Commenting on the mass killings in Guyana, the official newspaper of that country's ruling party, "The New Nation," editorialized:

"That so many people should want to leave the 'comfort' of the United States to come and settle in Guyana's hinterland reflected adversely on the 'American way of life.' That they could have done so successfully would have caused great anger and dissatisfaction in many quarters."

* * *

This opinion piece was accompanied by a cartoon showing a machete labeled "international conspiracy" cutting down a young plant, with the words "Peoples Temple" written on its leaves.

Hogwash.

What Jim Jones' settlement in Jonestown, Guyana, demonstrated was the truth of Lincoln's statement to a White House visitor that some of the people can be fooled all of the time.

Jones was a sex pervert who admired Mao Tse-tung and was fascinated by Marxism since his teen years. A man who once slammed a Bible on a table saying, "I've got to destroy this paper idol," he used paranoia to induce the loyalty in his sycophants that made them follow him to the grave — at least those who willingly killed themselves.

Jones convinced his supporters that without him they would be killed or imprisoned by the Ku Klux Klan, the CIA, or any number of unspecified forces of evil.

He told blacks that if they did not go with him to the jungle in Guyana they would be put in U.S. concentration camps. Whites were told they were on a CIA "enemies" list. This use of hate-objects to induce support for his own pseudo-religious dictatorship was something right out of George Orwell's "1984."

Remember the use Big Brother made of Emmanuel Goldstein, the "Enemy of the People" whose picture flashed periodically on the giant telescreen?

As Orwell described it:

"The program of the Two Minutes Hate varied from day to day, but there was none in which Goldstein was not the principal figure. He was the primal traitor, the earliest defiler of the Party's purity. All subsequent crimes against the Party, all treacheries, acts of sabotage, heresies, deviations, sprang directly out of his teaching. Somewhere or other he was still alive and hatching conspiracies; perhaps somewhere beyond the sea, under the protection of his foreign paymasters; perhaps even — so it was occasionally rumored — in some hiding place in Oceania itself."

* * *

The horrible thing about the Two Minutes Hate was that "it was impossible" to avoid reacting to Goldstein.

"A hideous ecstacy of fear and vindictiveness, a desire to kill, to torture, to smash faces in with a sledge hammer, seemed to flow through the whole group of people like an electric current, turning one even against one's will into a grimacing, screaming lunatic."

But when the hostile figure of Goldstein melted into the face of Big Brother, black-haired, black-mustachioed, full of power and mysterious calm:

"At this moment the entire group of people broke into a deep, slow, rhythmical chant of 'B-B! ... B-B! ... B-B!' over and over again, very slowly, with a long pause between the first 'B' and the second — a heavy, murmurous sound, somehow curiously savage, in the background of which one seemed to hear the stamp of naked feet and the throbbing of tom-toms ... it was a sort of hymn to the majesty of Big Brother, but still more it was an act of self-hypnosis, a deliberate drowning of consciousness by means of a rhythmic noise."

Jim Jones is not the first revolutionary who promised utopia but delivered death. As Joseph Conrad put it incisively in his novel, "Under Western Eyes":

* * *

"In a real revolution the best characters do not come to the front. A violent revolution falls into the hands of narrow-minded fanatics and of tyrannical hypocrites at first. Afterwards come the turn of all the pretentious intellectual failures of the time. Such are the chiefs and the leaders...

"The scrupulous and the just, the noble, humane and devoted natures, the unselfish and the intelligent may begin a movement — but it passes away from them. They are not the leaders of a revolution. They are its victims: the victims of disgust, of disenchantment — often of remorse. Hopes grotesquely betrayed, ideals caricatured — that is the definition of revolutionary success.

"There have been in every revolution hearts broken by such success."

* * *

A sign behind the "throne" of Big Brother Jones said it all: "Those who do not remember the past are condemned to repeat it." Indeed.

'Moonie' Laywer Calls for Jonestown Probe

Oakland attorney Ralph L. Baker, who defended members of the Rev. Sun Myung Moon's Unification Church against "de-programming" by their parents, announced the formation of a civilian task force to investigate the Peoples Temple actions in Jonestown, Guyana.

He said, at a press conference in his office, that an "anti-religion movement advocating violent de-programming" is spreading across the U.S., adding:

"These people are attempting to exploit the Jonestown horrors as a means of taking away the constitutional rights of other groups."

"The de-programmers are now saying (because of Jonestown) 'I told you so, I told you so,' " according to Baker.

Baker said he is a member of an organization called the Alliance for the Preservation of Religious Liberties, and said the group is going to probe the "internal and external factors and stresses" that resulted in the mass suicides in the Peoples Temple's Guyana settlement.

Baker said the alliance was organized in 1976, and is a human rights organization with offices in major U.S. cities. The alliance, he said, is made up of theologians, religious leaders, attorneys, and members of both established and new religions.

Baker appealed that people join the alliance and help investigate Peoples Temple. He said it was important that such an investigation be conducted by lay persons, because "people have lost confi-

dence in government investigative agencies."

He said there were some "gnawing" questions about the Jonestown situation, among them: why Peoples Temple moved to South America, what political ties the church had and whether the CIA had spies at Jonestown who knew beforehand what was going to happen.

Baker said Jim Jones' Peoples Temple — unlike other religious groups — "was Marxist and using religion as a shield."

Government's Jonestown role being investigated

By Brenda Payton

An Oakland attorney who represents the Unification Church has begun an investigation into the government's role in the Jonestown tragedy.

Ralph Baker, speaking for the Alliance for the Preservation of Religious Liberties (APRL), and who also is counsel for members of the Rev. Sun Moon's Unification Church, said the alliance is conducting a citizens' investigation.

"We intend to find out if the government was harassing the Peoples Temple as the members alleged and the way it harassed Dr. Martin Luther King Jr.," Baker said. He said he was suspicious because government agencies apparently knew a lot about the conditions in Jonestown and didn't take any action.

The APRL will set up an investigative task force of psychologists, lawyers, investigators and theologions. Baker said the group will be headed by Walter Bowar, author of the book "Operation Mind Control."

The APRL is looking for the answers to some of the questions raised by Jonestown, Baker said, to avert the exploitation of the tragedy by forces trying to undermine religious freedom.

He said deprogrammers — people who try to get members of the Unification Church (Moonies) and the Hare Krishnas away from those organizations by force — are trying to take advantage of the situation.

They are saying I told you so, he said. "Unless we get the full facts, these criminals will continue to take advantage of the tragic situation. They are a threat to anyone who believes in the Constitution of the United States."

Although he said he could understand how the Jonestown tragedy would worry the relatives of members of minority religious groups, he warned against generalizing. "The Moonies or Hare Krishnas would never do something like this. I can guarantee you 100 percent they won't commit suicide," Baker said.

He said there is no evidence that Moon church members or the Hare Krishnas are held against their will.

"There is no evidence that there is a fear of leaving the groups," he said. "If there were, then I think the groups should be investigated."

Baker represented five adult Moonies who were placed in guardianship by a state court. That decision was later reversed by a higher court but four of the five decided to remain outside of the church.

Baker said the investigation will attempt to find out why the Peoples Temple moved to Guyana, whether the group was really a Marxist political organization using religion as a front, and whether the CIA or government pressure had anything to do with the mass suicides — murders.

341

Jones Cult Spotlights Freedom Of Religion

By JOHN RUTHERFORD

Freedom of religion is under the spotlight as the result of the perversity of the Rev. Jim Jones and his suicide cult.

Jones was treated with deference while he was building his organization. One reason was that authorities felt themselves inhibited from too much involvement in the activities of his Peoples Temple out of a regard for what is often referred to as separation of church and state.

The actual wording of the religious guarantee of the First Amendment reads: "Congress shall make no law respecting an establishment of religion, or prohibiting the free exercise thereof." Courts have extended this constitutional order to the states through interpretation of a later amendment.

Historically, the concept of freedom of religion was preached by Baptists who have "no creed but Christ" and who emphasize the teachings of Jesus. Most Jews of his day tolerated strangers who tolerated them, but he expanded on the concept. Those teachings include the admonishment to render unto Caesar what is Caesar's and to God what is God's — in other words, separation of church and state.

How should this have been applied to Jones?

The Founding Fathers clearly did not intend to condone irreligiousness in the name of religion, but drawing the line has been difficult, particularly when con artists seek to confuse and subvert.

The Jonestown murders-suicides have led one U.S. senator to question the tax-exempt status of organizations like the Peoples Temple. The "free exercise" of religion was meant for individuals but, in one way of thinking, the tax exemption is actually a respecting of an establishment of religion.

And did Jones, in physically preventing persons from leaving his flock, deny those persons their religious liberty?

Was he actually trying to create his own nation in California run by a theocratic and hence unconstitutional government?

Was this why he established his colony in Guyana?

A casulty of the Jones massacre may be an unconstitutional persecution of all cults, whether or not they are truly religious.

Peoples Temple to Dissolve Itself

UPI, AP, Washington Post

San Francisco, Calif. — The tiny remnant of the Peoples Temple congregation, still isolated and despairing over the loss of its leader and more than 900 members in Guyana, moved Tuesday to dissolve the church and write an end to the strange cult's 13 year history.

Papers on file in San Francisco Superior Court said it was "practically and morally impossible for the corporation to continue its existence."

At the behest of its attorney, Charles Garry, and appeals from community leaders, the directors of the Temple asked that $1 million in assets be set aside for burial expenses of the sect members who were murdered or killed themselves.

Court Jurisdiction

Under California law, the court is expected to issue a decree that the corporation be dissolved. All assets will be put under jurisdiction of the court and, after any bills or claims are settled, the remaining assets will be disposed of.

It is not known what assets are available to the court. Some former members have reported the existence of $10 million or more in bank accounts in Switzerland and Panama. "We are ready to turn over everything, anywhere in the world," said Garry.

In Guyana, the government has denied reports that the Peoples Temple influenced senior cabinet members to stop a local investigation of Jonestown before the mass murder-suicide.

In its first reaction to a series of stories by The Associated Press, the Guyanese government also denied that:

The Peoples Temple was invited to participate in Guyanese politics to help the ruling People's National Con-

Turn to page 18, col. 1

From Page 1

gress Party win an important referendum last July.

Home Affairs Minister C. Vibert Mingo promised to intervene in a judicial hearing on the custody of 6 year old John Victor Stoen, whom Peoples Temple leader Jim Jones brought to Guyana two years ago, or that Mingo promised Jones protection against arrest in the case.

Former Minister of Foreign Affairs Fred Wills was a political adviser to Jones and that Jones contacted the Cuban Embassy to approach orders of Jones. Paula Adams, 29, of Ukiah, Calif., refused to identify the official but said the affair was "a completely personal relationship outside the Peoples Temple."

A survivor of the tragedy confirmed Tuesday that she had a sexual affair with a high Guyanese official, but denied that she did it on the Prime Minister Forbes Burnham seeking Wills' reinstatement after he was fired for issues not related to Jonestown.

In related developments:

The San Francisco Examiner reported Tuesday that arrest warrants have been obtained by the FBI for eight church members on charges resulting from the slaying of Rep. Leo Ryan (D-Calif.).

The House International Relations Committee, which inherited Ryan's investigation of the Peoples Temple, has laid plans for an inquiry covering the past, present and future of the cult, including its members, its money and its relations with US and Guyanese officials. The plan still has to be approved by Chairman Clement J. Zablocki (D-Wis.), who has pledged to complete the investigation begun by Ryan.

Phil Kerby

Sanity — A Condition of Survival

We are confronted in a distant jungle and in the magnificence of the City Hall of San Francisco with the mystery of human existence and the riddle of that inexplicable creature, man.

The historians say that mass suicide is not unprecedented. The trail they trace of similar but not identical epi-

Phil Kerby is an editorial writer for the Los Angeles Times.

sodes of self-destruction leads through the centuries and many cultures to the South American settlement.

The rootless, the dispossessed, the forlorn withdraw from a society they see as totally evil, and, when their vision dims, turn upon themselves and seek redemption in death and the promise of new life.

The psychiatrists, the priests of modern culture, tell us of the mental confusion that causes people to join a messianic cult. Many are emotionally crippled from the wounds of life. Others feel a rage at their incapacity to shape the events that control their lives.

They find some sense of personal worth in joining a band of other disaffected souls, but one step from intractable reality leads to another, and, finally, they live in an illusory realm of their own creation. In special circumstances in times of extraordinary social dissolution, mass delusion results in mass catastrophe.

The cry of the lost of the earth echoed in a note found on the body of the leader of the Peoples Temple, apparently from a follower in agreement with his decision for destruction:

"For my part — I am more than tired of this wretched, merciless planet and the hell it holds for so many masses of beautiful people — I thank you for the only life I have ever known."

The wail from the jungle sent a primeval shudder through the world.

From what I have read, all the interpretations that immediately followed attempted to draw a line between "them" and "us." But under examination, the line, if it exists, is a frail and wavering thread.

In this age of science and enlightenment, madmen have ruled not just cults of hundreds but mighty nations and have caused the deaths of millions in internal struggles and more millions in wars. The defenseless by the hundreds of thousands have been targeted for death by other leaders who never showed any visible doubt of their own humanity. In Cambodia, the destruction of life sweeps across the desolate land, and the streets of the civilized cities of the West are empty of protest.

Violence seeps into the psyche of nations, and the weak and deranged react to the signals. The daily rattle of gunfire is heard in our land, and the annual toll mounts to the thousands. Only occasionally does the terror impinge on the national consciousness: when a president falls, when his brother dies, when a civil rights leader crumples on the balcony of a motel. And now the mayor of San Francisco, still mourning his city's casualties in Guyana, is shot dead, and along with him a colleague — martyrs of violence, victims of a young man, who, in one moment of primitive rage, brought tragedy into the lives of two families and his own.

Somehow the cord that should bind us all in our common fate is severed again and again. Expressions of grief and foreboding follow the terrifying news, but the events of recent days and recent years fade before the ultimate terror of the last half of the 20th century: a dozen fallible human beings, perhaps fewer, have the power to destroy all life on earth, and, mesmerized, we submit to the horror of potential doom without revulsion.

Where then, precisely where, do we draw the line between our sanity and the insanity of Guyana? Where do we draw the line between the jungle and the chancelleries of the world?

Sect Request Denied

An attorney argued Wednesday that the trial of the leader of an alleged religious sect on sexual assault charges should be delayed indefinitely because of recent negative news reports concerning religious cults.

The attorney, Daniel Kondos, said that because of the publicity surrounding the recent murder of US Rep. Leo Ryan and the mass murder-suicides at the Peoples Temple in Guyana, as well as other publicized events concerning religious groups, that his client could not obtain a fair trial "anywhere in Western civilization."

His client is Socrates Sirisun, 27, who told authorities earlier that he was president of the Cultural Educational Research Institute in Bay View. He claimed a local following of more than 400.

Since Sirisun was charged this summer, the group has disbanded.

Reserve Circuit Judge Elliott Walstead said, "I don't see any reason to adjourn this case because of any particular passion.

"I think I read the newspapers and watch telvision as much as anyone ... and I've never heard of this man (the defendant)," Walstead said.

He said matters that might prejudice the trial could best be handled at the time of trial by the judge hearing the case.

Circuit Judge Ted E. Wedemeyer Jr. will preside at the trial, scheduled to begin Thursday. Walstead heard the motion because Wedemeyer is out of town.

Kondos had subpenaed representatives of The Milwaukee Journal, the Milwaukee Sentinel, and the three local network affiliated television stations. Walstead said it was not necessary for them to appear in court.

Sirisun is charged with having sexual relations with a 14 year old girl.

A vice squad sergeant said police had learned of the alleged activity when a 15 year old girl ran away from home after telling her mother that she and her 14 year old sister had had sexual relations with Sirisun.

345

Grand Jury Calls
17 From Temple

AP and UPI

Seventeen Peoples Temple followers, including two adopted sons of temple leader Jim Jones, were subpenaed Thursday to tell a San Francisco grand jury what they know about the slaying of Rep. Leo Ryan (D-Calif.) at a jungle airstrip in Guyana.

It was the first legal action taken against any of the 44 temple members who have returned thus far.

One of the 17, Laura Johnston, a nine year member of the cult, told reporters that

---

The Guyanese people are being kept in the dark about the Jonestown tragedy; story on Page 10 of Accent.

---

all those who arrived in New York Wednesday night had been subpenaed to appear in Federal Court in San Francisco before a grand jury investigating Ryan's death.

At least seven Peoples Temple members said they were to appear in San Francisco on either Dec. 8, 9 or 13.

One man, Paul McCann, was served with papers ordering him to appear Friday in San Francisco shortly after he arrived at Kennedy International Airport.

The other 15 men and one woman were immediately whisked away by more than 60 agents of the FBI and Secret Service for questioning in an airport hangar. The interviews lasted almost nine hours. Interviews with 27 survivors who returned on earlier flights had lasted approximately 90 minutes.

None of those aboard Wednesday's flight was in Jonestown when the slaying of Ryan and the subsequent mass suicide of sect members occurred. They were 150 miles away at the Peoples Temple headquarters in Georgetown.

McCann asked for a lawyer at the beginning of the questioning and was taken to Port Authority police headquarters.

David Zapp, an associate of lawyer William Kunstler, was brought in to represent McCann, and the FBI then spoke with both of them. During the interview, an assistant US attorney served McCann with the subpena.

Zapp said the FBI told McCann not to request a lawyer and quoted an agent as saying, "You know that's going to make you look guilty."

"This guy is frightened," Zapp said. "There is absolutely no reason why he asked for a lawyer other than just to have a lawyer."

McCann said he went to Jonestown 1½ years ago and was working at a sawmill in Georgetown when the deaths occurred.

Meanwhile, a police official in Georgetown said Thursday that about $1 million had been found in and near Jonestown and predicted more would be found.

In other developments Wednesday:

THREATS DISMISSED — The US State Department said American officials in Guyana received direct warnings last summer from the Peoples Temple that its members might commit mass suicide but the department says the threat was dismissed as a "psychological ploy."

It was the first official acknowledgement by the US that representatives of the Peoples Temple carried the suicide threat directly to American officials.

HIT LIST — A purported Peoples Temple hit list, naming enemies of the cult who should be the targets of assassinations, was based on rumors, speculation and hearsay, investigators said. The San Francisco Examiner reported that no documents had been found by the San Francisco district attorney's office to substantiate the existence of such a list.

Cult News Had Wide Following

By George Gallup

(c) Field Enterprises, Inc.

Princeton, N.J. — The story of the mass murders and suicides in Guyana was the most widely followed event of 1978, with a remarkable 98% of Americans saying they had heard or read about it.

Few events in the 43 year history of the Gallup Poll have been known to such a high proportion of the US public, except such events as the attack on Pearl Harbor in 1941 and the dropping of the atomic bomb on Hiroshima and Nagasaki in 1945.

For weeks in the aftermath of the grim developments on Nov. 18, historians, religious experts, psychiatrists and others have sought for motivations and have asked how the tragedy could have happened and whether it might happen again.

Amid this speculation, the Gallup Poll sought to find what Americans in all walks of life think are the main reasons people become involved in cults of this kind.

This question was asked first:

"Have you heard or read about the mass suicides in Guyana among members of a cult called the Peoples Temple?"

The results, in percentages:

Nationwide 98
College background 99
High school 98
Grade school 96

This question was asked next:

"Why do you think people become involved in cults of this kind?"

Here, in percentages, are the key reasons given:

Need for leadership, a father figure .. 15
Have unhappy lives,
  a feeling of hopelessness 13
Gullible 13
Need to have a sense of belonging,
  a sense of community 12
Searching for a deeper meaning to life,
  their lives are spiritually empty 12
They are mentally disturbed 11
A failure of churches, people
  are disillusioned with the churches .. 7
They are brainwashed 7
To escape from reality 7
Need for something to believe in 6
Insecurity 4
Homes have broken up/failed 4
Lack motivation, ambition, direction;
  have nothing better to do with their
  lives 3
The devil, false prophets 3
Lack of education 3
They are confused 2
Influenced by drug culture 2
Other reasons 2
No opinion 12

The results are based on interviews with adults in more than 300 localities across the nation Dec. 8-11.

Peoples congregation is dissolving church

United Press International

SAN FRANCISCO — The tiny remnant of the Peoples Temple congregation, despairing over the loss of their leader and more than 900 members in Guyana, moved to dissolve the church yesterday.

Papers on file in San Francisco Superior Court said it is "practically and morally impossible for the corporation to continue its existence."

At the behest of their attorney, Charles Garry, and appeals from community leaders, the directors of the temple asked that $1 million in assets be set aside for burial expenses of the sect members who committed suicide.

Under California law, all assets will be put under jurisdiction of the court.

Some former members have reported the existence of $10 million or more in bank accounts. But those remaining in the temple said they have no knowledge of such accounts.

"We are ready to turn over everything, anywhere in the world," said Garry.

In a related development, more than a dozen survivors of Jonestown, including two youths believed to be the adopted sons of cult leader Jim Jones, arrived in New York last night accompanied by an armed US sky marshal. Among the passengers listed by the FBI were Timothy Glen Jones, 19, and James W. Jones Jr., 18.

348

'How did your children become involved in People's Temple?'

The shocking tragedy in Jonestown, Guyana directly touched the lives of the Rev. and Mrs. John V. Moore of Reno, Nevada. Two of their daughters and a grandson were members of the People's Temple residing in Jonestown, and are presumed to have died there. Mr. Moore delivered the sermon which follows at the First UMC in Reno, where he is pastor, on the Sunday following news of the Mass Murder-Suicide in Guyana, noting: "I am preaching this morning because we alone can make our unique witness, and today is the day to make it."

By JOHN V. MOORE

During these past days we have been asked frequently: "How did your children become involved in People's Temple?" There is no simple answer. We are given our genetic ancestry. We are given our families. We are all on our personal journeys. All of these, along with the history of the race, converge upon the present wherein we make choices. Through all of this, providence is working silently and unceasingly to bring creation to wholeness.

I will talk only of our children's personal histories. The only way you can understand our children is to know something of our family. In our family you can see the relationship between the events of the sixties and this tragedy, just as there is a relationship between the self-immolation of some Americans during those years and the mass murder-suicide of last week.

Our children learned that mothering is caring for more than kin. Dad talked about it from the pulpit. Mother acted it out. More than 15 teenagers and young adults shared our home with our children. Some were normal, but others had problems. One did not say a word for three months. At least two others were suicidal. One young man had come from a home where his father had refused to speak to him for more than a year. From childhood our girls saw their mother respond to people in need—from unwed mothers to psychotic adults and the poor.

Carolyn loved to play, but as president of the MYF she pushed the group to deal with serious issues. She had a world vision. She traveled to Mexico with her high school Spanish class. Four years later she spent a year studying in France. At college she majored in international relations. As a member of People's Temple, she stood with the poor as they prepared for and stood in court. She expressed her caring both in one-to-one relationships and as a political activist.

From 1963 until 1972 when Annie left home, Annie and Becky walked with us in civil rights and anti-Vietnam War marches. We were together in supporting the farm worker's struggle to organize. They stood in silent peace vigils. In high school they bore witness to peace with justice in our world. Their youth group provided a camping experience for foster children. When Annie was 16, she worked as a volunteer in Children's Hospital in Washington, D.C. She worked directly with the children, playing with them, playing her guitar and singing. The children loved her. She decided that she wanted to work in a burn unit, which she did at San Francisco General Hospital before going to Guyana.

Our children, took seriously what we believed about commitment, caring about a better, more humane and just society. They saw in People's Temple the same kind of caring people and commitment to social justice that they had lived with. They have paid our dues for our commitments and involvement.

What went wrong?

The second question we have been asked is: "What went wrong?" What happened to turn the dream into a nightmare? I shall mention two things that were wrong from the beginning. These are idolatry and paranoia. I speak first of idolatry.

The adulation and worship Jim Jones' followers gave him was idolatrous. We expressed our concern from the first. The First Commandment is the first of two texts for my sermon. "Thou shalt have no other gods before me." Our children and members of People's Temple placed in Jim Jones the trust, and gave to him the loyalty, that we were created to give God alone.

It's not that they were so different from other mortals, for idolatry has always been easy and popular. The more common forms of idolatry are to be seen when people give unto the state or church or institution their ultimate devotion. The First Commandment says "No!" and warns of disastrous consequences for disobedience. The truth is that the Source of our lives, the One in whom we trust and unto whom we commit our lives, is the Unseen and Eternal One.

To believe the First Commandment, on the other hand, affirms that every ideal and principle, every leader and institution, all morals and values, all means and ends, are subordinate to God. This means that they are all subject to criticism. There was no place for this criticism in People's Temple.

The second thing that was wrong was paranoia. This was present through the years that we knew People's Temple. There is a thin line separating sensitivity to realities from fantasies of persecution. Jim Jones was as sensitive to social injustice as anyone I have ever known. On the other hand, he saw conspiracies in the opposition. I remember painfully the conversation around the table the last night of our visit to Jonestown. Jim and other leaders were there. The air was heavy with fears of conspiracy. They fed each other's fears. There was no voice to question the reality of those fears.

As their fears increased, they increased their control over the members. Finally their fears overwhelmed them.

Our relation to that tragedy

The death of hundreds and the pain and suffering of hundreds of others is tragedy. The tragedy will be compounded if we fail to discern our relation to that tragedy. Those deaths and all that led up to them are infinitely important to us. To see Jonestown as an isolated event unrelated to our society portends greater tragedy.

Jonestown people were human beings. Except for your caring relationships with us, Jonestown would be names, "cultists," "fanatics," "kooks." Our children are real to you, because you know and love us. Barbara and I could describe for you many of the dead. You would think that we were describing people whom you know, members of our church. If you can feel this, you can begin to relate to the tragedy.

If my judgment is true that idolatry destroyed Peoples Temple, it is equally true that few movements in our time have been more expressive of Jesus' parable of the Last Judgment of feeding the hungry, caring for the sick, giving shelter to the homeless and visiting those in prison than People's Temple. A friend said to me Friday, "They found people no one else ever cared about." That's true. They cared for the least and last of the human family.

The forces of life and death—building and destroying— were present in People's Temple. Death reigned when there was no one free enough, nor strong enough, nor filled with rage enough, to run and throw his body against a vat of cyanide spilling it on the ground. Are there people free enough and strong enough who will throw themselves against the vats of nuclear stockpiles for the sake of the world? Without such people, hundreds of millions of human beings will consume the nuclear cyanide, and it will be murder. Our acquiesence in our own death will make it suicide.

The forces of death are powerful in our society. The arms race, government distant from the governed, inflation, cybernation-unemployment are signs of death. Nowhere is death more visible than in the decay of our cities. There is no survival for cities apart from the creation and sustenance of communities within. Cities governed by law, but without a network of communities which support members and hold them accountable, these cities will crumble, and will bring down nations.

This is what made the Jonestown experiment so important for us. It was an effort to build this kind of common life. Its failure is our loss as we struggle against the forces of death in our cities.

God is making all things new

I have talked of history and our personal histories, of our journeys and our choices. Providence is God's working with and through all of these. God has dealt with tragedy before, and God is dealing with tragedy now. We are witnesses to the resurrection, for even now God is raising us from death. God whom we worship is making all things new.

Our Lord identified with the least of humans. Christ is present in the hungry and lonely, the sick and imprisoned. Christ, the love and power of God, is with us now. In Christ we are dying and are being raised to new life.

My last words are of our children. We have shared the same vision, the vision of justice rolling down like a mighty stream, and swords forged into plows. We have shared the same hope. We have shared the same commitment. Carolyn and Annie and Kimo served on a different field. We have wished that they had chosen ours, but they didn't. And they have fallen. We will carry on in the same struggle until we fall upon our fields.

No passage of scripture speaks to me so forcefully as Paul's words from Romans: "Nothing, absolutely nothing can separate us from the love of God we have known in Christ Jesus our Lord." This week I have learned in a new way the meaning of these words of Paul: "...love never ends."

Now may the Word which calls forth shoots from dead stumps, a people from dry bones, sons and daughters from the stones at our feet, babies from barren wombs, and life from the tomb, call you forth into the new creation.

After loss of three children, father looks at cult in different perspective

BOISE, Idaho —(NC)— Mike Carter, a Garden City, Idaho, man who lost seven members of his family in the Jonestown, Guyana, tragedy is in a reflective mood now.

At one time he was supportive of the People's Temple, believing that the group was doing good work among the poor. Now he sees it differently.

Four years ago Carter's eldest son, Tim, joined the People's Temple in San Francisco. Later another son, Michael, and Carter's only daughter, Terri, joined the group led by the Rev. Jim Jones.

Carter said Tim joined after serving in the army because he wanted to help people. He told Fr. Angelito Peries, associate pastor of Boise's St. Mary parish, that his children were happy in the People's Temple, but said that in

his opinion that it was not a religious group.

People's Temple is an organization based on human relationships, Carter, who is a member of St. Mary's parish, told Father Peries. The People's Temple offered members a way to express their enthusiasm and to find freedom. It looked good at first, Carter said, but later the group became more rigid, with Jones and other leaders becoming increasingly fanatical.

Carter said he did not like the rigidity and fanaticism of the leaders, but felt that on the whole the group was doing good things for his children.

All three Carter children married other People's Temple members and had children of their own. Tim Carter and his wife were taking care of four homeless native children in Guyana, Carter told Father

Peries. Letters from Guyana told of continuing happiness.

To Carter it looked like a life based on his family's life when the children were younger.

All three young Carters attended a parochial elementary school in San Mateo, Calif. They were happy children with a good family life, Carter said. His wife, now deceased, was a "very giving" Jewish woman.

The Carter children held no animosity toward the Catholic Church after deciding to dedicate their lives to the People's Temple. Young Mike Carter attended Mass frequently with his father when he visited Boise. All the Carter children were formed by the values of their Catholic upbringing, Carter said.

But now Terri is dead. So is her husband and young son and the wives and children of the two Carter men. Tim and

Mike were released last weekend after being held for questioning by authorities in Guyana concerning the murders of Congressman Leo Ryan and several other Americans, the event which set off the bizarre murder-suicide of more than 900 members of the cult.

Now that he has had some time to reflect on what has happened to his family and the People's Temple, Carter had some advice for young people looking for a place to put their own "enthusiasm" and "desire for freedom" to the service of others: Reflect on your own desires and the potential of the group you are thinking of joining. Young people should not make the kinds of commitments the Carters made to the People's Temple until they have reflected on it and are certain where they are going, he said. Maybe in that way similar tragedies can be avoided, he added.

Federal crackdown on cultists could threaten religious liberty

By Richard McMunn
OSV news analysis

That a spell-binding "religious" leader can lead U.S. citizens to a foreign country, incite the murder of innocent people and then lead his followers into completion of a grisly suicide pact is cause for serious concern. But over-reacting to that concern is a very real danger, argues Dr. William Whalen, a nationally recognized researcher and writer on the subject of cults.

Why didn't the government do something, people asked as the stark and ugly reality of the events in Guyana began to hit home. And since then, many editorialists and columnists have jumped into the fray demanding a federal crackdown of "freak religions."

But, as Dr. Whalen, of Indiana's Purdue University, points out, it must be remembered that adherents of cults are a very small minority in the American religious scene. Their numbers are few but their actions are dramatic and create headlines.

More importantly, he argues, any government action toward any religious group is a touchy subject, because the freedom of religion is constitutionally guaranteed. That doesn't mean, he explains, that there aren't abuses of religious freedom.

For example, a self-styled healer would probably be jailed for practicing medicine without a license. But as soon as he assumes the cloak of religion and becomes a faith healer he is virtually above the law.

Only in rare instances is the government willing to intervene. The courts have ordered medical care for minor children of parents who have refused to allow treatment, on the basis of religious conviction.

Dr. Whalen is worried that incidents such as these, combined with the tremendous impact of the Guyana tragedy, have so inflamed public opinion that government officials might feel compelled to take rash steps. If government is forced into a position of defining religion; is forced to set up standards to define the limits of church freedom, "the implications for religious liberty could be grave," he insists.

Still, something must be done. But what?

The effect of cults in our society can be minimized, if not eradicated, through public exposure of the nature of cults, Dr. Whalen believes. If the media can expose the "offbeat" cults for what they really are, they will no longer prove attractive for many people, especially the young, those between ages 18-25 who are most susceptible, he says.

But there is a problem here. Cults draw on tremendous financial resources, and have adopted the practice of instigating libel suits when they receive even the slightest hint of public criticism. They seldom win these suits, but the spectre of expensive litigation scares away all but the largest broadcasters and publishers, Dr. Whalen explains. Unfortunately, cults can be the most dangerous when they are isolated, out of the scrutiny of the public eye.

The government could take action in this area, he believes. A major step would be to revise civil law to prevent wealthy cults from avoiding adverse publicity with the use of expensive, nuisance law suits.

Parents, too, can play a major role, he says. The main thing for parents is to keep the communication lines with their children open. Young people must feel free to fully air their problems and questions at home so that they don't turn to cults in their search for that kind of atmosphere.

Moreover, he insists, parents should never threaten their children, telling them to drop cult associations or risk having a car, for example, taken away from them.

The mainline churches must adopt exactly the same attitude demanded of parents, Dr. Whalen believes. And he says the churches must move to create more programs that will challenge the idealism of young people.

Young people, he says, are most often attracted to cults because they are unhappy and confused about life and community as they have experienced these concepts. They are attracted by the austere, ascetic, ultra-straight lifestyle the cultists try to sell.

The important thing to remember, Dr. Whalen said, is that cults stand little chance of getting a permanent grip on young people if cults can be publicly exposed, if the young people can openly grapple with their problems within their families, and if young people can find something to relate to within mainline church bodies.

351

First Cult Bodies Leave Air Base

Dover, Del. —AP— The bodies of victims of the mass murder-suicide at the Peoples Temple commune in Guyana began leaving Dover Air Force Base Saturday afternoon.

William Torbert, a Dover mortician, said he understood that about 10 local funeral homes would be handling the bodies. He said a number of the families of the victims had requested cremation of the remains.

An Air Force spokesman said the number of transfers Saturday and Sunday would depend on how quickly the families of the 592 victims identified by Friday afternoon made arrangements with the funeral homes.

Most of the bodies are expected to be shipped to the West Coast, the home of many commune members before they moved to the South American jungle settlement.

Gramm says US does too much for 'kooks'

Jonestown retrieval criticized

By LARRY NEAL
Star-Telegram Austin Bureau

WASHINGTON — U.S. Rep.-elect Phil Gramm, D-College Station, figures the "kooks" who died at Jonestown are being treated a bit too well by the U. S. government.

The multi-million dollar body retrieval and identification operation staged by American authorities has rankled both his constituents and himself.

He said his office back in the district is wading through thousands of letters and the No. 1 item on peoples' minds in the expensive airlift of corpses back to the United States from the mass suicide-massacre site.

Families of those 900 who died, when capable, or Jonestown founder Jim Jones' People's Temple should pay the freight, he contends.

"We treat kooks better than we do average, law abiding, taxpaying citizens," he said.

"The average guy in the street would not be brought back" if he died overseas, he said.

Gramm said while he was "not unsympathetic" to the plight of the families of those who were killed or who killed themselves, that there is "a real question of whether the taxpayers should pay" to bring their bodies back.

The other top item listed by the letter writers, said Gramm, is another matter of expenses — the appropriation of money to put the controversial Panama Canal treaties into full effect.

And "I'm not going to vote for it," Gramm vowed.

"I don't pay people to take away my property," he explained.

● ● ●

353

'Jim Jones had a charisma that could take anybody in'

SAN FRANCISCO (UPI)—The neighborhood is a bleak patchwork of empty lots and mean streets littered with broken glass. At the corner barbershop they sell the Black Panther newspaper along with $3 haircuts.

Old men crowd a treeless park, drinking cheap wine and talking sports. A few blocks away stands a public housing project where broken windows are everywhere and hope is as dim as the hallway lighting.

And behind a ragged chain link fence, large crates labeled "Peoples Temple Agricultural Mission, Port Kaituma NWD, Guyana" still await shipment to a death village where hundreds from this sprawling neighborhood perished.

THIS IS SAN FRANCISCO'S Fillmore District, a largely black inner-city neighborhood where the Rev. Jim Jones' preachment of race war and black genocide flourished amid the hopelessness and naivete of the poor and the aged.

When the return of the bodies from Guyana and Dover Air Force Base is completed, local churchmen expect the total number of Fillmore residents who died in the Guyanese jungle to exceed 300.

Although Jones and the People's Temple attracted idealistic whites and even middle-class blacks from other cities, most of the flock was drawn from lower-income blacks from the Fillmore.

"People's Temple was 90 per cent black, and most of them were from the San Francisco area," said Al Mills, who acted as the Temple's membership director until he quit to join an anti-Temple group in Berkeley.

JONES' ENORMOUS APPEAL to ghetto blacks, ex-members said, grew out of his strong civil-rights record, fiery pulpit denunciations of racism and his ruthless manipulation of blacks' fundamentalist religious beliefs.

Sometimes, Jones even went so far as to barge into other ghetto churches during Sunday services and denounce their speechless ministers for "keeping mistresses and driving Cadillacs while the people starved," according to ex-member Phil Kearns.

Frequently, frenzied worshipers would stream past their stunned ministers to follow Jones out of the church and into his People's Temple, Kearns said.

Like a leisure-suited Elmer Gantry, Jones' sermons on impending race war and his "revelations" of a socialist haven in Guyana where food was plentiful and racism nonexistent electrified the naive and inspired the oppressed.

"Jim Jones had a charisma that could take anybody in," said Mills. "The devastating thing was that the people who usually fell for it were poor blacks."

Mills said Jones used a compelling mixture of Bible-belt oratory, threats of physical beatings and pure medicine-show hokum to galvanize blacks who had grown up in the Deep South's "holy-roller" religious tradition.

"He got the blacks with religion—with the phony faith healings, the pentecostal mumbo-jumbo. These were people who believed in the Second Coming of Christ, and that's what Jones gave them," said Mills.

Church tried to help Guyana cult members

BY NANCY FRAZIER
NC News Service

In the wake of the Nov. 18 tragedy that left more than 900 members of the People's Temple cult in Guyana dead in a mass suicide-murder, efforts of Catholics to assist cult members and their families before and afterward became clear.

The economic benefit to Guyana from cult's agricultural colony were also noted.

Commentators on the events included L'Osservatore Romano, the Vatican daily, and The Catholic Standard, an independent weekly in Georgetown, Guyana.

According to Father Robert Barrow, Jesuit superior in Guyana, many of the People's Temple members once belonged to the Catholic or Protestant churches. But there was a "sense of remoteness with the group, both because of the distance to the settlement, and because all of them were U.S. citizens and no Guyanese were involved," he added.

Before it was discovered that nearly all the cult members had died in the mass suicide-murder, the Jesuits had offered "to counsel members of the People's Temple who might decide to come to us."

Rep. Leo Ryan (D.-Calif.), who was killed along with four other U.S. citizens during an ambush as the group tried to board two small planes headed for Georgetown, the capital of Guyana, after a visit to the colony, was a baptized Catholic who had recently indicated he did not want to be listed in head counts of Catholic congressmen. It was his death and the others that apparently led the Rev. Jim Jones, leader of the People's Temple, to order the mass suicide-murder.

ONE Catholic who had been invited to visit Georgetown but never made the trip because of a lack of transportation was Mercy Sister Mary Liguori, a Philadelphia nun serving as a surgeon in Georgetown.

She said she had been invited to serve as a medical consultant to the Jonestown community in October and had agreed to travel to the camp on Sundays, but the cult had never been able to provide a

(Continued on Page 11)

(Continued from Page 1)

plane for the trips.

Among participants in one of the most grisly segments of the Guyana tragedy — the identification and processing of 912 bodies flown into Dover Air Force Base in Delaware — were two Catholic and five Protestant chaplains.

"We are trying to first offer support," said Holy Ghost Father John Egan, assistant base chaplain. "We are also available 24 hours a day to the volunteers, many of whom are encountering death for the first time." A Mass and ecumenical service were celebrated three times Nov. 26 for the volunteer workers who were employed in shifts.

THE EVENTS at Jonestown drew comment from a number of sources, including Catholic editorialists. Writing in L'Osservatore Romano, Franciscan Father Gino Concetti said that ignoring the church founded by Christ on a hierarchial basis leads, in religious matters, to "mad adventure."

"One may not and one must not believe in the 'false prophets' who proliferate in every age," said the front-page comment by Father Concetti, a staff member of L'Osservatore Romano.

"Taking advantage of the needs and good faith of people to affirm one's own credo is inhuman," the Vatican daily added. "Only true religion frees and redeems man. False ones oppress him, close him in a vise to the point of strangulation, first psychological and then physical. That's just what happened in the jungle of Guyana."

The Catholic Standard, an independent Catholic weekly in the Georgetown Diocese, said the people of Guyana expect answers about why Guyanese and U.S. authorities failed to heed clear warnings about the tragedy that was brewing at Jonestown.

"A number of questions require full and serious answers if both governments are to be exonerated from some responsibility for what occurred in Jonestown," said an editorial signed by Jesuit Father Andrew Morrison, editor. "The problem question is not so much why people came to the People's Temple, but why they stayed . . ."

WHY DID the Rev. Jim Jones choose such a remote area for his religious colony? Why did the Guyanese government, which now regrets the adverse publicity, welcome his group in 1974?

Close associates of Mr. Jones said he was trying to establish a refuge from nuclear holocaust, believing that Guyana would be safe. He also moved from his San Francisco headquarters as cult membership declined because services became strange and the discipline gave way to brutal beatings.

To Guyana, anxious for foreign investments and friendly contacts in the United States, Mr. Jones could exhibit his fortune (estimated at $15 million) collected from the members' savings, properties and earnings. He also could talk of having friends in high places, and of his tenure in the San Francisco housing authority.

70 at Jonestown Got Injections

(c) New York Times Service

New York, N.Y. — At least 70 of the Peoples Temple cult members who died in the mass murder-suicide at Jonestown, Guyana, were given cyanide by injection, according to well placed Guyanese officials.

According to these sources, the findings raise the possibility that the victims were murdered. They said the placement of the injections, high on the upper arm, made it unlikely that they were self-administered.

Most of the 70 injected were adults; among them was Christine Miller, the one woman identified by survivors as having been openly against the mass suicide plan of the cult leader, the Rev. Jim Jones.

356

'My daughters died in Guyana'

Personal view/John V. Moore

MY WIFE Barbara and I were on a retreat on Sunday, Nov. 19, when I received a phone call from my sister telling me of the murder of Rep. Leo Ryan and others in Guyana. A friend drove us home and said to me, "John, this is your calling."

I knew what he meant. I knew I had been called to bear witness to the word of God. My daughters Carolyn and Ann and Carolyn's 3-year-old son Jim-Jon were living in the People's Temple commune in Guyana.

Were living. Since then, the deaths of all three have been confirmed.

During these past days my wife and I have been asked frequently, "How did they become involved in People's Temple?" There is no simple answer. We are given our genetic ancestry. We are given our families. We are all on our personal journeys. All of these, along with the history of the human race, converge upon the present wherein we make choices.

THE ONLY WAY you can understand my children is to know something about our family. You'll see the relationship between the events of the 1960s and this tragedy, just as there is a relationship between the self-immolation of some Americans during those years and the mass murder-suicide in Guyana.

Our children learned that mothering is caring for more than kin Dad talked about it from the pulpit. Mother acted it out More than 15 teen-agers and young adults shared our home with our children Some were normal, others had problems One didn't say a word for three months At least two others were suicidal

From childhood our girls saw their mother respond to people in need, from unwed mothers to psychotic adults and the poor

Carolyn had a world vision She traveled to Mexico with her high school Spanish class. She studied a year in France In college she majored in international relations. Ten years ago she joined People's Temple to stand with the poor, both in one-to-one relationships and as a political activist.

Annie walked with us in civil rights and anti-Vietnam War marches. We stood together in supporting the farm workers struggling to organize. When she was 16 she worked as a volunteer in a children's hospital in Washington, D.C., playing with the young patients, playing her guitar and singing. The children loved her. She wanted to work in a burn unit, which she did at San Francisco General Hospital before going to Guyana with Carolyn in 1977.

Our children took seriously what my wife and I believed about working to create a better, more humane and just society. They saw in People's Temple the same kind of caring and commitment that they had lived with in our home as children. They have paid our dues for our commitments and involvement.

I AM ASKED a second question: What went wrong?

Two things were wrong with People's Temple from the beginning: idolatry and paranoia.

The adulation and worship of Jim Jones by his followers was idolatrous. My wife and I expressed our concern to our daughters from the first. The commandment says, "Thou shalt have no other gods before me." But our children gave to Jim Jones the trust and loyalty that should belong to God alone. It's not that they were so different from other mortals, for idolatry has always been easy and popular.

The paranoia existed all the years that we knew People's Temple. There's a thin line separating sensitivity to realities from fantasies of persecution. Jim Jones was as sensitive to injustice as anyone I have ever known. On the other hand, he saw conspiracies in any opposition. I remember painfully the conversation around the table in May, when my wife and I visited Jonestown. Jim and other leaders were there. The air was heavy with fears of conspiracy. All Jim talked about was conspiracy. The people fed each other's fears. And there was no voice to question the reality of those fears.

As their fears increased, so did the leaders' control over the members. Finally, the fears overwhelmed everyone.

The death of hundreds and the pain of hundreds of others is a tragedy; and that tragedy will be compounded if we fail to discern our relationship to it. The people of Jonestown were human beings who became involved because they cared about feeding the hungry, soothing the sick, sheltering the homeless. My wife and I could describe for you many of the dead, and you'd think we were describing people you know, members of your church—not "cultists," "fanatics," "kooks." If you can feel this, you can begin to relate to the tragedy.

THE FORCES OF LIFE and death, building and destroying, were present in People's Temple. Death reigned when there was no one free enough, nor strong enough, nor filled with sufficient rage to throw his body against a vat of cyanide, spilling it on the ground. Are there people free enough and strong enough who will thrown themselves against the vats of nuclear stockpiles for the sake of the world? Without such people, hundreds of millions of human beings will consume nuclear cyanide. And acquiesence in our own death will make it suicide.

The forces of death are powerful in our society: the arms race, government distant from the governed, inflation, the decay of our cities. There is no survival for cities apart from their communities; cities governed by law, but without a network of communities that support the lawmakers and hold them accountable, will crumble, and will bring down nations.

THE JONESTOWN EXPERIMENT was an effort to build a new kind of life based on caring and commitment to others. Its failure is our loss as we struggle against the forces of death.

My children and my wife Barbara and I shared a vision. We shared a hope. But Carolyn and Annie and little Jim-Jon served on a different field. Barbara and I wished they had chosen ours, but they didn't. And they have fallen. We will carry on in the same struggle until we fall upon our fields.

The Rev. John V. Moore is pastor of First United Methodist Church in Reno, Nev. This is excerpted from a sermon he gave on Nov. 26, shortly after he learned his daughters and grandson died in Guyana.

Jonestown Escapee Followed 'Moses' 22 Miles to Safety

Tinton Falls, N. J. —UPI— His name was Richard Clark, but they called him Moses as he led a small group of people out of Jonestown only hours before the mass suicides began in the Guyanese jungle.

Leslie Wilson, 21, said Tuesday that she had carried her 3 year old son, Jakari, on a 22 mile exodus out of the jungle, after Clark secretly gathered a group of people who wanted to leave the People's Temple.

Mrs. Wilson lost her husband, Joseph, 24, her mother, her sister and her brother-in-law in the Jonestown tragedy that ended in the deaths of more than 900 people.

Joseph Wilson's mother, Ann Freeland, who has never been to Guyana, lost 11 relatives including her son, two sisters and several nieces and nephews.

Mrs. Wilson, now at her mother-in-law's home here, said she wanted to leave Jonestown from the moment she arrived there from San Francisco 1½ years ago.

No Way Out

"Why did I stay? There was no way to get out. You had to plan it awfully carefully," Mrs. Wilson said.

But two weeks before the fatal visit of Rep. Leo Ryan, Mrs. Wilson began expressing her discontent to Clark's wife at the medical department where they both worked.

"There were very few people you could talk to. It was one of the worst crimes you could commit at Jonestown. Clark was the only one who knew who wanted to leave. He never told anyone. Either you trusted him or you didn't," Mrs. Wilson said.

"Then, one day, he said it was go," Mrs. Wilson said.

She said there was no sense in asking her husband and other family members because she knew they would not leave.

The group of about 11 persuaded a guard at Jonestown to let them go on a picnic, and they headed into the jungle following a set of railroad tracks, according to Mrs. Wilson.

Heard First Reports

Eight hours later, they arrived at the police station at Matthews Ridge and began hearing the first reports of suicide.

"We called him (Clark) Moses because he led us out," said Mrs. Wilson. She declined to reveal where Clark was now.

"I think more would have followed if more had known we were leaving," Mrs. Wilson said.

"I would never have chosen to leave with Leo Ryan. Walking out was a risk, but it was more of a risk to leave with Leo Ryan," she said.

Now, both Mrs. Freeland and Mrs. Wilson are waiting for the return of Joseph Wilson's body from Dover, Del.

"It is terribly hard. Everyone is waiting for that phone call. The waiting, the anticipation has been great, almost unbearable," said Mrs. Freeland, who is an elementary school teacher and associate pastor in Fair Haven, N. J.

Both women say they appreciate the generous gestures of friends, neighbors and relatives who are helping them deal with their grief.

"I've always been taught that death is something you have to deal with. I'm not upset to the point where I can't function. I feel a loss, a great loss. But I can't let it throw me back because I have a child to raise," Mrs. Wilson said.

"Jim Jones was the most egotistical person I've met in my life. He always wanted to go down in history. He did," Mrs. Wilson said.

Jonestown Physician Called a Sadist by Settlement Survivor

TINTON FALLS, N.J.—A survivor of the Jonestown tragedy says the doctor who purportedly mixed the poisonous fruit drink that killed hundreds of followers of the Rev. Jim Jones was a sadist who enjoyed watching people in pain.

Leslie Wilson, 21, who worked in the medical department at Jonestown, said Dr. Lawrence Schacht of Houston did little to relieve pain when people became ill.

"He was a sadist. He liked to see people in pain. He didn't do anything to relieve pain," Wilson said.

She returned from Guyana last week after leaving the settlement about eight hours before the mass suicides and murders began.

In San Francisco, a federal grand jury probe into the ambush killing of Rep. Leo J. Ryan (D-Calf.) was postponed by a federal judge who said subpoenaed survivors of the Peoples Temple settlement in Guyana needed time to recover from shock before testifying.

In Washington, a State Department spokesman said the department is "Leaning toward releasing a full list of the more than 900 victims, possibly by the end of this month. Several persons, including some reporters, have sought the names through the Freedom of Information Act but have had their requests temporarily rejected.

U.S. lists Jonestown victims who lack kin

WASHINGTON (AP)—The State Department Saturday released a list of victims of the Jonestown (Guyana) mass suicide who have no known next of kin.

Anyone knowing whereabouts of relatives may contact the department by phoning 202-632-3712.

Here are the names and ages of the victims:

Oreen (also known as Poplin) Armstrong, 84; Geneva M. Beal, 38; Daniel J. Beck, 10; Alfred Bell, 69; Beatrice C. Bell, 23; Elsie I. Bell, 60.

Donald R. Bower, 51; Kenneth B. Bowie, 18; Anthony Bowman, 14; Delores Bowman, 30; Luella H. Brown, 59.

Loreatha Buckley, 21; Ruthie (also known as Quinn) M. Cain, 38; Mary Francis Canada, 77; David Lee Chaikin, 15; Jose E. Chambliss, 76.

Sandra Yvette Cobb, 22; Arvelle Cole, 66; Mary Coleman, 84; Alma Coley, 54; Corlis D. Conley, 19.

CYNTHIA DAVIS, 29; Frances B. Davis, 50; Margaret V. Davis, 20; Lore B. Farris; Thomas R. Fitch, 29.

John L. Gardener, 18; Eugenia Gernandt, 55; Viola May Godshalk, 57; Dorothy L. Harris, 17; Josephine Harris, 70.

David B. Jackson, 86; Karen Jackson; Luvenia Jackson, 81; Ralph E. Jackson, 26; Thelma Jackson, 42.

Margaret James, 60; Daren Richard Janero, 14; Love (or Lave) Jay; Denise Johnson, 17; Helen Johnson, 51

Karl Johnson; Robert Johnson, 75; Rosa Johnson; Verna L. Johnson, 20; Ava P. Jones, 27.

Lew E. Jones, 22; Mary T. Jones, 24; Valerie Y. Jones, 20; Marie Kay; Elaine R. Keeler, 34.

Elfreida Kendall, 69; Lossie M. Lang, 74; Carrie O. Langston, 55; Henry L. Logan; Carolyn S. Looman, 35.

Love L. Lowe, 70; Lillian Malloy, 73; Irene Mason, 86; Virginia Middleton, 63; Lucy J. Miller, 65.

LUCY S. MILLER; Beverly D. Mitchell, 16; Tony L. Mitchell, 13; Betty K. Moore, 28; Leola K. Morehead, 52.

Lydia Morgan, 30; Lugenia Morrison, 51; Yvonne Morrison, 19; Joyce F. McIntyre, 21; Levatus V. McKinis, 72.

Earl McKnight, 83; Theodore D. McMurry, 20; Enola M. Nelson, 58; Winnieann Z. O'Bryant, 79; Marie Ollie.

Edna M. Oman; Victoria G. Parker, 8; Lucille E. Payney, 79; Lenora Perkins, 65; Amanda Poindexter, 97.

James R. Pugh, 61; Benjamin O. Robinson, 25; Anthony E. Rochelle, 6; Kay Rosas, 38; D'Andrea Moton Russell, 30.

Alida R. Santiago, 20; Karen L. Scott, 19; Rose O. Sharon, 71; Kivin Smith, 30; Dorrus H. Solomon, 21.

Wanda K. Souder, 25; Aurora M. Stewart, 11; Adeleine M. Strider, 74; Evelyn Thomas, 39; Etta Thompson, 79.

Larry H. Tupper, 19; Bruce E. Turner, 24; Deanna K. Wilkinson, 28; Curtis L. Winter, 63.

Cult intended to give millions to Russ

By Timothy McNulty
and Michael Sneed

Chicago Tribune Press Service

MATTHEWS RIDGE, Guyana—A sealed envelope from the People's Temple that accompanied $634,867 in cash earmarked for the Soviet consulate in Georgetown included a letter directing that an additional $7.3 million go to the Soviet government, it was disclosed Sunday at an inquest here.

Text of two cult letters on page 18

Text of two cult letters on page 18

The letter, revealed in testimony by Guyanese assistant police Commissioner Cecil Roberts, was written in the name of Annie McGowan, a 70-year-old cult member who died in the Nov. 18 mass murder-suicide in Jonestown. The letter was signed by McGowan and included account numbers of two Swiss banks in Panama, where the $7,284,536 is reportedly on deposit.

Including the newly disclosed secret funds, the known cash assets of the People's Temple amount to more than $8 million, including more than $1 million in cash found in the Jonestown area.

There also is speculation here that millions more may be found in a Venezuelan bank account opened in the name of Jim Jones' mistress, Maria Katsaris, who also left a will leaving her money to the Soviet Communist Party. Her passport showed she made seven trips to Venezuela in the six months before her death.

McGowan also made several trips out of Guyana in the weeks before the Jonestown tragedy, authorities said. Her passport showed five trips to Venezuela and Panama dating to Oct. 2.

The letter and McGowan's passport were found in a suitcase that three cult survivors said contained cash they were ordered to deliver to Soviet officials just as the cult's death orgy began.

THE LETTER was seized along with the suitcase by Guyanan soldiers as evidence for the coroner's jury inquest here. The inquest was concluded Sunday and a verdict is expected Wednesday.

The suitcase also reportedly contained five other documents, including letters instructing bank officials in Panama to send cashier's checks to the Soviet consul in Georgetown.

It was learned that one of the letters, which referred to the closing of an account in Panama, was dated Nov. 6, indicating that plans were being made to dispose of the funds 12 days before the mass suicide-murder in Jonestown.

There is some doubt among investi-

Continued on page 18, col. 1

Text of People's Temple letters

Chicago Tribune Press Service

MATTHEWS RIDGE, Guyana—The following papers were seized by Guyanan authorities as evidence for an inquest here Sunday. Both letters —dated Nov. 12, the day of the Jonestown carnage—direct how money deposited in banks in Panama and Venezuela is to be turned over to the Communist Party of the Soviet Union.

Mr. Fedor Timofeyev, consul
43 Chandre Nagar Street
Prashed Nagar
Georgetown, Guyana
Dear Comrade Timofeyev,

The following is a letter of instruction regarding all our assets, which we want to leave to the Communist Party of the Union of Soviet Socialist Republics. Enclosed in this letter are letters which instruct the banks to send the cashiers checks to you. I am doing this on behalf of the People's Temple because we, as Communists, want our money to be of benefit for help to oppressed peoples all over the world or in any way that your decision-making body sees fit.

There are two basic accounts which are in fixed time deposits. One is located in the Swiss Bank Corp., P.O. Box 3370, Panama 4, Panama. In this account are two deposits. One is for $557,000 and it is on a 30-day rotation so it can be withdrawn almost immediately, which the letter of instruction so instructs. The other is for $1,486,000, and it matures on July 6, 1978, so at that time you should receive a cashiers check for that amount.

The other account is located in the Union Bank of Switzerland, P.O. Box 6792, Panama 5, Panama. In this account are seven fixed-time deposits. The following is a list of the amounts and dates due [not including interest earned]:

$300,000, May 31 1979
$200,000, July 5, 1979
$1,622,000, July 25, 1979
$1,000,000, Aug. 21, 1979
$82,536, Aug. 29, 1979
$1,036,000, Sept. 21, 1979.
$1,000,000, July 20, 1979

The account number for the account at the Union Bank of Switzerland is 121-00-191a. The account number for the account at the Swiss Bank Corp. is 3357

With the enclosed letters you should have no difficulty in receiving the checks upon the above-mentioned maturity dates.

Signed cooperatively yours,
Annie J. McGowan

[Editor's note: Either the July 6, 1978, date or the reference to "matures," is in error, since the letter was dated Nov. 18, 1978.]

Handwritten note by Maria Katsaris, dated Nov. 18, 1978:

I, Maria Katsaris, leave all the money in the Banco Union de Venezuela in Caracas to the Communist Party, Soviet Union. The person to contact is Mr. Hedderich in Main Branch of Banco Union. This is my final wish before I die.

Maria Katsaris

Witness: Jim McElvane, Marilyn Bogue

Cult letter directs gift of $7.3 million to Soviets

Continued from page one

gators that the money belonged to Mc-Gowan. A senior government official said the Rev. Jim Jones preferred to use his followers as conduits for cult funds rather than make transactions in the name of the temple. Directions for the handling of the $7.3 million were apparently engineered by Jones, the official said.

"If this ploy was used to hide Temple funds, there could be millions stashed away in Maria Katsaris' bank account," Roberts said. "She was the banker, the key to everything. She knew where all the money was."

But attempts to determine the amount of money in the Venezuelan account have been unsuccessful, Roberts said.

The cash confiscated by the Guyanese army is being held by police here. "The money will remain here until a determination is made to whom it belongs, and the validity of the will is now a question for the lawyers," Roberts said.

The signing of Katsaris' will was witnessed by two persons, Marilyn Bogue and Jim McElvane, both of whom died at Jonestown.

MICHAEL CARTER, one of the three men who fled Jonestown with the suitcase bearing the will, described Mc-Gowan as "a very active senior."

"That was amazing about her," he said. "She was very old but very alert. She'd tell funny jokes all the time. She was a real sweet old lady."

McGowan, heavy-set, and about 5 feet, 6 inches tall, spent much of her time on sewing projects in Jonestown, including toys and dolls, he said.

A Guyanese police official said that among the papers in the suitcase was a will written by Jones' mistress, Maria Katsaris, leaving an unknown amount of money in the Banco Union de Venezuela, a bank in Caracas, to the Soviets.

KATSARIS "was a key to everything —she was the banker," a government source told The Tribune. "She knew where all the money was. She took care of the money."

During the first week of November, Katsaris and McGowan made several trips to Venezuela and Panama, according to documentation on their passports.

Katsaris, whose body was found lying on a bed in Jones' three-room cottage after the mass murder-suicide, bequeathed the money to the Communist Party in the Soviet Union, according to the will, which was dated Nov. 18 and witnessed by a man and a woman now dead.

McGowan's name was on the list of 613 cult victims identified by U.S. Air Force mortuary authorities, but she is listed as "unknown" in terms of place of birth, surviving family, and other identifying characteristics. However, her passport, one of several still retained by Guyanese authorities, says she was born on April 6, 1908, in Mississippi. The signature on the McGowan letter matches that on her passport, authorities say.

THE THREE cult survivors—Mike Prokes, 30, of San Francisco; Michael Carter, 20, of Boise, Idaho; and his brother, Tim Carter, 30, of San Francisco—said Katsaris gave them the large brown suitcase containing the cash with instructions to deliver it to "the embassy."

Guyanese officials originally said the amount totaled $500,000, but authorities now say it was $634,867 in U.S. currency and $137,661 in Guyanese currency. Officials said they also found more than $300,000 in U.S. currency about 2½ miles from the site of the airport massacre during the first week of this month.

Katsaris gave Prokes and Michael Carter each a handgun and instructed them to shoot themselves if captured, Michael Carter said.

The three said Katsaris did not specify to which embassy they were to go, and they did not know what the suitcase contained until they opened it to see why it was so heavy.

THE THREE said they took turns carrying the suitcase from Jones' cabin but, because it was so heavy, they opened it with the idea of lessening their load—and found they were carrying the cash.

They said they buried as much of the money as they could in the soil, loosening the dirt with the heels of their boots, and then covered the spot with banana leaves.

A few hours later, with the half-full but still-heavy suitcase, the men rested. That is when they opened the suitcase again and found the letter addressed to the Soviet embassy, they said.

Shocked by what they had found, they left the suitcase and the cash in a pigsty and headed toward Port Kaituma, they said.

The three came to authorities with $40,000 in their pockets.

TIM CARTER told police that he, his brother, and Prokes had been told privately by Katsaris that there was "going to be trouble" and that they were to meet her for "an assignment" at Jones' house in an orchard as most of the cult members were assembling in the commune's pavilion.

Katsaris put the cash into the suitcase in Jones's house, Tim Carter said.

362

Jones' son admits killings of 4 cultists

From Sun-Times Wires

GEORGETOWN, Guyana—The son of cult leader Jim Jones testified Monday that he killed four cultists the night that Jones and more than 900 of his followers perished in a suicide-murder ritual.

"Yeah, I killed them and was just trying to throw it off on Chuck [Beikman]," Stephan Jones, 19, said at a pretrial hearing for Beikman, who is accused of the murders.

Beikman looked startled at the unexpected confession, but said nothing.

A member of the California-based Peoples Temple discounted Jones' statement and Jones later told reporters he made the statement because "I was mad. I'm tired of being pushed around."

BUT POLICE PICKED Jones up Monday night for questioning about the statement. Police said Jones might remain at the police station overnight, but he had not been jailed and there was no arrest warrant or charge against him.

Cult member Paula Adams told reporters Jones wasn't in the cult's Georgetown house Nov. 18 when the killer slashed the throats of Sharon Amos, 42, and three of her children.

She said Jones "wasn't even there when it happened. I should know, I was there. He's doing this because he feels guilty about what his father did. How does a son pay back the guilt of his father?"

She was interviewed outside the courtroom and said she was among about 45 cultists in the Georgetown house when the victims were murdered in a bathroom.

JIM JONES AND SOME 900 followers were killed or took their own lives at the Peoples Temple settlement at Jonestown, 150 miles north of Georgetown.

In Washington, a Justice Department spokesman said Monday that the United States has taken steps to prevent the removal from secret bank accounts in Switzerland and other countries of more than $10 million stashed away by Jones and his cult.

Terrence Adamson said the United States has traced "more than enough funds to cover any government expenses" in connection with the Nov. 18 mass suicide-murder.

To recover the funds, the United States must first prove it has a valid claim to the money, which is still in the accounts, Adamson said.

THE SOVIET EMBASSY in Georgetown said Monday it knows nothing of reports the Peoples Temple ordered more than $7 mil-
lion in those accounts turned over to a Soviet official.

The spokesman denied knowledge of letters released Sunday that contain instructions to Swiss banks in Panama and Caracas, Venezuela, to turn the money over to Soviet Consul Feodor Timofeyev.

Stephan Jones made his startling statement when the prosecutor, Carlton Weithers, asked if he had been part of a conspiracy to commit murder.

During a recess after Jones' outburst, Weithers said, "There are no legal implications to Jones' statement. It just makes him less credit-worthy as a witness."

Weithers also said he would review the matter to determine if he would ask that Jones be named a co-defendant in the case. Jones had testified earlier that, as Adams claimed, he was not present when the murder took place.

BEIKMAN, 42, HAS been charged with murder and the hearing is to determine if there is sufficient evidence to bring him to trial.

He also is charged with the attempted murder of 12-year-old Stephanie Amos, who survived a 4-inch gash to her throat.

A murder conviction carries a death sentence.

Beikman's attorney also succeeded in having a statement by his client barred as evidence. In that statement, Beikman admitted being in the room where the murders occurred, but denied cutting anyone's throat.

When Jones was questioned during a recess, he said he made the statement because "I was being accused of conspiracy to murder my family, my loved ones and I was mad. I'm tired of being pushed around."

Beikman's hearing was adjourned until Tuesday.

A SIMILAR PRETRIAL hearing is to resume Wednesday in the case of Larry Layton, 32, who is accused of murdering Rep. Leo J. Ryan (D-Calif.) and four others. They were gunned down Nov. 18 in an airstrip ambush as the congressman was leaving Jonestown after visiting the commune to investigate allegations of mistreatment of cult members.

The government said Monday night that 18 more survivors of the Peoples Temple suicide-murders were free to leave the country.

That would leave 24 Americans of the San Francisco-based cult still detained for legal proceedings.

U.S. Acting to Secure Temple's $10 Million In 3 Banks in Panama

By JOHN M. CREWDSON
Special to The New York Times

SAN FRANCISCO, Dec. 19 — The Justice Department has located more than $10 million in funds deposited by the People's Temple in banks in Panama and has taken steps to freeze the money, a Government source said today.

The funds, which are on deposit in several Panamanian branch offices of Swiss banks, are believed to represent the majority of the assets amassed by the Temple's late founder, the Rev. Jim Jones.

The Government source said that he was uncertain just how the Justice Department had learned of the deposits, but added that "when we found out about it, we started diplomatic contact" with the Panamanian Government on the question of keeping the deposits intact.

U.S. Seeks to Recover Costs

The United States seeks to recover about $3.5 million in Federal funds spent in the last month for the removal of the bodies of hundreds of Mr. Jones's followers from the cult's settlement at Jonestown, Guyana.

Noting that the United States had taken "steps" to freeze the deposits, the government source said "that doesn't mean we can just run down there and get the money — there's probably going to be litigation in the Panamanian courts."

But he said that the United States had been assured that none of the temple members who are still alive could claim the assets until the legal question of ownership had been decided.

Correspondence found at Jonestown, in a suitcase containing several hundred thousand dollars in cash, bequeathed $7 million to the Communist Party of the Soviet Union.

That correspondence reportedly mentioned accounts in the name of the People's Temple or its members at branches in Panama of the Swiss Bank Corporation (Overseas) S.A., the Swiss Banking Corporation and the Union Bank of Switzerland.

The Justice Department has been searching for the temple's funds almost from the day that Mr. Jones and more than 900 of his followers died, most of them apparently by suicide. The mass deaths came a few hours after Representative Leo J. Ryan, a California Democrat, and three newsmen reporting on his visit to the Guyana settlement were slain.

State Dept. Sought Funds

Other sources have said that the State Department had asked the Justice Department to attempt to locate and report on the cult's funds, which according to some former Temple officials might total as much as $15 million.

The reason for the request, the sources said, was to determine whether sufficient funds would be available to compensate the United States for removing the bodies from Jonestown and transporting them to an Air Force facility at Dover, Del.

Late last month, a Federal grand jury here that is seeking evidence on several aspects of the temple's activities, including the possible existence of a conspiracy to murder Mr. Ryan, began issuing subpoenas for the records of banks in several countries, including Canada, where the cult was known to have kept its money.

Some of those banks are known to have been in Switzerland, and The New York Times last week quoted a Government official as saying that some or all of the temple's accounts in Switzerland had been emptied.

A Justice Department spokesman said that one of the former temple officials, Terri Buford, and her lawyer, Mark Lane, reportedly had traveled to Switzerland to remove some of the funds from a Zurich bank.

Mr. Lane denied, however, that either he or Miss Buford, who has said she withdrew from the People's Temple several months ago, had made such a trip or had withdrawn any money.

The lawyer said that his client had told the United States attorney here on Dec. 6 that most of $7.5 million in temple assets with which she was familiar had been transferred from a bank or banks in Switzerland to branch offices in Panama.

Mr. Lane is understood to have been seeking immunity from prosecution for Miss Buford, but it is not known whether such immunity has been granted.

Body of Cult's Leader
Is Cremated in Jersey;
Ashes to Be Scattered

CLARKSBORO, N.J., Dec. 19 (UPI) —
The body of the Rev. Jim Jones, the
leader of the People's Temple, was cremated Tuesday in southern New Jersey,
the manager of the crematory said.

A silver hearse carried Mr. Jones's
body from a funeral home in Dover, Del.,
to Eglington Crematory here, said the
manager, George Smith. The body, in a
coffin covered with a cardboard box, was
cremated shortly before 11 A.M., he said.

Mr. Jones's ashes were to be returned
to the Torbert Funeral Home in Dover
and later scattered over the Atlantic
Ocean from an airplane or boat, Mr.
Smith said.

Other Cremations Expected

He added that the bodies of other members of the Jones family who died at the
cult's commune in Guyana were expected
to be cremated here because of legal ob-
stacles in Delaware.

The bodies of the more than 900 persns
who died at the commune on Nov. 18 were
flown by the Federal Government to
Dover Air Force Base for identification
and other processing. Autopsies have
been performed on seven of the bodies at
the base's mortuary.

The autopsy on Mr. Jones's body
showed that he had "died from a contact
wound to the head which is not inconsist-
ent with a suicide," but which could also
indicate murder, said John Russell, a
Justice Department spokesman. An autopsy on the body of Anne Elizabeth
Moore, a cult member, found that she had
died of a "gunshot wound to the head
caused by a high-powered rifle or large-
caliber handgun," Mr. Russell said.

The causes of the deaths of the other
five cult members, including Mr. Jones's
mistress and the chief physician of the
commune, were undetermined pending
the results of tests, he said.

Jim Jones' memoirs reveal he believed in communism

New York Times Service

GEORGETOWN, Guyana — Jim Jones, whose People's Oemple settlement here espoused more socialism than religion, was a communist from the early 1950s on, according to a rambling, disjointed personal history found among his effects and published by the government-owned newspaper here.

Carl Blackman, editor of the Chronicle, Guyana's largest newspaper, said the 1974 document appeared to be Jones' personal writing and throughts.

The document implied throughout that Jones was always a communist and that he used his religious connections only to further communist ends and to politicize congregations.

Interviews with members of the People's Temple who survived the Nov. 18 death ritual indicated that the group had not been formally religious for several years, even though it registered as a religion with the State of California and paid federal income taxes based on rules for religious organizations. Survivors said they heard a great deal of socialist rhetoric.

Several survivors, like former farm manager Jim Boge, suggested that Jones' attachment to religion was not to the substance but to the technique. Jones, he said, had found evangelical speaking, music, faith healing and other tent-meeting techniques useful in attracting and controlling the many working-class members, particularly the aged, whose Social Security and government support checks were an important resource.

ACCORDING to the document, Jones, while studying at Indiana University "somewhere along in 1949-1950," became convinced there was a conspiracy in the United States to ostracize communists.

"And if you had any communist connections, your grandma or your cousin, or your trade union, you wouldn't get into this country (the United States). Immigration barriers were horrible. But Nazis kept coming in by the umpteen thousands. That is why I became very pro-Jewish. The strongest on the communist side were Jews. '

He recalled, "I was in a coma when the Rosenbergs (Julius and Ethel Rosenberg, convicted of treason in the sale of atomic secrets to the Soviet Union) were being executed. I was ready to die, infectious hepatitis." Jones said he would have "marched till there were holds in my shoes trying to petition" to save them and that he kept asking his wife, Marceline," "Are they dead yet?"

"I just died a thousand deaths. I wish I could have died then. Hell, you can have only so many revolutionary deaths," he wrote. Sometime after the Rosenbergs were executed, Jones said, "I quit crying. Don't cry anymore. Rough being a communist. Lot of persecutions would make good stories but I don't know how to get them out, too painful."

THE DOCUMENT continued: "I'd get picked up hitchhiking, talking communism — car would come to a screeching stop, and I'd be ordered out of the car, middle of nowhere. Happened not once but dozens of times."

It said that talking about communism was what put Jones in touch with a man he called Martin, a Methodist superintendent, who put him into his first church.

"He said I want you to take a church. I said, you giving me a church. I don't believe anything. I'm a revolutionary . . . and he appointed me, a communist, to a church, and I didn't even meet him through the party, I met him in a used car lot. This was in 1953," the document said.

At Jonestown there were no religious placards or outwardly religious trappings. There was a map of the Soviet Union, and a sign over Jones' mother's grave read: "Lynette P. Jones, in commemoration of a true fighter for the just, who gave the ultimate, a son, so he could serve the people in the struggle for justice, for freedom from oppression and for the foundations of socialism."

THE REV. DR. NELSON SMITH OF BIRMINGHAM

Minister looking for answers at Jonestown

BY RICHARD FRIEDMAN
News staff writer

The chilling mass suicide in Jonestown confronts Americans with deep and basic questions about their society, says a Birmingham clergyman now in Guyana.

"Jonestown needs to be studied continuously," believes the Rev. Dr. Nelson Smith, pastor of Birmingham's New Pilgrim Baptist Church and national chaplain for the Southern Christian Leadership Conference (SCLC).

The Guyanan tragedy should be studied by Americans especially, because most of the victims came from the U.S., Smith said Thursday in an interview from his Georgetown hotel, where *The News* reached him with a telephone call from Birmingham.

Smith arrived in Guyana early Wednesday. He is traveling with the Rev. Dr. Joseph Lowery, SCLC president, and the Rev. Dr. H.B. Gibson, a New York City clergyman.

The Birmingham clergyman said he

went to Guyana with some questions in mind. He wants to know, for example, why so many people would want to leave America for Jonestown.

SMITH ALSO notes that many were members of churches in the U.S. and wonders where the churches and the country failed those who turned to the Rev. Jim Jones and his Guyanan compound.

The tragedy raises important theological questions, he added, since it was "all done in the name of religion."

As of Thursday afternoon, bad weather had stopped Smith and the others from going to the Jonestown compound itself. He planned, if possible, to take the hour and a half helicopter ride to the village Friday morning.

Smith met with one Jonestown survivor and planned to meet with another. He would not reveal more details, saying the information was private.

"The trip has been quite rewarding," he said. In Guyana, he found a beautiful country, with a broad mix of people. "Apparently, they get along so well," he said.

Already, he believed, he could be more reflective about the Jonestown tragedy, though he said he was not quite ready to put his thoughts into words. "Let me reflect a little more on what I've found."

Smith believes his group is the first black group to investigate the tragedy. As a black clergyman, it was important for him to go, he said, because many who died were black and had left churches.

NOW, HE MUST PONDER the meaning of Jonestown. Smith and the others plan to report to a conference of black church leaders in San Francisco in early February.

From the moment the tragedy unfolded, says Smith, he's had an urge to learn more about what happened. "There's a message here," said Smith.

How many more Americans, he wondered, are searching for something? And how many more, he fears, may yet find a leader like Jim Jones?

Pressure for suppression of cults likely in wake of Jonestown horror

BY FR. JOHN B. SHEERIN
NC News Service

The Jonestown mass murder-suicide calamity was a shocker of the first magnitude.

It is a reminder that life is not always a paradise, not even in a rural setting that looks like a garden of paradise.

One American consular official in Guyana said he had thought at first that the jungle colony was little more than "an off-beat religious retreat." He was certainly surprised to find this tropical community rife with terror, deception, intimidation, large-scale murder, suicide, and brutal Marxist police-state methods for keeping the cult members in line.

The horror is over but undoubtedly there will be an aftermath in lurid press items about conflicting claims to property of the victims, real and personal, as well as rumors of the prosecution of certain survivors.

Like the vast tangled web of claims after an airplane disaster, this incredible mass murder-suicide involving 912 deaths will be the subject of discussion and lawsuits for long months to come.

ALREADY we have been hearing gossip and forecasts of what the future has in store. I heard a talk-show in Washington recently in which a very articulate caller demanded that hereafter the U.S. government should change its policy and stay completely out of the domestic affairs of other countries.

This was his way of leading up to the theme that Congressman Ryan had no business in going to Guyana to investigate the People's Temple community. That the human rights of Americans were involved did not seem to dawn on this caller.

I heard another talk-show in Washington in which the theme was the imperative need of cracking down on all religious cults pronto. Even before the massive horrors happened in the jungle colony, the U.S. State Department was under attack by critics who asked for action on their complaints about the cult.

When the calamity actually occurred, the critics contended that the State Department had been negligent in preventing the deaths.

The department reacted angrily, insisting that the U.S. consular officials had interviewed 75 members of the People's Temple in Guyana before the massacre and that not one had confirmed the allegations of the State Department had been receiving.

Ex-members of the cult responded they were browbeaten by the Rev. Jim Jones and forced to conceal their real views from consular officials. In fact, a former aid of Mr. Jones said in an affidavit that "Jones had instructed us that he had a spy working in the U.S. embassy and that he would know if anyone went to the embassy for help."

WHAT may come out of all this exchange between the State Department and the parents of the dead children is a new set of policies regarding complaints about "brainwashing," "kidnapping," "mind programming" and other violations of human rights.

Moreover, we might see some new legislation regarding the religious freedom of religious cults.

Of course, the Congress will not dare to tamper with First Amendment rights to freedom of religious belief. But it may possibly lay down some new directives about freedom to act under the First Amendment rights.

A Justice Department lawyer, Robert Keuch, said the U.S. government will be scrupulously careful about restricting religious activities. The right of freedom to believe is absolute, whereas freedom to act may be subject to regulation "but only to prevent grave and immediate dangers to interests which government may lawfully protect."

Keuch pointed out that members of cults are usually competent, consenting adults. Even if a sect requires its members to work long hours, to undergo indoctrination with little food or sleep, it is doubtful that the courts would look on such activities as a grave and present danger to society or to its members, at least not to the extent of inflicting on cult members criminal punishments.

At any rate, I think we will be hearing a lot about the need of suppressing cults in the near future.

It is well to keep in mind that Jonestown in the last few years was a Marxist colony and Mr. Jones enjoyed a personal cult or following but not a religious cult.

Many survivors of Jonestown stated that Mr. Jones had not conducted any religious services or discussions at the colony.

Cult Kept Huge Cache of Mind Warping Drugs

By Richard T. Pienciak

Georgetown, Guyana —AP— The Peoples Temple commune at Jonestown was stocked with thousands of doses of dangerous drugs smuggled into Guyana. Two Jonestown survivors said at least some of the drugs were used to brainwash or control would-be defectors.

An inventory of the drugs found in Jonestown shows large supplies of depressants. Survivors and law enforcement officials here said at least some of these were used to control the behavior of persons viewed as dangerous by the Rev. Jim Jones.

Included in the drug warehouse were Quaaludes, Demerol, Valium, morphine and 11,000 doses of a drug, Thorazine, used to calm manic depressives and others with extreme mental problems.

Profile of Drug Supply

Checks with medical officials and medical journals produced a profile of a drug supply that promotes suicidal tendencies, hallucinations, blurred vision, confusion, speech disturbances, involuntary movements and emotional highs and lows.

Because there are no records, it is impossible to say how frequently or extensively the drugs were used, but there was enough of some drugs to give the nearly 1,000 Jonestown residents 22 doses.

Various visitors to Jonestown have reported indications that these drugs were used liberally — perhaps forcefully on children and others — in the ritual in which more than 900 persons went to their deaths from drinking a cyanide laced soft drink.

Dr. Joyce H. Lowinson, a psychiatrist and member of President Carter's Strategy Council on Drug Abuse Prevention, said the list indicated "there were a lot of psychotic patients, or they (Peoples Temple) were using them to control people."

Control Defectors

Dale Parks, a nursing supervisor at Jonestown who is a trained therapist for respiratory ailments, said he knew some of the drugs were used to control would-be defectors in the commune's "extended care unit." But he professed

Turn to Guyana, page 14, col. 4

From Page 1

shock at the extent of the drugs found there, saying, "Oh my God, I don't believe it."

Parks fled Jonestown Nov. 18 with Rep. Leo Ryan, a California Democrat. A short time later, Ryan, three American newsmen and Parks' mother were slain at a remote airstrip.

"There's no way that many people were receiving treatment," Parks said in reference to the amount of drugs found in Jonestown. "I know they were using things to keep people under control, but not like this."

Separate Facilities

According to Parks, the control sessions took place in the extended care unit, eight beds separate from the regular medical facilities.

"If a person wanted to leave Jonestown or if there was a breach of rules, one was taken to the extended care unit," he said. "It was a rehabilitation place, where one would be reintegrated back into the community. The people were given drugs to keep them under control."

After a few days or weeks, the patients lost their desire to leave and no further behavioral problems were anticipated, Parks said. Asked about the use of drugs for brainwashing, he said, "It is a reasonable assumption that such went on in the extended care unit."

Another former Jonestown resident, who refused to let his name be used, said, "People who wanted to leave were fed drugs like Thorazine so they would come to their senses."

Some of the drugs were especially dangerous, such as Demerol. Therapeutic doses of it have precipitated unpredictable, severe and occasionally fatal reactions, according to medical journals.

Many of the drugs were not to be used on children; many were not to be used on the elderly. The fact that there were large numbers of both those groups at Jonestown point out even further the overstocking of these sensitive and potentially destructive items, medical officials said.

A partial drug inventory showed that the majority of the drugs were manufactured by US firms. They apparently were smuggled into Guyana by the Peoples Temple to get around the country's strict import regulations on pharmaceuticals.

Checks with some of the US firms that manufactured the drugs found at Jonestown brought denials of any involvement.

Temple Members Refuse to Testify

San Francisco, Calif. —UPI— Several members of the Peoples Temple who were in Guyana at the time of the assassination of Rep. Leo Ryan and the mass murdersuicides at Jonestown took the Fifth Amendment Wednesday when they appeared before a federal grand jury investigating the temple.

Tim Jones, 19, an adopted son of the Rev. Jim Jones, and Paul McCann, whose wife and three children died at Jonestown, refused to answer questions on the ground that they might incriminate themselves.

The grand jury is investigating whether the deaths of Ryan and four other persons in Guayana involved a conspiracy among temple members.

Profiles of Seven Whose Faith in Jim Jones Carried Them to Death in Guyana

The Rev. Jim Jones, who founded the People's Temple in Indianapolis in 1953 and perished with it last month in the tropical jungle that became its last refuge, had been followed there by young and old, black and white, the privileged the and poor, the well-educated and the barely literate. Following are closer looks at seven of the more than 900 who died at Jonestown, Guyana, on Nov. 18.

Jann Gurvich, 25; Poet Moved to Politics

Jann Gurvich read Shakespeare, studied law and translated Sanskrit. Everyone who knew her described her as brilliant.

But in a letter she wrote to the Rev. Jim Jones four months before she died in Jonestown, Guyana, the 25-year-old woman declared that that was "just not so."

"I'm educated but I'm not gifted with any extraordinary intelligence, and there's a big difference," she said.

Miss Gurvich grew up in New Orleans in a conservative, upper-middle-class family. Her father, Louis, operates the largest private patrol and detective agency in New Orleans.

The family decided that she should go to the best schools, and for 13 years Miss Gurvich attended a private academy in New Orleans, the Ecole Classique. Mr. Gurvich described it as white, upper-class and "quaint." It was there, he remembered, that she took fourth place in a statewide French contest.

It was also there, her father believes, that were planted the first seeds of the political radicalism she would later embrace: "Instead of turning out conservative, as you might expect from a school like that, she felt she had been given privileges that poorer blacks, for example, were denied."

In 1971, Jann Gurvich entered Newcomb University, which is affiliated with Tulane University in New Orleans. She was an honors student, and she become involved in the civil rights and antiwar movements on campus.

The next year she transferred to Vassar, but became ill and stayed just one semester. She went on to the University of California at Berkeley, where she majored in comparative literature and took her undergraduate degree in 1975.

Friends who knew her then said that she gradually began to read literature less and politics more and to express vaguely defined wishes "to be part of something" and "to be of service to society." She left behind her poetry and entered the Golden Gate University Law School in San Francisco.

Miss Gurvich, friends said, had a succession of boyfriends but no serious relationships. She spent so much time with her law studies and political causes, such as support for Chilean refugees, that she did not eat properly. Her health began to fail and, as school gave way to politics, so did her grades.

At some point she discovered Jim Jones and his peculiar brand of fundamentalist religion and Marxism seemed to fill a void. Carmen Garrett, a law-school classmate, recalled that "all she talked about was the People's Temple."

On Aug. 22, 1977, Jann Gurvich took a bus to Miami and got aboard an airplane for Guyana. As she left, she told Mrs. Garrett that she would try the life in Jonestown for two years, then return to to finish her legal studies.

But in the last letter that Mrs. Garrett received from her friend, a few weeks before Jim Jones, Jann Gurvich and most of the rest of Jonestown's residents died, the young woman said that she had decided to abandon the law to spend her life teaching children.

It had been the greatest joy of her life, she wrote, to teach the children of Jonestown and watch them grow up free.

The Willis Sneeds; They Cared for the Infirm

For most of their lives Willie and Clevyee Sneed didn't have much of their own, but those who knew them say they shared a passion for taking care of the infirm and those who had evenless.

Willie Delois Sneed, 59 years old when he died in Jonestown, was born in East St. Louis, Ill., and went to school there. His wife, Clevyee Louise, one year younger, was born in Covington, Tenn., and studied for a year at Le Moyne College in Memphis.

In the late 1950's, the couple moved to southern California. Mrs. Sneed took a day job as a nurse's aide at Victory Hospital in North Hollywood and another in the evening at a small sanitarium in West Los Angeles.

She liked the work, and after a few years of scrimping and saving she and her husband acquired a financial interest in the sanitarium. It was a financial success, and in 1967 they took over a larger facility, the 100-bed Fair Oaks Convalescent Home in Pasadena, Calif.

By then Mrs. Sneed, who is remembered by friends as an exceedingly pleasant and warm person, had become licensed as a vocational nurse. Although she shared the ownership of Fair Oaks with her husband, it was she who saw to the operation of the home while Mr. Sneed kept his job as a maintenance man for the Bank of America.

But Los Angeles health department officials say that Mrs. Sneed's concern for the sick and aged exceeded her abilities, and records there show that Fair Oaks was cited for a number of violations over the years.

The Fair Oaks home, officials said, was simply not managed well. There were not enough nurses, the medication control log was never up to standards, diets were found inadequate, the home itself fell further and further into physical decay.

But Fair Oaks was at least a financial success. The Sneeds drove a blue Cadillac and seemed to neighbors to have acquired some money. The Sneeds were well respected in Pasadena's large black community, where they lived in a neat, stucco, ranch-style house on a pleasant, tree-lined street. Through it all, they seemed never to lose sight of their religion.

The office at Fair Oaks was filled with religious pictures and objects, and one county official remembered an incident that showed the depth and nature of Mrs. Sneed's religious commitment.

His department's attention had been attracted to Fair Oaks because no funeral arrangements had been made for a patient who died a few days earlier. The official went to investigate and found the body surrounded by members of the immediate family, who were meditating over it.

The corpse had not been moved, Mrs. Sneed told him firmly, at the request of the family, whose church did not permit such a thing. She added, just as firmly, that she herself was a member of the church.

No one knows whether the Sneeds had joined the People's Temple at that point. But join they did and, with the State of California threatening to put them out of business, sold their failing rest home to a corporation in Seattle.

Whether they were driven to Jonestown by the loss of the home or by a thirst to finally succeed at being of service to the disadvantaged, no one can say. But whatever their reasons, Willie and Clevyee Sneed were disappointed for the last time in the Guyana jungle. Friends of the Sneeds in Jonestown say they were not at all happy there.

[Handwritten letter:]

Dear mommie + Daddy

How are you feeling,

as for myself Im very well and my diabetes is much better then ever.

How is g'unior doing please tell his i've ask about him and think of you all very often. I'm working still and in joy that very much The dogs are very under- standing I love them and the cats are my heart warmer I also love them. well iam here in Jones Town Guyana with all my friends from San Francisco were all very happy. much much happy. Love to you

From Elaine
Roslyn Pat

Constance Frohm, 23; Religious and Rootless

When Constance Frohm was attending high school in Houston a few years ago, she must have found the work easy. Her grades, teachers remembered, were well above average, even though she seemed to spend less time studying than writing the poetry for which she was known best.

"She was a very good student," Mary Getty, who taught a creative writing course for seniors at Houston's Austin High School, recalled. "She could finish her work and then start writing these poems. They were all about goodness, God or the bright Hereafter."

"I asked her once why she never wrote about other things, and she told me, 'My mind is mostly with God.'"

Even as a teen-ager, Constance Frohm lacked roots. She did not live at home with her mother, Mrs. Genevieve Rayford, but with a communal religious group. She told her teachers often of moving from place to place in Houston's black neighborhoods because members of her fundamentalist religious group were not permitted to live with a family for long, certainly not long enough to become close friends.

Mrs. Rayford, who still lives in Houston, refused twice to discuss any aspect of her daughter's life or her death. But records show that Constance was born Feb. 9, 1955, in Louisiana.

In 1973, the year when Constance Frohm graduated from high school with a high "B" average, she was living with N. C. Crain, a Baptist preacher, and his wife. It was that year that Jim Jones held a national convocation of People's Temple members in Houston, and during his stay they were preached at Mr. Crain's church.

A few months later, Miss Frohm left Houston and moved to California, where the Temple was based. The relatives and friends she left behind did not hear much more about her until her body was identified in Guyana.

The Rev. Bill Lawson, a Baptist pastor who conducted a memorial service for Constance Frohm in Houston earlier this month, said that she had seemed to be "a fiercely loyal girl."

"When her family didn't fill her needs, she clung to the pastors, and then transferred her loyalty to Jim Jones. I think she would have been loyal enough to commit suicide," he said.

"I can see why she would get into a group like that, the kind that looked to a brighter time and a better life. She always wrote about a better thing, a happier life. I guess because she didn't have one here."

Richard Tropp, 36; Scholarly, 'Private' Man

When Richard Tropp was pursuing undergraduate studies in English at the University of Rochester in his native New York in the mid-1960's, he left an indelible impression.

"Mr. Tropp," one faculty member there wrote, "is one of the three or four most brilliant students I've ever taught. Truly exceptional."

A member of the history faculty concurred. "Brilliant talents and great independence. He has the capacity to become a great teacher and a fine writer."

Within the People's Temple, according to former members, Dick Tropp's writing talents were put to good use by Jim Jones, who made him chief of the Temple's letter-writing unit, an efficient machine that ground out tens of thousands of missives to the politically powerful and otherwise influential people Mr. Jones wanted to cultivate.

Although Dick Tropp, the 36-year-old son of Jewish parents, was not reluctant to flaunt his academic credentials to the world outside — he received a master's degree in English from the University of California at Berkeley in 1967 — he was defensive about them with other Temple members.

After graduating from Berkeley, Dick Tropp taught English at Fisk University in Nashville and then at a junior college in Oakland, Calif.

In 1969, the year that he joined the People's Temple, Mr. Tropp moved to Ukiah, the northern California community where Jim Jones then had his base. He taught at a private ranch school for a year and then took a job as a machine operator, giving his earnings to the Temple's treasury.

In the fall of 1972, he joined the faculty of nearby Santa Rosa Junior College. Colleagues described him variously as an accomplished professional, a delightful person and a "private man."

During his years at Santa Rosa, Dick Tropp became increasingly involved with Mr. Jones and the Temple, as did his sister, Harriet, 28, who died with her brother at Jonestown, and his wife, Kathy, who is believed to be living in San Francisco.

If a Temple student fell into academic difficulty, she said, Dick Tropp was the one to smooth things out. But he also reported their failings to other Temple officials, who sometimes prescribed "counseling" or discipline.

When Jim Jones left California for Guyana in the summer of last year, Mr. Tropp went along, but, like many of Mr. Jones's other followers, apparently only to see how he liked the communal life in the jungle.

He did not resign his teaching post but quietly took a year's leave of absence, telling his associates only that he was engaging in unspecified religious missionary work.

No one at the college knew he had gone to Guyana until he wrote from Jonestown, asking that some of the well-thumbed books he had left behind be forwarded to him there.

Elaine Keeler, 27; Sought 'Promised Land'

"Well here I am in Jones Town Guyana with all my friends from San Francisco we're all very happy," Elaine Keeler wrote to her "Dear Mommie and Daddy" last month.

The letter arrived at the home of Mr. and Mrs. Irving Keeler at 2569 Seventh Avenue, near 148th Street, Elaine, who was born in New York 27 years ago, visited her parents there in August and September. She told them then that she was going to Guyana, and she tried to reassure them about the People's Temple and its leader, the Rev. Jim Jones.

A week after the letter arrived Elaine was dead and her parents were plunged into anguish. They succeeded in having her body found, identified and brought here for burial.

"She said Guyana was the Promised Land," Elaine's mother, Ellen Keeler, said in an interview in her office at Modern Photography magazine, where she is an editorial assistant. Mr. Keeler is a bridge operator.

"'It's so far away, so farfetched,'" Mrs. Keeler said that she and her husband told their daughter. "'Why don't you come home instead?'"

"We tried to argue, but she said no, because Jim said so. She insisted that it was the Promised Land. If you went there, you wouldn't want to leave. It has fresh fruit, fresh air and Jim said it is the only place on earth an atomic bomb cannot do any damage.

"She was the fourth generation of our family to go to the Abyssinian Baptist Church. Our family was never interested in 'off-beat' kinds of religions. We were against it."

Elaine joined the People's Temple three years ago in San Francisco. She had left her parents' home here to "be on her own," according to her mother.

Not long after joining the People's Temple, Elaine went to live in its Redwood Valley commune. She wrote her parents "how she was taking care of animals and the elderly, what compassion the church had, how beautiful all the brothers and sisters were, no racial barriers, everyone the same," Mrs. Keeler said.

The Keelers' only other child, Irving Jr., a high school teacher in Queens, went to California to check on his sister. He reported to his parents that his sister looked well.

When Elaine came back for a month's visit with her parents last summer, "We saw only positive changes," the mother said. "She was calmer, more receptive to her parents, solicitous about her grandmother, willing to do what she was told, willing to do housework."

In her final brief letter to her parents, Elaine, who had hopes of taking up veterinary medicine, wrote: "The dogs are very understanding. I love them and the cats are my heart-warmer. I also love them."

Mrs. Keeler does not know how her daughter died. She has not received a death certificate. She assumes that Elaine was not shot, because among the documents accompanying the body

to New York was one reporting that there were "no obvious signs of trauma."

Elaine Roslyn Keeler, sometimes called "Pat," was born in Morrisania Hospital in the Bronx May 8, 1951. Her parents were then living at 2415 Williamsbridge Road, the Bronx. They moved to Berkeley, Calif., when she was 4 years old. She attended Longfellow Elementary and Willard Junior High Schools there and graduated from Berkeley High School.

She came back to New York with her parents in 1963 and lived with them until 1974, when she moved to California. Surviving Miss Keeler, in addition to her parents and her brother, is her grandmother, Lydia McCloud, also of Manhattan.

Ellen Dupont, 48; All Her Marriages Failed

By the time Jim Jones found her lying drunk outside his People's Temple in Ukiah, Calif., Ellen Peterson Kerns Dupont had failed at three marriages and had long since released her dreams of becoming a writer.

But Mr. Jones had a talent for kindling dreams, and Ellen Dupont later told her daughter, Jeanette, that the preacher with the beneficent smile had been the first man to recognize her literary talents.

"The People's Temple offered my mother all the things she had been looking for," Jeanette said of the woman who had struggled between jobs and household chores to write poems about the pain of raising four children alone.

Ellen Peterson was born in Tucson, Ariz., in November 1930, the third child of a construction worker. She was pretty and popular in high school, was a good student and had ambitions of attending college until, a year after her graduation, she met and married Rollin Kerns, a sailor.

Mr. Kerns was away for long periods and his wife grew frustrated and lonely. Finally, in 1960, the couple was divorced and the mother and children left their comfortable, middle-class home near Norfolk, Va., for what was to be a far more chaotic life in California.

"I think that's when my mother's problems began," Jeanette said. "Before the divorce, my mother had been a meticulous housekeeper who never drank and who had the time and energy to teach us everything from swimming to playing the guitar. After the divorce she was devastated. She had to work at low-paying jobs she hated because all my father could afford to send her was $200 a month."

After two years on her own, Ellen Kerns married Donald Dupont, a widowed engineer with five children. Mr. Dupont purchased a beautiful home in Lancaster, Calif., but the marriage broke up after only a year over differences on raising the children.

Lessons for Society from the Jonestown Tragedy

The murders and mass suicides which took place recently in Jonestown, Guyana are one of the most stunning and tragic stories of all time. Nothing else like it apparently has ever happened in history. The sadness of it is indescribable. Our purpose here is to cite briefly lessons which society can learn from the event. Among these are:

(1) The unbelievable can happen. Until the Jonestown catastrophe it seemed unthinkable, impossible, that hundreds of adults and young people would take their own lives and that parents would commit the horrible act of taking the lives of their children, including the little babies. As Tom Brokaw said on NBC's "Today" program, "It was hard for the mind to take this in." Sinclair Lewis' novel, *It Can't Happen Here*, point of which was that dictatorship could happen here in America, conveys the fact of the possibility of many more unbelievable occurrences. Indeed it is possible for the horrors of Jonestown to happen again.

(2) Religion can be perverted from its divine intent. This fact is as old as the attempt of Simon the magician to secure the power of the Holy Spirit for his own ends (Acts 8:18 ff.), but the lesson needs to be kept in people's minds. The tragedy in Jonestown, a community established in the name of religion and by a religious leader, underscores this fact a thousand times. The Christian religion, whose Lord came to bring his followers abundant life, in the instance of Jonestown was perverted to mean death, and Christ's principle of love in the end there was set aside for the method of violence.

(3) The Jonestown tragedy emphasizes the value and strength of institutional religion as contrasted with cult religion centered around a self-designated individual leader. The branches of government need a system of checks and balances such as those richly provided in the Constitution of the United States. Checks and balances also are needed in religious organizations. These are provided in the institutional church. The People's Temple founder, the Rev. Jim Jones, according to United Methodist Communications, had failed to measure up to the requirements for admission to one institutional church, the United Methodist, the Indiana Conference having refused him admission as a candidate for the Methodist ministry because, it is reported, he apparently did not meet the psychological tests. He later became a part of an institutional church, the Disciples of Christ, and was apparently in good standing as a minister in that denomination until his death. Nevertheless he had quite evidently departed from the mainline path and pattern of his denomination and had become in effect a rule unto himself, going his own individualistic way.

(4) The business of Christianity is not fleeing the world, as the Jonestown community was doing in settling in Guyana, but remaining in the world and seeking to change it. The eminent church historian, Professor Roland H. Bainton, several years ago made this observation in reference to the ineffectiveness of the monasteries, which the church of the Middle Ages established. As Jesus expressed it in his petition for the disciples in his prayer in the Upper Room, "As thou didst send me into the world, so I have sent them into the world" (John 17-18).

(5) Church and world are not to go "witch-hunting" as a result of the Jonestown tragedy. That the leader there went awry does not mean at all that anybody is to be deprived of freedom of religious belief and practice. According to the *New York Times*, several spokesmen, including representatives of the United Church of Christ, the Union of American Hebrew Congregations, the National Council of Churches and the Carter Administration, have warned against "open season on the cults" and have urged the spirit of tolerance in this situation. Dr. Everett C. Parker of the United Church of Christ reminded that "anytime *your* civil rights are threatened, *mine* are the next to go."

(6) Every church, general and local, and every Christian disciple needs constantly to allow the light of the judgment of Christ to flow in upon purposes, plans, programs, performances so that it is Christ who reigns in institutional and individual Christian discipleship.

(7) Guyana is one place on the globe where tragedy occurred. Around the world and right around where most people are many tragedies are taking place — war, poverty, prejudice, greed, people dwelling in fear, people without the gospel, people without medical ministrations, hosts of other ills in the life of mankind. Society is warped and perverted in its own way as long as it accepts, in any way fosters, and does not act mightily to remove these blights.

Body of massacre victim returned to Evanston

By LORRAINE BANNON

Lore Bee Parris, was a familiar sight in Evanston in the early and mid-'70s. She always wore a long, bright white dress, carried a Bible everywhere she went, and regularly fed the pigeons at the Ridge Av., Emerson St. and Green Bay Rd. inter section.

Then she disappeared.

Mrs. Parris left Evanston in 1977 for California without telling her family or friends. "We couldn't get her on the phone," (at her apartment at Ebenezer-Primm Towers) recalled Jutta Hayes, wife of Mrs. Parris' stepson, Wayne. "Finally we got a call from her, saying she was in California with 'some people from church.' "

The "people from church" were the Rev. Jim Jones' People's Temple. From California she went to Guyana. And on the Friday before Christmas the Hayeses learned that Mrs. Parris, an ordained Baptist minister, had died in the "Jonestown massacre."

NEWS THAT the 68-year-old woman was one of the victims was uncovered by Melvin Smith of Evanston, editor of the CCC newsletter, who spent five weeks in a nationwide inquiry and investigation of the Jonestown dead. Mrs. Parris' death was con firmed by the U.S. State Department.

Mrs. Parris' body, along with hundreds of others of Jim Jones' dead followers, was shipped by the State Dept. to Dover, Del. where it was embalmed and awaited burial arrangements, which were left up to the families of massacre victims. Smith offered to raise money to pay the burial expenses, but the Hayes couple made their own arrangements.

There will be a closed-casket funeral service at 10 a.m. today in House of Thompson chapel. Burial will be in Sunset Memorial Cemetery, Northbrook.

Jutta Hayes said that she and her husband have not been told how Mrs. Parris died. "I can't believe she killed herself. I can't believe she would take her own life," she repeated.

JUTTA HAYES told of the letters she and her husband received from Guyana in which Mrs. Parris said she was "down here with Christian people I love." "The letters were positive. She said she was going to learn Spanish."

Wayne Hayes added that he did not recall his step-mother ever mentioning Jones' name in the letters.

Mrs. Parris helped to raise Wayne Hayes, whose own mother deserted him in infancy. Wayne grew up in Evanston, attended Foster (now King Lab), Haven Middle School and Evanston Township High School. He and his wife live in Chicago.

Mrs. Parris, who was born in Chicago, was ordained a minster by the Baptist Church of the Good Shepherd in St. Louis Mo., where she had lived before coming to Evanston. She arrived sometime in the '50s.

"She was deeply religious and a dear woman," said Jutta Hayes.

One year after Jonestown, cults still unchecked

Kenneth Wooden

Some survivors still believe in Jones; Kids are author's one-man crusade; Page 2

The Rev. Jim Jones, murderer of 276 children, left us a mocking message when he died one year ago in Guyana.

The message is still there, painted on a board above the throne where Jones presided over the deaths of the children and 635 other human beings in the Jonestown settlement on Nov. 18, 1978:

"Those who do not remember the past are condemned to repeat it."

I think we as a nation have not remembered well enough what happened there in Jonestown, or how and why it happened.

Jones was a madman who skillfully used psychological techniques and financial chicanery to lure hapless and innocent people into joining his cult, the Peoples Temple, and to hold them as hostages to his will.

AFTER THE JONESTOWN tragedy, it was surely legitimate to examine the tactics of other cults that have proliferated across the country during the decade now ending. There were, and are, obvious questions to be asked. But timid politicians have refrained from asking them.

President Carter has warned against "excessive" governmental interference with religious groups, even though the courts have ruled that the cult issue has nothing to do with religious freedom.

There has been total silence from California Gov. Edmund G. Brown Jr., in whose state the Peoples Temple was founded and who in fact was the legal guardian of many of the slaughtered children.

Two hasty federal investigations have been conducted, and found no one at fault.

Established religious leaders have joined forces with civil libertarians to frustrate state legislative investigations of groups including the Unification Church, the Love Family (Church of Armageddon), the Children of God, Scientology, Foundation Faith Ministries and The Way, International.

THE PEOPLES TEMPLE was unique. I do not mean to suggest that the leaders of these other groups share Jones' murderous motives. But the groups do employ many of the methods used by Jones to manipulate and dominate his disciples:

● Jones coerced his followers into signing over their properties and personal valuables to the Peoples Temple.

Love Family has maneuvered its renamed members into signing notarized statements reading: "LAST WILL AND TESTAMENT. I hereby bequeath all my worldly assets to the Church of Armageddon ... and further decree that the Church has full power of attor-

ney concerning my old name."

● Jones refused to allow children to leave Peoples Temple when their parents defected.

After he left Love Family, Steven Earl Fisher was told that "I need no longer be concerned about my son, because the Love Family was his total and absolute guardian."

● Jones and his lieutenants harassed and threatened ex-members and kept them in constant fear.

In Fairfax, Va., a state judge ordered members of The Way, International, to stop harassing the Bell family, who successfully won back their daughter from that sect. The father told Judge Burch Millsap: "They want my daughter back. We're frightened to death."

● Guyanan police reported that documents from the office of Rep. Leo J. Ryan (D-Calif.) were found in Jonestown, suggesting that Peoples Temple burglars broke into the late congressman's California office before he flew to his death in Guyana.

Two Church of Scientology members face federal trial on charges of removing records and other documents from Justice Department and Internal Revenue Service offices in Washington, D.C.

● Jones controlled parents and children by destroying the family unit and promoting himself as the members' one and only "father."

The "120 Day Training Manual" of the Unification Church describes parents who desire their children returned as "Satanic."

● Peoples Temple children were forced to beg on street corners.

Teen-age members are instructed to beg money for "spiritual uplift" by HARP (High School Assn. for Research of Principle), a front organization for the Unification Church.

● Peoples Temple children were routinely abused, neglected and denied medical attention—resulting in at least one needless pre-Jonestown death.

A young mother of the Foundation Faith Ministries, a Southern cult, was ordered to leave her gravely ill 2-month-old baby at the foundation's headquarters and go beg for money at the Atlanta airport for six straight days. Upon her return, she found the baby had died.

● Jones used authoritarian brainwashing techniques to recruit and indoctrinate children and adults.

THE MESSAGE FROM JONESTOWN: Amid the bodies and Jim Jones' throne, a paraphrase of the famous warning of writer-philosopher George Santayana. (AP)

A Unification Church defector told New York legislators of church plans to place members in teaching positions in public schools, where classes would be structured to use brainwashing techniques on pupils.

● To undermine the family unit, Jones encouraged and compelled Peoples Temple members to engage in bizarre sexual practices.

Children of God leaders have been accused of forcing members to engage in illicit and incestuous sex, and of sending young female members into the streets to lure male recruits with offers of sex.

Despite all this, our President and other politicians will speak no evil of the sects.

Their silence parallels the stillness of Jonestown.

THE HUMAN LOSS can never be measured: The baby shoes that will never be bronzed ... the dolls that will never be loved ... the sneakers that will never wear out at the toes nor be covered with dust from play. The toys and games, like the children, are lost in the larger political games of Washington and California and other states across America.

Candlelight memorial

A candlelight memorial service and vigil for the slain children of Jonestown will be held Sunday night at the First Congregational Church of Christ in Washington, D.C., sponsored by the Committee of Remembrance For the Children of Jonestown and Their Loved Ones.

The committee will sponsor similar observances Sun-

day in cities across the country, including one following morning services at Quinn Chapel A.M.E. Church at 24th and Michigan in Chicago.

Formation of the committee—by Chicagoan Kaye Jarrett—was inspired by a series of Sun-Times articles last June in which Sun-Times special correspondent Kenneth Wooden detailed the horrors of Jonestown and proposed a candlelight vigil for the children in Washington on the anniversary of their deaths.

374

Some Jones followers still believe in him

Lidia Wasowicz

SAN FRANCISCO—The church founded by the Rev. Jim Jones—whose final exhortation to his faithful one year ago left 913 bodies lying bloated in the jungles of Guyana—has been ordered dissolved and all its property has been sold at auction.

The old former synagog where Jones once delivered his fiery sermons and performed his "miraculous" healings belongs to a Korean evangelist now, and all physical signs of the Peoples Temple have been removed.

But not all traces of the death church have disappeared. Some of its members still believe in Jones' preachings and teachings. Some pay furtive visits to the old brick building in the Fillmore district ghetto where Jones drew them in.

"They never come inside. They just sort of stop on the sidewalk and look at the building, sometimes for a long time, then walk away," says Elder Ho Bae, who bought the structure for $300,000.

PROFITS FROM THE AUCTION, as well as cash found in the sect's bank accounts in Guyana, Panama and around the Caribbean, total $11 million, according to the court-appointed receiver for the church, Robert Fabian.

Charles Touchette, one of the survivors, cites estimates of the sect's worth—including secret bank accounts and the Jonestown assets—as high as $66 million, which still isn't enough to satisfy the many claims against the church.

In all, $1.78 billion is sought in 679 claims filed against the Peoples Temple by a number of businessmen and by survivors and relatives of those who died. Fabian is to decide how the money should be divided.

"The Guyanese government has filed so many suits, we don't expect to see any of the $3 million that's in that country," he says.

IN A CROSS-SUIT IN GUYANA, eight survivors—including Larry Layton and Charles Beikman, who face charges in the deaths—have asked to be declared the only heirs to Jones' fortune.

Litigation is expected to take months.

Meanwhile, the survivors struggle to take their place in the world Jones denounced.

The majority of the 81 who survived the death rite have settled in the San Francisco area, where in 1971 the mesmerizing preacher had set up the headquarters for his mostly black congregation.

"After an initial period of confusion and culture shock, they are doing extremely well in what for them is starting from scratch," Dr. Chris Hatcher says.

Hatcher, a psychiatrist at the University of California's Langley-Porter Institute, was appointed by San Francisco Mayor George Moscone—who was slain nine days after the mass suicides—to help the survivors resettle.

"FEAR, HOSTILITY, ANGER AND mistrust dominated the days immediately following the tragedy. Jones had predicted that those who survived would be haunted by society for the rest of their lives, that they'd never be allowed to escape the label of Jonestown," Hatcher says.

"And social reaction reinforced those predictions."

One former temple member applying for a job as a car salesman said later the interview ended abruptly and he was thrown out of the office as soon as the manager learned of his background.

But most survivors have managed to find jobs. Only two of the dozen former temple members interviewed by UPI were without work, and one of them was a 68-year-old retired janitor.

"It's amazing how these people are surviving. For them, it's like recovering from an earthquake that destroyed their family, property, all they had," says Yvonne Golden, principal of Opportunity II High School, once attended by as many as 100 Peoples Temple children.

Bea Orsott: "I was so mad when I found out I missed the end. I wish I had been there to share in the final moment of unity. I don't know how those who were there Nov. 18 and left can live with themselves."

Two former temple members, including a 17-year-old Jonestown survivor, are graduating from the school this year. "and they're doing just beautifully."

Many have gone to extremes to find privacy, but some still defend Jones and his final command triggering the mass deaths, including his own.

"Jim had no other choice. He knew his people would rather take their life than go against what they believed. I was to have left for Jonestown in a few weeks. If I'd been there, you wouldn't have to ask me twice to kill myself," Judith Merriam, a private duty nurse, says.

"The government would have come in and arrested everybody and brought them back to the United States, where our children would be taught racism and our seniors would be placed in convalescent hospitals. Jim always made the right decisions, even in the end."

Her eyes misty, her voice husky, she whispered, "I'll show you something I've never shown to anyone outside the Temple before."

FROM INSIDE HER BLOUSE, she removed a faded snapshot of a smiling Jones with a raven perched on his finger.

"I put this picture over my chest when I get a pain there, and the pain goes away. That's what Jim did for the poor, the elderly, the oppressed. He lessened their pain."

Bea Orsott, a former legal secretary for the Internal Revenue Service, was in a dentist's chair in Georgetown when her husband and other Temple members drank the cyanide-laced soft drink.

"I was so mad when I found out I missed the end. I wish I had been there to share in the final moment of unity. I don't know how those who were there Nov. 18 and left can live with themselves."

Sandy Bradshaw, 33, a former probation officer who was alleged by some Temple defectors to head a Peoples Temple "hit squad" in the Jonestown aftermath, says she, too, would have died willingly.

"It was the best life we've ever known. . . . I wish in having shared so much life with them, I could have shared in their death," she says, wiping away her tears.

LIKE SEVERAL OTHER SURVIVORS, Bradshaw, who works as a defense attorney, says she thought of killing herself.

"But Jim taught us to help others, so that's what I'm trying to do now. Some people will themselves to die. I've willed myself to live."

Even in view of the deaths, Opportunity II Principal Golden says, "I cannot say a bad word against Jim. The Temple children were always the best, most mature students."

"I still weep when I read these," she said, pointing to a stack of letters on her desk.

"I am writing to tell you of a beautiful life we all live here in Guyana," Linda Mitchell, 17, had written just a few weeks before her death. "This, my friend, is the only way to live."

Kids are author's one-man crusade

Rudy Maxa

WASHINGTON—Nearly a year after the horror of the Jonestown (Guyana) mass suicide-murder, 210 of the 276 children who died there are still unidentified.

Some children were wards of the state of California. No one has yet explained why government officials overlooked the fact that the state wards wound up living in the jungles of Guyana while federal payments earmarked for their care fattened the coffers of Jim Jones' cult.

"The FBI told me they didn't have the time or money to identify all the victims, and it wasn't a priority," says author Kenneth Wooden, who wrote the article on the first page of today's Views section. "And that's in keeping with the way kids are treated around the country.

Those with the lack of power are at the bottom of the list."

Wooden, 44, who lives in Bucks County, Pa., knows about forgotten children. His 1976 book, "Weeping in the Playtime of Others," was a highly acclaimed account of institutionalized violence against youngsters in reform schools and detention centers. In recent years he has worked with CBS' "60 Minutes" on reports of child pornography, child neglect and interstate commerce of children.

Last spring, a tip led him to investigate the role children played in Jones' hellish empire. The Chicago Sun-Times published his findings in a seven-part series that detailed in wrenching fashion the financial boon children represented to Jones; the use of children as prostitutes to curry favor with at least one politician, and the value of children in keeping parents under Jones' rule.

Wooden has been lobbying for months in Washington to speed up the identification of the young victims of Jonestown. "It's crucial for the identification process to be carried out," argues Wooden, "because there are some people in California who share some heavy responsibility for not monitoring those kids—to say nothing of the fact that parents would like the bodies of their children back

for a decent burial." Most were buried by bulldozer in a mass grave in Guyana.

Before burial, however, government officials did fingerprint, X-ray and photograph the bodies, and Wooden is working through California courts to become legal guardian of the unidentified victims in order to gain access to those documents.

Wooden's efforts are a labor of love born out of his childhood in Burlington, N.J. He was a punk and arsonist who graduated from high school unable to read. Drafted to fight in Korea, Wooden was introduced to classical music and books by fellow soldiers with college educations.

He married the woman who tutored him through Glassboro State College. After four years of teaching high school history and a few years of political organizing, he was appointed by former New Jersey Gov. William Cahill to help study the state's penal system.

"I came full circle," he remembers. "I saw kids locked up, and it reminded me of Ken Wooden, a real high school vandal. There but for the grace of God. . . ."

And then the rebel knew he had a cause.

Rudy Maxa writes for the Washington Post.

JONESTOWN

How Jim Jones "Conditioned" His Sheep For Death

". . . For false christs and false prophets will arise, and will show great signs and wonders, so as to lead astray, if possible, even the elect." Matthew 24: 24-25.

By Joe Shea

Father Divine was a black "religious" leader of the '30s. He had several wives and lovers, some white and some black. One of them, Ruth Boaz, a white woman, joined Divine in 1932 and stayed with that self-styled "messiah's" Kingdom of Divine for 30 years. She finally broke free of his influence and wrote an in-depth article describing her years of virtual slavery and the Kingdom's tight-knit hierarchy.

"Father Divine used to dramatically return all contributions and donations sent to him by outsiders," revealed Ruth Boaz in a searing story of her deception printed in *Ebony* magazine in 1962. "By so doing," Ruth Boaz wrote, "he cleverly built up an image of a man who demands nothing and takes nothing. Secretly, however, he collected millions from his consecrated followers."

She said that Divine organized his Kingdom of Divine on a cooperative basis around 1932, at the height of the Depression, when people were desperate for anything to believe in.

"An odd collection of neurotics, misfits and fanatics held together by a fearful discipline and a mystical, unquestioning belief in the small, shrewd Negro who is their leader," she wrote of the world-wide Father Divine organization, which counted several hundred whites in Switzerland, and an equal number in Australia, among its followers.

"The grip of Father Divine upon his followers is so inexorable that very few ever escape," she wrote in *Ebony*. "Only a few have succeeded in shaking themselves free from the spiritual shackles of this man. A

(Please turn to page 3)

Miracle cures of diseases, broken bones and drug problems, especially alcohol addiction, are frequently claimed by various groups preying on the unsuspecting. Jim Jones went even further: After a People's Temple service, Jones went out for a stroll, flanked by his lawyer, his bodyguard and several churchgoers.

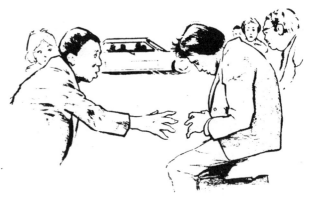

Suddenly, from around a corner, a black limousine appeared and attacked Jones with a burst of machine gunfire.

Covered in blood and apparently beyond all hope of recovery, Jones was carried back into his temple by his assistants.

A "miracle!" Jim Jones was quickly "restored to health." In less than 30 minutes, he removed his shirt, covered with tomato sauce in true Hollywood fashion, and reappeared "whole once more."

Jones' "miracles" were so elaborately staged that they convinced even the most skeptical viewers. His professional make-up artists transformed six young women into six wrinkled, arthritic old women.

He lay hands on her and "melted" off the woman's old age.

After about six months, Jones pretended to notice one of the women for the first time. He said, "I see that you are suffering from arthritis in your old age ... Because of your great faith in me, I am going to restore your youth."

AN INNER CIRCLE OF "ANGELS"

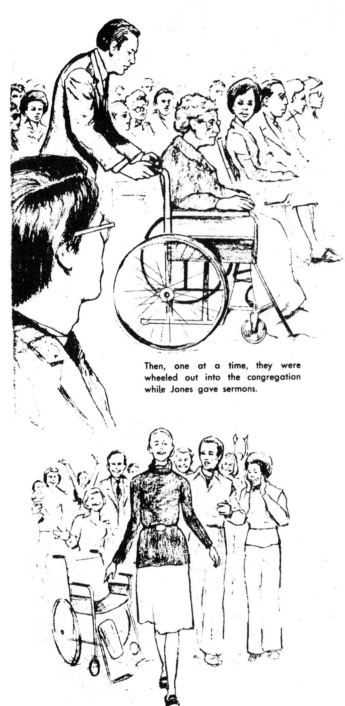

Then, one at a time, they were wheeled out into the congregation while Jones gave sermons.

Amidst thunderous "alleluias" from the audience, the "rejuvenated" woman discarded her wheelchair and strode happily down the aisle. At five other meetings, Jones worked the same "miracle."

In Jim Jones' case, the answer lay partly in a highly-polished blend of illusion, trickery and carefully-manufactured images whose dramatic quality captivated the attention of spellbound worshippers at his Geary St. headquarters in the slums of San Francisco.

(Continued from page 1) number have actually left the movement, but live in a form of mental bondage conditioned by a strange, nameless fear."

Those words, written in the 1960s, are chillingly prophetic to Americans who remember the awful carnage at Jonestown, Guyana, a little over a year ago. Like Father Divine, Jim Jones amassed a group of followers who were so well conditioned by him and his inner circle of "Angels" that thousands of them turned over their savings, property and weekly earnings to his "People's Temple."

How do men like Father Divine and Jim Jones "condition" their followers so deeply that they obey their every command, however strange and destructive? In Jim Jones' case. the answer lay partly in a highly-polished blend of illusion, trickery and carefully-manufactured images whose dramatic qualities captivated the attention of spellbound worshippers at his Geary Street headquarters in the slums of San Francisco.

Before Phil Tracy and Malcolm Kilduff of *New West* magazine exposed this vicious, capricious, violent

(Please turn to page 4)

Twin Circle, Sunday, January 27, 1980

PRACTICE MADE PERFECT

(Continued from page 3)
fraud in an article that dozens of Jones' business and political cronies tried to suppress, he led thousands of his congregation to believe that he could perform miracles, heal himself and others, restore lost youth and even eavesdrop on other persons' thoughts.

How Did He Do It?

Basically, Jones was a master showman. Using techniques that probably were picked up from his many friends in show business, he played on what one disillusioned follower called the "incredible vulnerability of the human mind" to astound and convince his constantly-expanding congregation.

Jones made a practice, for instance, of telling followers that his enemies, the CIA and Ku Klux Klan or Mafia, were out to get them and him. By constant repetition of this idea, he got followers constantly on guard and nervous about strangers.

But Jones went even further. On a sunny day, Jones strolled proudly with his followers and assistants in front of his temple. As they walked down the street, two sleek black Cadillac sedans pulled up to the curb beside him. The windows slowly rolled down, revealing menacing thugs in dark suits, hats pulled down over their eyes, armed with pistols and rifles.

Abruptly they opened fire. Blood exploded all over Jones' body, and he fell to the street. Amid screams and shouts from the crowd of worshippers, his close assistants carried him into the temple and left him in seclusion. While the congregation wailed outside, and suspense grew, Jones waited. Fifteen minutes after his shooting, he re-emerged from seclusion, miraculously "healed" by his own hands. Later, he was to place the bloody, bullet-riddled shirt he wore in a glass case in the People's Temple lobby as a reminder to devotees of his awesome powers.

The secret, of course, was a blood 'n guts Hollywood illusion you may remember from the movie, "Bullit," in which a man is gunned down by machine gun at close range as he jumps up from bed. Packets of ketchup were wired to a battery-operated device worn by the actor, which exploded small gunpowder charges when activated out of sight of the camera.

Rabbi Doctor Elmer Berger of New York says: "Communists and other extremists like Jim Jones are also master showmen and expert fight promoters. They have long made a practice of painting swastikas on Jewish temples and cemeteries. When an indignant rabbi complains, the communists arrange for a small bomb to go off at the rabbi's house so as to produce a 'media' event and syndicated story about 'right wing extremists' violating civil rights."

American conservatives received a similar blow in 1962. Led by Senator Joseph McCarthy, many Irish at that time were joining the Republican Party. But then Fair Play For Cuba Committee member Lee Harvey Oswald of New Orleans used the English-German, Protestant Republican city of Dallas as the locale to assassinate Catholic President Kennedy and wound Governor Connally, then both popular Irish Democrats.

The Old Grow Young

Dallas was immediately labeled the city of hatred, when actually a parade was being held in honor of President Kennedy when Oswald killed him.

Jones' illusions sometimes took months of careful planning and preparation. One elaborate ruse he dreamed up, for instance, required that a group of six hand-picked young women attend People's Temple services over a period of months in wheelchairs, with makeup applied to make their faces look aged and wrinkled.

Jones fed the women into the congregation one at a time, allowing others to get used to and accept their presence. First one old woman in a wheelchair, then two, then four, and finally six began appearing regularly at Jones' sermons, where he would frequently remind worshippers of his powers. Finally, he pretended to notice one of the women for the first time.

"I see that you are suffering from arthritis in your old age," he would begin. "And yet I can see by your face that you have perfect belief in me. Because of your great faith, I am going to restore your youth," he would announce. Approaching the woman, he would "lay hands" on her, and stunned onlookers, as years melted off the woman's face. To shouts of "Alleluia!" and the sound of the weak-hearted fainting, the woman would rise from her wheelchair to embrace Jones and stride happily through the aisles. Week after week, until all the original group were "rejuvenated," Jones worked "miracles."

Jones also conditioned them to expect and believe in virtually anything, as he was later to prove by the horrible mass suicide that followed Rep. Leo Ryan's fact-finding mission to Jonestown. Time and again, Jones would sound the alarm and order followers to line up and "practice" a suicide plan to be used if the colony were attacked. He never told people whether they were actually practicing or not until after they proved their allegiance by sipping a cup of "poison."

At the end, practice made perfect: more than 900 of Jones' followers marched like willing robots to their death.

Spies Everywhere

How did Jones accomplish one of his most useful tricks, seeming to read other people's thoughts? The secret lay in the large number of informers he placed on their guard throughout the People's Temple building and also in the surrounding cities.

These persons, usually innocuous-seeming people who had been born or raised in the community and fit in well, would gather small bits of information about people and events as they overheard them on the streets, in bars, at parties and political, religious or community meetings.

At the temple, they would pass the bits of information on to one of Jones' key lieutenants, who added bits and pieces together and came up with larger pieces of information that he then presented to Jones. The informers were rewarded by special attention and other small favors that maintained their loyalty.

When Jones confronted a church member with a wayward tongue, or a politician with an unfortunate "leak" among his office staff, he would astound the person by reeling off their statements and secrets with incredible accuracy.

(Part II will appear next week in Twin Circle)

> At the end,
> practice made perfect:
> more than 900 of Jones'
> followers marched like willing
> robots to their death.

379

Probe urged

Persistent rumors of CIA involvement in the 1978 mass suicide in Jonestown, Guyana, should be explored further, the staff of a House subcommittee said Thursday.

Nothing new came of hearings into the tragedy earlier this year, concluded the House Foreign Affairs subcommittee on international operations.

The allegations of CIA involvement, said the staff, "are largely speculative and unsubstantiated." However, the staff told the chairman, Rep. Clement Zablocki (D-Wis.), that the House Intelligence Committee should examine the allegations again.

Rep. Leo Ryan (D-Calif.) and other members of an American delegation were shot to death in November, 1978, by members of the People's Temple, a California-based religious cult led by the Rev. Jim Jones. The delegation had gone to Guyana to investigate Jones' cult.

Shortly after Ryan was killed, more than 900 cult members committed suicide or were killed by drinking a cyanide-laced drink at the Jonestown colony.

Claim against Temple assets denied

A US government claim against the assets of the defunct Peoples Temple has been denied by a Superior Court judge in San Francisco who is on record as saying that the money is needed more by survivors of those who died in the 1978 mass murders and suicides in Guyana.

The $1.9 million claim was denied without comment by Judge Ira Brown. The case now will be fought out in Federal Court.

The government says the money is needed to offset the cost of returning to the US the bodies of 900 Temple members who died in the Temple's jungle settlement at Jonestown.

CIA CHARGED WITH AIDING JIM JONES

THE CIA has been accused of using notorious People's Temple cult leader Jim Jones to conduct mind-control experiments for them in a legal action being brought by the families of the two men who were slaughtered just before the Guyana massacre.

Marvin Lewis, an attorney for the families of Congressman Leo Ryan and NBC reporter Don Harris, both murdered at a deserted airstrip outside Jonestown before the mass suicide of 900 cult members, also questions whether the deaths were indeed suicides and whether or not all who died were cult members.

"There are just too many un-answered questions," said Lewis, who is requesting that the U.S government not be reimbursed with more than $1 million from People's Temple funds for the transportation and burial of the Jonestown victims until possible CIA involvement is investigated.

"We know there were tons of drugs found at the scene — drugs that could only be obtained under a doctor's prescription," said Lewis.

"Somebody had to be allowing them to get to Guyana."

Among the other questions Lewis and the families want answered are: If all the members committed suicide, why did the autopsies of the victims show that they were injected with cyanide in the back.

How did Jones' massive cache of weapons and drugs build up unnoticed by the American intelligence community?

Why did the Army record only 301 bodies when they first started tagging the victims?

Said Lewis, "In my opinion, injections in the back could not have been self-inflicted. Furthermore, the Army said their initial count was incorrect because many bodies were buried beneath other bodies and were hidden from view. In that case how could 301 adult bodies cover more than 500 other bodies?"

A reply on Jonestown

Because of reports that there might have been some involvement of the Central Intelligence Agency in the tragedy in Jonestown, Guyana. where more than 900 persons committed suicide two years ago, Zablocki requested an investigation by the House Intelligence Committee.

In a reply, Rep. Edward P. Boland (D-Mass.) said the committee found "no evidence at all to suggest that the CIA knew anything about the Jonestown tragedy before it occurred. or that the agency had any connection with either Jim Jones or the Peoples Temple."

Suit Says U.S. Conspired In Mass Cult Deaths

SAN FRANCISCO, Oct. 14 (UPI) — Survivors of the People's Temple mission and relatives of the dead followers of the Rev. Jim Jones sued the Federal Government today, contending that it conspired in the deaths of more than 900 members in the mass murder-suicide at the cult's camp in Guyana.

The suit says former Secretary of State Cyrus R. Vance and Adm. Stansfield Turner, former Director of Central Intelligence, participated in a conspiracy with Mr. Jones to control temple members who held socialist beliefs.

The suit says Mr. Jones was a C.I.A. operative from 1963 until his death with the other temple members in 1978.

Jonestown: only a bad memory

By Don Bohning
© Knight-Ridder News Service

GEORGETOWN, Guyana — People in Guyana don't talk much about Jonestown any more.

The jungle is erasing remnants of a madness they would rather forget.

"Jonestown has been administered in a rather desultory fashion," said Christopher Nascimento, a Cabinet minister. "It does not figure in the minds of the Cabinet as an important place."

Resurrection unlikely

No longer is there talk of making it a tourist attraction or an agricultural cooperative. "Jonestown," Nascimento said, "has no significance in the economic development of Guyana."

Jonestown appears to have been abandoned, its resurrection unlikely in any form. It is difficult even to find which agency or individual has responsibility for administering what remains of Jonestown.

The jungle has helped erase the notoriety, reclaiming much of what it had given up to the Rev. Jim Jones and his Peoples Temple followers who fled California in the mid-1970s to establish the remote, 3,852-acre commune that bore his name.

Jonestown. Nov. 18, 1978.

Before that day was over, 918 men, women and children would die, victims of a mad American preacher who thought he had found paradise in the South American jungles.

Additional victims

As his paranoia closed in about him, Jones presided over the ritualistic poisoning, with cyanide-laced punch, of himself and 908 of his followers in the isolated Guyana community.

Nine others, among them three newsmen and a California congressman, also were to die that day, additional victims of Jones' madness.

For Guyana, a former British colony of 800,000 people on the southeast coast of South America, what remains is a bad memory that the government is encouraging to fade.

Government permission is needed to visit the site, 130 miles to the northwest of Georgetown, the coastal capital. Even if permission is obtained, the logistics of getting there present another major obstacle.

The nearest landing strip is Port Kaituma, 6 miles away over a road that becomes virtually impassable during the rainy season — if a vehicle can be found to take a visitor to Jonestown.

'Has been forgotten'

Once there, there is little to see except the abandoned remnants of what Jones had wrought.

"Jonestown," one recent non-Guyanese visitor to the jungle community said, "has been forgotten, and the government intended it to be that way."

He reports shoulder-high grass along the unkept walkways of the community, now inhabited only by a three-man police detachment and the creatures of the jungle.

The livestock is gone. The banana plants and cassava, the principal root crop once cultivated in Jonestown, are untended. The tidy cabins, with their tin roofs gleaming under a tropical sun, remain but are unused.

At the main pavilion, where Jonestown residents drank the poison potion, several of the religious slogans are still in place, along with George Santayana's dictum, "Those who do not remember the past are condemned to repeat it."

Nascimento said that much of the Jonestown infrastructure remains intact but that heavy machinery that was usable elsewhere has been taken away.

Stanley Hamilton, permanent secretary in the recently created Ministry of Regional Development, acknowledges that Jonestown comes under his ministry's jurisdiction, although he said that he never has been there. "Jonestown," he said, "is an experience we would like to forget."

Hamilton said there are no plans for its use or development. "Until the legal aspects are settled there is no sense in doing anything with it," he said, "and I suppose that will take some time to resolve."

Among the pending court actions is one involving Peoples Temple member Larry Layton, on trial in California in connection with the Port Kaituma slaying of California Rep. Leo Ryan, whose visit to Jonestown touched off the suicide-murders.

Layton was tried and acquitted in Guyana of attempted murder, then returned to the United States to face charges. A September trial in San Francisco ended in a hung jury. A second trial is to begin on Dec. 1.

But there is virtually no mention of the Layton trial or anything else relating to Jonestown in the Guyana media.

Hamilton said that he is uncertain even if there are policemen assigned to Jonestown.

Police Commissioner Lloyd Barker, after telling a reporter that anything about Jonestown will have to come from his superiors in the Ministry of Home Affairs, confirmed: "There are three policemen at Jonestown whose duty is the preservation of property."

Occasional visitors — "curious people and now and then a government official" — go to Jonestown, he said.

"Everything of significant value has been removed from Jonestown," another official said. "The site literally has been abandoned, and there are no current plans for action."

For Guyana President Forbes Burnham, Jonestown is "an American tragedy that was acted out in Guyana and for which we get the blame."

Burnham acknowledged that the jungle is taking Jonestown over. "Some people had suggested that we sort of make it a special place for tourists, but we don't have the money to develop it," he said.

The entire area, including Jonestown, Burnham said, is slated for an extensive agricultural project that will cover about 40,000 acres, "but, at the moment, I can't get Guyanese to go in there to work," he said.

Burnham, a London-educated lawyer who numbers among the English-speaking Caribbean's most politically astute and articulate leaders, clearly is exasperated with the notoriety that Jonestown brought Guyana.

"I suppose that Guyana will go down in history for Jonestown and nobody will remember that Bishop "Jim" Jones got a letter from Mrs. (Rosalynn) Carter and that Walter Mondale met Ptolemy Reid, who was then deputy prime minister, and asked him, 'How is my friend Jim Jones?' Nobody remembers that," Burnham complained. "All they remember is Guyana. I even hear that some whippersnapper said that I go around dressed in white robes.

"Now how do you conquer all that? Do you have time? Can you run a country and conquer all that?"

He added, "The dust has settled. People are beginning to understand what the facts are, but at the time Guyana was a terrible place and the man Burnham believes in all these necromancies and all that sort of thing. That was the word. Read the books."

$1.6 million settlement near in cult suits

From Sentinel wire services

San Francisco, Calif. — Lawsuits filed against the Peoples Temple by the families of slain US Rep. Leo Ryan (D-Calif.), NBC correspondent Don Harris and wounded Ryan aide Jackie Speier have been tentatively settled for nearly $1.6 million.

The proposed settlements, if approved June 11 by a Superior Court judge, won't be paid until all other 760 claims against the Peoples Temple also are settled. The three settlements were detailed in court documents filed Wednesday.

About $1.8 billion in claims are on file before Robert Fabian, a former Bank of America legal counsel appointed by the court as a receiver for the Temple. The Temple's assets are estimated at $7.9 million.

Ryan, Harris and three others were slain and Speier was wounded in 1978 at the Port Kaituma airstrip in Guyana during a fact-finding mission to the cult's Jonestown jungle commune.

Temple member is home

Charles Beikman, the last People's Temple survivor to leave Guyana, is living in Indiana, not far from where the Rev. Jim Jones founded the Temple in the 1950s.

Beikman, 49, was freed last week from a Guyana prison where he was serving a term for attempted murder for a 1980 incident that followed the suicide of Jones and more than 900 others at Jonestown, the religious settlement in Guyana. Beikman moved in with a brother in suburban Indianapolis after his release.

Beikman was sentenced in 1980 to five years in prison for attempting to murder 9-year-old Seraphine Jones, the adopted granddaughter of Jones. He was released early for good behavior.

Another part of Peoples Temple story ends

Four years and four months after more than 900 followers of cult leader Jim Jones died in Guyana, final checks from the Peoples Temple's assets are being sent to their survivors.

The checks, ranging from 36 cents to about $7,500, are being mailed to 577 people whose claims were approved in a settlement last year.

Nearly all the assets already were dispensed in two previous mailings in August and November. The final checks total $184,118.

Robert Fabian, a court-appointed receiver in San Francisco, was authorized last week by Superior Court Judge Ira Brown to make the final payment and give any leftover money to Glide Memorial Church in San Francisco.

"There might be about $5,000 to $10,000 left over when all the checks are written," Fabian said. "The (state) attorney general has the power to say who gets any money. I recommended Glide Memorial, and he agreed, because it is set up to serve the poor, which is what the Peoples Temple said it intended to do."

Fabian said total settlements to the 577 claimants came to $9.5 million.

The suicide-massacre at Jonestown, Guyana, on Nov. 18, 1978, began with the airport slaying of US Rep. Leo Ryan, three reporters and a Temple member. Ryan had traveled to the Guyana to investigate reported abuse of Temple members.

Hours after the murders, more than 900 cult members drank a cyanide-laced drink at their jungle commune. Jones died of a gunshot wound.

Fabian began with $295,000 in Temple assets when he was appointed receiver in February 1979. He found an additional $10 million in assets in bank accounts and property holdings in Central American and Caribbean countries, including $7 million in Panama, $600,000 in Guyana and $80,000 in Grenada.

The assets grew to about $13.1 million in four years as Fabian rolled them over in short-term bank certificates of deposits.

'Remember Jim Jones? I'm his son'

By Paul Galloway

SAN FRANCISCO—He hasn't changed his name or tried to hide his identity. In a way, there is no reason to; his last name is common enough, and his looks and size differ enough that people don't automatically connect him to his father.

Yet it is more than that. It is because he doesn't want to avoid the past; he wants to confront the stigma, he wants to talk about who he is and about what happened and about the people who died. Especially about the people who died.

He doesn't want to talk about it with strangers, however. He still feels some anxiety when he deals with people he doesn't know: a garage mechanic, a salesperson, someone he has just met. The feeling is beginning to recede, but it is still there.

It is a fear that they will discover who he is and when they do, there will be harsh words—an ugly scene—or the kind of icy rejection he got when he applied for work after his return from Guyana.

The jobs he sought involved physical labor, something in a warehouse or in construction, and the first four or five times it was exactly the same:

The personnel man who conducted the interview would ask about his previous experience.

"I'VE WORKED ON docks, loading and unloading boats," he would answer. "I've cleared land and cut timber, and I've been a carpenter. I've built houses."

"Where did you get your experience?" the personnel man would ask.

Despite his paranoia—this feeling that even though he was innocent, he would be *caught*—he would answer truthfully. It was a matter of honor.

"Jonestown," he would say.

And this expression—part surprise, panic and repugnance—would pass across the personnel man's face, and he would reply, abruptly, as if what he was saying were perfectly believable, "Well, I'm sorry, but that position has been filled."

It was not until he lied and said that he had acquired his skills as a Vista volunteer that he was finally hired.

For Stephan Gandhi Jones, Jonestown will never go away. It is a legacy he can never leave behind. It is a memory that he will always carry with him.

His father will be there, too, of course, a presence that will follow him like a malevolent shadow. The ghost of his father, whom he once loved and whom he grew to hate, will always be a part of Steve Jones.

THE REV. JIM JONES has been dead for more than five years now, as have the 913 members of his Peoples Temple who perished with him—*because* of him. It was Nov. 18, 1978,

when that monstrous, incomprehensible ritual of murder and suicide took place at dusk in a South American jungle.

The aftershocks continue. A few weeks ago in Los Angeles, a 28-year-old man named Tyrone Mitchell began firing into the playground of a school across the street from his apartment. A 10-year-old girl was killed and several others were

Continued on page 4

Jim Jones' son confronts the ghosts of Jonestown

Continued from first Tempo page

wounded.

People who knew Mitchell told police that he had been deeply affected by the deaths of his parents, his sisters and brother in Jonestown. When reporters found out about the link to Peoples Temple, the phone began to ring again in Steve Jones' apartment in a suburb south of San Francisco.

He understands; he is accustomed to it. It happens each November just before the anniversary. He thinks it helps him to talk about "the tragedy," and, more important, he wants to explain how it could happen, he wants to make everything clear to all of us in the outside world.

"I've never made a cent off talking about this, and I never will," he says. "The reason I am talking is I want people to know what kind of people were down there.

"I could not stand my father. I fought him all the time. I hated that man. I was in Jonestown for the love of the people there."

HE WAS 19 when the mass deaths occurred at the jungle settlement he had helped to build. He survived because he was 150 miles away, in Georgetown, the capital of Guyana. He had gone there with the Peoples Temple basketball team to play the Guyanese national team. When Rep. Leo Ryan, the California Democrat, and his party arrived for their fatal visit, Jim Jones had ordered his son back to Jonestown.

"I flatly refused," Steve says, "which, by the way, was unheard of."

The only child born to Jim and Marceline Jones, he will be 25 in June. He is married to a former Temple member who left before the mass exodus of the sect, in 1977, from San Francisco to Jonestown.

Steve Jones is tall and strikingly handsome, so handsome that people have urged him to become a model or an actor. But that is not him, he says. He installs office systems; he says he thrives on physical work, needs it, purposely turns down management jobs he has been offered because he can't make himself give orders.

His height is 6 feet 5 inches, he weighs 196 pounds, his hair is raven, as his father's was. He is trim and muscular; he swims daily and lifts weights. He says his only addiction is to exercise.

THE BOUNDARY between the boy he was and the man he has become is as distinct as a scar. Steve Jones the man has been forged by the searing horror of that November day in 1978, a day of grief that also released him from his father's closed, twisted world.

when he went there in February, 1977, as a member of the construction party sent ahead to erect an encampment that would be safe from the increasing scrutiny of the press and the authorities.

For a few months, he was happy. "He wasn't around. He was thousands of miles away, back in San Francisco, and I could be my own person. We were working 18 hours a day, and I loved it. We were clearing jungle, and we were putting up walls and carrying them out and putting them up."

This crew of fewer than 50 built most of Jonestown in an intense, eight-month period—300 acres cleared, more than 50 cottages, five huge dormitories, schools, larger cabins and a peaked-roof pavilion, which would become the center of the killing ground.

The atmosphere was relaxed, horseplay broke the tedium and there were none of the endless, tiresome meetings required when "Father," as Jim Jones was called, was present.

At night they watched movies. "Shane" was popular; everyone knew "Shane" by heart. There were a couple of Dirty Harry films, some Bruce Lee epics and "Z," the Costa-Gavras film about a right-wing dictatorship that Steve had already seen at least 30 times because it was his father's favorite.

THERE WAS TIME, too, to go into the jungle. From the outside, it is an emerald canopy of stillness and silence; inside, it is an enchanted chamber of sound and light and life.

"I liked going into the bush before morning light, he says. "I would sit and watch the jungle come alive. If you walked in, you'd think there was nothing living there, but there is a lot going on if you become part of the scenery," he says.

The solitude also gave him time to think. "It wasn't until I was in Jonestown alone that I really began seeing my father for what he was."

By July, 1977, most of the 950 Peoples Temple members had arrived—a large number of them elderly, two-thirds of them women, 70 percent of them black, 300 under the age of 18.

Everyone was again under the oppressive control of Father, whose drug dependency was now glaringly obvious. For Steve and others, his father's deterioration was a cause for hope. "He couldn't keep hidden in Jonestown what he could hide in the United States," he says.

The words were slurred on the loudspeaker as Father read his version of the news. When he claimed not to have slept for days, Steve and others laughed.

stand how people could become part of Peoples Temple and what kept people there," he says.

"FIRST, THERE were camaraderie and love and a total absence of racial bigotry. There was this feeling of togetherness and purpose. As time went by, it became your family.

"A lot of people came into the Temple with a kind of idealism from the '60s, looking for a way to do something for mankind. It seemed like the more sensitive you were, the more susceptible you were."

Steve also stayed because of his mother. "She was loved by everyone. They feared my father, and they loved her. He tried to keep her in California, but whenever she made one of her visits, she spent her time undoing his injustices. Somewhere along the line she was no longer Marceline Jones, she just lived for everybody there. It was a horrible irony that she was there at the end."

tion is "Raven," by Tim Reiterman, who was with Rep. Ryan, and John Jacobs. "They worked hard, and they got it right," he says. But he has not finished the book; he cannot bring himself to read the final chapters, about the deaths.

Although he says he never prays and is an agnostic, he is absorbed with morality, with doing the right thing, with being caring and considerate. Some may find the way he views his past as curious or perhaps noble.

"I'VE HAD A good life," he says. "I wouldn't trade it with anybody. I am grateful when I look at some people my age and say, 'My God, I could be like them if I hadn't experienced what I have.'

"From everything I have experienced I have grown a little, and growth is important to me. Somewhere along the way I have learned to like myself, and I'm glad."

Finally, the bitterness is lifting. He notices it in the way the dreams are changing. Now the people are no longer in Jonestown, and their personalities and their appearances have changed with the years. They are aging along with him, but by the end of the dream he is sure they are alive. Much of the time he is searching for them, until the anxiety wakes him.

The first positive dream about his father was the last one he had. "There had been some kind of catastrophe—some Armageddon. He had always preached that he would take us to a safe place when this happened, where we would survive and build a new community.

"I was with a group who had been sent ahead to find this place. We had found it, and I was running down this path and I saw all of them from afar. He was leading all of them. He was walking in front with a staff in his hand and it was obvious the people wanted to be with him and he was loving and gentle.

"He looked older. His hair wasn't dyed anymore, and it was graying. He seemed more like a wise man or a prophet, which is the way he built himself up in the very early years."

Stephan Jones is quiet for a moment, then he says. "It sounds ridiculous, but it was like I had found peace. I had dealt with it. The turmoil I had had for so many years was gone."

'I have changed so much,' he says. 'People who haven't seen me in a long time can't believe the difference. Before, I was angry and frustrated all the time, and now the rage I had is gone.'

In the early days, there were good times in what Jim Jones called his 'rainbow' family of Steve and his adopted siblings—a brother who was black and a brother and sister who were Korean. 'He was not a bad father,' he says. 'There were times when he would play with us and talk to us, but they got fewer and fewer and then not at all.'

His father's image was stained when Steve was 9 or 10 and he heard his parents arguing because his mother had flushed his father's pills down the toilet. It became irreparably torn a few months later, when his father brought him along on a sexual liaison with Carolyn Layton, one of the Temple members.

He could hear the woman sing while she and his father made love in the next room, and he was devastated. Later, his mother told him that she knew about his father's affair. She even recited the words to the song that Layton sang; his father had boasted to her about it.

JIM JONES WOULD become open in his sexual couplings, indulging himself in his home with a variety of lovers. 'I've seen TV shows where a kid is damaged because once he walked in when his father was with somebody else,' Steve says. 'This happened more than once with me, and not only did I walk in on him with somebody else but I walked in on him with women and men.'

The discrepancies between the public and private Jim Jones caused resentment and confusion. 'I believed my father had some kind of power. I mean, he came on so strong, and he was so confident and ... was built up to be this perfect man. People believed in him, and I wanted to believe.'

It was unsettling and exciting when Jim Jones told his son that they were the only two in the world with this mysterious power. 'He took me out one night when I was 12 or so and pointed to a star and said that since we came from... my father always took his fantasies too far. He always implied that I would inherit his psychic powers and take over from him one day.

'As a kid, I said, 'Oh, great!' It was like becoming Superman.'

Now he is apprehensive about the thought. He worries about his potential for leadership. 'I'm afraid of the way I can influence and manipulate people. I do have a presence. It's my size and my ability to speak. I can influence everybody, of course, but there are times when I notice that I can and I pull back.

'Who's to say what I could have ended up becoming if my father hadn't lived before me and I hadn't seen what can happen with this kind of ability?'

MANY OF HIS memories of Jonestown are pleasant. He loved the jungle, he loved the freedom he felt

THE ABSURDITIES were becoming more evident, skepticism among the followers was growing, the leader was being derided in private. 'A great majority of the people were not 100 percent behind him,' especially in the later months.

Steve retreated to the bush during the day, but in camp he and his father were arguing constantly, often in public, exchanging curses and insults. 'He ordered me put under surveillance,' Steve says. 'Toward the end, I don't think he looked at me as his son anymore. I was more like his nemesis.'

The last time they talked privately

> 'Who's to say what I could have ended up becoming if my father hadn't lived before me and I hadn't seen what can happen with this kind of ability?'

was after his father staged a heart attack. 'There were at least 40 people in his house,' he says. 'He had everybody leave the room but me. He said, 'It doesn't hurt to cry.' He meant I could cry about his heart attack, which I didn't buy for a minute. I said I didn't feel like crying. This was his last effort to patch it up with me. He knew the rift between us was causing trouble. It was encouraging others to rebel.'

An aide then entered with a syringe. Jones said the injection was B-12 vitamin, but in a matter of minutes, he was incoherent.

There were scenes in Father's house when Jones would make it appear that he had returned to a former life. Steve would be called there and find his father raving and berating his mistresses. Once, he threw his father to the floor in disgust.

'HE SPOKE IN this terrible Russian accent, like he was Lenin in the middle of the Revolution. He wasn't delusional. He knew what he was doing. Just sitting here thinking about it makes me angry.'

The Lenin incarnation was calculated, for Jones' message was far more political than religious. His was an illogical mix of socialism and traditional manipulative techniques employed by cult leaders.

'It's a lot simpler than people have made it. It may have seemed like he was this good man who went insane, but I think he was a manipulator before I was born. It was an ego out of control. The more he became respected and idolized and even worshipped, the more out of hand he became.'

Many were inclined to ignore the craziness or to blame it on his fanatical staff. 'The most important thing for me is to have people under-

The day before the tragedy, the congressman, accompanied by a contingent of reporters and families who wanted to persuade Temple members to leave, flew into the tiny Port Kaituma airport for an inspection of Jonestown.

'The three worst things to my father were the U.S. government, the press and defectors,' he says, 'and they hit this drug-crazed man with all three at once. If they had waited another six months ...'

HIS VOICE TRAILS off for a moment before he resumes. The subject is the White Nights, the bizarre rehearsals for mass suicide. They were numerous, and always, Jones had found a way to stop them.

It is futile to make sense out of something that makes no sense, but he tries. 'I am convinced my father liked living. He was a coward. Given an alternative, he was not going to take his own life.

'You didn't take White Nights seriously—you never thought he'd go through with it.' He pauses. 'Although every time one of them started I got butterflies in my stomach.'

The Jonestown team had played well but lost by 10 points to the Guyanese team, and on Nov. 18, Steve and some teammates treated themselves to a movie. John Saxon was in it, and it was about hit men.

He didn't get to see the end because of a message to come to the Temple office in Georgetown; something terrible was happening in Jonestown.

He would serve three months in prison while Guyana prosecutors tried unsuccessfully to implicate him in a murder-suicide involving the leader of the Temple's Georgetown cadre, and his cell would be the crucible in which he would start to come to terms with his loss.

'I LOST MY family, my friends, I lost everything. It was like you took a vacation to Europe and found out the United States had sunk while you were away. I had nothing.

'I helped build Jonestown. My life was completely sunk into Peoples Temple. I was born into it. Nothing else existed. Everything else was the outside, and I was led to believe that all outsiders hated us because of our beliefs.'

At night he killed rats and cockroaches; he lost 20 pounds from the putrid food; he was threatened and called the Liquidator by the other inmates, who were black, but he found he could endure.

He returned to the San Francisco area, was married and began to build bridges to people. Only after getting to know someone, he has a way of letting them know. 'I'll say, 'You remember Jonestown? Well, my name is Stephan Jones.' He pauses. 'Then I say, 'I'm his son.' 'I've never had counseling,' he says. 'For me, my therapy was prison. I found I could be totally alone and at peace with myself.'

He is critical of the books and movies that have appeared about Jonestown and his father. The excep-

Probe of cult termed inadequate

Sacramento, Calif. —AP— The political influence of the Rev. Jim Jones may have played a part in halting a state investigation of the Peoples Temple before the group's mass murder-suicide in Guyana, a state attorney general's report concluded Tuesday.

The report also said the lives of 22 children might have been saved had the state of California warned judges — who awarded guardianships over the children to Temple members — about instances of child abuse in the cult.

The report by Deputy Atty. Gen. John Moy said no evidence of criminal responsibility by the state could be established in the deaths of the children among the 900 who died in November, 1978, because federal officials knew of allegations of abuses there.

But Moy criticized the investigation by the Department of Social Services into published reports that children were being mistreated.

Social Services Director Marion Woods issued a statement denying political influence on his department. Woods said the report didn't mention the attorney general's reponsibility to prevent child abuse.

The state investigation was begun by the Health Department after a 1977 article on the cult in New West magazine, Moy said.

He said the earlier report, though it omitted details of beatings and punishments described in the magazine, contained enough information about abuses to justify fuller investigations. But they were never made, he said.

Moy said several officials quoted Mari Goldman, then a top licensing official at the Department of Social Services, as saying at a 1978 meeting that Peoples Temple was "highly publicized, too political" and that her staff had higher priorities for investigation.

Goldman ridiculed the contention.

Guyana trial opens

Georgetown, Guyana —AP— The first witness in the trial of Larry Layton, accused in the airstrip shootings that preceded the mass deaths at Jonestown, testified Tuesday that the former Peoples Temple member "ripped out his gun and began firing inside the airplane."

The witness, Vern Gosney, was one of those trying to flee Jonestown at the time.

Layton is accused in the murder of Rep. Leo Ryan (D-Calif.), three journalists and a defecting cult member at the airport. But this trial is considering only charges that he attempted to murder two cult defectors who were wounded at the same time. Layton pleaded not guilty.

Layton Sentenced to Life in Ryan's Death

By DAN MORAIN,
Times Staff Writer

SAN FRANCISCO—Larry Layton was sentenced Tuesday to life in prison for his role in conspiring to murder Rep. Leo Ryan in Guyana in 1978.

But Layton, saying he wishes he could ease the pain of survivors of the Jonestown massacre, could be freed within five years.

U.S. District Judge Robert F. Peckham recommended that parole authorities consider releasing Layton in five years. He also gave the former Peoples Temple follower credit for spending a year and 49 days in jail while his trial was pending—thereby reducing the potential sentence by that amount of time.

Peckham said he was particularly struck by pleas for leniency from four jurors, two prosecution witnesses and survivors of an attack by Layton at an airstrip outside the Guyanese encampment of Jonestown.

Although he called it a "very grave crime," Peckham said Layton has shown "great remorse," and his actions in 1978 reflected how the cult leader, the Rev. Jim Jones, destroyed the will of his followers.

"Although Larry Layton must be held responsible for his actions, a just sentence requires consideration of the environment in which Layton and other members were virtually imprisoned," Peckham said.

Layton, 41, is the only former Peoples Temple member who was tried in the United States in connection with the slaughter on Nov. 18, 1978.

One of three family members who joined the cult, he was convicted Dec. 1 of conspiring with Jones to murder Ryan, a crusading San Mateo Democrat, and of conspiring in the attack on Richard C. Dwyer, then deputy chief of the U.S. mission in Guyana. Dwyer, who was wounded in the attack, has retired from the Foreign Service.

In all, Layton was convicted of four charges—conspiracy and aiding and abetting in the shootings of Ryan and Dwyer. The conspiracy to murder Ryan carried a mandatory life sentence, though federal law makes him eligible for parole in 10 years. Peckham sentenced Layton to 15 years in prison for the other three counts, but said the terms will run concurrently with the life term.

Layton, expressionless for most of the hearing and dressed casually in a light blue sweater, said he extended his "most sincere regrets" to the families of the victims.

"I only wish there was something I could do to ease the pain," he said, fighting to keep his voice from breaking.

Robert Bryan, who took over the case after Layton's conviction, said he hopes to win a new trial for Layton. He said Layton was insane at the time and was drugged by Jones with a mood-enhancing stimulant. He called Layton "the ultimate victim of Jim Jones."

U.S. Atty. Joseph Russoniello did not criticize Peckham's sentence, but in urging that Layton serve 20 years before being eligible for parole, he cited Layton's suggestion to Jones that Layton use dynamite to blow up Ryan's plane and its unwanted outsiders—a fact that was not revealed until Tuesday.

Layton was also quoted in a sentencing report to Peckham as saying that a cultist close to Jones had asked that he stop Ryan from leaving and gave him a gun. Layton's two ex-wives—both had been lured from Layton by Jones—also encouraged him to somehow stop Ryan, Russoniello said.

"I am taking solace in knowing that Larry Layton is going to pay back society for having assassinated the first congressman ever in this country," said Assemblywoman Jackie Speier (D-San Mateo), who had accompanied Ryan on the trip as an aide.

Ryan traveled to Guyana after winning his fourth congressional term to investigate reports from cult defectors—including Layton's sister, Debra—that the cult was holding members against their will.

He had completed his mission and was trying to take off from an airstrip six miles from the jungle compound of Jonestown when a trailer filled with eight armed Jones devotees pulled onto the runway and began firing.

Ryan, three journalists and a defector were killed. Dwyer, Speier and nine others were wounded. Layton was already aboard one of the two planes, posing as a defector. He pulled out a gun and shot and wounded two cult defectors.

Jones had ordered the ambush out of fear that Ryan would expose the cult. With Ryan dead, Jones concluded that the United States would retaliate, so he exhorted his followers to kill themselves by drinking cyanide-laced punch. Those who refused were shot; children were injected with poison. In all, 913 died. Jones died of a gunshot wound to the head.

Layton was arrested shortly after the killings by Guyanese authorities and signed a confession taking responsibility for the airstrip deaths—a confession that his lawyers maintained was coerced. Although he was acquitted in Guyana, he was returned here to face charges related to the shootings of Ryan and Dwyer, who were protected under U.S. law.

Layton's first trial ended in a hung jury in 1981, with 11 of the 12 jurors voting to acquit him. In between his trials, he lived under an assumed name in Eureka and, more recently, in San Francisco, where he sold real estate and took computer classes. Layton's mother, also a Peoples Temple member, died of cancer in Jonestown two weeks before the massacre. Layton's lawyer said that made Layton more susceptible to Jones' spell.

Jones, who founded his church in Indiana and moved here in 1970, relocated to Guyana, a former British colony in South America, in 1977 after critical press accounts about his politically prominent sect.

Final accounting near for Peoples Temple

San Francisco, Calif. —UPI— The time has come for the final accounting in the strange saga of the ill-fated Peoples Temple and its bizarre leader, Jim Jones.

Robert Fabian — appointed to the task of unraveling the financial affairs, finding all the property owned by the cult and distributing its assets — said he hoped to wrap up his duties this month.

"I expect to have the job done by the end of June," Fabian said in an interview.

Fabian, appointed by the San Francisco Superior Court to find all the assets of the Peoples Temple and its mysterious mission in the jungle of Guyana, located about $10 million in cash and property. He must settle claims that totaled $1.8 billion.

Jones founded his church in California and led more than 900 members to the Jonestown mission in Guyana in the late 1970s.

A trip by Rep. Leo Ryan (D-Calif.) to investigate Jonestown in 1978 led to a shootout on a jungle airstrip in which Ryan and three other people were killed. That was followed by a grim ritual suicide of more than 900 cult members and the death of Jones.

There were bank accounts in the United States and abroad, and property in California. Claims were filed by the federal government, by Ryan's family and the families of other victims, and by scores of families who lost members in the tragedy.

Fabian, 68, a lawyer who came out of retirement to serve as referee over the assets, has been praised for settling the accounts in relatively quick time considering the confusion left by the Jonestown tragedy.

He is also credited with adding $3 million to the $10 million assets of the church by wise investment of the funds in his custody.

A hearing is scheduled for June 15 on the organization's financial statement for the first four months of 1983.

Fabian said he must "file tax returns and complete transfer of whatever little money is left to Glide Memorial Church and the San Francisco Council of Churches. Then the books will be closed.

The Council of Churches will be reimbursed for the money spent to transport 545 unclaimed or unidentified bodies of those who died in the Jonestown massacre from Dover, Del., to the San Francisco Bay area for burial.

Fabian said his job included accompanying bodies from Delaware, where the Air Force had flown them from Guyana. He conducted auctions to sell buses and the cult's headquarters in San Francisco. He tracked down Peoples Temple bank accounts around the world.

The court had about 750 claims filed by families of the dead, the government, people who had donated property to the temple and former church members.

Many of the claimants were poor people victimized by Jones, said Fabian.

Federal statutes decreed that, before any money could be paid out to other claimants, the federal government had to be reimbursed for the money spent returning the bodies of victims to the United States. The government asked for $4.3 million but settled for $1.6 million in August 1981.

Pain is still intense 10 years after Jonestown

By Lisa Levitt Ryckman
Associated Press

SAN FRANCISCO — John Victor Stoen died in a South American jungle 10 years ago, the object of a struggle over which he had no control, a victim of an evil he would never understand.

The last taste in his mouth was grape Flavor-Aid poisoned with cyanide.

John Victor Stoen was 6 years old.

On Nov. 18, 1978, 912 members of the Peoples Temple committed suicide or were murdered at the urging of the Rev. Jim Jones, the madman whom children and seniors alike called "Father."

At least 276 of the dead were children, including three dozen babies born in the Guyanese jungle encampment known as Jonestown. A decade later, memories of innocents lost still evoke the most intense, enduring pain for many relatives and survivors of the cult called the Peoples Temple.

"After he died, he came to me in a dream," Grace Stoen said of her dead son. "He said, 'I just want you to know, I really, really love you. And it's OK.'

"I'm sure that was my subconscious saying to me, 'Hey, you tried to get him back.' "

The brief, bizarre life of John Victor Stoen, a topic his parents have rarely discussed with anyone in the past 10 years, provides a cautionary tale as strange as it is tragic. Jonestown, the agricultural mission that was supposed to be paradise, has come to be synonymous with destructive cults, but millions of Americans have ignored its warnings.

"For every child who died in Jonestown, many more have died since in similar circumstances," asserts Cynthia Kisser, executive director of the Chicago-based Cult Awareness Network. The national non-profit group, formed in the aftermath of Jonestown, estimates that 2,500 destructive cults operate in the United States and have affected 3 million people.

"In recalling it 10 years later, a whole lot has not changed in terms of how we deal with cults in this country," said Jackie Speier, who was critically wounded in an ambush by Temple gunmen at the Port Kaituma airstrip just hours before the mass murder-suicides at nearby Jonestown.

Speier was then an aide to U.S. Rep. Leo Ryan, who was killed in the attack along with three journalists and a Temple defector. Ryan, responding to worried California constituents, had gone to Jonestown to investigate allegations of abuse and imprisonment.

After Ryan's death, one of his five children joined the anti-cult movement; another joined a cult.

"Do people learn lessons until it absolutely hits them smack-dab in the face?" said Speier, who now holds the California Assembly seat Ryan held 18 years ago. "Before your son or daughter is transformed by an experience they call religious and go off to join a particular group, do you even consider the idea of cults?"

Certainly it had never occurred to John Victor Stoen's mother, Grace. In 1970, when she attended her first Peoples Temple meeting at Redwood Valley near Ukiah with her future husband, she was a naive 19-year-old from San Francisco. Tim Stoen, a strait-laced, bespectacled Stanford University law school graduate 12 years her senior, believed in the possibility of utopia. He believed Jim Jones was the man who could create it.

"When I would come to the Temple, people would come to me and say, 'Before I came here, I had nothing in my life. Now I have a family, now I have people who care,' " recalled Stoen, who eventually became the Temple's attorney and church board chairman at Ukiah. "That's what sustained me for seven years."

John Victor Stoen was born into the cult, taken from his parents as a toddler to be raised communally and revered by Jones' inner circle as the very reincarnation of Jones himself, spouting socialist platitudes while still in diapers.

Ultimately, Jones alleged he was John Victor's biological father and defied court orders to relinquish him. The precocious, black-haired child became the object of a bitter custody battle no one would win.

During six years in the Temple, Grace Stoen rose to the respected position of head counselor, worked grueling hours on little sleep, watched her marriage disintegrate and saw her child taken beyond her reach. As Jones' public humiliations and beatings of Temple members increased, so did her resolve to leave.

"Jim said, 'If anybody ever leaves, they'll be killed.' I really believed that," she said. "But I thought, at least if I go I'll die, and I won't have to live like this anymore."

She left Ukiah in the summer of 1976 with Walter Jones, another Temple member. John Victor stayed behind, in San Francisco.

"I wanted to take John, but I didn't have him physically, and I felt like I didn't have him psychologically," she said. "All the time John was alive, people were telling me I wasn't good enough for him, that he was more intelligent than I, that I wasn't a good mother.

"Later, my attorney (in the custody fight) said, 'No one is ever going to understand how you could leave that child.' I shouldn't have left him. But I didn't even feel like I was his mother."

Three years before his wife left, Stoen helped Jones draft a plan for a Caribbean agricultural mission where Temple members could escape persecution by police or press. In 1974, the first settlers began beating back 300 acres of Guyanese jungle that would become Jonestown, convinced they were creating a socialist paradise where they could live in peace and freedom.

When Tim Stoen arrived in Guyana in early 1977, only 50 Temple pioneers lived there, his son among them. Within months, Jones' paranoia had escalated to the point where he and his top aides began plotting a mass exodus to Guyana; by July, Jonestown's population was close to 600.

It was Grace who convinced a confused, conflicted Tim that it was time to leave the Temple.

"She said, 'They're turning John against me. Jim Jones is telling John I never loved him.' Immediately when she said that, it was like the skies opened," said Stoen, who left the Temple in November 1977. "I decided that no matter how pure and wonderful this philosophy is, nothing can justify violating a child's love for his mother."

Together, the Stoens went to court to try to wrest their son from Jim Jones' control. They formed a group called "Concerned Relatives," involving about 50 people worried about family members in Jonestown.

"The reason he kept John was not because of his love for John but because of his hatred for Grace and me," said Stoen, who was reviled by other cult members for the intensity of his fight to retrieve his son, which they saw as a direct attack on Jones. Stoen's obsessive commitment to the Temple and Jones had ended, replaced by a fanatic desire to save his only child.

"I said to myself, 'John, you're going to be proud of me because of what I'm doing for you. I'll get you out of there,'" Stoen said. "I kind of expected to die, but I just wanted to die saving John."

Stoen did not die, and he could not save his son. Stanley Clayton, a Temple member who escaped Jonestown while people writhed in death throes around him, told journalists Tim Reiterman and John Jacobs that he saw John Victor crying and protesting as he was led to Jones' house, where he would die.

"Is that my son doing all that crying?" asked Jones, who had spotted John. "My son shouldn't be crying."

Some of Jones' last words, preserved on tape, were for Stoen: "We win when we go down. Tim Stoen has nobody else to hate. Then he'll destroy himself...."

Tim Stoen did not self-destruct. For the 10 years since John's death, he has led a solitary life in California and Colorado. Grace married Walter Jones, her fellow defector, and began a new life.

In a sense, the Stoens were more fortunate than other relatives. Witnesses to the aftermath told them they saw John Victor's body in Jones' house at the jungle compound. His body was shipped back and buried by his parents.

Many other bodies were never identified. The government made lists of unidentified and presumed dead. The unknowns were buried in a mass grave in Evergreen Cemetery in Oakland.

The Stoens, at least, knew for certain.

Others, such as George Brady, who was able to bury his former wife, Michaeleen, and daughter, Michelle, but never received the body of a second daughter, Georgiann, may always wonder.

"I realize it's very remote that she might still be alive, but every time I go to the cemetery, I realize she's not there. So where is she?"

Brady wrote in a recent letter to a reporter, asking for help in locating his namesake.

Pieces of Georgiann's brief life are tucked amid the voluminous

'A whole lot has not changed in terms of how we deal with cults in this country.'

ASSEMBLYMAN JACKIE SPEIER

Temple records preserved in more than 100 boxes at the California Historical Society library. There's a photo ID card showing a bright-eyed, snub-nosed child with sunburned cheeks; release forms, signed by her mother, granting permission for the trip to Guyana; and the girl's own signature on a letter to a friend's mother: "Georgiann Brady, Father's child."

"Father" referred not to George Brady, but to Jim Jones. Georgiann Brady was 12.

When the end came in Jonestown, the children died first. Parents held squirming babies while a nurse squirted poisoned punch into their mouths with a syringe. When the screams of pain had ceased, the smallest bodies formed the bottom layer of corpses piled three-high.

"The sequence of death would be children, young adults, adults, the elderly," Reiterman and Jacobs wrote in "Raven: The Untold Story of the Rev. Jim Jones and His People," their definitive book on Jones and Peoples Temple. "Such a clever way to make sure all died: What would the adults have to live for after they watched the next generations die?"

Grace Stoen has started another generation. "Because of John, I always knew I wanted children," said Stoen, now 38 and the mother of a 4-year-old girl and 2-year-old boy. She saved the newspaper clippings, and someday she'll tell her children about the son she lost.

Occasionally, she has spoken to high school classes about her cult experience.

"I do it sometimes because I feel people can relate to me," she said. "They say, 'Hey, she looks normal, she looks like someone I could know.' Because I think people would like to think, 'Oh, these were just a bunch of weird people.' When people say that, I say, 'You know, there were people just like you in the Peoples Temple, who looked just like you.'"

Tim Stoen looks at framed photos of John every day. For the San Francisco attorney, a youthful 50, there has been no new marriage, no child to ease the pain, to create new memories.

"I feel responsible for the fact an innocent 6-year-old boy died, and that's the heaviest burden in my life," Stoen said, and the tears come.

"I would go through all the misery of this experience again just to hold John in my arms for an hour."

10 years after Jonestown, victim's kin fears recurrence

By Guy Darst
Associated Press

WASHINGTON The mass suicide of hundreds of cult followers 10 years ago at Jonestown, Guyana, could happen again, the daughter of a congressman murdered there said Sunday.

"We need to keep working, keep educating, keep helping so the question, 'How could something like Jonestown have happened again?' is a question our children will never have to answer," Patricia Ryan of Washington said at a 10th anniversary memorial service for the Jonestown victims.

Her father, Rep. Leo Ryan, D-Calif., was killed by followers of the Rev. Jim Jones on Nov. 18, 1978. Guyanese officials investigating the deaths of Ryan and four journalists at a jungle airfield found that Jones and almost all his followers were dead.

An investigation revealed that most had committed suicide by taking poison. However, some had been shot, some injected with poison and others forced to drink the deadly beverage prepared for the mass suicide.

In all, 912 people died at the People's Temple.

In an interview after her remarks at the service on the steps of the Jefferson Memorial, Ryan was asked if the massacre could happen again.

"Sure," she replied, "if a leader decides to use the control he has over his followers."

In her talk, she said experts "estimate that more than 10 million people may be involved in destructive cults today ... That's 10 million people whose minds have been taken away from them ... 10 million people who have lost all sense of what is real."

Cults, she said, are a problem that "target the young, the vulnerable and the friendless. But it also captures the minds of bright, apparently normal people who fall prey to seductive and deceptive promises of a better life and easier answers."

The experts she quoted had higher estimates than many. The Cult Awareness Network, one of the sponsors of the service, has estimated that there are 3 million cult members nationwide.

Jane Wills, a former cult member who spoke at the ceremony, recalled that while watching news coverage of the deaths on television she and her husband "wept at the sight of the bodies" because they knew how difficult it is to break free of cults. They had just left a cult called the Children of God, she said.

"I would have taken the poison devoutly," she said. But 10 years after her break, "I treasure the freedom God has given me to think for myself."

The service marks the beginning of a week of remembrances that wind up with a candlelight service in San Francisco, where Jones' temple started.

Survivor

A decade after Jonestown horrified
the world, an 86-year-old woman
struggles each day with her memories

By Wes Smith

Lately, it has been on her mind a lot, she said, persistent, frightening images that bedevil an elderly woman in a wheelchair in a church-owned nursing home in Indianapolis.

Flashes of jungle and death. Her sister prone on the ground outside a pavilion. Hundreds of other bodies, infants, children, teenagers, men and women. Hypodermic needles in the jungle grass.

"I try not to think about nothin'," she said. "Here lately it has been on my mind quite a bit, and I try my best not to think about it. It's water over the bridge ... nothing I can do about it. . . ."

Hyacinth Thrash was born in 1902 and grew up in Alabama. She and her sister Zipporah, or "Zip," moved North looking for a better life when they came of age. They went to Indianapolis and settled into the tiny niche of opportunity then available for uneducated black women.

It was not much, but the Thrash sisters knew how to live on not much. They worked as maids, elevator operators, seamstresses. They grew and canned their own foods and made their own clothes.

They looked to God for the daily inspiration to continue, but there were not a lot of churches in Indianapolis back then that welcomed blacks. At one time, the town had welcomed the Ku Klux Klan.

In 1957 they found a church on television in a local broadcast by a local minister, Rev. Jim Jones, from Lynn, Ind. His church was called the People's Temple. He was a white man backed by a black choir.

Jones often spoke of "we blacks" and claimed falsely that he was of mixed parentage. He and his wife, Marceline, had adopted children of mixed race, including Asians and blacks. He conducted services in a former synagogue and sold monkeys as pets door to door to raise money for his ministry.

And he appealed to people such as the Thrash sisters. poor but willing to give.

"He was trying to do things that the Bible said was right," Hyacinth Thrash recalled.

"He was a nice man going all out for blacks, helping them in different ways and trying to integrate things that wasn't integrated."

When a local barber refused to serve a black man while cutting Jones' hair. the minister got up and walked out with half a haircut, Thrash said.

When a local restaurant refused to serve a black man at the counter. Jones took his plate out to the curb and sat with the man.

And when a local hospital treated blacks only in its basement. Jones moved his hospital bed down to the basement with them.

"He made them move all the people up," Thrash said. "He helped us all get good jobs, and he tried to get all the churches around to unite."

Jones' desegregation efforts won him the loyalty and support of many Indianapolis blacks, among them the Thrash sisters. He also acquired political power and clout in the early 1960s as chairman of the Indianapolis Human Rights Commission, appointed to heal old racial wounds.

He healed his followers, too, Hyacinth Thrash said. A young girl received a new kidney through his prayers, she said.

She benefited, too, from his powers, she said. In 1963, when the doctors told Thrash that she had breast cancer, Jones had his congregation of about 1,000 pray for her on a Sunday night, "and it was gone by Wednesday.

"The doctors said it was a miraculous

See Jonestown, pg. 2

Continued from page 1

thing. They asked me where it went, and I said, 'Do you believe in divine healing?' They laughed. But they didn't say anything else about it."

Although he had a strong following among those whose rights he championed, Jones also inspired enemies. After threats of bombings at churches he visited, he moved to open fields.

Indianapolis eventually became too hostile for Jones, at least in his mind, so in 1965 he told his followers that he would move to the coastal city of Redwood Valley, Calif., in Mendocino County about 90 miles north of San Francisco. Jones claimed to have a hiding place safe from racists and nuclear war there.

Thrash's sister Zip and about 70 other families from the Indianapolis congregation quickly followed. Hyacinth, a skeptic at heart, held back leaving the home she had labored to own.

"But I finally went because my sister kept after me to go. Redwood Valley was a beautiful place," she said. "We bought our own ranch house and almost had

By this time, the Thrash sisters had turned over all of their finances and possessions to their minister and also had agreed to tithe their Social Security checks and other assets to his church, Hyacinth said.

"Everything he asked for, we gave him," she said. "Sometimes you do things that you never think you would do."

Jones built a redwood chapel in Redwood Valley that was paid for by his followers' donations and by their wages earned in the surrounding orchards. As his influence spread in the area, he acquired political power. He became chairman of the Mendocino County grand jury in 1966 by judicial appointment.

He also founded churches in San Francisco and Los Angeles in 1971. He focused on San Francisco, where he resumed his desegregation efforts and again established political muscle by charming liberal politicians with his 80 percent black congregation.

Membership in his church reached 20,000 in California by the early '70s, and his church had 13 buses used to transport large groups on short notice to demonstrations or political rallies that Jones supported.

After helping George Moscone, who later would be murdered in City Hall, win the mayoral election by a slim margin, Jones was rewarded with the job of heading the San Francisco city housing authority.

In 1977 Jones came under attack in magazine and newspaper articles detailing his ever-increasing financial empire and alleged beatings of church members. Among those holdings were 27,000 acres in the jungle of Guyana.

"He said he wanted to go and work with the Guyanese," Thrash said. "He said they had just gotten their freedom from Great Britain, and he wanted to help them for a few years and then come back and build a big care home for all of us.

"I knew I would retire soon, and we thought that was nice," she said. "We was brainwashed, too. We just all followed him out there. You know how people get excited and things. . ."

Hyacinth Thrash disliked Guyana from the start, she said.

"I didn't like it from when I first got off the flatbed truck. I didn't like it at all."

When she and her sister arrived in Georgetown around midnight, the rain was falling like they had never seen it come down in Alabama, Indianapolis or California. Zip cried.

They were taken from Georgetown to Jonestown by river boat, a journey of 11 hours, and then a 2-hour ride in the bed of a dump truck through the jungle. Their journey ended at the doorstep of a thatched house elevated on blocks. It leaked.

The jungle seemed to grow up through the clouds, clamping a lid on their lives. The sister prayed and praised the Lord. It was not their way to complain.

A cottage was built for the sisters and two other elderly women, one of whom had suffered a stroke.

They raised hogs and chickens that were butchered and sold or fed to others. Sweet potatoes, bananas and other fruits grew around them in abundance, but they rarely were given anything so substantial to eat. Meals were brought to the four women, who were generally isolated. They were not allowed in the mess hall with the others. White rice and gravy for breakfast was their best meal.

Hyacinth began to suspect that Jones was trying to starve the old folks, she said.

One of the women who visited them from the camp, and washed Hyacinth's hair for her, told the women she had seen something disturbing one day and made them promise not to tell anyone if she told them. They promised.

"I saw a big thing of cyanide,' she said," Hyacinth recalled.

Hyacinth suggested that maybe it was meant to poison the rats that attacked the camp from the jungle.

"She said maybe so." Thrash said. "One time after that, I told the same woman that I was gonna have to get some new rubber tips for my walker, and she said, 'You may not need them.'

"I said, 'Why not? I'm not gonna get healed.'

"And she didn't say any more."

On another ominous occasion, one evening after they had enjoyed a stew, Jones told them that they had just eaten a mercenary who had come to attack them but had been shot.

The women were unsure if it was a joke.

Their cottage was on a hill overlooking Jones' living quarters, and the women came to realize that Jones and his inner circle were eating fresh-baked goods and big meals. Their leader also had a fan and air conditioner that were greatly coveted by his suffering congregation, she recalled. Her skin peeled from the heat.

They could also see that their "Father," as he called himself, was attended to by nurses who sometimes wore only bikini tops and bottoms. Hyacinth became disgusted at their minister's preoccupation with sex.

"I realized after about half a year that things had gone haywire," she said. "I quit going to church meetings because they was just sex meetings. I quit going, and he didn't even send for me.

"I got sick of him talking about sex. They had nights when they had the homosexuals talk about their sex and then the lesbians talk about their sex. I thought 'Boy, oh, boy.'

"Anybody would get fed up with that, but there wasn't any way we could leave."

Their minister of 20 years, the man they had given everything and followed across the world, had given up on God, she said.

When the toilet paper ran out, Jones told the women to use pages from the Bible. Hyacinth Thrash refused to follow such blasphemy.

Jones began preaching about threats from the outside and suicide. He conducted a "Kool-Aid drill," she said, that made the old women in the cottage laugh.

The day U.S. Rep. Leo Ryan of San Francisco came, Hyacinth saw his plane overhead but did not go down with the others to meet him. Zip and the other two women did. Zip came back and said the congressman seemed satisfied that no one wanted to leave, until one woman stepped forward and stirred up a "hornet's nest."

The congressman said any who wanted to leave could go with him on the plane. He said he would come back for those who could not get on the plane now, Zip told her sister.

As Zip relayed that information, Jones' voice came over the loudspeaker. He ordered everyone to the pavilion.

Zip and the other two women went down, Zip had remained faithful to her minister, to the point that Hyacinth had quit confiding her fears, for fear that Zip would squeal to Jones.

Hyacinth stayed behind. "I wouldn't go. I said I wasn't going and I meant it. I was through with him that night. If someone had knocked me in the head . . . I wasn't afraid," she said.

When she heard shots, Hyacinth hid beneath her bed. She later would learn that the congressman and four others had been killed when Jones' followers opened fire at the airport as members tried to leave with Ryan.

"They were calling for one woman I knew, and I thought she had probably run away. I got scared and went underneath the bed until it all ceased. I didn't hear but one shot. I thought they were trying to scare her to come. . . ."

She was weary, so she came out from hiding and climbed in her bed, which was behind the cottage door. She slept until 7 the next morning.

"I guess they started killing about 7 in the night," she said.

She rose in the morning and used her cane to get down to the pavilion in search of her sister.

"The first people I saw were Guyanese boys at the pavilion. They were combing the jungle. I walked with my cane between the two boys. I don't know how I felt or what I thought. I was just blank.

"I walked around there pinching myself to see whether I was walking around alive or dead.

"I seen my sister right away. She was lying outside the pavilion with the others. I saw needles everywhere. I didn't go inside the pavilion, but I seen them on the ground there.

"It's something I never thought I'd see in my lifetime."

She has collected her memories in an as-told-to book with writer

'I seen my sister right away. She was lying outside the pavilion with the others. I saw needles everywhere.'

Marian K. Towne, but no publisher has taken an interest in it, she said. She has given up on it.

She would just as soon rid her mind of it altogether. But that has proved difficult.

The angels camped around her to deliver her from the fate that befell Jones and more than 900 others who committed suicide or were forced to drink or be injected with cyanide-laced fruit juice at the People's Temple in Jonestown 10 years ago, Hyacinth Thrash said.

"I used to always say, and I say now, that God is a good God, and if you follow God like you should, he won't let you get into anything like that. He will let you have some warning.

"The devil is so busy, he can get you doing wrong when you think you are doing right.

"Now every time I see a preacher on TV, I pray for God to show me if he is right or wrong, and God does.

"I don't think I would ever go wrong again."

'Everything he [Jones] asked for, we gave him. Sometimes you do things you never think you would do.'

THE UNITED METHODIST

VOLUME 135   NUMBER 25

Send P.O. Form 3579 to P.O. Box 660

10 years after, Jonestown

UM family says their loss, tragedy serve as reminders that 'forces for good, death are closely intertwined'

EDITOR'S NOTE: Nov. 18 is the 10th anniversary of one of this century's most bizarre episodes: the mass suicide-murder of 912 people, all U.S. citizens but one, at Jonestown, Guyana. The victims were members of Peoples Temple, a (Christian Church) Disciples of Christ congregation based in San Francisco, and followers of its charismatic leader, the Rev. Jim Jones.

The congregation moved to Guyana, an English-speaking country the size of Idaho on the northern coast of South America, in 1977. There church members built a community—Jonestown—on 3,800 acres of jungle 30 miles from the Venezuela border. The community was an attempt to create a "new society" based on socialism and freedom from race, age and sex discrimination.

Most of the 912 died from being injected with or drinking lethal doses of cyanide poison. A few died from gunshot wounds.

Three of Jonestown's victims were members of the family of a United Methodist pastor, the Rev. John V. Moore, a clergy member of the California-Nevada Annual Conference. Mr. Moore and his wife, Barbara, lost two of their three daughters, Carolyn and Annie, and a grandson, Kimo. At the time of their deaths, Carolyn was 33; Annie, 24; and Kimo, 4.

The following article is based on a recent two-hour interview with Mr. and Mrs. Moore and their surviving daughter, Rebecca, and on books and articles about Jonestown written and/or edited by Rebecca and her husband, Fielding M. McGehee III.

By STEPHEN L. SWECKER
Associate Editor

It's been 10 years since two of her daughters and a grandson died at Jonestown, Guyana. It could have been yesterday.

"Jonestown and Jim Jones are forever present in our lives," Barbara Moore recently wrote. She told a story that echoes with the ache of that unending presence.

In January, she said, she was called for jury duty in Davis, Calif., where her husband is pastor of Davis United Methodist Church. After routine questioning by the attorneys in the case, it appeared that she was accepted to serve on the jury.

Following a lunch break, she returned to the courtroom with the other jurors. The judge entered the room and abruptly asked, "Is there a person in this courtroom whose daughters died in the Jonestown massacre?" A stunned Barbara raised her hand.

"You're dismissed," the judge said.

Too shocked to say anything or to question Jonestown's relevance to the theft case being tried, Barbara left the courtroom—"with as much dignity as I could muster," she said.

"I understood then, as I do now, that reminders will occur over and over in my life," she said.

Reminders self-imposed

Ironically, many of the Moore family's "reminders" of the 1978 deaths of 912 members of the Peoples Temple, a Christian Church (Disciples of Christ) congregation that had left San Francisco for Guyana, have been self-imposed.

Primarily because of 37-year-old daughter Rebecca's efforts to obtain hard-to-get information about the massacre at Jonestown, the community that church members built in the South American jungle, the Moores have been engaged in ongoing investigation of and reflection about the event that claimed their three kin.

As a result of their quest for insight and understanding of the deaths of Carolyn, Annie and Carolyn's son, Kimo, no fewer than five books about Peoples Temple and Jonestown have been written or edited by Rebecca and her husband.

More than books, however, have resulted from their 10-year quest for facts and insight about the Jonestown deaths.

The Moores have emerged from their experience free of bitterness. In addition, their willingness to reflect with others about that experience has added a new dimension to their sense of ministry.

Little comfort, few details

Their investigations have yielded little comfort and few certain details about Carolyn, Annie, and Kimo's last hours.

What they do reveal is that Carolyn—who had an affair with the Rev. Jim Jones, leader of the Peoples Temple, and served as one of his most trusted assistants—died with him in his Jonestown cabin. She was poisoned.

Annie, a nurse who some witnesses said helped distribute the poison, may have been the last person to die at Jonestown, perhaps from a self-inflicted gunshot wound to the head. Jim Jones also died as the result of a gunshot.

The widespread assumption of 10 years ago—since reconfirmed by the Moores' reconstruction of events—is that the suicides resulted from a paranoia-induced certainty by Jonestown residents that the end was near because of a U.S. government plot to destroy the settlement.

The feared "conspiracy" was confirmed to them when a U.S. congressman, Rep. Leo Ryan, visited the town to investigate reports of malnourishment and mistreatment of residents.

Peoples Temple members killed the congressman as he was about to board a plane to leave with a few discontented Jonestown residents. That incident triggered the mass deaths, which had been "rehearsed" many times, according to Rebecca.

Why spend 10 years investigating such gruesome and personally painful events and writing and talking about them with whomever is interested?

"We didn't really choose to get so involved," said Rebecca, community relations director for United Way of Northern Nevada and a member of First United Methodist Church in Reno. "But we saw it as important to get the story out. Events chose us."

PORTER

275, Dallas, TX 75266-0275   NOVEMBER 18, 1988

massacre remembered

She expressed particular frustration that few scholars have dealt with Peoples Temple and Jonestown. Most look upon the two as "aberrations" that don't fit neatly into conventional history, she said.

But that's precisely the point, according to her father, John. He has called the Jonestown a "mirror" on the human condition.

The massacre and the events leading up to it, he says, are reminders of life's deep ambiguities, namely that possibilities for good and the "forces of death" often are closely intertwined.

Much of what John says and writes today about the Peoples Temple follows the outline of a widely circulated sermon he preached a week after the 1978 event entitled, "A Witness to Tragedy and Resurrection."

'Went wrong' in two ways

He frankly acknowledged then as now that Jonestown "went wrong" in two fundamental ways: The adulation of Jim Jones by his followers was "idolatrous," and the "paranoia" of Jones and his followers, which fed fears of a U.S.-government conspiracy against Peoples Temple, hopelessly blurred the thin line between fantasy and reality.

But the situation was not entirely evil, he said. The people of Jonestown were engaged in worthwhile social experimentation, judging partly from a favorable impression he and Barbara gained from a visit there months before the suicides.

"We wanted to affirm the humanness of all the people there," he said of the family's willingness to share its experience openly.

"The media were speaking of all the kooks and nuts. But we knew the people and were pained and perplexed by that. We knew them as whole persons.

"Once we started down that path (of dealing openly with the tragedy), it became part of the healing process for us. We've tried not to be defensive."

All three Moores distinguish between their negative feelings about Jim Jones personally and their positive assessment of things he and his followers did to promote racial justice and to help poor people.

'He was a creepy person'

"I can say unequivocally that I never liked Jim Jones," Barbara said. "He was kind of a creepy person who was warped by his hatred of injustice and his life-isn't-fair attitude."

John, recalling when he served as a campus pastor in Davis in the late 1960s and knew Jones as a fellow minister, said, "He couldn't work with anyone. You either did it his way or you didn't do it at all."

During the years in Davis and afterwards, Jones was an occasional visitor in the Moore home. The relationship continued after he fathered a son by Carolyn out of wedlock.

The affair between Jim Jones and their oldest daughter was always a source of discomfort for John and Barbara. They said they frequently raised the question of marriage and noted that Jones already had a wife.

The Moores were especially disappointed when, in 1972, youngest child Annie joined Peoples Temple in San Francisco (Carolyn had joined in 1968). Upon learning of Annie's decision, John exclaimed, "My God, isn't one child enough?"

"I guess we always tried to affirm our children's right to make their choices and to bear the consequences, and we would bear them along with them," John said.

Hard question remains

But the hard question remains: How could the offspring of a happy, close-knit family that both taught and actively lived out their Christian faith be attracted to Peoples Temple?

Rebecca put it this way: "We had a childhood that made us open to new ideas, open to social issues, and that openness made us vulnerable to people who worked to right wrongs."

Then she added: "People from close-knit families are most vulnerable to groups that offer such closeness, even more vulnerable than people who come from miserable families."

In his 1978 sermon, John answered the question in slightly different terms:

"Our children took seriously what we believed about commitment, caring about a better, more humane and just society. They saw in Peoples Temple the same kind of caring for people and commitment to social justice that they had lived with. They have paid our dues for our commitments and involvements."

During the recent interview, John wondered aloud where in the United Methodist Church and other mainline churches people can be "involved with the same intensity" as his daughters were with Peoples Temple. "Perhaps as a missionary," he suggested.

Church relationship is positive

However, the Moores harbor no reservations about how the church has related to them during and since the tragedy.

"Our relationship with the church has continued in a positive way," Barbara said. "We've been affirmed and validated by our United Methodist friends. Even if they didn't understand, they affirmed us and our children."

Today, John and Barbara attempt whenever possible to help others, particularly young people, who have gone through or are going through painful experiences with "new religious groups," as they prefer to call them.

"Cult" has a negative connotation that doesn't do justice to the complex mixture of good and bad in most such groups, John said.

"I think some good has come out of our experience in that respect," John says of his and Barbara's work with people who are re-entering society after being involved with new religious groups.

"We've decided we want to deal with what's important with the years left to us. There's so much in the church that is superficial and sentimental. But our days are limited. We can spend time on things like that or dealing with people and their needs."

And how will they celebrate Thanksgiving 10 years after the event that "changed their lives with a vengeance," as Rebecca put it?

"We're great party people; we like a good time," Barbara said. "We'll celebrate Thanksgiving as we always have, giving thanks for all good things and expressing concern for others."

John added: " . . . and for all the good years we had with Carolyn and Annie."

ittle Remains of Peoples Temple Outpost Where 913 Died

10 Years Later, Jonestown Is a Site of Silent Desolation

By WILLIAM R. LONG, *Times Staff Writer*

JONESTOWN, Guyana—In 10-ear-old photographs, the ground 'ound the Jonestown pavilion is 'vered with bodies of men, wom-a and children. More than 900 .ople had received a fatal potion f poison in Jim Jones' grisly ritual f suicide and murder.

Today, the infamous spot is cov-red with a dense mat of green eeds, flanked by a large bougain-illea bush that blooms in a cascade ' bright purple. Little remains of .e pavilion. Only three of its many upport poles still stand to mark .e spot. Charred timbers and .anks lie scattered under the tan-.e of waist-high weeds, rotting on .e moist tropical soil.

Gone too the ceremonial stage here Jim Jones worked his dark .arisma, gone his priestly throne 'nd the sign that warned his fol-.wers: "Those who do not learn om the past are condemned to 'peat it."

Then an American communal .periment in the tropical wilder-.ss of South America, Jonestown .ded its horror on Nov. 18, 1978. ow an abandoned historical site in .e Guyanese jungle, Jonestown is ding away under a mantle of eeds, brush and decay.

The Guyanese government ap-pears content to let time and isolation dim the enormity that happened here. Authorities are do-ing nothing to preserve what little is left of the former settlement.

No Guyanese investigation was ever made into the rise and fall of Jonestown and its implications for this former British colony on the Caribbean's southeastern edge. Of-ficials here have preferred to dis-miss the subject, calling Jonestown an American problem.

For years, the Guyanese govern-ment gave no cooperation to out-siders who wished to come and see the hard-to-reach site in the coun-try's remote northern hinterlands. Only recently has the Ministry of Information helped to arrange vis-its when requested by foreigners.

To mark the 10th anniversary of the tragedy, several American journalists came for a look. They found the 300 acres of once-pro-ductive land overgrown with weeds and brush. It is a scene of silent desolation, unclaimed either by man or by the tropical forest that forms a high wall around it.

Many fruit trees are dead or dying for want of cultivation and care. Others produce bananas, or-

anges and tangerines that fall un-harvested on the ground. Palms that were just getting started when Jonestown died now rise tall over the wasted land.

Of nearly 100 wooden buildings that once housed a bustling com-munity, none is left standing. Bro-ken machinery, vehicle carcasses and other metal remnants have turned crumbly with rust.

Residents of Port Kaituma, an impoverished town on a jungle river 7 miles from Jonestown, say the abandoned settlement burned down in a brush fire sometime after 1983. What year the fire took place was not clear from interviews, but everyone seemed to agree that it was not caused by arson.

"Just dry grass got fire," said Laurence Inverary, 31, a former policeman.

No Resettlement

In 1980, Inverary said, he lived in Jonestown as a police guard for government livestock that used to graze the clearings. But no farmers have ever tried to resettle the land, he said. Asked why, he hesitated before responding. "They might be afraid."

Mortimer Kansinally, a police-

man in Port Kaituma, confirmed the lingering fear.

"From the incident, everybody afraid of the old place," said Kan-sinally, 40. "They don't know if things still about." He said some people imagine that Jonestown is haunted by *jumbies*—evil spirits in Caribbean folklore.

Kansinally, a slightly built man with a gold tooth and a red stocking cap, said he was at the Port Kaituma airstrip in 1978 when the Jonestown nightmare began.

Rep. Leo Ryan, a Northern Cali-fornia congressman, had come to Jonestown on Nov. 17 to investi-gate allegations that members of Jones' Peoples Temple were being kept here against their will. Ryan was accompanied by American journalists, members of his staff and relatives of temple members.

The group spent the night in the settlement, and as it prepared to leave the next day, more than a dozen residents said they wanted to defect. Jones had been angered by previous defections, which he de-scribed as part of a conspiracy to destroy his tight-knit organization. Tension was high in Jonestown as Ryan prepared to leave in a truck on Nov. 18. A temple member

grabbed the congressman and briefly held a knife to his throat, but Ryan was not hurt.

Later, however, a death squad from Jonestown opened fire on the group at the Port Kaituma airstrip. Keith Thorne, 52, a shopkeeper in Port Kaituma, said he saw the group gunned down.

"They were all, first, around the plane, then started wild shooting," Thorne recalled. Ryan and four other people were killed. Ten were wounded.

"It was an awful sight to see," said policeman Kansinally.

Called for Mass Suicide

Something even more awful be-gan late that same afternoon in Jonestown. Jones called everyone to the pavilion and told them that the settlement would soon be under attack. He said they had no choice but to "take the potion like they used to take in ancient Greece."

The Jonestown potion was made with a patented grape flavoring named Fla-Vor-Aid and lethal po-tassium cyanide. First children, then adults, drank it from paper cups. Children who refused the poison were held while it was

Please see JONESTOWN, Page 23

JONESTOWN: Guyana Lets Settlement Decay

Continued from Page 22

squirted into the backs of their mouths with syringes. Adults who resisted were injected.

At the end, Jones and a close aide, Annie Moore, died of shots to the head from a 38-caliber pistol that was found beside their bodies.

When it was over, the bodies of Jones and 912 followers lay in tangled clusters over the pavilion area, a ghastly scene that would shock the world. Two men sneaked away during the the death ritual and survived to describe it.

Since then, much has been written about Jones' troubled youth, his early years as an unorthodox and demanding religious leader, the growth of his Peoples Temple cult in San Francisco and Los Angeles and its exodus to Guyana in 1977. It is clear that deep-rooted obsessiveness, paranoia and megalomania propelled Jones to his final act of horror.

"It was not the temple's enemies that brought down the temple, but Jones' destructive personality," wrote Tim Reiterman in "Raven," a 1982 book on Jones.

In the early 1970s, reports from Peoples Temple defectors began to raise questions about the secretive sect and its leader, who was a member of the San Francisco Housing Authority. In response, Jones began planning for the creation of a Caribbean sanctuary.

In many respects, Guyana was a logical place for Jones to seek a fresh beginning for the Peoples Temple. He called himself a socialist, as did the then-leader of Guyana's government, Forbes Burnham. Although Jones was white, most of the sect's members were black, as was Burnham, most of his government and about 40% of the Guyanese population.

Guyana welcomed projects for settling its undeveloped hinterlands and increasing the country's agricultural production, which must be supplemented by food imports. Most of Guyana's 755,000 residents are clustered along the Caribbean coast, while most of its Idaho-sized territory is unused except by native Indians and gold prospectors.

The government especially wanted settlers in the northwestern district where Jones was offered a lease, because it is near the border with Venezuela, which claims historic rights to more than half of Guyana's territory.

Jonestown's first settlers moved to the site permanently in 1975. Late in 1976, journalists in the United States began investigating reports of beatings, mysterious deaths and deviant sexual practices in the Peoples Temple. Under increasing pressure, Jones began moving most of his membership from San Francisco and Los Angeles to Jonestown in May, 1977. He moved himself in August.

Although it was not self-sufficient in food or other supplies, Jonestown quickly became a fully functional community, with electrical generators, tractors and other vehicles, schoolrooms, wood and metal shops, chicken coops and pigsties. In all, an estimated $5 million was invested in the project.

Defectors said Jonestown was a concentration camp whose residents were subjected to psychological pressure, forced labor and physical mistreatment. From his fan-backed seat of power in the pavilion, Jones presided over long and emotional sessions called "white nights," dwelling on sex and love, revolution and socialism, traitors and enemies, death and suicide.

Brindley Benn, leader of a leftist opposition group in Guyana, began demanding an official investigation of Jonestown after U.S. press reports cast increasing suspicion on Jones and his practices.

'State Within a State'

"He had the government in his pocket," Benn said in a recent interview. In a political news sheet that he edited, Benn expressed fear that Jonestown was becoming a "state within a state," he recalled. But he said that Lloyd Barker, then the Guyanese police commissioner, claimed "there was nothing to worry about."

In a separate interview, Barker said: "I know there were some rumors there, especially people of the opposition. It was felt that an investigation was needed. I never felt professionally that there was any need."

Barker added that he knew Jones personally. "I think he was very intelligent, a very honest human. He had a type of esprit de corps that was required in the type of business he was doing."

Asked what lasting impact the deaths at Jonestown had had on Guyana, Barker said that before the tragedy, Guyana was so little known that the U.S. Postal Service often sent letters addressed for this country to Africa, the clerks apparently thinking the country' name sounded African. "After the Jonestown incident, people were getting their letters properly," he said.

Still, Guyana would like to be known for its spectacular Kaieteur Falls, or the ornate wooden buildings of its capital. Instead, Guyanese are haunted by Jim Jones.

"They groan every time Jonestown is mentioned," said a foreign diplomat in Georgetown. "I think it has proved to be a major embarrassment to the country."

The main long-term impact of Jonestown on Guyana may have been to dampen development of the country's interior, according to Courtney Gibson, a journalist who once edited the governing party's newspaper.

"If Jonestown had gone well, if that disaster had not happened, I think the government's hinterland development project would be moving at a much more rapid rate," he said.

Patrick Denny, an Information Ministry official, said the government kept military or police guards at Jonestown until at least 1983.

"They were just minding some goats and things like that," he said, but no revival of the agricultural project was attempted.

"I think the real idea was to just let the jungle take it back, because you certainly weren't going to get any Guyanese to go in there and live," Denny said.

Why not? "Jumbies," he said, smiling.

As the 10th anniversary of the tragedy approached, the government acknowledged outside interest with apparent resignation and lowered the barriers that had made it difficult to reach Jonestown. The airstrip at Port Kaituma was unofficially reopened, and a government plane was made available for trips in.

Only Remnants Left

After riding on a tractor over a rarely used track through the jungle from the airstrip to Jonestown, one group of visitors spent nearly three hours looking around the site. Spread through the weeds and brush of the biggest clearing were the rusted shells of two trucks, a dismembered tractor, a shoe-making machine, a wood-milling machine, a large storage tank, a concrete mixer, an air compressor, several engine blocks, pieces of aluminum roofing and a generator. The visitors found what was left of the pavilion, then the area of the married couples' cottages.

Finding a large metal object, someone used a machete to hack some weeds away. "It's a filing cabinet," Gouveia announced. Jim Jones' filing cabinet, now empty, broken and rusted. Not much more was left.

FRANK BURSINGER / Los Angeles Times

Jonestown myths leave people unaware, vulnerable

By Lisa Levitt Ryckman

SAN FRANCISCO — Threads of an invisible Jonestown have been so successfully woven into society's fabric that most people remain unaware of the proliferation and destructive power of cults in America.

"People think the cult problem died in Jonestown,," said Patricia Ryan, daughter of U.S. Rep. Leo Ryan, who was killed by Peoples Temple gunmen hours before 912 people swallowed poison at the cult's jungle compound. "But problems like this are happening everyday on a smaller scale. Cults are a huge problem."

A decade since the shock and horror of the Jonestown massacre on Nov. 18, 1978, myths persist about cults and the people who become trapped in them.

The two most pervasive misconceptions: that cult members are glassy-eyed flower peddlers, easily recognizable from everybody else, and that people who become involved in cults were emotionally weak or defective to begin with.

"People don't realize that destructive cults blend in very well with society. They don't realize they may be working with someone in a cult, that they may have relatives in a cult," said Cynthia Kisser, executive of the Chicago-based national Cult Awareness Network, a clearinghouse for information about cults.

Ryan learned that lesson firsthand. Now a network board member, she became involved with the anti-cult effort after her younger sister joined Bagwan Shree Rajneesh's group. Ryan's sister went to India at a friend's urging, promising her family she wasn't getting involved in a cult. A month later, she had joined.

"Perfectly normal people get involved, but more vulnerable are people who are idealistic or people who may be going through some kind of life crisis," Ryan said.

"There's this attitude that 'I could never be recruited into a cult, I could recognize it as a cult and avoid it,'" said Kisser, who estimated that 2,500 cults now operate in the United States and that 3 million people have been affected by them.

Trying to do good

The public should remember that most of the Rev. Jim Jones' followers were good people who wanted to do good, said journalist Tim Reiterman, who spent more than four years investigating the Peoples Temple before and after the mass death, and who was wounded in the Port Kaituma airstrip ambush that killed Ryan and four others.

The Peoples Temple had its share of former drug addicts and ex-cons; it also attracted college professors, white-collar professionals and Ivy League lawyers. Between these extremes were decent, hard-working, middle-class folk who believed in interracial harmony and helping others.

"People still have the tendency to dismiss the people of the Peoples Temple as a bunch of crazies and kooks and worse. But when you've spent a whole lot of time with the subject, you understand they're a whole lot like the rest of us," said Reiterman, who wrote eloquently about Jones and the Temple in his 1982 book with co-author John Jacobs, "Raven: The Untold Story of the Rev. Jim Jones and His People."

For some followers, the beginning was Indiana in the 1950s, when Peoples Temple was an interracial ministry with heavy evangelical and Pentecostal over-

See JONESTOWN, page 5C

Jonestown

From page 1C

tones. Eventually, the Temple became less a religious group than a political one, and always, it was the handsome, charismatic Jones who inspired his diverse flock.

"There was no way to separate (his) warped world from his idealized vision and his social conscience, nor the real threats from his paranoia, his benevolence from his cruelty, his genius from his madness," Reiterman and Jacobs wrote.

A master manipulator, Jones used classic mind-control techniques on his followers, including isolation, fear and denial of sleep, protein and privacy. By Nov. 18, 1978, the leader's paranoid belief that death was the only way to avoid destruction by outside forces had been adopted by many people far more rational than Jones.

"They were drawn to Jim Jones as a father, as a priest, as a hero, as someone who could complete their lives," said California Assemblywoman Jackie Speier, who also was wounded at Port Kaituma. "In one way or another, we're all seeking that."

Cult Awareness Network

The fact that search continues is reflected in the volume of calls providing or requesting information of the Cult Awareness Network: 10,000 this year, twice as many as 1987. The kinds of groups eliciting the most inquiries include satanic, Bible-based, New Age and self-awareness, Kisser said.

The network believes destructive cults meet four criteria: the use of deceptive recruiting; financial exploitation of recruits for the group or leader's benefit; use of mind control or brainwashing techniques, and a feeling by members of being trapped.

The Peoples Temple fulfilled those, as do others now. Public ignorance and denial of that fact make another Jonestown a real possibility, Kisser said.

"We do have these deaths occurring regularly, but it's one here and two there," she said, citing last month's beating death of 8-year-old Dayna Lorae Broussard, whose father, Eldridge Broussard, founded the Ecclesia Athletic Association.

Through Ecclesia, more than 50 children were moved from inner-city Los Angeles to a house near Portland, Ore., where authorities said the youngsters were beaten and starved.

"For every child who died in Jonestown, many more have died since in similar circumstances," Kisser said. "Tragedies are being perpetrated one person at a time."

Associated Press

405

'Those people should have lived'

Jonestown survivor endures memories so young will know

By Brian Smith
New York Times News Service

INDIANAPOLIS — Hyacinth Thrash's scars are the kind that do not show. In her cozy room at Mount Zion Geriatric Center, she reclines in a wheelchair and tries to forget the unforgettable: Jonestown.

Ten years ago Saturday, 913 members of the Peoples Temple, including their charismatic leader, Jim Jones, and at least five Thrash. Her sister, Zipporah Edwards, and several friends were among the dead.

Most committed suicide, at Jones's behest, by drinking a cyanide-laced liquid.

A few people escaped into the nearby jungles, but by the next morning, only one person in Jonestown remained alive: Thrash. Her sister, Zipporah Edwards, and several friends were among the dead.

Thrash, now 86, said the nine previous anniversaries were easier to endure. "This one has worried me more than any of them," she said. "Lately, I haven't been sleeping too well."

That is hardly surprising. Over the last few weeks, she has dredged her memory repeatedly before a parade of local reporters, reciting her survival story countless times.

Somehow, her raspy voice stays steady, even when recounting the most horrifying details, and her manner remains pleasant and co-operative.

But discussing Jonestown is not the same as seeing it again, as she discovered Wednesday when a television newscast showed the bodies.

"I just don't feel too good thinking about it," she said moments after the newscast.

"When I see all those people, it makes me nervous," she said. "We had a nice bunch of people there. It was just like a big family. All those people should have lived a long life, especially those babies."

She talks a lot about babies and children. One reason she so willingly relives the agonizing memories is that she wants to prevent young people from falling prey to similar cults.

"I like to witness to the kids," she said. "The young generation needs to know. I think the kids will read about it, and it might keep somebody else from falling into the same trap."

Although her ordeal centered on a church, Thrash has remained steadfast in her religious faith.

"God saved me," she said of her survival in Jonestown.

Her bitterness is directed at Jones, whom she once admired for his civil rights work in Indianapolis.

In the 1960s, Jones espoused the cause of underprivileged blacks.

"He was nice at that time," said Thrash, who had endured racial prejudice as a child in the South.

With her sister's encouragement, she joined the Peoples Temple. At Jones's urging, she sold her Indianapolis home for $35,000 and gave him the proceeds.

A few years later, when the church moved to California, she bought and sold another home, again giving the money to Jones.

But by 1977, when he led his followers to Guyana, Jones had become erratic, showing contempt for Christianity, said Thrash.

"He changed in so many ways," she said. "He said there was no Jesus, there was no God — that he was the onliest God. I think he got possessed of the Devil."

Thrash grew increasingly disenchanted with him. On the night of the mass suicide, when Jones summoned his followers to the town pavilion, Thrash refused to go, declaring to her sister that she was "sick of Jim Jones." Her sister went ahead.

Later, Jones' security guards combed the community for stragglers but overlooked Thrash, who had turned out her lights and crawled under the bed.

She hid there for about five minutes, then, unaware of the holocaust that was unfolding, undressed and went to bed.

The next morning, on the way to breakfast, she discovered 15 bodies. Panic yielded to calm, she said, when God told her He was with her.

She returned to her cottage, where Guyanese authorities found her the next day.

After returning to the United States, she spent the first five years living with relatives and the last five in the nursing home.

Thursday, sitting in her corner room, Thrash seems safely removed from the Jonestown nightmare. But perhaps she will never be.

"This is nice, but there's no place like home," she said.

"If I'd kept my California home, I'd be out there now."

Still, she said, "I have things to be happy about"

"I'm not going to let it drive me crazy," she said.

"I know it was terrible and it happened, but you know, time goes on. You can't give up on life over that."

CULTS AND NEW RELIGIONS